Organizations

Behavior
Structure
Processes

Organizations

Behavior
Structure
Processes

Tenth Edition

James L. Gibson
Professor Emeritus
College of Business and Economics
University of Kentucky

John M. Ivancevich
Hugh Roy and Lillie Cranz Cullen Chair
and Professor of Organizational Behavior and Management
University of Houston

James H. Donnelly, Jr.
Thomas C. Simons
Professor of Business
College of Business and Economics
University of Kentucky

Boston   Burr Ridge, IL   Dubuque, IA   Madison, WI   New York   San Francisco   St. Louis
Bangkok   Bogotá   Caracas   Lisbon   London   Madrid
Mexico City   Milan   New Delhi   Seoul   Singapore   Sydney   Taipei   Toronto

McGraw-Hill Higher Education

A Division of The **McGraw-Hill** *Companies*

ORGANIZATIONS

Copyright © 2000, 1997, 1994, 1991, 1988, 1985, 1982, 1979, 1976, and 1973 by the McGraw-Hill Companies, Inc. All rights reserved. Printed in the United States of America. Except as permitted under the United States Copyright Act of 1976, no part of this publication may be reproduced or distributed in any form or by any means, or stored in a data base or retrieval system, without the prior written permission of the publisher.

This book is printed on acid-free paper.

domestic   1 2 3 4 5 6 7 8 9 0 VNH/VNH 9 0 9 8 7 6 5 4 3 2 1 0 9
international   1 2 3 4 5 6 7 8 9 0 VNH/VNH 9 0 9 8 7 6 5 4 3 2 1 0 9

ISBN 0-07-229587-2

Publisher: *Craig S. Beytien*
Senior sponsoring editor: *John E. Biernat*
Editorial coordinator: *Erin Riley*
Marketing manager: *Kenyetta Giles Haynes*
Project manager: *Margaret Rathke*
Senior production supervisor: *Lori Koetters*
Senior designer: *Michael Warrell*
Supplement coordinator: *Becky Szura*
Compositor: *Black Dot*
Typeface: *10.5/12 Garamond*
Printer: *Von Hoffmann Press, Inc.*

Library of Congress Cataloging-in-Publication Data

Gibson, James L.
    Organizations : behavior, structure, processess / James L. Gibson,
John M. Ivancevich, James H. Donnelly, Jr.—10th ed.
      p. cm.
    Includes bibliographical references and indexes.
    ISBN 0-07-229587-2 (alk. paper)
  1. Organization. 2. Organizational behavior. 3. Leadership.
4. Organizational effectiveness. I. Ivancevich, John M.
II. Donnelly, James H. III. Title.
HD58.7.G54 2000
658.4–dc21   99–24416

INTERNATIONAL EDITION ISBN 0-07-116950-4

Copyright © 2000. Exclusive rights by The McGraw-Hill Companies, Inc. for manufacture and export. This book cannot be re-exported from the country to which it is consigned by McGraw-Hill. The International Edition is not available in North America.

www.mhhe.com

The 10th edition, like the previous ones, is based on the proposition that managing people and their behavior in organizations is one of the most challenging tasks anyone could face. There is nothing boring about managing organizational behavior. Traditional approaches that worked a decade ago or even a few years ago are correctly questioned, modified, or rejected. This book will provide an opportunity for you to look inside organizations and to develop your own perspective and skills for managing organizational behavior. Your own perspective and approach will serve you in the positions you hold, the challenges you face, and the career choices you make in the 21st century.

The 10th edition of *Organizations: Behavior, Structure, Processes* presents theories, research results, and applications that focus on managing organizational behavior in small, as well as large and multinational organizations. Through the successful history of the book, feedback from students and teachers has indicated that we have succeeded in presenting a realistic view of organizational behavior.

A consistent theme throughout the book is that effective management of organizational behavior requires an understanding of theory, research, and practice. Given this theme, we view our task as the presentation and interpretation of organizational behavior theory and research so that students can comprehend the three characteristics common to all organizations—behavior, structure, and processes—as affected by the actions of managers. Accordingly, we illustrate how organizational behavior theory leads to research and how both theory and research provide the basic foundation for practical applications in business firms, hospitals, educational institutions, government agencies, and other organizations.

Special features of this edition

Interestingly, this edition has both more and less than previous editions. It is shorter than the previous edition because we have shortened the length of most chapters. But it also has a significant amount of new material on information technology, e-commerce, the new economy, diversity, ethics, global management, organizational culture, teams, team building, and total quality management (TQM). Coverage of some of these topics began a few editions back and is further expanded in this edition. Let us briefly review some of the changes in this edition.

- The book uses real-world situations and examples to illustrate how the theory and research lessons can be applied in work settings. Students prefer to have real examples to support what academics and researchers are proposing or stating. The real world is reflected in the chapter content, the Close-Up boxes, and the cases.

- Learning more about real companies is made easier by providing in each chapter World Wide Web addresses. Each Web site for a company has a unique address called the Uniform Resource Locator (URL). By accessing these addresses students can enter the company's domain. Many of the addresses are hyperlinked or connected to other pages on the World Wide Web. This feature will allow students to stay very current on what is going on within the companies listed. Using these addresses will enrich what is occurring in the classroom. We have found that students learn from visiting the sites and exchange other addresses that take them to new sites.

- Each year organizations become more involved in global business, global joint ventures, and global negotiations. This edition pays particular attention to global business and issues in each chapter.

- Diversity needs to be examined in all organizations. Thus, diversity management is presented, debated, and analyzed throughout the text.

- Teams, group dynamics, and group decision making are each important topics that we have emphasized more in this edition.

- One of the characteristics of every one of our new editions is that the latest thinking, debate, and insight are included. This new edition adheres to this concept of currency. Content is updated in such areas as cultural diversity, competitiveness, globalization, empowerment, organizational learning, performance-based rewards, managing information technology, virtual organizations, electronic commerce, strategic decision making, innovation, flexible organizational and job design, contingency theory, ethical dilemmas, sexual harassment, politics and change, communication skills, enterpreneurship, and motivation.

- Coverage of ethics has been greatly expanded. Ethical issues are covered in many parts of the book as well as in our Close-Up boxes and end-of-chapter material.

- Our Close-Up boxes remain a favorite of students and teachers. Each chapter has two boxes. They report actual applications of the concepts and theories presented in the chapter. Wherever appropriate and feasible, we've adopted these two features to reflect the important issues of ethics, diversity, and international organizational behavior.

- Every chapter has been completely revised and updated. The content in the field of organizational behavior and management is constantly changing and is expanding. We want to capture currency along with a sense of history. Thus, the revision work concentrated on using current concepts along with proven approaches to managing behavior within organizations.

- Continuing attention to teaching also went into preparing the supplements for our book. We believe these are the best available. In developing and testing our supplements, we continually focus on the needs of both students and instructors. We want our supplements to add to students' understanding while simultaneously enabling the instructor to teach an exciting course. Our Instructor's Manual, Lecture Resource Manual, Test Bank, Computerized Test Service, and Pow-

erPoint® Presentation Software comprise a total system to enhance learning and teaching. Furthermore, we have increased the number of objective questions in the Test Bank to approximately 100 per chapter.

Organizations: Behavior, structure, and processes on the Web

There are numerous resources relevant to this course and its topic areas that can be found on the World Wide Web. Listed below by topic are some of the thousands of sites that can enhance your learning. We provide these addresses and encourage you to take a look at those sites that suit your interest.

Communications
www.genelevine.com/papers/18.html
st1.yahoo.com/forleaders/emcom.html
www.leadsolutions.com
www.acertraining.com.au/peopleskills.html
www.members.tripod.com/~cooperate/
impcom.html
www.ee.ed.ac.uk/~gerard/Management/
art7.html

Conflict Resolution
www.geocities.com/Athens/8945/sycho.html
www.cmhc.com/psyhelp/chap13.html
www.commnet.edu/QVCTC/classes.conflict.
author.html
web.utk.edu/~susanart

Goal Setting
www.andersonplan.com.au/wb/goals1.
html#Smart
www.mindzone.net/special_report.html
www.mindtools.com/page6.html
www.gapmtn.com/goalsetting.html
www.adv-leadership-grp.com
www.bouldercycling.com
www.gsu.edu/~gsolnmm/

Motivation
www.qmtheory.com
www.engr.uark.edu/~whl/herzberg.html
www.com/criv/motivate.html
www.mcrel.org/products/noteworthy/
barbaram.html/
www.epic.com/MOTIV/MOTIVTIP>HTML
www.motivateus.com/
www.themms.com

//miinc.com
www.consumermotivation.com

Empowerment
www.empowerment-now.com
www.innovint.com
www.peoplepositive.com
//members.aol.com/empower16/steps.html
www.empowermentworks.com/
index.html#programs
www.timsystem.com/timesystem/methods/
book/empowerm.html
www.city.grande-prairie.ab.ca/self_emp.html

Leadership
www.oise.on.ca/%7Ebwillard/leadaid.html
www.leadershipmanagement.com/
www.onnow.com/events/3769.shtml
www.cmd-glg.com/
www.communityleadership.org/overview.html
www.emergingleader.com
www.balacreates.com
www.newleadership.com
www.lios.org/
www.np.ac.sg
www.leadership.mindgarden

Teams
www.oeg.net/twkmod.html
www.teamresources.com/
www.yorkteam.com/custom.html
www.paintballarena.com/action.html
www.iain.co.uk/mrt.html
www.hummerextreme.com/
CorporateMainMenu.html

Stress
www.onhealth.com/ch1/in-depth/item/
0.1007.2557.00html
www.health-net.com/stress.html
//primusweb.com/fitnesspartner/library/
weight/stresmgt.html
www.mediconsult.com/stress/shareware
www.mindtools.com/smpage.html
www.stressfree.com
www.gday-mate.com
www.lindaland.com/stressbook/bookindex.html
www.arc.sbc.edu/stress.html
//hammock.ifas.ufl.edu/txt/fairs/30922
www.tcfn.org/cbestheart/articles/workst~1.html
//fitlife.com/health/stress.shtml

Framework of this edition

This book is organized and presented in a sequence based on the three previously cited characteristics common to all organizations: behavior, structure, and processes. This framework has been maintained based on the responses from numerous users of previous editions. However, in this edition, each major part has been presented as a self-contained unit and can therefore be presented in whatever sequence the instructor prefers. Some instructors present the chapters on structure first, followed by those on behavior and processes. The text is easily adaptable to these individual preferences. The book concludes with an Appendix which reviews research procedures and techniques used in studying organizational behavior.

Contributors to this edition

Macgorine A. Cassell, Fairmont State College; James W. Fairfield-Sonn, University of Hartford; Mitchell J. Hartson, Florida Institute of Technology; Mary Giovannini, Truman State University; and Monty L. Lynn, Abilene Christian University.

Reviewers of previous editions

Jeffrey Glazer, San Diego State University; Eugene H. Hunt, Virginia Commonwealth University; William D. Murry, SUNY at Binghamton; Stanley J. Stough, Southeast Missouri State University; William E. Stratton, Idaho State University; Harold Strauss, University of Miami; Harry A. Taylor, Capitol College; Betty Velthouse, University of Michigan-Flint; and Diana Ting Liu Wu, Saint Mary's College of California. Ginger Roberts was invaluable in making sure everything was done correctly. Of course, we are responsible for any errors that may be present.

James L. Gibson
John M. Ivancevich
James H. Donnelly, Jr.

CONTENTS IN BRIEF

CONTENTS

Part 1

Introduction

Chapter 1

Chapter 2

Part 2

Behavior within Organizations: The Individual

Chapter 4

Part 3

**Behavior within Organizations:
Groups and Interpersonal Influence**

Chapter 8

Chapter 9

Part 4

The Structure and Design of Organizations

Chapter 13

Organization Structure

Chapter 14

Designing Productive and Motivating Jobs   348

Part 5

The Processes of Organizations

No. 1

Introduction

Chapter 1

The Study of Organizations

Learning Objectives

After completing Chapter 1, you should be able to:

Define
The term *organizational behavior*.

Explain
The contingency approach to managing individuals' behavior within an organizational setting.

Identify
Why managing workplace behavior in the United States is likely to be different from managing workplace behavior in another country, such as Germany.

Compare
The goal, systems, and multiple-constituency approaches to effectiveness.

Describe
The type of environmental forces that make it necessary for organizations to initiate changes.

Years ago when change was slow, markets were concentrated in a handful of countries, and stability was the

rule rather than the exception, an organizational approach that emphasized top-down hierarchy, rules and regulations, and authority in the hands of executives dominated.[1] Ford Motors, Sears Roebuck, General Electric, and IBM, organizational giants that dominated the market, used a rigid hierarchy system from top management to operating-level employees to accomplish their goals. In the 1970s everything in the environment such as government regulations, information technology, global competitors, union strength and influence, and customer demands and needs changed, and pressures for change in how organizations operate dramatically increased. Unfortunately, as we move into the 21st century, many organizations have failed to change or adapt to their more turbulent environments.

This book is about organizations and how they operate in a world that is rapidly changing. We will focus our attention throughout this book on people working within organizations or interacting with them from outside. People working together or contributing individually within organizations, large and small, have built pyramids, city-states, spacecraft, running shoes, automobiles, and entire industries. Each of us spends much of our life working for or conducting transactions with organizations—restaurants, schools, medical clinics, Federal Express, General Motors, the Internal Revenue Service, and Walt Disney are a few examples.

Jack Welch the chief executive officer (CEO) of General Electric, has become a role model for managers worldwide as he gradually restructured his firm.[2] Welch evolved from a hard-edged authoritarian to a more people-sensitive leader. Welch's regard for people and their importance is reflected in his statement:

The talents of our people are greatly underestimated and their skills are underutilized. Our biggest task is to fundamentally redefine our relationship with our employees. The objective is to build a place where people have the freedom to be creative, where they feel a real sense of accomplishment—a place that brings out the best in everybody.

People and how they work individually and together is what this book will focus upon. The story of Aaron Feuerstein in the Close-up clearly shows that putting people first can have dramatic positive effects for an organization.

Another characteristic of the book is that it is globally oriented. People working in organizations, producing goods and services, and contributing to a society is not a phenomenon of the United States only. Americans are no smarter than Germans, nor are they better workers than Brazilians. The fact that the United States became such a productive nation is largely the result of the application of sound management practices and techniques. Americans planned efficiently, organized systematically, and led workers effectively. Also, Americans came up with new techniques, new methods, and new styles of management that fit the time, the workforce, and the mission. In the first half of this century, productivity improvement was a state of mind.

As we move into the 21st century, managers around the world must recapture the feel, the state of mind, the passion, and the desire for being effective, producing high-quality products, and providing the best service possible. The importance of managing human resources hasn't been questioned. But attention to the details of managing people has slipped badly in the past two decades. Managing people effectively in organizations is the most essential ingredient for retaining a comfortable standard of living, remaining one of the world's economic leaders, and improving the quality of life for all citizens.[3] The quality of life is connected to the quality of work.

Whether we're talking about a pizza parlor in East Orange, New Jersey, a glass manufacturing plant in Monterrey, Mexico, or a cooperative produce shop in Vilnius, Lithuania, management within an organizational setting is important. The clerk in the Lithuanian produce shop wants to earn a fair day's pay for his work, the company president in Mexico has to purchase the best equipment to compete internationally, and the pizza parlor owner must motivate people to work. These individuals' work behaviors occur within organizations. To better understand these behaviors, we believe that we must formally study people, processes, and structure in relation to organizations.

C L O S E — U P

Putting People First

On December 11, 1995, a devastating fire swept through a mill complex in the heart of Lawrence, Massachusetts. Malden Mills, one of the few remaining textile firms operating in New England, owned the factory. The destruction threatened the 1,400 jobs at the mill. A thousand other jobs at plants in the community were also threatened. However, on the morning after the fire, the owner of Malden Mills, Aaron Feuerstein, promised his employees that their jobs were secure. Malden Mills would rebuild the ruined plant and would continue to provide full paychecks and medical benefits through the holiday season.

The fire and its aftermath generated a lot of national attention. Feuerstein's actions were praised and he was

regarded as a sensitive, caring leader. A few months later, a welder at the plant, declared of Feuerstein, "With what he's doing with Malden Mills, it's an honor to work in this place."

Putting people first was something that Feuerstein did with ease. In a region of the United States that had witnessed downsizing, reengineering, and outsourcing, Feuerstein's behavior was embraced, applauded, and held in high regard. Feuerstein had faith in his workers and showed how important they were to him.

Source: Adapted from Richard K. Lester, *The Productivity Edge* (New York: Norton, 1998), pp. 213–214 and *Boston Globe,* June 9, 1996, p. 85.

An **organization** is a coordinated unit consisting of at least two people who function to achieve a common goal or set of goals. This is what this book is about—organizations, large and small, domestic and global, successful and unsuccessful. Looking inside the organization at the people, processes, and structure will help enlighten the observer and will also reveal the inner workings of this unit that has been a main contributor to the standards of living enjoyed by people around the world.

Organizations

Entities that enable society to pursue accomplishments that can't be achieved by individuals acting alone.

Studying Organizational Behavior

Why does Ric Nunzio always seem to hire older employees for his pizza parlor? Why is Mary Beth Wheeler the best decision maker in selecting what piece of equipment to purchase? Why does Val Kupolus always complain that he's not paid enough to sell produce at the Vilnius produce stand? Such questions are studied, analyzed, and debated in the field called **organizational behavior.** The formal study of organizational behavior (also referred to as OB) began around 1948 to 1952. This still emerging field attempts to help managers understand people better so that productivity improvements, customer satisfaction, and a better competitive position can be achieved through better management practices.

The behavioral sciences—especially psychology, sociology, political science, and cultural anthropology—have provided the basic framework and principles for the field of organizational behavior. Each behavioral science discipline provides a slightly different focus, analytical framework, and theme for helping managers answer questions about themselves, nonmanagers, and environmental forces (e.g., competition, legal requirements, and social/political changes).

Organizational Behavior

The field of study that draws on theory, methods, and principles from various disciplines to learn about *individuals'* perceptions, values, learning capacities, and actions while working in *groups* and within the *organization;* analyzing the external environment's effect on the organization and its human resources, missions, objectives, and strategies.

Our multidisciplinary definition of organizational behavior illustrates a number of points. First, OB indicates that behaviors of people operate at individual, group, and organizational levels. This approach suggests that when studying OB we must identify clearly the level of analysis—individual, group, and/or organizational—being used. Second, OB is *multidisciplinary;* it uses principles, models, theories, and methods from other disciplines. The study of OB isn't a discipline or a generally accepted science with an established theoretical foundation. It's a field that only now is beginning to grow and develop in stature and impact. Third, there's a distinctly *humanistic orientation* within organizational behavior. People and their attitudes, perceptions, learning capacities, feelings, and goals are important to the organization. Fourth, the field of OB is *performance oriented*. Why is performance low or high? How can performance be improved? Can training enhance on-the-job performance? These are important issues facing managers. Fifth, the *external environment* is seen as having significant impact on organizational behavior. Sixth, since the field of OB relies heavily on recognized disciplines, the *scientific method* is important in studying variables and relationships. As the scientific method has been applied to research on organizational behavior, a set of principles and guidelines on what constitutes good research has emerged.[4] Finally, the field has a distinctive *applications orientation;* it concerns providing useful answers to questions that arise in the context of managing operations.

Organizational behavior has evolved into an applied set of behavioral science concepts, models, and techniques. The predominant contributors to OB—psychology, social psychology, sociology, political science, and anthropology—have contributed to our understanding and use of OB in organizational selling. Figure 1–1 presents an illustration of some of the major contributions of the behavioral sciences to the study and application of OB.

To help you learn how to manage individuals and groups as resources of organizations, this book focuses on *the behavior of individuals and groups, organizational structure and job design, and processes.* Developing the model presented in this book required the use of several assumptions. These assumptions are explained briefly in the following paragraphs, which precede the model.[5]

Figure 1–1

Contributions to the Study and Application of OB

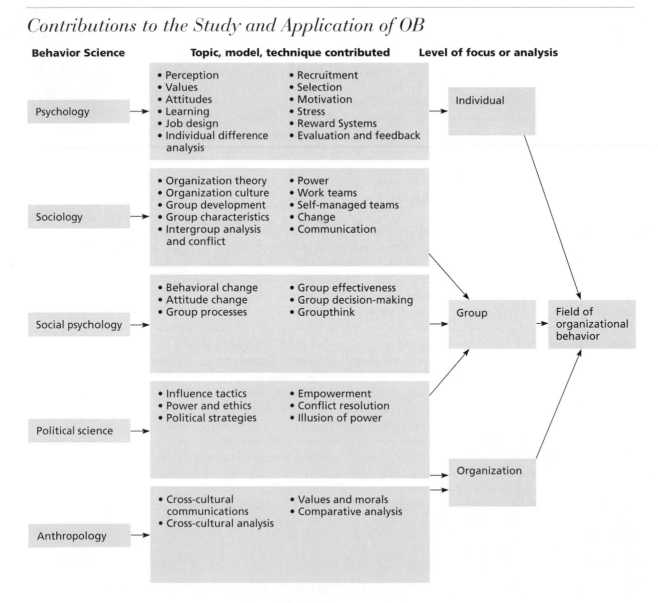

Learning about behavior within organizations can help provide skills of observation, prediction, and implementation. Also, any reader interested in pursuing a career in management will want to know as much as possible about behavior and how to properly apply leadership principles in an organizational setting.

Organizational behavior follows principles of human behavior

The effectiveness of any organization is influenced greatly by human behavior. People are a resource common to all organizations. The pizza parlor, the glass manufacturing plant, and the produce stand employ and interact with people.

One important principle of psychology is that each person is different. Each has unique perceptions, personality, and life experiences. People have different ethnic backgrounds, different capabilities for learning and for handling responsibility, and different attitudes, beliefs, and aspiration levels. We've moved from an era in which large portions of the workforce were middle-aged men who spoke only English to an era of diversity. Today's workforce doesn't look, think, or act like the workforce of the past.[6] To be effective, managers of organizations must view each employee or member as a unique embodiment of all these behavioral and cultural factors. Many culturally diverse individuals are spread throughout the workforce.

Organizations are social systems

The relationships among individuals and groups in organizations create expectations for individuals' behavior. These expectations result in certain roles that must be performed. Some people must perform leadership roles, while others must participate in the roles of followers. Middle managers, because they have both superiors and subordinates, must perform both roles. Organizations have systems of authority, status, and power, and people in organizations have varying needs from each system. Groups in organizations also have a powerful impact on individual behavior and on organizational performance.

Multiple factors shape organizational behavior

A person's behavior in any situation involves the interaction of that individual's personal characteristics and the characteristics of the situation. Thus, identifying all of the factors is time-consuming and difficult; frequently, the task is impossible.

To help us identify the important managerial factors in organizational behavior, we use the **contingency** (or *situational*) **approach**. The basic idea of the contingency approach is that there's no one best way to manage; a method that's very effective in one situation may not work at all in others. The contingency approach has grown in popularity because research has shown that given certain characteristics of a job and certain characteristics of the people doing the job, some management practices work better than others. Thus, the Mexican glass manufacturing plant's manager of operations faced with a poorly performing group doesn't assume that a particular approach will work. In applying the contingency approach, he diagnoses the characteristics of the individuals and groups involved, the organizational structure, and his own leadership style before deciding on a solution.

Contingency Approach

Approach to management that believes there's no one best way to manage in every situation and managers must find different ways that fit different situations.

Structure and processes affect organizational behavior and the emergent culture

Structure

Blueprint that indicates how people and jobs are grouped together in an organization. Structure is illustrated by an organization chart.

Processes

Activities that breathe life into organization structure. Common processes are communication, decision making, socialization, and career development.

www.nikebiz. com

www.wal-mart. com

An organization's **structure** is the formal pattern of how its people and jobs are grouped. Structure often is illustrated by an organization chart. **Processes** are activities that give life to the organization chart. Communication, decision making, and organization development are examples of processes in organizations. Sometimes, understanding process problems such as breakdowns in communication and decision making will result in a more accurate understanding of organizational behavior than will simply examining structural arrangements.

The pattern of basic assumptions used by individuals and groups to deal with the organization and its environment is called its *culture*. In straightforward terms, the organization's culture is its personality, atmosphere, or "feel." The culture of an organization defines appropriate behavior and bonds, it motivates individuals, and it governs the way a company processes information, internal relations, and values. It functions at all levels from the subconscious to the visible. A firm's culture has been likened to one of those ink blots in which we see what we want to see.[7] A firm's culture results in shared thoughts, feelings, and talk about the organization. Nike employees share norms about dress code, business practices, and promotion systems. Wal-Mart associates share emotions about working for the chain and coming to work on time with a positive attitude. It's the sharing that bonds employees together and creates a feeling of togetherness.[8]

Cultures of organizations can be positive or negative. An organization's culture is positive if it helps to improve productivity. A negative culture can hinder behavior, disrupt group effectiveness, and hamper the impact of a well-designed organization.

Effective managers know what to look for in terms of structure, process, and culture and how to understand what they find. Therefore, managers must develop diagnostic skills; they must be trained to identify conditions symptomatic of a problem requiring further attention. Problem indicators include declining profits, declining quantity or quality of work, increases in absenteeism or tardiness, and negative employee attitudes. Each of these problems is an issue of organizational behavior.

A Model for Managing Organizations: Behavior, Structure, and Processes

Figure 1–2 shows how the many topics covered in this book can be combined into a meaningful framework for studying organizational behavior.

The organization's environment

Figure 1–1 draws attention to the organization's environment; that is, to the relationships between organizations and the society that creates and sustains them. Within a society, many factors influence an organization, and management must be responsive to them. Every organization must respond to the needs of its customers or clients, to legal and political constraints, and to economic and technological changes. The model reflects environmental forces interacting within the organization. Throughout our discussion of each aspect of the model, we identify and examine the relevant environmental factors.

Figure 1–2

Plan for the Book

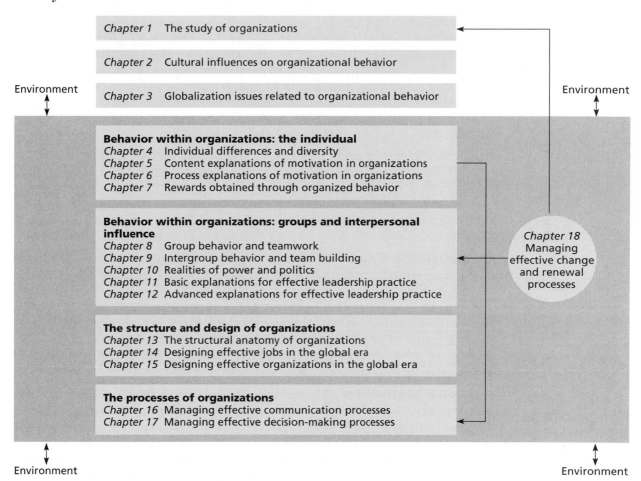

Economic and market circumstances and technological innovations make up an organization's environment, as do federal, state, and local legislation and political, social, and cultural conditions external to the organization. Together, these components of an environment influence how an organization operates, as well as how it is structured.

Managers increasingly work in an unpredictable economic environment. It is now important for managers to respond quickly to changing economic conditions in other countries. Also, the dramatic and unexpected consequences of technological innovations require astute management attention and action. For example, since the transistor was invented in 1947, digital technology has been coming faster and more often. Computing devices are getting smaller, cheaper, and more powerful. These devices, combined with databases, multimedia interfaces, and software, are impacting every profession, company, and business practice. Daimler-Benz, for example, has already designed an Internet-ready car and in Germany offers wireless on-board computers that use global positioning satellites to give vocal directions to any destination.

Increased government regulations have impacted management's actions in production and employment practices. Foreign trade tariffs, occupational safety and health guidelines, and equal employment opportunities influence the way a firm conducts business.

Behavior within organizations

THE INDIVIDUAL   Individual performance is the foundation of organizational performance. Understanding individual behavior is, therefore, critical for effective management, as illustrated in the following account:

Ted Johnson has been a field representative for a major drug manufacturer since he graduated from college seven years ago. He makes daily calls on physicians, hospitals, clinics, and pharmacies. Ted's sales of his firm's major drugs have increased, and he has won three national sales awards given by the firm. Yesterday, Ted was promoted to sales manager for a seven-state region. He'll no longer be selling but instead will be managing 15 other representatives. His sales team includes men and women, Caucasians, Hispanics, Blacks, and Asians. Ted accepted the promotion because he believes he knows how to motivate and lead salespeople. He comments, "I know the personality of the salesperson. They are special people. I know their values and attitudes and what it takes to motivate them. I know I can motivate a sales force."

In his new job, Ted Johnson will be trying to maximize the individual performances of 15 sales representatives. In doing so, he will be dealing with several facets of individual behavior.

Individual Characteristics   Because organizational performance depends on individual performance, managers such as Ted Johnson must have more than a passing knowledge of the determinants of individual performance. Psychology and social psychology contribute relevant knowledge about the relationships among attitudes, perceptions, personality, values, and individual performance. Learning to manage cultural diversity, such as that found among Ted's 15 sales representatives, has become more and more important in recent years. Managers can't ignore the necessity for acquiring and acting on knowledge of the individual characteristics of both their subordinates and themselves.

Individual Motivation   Motivation and ability to work interact to determine performance. Motivation theory attempts to explain and predict how individuals' behavior is aroused, sustained, and stopped. Unlike Ted Johnson, not all managers and behavioral scientists agree on what is the best theory of motivation. In fact, the complexity of motivation may make an all-encompassing theory of how it occurs impossible. But managers must still try to understand it. They must be concerned with motivation because they must be concerned with performance.

Rewards and Appraisal   One of the most powerful influences on individual performance is an organization's reward system. Management can use rewards to increase present employees' performance. It can also use rewards to attract skilled employees to the organization. Performance appraisals, paychecks, raises, and bonuses are important aspects of the reward system, but they aren't the only aspects. Ted Johnson makes this point clear in the preceding account when he states, "I know what it takes to get them to perform." Performance of the work itself can provide employees with rewards, particularly if job performance leads to a sense of personal responsibility, autonomy, and meaningfulness. These intrinsic rewards are also supplemented with extrinsic rewards, or what an organization, a manager, or a group can provide a person in terms of monetary and nonmonetary factors.

GROUPS AND INTERPERSONAL INFLUENCE   Group behavior and interpersonal influence are also powerful forces affecting organizational performance, as the following account shows:

During her two and one-half years as a teller in a small-town bank in Fort Smith, Arkansas, Kelly McCaul developed close personal friendships with her co-workers.

These friendships existed outside the job as well. Two months ago Kelly was promoted to branch manager. She was excited about the new challenge. She began the job with a great deal of optimism and believed her friends would be genuinely happy for her and supportive of her efforts. But since she became branch manager, things haven't been quite the same. Kelly can't spend nearly as much time with her friends because she's often away from the branch attending management meetings at the main office . Kelly senses that some of her friends have been acting a little differently toward her lately.

Recently Kelly said, "I didn't know that being a part of the management team could make that much difference. Frankly, I never really thought about it. I guess I was naive. I'm getting a totally different perspective on the business and have to deal with problems I never knew about."

Kelly's promotion has made her a member of more than one group. In addition to being part of her old group of friends at the branch, she's also a member of the management team. She's finding out that group behavior and expectations have a strong impact on individual behavior and interpersonal influence.

Group Behavior   Groups form because of managerial action and because of individual efforts. Managers create work groups to carry out assigned jobs and tasks. Such groups, created by managerial decisions, are termed *formal groups*. The group that Kelly McCaul manages at her branch is a group of this kind.

Groups also form as a consequence of employees' actions. Such groups, termed *informal groups*, develop around common interests and friendships. Kelly's bowling group is an informal group. Though not a part of the organization, groups of this kind can affect organizational and individual performance. The effect can be positive or negative, depending on the group members' intentions. If the group at Kelly's branch decided informally to slow the work pace, this norm would exert pressure on individuals who wanted to remain a part of the group. Effective managers recognize the consequences of individuals' needs for affiliation.

Intergroup Behavior and Conflict   As groups function and interact with other groups, each develops a unique set of characteristics, including structure, cohesiveness, roles, norms, and processes. The group in essence creates its own culture. As a result, groups may cooperate or compete with other groups, and intergroup competition can lead to conflict. If the management of Kelly's bank instituted an incentive program with cash bonuses to the branch bringing in the most new customers, this might lead to competition and conflict among the branches. While conflict among groups can have beneficial results for an organization, too much or the wrong kinds of intergroup conflict can have negative results. Thus, managing intergroup conflict is an important aspect of managing organizational behavior.

Power and Politics   Power is the ability to get someone to do something you want done or to make things happen in the way you want them to happen. Many people in our society are uncomfortable with the concept of power. Some are deeply offended by it. This is because the essence of power is control over others. To many Americans and a growing number of people around the world, this is an offensive thought.

But power does exist in organizations. Managers derive power from both organizational and individual sources. Kelly McCaul has power by virtue of her position in the formal hierarchy of the bank. She controls performance evaluations and salary increases. However, she may also have power because her co-workers respect and admire her abilities and expertise. Managers must become comfortable with the concept of power as a reality in organizations and managerial roles.

Leadership   Leaders exist within all organizations. They may be found in formal groups, like the bank's Kelly McCaul, or in informal groups. They may be managers or nonmanagers. The importance of effective leadership for obtaining individual, group, and organizational performance is so critical that there has been much effort to determine the causes of such leadership. Some people believe that effective leadership depends on traits and certain behaviors, separately and in combination; other people believe that one leadership style is effective in all situations; still others believe that each situation requires a specific leadership style.

Quality and leadership concepts have been found to be inseparable. Without effective leadership practices, instilling concern about customer-focused quality is difficult, if not impossible.

The structure and design of organizations

To work effectively in organizations, managers must clearly understand the organizational structure. Viewing an organization chart on a piece of paper or framed on a wall, we see only a configuration of positions, job duties, and lines of authority among the parts of an organization. However, organizational structures can be far more complex, as the following account shows:

> *Dan Sharky was appointed vice president of quality at a small manufacturing shop in Orange, New Jersey. He has spent about three months studying the organization which produces generator parts sold throughout the United States, Canada, Mexico, Poland, Hungary, and Russia. Dan wants to instill more of a teamwork concept and an interest in quality improvement. This would be quite a change from the present rigid departmental structure that now exists in the company. His unit leaders are Hispanic, Italian, German, and Vietnamese. They each have voiced opinions that management discriminates against them and isn't ethnically aware. Dan wants to correct this perception and wants each unit leader to be a part of his team. He must change perceptions, redesign the organization, develop a team spirit, and produce high-quality products in an increasingly competitive market.*

An organization's structure is the formal pattern of activities and interrelationships among the various subunits of the organization. Our model includes two important aspects of organizational structure: job design and organizational design.

JOB DESIGN   Job design refers to the process by which managers specify the contents, methods, and relationships of jobs to satisfy both organizational and individual requirements. Dan must define the content and duties of the unit leader's position and the relationship of the position to each member of his team.

ORGANIZATIONAL DESIGN   Organizational design refers to the overall organizational structure. Dan plans to change the philosophy and orientation of the teams. This effort will create a new *structure* of tasks, authority, and interpersonal relationships that he believes will channel the behavior of individuals and groups toward improved quality performance.

The processes of organizations

Certain behavioral processes give life to an organizational structure. When these processes don't function well, unfortunate problems can arise, as this account shows:

> *When she began to major in marketing as a junior in college, Sandy Sherman knew that someday she would work in that field. Once she completed her M.B.A., she was more positive than ever that marketing would be her life's work. Because of her excellent academic record, she received several outstanding job offers. She accepted the offer*

from one of the nation's largest consulting firms, believing that this job would allow her to gain experience in several areas of marketing and to engage in a variety of exciting work. Her last day on campus, she told her favorite professor, "This has got to be one of the happiest days of my life, getting such a great career opportunity."

Recently, while visiting the college placement office, the professor was surprised to hear that Sandy had told the placement director that she was looking for another job. Since she'd been with the consulting company less than a year, the professor was somewhat surprised. He called Sandy to find out why she wanted to change jobs. She told him, "I guess you can say my first experience with the real world was a 'reality shock.' All day long, I sit and talk on the phone, asking questions and checking off the answers. In graduate school, I was trained to be a manager, but here I'm doing what any high school graduate can do. I talked to my boss, and he said that all employees have to pay their dues. Well, why didn't they tell me this while they were recruiting me? A little bit of accurate communication would have gone a long way."

Our model includes two behavioral processes that contribute to effective organizational performance: communication, and decision making.

COMMUNICATION Organizational survival is related to management's ability to receive, transmit, and act on information. The communication process links the organization to its environment as well as to its parts. Information flows to and from the organization and within the organization. Information integrates the activities within the organization. Sandy Sherman's problem arose because the information that flowed *from* the organization was different from the information that flowed *within* the organization.

DECISION MAKING The quality of decision making in an organization depends on selecting proper goals and identifying means for achieving them. With good integration of *behavioral* and *structural* factors, management can increase the probability that high-quality decisions are made. Sandy Sherman's experience illustrates inconsistent decision making by different organizational units (human resources and marketing) in hiring new employees. Organizations rely on individual decisions as well as group decisions. Effective management requires knowledge about both types of decisions.

Since managerial decisions affect people's lives and well-being, ethics play a major role.[9] Was Sandy provided with realistic and truthful information about the job? If not, was there a breach of ethics on the part of the recruiter? Since managers have power by virtue of their positions, the potential for unethical decision making is present. With all of the newspaper and TV accounts of scandals around the world in business, government, medicine, politics, and the law, there's evidence that ethics in terms of decision making need serious attention.

Ethics suggest that managers when faced with a problem, situation, or opportunity requiring a choice among several alternatives, must evaluate their decision on what course to follow as good or bad, right or wrong, ethical or unethical.[10] Conflict between an individual manager's personal moral philosophy and values and the culture and values of an organization regularly arise and make decision making a difficult endeavor. At Levi Strauss, ethics-centered management has become a part of the firm's value system as discussed in the Close-Up box on page 14.

Managerial decision making is permeated by ethical issues. Managers have power and authority and when these factors exist there is potential for wrong and right, good and evil. A few indications that managerial decisions are linked to ethics are:[11]

- Managers make decisions that affect the lives, careers, and well-being of people.
- Managers make decisions involving the allocation of limited resources.

- Managers design, implement, and evaluate rules, policies, programs, and procedures.
- Managers in making decisions display to others their moral and personal values.

Examples of managerial decision making and their link to ethics will become obvious throughout the book. Skilled managers making decisions consider ethics to be an important factor to consider when making choices that impact individuals, groups, and organizations.[12]

Perspectives on Effectiveness

Managers and others who have interests in whether organizations perform effectively can focus on one or all of three perspectives. The most basic level, *individual effectiveness,* emphasizes the task performance of specific employees or members of the organization. The tasks to be performed are parts of jobs or positions in the organization. Managers routinely assess individual effectiveness through performance evaluation processes to determine who should receive salary increases, promotions, and other rewards available in the organization.

Individuals seldom work alone, in isolation from others in the organization. Usually, employees work in groups, necessitating yet another perspective on effectiveness, *group effectiveness.* In some instances, group effectiveness is simply the sum of the contributions of all its members. For example, a group of scientists working alone on unrelated projects would be effective to the extent that each individual scientist is effective. In other instances, group effectiveness is more than the sum of individual contributions (for example, an assembly line that produces a product or service that combines the contributions of each individual working on the line). The term *synergy* refers to instances when the sum of individual contributions exceeds the simple summation of them.

The third perspective is *organizational effectiveness.* Organizations consist of individuals and groups; therefore, organizational effectiveness consists of individual and group effectiveness. But organizational effectiveness is more than the sum of individual and group

---

C L O S E — U P

Is the Levi Strauss & Co. Ethical Approach Sound Management?

Levi Strauss & Co. is a company that has a reputation for being progressive, socially responsible, visionary, or flaky. The perspective one takes in viewing or analyzing the company depends on how the person feels about the successes and failures of the firm. Instead of making a judgment about the quality of the company's management thinking and application, we offer a few of the firm's positions on various concepts. Make your own judgment after considering the position taken by the company.

Diversity Levi Strauss & Co. values a diverse workforce (e.g., age, sex, ethnic group, religious affiliation). Diversity will be sought, rewarded, and recognized whenever possible.

Ethical practices Management will model standards of acceptable ethical behavior. These behaviors will be practiced throughout the firm.

Empowerment Levi Strauss & Co. will increase the authority and responsibility of employees closest to its customers.

Communications In every memo or interaction, Levi Strauss & Co. managers must strive to clearly communicate what is expected of employees to accomplish goals.

Levi Strauss & Co. believes that organizations can be diverse, ethical, participative, and profitable. No American company to date has embraced these concepts as intensely as Levi Strauss has in the past decade.

Source: Levi Strauss & Co. Annual Reports, 1995 and 1994; "Managing by Values: Is Levi Strauss' Approach Visionary—or Flaky?" *Business Week,* August 1, 1994, pp. 46–52.

 www.levistrauss.com

Figure 1–3

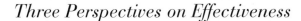

Figure 1–3

Three Perspectives on Effectiveness

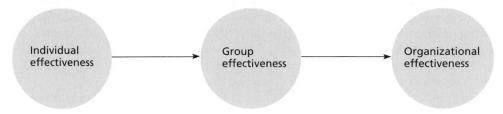

effectiveness. Through synergistic effects, organizations obtain higher levels of effectiveness than the sum of their parts. In fact, the rationale for organizations as a means for doing society's work is that they can do more work than is possible through individual effort.[13]

Figure 1–3 reveals the relationship among the three perspectives on effectiveness. The connecting arrows imply that group effectiveness depends on individual effectiveness, while organizational effectiveness depends on individual and group effectiveness. The exact relationships among the three perspectives vary depending on such factors as the type of organization, the work it does, and the technology used in doing that work. Figure 1–3 recognizes the three perspectives' synergistic effects. Thus, group effectiveness is larger than the sum of individual effectiveness because of the synergies realized through joint efforts.

Management's job is to identify the *causes* of organizational, group, and individual effectiveness. The distinction between causes of effectiveness and indicators of effectiveness can be difficult for both managers and researchers.[14] The term *effectiveness* derives from the term *effect* and we use the term in the context of cause-and-effect relationships. As Figure 1–4 shows, each level of effectiveness can be considered a variable caused by other variables. For example, a person's motivation, ability, skill, knowledge, attitude, and stress level causes him or her to be effective. There are of course many other factors that cause an individual to be effective. The variables in Figure 1–4 are only a sample for illustrative purposes.

Figure 1–4

Causes of Effectiveness

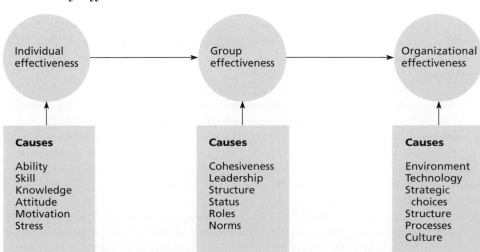

Management and organizational behavior literature has reported various theories and research on causes of effectiveness at each of the three levels of analysis. For example, causes of individual effectiveness include ability, skill, knowledge, attitude, motivation, and stress. These individual differences account for differences in effectiveness in individual performance. Some of the more usual causes of differences in group and organizational effectiveness are also noted in Figure 1–4.[15] These and other potential causes of effectiveness are discussed at length in subsequent chapters. But the reality of organizational life is that there are few unambiguous cause-and-effect relationships. In most instances, evaluation judgments must take into account multiple causes and circumstances.[16]

How then can managers increase and maintain individual, group, and organizational effectiveness? The following section addresses this question by describing the nature of managerial work.

The Nature of Managerial Work

Many individual writers (far too many to survey completely) have contributed theories describing what managers do or prescribing what they should do.[17] Here we'll rely on the ideas of a group of writers who constitute the Classical School of Management.[18] We refer to these writers as *classical* because they were the first to describe managerial work. Writers of the Classical School proposed that managerial work consists of distinct, yet interrelated, *functions* which taken together constitute the *managerial process.* The view that management should be defined, described, and analyzed in terms of what managers (functions and processes) do has prevailed to this day, but with considerable modification as management functions and processes change in response to changing times and circumstances.

Henry Mintzberg's influential study identified three primary and overlapping managerial roles: interpersonal role, decisional role, and informational role.[19] Each role has several related activities that distinguish one role from the others. But interpersonal role activities clearly involve the manager with other people both inside and outside the organization. Decisional role activities involve the manager in making decisions about operational matters, resource allocation, and negotiations with the organization's constituencies. The informational role involves the manager as a receiver and sender of information to a variety of individuals and institutions.

The concept of management developed here is based upon the assumption that the necessity for managing arises whenever work is specialized and undertaken by two or more persons. Under such circumstances, the specialized work must be *coordinated,* creating the necessity for managerial work. The nature of managerial work is then to coordinate the work of *individuals, groups,* and *organizations* by performing four management functions: *planning, organizing, leading,* and *controlling.* Figure 1–5 depicts management's contribution to effectiveness.

The list of management functions can be increased to include other functions, but these four can be defined with sufficient precision to differentiate them and, at the same time, to include others that management writers have proposed. For example, some managers and organizations include functions such as decision making, staffing, coordinating, implementing, and executing. Remember, management and organizational behavior aren't exact sciences with uniform language and definitions. The various definitions of *management* reflect the specific expectations of the people who practice management in specific organizations.[20]

While the list we propose might be arbitrary, managers at all levels of the organization generally perform these functions. The relative importance of one function vis-à-vis another function differs depending upon where the manager is in the organization and

Figure 1–5

Management's Contribution to Effectiveness

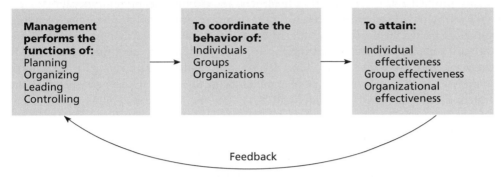

what problems and issues the manager faces. But the ability to discern the relative importance of planning, organizing, leading, and controlling may distinguish effective managers from ineffective managers.[21]

Planning effective performance

The planning function includes defining the ends to be achieved and determining *appropriate means to achieve the defined ends.* The necessity of this function follows from the nature of organizations as purposive (end-seeking) entities. Planning activities can be complex or simple, implicit or explicit, impersonal or personal. For example, a sales manager forecasting demand for the firm's major product may rely upon complex econometric models or casual conversations with salespersons in the field.

The intended outcomes of planning activities are mutual understandings about what the organization's members should be attempting to achieve. These understandings may be reflected in the form of complicated plans specifying the intended results or they may be reflected in a general agreement among the members.

Planning involves specifying not only where the organization is going but also how it's to get there. In specific terms, alternatives must be analyzed and evaluated in terms of criteria that follow from the mission goals. Thus, managers by their own decisions can affect how they and their organizations will be evaluated. They determine what ends are legitimate and, therefore, what criteria are relevant.[22] And once appropriate means are determined, the next managerial function—organizing—must be undertaken.

Organizing effective performance

The organizing function includes all managerial activities that translate required planned activities into a structure of tasks and authority. In a practical sense, the organizing function involves (1) designing the responsibility and authority of each individual job and (2) determining which of these jobs will be grouped in specific departments. For example, managers of an engineering firm must determine what each engineer should do and what group each engineer will be assigned to. The organizing function's outcome is the organization structure.

The organization structure consists of many different individuals and groups performing different activities. These different activities must be integrated into a coordinated whole.[23] It's management's responsibility to devise integrating methods and processes. If the differences among jobs and departments aren't too great, then the simple exercise of authority is sufficient to integrate the differences. For example, a small yogurt shop's manager can easily integrate ordertakers' work by issuing directives. But the manager of a multiproduct, multidivisional organization must rely on more complex cross-functional teams, product and customer service managers, and electronic communications.[24]

The interrelationships between planning and organizing are apparent. The planning function results in determining organization ends and means; that is, it defines the "whats" and "hows." The organizing function results in determining the "whos" (who'll do what with whom to achieve the desired end results). The structure of tasks and authority should facilitate the fulfillment of planned results if the next management function, leading, is performed properly.

Leading effective performance

The leading function involves the manager in close day-to-day contact with individuals and groups. Thus, the leading function is uniquely personal and interpersonal. Though planning and organizing provide guidelines and directives in the form of plans, job descriptions, organization charts, and policies, it's people who do the work. And people are variable entities. They have unique needs, ambitions, personalities, and attitudes. Each person perceives the workplace and his job uniquely. Managers must take into account these unique perceptions and behaviors and somehow direct them toward common purposes. One thoughtful and sensitive observer of leadership behavior has encouraged managers to become more knowledgeable about human psychology as a means to more effective performance.[25]

Leading involves day-to-day interactions between managers and their subordinates. In these interactions the full panorama of human behavior is evident. Individuals work, play, communicate, compete, accept and reject others, join groups, leave groups, receive rewards, and cope with stress. Of all the management functions, leading is the most human-oriented. It's not surprising that the overwhelming bulk of organizational behavior theory and research relates to this function. And while much of the literature and conventional wisdom affirms the importance of leadership, we must recognize that there's evidence suggesting that leadership's importance is overrated.[26]

Leaders in executive positions represent the organization to its external constituencies. In this role, effective executive leaders use words and symbols to express the organization's abstract ideals and what it stands for. The organization's mission statement provides a starting point for performing this leadership role. But without the ability to use powerful language and metaphors, the executive leader will fail even if she has effective interpersonal skills.[27]

Controlling effective performance

The controlling function includes activities that managers undertake to ensure that actual outcomes are consistent with planned outcomes. Managers undertake control to determine *whether* intended results are achieved and if they aren't, *why* not. The conclusions managers reach because of their controlling activities are that the planning function was (and is) faulty or that the organizing function was (and is) not faulty, or both. Controlling is, then, the completion of a logical sequence. The activities that constitute controlling include employee selection and placement, materials inspection, performance evaluation, financial statement analysis, and other well-recognized managerial techniques.

The controlling function involves explicit consideration of effectiveness at all three levels: individual, group, and organizational. Performance evaluation involves comparisons of actual personnel performance against standards of performance. Managers judge as effective those employees who meet performance standards. Likewise, when supervisors focus on organizational groups such as production, sales, and engineering departments, they make judgments about whether these units have performed as expected (whether they've been effective). And at the highest level of performance, top managers judge the effectiveness of organizations.

The functions of management require technical and administrative skills. They also require human relations skills, the ability to deal with and relate to *people*. Organizational behavior literature stresses the importance of people. Many observers and practitioners of management believe that managing people effectively is the key to improving effectiveness of groups and organizations.

At every level, managers of organizations have the primary responsibility for attaining effective performance. We've seen that they can meet this responsibility by practicing with skill the four functions of management to identify the causes of effectiveness—accentuate the positive ones and eliminate the negative ones. But we must now think about the concept of effectiveness per se. What is it? How can we know it when we see it?

Three Ways to Think about Effectiveness

Thus far, we've assumed a definition of *effectiveness*. But effectiveness means different things to different people, whether in a theoretical or practical sense. Differences in its meaning reflect one's adherence to the goal approach, the systems theory approach, or the stakeholder approach.[28] Managers must be able to use each of these approaches to effectiveness when appropriate.

Goal approach to effectiveness

The **goal approach** to defining and evaluating effectiveness is the oldest and most widely used evaluation approach.[29] According to this approach, an organization exists to accomplish goals. An early and influential practitioner and writer in management and organizational behavior stated, "What we mean by effectiveness . . . is the accomplishment of recognized objectives of cooperative effort. The degree of accomplishment indicates the degree of effectiveness."[30] The idea that organizations, as well as individuals and groups, should be evaluated in terms of goal accomplishment has widespread commonsense and practical appeal. The goal approach reflects purposefulness, rationality, and achievement—the fundamental tenets of contemporary Western societies.

Goal Approach to Effectiveness

Perspective on effectiveness that emphasizes the central role of goal achievement as a criterion for assessing effectiveness.

Many management practices are based upon the goal approach. One widely used practice is management by objectives. According to this practice, managers specify in advance the goals that they expect their subordinates to accomplish and then evaluate periodically the degree to which they accomplish them. The actual specifics of management by objectives vary from case to case. In some cases, the manager and subordinate(s) discuss the objectives and attempt to reach mutual agreement. In other instances, the manager simply assigns the goals. Management by objectives can be useful whenever there's a strong relationship between job behavior and a measurable outcome, the objective.

The goal approach, for all its appeal and apparent simplicity, has problems.[31] A few recognized difficulties include:

1. Goal achievement isn't readily measurable for organizations that don't produce tangible outputs. For example, a college's goal is to provide a liberal education at a fair price. The question is, how would we know whether the college reaches that goal? What's a liberal education? What's a fair price?

2. Organizations attempt to achieve more than one goal, but achieving one goal often precludes or diminishes their ability to achieve other goals. A firm states that its goal is to maximize profit and to provide absolutely safe working conditions. These two goals are in conflict because one is achieved at the expense of the other.

3. The very existence of a common set of "official" goals to which all members are committed is questionable. Various researchers have noted the difficulty of obtaining consensus among managers as to their organization's specific goals.[32]

One of the narrowest views of effectiveness defines it as "the financial viability of an organization."[33] A financially viable organization can pay its bills as they're due; the more effective organization will have funds in reserve. This view's proponents state that even though it's narrow, it's still useful because it overcomes the limitations of the wider idea of the goal approach. For example, measuring financial viability is relatively easy compared with measuring management's "real" goals. Return on assets and return on equity are straightforward and readily available measures of firms' financial viability. Nonbusiness organizations have similar measures. Educational institutions can measure financial viability as revenue per student; government agencies can measure it as revenue per employee.[34] The idea that organizational effectiveness can be defined and measured simply has considerable appeal.

The goal approach exerts a powerful influence on the development of management and organizational behavior theory and practice. It's easy to say that managers should achieve the organization's goals. It's much more difficult to know how to do this. The alternative to the goal approach is the systems theory approach. Through systems theory, the concept of effectiveness can be defined in broader terms that enable managers to understand the causes of individual, group, and organizational effectiveness.

Systems theory approach to effectiveness

The term *system* is used in everyday conversations. A variety of meanings and interpretations are used to describe accounting systems, inventory control systems, a car's ignition system, an ecological system, and the U.S. tax system. Each system consists of elements or characteristics that interact. Thus, a **system** is a grouping of elements that individually establish relationships with each other and that interact with their environment both as individuals and as a collective.[35] Systems theorists propose that systems can be categorized three ways: (1) conceptual systems (a language); (2) concrete systems (machines); and (3) abstract systems (culture of an organization).

Systems

A grouping of elements that individually establish relationships with each other and that interact with their environment both as individuals and as a collective.

Managers in organizations use the notion of a system to view their internal and external world and how the parts relate and interact with each other.

By viewing the individuals, groups, structure, and processes of organizations in terms of a system, managers are able to identify common and uncommon themes that help explain the behavior and effectiveness of people. Identification of themes or patterns is important because it helps explain how effective an individual, group, or entire organization is in terms of goals.[36]

Systems theory enables us to describe organizations' internal and external behavior. Internally we can see how and why people inside organizations perform their individual and group tasks. Externally we can assess organizations' transactions with other organizations and institutions. All organizations acquire resources from the larger environment of which they're part and, in turn, provide the goods and services demanded by the larger environment. Managers must deal simultaneously with the internal and external aspects of organizational behavior. This essentially complex process can be simplified, for analytical purposes, by employing the basic concepts of systems theory.

In the context of systems theory, the organization is one element of a number of elements interacting interdependently. The flow of inputs and outputs is the basic starting point in describing the organization. In the simplest terms, the organization takes resources (inputs) from the larger system (environment), processes these resources, and returns them in changed form (output). Figure 1–6 displays the fundamental elements of the organization as a system.

Systems theory also stresses the organization's connection to the larger system of which it is a part. Every organization is part of an industry (a larger system), a society (a yet larger system), and, increasingly, a global economy (perhaps the largest system of all). All these systems make demands on their parts. These demands include more than simply demand for products of acceptable quality and quantity. Organizations must also satisfy the demands that their actions contribute to viable environments by promoting clean air and water, internal national stability by rebuilding riot-torn U.S. cities, and global political stability by investing in Eastern European economies. Thus, the organization can't simply produce a product or service to satisfy its customers; it must also produce actions and behaviors to satisfy other important components of the larger environment, the larger systems.

Systems theory can also describe behavior of individuals and groups. The "causes" of individual behavior are "inputs" arising from the workplace. For example, the cause could be a manager's directive to perform a certain task. The input (cause) is then processed by the individual's mental and psychological processes to produce a particular outcome. The outcome that the manager prefers is, of course, compliance with the directive, but depending upon the states of the individual's processes, the outcome could be noncompliance. Similarly, we could describe the behavior of a group in systems theory terms. For example, the behavior of a group of employees to unionize (outcome) could be explained in terms of perceived managerial unfairness in the assignment of work (input) and the state of the group's cohesiveness (process). We use the terms of systems theory throughout this text to describe individuals' and groups' behavior in organizations.

SYSTEMS THEORY AND FEEDBACK   The concept of the organization as a system that's related to a larger system introduces the importance of feedback. As noted already, the organization depends on the environment not only for its inputs but also for the acceptance of its outputs. Thus, the organization must develop means for adjusting to environmental demands. The means for adjustment are information channels that

Figure 1–6

The Basic Elements of a System

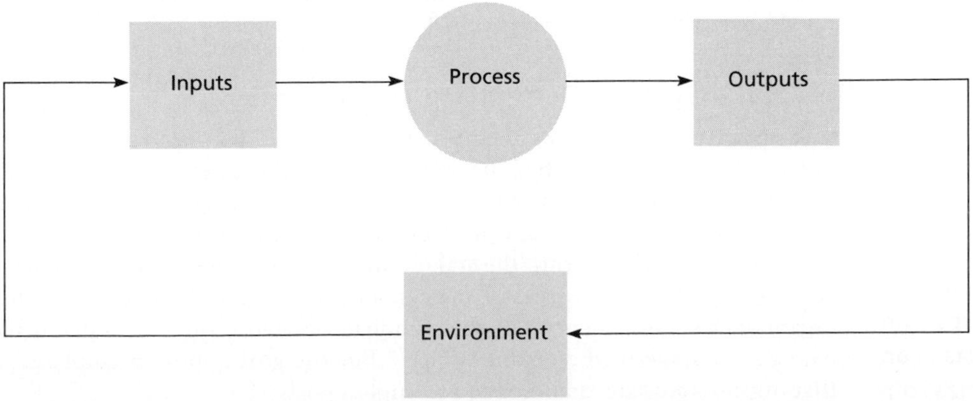

enable the organization to recognize these demands. For example, in business organizations, market research is an important feedback mechanism.

In simplest terms, *feedback* refers to information that reflects the outcomes of an act or a series of acts by an individual, group, or organization. Throughout this text, we'll see how important feedback is for reinforcing learning and developing personality, group behavior, and leadership. Systems theory emphasizes the importance of responding to the content of the feedback information.

EXAMPLES OF THE INPUT-OUTPUT CYCLE   The firm has two major categories of inputs: human and natural resources. Human inputs consist of the people who work in the firm: operating, staff, and managerial personnel. They contribute their time and energy to the organization in exchange for wages and other rewards, tangible and intangible. Natural resources consist of the nonhuman inputs to be processed or to be used in combination with the human element to provide other resources. A steel mill uses people and blast furnaces (along with other tools and machinery) to process iron ore into steel and steel products. An auto manufacturer takes steel, rubber, plastics, fabrics, and (in combination with people, tools, and equipment) makes cars. A firm survives as long as its output is purchased in the market in quantities at prices that enable it to replenish its depleted stock of inputs.

A university uses resources to teach students, to do research, and to provide technical information to society. A university's survival depends on its ability to attract students' tuition and taxpayers' dollars in sufficient amounts to pay the salaries of its faculty and staff and the other costs of resources. If a university's output is rejected by the larger environment so that students enroll elsewhere and the government uses tax dollars to support other public endeavors, or if a university is guilty of expending too many resources in relation to its output, it will cease to exist. Like a business, a university must provide the right output at the right price if it's to survive.[37]

As a final example, we'll describe a hospital in terms of systems theory. A hospital's inputs are its professional and administrative staff, equipment, supplies, and patients. Patients are processed by applying medical knowledge and treatment. To the extent that its patients are restored to the level of health consistent with the severity of their disease or injury, the hospital is effective.

Systems theory emphasizes two important considerations: (1) the ultimate survival of the organization depends on its ability to adapt to the demands of its environment; and (2) in meeting these demands, the total cycle of input-process-output must be the focus of managerial attention. Therefore, criteria of effectiveness must reflect both considerations and we must define *effectiveness* accordingly. The systems approach accounts for the fact that resources have to be devoted to activities that have little to do with achieving the organization's goal.[38] In other words, adapting to the environment and maintaining the input-process-output flow require that resources be allocated to activities that are only indirectly related to the organization's primary goal.

Stakeholder approach to effectiveness

Stakeholder Approach to Effectiveness

Perspective that emphasizes the relative importance of different groups' and individuals' interests in an organization.

The application of systems theory concepts to the discussion of organizational effectiveness identifies the importance of the external environment. Systems theory also identifies the importance of achieving a balance among the various parts of the system of which an organization is but one part. In practical and concrete terms, the **stakeholder approach** means achieving balance among the various parts of the system by satisfying the interests of the organization's constituency (all those individuals and groups of individuals who have a stake in the organization).[39] But the goal approach emphasizes that organizations are chartered to accomplish goals.

Individuals and groups of individuals having stakes in an organization include its employees (nonmanagers and managers), stockholders, directors, suppliers, creditors, officials at all levels of government, managers of competitive and cooperative organizations, and the general public. Each of these individuals and groups of individuals expects the organization to behave in ways that benefit them; these expectations may or may not be compatible with those of other individuals and groups. Given that an organization can be judged effective or ineffective depending upon who's making the judgment, how can managers ever achieve effectiveness in the sense of satisfying all the claims of the organization's constituencies?

One approach would be to state that there's no way to determine the relative importance of the constituent claims and that there are as many evaluations of effectiveness as there are individuals making judgments. This relativistic view assumes that all claims on the organization are valid and that no basis exists for ordering their importance, so no basis exists for making an overall judgment of organizational effectiveness.[40]

How then is management to act? One answer is provided by the idea that each of the stakeholder controls resources that are valuable to the organization. At any point in time, the resources they control are more or less important, and the organization is effective to the extent that it satisfies the interest of the group controlling the most important resource.[41] Thus stockholders' interests supersede employees' interests when the organization must acquire equity funds in order to survive. Or a government regulatory agency's interests supersede stockholders' interests when safety regulations require investment in safe working conditions. This view can be extended to a concept of the organization as an arena in which the different groups negotiate their claims by developing coalitions capable of combining the power of each member of the coalition. Managers of the organization achieve effectiveness by identifying the most powerful coalitions and satisfying the demands of the most influential members of those coalitions.

Whether the organization is effective when satisfying the most powerful group involves value judgment. And we shouldn't lose sight of the fact that all judgments of effectiveness involve value judgment. To state that one should satisfy the most powerful group at the expense of the least powerful group is to make a personal statement of what's ultimately important. Since many different sources of value judgments exist, we shouldn't expect any final answer to the question, Is the organization effective? Nor should we expect any final answer when the focus is individual and group effectiveness. Values reflect human judgments about what's important, but those judgments shift with individuals, place, and time.

One study of the applicability of multiple-constituency theory suggests that it may in fact integrate both the system and goal approaches to effectiveness.[42] The study documents that some constituencies favor outcomes related to means (the process element in systems) while others favor outcomes related to ends (the outcome element in systems). Thus, it's possible to use the multiple-constituency theory to combine the goal and systems approaches to obtain a more appropriate approach to organizational effectiveness. But even if we can resolve the differences between the goal and system approaches with respect to what different constituencies desire from organizational performance, we still must recognize that these desires can shift with time.

Organizational development and change

Sometimes effectiveness can be achieved only by making significant changes in the total organization. Organizational development is the process of preparing for and managing organizational change. Organizational change is the planned attempt by management to improve the overall effectiveness of individuals, groups, and the organization by altering structure, behavior, and processes. If the change is correctly implemented, individuals and groups should move toward more effective performance. Concerted, planned, and evaluated efforts to improve effectiveness have potential for success.

www.ibm.com

www.harley-davidson.com

An examination of the stories of how IBM changed or how Harley-Davidson changed from companies that were losing market share and profits to become beacons of success reveals two important patterns. First, successful change is associated with a multistep process that creates power and motivation to continue. Second, the change process is driven by top-quality leaders who exert a lasting influence on the changes being made. These leaders establish direction, align people with their visions, and inspire people to overcome political, personal, and bureaucratic barriers to change.

As changes occcur in the workforce, technology, economy, competition, social trends, and world politics it is inevitable that leaders will have to initiate organizational development interventions. Chapter 18 will examine alternative approaches and interventions of change. Since competition is becoming stronger each day organizations have no choice—they must change. In all industries, a standard of continuous improvement and learning is becoming the norm around the world.

Each of you reading this book has a viewpoint, a set of assumptions, or some specific ideas about why people behave as they do. Each person attempts to explain, predict, or analyze the behavior of others. How valid and how good are these viewpoints? To help you learn how to develop valid viewpoints, this book will provide suggested frameworks and explanations about behavior of people working in organizations.

Think about the following statements and your personal beliefs:

1. Satisfied workers produce the highest quality output.

2. Women employees work harder for female managers than for male managers.

3. Enriched jobs are preferred by the vast majority of 50- to 60-year-old employees.

4. American managers are more stressed about their jobs than their Japanese counterparts.

5. Positively cohesive work groups are usually more productive than noncohesive work groups.

6. Women are more motivated by the amount of pay they receive than men.

7. Personality conflicts are outdated and aren't problems in most work settings.

8. Organizations with no structure are more autonomous, more productive, and more cost conscious.

9. Leaders are born.

10. Most million-dollar training programs are carefully evaluated for their effectiveness.

These broad comments are subject to debate. None of them are perfectly true or false. This reflects how difficult behavior is to understand and analyze. As you progress through the course, test your own views against what you read and discuss. Improving your ability to understand, explain, and predict behavior is the road we'll follow in the rest of the book.

Even those students with no interest or motivation to serve as managers will benefit from learning more about behavior in general and organizational behavior specifically. Working for others, starting your own organization, or doing business with organizations (e.g., the Internal Revenue Service, the public utility company, the school in your community) will require an awareness and understanding of the behavior of people. Through a better awaremess and understanding the transactions each of us have in society can be more positive and beneficial than simply remaining uneducated about behavior.

Figure 1–7   Relationships among the Management Functions and Individual, Group, and Organizational Effectiveness

	Sources of Effectiveness		
MANAGEMENT FUNCTIONS	INDIVIDUALS	GROUPS	ORGANIZATIONS
Planning	Objectives	Goals	Missions
Organizing	Job designs	Department or unit	Integrative methods
	Delegated authority		and processes
Leading	Person-centered influence	Group-centered influence	Entity-centered influence
Controlling	Individual standards of performance	Group standards of performance	Organization standards of performance

Managerial Work and the Behavior, Structure, and Processes of Organizations

The concept of managerial work that we've developed so far is brought into perspective and summarized in Figure 1–7. This text's focus is the *behavior of individuals and groups in organizations.* The purpose of managers in organizations is to coordinate behavior so that an organization is judged effective by those who evaluate its record. Those who evaluate organizations can be concerned with any number of specific or general criteria and with either output, process, or input measures.[43] To coordinate behavior and to satisfy evaluators, managers engage in activities intended to *plan, organize, lead,* and *control* behavior. Major factors in determining individual and group behavior are task and authority relationships.[44] Therefore, managers must design organizational *structures* and *processes* to facilitate communication among employees.

Thus, it would seem that the relationships between management, organizations, and effectiveness are straightforward. Effective individual, group, and organizational performance should be the result of effective planning, organizing, leading, and controlling. However, as will become obvious, organizations and people are not that simple. Managing culturally diverse people in organizations to achieve meaningful goals of individual, group, and organizational effectiveness in a rapidly changing and complex environment is challenging, rewarding, and frustrating. This book will portray the challenge, reward, and frustration in a realistic and contemporary way.

Summary of Key Points

• This book focuses on the developing field of management known as *organizational behavior.* Organizational behavior studies the behavior of individuals and groups in organizational settings. The framework within which this book's contents are presented is based on three characteristics common to *all* organizations: the *behavior* of individuals and groups, the *structure* of organizations (that is, the design of the fixed relationships among the jobs in an organization), and the *processes* (e.g., communication and decision making) that make organizations "tick" and give them life. The model in Figure 1–1 has evolved from our concept of what all organizations are.

• A major interest is learning about the behavioral sciences that have produced theory and research concerning human behavior in organizations. However, no attempt has been made here to write a book that teaches behavioral science. The continuous theme throughout the book is the management of organizational behavior. Given this theme, the task is to interpret behavioral science materials so that management students can comprehend the behavior, structure, and process phenomena as these are affected by managers' actions. We intend to provide readers with a basis for applying the relevant contributions of behavioral science to the management of organizations.

- An overriding consideration documented in many studies of managerial work is that the managerial process is inherently a human process—people relating to people. Recognizing this fact establishes the importance of understanding human behavior in the workplace. The behavior of individuals and groups is important for achieving effective organizational performance, but behavior of managers themselves must also be understood.

- The nature of managerial work derives from the necessity to coordinate work in organizations. By their nature, organizations exploit the benefits of specialization, but by its nature, specialization requires coordination. Managers coordinate specialized work by applying planning, organizing, leading, and controlling functions. These functions require that managers determine and influence the causes of individual, group, and organizational effectiveness.

- Two competing concepts of effectiveness derive from two competing theories of organizations. Goal theory is based on the idea that organizations are rational, purposive entities pursuing specific missions, goals, and objectives. Accordingly, how well they function (i.e., how effective they are) is reckoned in terms of how successful they are in achieving their purposes. Systems theory assumes that organizations are social entities existing as parts of larger environments and that, to survive, they function to satisfy the demands of those environments.

- The stakeholder perspective on organizational effectiveness recognizes that organizations exist to satisfy the demands of many different individuals and institutions (constituencies). Each constituency has expectations that the organization must satisfy through its performance.

Discussion and Review Questions

1. Think of an organization (e.g., bank, grocery store, school) you most recently visited. Describe the types of indicators you noted that would help you determine the firm's culture.

2. We sometimes encounter red tape and inefficiency in a generally unresponsive and ineffective organization. One of management's goals is to achieve the opposite: an efficient and effective organization. What management skills are needed to help an organization become effective?

3. Can an organization's effectiveness ever be evaluated in absolute terms? Or must we always state effectiveness criteria in relative terms? Explain and give examples to support your argument.

4. What contribution does the concept *multiple constituency* make to our understanding of organizational effectiveness? In particular, does the concept make it easier or harder for a manager to know when she has accomplished effective performance for her group or organization? Explain.

5. What role can the field of organizational behavior play in a country such as Hungary that is undergoing restructuring, reform, and privatization?

6. Should a manager of a small firm (say, 25 employees) be concerned about establishing an organization structure? Explain.

7. Describe how a manager that worked for 15 years in Los Angeles would apply a contingency management approach when he's transferred to a similar managerial position in the firm's Barcelona, Spain, office.

8. In your judgment, what are the most effective organizations in contemporary American society? Why are they the most effective? Give evidence to support that opinion.

9. If you were a training director responsible for instructing first-line supervisors in the techniques of supervision, how would you evaluate your training program's effectiveness? Is the goal model of effectiveness useful? Is the systems model useful?

10. One writer on management theory states that management is aptly defined as "getting work done through other people." Compare this concept of management with the one proposed in this chapter.

C A S E   F O R   A N A L Y S I S

McDonald's: Can It Regain Its Effectiveness?

The McDonald brothers' first restaurant was founded in 1937 just east of Pasadena, California. It didn't even serve hamburgers, had no playground, and no Happy Meals. The most popular menu item was the hot dog. Ray Kroc built McDonald's into a mammoth business that still has 42 percent of the U.S. fast-food burger market. For decades McDonald's growth and profit margins were the envy of the world. McDonald's was considered an effectivie business with tremendous potential for growth domestically and internationally.

Consumer tastes constantly change and adults began to get bored with the McDonald's menu in the 1960s. Responding to environmental pressure such as changes in consumer tastes, McDonald's introduced a new sandwich called the Big Mac. As consumers grew weary of beef McDonald's introduced bite-sized chunks of chicken in the early 1980s and within four years was the nation's second-largest poultry seller.

McDonald's changed as the environment demanded. It became the most recognized brand name and built thousands of golden arches stores. McDonald's wanted to provide consumers what they wanted at a fair price and of the best quality. However, in the 1990s McDonald's has tried pizza, fajitas, pasta, fried chicken, and low-fat sandwiches and they have all been failures.

For a company that enjoyed significant growth for five decades based on its ability to read environmental trends, the failures have been shocking. McDonald's has been unable to capitalize on its brand name or move beyond hamburgers and french fries. During a period when Americans are eating out more, McDonald's has failed to capture a growing portion of the market.

The problems facing McDonald's in the United States are spreading to its overseas markets. The easy markets such as London and Moscow have been entered. Now the firm is entering less bustling markets in Eastern Europe and Latin America. McDonald's is also faced with the quality-control problem of building more and more stores without carefully checking product quality. In a survey for *Restaurants & Institutions* magazine in which 2,800 consumers graded chains based on the taste of their food, McDonald's ranked 87th out of 91. Consumers around the world want taste and quality when selecting a restaurant.

The organizational effectiveness of McDonalds is now a serious concern among franchisers, executives, and stockholders. How or whether McDonald's can make the necessary changes to again be the growth-oriented organization it once was is questionable. McDonald's management has to identify the causes of the lost luster and then take specific steps to correct the problems.

Discussion Questions

1. How can McDonald's use its powerful brand name to help improve effectiveness?

2. Is quality and taste important to you when selecting a restaurant? Explain.

3. What environment forces are the most different as we enter the 21st century when compared to the 1950s and 1960s?

Source: David Leonhardt, "McDonald's: Can It Regain Its Golden Touch?" *Business Week,* March 9, 1998, pp. 70–77.

 **www.mcdonalds.com**

Chapter 2

Cultural Influences on Organizational Behavior

Learning Objectives

After completing Chapter 2, you should be able to:

Define
The terms *organizational culture* and *socialization*.

Explain
Why it is too simplistic to assume that managers can state that they are creating a firm's culture.

Describe
The relationship between a society's culture and an organization's culture.

Explain
Why valuing diversity has become an important leadership requirement.

Identify
Specific practices and programs used by organizations to facilitate socialization.

In most cases a person will move from one firm to another, or even from one department to another within the same firm and, consequently, will experience differences between the environments. Attempting to adjust to these different environments involves learning new values, processing information in new ways, and working within an established set of norms, customs, and rituals. The adaptation to new environments is a common occurrence. Although adaptation is difficult, it can be better understood by learning about organizational culture.[1]

Organizational Culture

If a person walks into the Broadmoor Hotel in Colorado Springs, the Breakers Hotel in West Palm Beach, or the St. Francis Hotel in San Francisco, there is a certain atmosphere, feeling, and style that is unique. These hotels have a personality, a charm, a feel. They have a cultural anchor that influences the way customers respond and the way employees interact with customers.

McDonald's also sends off a powerful cultural message.[2] The 24,000 restaurants in 114 countries in McDonald's network all pay attention to quality, service, and cleanliness. Ray Kroc, the founder, instilled these cultural values in McDonald's. He had a significant influence on what McDonald's is throughout the world from Tokyo to Chicago to Moscow. Kroc projected his vision and his openness about what McDonald's would be to customers. He gave McDonald's a purpose, goals, and a cultural base.

Whether the discussion focuses on a grand hotel that exudes culture or a McDonald's restaurant that projects its founder's vision of the business, culture is a part of organizational life that influences the behavior, attitudes, and overall effectiveness of employees.

Organizational culture defined

Despite being an important concept, organizational culture as a perspective from which to understand the behavior of individuals and groups within organizations has its limitations. First, it is not the only way to view organizations. We have already discussed the goal and systems views without even mentioning culture. Second, like so many concepts, organizational culture is not defined the same way by any two popular theorists or researchers. Some of the definitions of culture describe it as

- Symbols, language, ideologies, rituals, and myths.[3]
- Organizational scripts derived from the personal scripts of the organization's founder(s) or dominant leader(s).
- A product; historical; based on symbols; and an abstraction from behavior and the products of behavior.[4]

Organizational Culture

What the employees perceive and how this perception creates a pattern of beliefs, values, and expectations.

Organizational culture is what the employees perceive and how this perception creates a pattern of beliefs, values, and expectations. Edgar Schein defined culture as

"A pattern of basic assumptions—invented, discovered, or developed by a given group as it learns to cope with the problems of external adaptation and internal integration—that has worked well enough to be considered valid and, therefore, to be taught to new members as the correct way to perceive, think, and feel in relation to those problems."[5]

The Schein definition points out that culture involves assumptions, adaptations, perceptions, and learning. He further contends that an organization's culture such as Walt Disney's or J.C. Penney's or Compaq Computer's has three layers. Layer I includes artifacts and creations that are visible but often not interpretable. An annual report, a newsletter, wall dividers between workers, and furnishings are examples of artifacts and creations. At Layer II are values, or the things that are important to people. Values are conscious, affective desires or wants. In Layer III are the basic assumptions people make that guide their behavior. Included in this layer are assumptions that tell individuals how to perceive, think about, and feel about work, performance goals, human relationships, and the performance of colleagues. Figure 2–1 presents the Schein three-layer model of organizational culture.

 www.disney.com

 www.jcpenney.com

 www.compaq.com

Asking McDonald's or Walt Disney employees about their firm's organizational culture is not likely to reveal much. A person's feelings and perceptions are usually kept at the subconscious level. The feelings one has about a stay at Motel 6 or a stay at the St. Francis Hotel are often difficult to express. The culture of a firm can be inferred by looking at those aspects that are perceptible. For example, four specific manifestations of culture at Walt Disney are shared things (wearing the Walt Disney uniform to fit the attraction), shared sayings (a "good Mickey" is a compliment for doing a good job), shared behavior (smiling at customers and being polite), and shared feelings (taking pride in working at Disney).

 www.pfizer.com

Pfizer is a large international pharmaceutical company that was incorporated in 1900. The New York–based firm is the maker of Ben-Gay, Visine, Viagra (impotence), and Zoloft (antidepressant). Pfizer is considered a great company in studies of most admired firms. Bruce Pfau, a vice president of the Hay Group of Philadelphia, states that firms such as Pfizer have unique organizational cultures. He states, "The corporate cultures of high-performing companies are dramatically different from those of average companies."[6] He believes companies like Pfizer stress teamwork, customer focus, fair treatment of employees, initiative, and innovation. The Close-Up (on page 32) presents some of Pfizer's values and philosophy.

Figure 2–1

Schein's Three-Layer Organizational Model

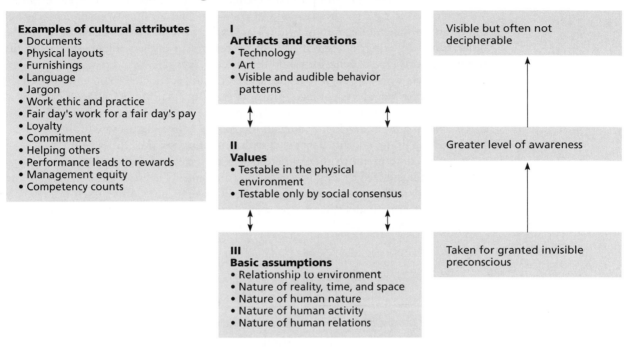

Examples of cultural attributes	**I**	
• Documents	**Artifacts and creations**	Visible but often not decipherable
• Physical layouts	• Technology	
• Furnishings	• Art	
• Language	• Visible and audible behavior	
• Jargon	patterns	

Examples of cultural attributes
- Documents
- Physical layouts
- Furnishings
- Language
- Jargon
- Work ethic and practice
- Fair day's work for a fair day's pay
- Loyalty
- Commitment
- Helping others
- Performance leads to rewards
- Management equity
- Competency counts

I
Artifacts and creations
- Technology
- Art
- Visible and audible behavior patterns

Visible but often not decipherable

II
Values
- Testable in the physical environment
- Testable only by social consensus

Greater level of awareness

III
Basic assumptions
- Relationship to environment
- Nature of reality, time, and space
- Nature of human nature
- Nature of human activity
- Nature of human relations

Taken for granted invisible preconscious

Source: Adapted from H. E. Schein, "Does Japanese Management Style Have a Message for American Managers?" *Sloan Management Review,* Fall 1981, p. 64.

Organizational Culture and Societal Value Systems

Organizations are able to operate efficiently only when shared values exist among the employees. **Values** are the conscious, affective desires or wants of people that guide their behavior. An individual's personal values guide behavior on and off the job. If a person's set of values is important, it will guide the person and also promote consistent behavior across situations. Values are a society's ideas about what is right or wrong—such as the belief that hurting someone physically is immoral. Values are passed from one generation to the next and are communicated through education systems, religion, families, communities, and organizations.[7]

A society's values have an impact on organizational values because of the interactive nature of work, leisure, family, and community.[8] American culture has historically given work a central place in the constellation of values. Work remains a source of self-respect and material reward in the United States. Work also serves as a place to achieve personal growth and fulfillment. As the demographics and makeup of the workforce become more culturally diverse, it will become extremely important for managers to learn about the value systems and orientations of the changing workforce.[9] Does the value mix change or is it different for African-Americans, Mexican-Americans, immigrants, physically challenged workers, and others who are increasing in numbers in the society and in the workforce? This is a question that empirical studies and extensive analysis and debate will need to cover more thoroughly in the next few decades.

Values

The conscious, affective desires or wants of people that guide their behavior.

Organizational culture and its effects

Since organizational culture involves shared expectations, values, and attitudes, it exerts influence on individuals, groups, and organizational processes. For example, members are influenced to be a good citizen and to go along. Thus, if quality customer service is important in the culture, then individuals are expected to adopt this behavior. If, on the other hand, adhering to a specific set of procedures in dealing with customers is the norm, then this type of behavior would be expected, recognized, and rewarded.

Researchers who have suggested and studied the impact of culture on employees indicate that it provides and encourages a form of stability.[10] There is a feeling of stability, as well as a sense of organizational identity, provided by an organization's culture. Walt Disney is able to attract, develop, and retain top quality employees because of the firm's stability and the pride of identity that goes with being a part of the Disney team.

It has become useful to differentiate between strong and weak cultures.[11] A strong culture is characterized by employees sharing core values. The more employees share and accept the core values, the stronger the culture is and the more influential it is on behavior. Religious organizations, cults, and some Japanese firms such as Toyota are examples of organizations that have strong, influential cultures.

CLOSE—UP

Pfizer

MISSION

Over the next five years we will achieve and sustain our place as the world's premier research-based health care company. Our continuing success as a business will benefit patients and our customers, our shareholders, our families, and the communities in which we operate around the world. In each of its global health care businesses, Pfizer will secure a leading position through excellence in the following areas:

- Research and Development
- Marketing Innovative Products
- Financial Performance

VALUES

To fulfill our purpose and achieve our mission, we abide by the enduring values that are the foundation of our business:

- Integrity
- Innovation
- Respect for People
- Customer Focus
- Teamwork
- Leadership
- Performance
- Community

Each of the values is outlined at www.pfizer.com. Only two of the values are presented in full here for illustrative purposes.

INTEGRITY

We demand of ourselves and others the highest ethical standards, and our products and processes will be of the highest quality. Our conduct as a company, and as individuals within it, will always reflect the highest standards of integrity. We will demonstrate open, honest, and ethical behavior in all dealings with customers, clients, colleagues, suppliers, partners, the public, and governments. The Pfizer name is a source of pride to us and should inspire trust in all with which we come in contact. We must do more than simply do things right—we must also do the right thing.

RESPECT FOR PEOPLE

We recognize that people are the cornerstone of Pfizer's success. We come from many different countries and cultures, and we speak many languages. We value our diversity as a source of strength. We are proud of Pfizer's history of treating employees with respect and dignity and are committed to building upon this tradition. We listen to the ideas of our colleagues and respond appropriately. We seek a business environment that fosters personal and professional growth and achievement. We recognize that communication must be frequent and candid and that we must support others with the tools, training, and authority they need to succeed in achieving their responsibilities, goals and objectives.

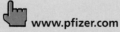 **www.pfizer.com**

An American firm with a notoriously strong and influential culture is Southwest Airlines. Herb Kelleher, one of the founders, is largely responsible for the strong culture. Along with Roland King, Kelleher rather impulsively decided to start an airline.[12] At Southwest, employees are expected to learn more than one job and help one another when needed. To show his own commitment, Kelleher often pitches in to help employees as he travels around doing business. Stories about Kelleher's pitching-in are legendary at Southwest. One tells of how Kelleher sat next to mailing operators through one night and later into the morning doing the same work they did. He often gets off a plane, goes down to baggage, and pitches in handling bags. The day before Thanksgiving one year, which is the busiest day of the year, Kelleher worked in baggage all day despite a pouring rain.[13]

The closeness of the employees at Southwest is expressed by having fun and working hard. One researcher who studied the airline concluded:

"The atmosphere at Southwest Airlines shows that having fun is a value that pervades every part of the organization. Joking, cajoling, and prank-pulling at Southwest Airlines are representative of the special relationships that exist among the employees in the company."[14]

The strong culture that has evolved at Southwest Airlines was created by the founder and the employees. They make it a distinct culture and influence everyone within the firm.

Popular best-selling books provide anecdotal evidence about the powerful influence of culture on individuals, groups, and processes. Heroes and stories about firms are interestingly portrayed.[15] However, theoretically based and empirically valid research on culture and its impact is still quite sketchy. Questions remain about the measures used to assess culture, and definitional problems have not been resolved. There has also been the inability of researchers to show that a specific culture contributes to positive effectiveness in comparison to less effective firms with another cultural profile.

Creating organizational culture

Can a culture be created that influences behavior in the direction management desires? This is an intriguing question. An experiment to create a positive, productive culture was conducted in a California electronics firm.[16] Top managers regularly met to establish the core values of the firm. A document was developed to express the core values as: "paying attention to detail," "doing it right the first time," "delivering defect-free products," and "using open communications." The document of core values was circulated to middle-level managers who refined the statements. Then the refined document was circulated to all employees as the set of guiding principles of the firm.

An anthropologist was in the firm at the time working as a software trainer. He insightfully analyzed what actually occurred in the firm. There was a gap between the management-stated culture and the firm's actual working conditions and practices. Quality problems existed throughout the firm. There was also a strictly enforced chain of command and a top-down only communication system. The cultural creation experiment was too artificial and was not taken seriously by employees.

The consequences of creating a culture in the California firm included decreased morale, increased turnover, and a poorer financial performance. Ultimately, the firm filed for bankruptcy and closed its doors.

The California electronics firm case points out that artificially imposing a culture is difficult. Imposing a culture is often met with resistance. It is difficult to simply create core values. Also, when a disparity exists between reality and a stated set of values, employees become confused, irritated, and skeptical. They also usually lack enthusiasm and respect when a false image is portrayed. Creating a culture apparently just doesn't happen because a group of intelligent, well-intentioned managers meet and prepare a document.

Cultures seem to evolve over a period of time as did McDonald's and Walt Disney's. Schein describes this evolution as follows:

> *"The culture that eventually evolves in a particular organization is . . . a complex outcome of external pressures, internal potentials, responses to critical events, and, probably, to some unknown degree, chance factors that could not be predicted from a knowledge of either the environment or the members."[17]*

A model that illustrates the evolution of culture and its outcome is presented in Figure 2–2. The model emphasizes an array of methods and procedures that managers can use to foster a cohesive culture. In examining this model, recall the California electronics firm and the limited methods it used to generate a quick-fix culture. In Figure 2–2 there is an emphasis on the word HOME, which suggests the importance of *h*istory, *o*neness, *m*embership, and *e*xchange among employees.

Influencing culture change

There is a limited amount of research done on cultural change. The difficulty in creating a culture is made even more complex when attempting to bring about a significant cultural change. The themes that appear in discussing change are:

Figure 2–2

The Evolution of a Positive Culture

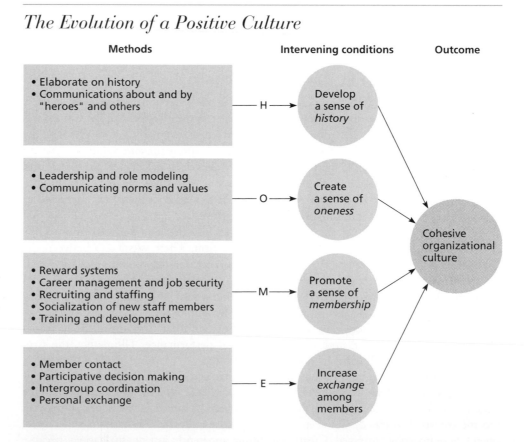

- Cultures are so elusive and hidden that they cannot be adequately diagnosed, managed, or changed.
- Because it takes difficult techniques, rare skills, and considerable time to understand a culture and then additional time to change it, deliberate attempts at culture change are not really practical.
- Cultures sustain people throughout periods of difficulty and serve to ward off anxiety. One of the ways they do this is by providing continuity and stability. Thus, people will naturally resist change to a new culture.[18]

These three views suggest that managers who are interested in attempting to produce cultural changes face a difficult task. There are, however, courageous managers who believe that they can intervene and make changes in the culture. Figure 2–3 presents a view of five intervention points for managers to consider.[19]

A considerable body of knowledge suggests that one of the most effective ways of changing people's beliefs and values is to first change their behavior (intervention 1).[20] However, behavior change does not necessarily produce culture change because of the process of justification. The California electronics example clearly illustrates this point. Behavioral compliance does not mean cultural commitment. Managers must get employees to see the inherent worth in behaving in a new way (intervention 2). Typically, communications (intervention 3) is the method used by managers to motivate the new behaviors. Cultural communications can include announcements, memos, rituals, stories, dress, and other forms of communications.

Another set of interventions includes the socialization of new members (intervention 4) and the removal of existing members who deviate from the culture (intervention 5). Each of these interventions must be done after careful diagnoses are performed. Although some individuals may not perfectly fit the firm's culture, they may possess exceptional skills and talents. Weeding out cultural misfits might be necessary, but it

Figure 2–3

Changing Culture Intervention Points

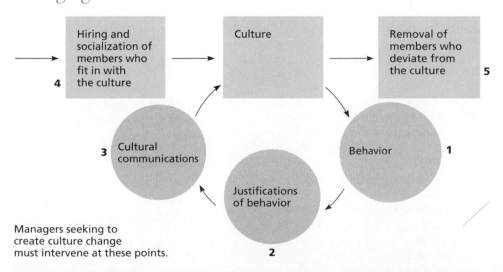

Source: V. Sathe, "How to Decipher and Change Culture," in R. H. Kilman, M. J. Saxon, R. Serpa, and Associates, eds., *Gaining Control of Corporate Culture* (San Francisco: Jossey-Bass, 1985), p. 245.

should be done only after weighing the costs and benefits of losing talented performers who deviate from the core cultural value system.

Changing an organization's culture takes time, effort, and persistence, especially in firms with strong cultures. Older, strong culture organizations have established stories, use symbols, conduct rituals, and even use their own unique language. In a strong culture organization the core values are widely shared, respected, and protected. As the following Close-Up illustrates, an organization that is steeped in history, stories, and traditions will exert significant influence on the employees. On the other hand, new companies or ones with weak cultures do not have the traditions, real or mythical, to have a dramatic influence on its employees.

Socialization and culture

Socialization

The process by which organizations bring new employees into the culture.

Socialization is the process by which organizations bring new employees into the culture. In terms of culture, there is a transmittal of values, assumptions, and attitudes from the older to the newer employees. Intervention 4 in Figure 2–3 emphasizes the "fit" between the new employee and the culture. Socialization attempts to make this fit more comfortable for the employee and the firm. The socialization process is presented in Figure 2–4.

The socialization process goes on throughout an individual's career. As the needs of the organization change, for example, its employees must adapt to those new needs; that is, they must be socialized. But even as we recognize that socialization is ever present, we must also recognize that it is more important at some times than at others. For example, socialization is most important when an individual first takes a job or takes a different job in the same organization. The socialization process occurs throughout various career stages, but individuals are more aware of it when they change jobs or change organizations.[21]

C L O S E — U P

Key Organizational Culture Factors

Myths and stories are the tales about the organization that are passed down over time and communicate a story of the organization's underlying values. Virtually any employee of Wal-Mart can tell you stories about Sam Walton and his behavior—how he rode around in his pickup truck, how he greeted people in the stores, and how he tended to "just show up" at different times. The Center for Creative Leadership has stories about its founder, H. Smith Richardson, who as a young man creatively used the mail to sell products.

Rituals are recurring events or activities that reflect important aspects of the underlying culture. Mary Kay cosmetics has spectacular sales meetings for its top performers every year. Top-performing saleswomen are awarded an array of gifts—automobiles, diamonds, and fur coats—for achieving

sales quotas. This ritual would be an indication of the value placed on high sales and meeting high quotas. Another kind of ritual is the retirement ceremony. Elaborate or modest retirement ceremonies may signal the importance an organization places on its people.

Language concerns the jargon, or idosyncratic terms, of an organization and can serve several different purposes relevant to culture. First, the mere fact that some know the language and some do not indicate who is in the culture and who is not. Second, language can also provide information about how people within a culture view others. Third, language can be used to help create a culture.

Source: Adapted from Richard L. Hughes, Robert C. Ginnett, Gordon J. Curphy, *Leadership* (Burr Ridge, IL: Irwin, McGraw-Hill, 1999), p. 458.

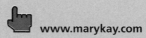 www.marykay.com

Figure 2–4

The Process of Organizational Socialization

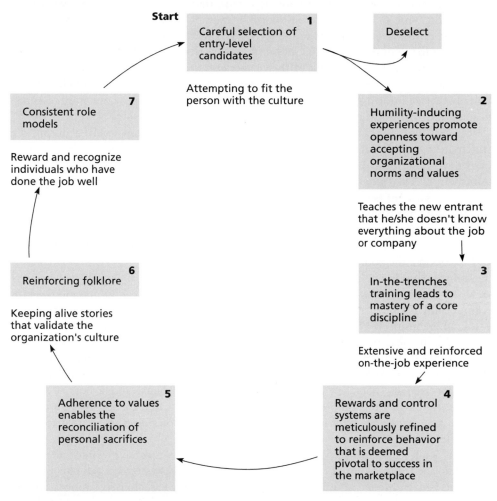

Source: Adapted from R. T. Pascale, "The Paradox of 'Corporate Culture': Reconciling Ourselves to Socialization," *California Management Review,* p. 38, Winter 1985. © 1985 by the Regents of the University of California. Reprinted with permission of the Regents.

Socialization stages

The stages of socialization coincide generally with the stages of a career. Although researchers have proposed various descriptions of the stages of socialization,[22] three stages sufficiently describe it: (1) anticipatory socialization, (2) accommodation, and (3) role management.[23] Each stage involves specific activities that, if undertaken properly, increase the individual's chances of having an effective career. Moreover, these stages occur continuously and often simultaneously.

ANTICIPATORY SOCIALIZATION   The first stage involves all those activities the individual undertakes prior to entering the organization or to taking a different job in the same organization. The primary purpose of these activities is to acquire information about the new organization and/or new job.

People are vitally interested in two kinds of information prior to entering a new job or organization. First, they want to know as much as they can about what working for the organization is really like. This form of learning about the organization is actually attempting to assess the firm's culture. Second, they want to know whether they are suited to the jobs available in the organization. Individuals seek out this information with considerable effort when they are faced with the decision to take a job, whether it be their first one or one that comes along by way of transfer or promotion. At these times, the information is specific to the job or the organization.

We also form impressions about jobs and organizations in less formal ways. For example, our friends and relatives talk of their experiences. Parents impart both positive and negative information to their offspring regarding the world of work. Although we continually receive information about this or that job or organization, we are more receptive to such information when faced with the necessity to make a decision.

It is desirable, of course, that the information transmitted and received during the anticipatory stage accurately and clearly depicts the organization and the job. However, we know that individuals differ considerably in the way they decode and receive information. Yet if the fit between the individual and the organization is to be optimal, two conditions are necessary. The first condition is *realism;* both the individual and the organization must portray themselves realistically. The second condition is *congruence.* This condition is present when the individual's skills, talents, and abilities are fully utilized by the job. Either their overutilization or underutilization results in incongruence and, consequently, poor performance.[24]

Transmitting the culture of a firm such as the Calvert Group is part of the job interview. Determining whether there is a congruence between the job applicant and the firm is important because the Calvert Group wants to hire employees who accept its way of conducting business. The Calvert Group is a Bethesda, Maryland, mutual funds company. The firm has pioneered the concept of socially responsible investing. Community involvement is significant at the Calvert Group.[25] The company gives workers 12 days a year off, with pay, to perform community service. The Calvert Group sponsors activities for senior citizens, homeless people, blood drives, Head Start, and a host of similar community-based programs. Becoming an employee who fits Calvert Group's culture requires a fit between a person's values and the organization's need to be involved with the community.

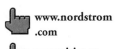
**www.nordstrom
.com**

**www.citicorp
.com**

**www.hewlett-
packard.com**

Firms such as Nordstrom's, Citicorp, and Hewlett-Packard have worked extremely hard, like the Calvert Group, to attract and retain employees who have values congruent with the firm's unique cultures. For example, Nordstrom has built so strong a culture around serving the customer (letting go any employee who fails to become socialized) that the entire employee manual is a 5-by-8 inch card with one rule on it: "Use your good judgment in all situations."[26]

ACCOMMODATION   The second stage of socialization occurs after the individual becomes a member of the organization, after he or she takes the job. During this stage, the individual sees the organization and the job for what they actually are. Through a variety of activities, the individual attempts to become an active participant in the organization and a competent performer on the job. This breaking-in period is ordinarily stressful for the individual because of anxiety created by the uncertainties inherent in any new and different situation. Apparently, individuals who experienced realism and congruence during the anticipatory stage have a less stressful accommodation stage. Nevertheless, the demands on the individual do indeed create situations that induce stress.

Four major activities constitute the accommodation stage: all individuals, to a degree, must engage in (1) establishing new interpersonal relationships with both co-workers and supervisors, (2) learning the tasks required to perform the job, (3) clarifying their role in the organization and in the formal and informal groups relevant to that role, and (4) evaluating the progress they are making toward satisfying the demands of the job and the role. Readers who have been through the accommodation stage probably recognize these four activities and recall more or less favorable reactions to them.

If all goes well in this stage, the individual feels a sense of acceptance by co-workers and supervisors and experiences competence in performing job tasks. The breaking-in period, if successful, also results in role definition and congruence of evaluation. These four outcomes of the accommodation stage (acceptance, competence, role definition, and congruence of evaluation) are experienced by all new employees to a greater or lesser extent. However, the relative value of each of these outcomes varies from person to person.[27] Acceptance by the group may be a less valued outcome for an individual whose social needs are satisfied off the job, for example. Regardless of these differences due to individual preferences, each of us experiences the accommodation stage of socialization and ordinarily moves on to the third stage.

ROLE MANAGEMENT   In contrast to the accommodation stage, which requires the individual to adjust to demands and expectations of the immediate work group, the role management stage takes on a broader set of issues and problems. Specifically, during the third stage, conflicts arise. One conflict is between the individual's work and home lives. For example, the individual must divide time and energy between the job and his or her role in the family. Since the amount of time and energy are fixed and the demands of work and family seemingly insatiable, conflict is inevitable. Employees unable to resolve these conflicts are often forced to leave the organization or to perform at an ineffective level. In either case, the individual and the organization are not well served by unresolved conflict between work and family.

The second source of conflict during the role management stage is between the individual's work group and other work groups in the organization. This source of conflict can be more apparent for some employees than for others. For example, as an individual moves up the organization's hierarchy, he or she is required to interact with various groups both inside and outside the organization. Each group can and often does place different demands on the individual, and to the extent that these demands are beyond the individual's ability to meet them, stress results. Tolerance for the level of stress induced by these conflicting and irreconcilable demands varies among individuals. Generally, the existence of unmanaged stress works to the disadvantage of the individual and the organization.

Characteristics of Effective Socialization

Organizational socialization processes vary in form and content from organization to organization. Even with the same organization, various individuals experience different socialization processes. For example, the accommodation stage for a college-trained management recruit is quite different from that of a person in the lowest paid occupation in the organization. As John Van Maanen has pointed out, socialization processes are not only extremely important in shaping the individuals who enter an organization, but they are also remarkably different from situation to situation.[28] This variation reflects either lack of attention by management to an important process or the uniqueness of the process as related to organizations and individuals. Either explanation permits the suggestion that, while uniqueness is apparent, some general principles can be implemented in the socialization process.[29]

Effective anticipatory socialization

The organization's primary activities during the first stage of socialization are *recruitment* and *selection and placement* programs. If these programs are effective, new recruits in an organization should experience the feeling of *realism* and *congruence*. In turn, accurate expectations about the job results from realism and congruence.

Recruitment programs are directed toward new employees, those not now in the organization. It is desirable to give prospective employees information not only about the job but also about those aspects of the organization that affect the individual. It is nearly always easier for the recruiter to stress job-related information to the exclusion of organization-related information. Job-related information is usually specific and objective, whereas organization-related information is usually general and subjective. Nevertheless, the recruiter should, to the extent possible, convey factual information about such matters as pay and promotion policies and practices, objective characteristics of the work group the recruit is likely to join, and other information that reflects the recruit's concerns.

Selection and placement practices, in the context of anticipatory socialization, are important conveyers of information to employees already in the organization. Of prime importance is the manner in which individuals view career paths in organizations. As noted earlier, the stereotypical career path is one that involves advancement up the managerial hierarchy. This concept, however, does not take into account the differences among individuals toward such moves. Greater flexibility in career paths would require the organization to consider lateral or downward transfers.[30]

Effective accommodation socialization

Effective accommodation socialization comprises five different activities: (1) designing orientation programs, (2) structuring training programs, (3) providing performance evaluation information, (4) assigning challenging work, and (5) assigning demanding bosses.

Orientation programs are seldom given the attention they deserve. The first few days on the new job can have very strong negative or positive impacts on the new employee. Taking a new job involves not only new job tasks but also new interpersonal relationships. The new person comes into an ongoing social system that has evolved a unique set of values, ideals, frictions, conflicts, friendships, coalitions, and all the other characteristics of work groups. If left alone, the new employee must cope with the new environment in ignorance, but if given some help and guidance, he or she can cope more effectively.[31]

Thus, organizations should design orientation programs that enable new employees to meet the rest of the employees as soon as possible. Moreover, specific individuals should be assigned the task of orientation. These individuals should be selected for their social skills and be given time off from their own work to spend with the new people. The degree to which the orientation program is formalized can vary, but in any case, the program should not be left to chance.

Training programs are invaluable in the breaking-in stage. Without question, training programs are necessary to instruct new employees in proper techniques and to help them develop requisite skills. Moreover, effective training programs provide frequent feedback about progress in acquiring the necessary skills. What is not so obvious is the necessity of integrating formal training with the orientation program.

Performance evaluation, in the context of socialization, provides important feedback about how well the individual is getting along in the organization. Inaccurate or ambiguous information regarding this important circumstance can only lead to performance problems. To avoid these problems, it is imperative that performance evaluation sessions take place in face-to-face meetings between the individual and manager and that in the context of the job the performance criteria must be as objective as possible. Management by objectives and behaviorally anchored rating scales are particularly applicable in these settings.

Assigning challenging work to new employees is a principal feature of effective socialization programs. The first jobs of new employees often demand far less of them than they are able to deliver. Consequently, they are unable to demonstrate their full capabilities, and in a sense they are being stifled. This is especially damaging if the recruiter was overly enthusiastic in "selling" the organization when they were recruited.

Assigning demanding bosses is a practice that seems to have considerable promise for increasing the retention rate of new employees. In this context, "demanding" should not be interpreted as "autocratic." Rather, the boss most likely to get new hires off in the right direction is one who has high but achievable expectations for their performance. Such a boss instills the understanding that high performance is expected and rewarded; equally important, the boss is always ready to assist through coaching and counseling.

Socialization programs and practices intended to retain and develop new employees can be used separately or in combination. A manager is well advised to establish policies most likely to retain those recent hires who have the highest potential to perform effectively. This likelihood is improved if the policies include realistic orientation and training programs, accurate performance evaluation feedback, and challenging initial assignments supervised by supportive, performance-oriented managers.

Effective role management socialization

Organizations that effectively deal with the conflicts associated with the role management stage recognize the impact of such conflicts on job satisfaction and turnover. Even though motivation and high performance may not be associated with socialization activities, satisfaction and turnover are, and organizations can ill afford to lose capable employees.

Retention of employees beset by off-job conflicts is enhanced in organizations that provide professional counseling and that schedule and adjust work assignments for those with particularly difficult conflicts at work and home. Of course, these practices do not guarantee that employees can resolve or even cope with the conflict. The important point, however, is for the organization to show good faith and make a sincere effort to adapt to the problems of its employees. Table 2–1 summarizes what managers can do to encourage effective socialization.

SOCIALIZATION STAGE	PRACTICES	**Table 2–1**
Anticipatory socialization	1. Recruitment using realistic job previews 2. Selection and placement using realistic career paths	A Checklist of Effective Socialization Practices
Accommodation socialization	1. Tailor-made and individualized orientation programs 2. Social as well as technical skills training 3. Supportive and accurate feedback 4. Challenging work assignments 5. Demanding but fair supervisors	
Role management socialization	1. Provision of professional counseling 2. Adaptive and flexible work assignments 3. Sincere person-oriented managers	

Mentors and socialization

In the medical field, young interns learn proper procedures and behavior from established physicians; Ph.D. students learn how to conduct organizational research from professors who have conducted studies. What about the process of learning or working with a senior person called a **mentor** in work settings? In Greek mythology, the mentor was the designation given to a trusted and experienced advisor. Odysseus, absent from home because of the Trojan Wars, charged his servant, Mentor, with the task of educating and guiding his son. In work organizations, a mentor can provide coaching, friendship, sponsorship, and role modeling to a younger, less experienced protégé. In working with younger or new employees, a mentor can satisfy his or her need to have an influence on another employee's career.

MENTORS

A friend, coach, advisor or sponsor who supports, encourages, and helps a less experienced protégé.

Research has indicated that a majority of managers reported having had at least one mentoring relationship during their careers.[32] Kram has identified two general functions of mentoring that she designated as career functions and psychosocial functions. The career functions include sponsorship, exposure and visibility, coaching, production, and challenging assignments. The psychosocial functions are role modeling, acceptance and confirmation, counseling, and friendship.[33]

Although mentoring functions can be important in socializing a person, it is not clear that a single individual must play all of these roles. New employees can obtain valuable career and psychosocial influence from a variety of individuals—managers, peers, trainers, and personal friends. At Ford Motor Company, a study was conducted to develop guidelines to socialize new management trainees.

Most mentor–mentee relationships develop over time. There appear to be several distinct phases of mentor–mentee relationships. Table 2–2 presents a four-phase model proposed by Kram. The reasons that cause movement in the relationship are described as turning points. Initiation, cultivation, separation, and redefinition cover general time periods of six months to more than five years.

The benefits that result from mentoring can extend beyond the individuals involved. Mentoring can contribute to employee motivation and retention and the cohesiveness of the organization.[34] The organization's culture can be strengthened by passing the core values from one generation to the next generation.

The increasing diversity of the workforce adds a new dimension to the mentor–mentee matching process. People are attracted to mentors who talk, look, act, and communicate like them. Gender, race, ethnicity, and religion can all play a role in matching. If mentor–mentee matching is left to occur naturally, women, African-American, Hispanics, and Asians may be left out.[35] The underrepresentation of these groups in management level positions needs to be evaluated in each firm that considers using mentor–mentee matching. One study showed that cross-gender relationships can be beneficial. The results of 32 mentor–mentee pairings (14 male–female; 18 female–female) found that male–female mentor matchings can be as successful as female–female mentoring.[36]

Socializing a Culturally Diverse Workforce

The United States society consists of people with many religions, many cultures, and many different roots: African, European, Asian, South American, Middle Eastern, and

Indian. Today, African-Americans, Asian-Americans, and Hispanics constitute about 21 percent of the American population. By the year 2000, about 51 percent of the total workforce will be female.

We hear a lot about diversity, but what it means is sometimes confusing.[37] Diversity is not a synonym for equal employment opportunity (EEO). Nor is it another word for affirmative action. **Diversity** is the vast array of physical and cultural differences that constitute the spectrum of human differences. Six core dimensions of diversity exist: age, ethnicity, gender, physical attributes, race, and sexual/affectional orientation. These are the core elements of diversity that have a lifelong impact on behavior and attitudes.

There are secondary forms of diversity that can be changed. These are differences that people acquire, discard, or modify throughout their lives. Secondary dimensions of diversity include educational background, marital status, religious belief, health disabilities, and work experience.

Valuing diversity from an organizational and leadership perspective means understanding and valuing core and secondary diversity dimension differences between oneself and others. An increasingly important goal in a changing society is to understand that all individuals are different and to appreciate these differences.[38] The Close-Up on diversity offers a few questions that may give you some idea about how much you know or do not know about other races, ethnic groups, and religions.

Diversity

The vast array of physical and cultural differences that constitute the spectrum of human differences.

Table 2–2	Phases of the Mentor Relationship	
PHASE	**DEFINITION**	**TURNING POINTS***
Initiation	A period of six months to a year during which time the relationship gets started and begins to have importance for both managers.	Fantasies become concrete expectations. Expectations are met; senior manager provides coaching, challenging work, visibility; junior manager provides technical assistance, respect, and desire to be coached. There are opportunities for interaction around work tasks.
Cultivation	A period of two to five years during which time the career and psychosocial functions provided expand to a maximum.	Both individuals continue to benefit from the relationship. Opportunities for meaningful and more frequent interaction increase. Emotional bond deepens and intimacy increases.
Separation	A period of six months to two years after a significant change in the structural role relationship and/or in the emotional experience of the relationship.	Junior manager no longer wants guidance but rather the opportunity to work more autonomously. Senior manager faces midlife crisis and is less available to provide mentoring functions. Job rotation or promotion limits opportunities for continued interaction; career and psychosocial functions can no longer be provided. Blocked opportunity creates resentment and hostility that disrupt positive interaction.
Redefinition	An indefinite period after the separation phase during which time the relationship is ended or takes on significantly different characteristics, making it a more peerlike friendship.	Stresses of separation diminish and new relationships are formed. The mentor relationship is no longer needed in its previous form. Resentment and anger diminish; gratitude and appreciation increase. Peer status is achieved.

* Examples of the most frequently observed psychological and organizational factors that cause movement into the current relationship phase.
Source: Kathy E. Kram, "Phases of the Mentor Relationship," *Academy of Management Journal,* December 1983, p. 622. Used with permission.

Management's ability to capitalize on diversity

Due to the changing demographics in the United States, differences in the employee pool are going to continue to increase over the next few decades. Managers will have to study socialization much more closely and intervene so that the maximum benefits result from hiring an increasingly diverse workforce. Studying the ethnic background and national cultures of these workers will have to be taken seriously. The managerial challenge will be to identify ways to integrate the increasing number and mix of people from diverse national cultures into the workplace. Some obvious issues for managers of ethnically diverse workforces to consider are:

*   Coping with employees' unfamiliarity with the English language.
*   Increased training for service jobs that require verbal skills.
*   Cultural (national) awareness training for the current workforce.
*   Learning which rewards are valued by different ethnic groups.
*   Developing career development programs that fit the skills, needs, and values of the ethnic group.
*   Rewarding managers for effectively recruiting, hiring, and integrating a diverse workforce.
*   Do not focus only on ethnic diversity but also learn more about age, gender, and workers with disability diversities.

CLOSE—UP

Learning about Diversity

Learning about other ethnic groups, races, and religions has become an important organizational issue in terms of showing understanding about the totality of other people. Let's simply list a number of points that students, managers, and people in general should know about.

*   What race are Hispanics?
    Black, white, brown? The correct answer is all of the above. Hispanic refers not only to a race but also to an origin or an ethnicity. There are Hispanic segments—Cubans, Puerto Ricans, Mexicans, Salvadorans, and others who are different in their indigenous ancestry, origins, accents, and many other characteristics.

*   What is Confucianism?
    Confucianism is the major religious influence on Chinese, Japanese, Korean, and Vietnamese cultures. Confucianism emphasizes response to authority, especially parents and teachers; hard work; discipline and the ability to delay gratification; harmony in relationships; and the importance of the group.

*   Does the term African-American apply to all blacks?
    No. Black Americans came from cultures other than just those in Africa. Caribbean, Central American, and

South American cultures have provided the United States with many talented blacks. Just as there is in the general population, there is great variety in lifestyle, career choice, educational level attained, and value systems across segments of the over 30 million Black American (includes African and other cultural backgrounds) population.

Should a manager know what the terms Hispanic, Confucianism, and African-American mean? We think so and believe that cultural and religious awareness are going to become more important as the workforce changes in terms of race, ethnic, and religious diversity. Managers and leaders in organizations need to develop a style and pattern of behavior that appeals to and reaches all segments of the diverse workforce. Although the United States has never had a homogeneous culture or population, it is now not possible to ignore the mix of diverse workers, colleagues, customers, suppliers, and owners facing the organization.

Sources: Adapted from John Naisbitt, *Global Paradox* (New York: Morrow, 1994), pp. 227–35; Marlene L. Rossman, *Multicultural Marketing* (New York: AMACOM, 1994), pp. 46–52.

Socializing involving an ethnically diverse workforce is a two-way proposition. Not only must the manager learn about the employees' cultural background, but the employee must also learn about the rituals, customs, and values of the firm or the work unit.[39] Awareness workshops and orientation sessions are becoming more popular every day. Merck has an educational program to raise its employees' awareness and attitudes about women and minorities.[40] The program emphasizes how policies and systems can be tailored to meet changes in the demographics of the workplace. Procter & Gamble has stressed the value of diversity. The firm uses multicultural advisory teams, minority and women's networking conferences, and "onboarding" programs to help new women and minority employees become acclimated and productive as quickly as possible. Ortho Pharmaceutical initiated a program to "manage diversity" that is designed to foster a process of cultural transition within the firm. Northeastern Products Company established an on-site English as a Second Language (ESL) program to meet the needs of Hispanic and Asian employees. A buddy system has been established at Ore-Ida. A buddy (English speaker) is assigned to a new employee (first language is not English) to assist him or her with communication problems.

The Seattle-Times Co. (publisher of a newspaper) 10 times a year conducts a two-day training session called "Exploration into Diversity." The training program covers such issues as diversity, multiculturism, and pluralism. The trainees define terms, discuss obstacles to achieving pluralism, present experiences, present concepts of stereotyping and prejudices, and cover methods to overcome obstacles. Follow-up sessions are also a part of the Seattle Times's approach to improving diversity awareness.[41]

Global competition, like changing domestic demographics, is placing a new requirement on managers to learn about unfamiliar cultures from which new employees are coming. The emphasis on open expression of diversity in the workforce is paralleled by a social movement toward the retention of ethnic roots. The "new ethnicity," a renewed awareness and pride of cultural heritage, can become an advantage of American firms operating in foreign countries.[42] Using the multicultural workforce to better compete, penetrate, and succeed in foreign cultures is one potential benefit of managing diversity effectively.

Socialization as an Integration Strategy

It is possible to view socialization as a form of organizational integration. Specifically, socialization from the integration perspective is a strategy for achieving congruence of organizational and individual goals. Thus, socialization is an important and powerful process for transmitting the organizational culture. The content of socialization strategies are practices and policies that appear in many places throughout this text. Here we can not only summarize our discussion of socialization processes but also cast some important organization behavior concepts and theories in a different framework.

Organizational integration is achieved primarily by aligning and integrating the goals of individuals with the objectives of organizations. The greater the congruity between individual goals and organization objectives, the greater the integration. The socialization process achieves organization integration by, in effect, undoing the individual's previously held goals and creating new ones that come closer to those valued by the organization. In its most extreme form, this undoing process involves debasement techniques such as those experienced by U.S. Marine Corps recruits, military academy plebes, and fraternity and sorority pledges.

Integration of organizational and individual interests can also involve ethical issues. These ethical issues are most evident when the two parties do not share the same information or hold the same legitimate power. Ethics involves moral issues and making choices. It is not realistic to assume that the organization and an individual will always make the same ethically based decision. Individuals are challenged to make moral decisions that are fair and the right thing to do. By examining an organization's code of ethics an individual can acquire some knowledge about how ethical issues are typically handled.

Rensis Likert is a spokesperson for the use of leader and peer socialization. While presenting his ideas on leadership theory, Likert stresses the importance of the leader who maintains high performance standards and group-centered leadership techniques. The leader sets high standards for his or her own behavior and performance and, through group-centered leadership, encourages the group to follow the example. If successful, the leader creates a group of high performance that is apparent to a new employee assigned to the group.

The common thread recommended to organizational leaders in any country is the active role played by the leader and the group members in integrating goals and objectives. Effective socialization, particularly during the accommodation and role management stages, requires joint and supportive efforts of leaders and subordinates alike. The remainder of the book attempts to illustrate that an understanding of organizational and national culture, socialization, and diversity has become an important requirement for achieving effectiveness. Competition, markets, and people are so complex that using the talents and skills of every single worker has become a valued competence of today's leaders within organizations.

Summary of Key Points

- *Culture* is a pattern of assumptions that are invented, discovered, or developed to learn to cope with organizational life. *Socialization* is the process by which organizations bring new employees into the culture.

- Simply declaring that "this" will be the culture is not realistic. Culture evolves over a period of time. It can be influenced by powerful individuals such as Ray Kroc at McDonald's or Walt Disney, but it typically evolves and becomes real when people interact and work together.

- Organizations can achieve effectiveness only when employees share values. The values of an increasingly diverse workforce are shaped long before a person enters an organization. Thus, it is important to recruit, select, and retain employees whose values best fit the values of the firm.

- Socialization is the process by which organizations bring new employees into the culture. There is a passing of values, assumptions, and attitudes from the older to the newer workers.

Discussion and Review Questions

1. Organizational culture is a difficult concept to define. How would you define the culture of an office or a manufacturing plant?

2. A growing number of Americans work for Japanese-owned firms in the United States. Do you think that these American employees are being influenced by the Japanese approach to management and the culture of Japan? Explain.

3. Identify the three socialization stages. Which of these stages is most important for developing high-performing employees? Explain.

4. Since the process of organizational socialization is inevitable, why is it important that it be managed?

5. How can a leader or founder help create a strong culture in an organization? Can any founder create a culture? Explain.

6. Research indicates that national cultures exist. Do you believe that in a heterogeneous nation, such as the United States, a national culture that is shared by society does exist?

7. What should managers of diverse workforces know about differences in values among individuals?

8. Point out three assumptions about the culture of the last (or present) firm by which you were employed.

9. Why is it so difficult to change an organizational culture that is considered strong or influential in impacting the behavior of employees?

10. Why is culture so difficult to measure or assess?

CASE FOR ANALYSIS

The Consolidated Life Case: Caught between Corporate Cultures

Part I

It all started so positively. Three days after graduating with his degree in business administration, Mike Wilson started his first day at a prestigious insurance company—Consolidated Life. He worked in the Policy Issue Department. The work of the department was mostly clerical and did not require a high degree of technical knowledge. Given the repetitive and mundane nature of the work, the successful worker had to be consistent and willing to grind out paperwork.

Rick Belkner was the division's vice president, the man in charge at the time. Rick was an actuary by training, a technical professional whose leadership style was laissez-faire. He was described in the division as "the mirror of whoever was the strongest personality around him." It was also common knowledge that Rick made $60,000 a year while he spent his time doing crossword puzzles.

Mike was hired as a management trainee and promised a supervisory assignment within a year. However, because of a management reorganization, it was only six weeks before he was placed in charge of an eight-person unit.

The reorganization was intended to streamline workflow, upgrade and combine the clerical jobs, and make greater use of the computer system. It was a drastic departure from the old way of doing things and created a great deal of animosity and anxiety among the clerical staff.

Management realized that a flexible supervisory style was necessary to pull off the reorganization without immense turnover, so they gave their supervisors a free hand to run their units as they saw fit. Mike used this latitude to implement group meetings and training classes in his unit. In addition he assured all members raises if they worked hard to attain them. By working long hours, participating in the mundane tasks with his unit, and being flexible in his management style, he was able to increase productivity, reduce errors, and reduce lost time. Things improved so dramatically that he was noticed by upper management and earned a reputation as a superstar despite being viewed as free spirited and unorthodox. The feeling was that his loose, people-oriented management style could be tolerated because his results were excellent.

A chance for advancement

After a year, Mike received an offer from a different Consolidated Life division located across town. Mike was asked to manage an office in the marketing area. The pay was excellent and it offered an opportunity to turn around an office in disarray. The reorganization in his present division at Consolidated was almost complete and most of his mentors and friends in management had moved on to other jobs. Mike decided to accept the offer.

In his exit interview he was assured that if he ever wanted to return, a position would be made for him. It was clear that he was held in high regard by management and staff alike. A huge party was thrown to send him off.

The new job was satisfying for a short time but it became apparent to Mike that it did not have the long-term potential he was promised. After bringing on a new staff, computerizing the office, and auditing the books, he began looking for a position that would both challenge him and give him the autonomy he needed to be successful.

Eventually word got back to his former vice president, Rick Belkner, at Consolidated Life that Mike was looking for another job. Rick offered Mike a position with the same pay he was now receiving and control over a 14-person unit in his old division. After considering other options, Mike decided to return to his old division, feeling that he would be able to progress steadily over the next several years.

Enter Jack Greely; return Mike Wilson

Upon his return to Consolidated Life, Mike became aware of several changes that had taken place in the six months since his departure. The most important change was the hiring of a new divisional senior vice president, Jack Greely. Jack had been given total authority to run the division. Rick Belkner now reported to Jack.

Jack's reputation was that he was tough but fair. It was necessary for people in Jack's division to do things his way and get the work out.

Mike also found himself reporting to one of his former peers, Kathy Miller, who had been promoted to manager during the reorganization. Mike had always hit it off with Kathy and foresaw no problems in working with her.

After a week, Mike realized the extent of the changes that had occurred. Gone was the loose, casual atmosphere that had marked his first tour in the division. Now, a stricter, task-oriented management doctrine was practiced. Morale of the supervisory staff had decreased to an alarming level. Jack Greely was the major topic of conversation in and around the division. People joked that MBO now meant "management by oppression."

Mike was greeted back with comments like "Welcome to prison" and "Why would you come back here? You must be desperate!" It seemed like everyone was looking for new jobs or transfers. Their lack of desire was reflected in the poor quality of work being done.

Mike's idea: Supervisors' Forum

Mike felt that a change in the management style of his boss was necessary in order to improve a frustrating situation. Realizing that it would be difficult to affect his style directly, Mike requested permission from Rick Belkner to form a Supervisors' Forum for all the managers on Mike's level in the division. Mike explained that the purpose would be to enhance the existing management-training program. The forum would include weekly meetings, guest speakers, and discussions of topics relevant to the division and the industry. Mike thought the forum would show Greely that he was serious about both his job and improving morale in the division. Rick gave the OK for an initial meeting.

The meeting took place and 10 supervisors who were Mike's peers in the company eagerly took the opportunity to "Blue Sky" it. There was a euphoric attitude about the group as they drafted their statement of intent. It read as follows:

TO: Rick Belkner
FROM: New Issue Services Supervisors
SUBJECT: Supervisors' Forum

On Thursday, June 11, the Supervisors' Forum held its first meeting. The objective of the meeting was to identify common areas of concern among us and to determine topics that we might be interested in pursuing.

The first area addressed was the void that we perceive exists in the management-training program. As a result of conditions beyond anyone's control, many of us over the past year have held supervisory duties without the benefit of formal training or proper experience. Therefore, what we propose is that we utilize the Supervisors' Forum as a vehicle with which to enhance the existing management-training program. The areas that we hope to affect with the supplemental training are: (a) morale/job satisfaction; (b) quality of work and service; (c) productivity; and (d) management expertise as it relates to the life insurance industry. With these objectives in mind, we have outlined below a list of possible activities that we would like to pursue.

1. Further utilization of the existing in-house training programs provided for manager trainees and supervisors; that is, Introduction to Supervision, E.E.O., and Coaching and Counseling.

2. A series of speakers from various sections in the company. This would help expose us to the technical aspects of their departments and their managerial style.

3. Invitations to outside speakers to address the forum on management topics such as managerial development, organizational structure and behavior, business policy, and the insurance industry. Suggested speakers could be area college professors, consultants, and state insurance officials.

4. Outside training and visits to the field. This could include attendance at seminars concerning management theory and development relative to the insurance industry. Attached is a representative sample of a program we would like to have considered in the future.

In conclusion, we hope that this memo clearly illustrates what we are attempting to accomplish with this program. It is our hope that the above outline will be able to give the forum credibility and establish it as an effective tool for all levels of management within New Issue. By supplementing our on-the-job training with a series of speakers and classes, we aim to develop prospective management personnel with a broad perspective of both the life insurance industry and management's role in it. Also, we would like to extend an invitation to the underwriters to attend any programs at which the topic of the speaker might be of interest to them.

cc: J. Greely
       Managers

The group felt the memo accurately and diplomatically stated their dissatisfaction with the current situation. However, they pondered what the results of their actions would be and what else they could have done.

Part II

An emergency management meeting was called by Rick Belkner at Jack Greely's request to address the "union" being formed by the supervisors. Four general managers, Rick Belkner, and Jack Greely were at that meeting. During the meeting it was suggested the forum be disbanded to "put them in their place." However, Rick Belkner felt that, if guided in the proper direction, the forum could die from lack of interest. His stance was adopted but it was common knowledge that Jack Greely was strongly opposed to the group and wanted its founders dealt with. His comment was, "It's not a democracy and they're not a union. If they don't like it here, they can leave." A campaign was directed by the managers to determine who the main authors of the memo were so they could be dealt with.

About this time, Mike's unit had made a mistake on a case, which Jack Greely was embarrassed to admit to his boss. This embarrassment was more than Jack Greely cared to take from Mike Wilson. At the managers' staff meeting that day, Jack stormed in and declared that the next supervisor to screw up was out the door. He would permit no more embarrassments of his division and repeated his earlier statement about people leaving if they didn't like it here. It was clear to Mike and everyone else present that Mike Wilson was a marked man.

Mike had always been a loose, amiable supervisor. The major reason his units had been successful was the attention he paid to each individual and how they interacted with the group. He had a reputation for fairness, was seen as an excellent judge of personnel for new positions, and was noted for his ability to turn around people who had been in trouble. He motivated people through a dynamic, personable style and was noted for his general lack of regard for rules. He treated rules as obstacles to management and usually used his own discretion as to what was important. His office had a sign saying, "Any fool can manage by

rules. It takes an uncommon man to manage without any." It was an approach that flew in the face of company policy, but it had been overlooked in the past because of his results. However, because of Mike's actions with the Supervisors' Forum, he was now regarded as a thorn in the side, not a superstar, and his oddball style only made things worse.

Faced with the fact that he was rumored to be out of the door, Mike sat down to appraise the situation.

Part III

Mike decided on the following course of action:

1. Keep the forum alive but moderate its tone so it didn't step on Jack Greely's toes.

2. Don't panic. Simply outwork and outsmart the rest of the division. This plan included a massive retraining and remotivation of his personnel. He implemented weekly meetings, cross training with other divisions, and a lot of interpersonal "stroking" to motivate the group.

3. Evoke praise from vendors and customers through excellent service and direct that praise to Jack Greely.

The results after eight weeks were impressive. Mike's unit improved the speed of processing 60 percent and lowered errors 75 percent. His staff became the most highly trained in the division. Mike had a file of several letters to Jack Greely that praised the unit's excellent service. In addition, the Supervisors' Forum had grudgingly attained credibility, although the scope of activity was restricted. Mike had even improved to the point of submitting reports on time as a concession to management.

Mike was confident that the results would speak for themselves. However, one month before his scheduled promotion and one month after an excellent merit raise in recognition of his exceptional work record, he was called into the office of his supervisor, Kathy Miller. She informed him that after long and careful consideration the decision had been made to deny his promotion because of his lack of attention to detail. This did not mean he was not a good supervisor, just that he needed to follow more instead of taking the lead. Mike was stunned and said so. But, before he said anything else, he asked to see Rick Belkner and Jack Greely the next day.

The showdown

Sitting face-to-face with Rick and Jack, Mike asked if they agreed with the appraisal Kathy had discussed with him. They both said they did. When asked if any other supervisor surpassed his ability and results, each stated Mike was one of the best, if not *the* best they had. Then why, Mike asked, would they deny him a promotion when others of less ability were approved. The answer came from Jack: "It's nothing personal, but we just don't like you. We don't like your management style. You're an oddball. We can't run a division with 10 supervisors all doing different things. What kind of a business do you think we're running here? We need people who conform to our style and methods so we can measure their results objectively. There is no room for subjective interpretation. It's our feeling that if you really put your mind to it, you can be an excellent manager. It's just that you now create trouble and rock the boat. We don't need that. It doesn't matter if you're the best now, sooner or later as you go up the ladder, you will be forced to pay more attention to administrative duties and you won't handle them well. If we correct your bad habits now, we think you can go far."

Mike was shocked. He turned to face Rick and blurted out nervously, "You mean it doesn't matter what my results are? All that matters is how I do things?" Rick leaned back in his chair and said in a casual tone, "In so many words, Yes."

Mike left the office knowing that his career at Consolidated Life was over and immediately started looking for a new job. What had gone wrong?

Epilogue

After leaving Consolidated Life, Mike Wilson started his own insurance, sales, and consulting firm, which specialized in providing corporate risk managers with insurance protection and claims-settlement strategies. He works with a staff assistant and one other associate. After three years, sales averaged over $7 million annually, netting approximately $125,000 to $175,000 before taxes to Mike Wilson.

During a return visit to Consolidated Life, three years after his departure, Mike found Rick Belkner and Jack Greely still in charge of the division in which Mike had worked. The division's size had shrunk by 50 percent. All of the members of the old Supervisors' Form had left. The reason for the decrease in the division's size was that computerization had removed many of the people's tasks.

Discussion Questions

1. Can a manager such as Jack have an impact on the culture of a workplace? Explain.

2. How was the forum perceived by Jack?

3. What norms of expected behavior did Mike violate, if any?

4. How could Mike have done a better job of diagnosing the culture at Consolidated Life after Jack had joined the firm?

Source: Joseph Weiss, Mark Wahlstrom, and Edward Marshall, *Journal of Management Case Studies,* Fall 1986, pp. 238–43.
    The authors thank Duncan Spelman and Anthony Buono for their helpful comments on this text.

E X P E R I E N T I A L   E X E R C I S E

Personal Appearance Could Mean Something

Personal appearance in some organizations is a part of the diversity equation. The following quiz developed by George Simons International in Santa Cruz, California, assesses your understanding of the notion of personal appearance.

Do you consider looks as part of the diversity equation? Take this quiz to find out how you would score in appearance-based situations.

1. When working inside the U.S. business community
   a. Ability, qualifications and performance are generally more important than perfect grooming.
   b. Fashion usually comes before comfort.
   c. Judgments are made on styles of dress more than achievements.

2. As a middle manager in your Mexico office, you will be expected to
    a. Dress stylishly. Good clothes and careful grooming are expected of both managers and staff.
    b. Dress for comfort. Mexicans will judge you on your credentials, not how you look.
    c. Dress well yourself and let your staff dress however they please.

3. Employees in your organization are all under 30. You like this young image and feel it sells your product. You
    a. Are justified in not hiring older people; they may not fit in.
    b. Should hire older people for inside work to create a balance in your staff.
    c. Should disregard these considerations and base your hiring solely on objectives and job-related criteria, without respect to age.

4. People labeled "fat" are less likely to be hired for a job, make less money when they are hired, and are less likely to be promoted. True or false?

5. Men value physical attractiveness and youthfulness in their mates more than women do; women, on the other hand, look for ambition, status and wealth in their prospective mate. True or false?

6. If you want to regularly acknowledge a women you work with
    a. Tell her how good she looks or dresses.
    b. Give her feedback on her work.
    c. Treat her like "one of the guys."

7. In a culture obsessed with looks, people with disabilities shed a bad light on the organizations who hire them. True or false?

8. Women of large body size make at least $_____ less per year than women of small body size.
    a. $500
    b. $11,280
    c. $6,700.

Completing the exercise

1. The class should be divided into groups of 4 to 6 to discuss your individual scores.

2. Since appearance is a personal area of human diversity, should it be a factor used in selecting employees?

Source: George Simons, "How Appearance Savvy Are You?" *Personnel Journal,* December 1995, p. 53.

Answers: 1. a, 2. a, 3. c, 4. True, 5. True, 6. b, 7. False, 8. c.

Chapter 3

Globalization

Learning Objectives

Define
What is meant by *globalization*.

Describe
What cross-cultural management study attempts to extend.

Discuss
The global skills managers must learn, practice, and refine to deal with a changing world.

Compare
How the characteristics of culture can influence the behavior and attitudes of employees.

Identify
Hofstede's original cultural dimensions.

In the world of business at the start of the 21st century, a clear picture of global interrelationships and interdependencies has emerged. Products, capital, and human resources are becoming interdependent as business entities increasingly consider their market areas as being global rather than simply domestic.[1] More and more enterprises search for markets, resources, and human assets in every corner of the globe. Today, fewer and fewer entrepreneurs and businesses find that they can prosper and grow solely within the confines of a domestic market.

As the globalization of business continues, organizations must be analyzed and managed in a new way. Simply considering how office workers behave and perform in Chicago and then attempting to generalize findings and conclusions to office workers in Madrid is not sufficient. American office workers and Spanish office workers definitely think and behave in different ways. Behavior, structure, and processes are all crucial to the successful operation of an enterprise. However, as globalization spreads, it is important to acknowledge, study, interpret, and manage differences across countries and groups of employees in these areas. In this chapter we examine organizational behavior from a globalization perspective, starting with an introduction of the requirements for the global manager who must operate in the 21st century. The chapter focuses primarily on culture and cultural variation, areas that managers must understand to compete effectively in a world that's undergoing rapid transformation.[2]

In his book, *The Work of Nations,* Robert Reich notes that "we are living through a transformation that will rearrange the politics and economics of the coming century. There will be no national products or technologies, no national corporations, no national industries."[3] Reich points out that many corporations are becoming "global webs" in which products are international composites. He also argues that a nation's commitment to developing its people is the prime way to ensure global competitiveness. If development of people is vital on a national basis, it is certainly vital on an organizational level.

Global Strategy

International businesses have existed for years. Today, however, economic and business activity includes global strategic alliances, worldwide production and distribution, and integration among nations such as the European Economic Community and the North American Free Trade Agreement. **Globalization** is defined as this interdependency of transportation, distribution, communication, and economic networks across international borders.

Globalization

The interdependency of transportation, distribution, communication, and economic networks across international borders.

Marketing scholar and researcher Theodore Levitt maintains that the existence of truly global markets demands a new type of corporation.[4] He believes the global corporation has replaced the multinational corporation as the most effective international competitor. The multinational corporation conducts its business in various countries, adapting its products and practices to local conditions by customizing products for specific markets. In contrast, the global corporation avoids the high relative costs of the multinational corporation by offering universal standardized products for a homogeneous world market.

Global strategies and approaches to managing diverse workers have become a new requirement for managers.[5] It is often the case that management practices in an organization relate to the nationality of its ownership rather than to the particular locations of its facilities.[6] However, it is no longer enough to simply assume that a motivational approach, job design technique, or performance review system will have similar results for all workers in all settings.[7] The evolution of business from being primarily domestic-based and oriented to more globally oriented will require new thinking and new managerial skills. Table 3–1 traces changes since 1945 (when a domestic orientation dominated the American manager's attitude) to the present in such areas as competitiveness, structure, and cultural sensitivity. The fourth phase of evolution, the global stage, emphasizes that firms need to understand their customers' (clients') needs, quickly translate them into products and services on a least-cost basis, and market them effectively. The ability to diagnose customer needs, manage cross-cultural transactions, manage multinational teams, and form and manage effective global alliances is crucial to succeeding in the fourth phase.

Cross-Cultural Management

The study of the behavior of individuals in organizations around the world.

Cross-cultural management involves the study of the behavior of individuals in organizations around the world. The study describes organizational behavior within countries and cultures; compares organizational behavior across countries and cultures; and attempts to understand and improve the interaction and behavior of co-workers, clients, suppliers, and alliance partners from different countries and cultures.[8] Cross-cultural management attempts to extend the study of domestic management to encompass global and multicultural considerations.

The global manager is a person who views markets, production, service, and opportunities globally and who seeks higher profits for the firm on a global basis. The truly global manager is at home anywhere in the world. He or she is considered open to national ideas and free of prejudices or attachments to one community, country, or culture. The global manager is aware of and understands the major cultural differences from country to country. This awareness and understanding is acquired by observation, learning, participation, and involvement with people from many different countries and cultures.

Leaders of global enterprises in such emerging markets as China, India, and Indonesia will need to possess local sensitivity and global knowledge. Currently, senior management ranks in emerging countries are filled with nationals from the company's home country.[9] Are today's global firms prepared to accommodate over 50 percent of their top

Table 3-1 Corporate and Cross-Cultural Evolution

	PHASE I DOMESTIC	PHASE II INTERNATIONAL	PHASE III MULTINATIONAL	PHASE IV GLOBAL
Primary orientation	Product/service	Market	Price	Strategy
Competitive strategy	Domestic	Multidomestic	Multinational	Global
Importance of world business	Marginal	Important	Extremely important	Dominant
Product/service	New, unique	More standardized	Completely standardized (commodity)	Mass-customized
	Product engineering emphasized	Process engineering emphasized	Engineering not emphasized	Product and process engineering
Technology	Proprietary	Shared	Widely shared	Instantly and extensively shared
R&D/sales	High	Decreasing	Very low	Very high
Profit margin	High	Decreasing	Very low	High, yet immediately decreasing
Competitors	None	Few	Many	Significant (few or many)
Market	Small, domestic	Large, multidomestic	Large, multinational	Largest, global
Production location	Domestic	Domestic and primary markets	Multinational, least cost	Global, least cost
Exports	None	Growing, high potential	Large, saturated	Imports and exports
Structure	Functional divisions	Functional with international division	Multinational line of business	Global alliances
	Centralized	Decentralized	Centralized	Coordinated, decentralized
Cultural sensitivity	Marginally important	Very important	Somewhat important	Critically important
With whom	No one	Clients	Employees	Employees and clients
Level	No one	Workers and clients	Managers	Executives
Strategic assumption	"One way"/ "one best way"	"Many good ways"	"One least-cost way"	"Many good ways" simultaneously

Source: © 1989 by Nancy J. Adler. See N. J. Adler and F. Ghadar, "International Strategy from the Perspective of People, and Culture: The North American Context; in A. M. Rugman, (ed.), *Research In Global Strategic Management: International Business Research for the Twenty-First Century: Canada's New Research Agenda,* Vol 1. (Greenwich, CN.: JAI Press, 1990), pp. 179–205. (3) Phases I–III are based on R. Vernon, "International Investment and International Trade Product Cycle," *Quarterly Journal of Economics,* May 1966, p. 87.

management teams coming from the home country? The qualifications for these needed top managers should include a sharp global vision. It is a global vision that will help firms provide the products and services for consumers who have been starved for choice for over 50 years in such emerging countries as China, India, Brazil, Indonesia, Ecuador, Nigeria, Hungary, and Mexico.

Providing acceptable products to the gigantic emerging markets of China, India, and Indonesia requires making timely and relevant decisions. For example, consumers in China appear to be very concerned about the price-performance equation. Philips Electronics introduced a combination video-CD player in China where there was no market for this product in the United States or Europe. More than 15 million units have been sold because the Chinese quickly adopted a positive view of the two (video and CD) for one bargain price.

Companies have learned that consumers in India are different from those in the West. Single-service packets, or sachets, are very popular in India. They allow consumers in India to buy only what they need, try out the products, and save their money. Products as varied as shampoos, pickles, cough syrup, and detergents are sold in sachets in India, and it is estimated that they make up 20 to 30 percent of the total sold in their categories.[10]

Global strategic skills

Managers operating in a globally shifting work environment will need a working knowledge of international relationships and foreign affairs, including global financial markets, international law, and exchange rate movements. Understanding global economies of scale, work ethics of employees, and host government policies and procedures will be required to formulate feasible, fair, legal, and effective strategies.[11]

Levitt's view of standardized world markets was presented earlier. Although the global market view is widely publicized, there is a need to be sensitive to local customs, preferences, and idiosyncrasies.[12] A few examples illustrate the strategic importance of local preferences and global standardization.

www.pg.com

www.kelloggs
.com

www.loreal.com

www.electrolux
.com

- Procter & Gamble's liquid detergent failed in Europe when it was introduced because European washing machines were not equipped for liquid detergent. Modifications to the detergent were made and sales subsequently improved.

- Kellogg's Cornflakes were misused as a snack when first introduced in Brazil. With educational advertising, Cornflakes gained acceptance as a breakfast food.

- L'Oréal markets its hair care and cosmetic products in more than 100 countries. It has adopted and implemented a strategy to produce local products adapted to local markets, while it reaps world economies of scale in research and development, raw materials sourcing, and productivity balancing.

- Electrolux has targeted three major markets: Europe, the United States, and Japan. Customers in these areas expect their large kitchen appliances (microwave ovens, washing machines, and freezers) to provide dependable service. Thus, Electrolux has manufactured similar products that are salable in all three areas. However, Electrolux managers are aware that strong local preferences exist. For example, with refrigerators, shelves on the door must take various sizes of milk, juice, and packages because consumer drinks do not come in standard packages even in developed countries. Thus, modifications in the Swedish firm's kitchen appliances are made to fit local standards.[13]

Nestlé has tailored products to what the Chinese consumer wants and needs—instant noodles, seasonings for Chinese cuisine, mineral water, and a popular live-lactobacillus health drink.[14]

These four examples suggest that global success requires striking a balance between capitalizing on resources and needs within a nation and capturing a vision of a globalizing world. Local requirements such as customer satisfaction must be met. But local managers also will need to think in global terms so that economies of scale and competition can be addressed.

Team-building skills

The increased complexity of global operations will require more use of work teams, including culturally diverse groups. The need for global teamwork is obvious when considering how accounting and auditing are conducted in various parts of the world. In one country, financial statements are used to reflect the economic conditions of a firm, and the audit is an accuracy check of the condition. In another country, the audit is conducted to make sure that legal requirements are met. Imagine how the audit could be interpreted in different countries and why teamwork is needed to assure a clear understanding of its use.

In operations management, it is important to develop systems, processes, and procedures across subsidiaries. Many companies have subsidiaries in different countries.

Determining if the system that is so valuable in one country can be applied or modified to fit another country requires teamwork.

Teams should not ignore or minimize either cultural differences or the difficulty faced in trying to develop multicultural teams.[15] In the context of a global organization, it becomes even more critical that team members become aware of their own stereotypes without allowing them to limit their expectations and actions. There is also an urgent need for teams to avoid cultural dominance (disproportionate power vested in members of one culture over those from other cultures). Managers should distribute power according to each member's ability to do the task, not according to some preconceived notion of relative cultural superiority.

Organization skills

The management philosophy of North America for the vast majority of the 20th century reflected Douglas McGregor's Theory X. He stated that Theory X held that workers are irresponsible and unwilling to work and must be persuaded to perform their obligations to their employers. Thus, the Theory X-based management approach to organization is to structure the job, closely supervise, and reward good performance and punish poor performance. This approach encourages a carrot-and-stick, hierarchically controlled approach to management. The emphasis is on short-term compliance and profitability. Is this really the way U.S. workers are? Certainly some American workers and workers in other countries fit the Theory X mold perfectly. However, others respond better to a Theory Y approach, the opposite of Theory X. Theory Y managers create an environment that encourages self-control and the willingness to take responsibility. They assume that most employees want to work and do not have to be coerced to do a good job. The employees who react positively to this style want autonomy, recognition, and an opportunity to display their skills, creativity, and commitment.

In addition to cultural diversity, managers must consider individual differences when organizing firms, units, and jobs. Minimum requirements for managers operating in a globally shifting world would include

- Creativity and inventiveness in designing organizations and jobs.
- High tolerance for ambiguity.
- Ability to coordinate finance, marketing, operations management, and human resource interdependencies.

Communication skills

In the global environment, managers will need to be able to communicate with diverse groups of people. The communication task would be easier if managers possessed multilingual skills and high levels of cross-cultural awareness and sensitivity.[16] Within the global business environment, strategy formulation, decision making, motivating, team building, organization and job design, leading, and negotiating are all based on managers' ability to communicate with each other and with subordinates. Achieving effective communication in a culturally homogenous setting is extremely difficult. However, it is much more challenging and difficult when a variety of nationalities, languages, and cultures are represented within the same organization.[17]

Cross-cultural communication often involves misunderstanding caused by misperception, misinterpretation, and misevaluation. When the sender of a memo, report, or policy comes from one culture and the receiver comes from another, the chances of an accurate transmission of a message may be quite low. People often understand and interpret the message differently.

Continually working to improve communication skills that work with culturally diverse employees will become mandatory. It will not be easy, but awareness of the difficulty of cross-cultural communication is a starting point.

Transfer of knowledge skills

The increased competitiveness throughout the world has placed a special emphasis on technological advances for product and process innovations. This emphasis has increased the need to transfer knowledge. Learning about a practice, technique, or approach in one country that can be transferred elsewhere is a skill that managers can apply on a regular basis.

For years, Americans appeared to be oblivious and arrogant about using knowledge, information, or techniques initiated and practiced in other countries. The quality movement initiated in Japan by an American, W. Edwards Deming, after World War II, however, has changed the historic practice of ignoring what other countries and companies are doing. Benchmarking (analyzing how a firm is doing against competitors) is now a widespread practice around the world. Benchmarking attempts to answer the question: How are we doing in terms of strategy, quality of product, compensation program, job design, or teamwork?[18]

Benchmarking

A standard of excellence or achievement against which a firm's products or practices are measured or judged.

The Japanese have become experts at transferring knowledge. Although U.S. manufacturers were the first to design both monochrome and color televisions with transistors replacing slower starting, shorter lived electron tubes, they failed to implement the newer technology in their main product offering. By 1963, most Japanese sets exported to the United States were transistorized.[19] On the other hand, although they had the capability earlier, U.S. producers did not move to complete transistorization of their monochrome sets until the late 1960s. The Japanese moved aggressively to solid-state color designs, first in their home market and then for export sales. Through learning and transfer of knowledge, they reduced the cost and improved the quality of TV sets.

Can any manager acquire all of the skills reviewed above? This question is difficult to answer. To develop these and other managerial skills will take a long time—perhaps an entire lifetime. Each of the skills needs to be understood and examined in terms of what will be needed to compete globally. The job of skill development, although difficult, will be exciting and challenging for any individual who takes pride in managing behavior, structure, and processes within organizations.

Culture

National culture

National Culture

A set of values, attitudes, beliefs, and norms shared by a majority of the inhabitants of a country.

A national culture is a set of values, attitudes, beliefs, and norms shared by a majority of the inhabitants of a country. These become embodied in the laws and regulations of the society, as well as in the generally accepted norms of the country's social system. People in a society learn what to notice and what not to notice, how to behave with each other, and how to handle responsibility, success, and failure. Most people are unaware of just how their culture has influenced their values, attitudes, beliefs, and norms.

In most countries, a dominant national culture exists. However, even the most homogenous nations such as Japan contain subcultures with distinct characteristics. In the United States, powerful subcultures exist among many groups such as the Amish in

Pennsylvania, the Cajuns in Louisiana, the Russian immigrants in Brighton Beach, New York, and the Pueblo Indians in Colorado. Strong national culture may create a state of conflict with subcultures that undermines the society and subgroups.

History and culture

A country's history provides insight into the development of a national culture. The U.S. culture has been shaped by such factors as Native Americans, pioneers, immigrants, its vast size, and a large base of natural resources. The importance of the individual has been embedded in American history and folklore for centuries.

The Atlantic and Pacific Oceans, separating the United States from other continents, have created a tendency toward isolation, a distrust of alliances, and a general lack of concern about political issues and policies in other countries. Americans have viewed their country as an island, separate from world conditions, problems, and politics.[20] However, as the world became more interdependent and transportation systems evolved, Americans were suddenly brought into contact with world problems such as hunger, religious conflict, collapsing regimes, environmental degradation, and territorial disputes.

National culture, subcultures, organizational culture, and history all influence behavior patterns of employees and the structures and processes found in organizations. The complexity of these patterns, structures, and processes requires careful analysis of many different variables. Despite such complexity, it is more important than ever for managers to attempt to unravel the dimensions that differentiate cultures. To motivate, lead, reward, structure, evaluate, and change behavior patterns, cultural variation must be studied and understood, particularly as it relates to performance, attendance, satisfaction, and ethical behavior. The accompanying Close-Up spells out ethical differences among American, German, and French managers.

Cultural Dimensions

There are many cultural dimensions that differentiate cultures. These cultural dimensions can influence behavior that can cause misunderstandings, disagreements, or conflicts.[21]

People's relationship to nature

In some countries, people attempt to control their natural environment. Americans and Canadians use manmade fertilizers and insecticides and technologically sophisticated equipment to improve crops and crop yield. Middle Easterners view life as being fated to happen. When a flood or typhoon wipes out a village, it's seen as God's will. Far Eastern countries attempt to deal with nature on nature's terms, to work in harmony with it.

These three perspectives can be referred to as dominance, preordained, and harmony. In terms of organizational practices, these three perspectives could result in significantly different responses to poor performance. In a culture in which dominance is practiced, poor performance often results in sanctions or punishment. In a preordained cultural setting, poor performance is expected from some people. In a harmony-oriented culture, poor performance is likely to be met with recognition that it or the system in which it occurs must be improved.

Individualism versus collectivism

Americans place a high premium on the concept of individualism that describes the attitude of independence of a person who feels a large degree of freedom in his personal life and decisions. In American culture, individualism may motivate personal accomplishment or striving for self-fulfillment. On the other hand, Germany and Japan are today categorized as *communitarian societies*.[22] This term reflects a premise that the individual is an integral part of the whole and that the best chance of self-fulfillment is in the context of the nation's goals. In an individualist society, it is generally accepted that each person's highest priority is his own welfare and that of his family.

As you might expect, the organization charts of firms in individualistic and collective societies differ. For example, in the United States, organization charts generally specify individual positions by title, job description, and job responsibilities.[23] By contrast, organization charts in more group-oriented societies only specify sections, units, or departments. In group-oriented societies, assignments are provided in collective terms.

CLOSE—UP

Ethical Differences

As they relate directly to perceptions, attitudes, and behaviors—factors that may vary tremendously across cultures—ethical issues must be examined and addressed in a multicultural context. In a study of 124 American, 72 French, and 70 German managers, each manager was asked to respond to a series of five vignettes that examined ethical situations related to coercion and control, conflict of interest, the physical environment, paternalism, and personal integrity. In most cases, the Americans' responses were different from those of their European counterparts. Here's one of the vignettes:

Rollfast Bicycle Company has been barred from entering the market in a large Asian country by collusive efforts of the local bicycle manufacturers. Rollfast could expect to net $5 million per year from sales if it could penetrate the market. Last week a businessman from the country contacted the management of Rollfast and stated that he could smooth the way for the company to sell in his country for a price of $500,000.

Managers from the three countries were asked how they would respond to the request for payment. Thirty-nine percent of the Americans were opposed to paying the money and said that a bribe was unethical or that it was forbidden under the Foreign Corrupt Practices Act of 1977, which makes it illegal to influence foreign officials through personal payment or political contribution. Only 12 percent of the French felt that way, and none of the Germans agreed. Fifty-five percent of the French and 29 percent of the Germans said that paying the money was not unethical but merely the price to be paid for doing business.

Part of the reason for these diverse answers is that neither France nor Germany has laws that make it a crime to bribe or corrupt a public or private official of another country. However, legal restrictions are not the only reasons for differences in managerial views of ethical behavior. Here's the conflict-of-interest vignette presented to the managers.

Jack Brown is vice president of marketing for Tangy Spices, a large spice manufacturer. Jack recently joined a business venture with Tangy's director of purchasing to import black pepper from India. Jack's new company is about to sign a five-year contract with Tangy to supply its black pepper needs. The contract is set at a price 3 cents per pound above the current market price for comparable black pepper imports.

Should Brown sign the contract? Once again, managers from the three countries were divided regarding what should be done and why. Most American managers felt that signing the contract would be dishonest or a conflict of interest. Many French managers agreed with this, but only one-third of the German responses indicated that they would sign the agreement.

Each country has its own interpretation of what constitutes ehtics. Americans are no more ethical than any other nationality. The laws and culture of each country establishes guidelines for conducting business. Americans as well as the French and German managers must learn how to conduct business with each other.

Source: Adapted from Richard M. Hodgetts and Fred Luthans, *International Management* (New York: McGraw-Hill, 1991), pp. 448–49. The study used as the basis for the Close-Up is Helmut Becker and David J. Fritzche, "A Comparison of the Ethical Behavior of American, French, and German Managers," *Columbia Journal of World Business,* Winter 1987, pp. 87–95; also see Alan Richter and Cynthia Barnum, "When Values Clash," *HRMagazine,* September 1994, pp. 42–45; James W. Kinnear, "The Ethics of International Business," *Vital Speeches of the Day,* July 1, 1995, pp. 561–65.

Time orientation

How is time viewed in a society? In many countries, employees are not accustomed to specific scheduling of work on an hourly basis. Time might be considered in terms of seasons rather than in hours or workdays. Americans are meticulous about time—arriving at work, starting a meeting, beginning a sporting event. Being late for a meeting in northern Europe might be considered so disrespectful as to sever a business relationship. On the other hand, in South America or various areas of Africa, being late is considered the norm.

Americans tend to perceive time as a resource that is scarce and must be used wisely. Therefore, this view of time results in impatience about delays plus attempting to fit as many activities as possible in the allotted time. In contrast, Eastern cultures view time as unlimited—an unending, inexhaustible resource. These differences in cultural views of time help explain behavioral differences among people from different societies and the problems that may result when individuals with different orientations must interact.

Activity orientation

In cultures such as the United States, emphasis is placed on taking action. Accomplishing results and being recognized for achievements are considered important. Managers in results-oriented cultures can motivate employees with promotions, merit-based raises, bonuses, and public recognition.

In contrast to a results-oriented culture is a *being culture.* The being culture emphasizes enjoyment, living with the flow, and being gratified for the moment. Employees in a being culture work for today, and when the job becomes troublesome or detracts from their enjoyment, they quit.

Understanding a culture's activity orientation can provide insight into how employees view work and leisure, what is rewarding, and how they make decisions regarding the job. The results-oriented culture suggests that employees work to accomplish specific goals. The being-oriented culture finds employees working to enjoy life more fully.

Informality

Americans do not ordinarily have a high regard for tradition, ceremony, and social rules. This informality has caused problems in business dealings and negotiations with people from other cultures. Latin Americans enjoy and respect pomp, circumstance, and ceremony. They tend to like public receptions, lavish meetings, and formal introductions. Americans faced with such events are often ill at ease.

In negotiations, Americans have acquired a reputation around the world for not wanting to first establish a relationship. Some consider the American style as brash, arrogant, and distant. Americans want to get to the problem, solve it, and get on with business. However, negotiators from the Middle East, Latin America, and southern Europe find it customary to converse first about unrelated areas and topics. They believe that first some degree of rapport must be established between negotiators. In many countries being blunt and informal is considered impolite and nonprofessional.

Language

Languages present barriers to conducting global transactions. There are over 3,000 languages spoken in the world. Culture reflects what the society values in its language. In some European and Asian countries, a number of languages are spoken. It is not correct, however, to conclude that when only one language exists, there will be only one culture. People in the United States and Australia speak English, but both countries have their own culture.

Canada provides a unique case of how language can play a significant role in business. Canada's heated controversy about the English and French languages has resulted in a joint government-industry committee producing typewriter and computer keyboards including accented French letters. Although the Canadian government is officially bilingual, English remains the dominant language.

When communication in organizations involves translation from one language to another, the problems of meaning that arise become significant. It is difficult to translate from one language to another. Many managers have been surprised to find that noddings and yes responses to their Japanese counterparts did not mean the deal was accepted. The Japanese word for yes, *hai,* can also mean "I understand you," or "I hear you." And indeed, in some countries nodding the head means disagreement while shaking the head means agreement, exactly the opposite of what is seen in most cultures.

Examples of language problems in business transactions have filled books. An example that illustrates barriers and misinterpretations involved a Monterey Park, California, medical office building with the numbers 941–943 emblazoned in three-foot characters. These are merely the building's address. However, to the many Chinese-Americans who pass by or see the building, the numbers have a different meaning. In Mandarin or Cantonese dialects, they sound like a common Chinese saying: "Nine die; one lives." To the Chinese, a medical building with such numbers suggests that the possibility for surviving is almost zero. Chinese numerology is an amalgam of linguistic interpretation and age-old superstitions that have been brought to America.[24]

Religion

In many cultures, religion is a dominant factor. As such, it can have a significant effect on how and what business is conducted, work schedules, and attitudes about ethics. Baptists and Adventists honor Sunday as a day of rest, whereas in Islamic countries, it's Friday, and in Israel, it's Saturday.

Islam also forbids "excessive" profit, which is considered exploitive. Islam preaches moderation and the sharing of wealth with others less fortunate. The concept of sharing wealth is manifested in one form called *zakat,* an annual tax of 2.5 percent collected from individuals and used for the benefit of the community. Banks in fundamentalist Islamic nations take equity in financing ventures, sharing profits as well as losses in the joint ventures.

Muslims are expected to pray facing the holy city of Mecca five times every day. Companies and managers must be aware of this religious ritual and might consider making adjustments that would permit employees to stop working during prayer time. Are American, British, or French managers aware of this ritual and are they willing to provide their Muslim workers with the opportunity to practice this religious ritual?

In certain countries, religion may require its followers to dress in a particular manner that may conflict with organizations' norms of appearance. These customs may have to be examined in terms of the individual, the religion, and the organization.

Cross-Cultural Research Findings

An increasing body of research attempts to empirically investigate cultural variation and its impact on behavior and styles of management. The research continues to attempt to deal with cultural dimensions that are difficult to reliably and validly measure and that are difficult to translate in various languages. The studies presented in the section aren't without their limitations and problems. However, they are major attempts to study cross-cultural issues.

Hofstede's research

Geert Hofstede, a Dutch researcher, decided to study how cultures in countries are similar and different. He developed a survey instrument and administered it to IBM offices in 40 countries. A total of 116,000 survey instruments were returned and analyzed. The initial Hofstede survey data resulted in four dimensions being identified as explaining differences and similarities in cultures: uncertainty avoidance, masculinity–femininity, individualism–collectivism, and power distance.[25]

UNCERTAINTY AVOIDANCE   This dimension concerns the degree to which people are comfortable with ambiguous situations and with the inability to predict future events with accuracy. People with weak uncertainty avoidance feel comfortable even though they are unsure about future events. Their attitudes are reflected in statements such as:

Uncertainty Avoidance

A dimension uncovered by Hofstede that concerns the degree to which people are comfortable with ambiguous situations and with the inability to predict future events with accuracy.

- Life is inherently uncertain and is most easily dealt with if taken one day at a time.

- There should be as few rules as possible, and rules that cannot be kept should be changed or eliminated.

In contrast, strong uncertainty avoidance people are uncomfortable when they are unsure what the future holds. Their attitudes are reflected by statements such as:

- The uncertainty inherent in life is threatening and must be fought continually.

- Having a stable, secure life is extremely important.

In cultures characterized by high uncertainty avoidance, behavior is motivated to some degree by fear of the unknown. People in such cultures attempt to reduce or avoid uncertainty by establishing rules, policies, and procedures. In Japan, for example, where lifetime employment has been somewhat common in large organizations, there is high uncertainty avoidance.

MASCULINITY–FEMININITY   Hofstede used the term *masculinity* to designate the degree to which a culture emphasizes assertiveness, dominance, and independence. People in a culture that has a high masculinity orientation believe that

Masculinity–Femininity

A dimension uncovered by Hofstede. High masculinity in a culture designates assertiveness, dominance, and independence. High femininity in a culture designates interdependence, compassion, and emotional opinions.

- Sex roles in society should be clearly differentiated; men are intended to lead and women to follow.

- Ambition and assertiveness provide the motivation behind behavior.

Femininity describes a culture's tendency to favor such values as interdependence, compassion, and emotional openness. People in a culture oriented toward femininity hold the following kinds of beliefs:

- Sex roles in society should be fluid and flexible; sexual equality is desirable.

- The quality of life is more important than personal performance and visible accomplishments.

Work in cultures can be divided on the basis of a masculine–feminine dimension. In masculine cultures, men possess jobs that contain power, authority, and responsibility. In feminine-oriented cultures, the roles of teaching, caring for patients, and helping the less fortunate are valued. There would also be a more equality-based norm between the sexes. Neither men nor women would be expected to be better managers or leaders. Individual talents and skills, and not gender, are the focus for acceptance and recognition in the feminine-oriented national culture country.

Individualism–Collectivism

A dimension uncovered by Hofstede. Individualism emphasizes pursuit of individual goals, needs, and success. Collectivism emphasizes group need, satisfaction, and performance.

INDIVIDUALISM–COLLECTIVISM   This dimension refers to the tendency of a culture's norms and values to emphasize satisfying individual needs or group needs. Individualism emphasizes pursuit of individual goals, needs, and success. It is assumed that if each person takes care of her or his personal needs, then the entire society will benefit. The individualism philosophy is that

- *I* is more important than *we.*
- Success is a personal achievement. People function most productively when working alone.

In contrast, the collectivist perspective emphasizes group welfare and satisfaction. The individual is willing in a collectivist culture to make personal sacrifices to better the stature, performance, and satisfaction of the group. The collectivism philosophy is that

- *We* is more important than *I.*
- Every member of society should belong to a group that will secure members' well-being in exchange for loyalty and occasional self-sacrifice.

People's attitudes and behaviors lie somewhere between these poles of individualism and collectivism. Individualists are committed to their own development, quality of life, and rewards. In collectivist national cultures, the group and its accomplishments take precedence over anything else. There is a strong sense of group commitment.

Power Distance

A dimension determined by Hofstede. It refers to the degree to which members of a society accept differences in power and status among themselves.

POWER DISTANCE   This refers to the degree to which members of a society accept differences in power and status among themselves. In national cultures that tolerate only a small degree of power distance, norms and values suggest that power differences should be minimal. Such cultures prefer participative management and worker involvement in decision making. Individuals in such cultures believe that

- Superiors should be readily accessible to subordinates.
- Using power is neither inherently good nor inherently evil; whether power is good or evil depends on the purposes for and consequences of its use.

On the other hand, in national cultures characterized by a large degree of power distance, norms and values based on hierarchical distribution predominate. People in these cultures use authority and power to coordinate individual work and behavior. Individuals in large power distance cultures believe that

- Power holders are entitled to special rights and privileges.
- Superiors and subordinates should consider each other to be different kinds of people.

Authoritarian manager styles are more likely to exist in a large power distance culture than in a small power distance culture. Decentralization, participation, and worker involvement are more likely to exist in a small power distance culture than in a large power distance culture.

Figures 3–1, 3–2, and 3–3 show how select countries cluster on the basis of Hofstede's proposed cultural differences. As shown in Figure 3–1, the Scandinavian countries are most feminine; the United States, slightly masculine; and Japan and Austria, highly masculine. In Japan and Austria, many people still believe that women should stay home and not pursue careers. The United States encourages women to work. In Sweden, women are expected to work.

Figure 3–1

Position of Selected Countries on Uncertainty Avoidance and Masculinity–Femininity

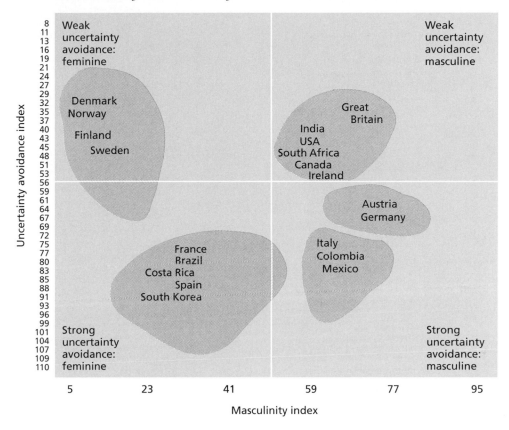

Source: Adapted from Geert Hofstede, "The Cultural Relativity of Organizational Practices and Theories," *Journal of International Business Studies,* Fall 1983, p. 86. Used with permission.

Figure 3–2 illustrates that a country such as Great Britain that is low on power distance and uncertainty avoidance has very little hierarchy and much interaction among people. Employees in high power distance and low uncertainty avoidance cultures such as India view their organizations as families. Employees in countries such as South Korea and Brazil tend to consider their organizations as pyramids of people. Roles and procedures in countries with small power distance and strong uncertainty avoidance, such as Germany, tend to work in highly predictable settings.

Figure 3–3 shows that the United States rates low on power distance. Japan and India rate high on power distance and low on individualism. In these countries bypassing or arguing with a superior would be considered insubordination.

Table 3–2 presents scores for the 40 initial countries studied by Hofstede on each of the four dimensions. Larger numbers indicate greater amounts of uncertainty avoidance, masculinity, individualism, and power distance. Note that the United States has the highest individualism score (91), a moderate masculinity score (62), a low uncertainty avoidance score (46), and a low power distance score (40).

Hofstede and other researchers have examined attitude information and concluded that eight basic clusters of nations exist (Figure 3–4).[26] The attitudes (work goals, needs,

Figure 3–2

Position of Selected Countries on Uncertainty Avoidance and Power Distance

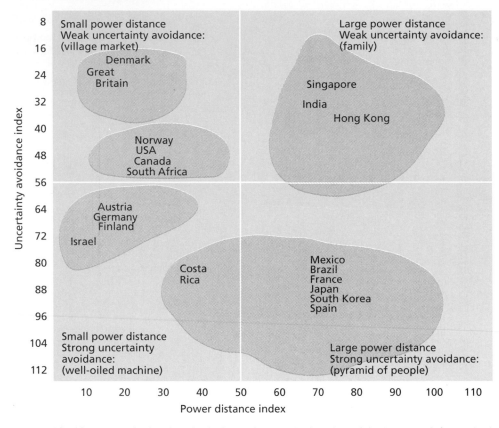

Source: Adapted from Geert Hofstede, "The Cultural Relativity of Organizational Practices and Theories," *Journal of International Business Studies,* Fall 1983, p. 84. Used with permission.

and values) of each nation in a cluster were more similar to each other than to attitudes found in other clusters. The United States cluster, called ANGLO, includes the English-speaking nations of Canada, New Zealand, Ireland, Australia, the United Kingdom, and South Africa. Four nations—Brazil, Japan, India, and Israel—did not fit into any of the eight country clusters.

www.ibm.com

Hofstede-inspired research

Since the original research on IBM employees, Hofstede and other researchers have continued to examine cultural differences and similarities. Bond studied students in 22 countries using a value survey.[27] He discovered a fifth cultural dimension labeled **Confucian dynamism.** It designated the extent to which people perceive the importance of the values of persistence, status, thrift, and feeling shame plus the unimportance of the values of personal stability, face saving, respect for tradition, and reciprocation of favors and gifts. Confucian dynamism indicates how strongly a person believes in ethical principles.

Confucian Dynamism

The extent to which people believe in the importance of the values of persistence, status, thrift, and feeling shame and the unimportance of the values of personal stability, face saving, respect for tradition, and reciprocation of favors and gifts.

Hofstede has proposed that not only management practices but also management theories are constrained by the national cultural environment in which they were created.[28] He claims that management as an activity and a class of people is an American invention. In the United States, the manager is a culture hero. However, other cultures have different views of management and managers.

In Germany, the engineer rather than the manager is the hero. An effective apprenticeship program both on the factory floor and in the office is in place. Germans expect their boss, or *Meister,* to assign their tasks and to be a technical expert. They do not, however, rely on a manager, American style, to motivate them.

The manager, U.S. version, is also missing in Japan. In the United States, the core of the enterprise is the managerial class. In Japan, the core consists of a permanent worker group. University graduates in Japan first join the permanent worker group and subsequently fill various positions. Japanese workers are to a large extent controlled by their peer group rather than by their manager.

Hofstede believes that history and cultural characteristics explain clearly why American managers behave as they do in terms of managerial practice, structuring of organization, designing jobs, decision making, and communications.[29] Nothing is inherently

Figure 3–3

Position of Selected Countries on Individualism and Power Distance

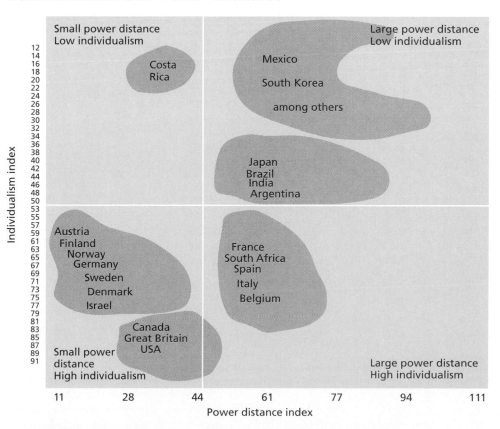

Source: Adapted from Geert Hofstede, "The Cultural Relativity of Organizational Practices and Theories," *Journal of International Business Studies,* Fall 1983, p. 82. Used with permission.

68

Part 1 Introduction

Table 3-2   Scores on Four Hofstede Dimensions

NATIONAL CULTURE	UNCERTAINTY AVOIDANCE	MASCULINITY–FEMININITY	INDIVIDUALISM–COLLECTIVISM	POWER DISTANCE
Argentina	86	56	46	49
Australia	51	61	90	36
Austria	70	79	55	11
Belgium	94	54	75	65
Brazil	76	49	38	69
Canada	48	52	80	39
Chile	86	28	23	63
Colombia	80	64	13	67
Denmark	23	16	74	18
Finland	59	26	63	33
France	86	43	71	68
Germany	65	66	67	35
Great Britain	35	66	89	35
Greece	112	57	35	60
Hong Kong	29	57	25	68
India	40	56	48	77
Iran	59	43	41	58
Ireland	35	68	70	28
Israel	81	47	54	13
Italy	75	70	76	50
Japan	92	95	46	54
Mexico	82	69	30	81
Netherlands	53	14	80	38
New Zealand	49	58	79	22
Norway	50	8	69	31
Pakistan	70	50	14	55
Peru	87	42	16	64
Philippines	44	64	32	94
Portugal	104	31	27	63
Singapore	8	48	20	74
South Africa	49	63	65	49
Spain	86	42	51	57
Sweden	29	5	71	31
Switzerland	58	70	68	34
Taiwan	69	45	17	58
Thailand	64	34	20	64
Turkey	85	45	37	66
United States	46	62	91	40
Venezuela	76	73	12	81
Yugoslavia	88	21	27	76

Note: Larger numbers signify greater amounts of uncertainty avoidance, masculinity, individualism, and power distance.

Source: Based on Geert Hofstede, "Motivation, Leadership, and Organization: Do American Theories Apply Abroad?" *Organizational Dynamics* 9 (1980), pp. 42–63.

Figure 3–4

Country Clusters Based on Employee Attitudes

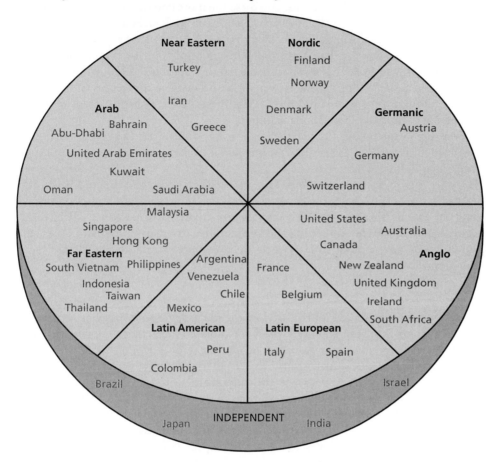

Source: Simcha Ronen and Oded Shenkar, "Clustering Countries on Attitudinal Dimensions: A Review and Synthesis," *Academy of Management Review,* July 1985, p. 449. Used with permission.

wrong or right in American managerial behavior, just as nothing is necessarily good or bad about Japanese, German, Mexican, or Nigerian managerial behavior. Each managerial or cadre group has its own peculiar idiosyncrasies.

A study of American and Japanese managers examined the influence of national culture on budget control practices in manufacturing firms. Budget control practices included communication and coordination processes used in budget planning, the time horizon used, the rules and procedures followed, the amount of budget slack built into the system, the degree of managerial control over the budget, and the budget performance evaluation period.[30] Since Japan has been identified as a highly collectivist nation and the United States has been found to be very individualistic, it was proposed that differences in budgetary control would be found. As hypothesized, U.S. companies, compared with Japanese companies, tend to use communication and coordination more widely, build more budget slack into considerations, and use a short-term performance evaluation. The findings are compatible with the view that the United States practices more hierarchically oriented management and uses a shorter term perspective for evaluation and review.

CRITIQUING HOFSTEDE   The original Hofstede research was conducted in only one organization, IBM, which limits its generalizability. In addition, questions are still raised about the validity and reliability of the measures used by Hofstede. Is he accurately measuring cultural dimensions? Are these the most important cultural dimensions? Can a survey measure cultural dimensions? Since culture is such a subtle characteristic, can it be measured at all? These are questions raised about any survey-based research.[31]

Cultural tendencies can lead to respondents' minimization or exaggeration of their feelings on a rating scale.[32] There is also the issue of subcultural influences on respondents. If Canadians completed the survey, wouldn't there be differences in responses in British Columbia as compared to Quebec? Are mean values, averaged across all subjects, accurate representations of a national culture?

There is also the problem of whether four or five dimensions can conceivably explain a national culture. What dimensions are missing, if any? Explaining such a complex phenomenon as culture is not an easy task.

Despite these criticisms and limitations, Hofstede's research and the studies that it has stimulated have called attention to national culture and its possible impact on behavior and style. He has finally introduced into the organizational sciences a word of caution about generalizing from one setting and one country to other settings and other countries. Hofstede has increased interest in conducting more internationally relevant organizational science, research, and applications.

Laurent's research

A French researcher, André Laurent, studied the philosophies and behaviors of managers in nine Western European countries, the United States, Japan, and Indonesia.[33] He was interested in determining how managers behaved in various work situations. He found unique patterns or styles of managerial behavior in each country.

Table 3–3 summarizes responses to the statement, "The main reason for hierarchical structure is so that everybody knows who has authority over whom." Most Americans and Germans disagreed with this statement. Americans and Germans believe that the purpose of hierarchy is to organize tasks so that work can be accomplished. By contrast, Italians, Japanese, and Indonesians generally agree with the statement. Hierarchy informs everyone who is in charge.

Laurent's subjects also reacted to the assertion; "In order to have efficient work relationships, it is often necessary to bypass the hierarchical line." Swedish managers saw very little problem with bypassing a chain of command. Finding the right person to accomplish the task was the top priority to Swedish managers. As Table 3–4 indicates, Italian managers considered bypassing to be a form of insubordination. Laurent found that most Italian managers handle bypassing by reprimanding offenders or redesigning the hierarchical reporting structure. Given this, how comfortably could a Swede or American work in an Italian-managed organization?

The notion of an American manager being a problem solver is supported by Laurent's research. He asked managers whether "it is important for a manager to have at hand pre-

---

Table 3-3   Hierarchy Is for Identifying Who Has Authority: Agreement Rate across Countries

UNITED STATES	GERMANY	GREAT BRITAIN	NETHERLANDS	FRANCE	ITALY	JAPAN	INDONESIA
18%	24%	38%	38%	45%	50%	52%	86%

Source: Based on André Laurent, "The Cultural Diversity of Western Conceptions of Management," *International Studies of Management and Organization,* vol. XIII, no. 1–2 (Spring–Summer 1983), pp. 75–96. Reprinted by permission of publisher, M. E. Sharpe, Inc., Armonk, N.Y.

Table 3–5   Bypassing the Chain of Command Is Acceptable: Percent Disagreement across Countries

SWEDEN	GREAT BRITAIN	UNITED STATES	NETHERLANDS	FRANCE	GERMANY	ITALY
22%	31%	32%	39%	42%	46%	75%

Source: Based on André Laurent, "The Cultural Diversity of Western Conceptions of Management," *International Studies of Management and Organization,* vol. XIII, no. 1–2 (Spring–Summer 1983), pp. 75–96. Reprinted by permission of publisher, M. E. Sharpe, Inc., Armonk, N.Y.

cise answers to most of the questions that subordinates may raise about their work." American, Swedish, and Dutch managers believe that managers are there to help solve problems. On the other hand, French managers believe that a person should not be in a managerial position unless he has precise answers to job-related questions. Figure 3–5 presents the differences in views about a manager's role.

These are summaries of only 3 of the 60 work-related issues studied by Laurent. Based on his study and review of the literature he, along with Hofstede, believes that managers' national origin significantly affects their views and style of managing. Just as there's an American bias in some managerial approaches, there's a Japanese bias in other

Figure 3–5

Manager's Role Varies across Cultures: Reactions to "Managers Have Precise Answers to Subordinates' Questions"

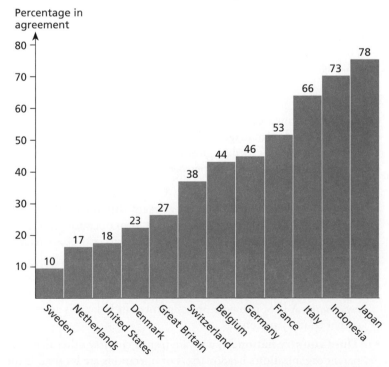

Source: Based on André Laurent. "The Cultural Diversity of Western Conceptions of Managements," *International Studies of Management and Organization,* vol. XIII, no. 1–2 (Spring–Summer 1983), pp. 75–96. Reprinted by permission of publisher, M. E. Sharpe, Inc., Armonk, N.Y

practices. No nation, group of managers, or set of researchers is perfectly free of any bias or ethnocentric tendencies. Cross-cultural understanding will only come about if managers and researchers are willing to increase their global perspectives and knowledge bases about diverse groups of employees. Global approaches to managing behavior, structure, and processes will eventually become a top priority around the world. The era of domestically bound approaches to managing what occurs in organizations is ending.

Cross-Cultural Transitions

Multinational Corporation

A firm with operations in different nations with each viewed as a relatively separate enterprise.

Global Corporation

An enterprise structured so that national boundaries become blurred. The best people are hired irrespective of national origin.

Although the terms are often treated as the same, Table 3–1 pointed out important distinctions between a **multinational corporation** and a **global corporation.** A multinational corporation (MNC) might have operations in different nations but each operation is viewed as a relatively separate enterprise. Key human resources are usually sent out from the company's home offices, and most decision making remains at corporate headquarters. Thus, although the MNC is largely staffed by people from the nation in which a particular facility is found, managers from the corporation's home country retain most authority.[34] The multinational corporation does not yet see its potential market as the world. Rather, it views each of its foreign operations as a specialized market for a particular product. In other words, each foreign subsidiary concentrates its efforts on the nation in which it is located.

In contrast to an MNC, the global corporation (GC) is structured so that national boundaries disappear and it hires the best persons for jobs irrespective of their national origin. The global corporation sees the world as its labor source as well as its marketplace. Thus, the global corporation will locate an operation wherever it can accomplish its goals in the most cost-effective way.[35] The true global corporation also believes in a world market for essentially similar products. Moreover, the national affiliation of an employee becomes rather unimportant. For example, Mars Inc.-Spain has had an English general manager, a French finance manager, and a Swiss human resource manager.[36]

Human resources for international assignment

Host Country Nationals

Workers from the local population.

Parent Country Nationals

Individuals sent from the country in which the firm is headquartered. Often called *expatriates.*

Third Country Nationals

Employees from a country other than where the parent company is headquartered.

Generally speaking, three sources provide employees for an international assignment. For key managerial and technical positions, all three sources of workers are frequently used in global organizations. Which source is used the most depends, however, on the perspective of the company. The organization might choose to hire

- **Host country nationals,** who are workers from the local population. A worker from Ireland employed by a U.S. firm operating in Dublin would be considered a host country national. Sometimes they are referred to as local nationals.

- **Parent country nationals,** who are sent from the country in which the organization is headquartered. These persons are usually referred to as *expatriates.* A U.S. manager on assignment in Ireland is an expatriate or parent country national.

- **Third country nationals,** who are from a country other than where the parent organization's headquarters or operations are located. If the U.S. firm employed a manager from Canada at facilities in Ireland, she would be considered a third country national.

The tendency to be ethnocentric (a belief that your nation's cultural values and customs are superior to all others) is strong for new and even for many well-established foreign organizations conducting business in the United States. There is an assumption that most executive-level positions in Japanese-owned businesses in the United States are occupied by Japanese nationals. Only about 31 percent of the senior management positions in such firms are occupied by U.S. managers. More commonly, local nationals are used for specific functions such as liaison, but Japanese organizations have a reputation among some people for showing little regard for these persons' career development. (See the end-of-chapter case.) In contrast, some researchers suggest that foreign companies in Japan hire local Japanese managers for nearly 80 percent of their management needs.[37]

The expatriate manager

Perhaps one of the most important tasks for the multinational or global corporation is managing the expatriate adjustment process. An **expatriate manager** is a manager from the corporation's home nation who is on a foreign assignment. The focus for the company will therefore be on the selection, training, appraisal, and compensation of the expatriate. Significant efforts will also be placed on career management as it relates to the expatriate's return to headquarters. The Close-Up at the bottom of page 74 illustrates some of the benefits and costs of being an expatriate manager.

Expatriate Manager

A manager from the firm's home nation who's on a foreign assignment.

Figure 3–6 lists the factors that seem to be most commonly associated with expatriate success and failure. Clearly, selection for expatriate assignments is a complex, sensitive task. Many factors related to a successful expatriate assignment are difficult to measure, and managers' success in domestic operations may have very little to do with their success overseas. One major reason that expatriate failure rates are so high for many companies is that these companies believe that a manager's domestic performance will always be related to her overseas performance. As a result, they frequently overemphasize technical competency and disregard more important factors when selecting the expatriate.[38]

As Figure 3–6 shows, the real keys to a successful expatriate choice are finding managers who are culturally flexible and adaptable, who have supportive family situations, and who

Figure 3–6

Factors in Expatriate Managers' Success and Failure

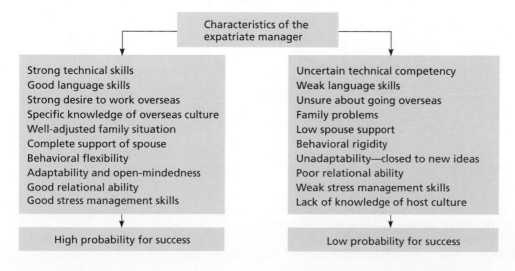

are motivated to accept the overseas assignment. Other factors such as cultural familiarity and language fluency are also apparently more important than technical competency.

Staffing an international joint venture with expatriates can be challenging since the partners in the venture might disagree about the necessary qualifications for a manager. For example, a Japanese partner might be looking for a manager who is a real team player while a U.S. partner might be seeking a highly aggressive self-starter for the same position. Such disagreements are one reason that joint ventures using one partner's management philosophies seem to work better than shared systems.[39]

Motivation to accept an overseas assignment is also a factor in the expatriate's success. Without a strong commitment to completing the assignment, the expatriate's chances of success are small. The organization can help create this motivation in several ways. Compensation programs that are attractive to the expatriate can help. Perhaps more important, however, is creating a system where the overseas assignment is beneficial to the expatriate's long-term career objectives. One of expatriates' most commonly mentioned concerns is that their position in the home offices may be jeopardized if they are away too long. That is, many expatriates believe that accepting a lengthy overseas assignment will derail any successful career path they had established in domestic operations.

A Supreme Court ruling has added a potentially interesting twist to instilling expatriates with the motivation necessary for successfully completing their assignments. In *Equal Employment Opportunity Commission v. Arabian American Oil Co.* (1991), Chief Justice Rehnquist argued that the case

> *presents the issue whether Title VII applies extraterritorially to regulate the employment practices of United States employers who employ United States citizens abroad. The United States Court of Appeals for the Fifth Circuit held that it does not, and we agree with that conclusion.*

Simply stated, the Supreme Court determined that equal employment opportunity protection afforded under Title VII (prohibiting discrimination on the basis of sex, race,

---

C L O S E — U P

Expatriate Managers

When Vittorio Levi decided to leave the warmth of Italy for a job in Sweden, everyone told him he was crazy. Scandinavians may dream of working in a Mediterranean climate, but Italians aren't supposed to be willing to go north. Nonetheless, Mr. Levi says he made the right choice when he joined Oy Nokia's Stockholm-based computer division as president.

Expatriate executives are no novelty, of course. As more companies try to compete globally, more executives are crossing borders—not just as a brief detour, but as a critical, and sometimes inevitable, stage in their careers. That trend is particularly pronounced in Europe, where plans for a unified market are spurring companies to reorganize.

Responsibilities are rapidly shifting from national to regional or pan-European units. At the same time, companies want to stay in touch with local tastes. So they need managers who can think big while understanding local nuances.

Mastering that tricky mix often means hiring what some companies call Euromanagers: people skilled at dealing with a variety of cultures and at bringing a diverse team together. And that means hiring and promoting more foreigners.

"You need as much cultural mix and diversity and experience as possible . . . if you are running a global company," says Bob Poots, personnel director for the European division of London-based Imperial Chemical Industries (ICI). ICI's executive ranks were predominantly British 20 years ago; now, only 74 of the company's top 150 executives worldwide are British.

That sort of change isn't easy to effect. The problem, headhunters and human resource managers say, is that Europe has a shortage of good senior executives who are willing to move. Tax and pension hassles, family ties, and simple chauvinism keep many top managers in their own backyards.

"It's easy to say 'Euromanager,'" notes Brian F. Bergin, president of the European division of Colgate-Palmolive.

religion, color, and national origin) may not extend to the typical expatriate manager's situation. Although any such decision cannot be overinterpreted since it addresses specific circumstances, the general notion of this ruling suggests that expatriates do not have the same degree of protection against discrimination as managers employed in the United States. This could potentially reduce many managers' interest in accepting such assignments.

The role of the expatriate's family shouldn't be underestimated when deciding about overseas assignments. Research indicates that a dissatisfied spouse can significantly affect the expatriate's performance. Some evidence even suggests that a spouse's inability to adjust to the overseas assignment is the single most common factor in expatriate failures.[40] For an expatriate with children, worries over schooling and leisure activities can add to the stress associated with the assignment. Eventually, if these worries aren't resolved, the assignment might end with the expatriate's early return to her parent country.

Because the family can be such an important factor in expatriate manager failures, the temptation for many companies may be to only send single managers. While this practice might eliminate one problem, it could easily create many others. For example, it's likely that a greater proportion of men than women are single in certain occupational groups. If a company only selects single persons for desirable overseas assignments, it might unintentionally discriminate against women.

Culture shock and the expatriate manager

A trip to a foreign culture can cause tourists and expatriate managers alike to go through a predictable series of reactions to their unfamiliar surroundings. Figure 3–7 illustrates the **culture shock cycle.** First, there is a period of fascination during which all of the different aspects of the culture are viewed with interest and curiosity. This first reaction to a new culture is generally a positive experience.

Culture Shock Cycle

A three-phase cycle (fascination and interest, frustration and confusion, and adaptation) that most individuals sent to another culture experience.

"In fact, [hiring them] is an extremely difficult task. But it's happening."

To help realign its management, Colgate appointed a pan-European human resources director, Peter Dessau, a Dane who moved to Brussels. His job is to encourage mobility among managers in the U.S. company's European units.

A barrier to the free flow of executives is prejudice. Especially among older executives, history weighs heavily. Asked why his company wasn't moving into the German market, the chief of a Dutch retailer replied without hesitation, "Because we [in the company] don't like Germans." The many differences in preferred management style that exist among European countries may contribute to these barriers as well.

To overcome these obstacles, companies are trying to be more flexible in managing people. Nokia, for instance, made it possible for the Italian Mr. Levi to keep his main residence in Turin. The company provides him with a small apartment in Stockholm and flies him home to Italy for about two weekends a month.

Mr. Levi says such benefits have helped him make a smooth transition. At age 52, he is older than most executives in their first senior position abroad. Though he doesn't expect to spend the rest of his career in Stockholm, he says his international job gives him a better understanding of Europe's political and economic transformation. "In a time of great change," he says, "you get a closer view if you are in a position like this than if you stay home in Italy with your friends."

Source: Bob Hagerty, "Companies in Europe Seeking Executives Who Can Cross Borders in a Single Bound." Reprinted by permission of *The Wall Street Journal,* © January 25, 1991, Dow Jones & Company, Inc., pp. B1, B8. All Rights Reserved Worldwide. See also Andrew Myers, Andrew Kakabadse, Tim McMahon, and Gilles Spony, "Top Management Styles in Europe: Implications for Business and Cross-National Teams," *European Business Journal,* 1995, pp. 17–27.

 **www.colgate.com**

Next, however, comes a period known as culture shock. Culture shock refers to the frustration and confusion that result from being constantly subjected to strange and unfamiliar cues about what to do and how to get it done.[41] Notice from the exhibit that culture shock doesn't typically occur during the earliest days of a trip overseas. Thus, while many expatriate managers' assignments begin very positively, their experiences often turn negative soon after.

The successful expatriate must cope effectively with culture shock. It's a period in which the manager may miss the familiar surroundings of the home office. Simple, daily events can become sources of stress and dissatisfaction. For example, being denied access to a favorite snack food or leisure activity because it's unavailable in the host country may not seem important, but to the expatriate on a lengthy overseas assignment, it can become extremely frustrating. What may be even more difficult to deal with is active resentment of the expatriate by the natives of the country, such as that which may be faced by African-American managers taking positions in South Africa.[42] Negative feelings such as this resulting from the perception that the expatriate is taking away a job that could be held by a native of the country may be overt or subtle but can influence many aspects of an expatriate's tour of duty.

The final stage of coping with a new culture is an adaptation stage. During this stage, the expatriate has made reasonable adjustments to the new culture and is able to deal effectively with it. Although this stage seldom returns the expatriate to the heights of excitement that he first experienced, a successful transition to a new culture does return the expatriate to manageable levels of a "normal" lifestyle.

Training the expatriate manager

Once the groundwork for a successful overseas assignment has been laid by choosing expatriates with good chances of succeeding, the next step toward ensuring success is for the organization to properly train and prepare these managers for their upcoming assignments. As with selection, expatriate manager training programs need to focus on issues that are not typically dealt with in domestic training programs.

Figure 3–7

The Culture Shock

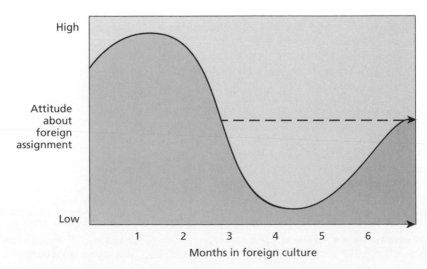

Figure 3–8

Phases of an Expatriate Manager Training Program

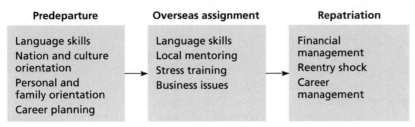

Predeparture	Overseas assignment	Repatriation
Language skills Nation and culture orientation Personal and family orientation Career planning	Language skills Local mentoring Stress training Business issues	Financial management Reentry shock Career management

Source: Adapted from Edward Dunbar and Allan Katcher, "Preparing Managers for Foreign Assignments," *Training and Development Journal,* September 1990, p. 47.

Intercultural training seems to improve the chances for success on an overseas assignment.[43] There are several different kinds of training to choose from, including "documentary" and "interpersonal" training. Documentary training involves relatively passive learning about another culture and its business practices; interpersonal approaches focus on intercultural role playing and self-awareness exercises. Both can be valuable forms of preparation for the expatriate manager.[44]

According to Tung,[45] two primary factors determine how much and what kind of training expatriate managers should receive. These are the level of contact with the host culture that the expatriate will encounter and the degree of dissimilarity between the home and host cultures. As either of these increases, the expatriate will require more in-depth training for the overseas assignment.

Figure 3–8 shows the content and structure of an integrated expatriate manager training program. Its three phases have specific objectives for helping the expatriate to be successful.

Predeparture training includes the critical activities of preparing the expatriate for the overseas assignment. Its purpose is to reduce the amount of culture shock that the manager and his family encounter by familiarizing them with the host country. Among the most important predeparture activities are language training and cultural orientation training.

Prospective global managers should prepare satisfactory answers to the following questions before going on an overseas assignment:

1. How will living abroad affect me and my family?
2. What will my spouse do in terms of work and home life?
3. Are my children prepared for living abroad?
4. What assistance and support will be available to us?
5. What will happen to our home and other personal property while we are gone?
6. What arrangements can be made for family pets?
7. How will we handle health care while we are overseas?
8. Can we expect to encounter any anti-Americanism? What about the threat of terrorism?
9. What security measures should we take?
10. What kinds of recreational opportunities are available?
11. Will language barriers present problems for me?
12. What is the proper form of dress for various occasions?
13. How will we handle transportation at the overseas location?
14. What kinds of food can we expect to eat?

Source: Adapted from Philip R. Harris and Robert T. Moran, "So You're Going Abroad Survey," in *Managing Cultural Differences,* 3d ed. (Houston: Gulf Publishing, 1991).

Table 3–5

Expatriate Self-Awareness: Being Prepared for Culture Shock

Self-awareness is an important aspect of preparing for an international assignment. Assessment techniques such as the one in Table 3–5 can be very helpful to the expatriate. Responding to these kinds of questions can help the manager to know just where she's most likely to encounter the ill effects of culture shock. This kind of advanced preparation can go a long way toward reducing the negative effects of being transplanted to a new culture.

The second phase of an expatriate manager training program occurs at the host country site. In other words, expatriate training does not stop just because the manager has her boarding pass in hand. As seen in Figure 3–8, language instruction continues to be a priority during this phase of training. In addition, mentoring relationships have proven to be effective expatriate training tools. Many organizations with several expatriates at the same overseas location have developed local support groups to help the entire family of a newly arriving expatriate. Some organizations even make participation and leadership in such support groups a part of senior expatriates' jobs.[46]

The final phase of an integrated expatriate training program occurs when the manager is preparing to return to the parent country. The process of being reintegrated into domestic operations is referred to as *repatriation*. And although it may seem straightforward, repatriation can cause culture shock similar to the shock that occurred when the expatriate originally went overseas. Some of the more critical issues that repatriation training must deal with are contained in Figure 3–8. These include the financial adjustments that must be made since the expatriate will frequently lose overseas living subsidies and salary premiums. Helping the manager to get back on career track is also important for repatriation.[47]

The Global Theme for Organizations: Behavior, Structure, and Process

The majority of theory, research, practice, and concepts that deal with organizations have been proposed by Americans, using American subjects (mostly male), with domestic firms.[48] However, globalization has now become a reality. The remaining chapters should be viewed in terms of this global transformation. American-made organizational prescriptions are not superior or inferior to the perspectives offered by others. They are, however, limited in their value. The United States is just one of many important countries in which organizations play a significant role in a nation's social-political, economic, and technological process.

The world's dramatic shifts require more than culture-bound approaches to managing behavior, structure, and processes. The more a country's history and culture deviate from America's, the more caution we need in evaluating the material in the rest of the chapters in this book. The cultural foundations and influences of this chapter are intended to assist readers in recognizing differences and similarities across cultures.

Summary of Key Points

- Globalization has become a reality. It describes the interdependency of transportation, distribution, communication, and economic networks across international borders.

- Cross-cultural management describes organizational behavior within and across countries and attempts to understand and improve the interaction and behavior of co-workers, clients, suppliers, and alliance partners from different cultures and countries.

- The American Society for Training and Development has aptly listed a number of skills that global managers will need to compete effectively in the 21st century. These skills are global strategy, cultural diversity management, team building, organization, communication, and transfer of knowledge.

- Culture consists of patterns of behavior acquired and transmitted within a society. Culture is learned, shared, transgenerational, an influence on perception, and adaptive.

- National culture consists of a set of values, attitudes, beliefs, and norms shared by a majority of the inhabitants of a country.

- Cultural dimensions that differentiate one culture from another include people's relationships to nature, individualism versus collectivism, time orientation, activity orientation, informality, language, and religion.

- Geert Hofstede, a Dutch researcher, has conducted a number of studies that examine national cultures. His initial studies have resulted in the identification of four dimensions that explain some differences and similarities in cultures. The dimensions are *uncertainty avoidance* (the degree to which people are comfortable with ambiguous situations and with the inability to predict future events with accu-

racy), *masculinity–femininity* (masculine cultures are assertive, with dominance practiced and independence valued; feminine cultures are interdependent, compassionate, and emotionally open), *individualism–collectivism*, and *power distance* (referring to the degree to which members of a society accept differences in power and status among themselves).

- Successful expatriate managers have strong technical and language skills, want to work overseas, are flexible, are supported by their families, and manage stress effectively.

- The culture shock cycle involves an initial period of fascination; then a period of shock, confusion, and frustration; and finally a stage that involves adaptation and the ability to cope with the new culture.

Discussion and Review Questions

1. In selecting expatriate managers, why would it be important to make sure that a candidate's family supports his assignment?

2. Are Americans any more or less parochial or ethnocentric than Japanese or French-Canadians? Explain.

3. Which countries do you believe are most like the United States? Do you agree with Hofstede's findings? Why?

4. What is meant by the term a *culture-bound theory of motivation?*

5. What is culture shock and how can it affect the behavior of a newly assigned expatriate manager?

6. What would you expect to find in terms of Hofstede's initial four dimensions when and if Russian managers are studied?

7. Describe the attitudes a manager would need to be successful and effective in managing in India, China, and Saudi Arabia.

8. Can domestic cultural diversity in the United States help American firms better understand and deal with global cultural diversity? Explain.

9. How does a national culture differ from what is referred to as an organization's culture?

10. Why is religion often incorrectly ignored in discussions and analyses of business, negotiations, and culture?

CASE FOR ANALYSIS

Employment Opportunities in Multinational Firms

When a foreign-owned firm enters a country, an inevitable concern of the natives of that country focuses on the hiring practices and opportunities for advancement in that organization. Often considerable attention will be paid to the number of home-country nationals that are employed and promoted by foreign companies. Also often, this scrutiny can take on a negative tone. For example, early in the 1990s a large number of Americans viewed Japanese corporations as hostile, powerful, and suspiciously nonwhite institutions. These Americans believed that Japan was about to conquer the United States economically. The sentiment was strong enough that a U.S. House Subcommittee on Employment and Housing convened from July 1991 to June 1992 to investigate charges that

Japanese corporations were "systematically discriminating against Americans in general and against American minorities and women in particular." The question was asked whether Japanese corporations in the United States had "glass ceilings" that limited promotion and job assignment of American employees.

To address this issue, 400 detailed questionnaires were sent to "workplace units" of Japanese corporations in the United States from December 1991 to February 1992. For this survey, a workplace unit was defined as a separate physical unit of operation that employed more than 20 persons at the time of the survey. The sample was selected on a random basis from a mixed pool of subsidiaries, manufacturing plants, branch operations, and joint ventures

Exhibit 1   Responding Japanese Firms in the United States by Employment Size

EMPLOYEES PER WORKPLACE	WORKPLACE UNITS	AMERICAN EMPLOYEES	JAPANESE EXPATRIATES	TOTAL	% JAPANESE
Fewer than 50	46	830	315	1,145	27.5
50–99	17	977	156	1,133	13.7
100–299	36	5,563	603	6,166	9.7
300–499	16	5,825	242	6,067	3.9
500–999	11	7,162	333	7,495	4.4
Over 1,000	18	45,081	1,104	46,185	2.4
Total	144	65,438	2,753	68,191	4.03

Exhibit 2   Racial Makeup of American Employees in Japanese Firms in the United States

	% CAUCASIAN	% AFRO-AMERICAN	% HISPANIC	% ASIAN	% OTHER
NONEXEMPT STATUS					
Total employees (46,884)					
Male (28,937)	76.4	8.6	9.9	4.6	0.5
Female (17,947)	72.1	11.1	9.6	7.1	0.1
EXEMPT STATUS					
Total employees (16,974)					
Male (12,456)	83.3	3.1	3.6	9.3	0.7
Female (4,518)	78.3	5.3	4.2	12.1	0.1

constituting the major Japanese business operations in the United States.

By the end of February 1992, 144 responses (36 percent) were received. From these responses, functional profiles of Japanese corporations in the United States and their human resource practices were developed by the researchers. Those 144 workplace units are distributed in terms of employment size in Exhibit 1.

Totaled together, the 144 respondents employed 65,438 Americans as of February 1992. From this it was estimated that at that time a total of about 850,000 Americans were employed directly by Japanese businesses in the United States. In contrast, an estimated 50,000 Americans were directly employed by Japanese businesses in the United States in 1982. Thus, between 1982 and 1992, at least 800,000 jobs were directly created by Japanese businesses in the United States (a conservative estimate). In addition to Japanese corporations in the United States, literally thousands of Japanese entrepreneurial shop owners and privately owned businesses have expanded their diverse mercantile activities in the United States. Many of them employ Americans.

Exhibit 2 analyzes 135 responding firms' racial profiles of American employees. Nonexempt status

employees were defined as the so-called rank-and-file employees. Exempt-status employees included managers, executives, and professionals who earned annual salaries but were ineligible for hourly overtime compensation. These classifications followed the categories specified by U.S. employment and labor laws.

The 1990 U.S. Bureau of the Census figures break down the nation's racial makeup into the following categories: white (Caucasian) 72.02 percent, Afro-American 12.1 percent, Hispanic 9.0 percent, Asian and Pacific Islanders 2.9 percent, others 3.9 percent, and Native Americans .08 percent. Using these figures as a basis of comparison, Japanese firms in the United States employed a large number of minorities, but these minorities tended to be Asian-American rather than Afro-American and Hispanic workers.

The larger representation of Asian-American minorities in the workforce of Japanese-owned firms is not entirely surprising. Many capable Asian-Americans may have found satisfactory employment with Japanese firms while they are often shunned by American firms. Thus the larger proportion of Asian-Americans over Hispanic and Afro-American minorities does not necessarily mean that Japanese firms avoid these groups. Furthermore, the reason why Japanese businesses appeared to employ a relatively smaller percentage of Afro-Americans than the general racial composite is that over one-half of Japanese businesses in the United States are engaged in headquarters administration, research and development, customer service, and sales functions. In American corporations, these particular areas also employ a relatively smaller percentage of Afro-Americans in general and fewer male Afro-Americans in particular.

Any person who investigates host country employees' complaints about foreign multinational firms is invariably struck by the common perception of glass ceilings blocking promotional opportunities. These problems are common to foreign multinationals in any country and are often aggravated by the workforce's proclivity to label missed promotions and other related disappointments as an employer's unfair practices. When their employers are foreign, host country employees invariably claim that many workplace promotional disappointments are due to foreign employers' discrimination against native employees.

Japanese companies in the United States have come under close examination based on employees' charges of discriminatory practices. Even when Japanese firms adopt the customary practice of sending their Japanese rotational executives to occupy the highest executive positions in their American subsidiaries, the American public and mass media are quick to point out that Japanese businesses are excluding Americans from these posts.

This may, however, not be the case. Contrary to the above perceptions, some surveys suggest that promotions and job security for certain executive positions are more often available in foreign subsidiaries in the U.S. than in U.S.-owned firms. In terms of the survey on Japanese-owned companies, Exhibit 3 illustrates that both male and female Americans were occupying executive ranks in more than a few firms. Americans were found in the three top executive level positions (chairman, president, and executive vice president), although these positions were overwhelmingly held by Japanese expatriates. However, the seemingly lower percentages of Americans in the top echelons of Japanese firms in the United States were in fact higher when compared to American firms' practices in Japan, German firms' practices in Japan, or German firms' practices in the United States.

Repeatedly in recent years, American executives have watched as Japanese companies took failing U.S. plants and unproductive, uncooperative workers and turned them into rousing successes. At a time when American manufacturers have been pushing production overseas, Japanese companies have opened about 2,000 factories in the United States. These successes are made possible by incorporating flexible manufacturing, zero-defect production, and quick customer response. Recent rebirths of American integrated steel firms have also been made possible through massive infusions of Japanese technology, capital, and manufacturing systems. Many Japanese factories throughout the United States (like Toyota's plant in Kentucky and Honda's in Ohio) are serving as models of quality manufacturing for American corporations. Adaptive management systems of Japanese manufacturing firms are providing prototypes of the "human resource–based" manufacturing and customer services for the high tech global age of the future.

This is not to say, however, that all is wonderful in foreign-owned organizations. Quite often tremendous

Exhibit 3   Japanese Expatriates and Americans in Executive Positions

	JAPANESE EXPATRIATES	TOTAL AMERICANS	FEMALE AMERICANS	% AMERICANS
TOP EXECUTIVE ECHELON				
Chairman	52	5	0	9.2
President	99	19	1	16.6
Executive VP	89	56	4	38.6
Branch manager	92	301	44	76.5
MIDDLE MANAGEMENT				
Senior VP	90	104	5	53.6
Vice president	185	391	32	67.8
General manager	193	329	18	63.0
Assistant or deputy VP	148	321	53	68.4
Manager	895	2,652	417	74.7

communication problems exist among employees, between employees and management, and between management in the host country and top management in the home country. There are often significant difficulties among American workers in adjusting to the culture typically prevalent in Japanese-owned companies, and among Japanese managers attempting to implement specific business practices for their American employees. For instance, the use of pay systems that focus on tangible rewards for individual performance still goes against the grain of many teamwork-oriented Japanese managers.

According to one survey done in the midst of the furor over Japanese hiring practices, over two-thirds of Japanese firms of all types in the United States had become more negative in their attitudes and their perception of political risks of further expansion in the United States. Much of this bad feeling about the United States as an inhospitable environment for Japanese business could be directly attributed to an atmosphere of "Japan-bashing." No doubt, some Japanese managers or some Japanese firms have treated some Americans badly or been less than culturally sensitive to their American employees. The opposite argument, it should be noted, can also be made both here and abroad for American-owned firms. The wronged parties, both American and Japanese, should be given full legal recourse and due process under the law and have state and federal officers to protect them, including the Equal Employ-ment Opportunity Commission (EEOC). The basic issue that continues to be addressed, however, is how host country nationals can be integrated into a foreign subsidiary to the benefit of the workers, the host country, and the organization as well.

Discussion and Review Questions

1. Do Japanese corporations in the United States have any more of a glass ceiling for the promotion of American employees than do other foreign-owned corporations in the United States?

2. What are some approaches that could be taken to facilitate the recruitment and retention of host country nationals for a multinational subsidiary?

3. Given that a glass ceiling for promotion for women appears to be more in existence in the United States and Japan than it does in other parts of Asia such as Hong Kong, what does this tell us in regard to the need for cultural awareness among managers in multicultural settings?

Source: Adapted from Yoshi Tsurumi, "Japanese Corporations in America: Managing Cultural Differences," *Pacific Basin Quarterly,* Fall 1992, pp. 3–9, 14–19; see also Michelle Martinez, "Foreign-Owned Companies Offer Opportunity for Fast-Track CFOs," *HRMagazine,* October 1995, p. 25; DeAnn Christinat, "Salary or Stability?," *CFO: The Magazine for Chief Financial Officers,* October 1995, p. 19; Anne Stuart, "Money Can't Buy You Love," *CIO,* October 1, 1995, p. 44; Anne Stuart, "My Owner Lies Over the Ocean," *CIO,* October 1, 1995, p. 39; Anne Stuart, "Long-Distance Relationships," *CIO,* October 1, 1995, pp. 37–44; William P. Cordeiro and Robert H. Turner, "20/20 Hindsight: Managers Must Commit to TQM," *Interfaces,* May/June 1995, pp. 104–12; Anonymous, "Japanese Companies Can't Seem to Adjust to U.S. Pay Practices," *HR Focus,* February 1995, p 14; Gillian Flynn, "Asian Markets Provide Women Ample Opportunity," *Personnel Journal,* November 1995, p. 30.

EXPERIENTIAL EXERCISE

Testing Globalization Knowledge

Objectives

1. To test your understanding of cultural differences.
2. To compare your understanding and international experiences with classmates.

Starting the Exercise

1. Each student should complete the seven-category survey.
2. Score your individual answers with the answer key.
3. Form into groups of five or six and compare international experiences. Did individuals with more international experience score better?

4. Within the group, discuss steps that could be taken to improve individual knowledge of cultural differences.

Going Global? Test Your Business Etiquette Knowledge. (Some Questions Have More Than One Answer.)

1. During business meetings, use first names in
    a. Great Britain, because everyone is so chummy.
    b. Australia, because informality is the rule.
    c. China, because the first name is the surname.
    d. Japan, because the last names are easy to mispronounce.

2. In China, offer expensive gifts to your hosts
   a. Every time they ask for one.
   b. When you need help getting out of the country.
   c. Never. If they can't reciprocate it, they'll lose face.

3. In which country is a business card an object of respect?
   a. Japan. An executive's identity depends on his employer.
   b. Taiwan. It explains a person's rank and status.
   c. France, especially cards describing a man's experience.

4. When doing business in Japan, never
   a. Touch someone.
   b. Leave your chopsticks in the rice.
   c. Take people to pricier restaurants than they took you to.
   d. All of the above.

5. Power breakfasts are inappropriate in all but
   a. Italy. The natives like to bring the family along.
   b. Mexico. People don't bother to get to work till 10 a.m. anyway.
   c. United States. We invented them.
   d. France. People are at their most argumentative in the morning.

6. In some countries, colors are key. Which is true?
   a. For Koreans, writing a person's name in red signifies death.
   b. In China and Japan, gifts wrapped in white or black should only be presented at funerals.
   c. Purple suits in Great Britain represent lack of taste.

7. Which of these choices are obscene gestures?
   a. The okay sign in Brazil.
   b. A hearty slap on the back in Switzerland.
   c. Doing anything with the left hand in Saudi Arabia.
   d. Thumb between second and third finger in Japan.

Answers: 1—b, c; 2—c; 3—a, b; 4—d; 5—c; 6—a, b; 7—a, c, d.

Source: Business World, May 1990, p. 27.

Southwest Airlines: Creating the Organizational Culture

For some organizations, the slogan "focus on customers" is merely a slogan. At Southwest Airlines, however, it is a daily goal. For example, Southwest employees responded quickly to a customer complaint: Five students who commuted weekly to an out-of-state medical school notified Southwest that the most convenient flight got them to class 15 minutes late. To accommodate the students, Southwest moved the depature time up by a quarter of an hour.

Southwest Airlines is an organization that has built its business and corporate culture around the tenets of total quality management. Focus on the customer, employee involvement and empowerment, and continuous impovement are not just buzz words to Southwest employees or to Herb Kelleher, CEO of Southwest Airlines in Dallas, In fact, Kelleher has even enlisted passengers in the effort to strengthen the interviewing and selecting prospective flight attendents. Focus groups are used to help measure passenger response to new services and to help generate new ideas for improving current services. Additionally, the roughly 1,000 customers who write to the company every week generally get a personal response within four weeks. It's no surprise that in 1994, for the third consecutive year, Southwest won the U.S. Department of Transportation's Triple Crown Award for best on-time performance, best baggage handling, and fewest customer complaints.

The airline industry

Southwest has been posting hefty profits in an industry that lost $4 billion between 1990 and 1993. Since the 1978 Airline Deregulation Act, constant fare wars and intense competition have contributed to a turbulent environment for the industry. Under deregulation, the government no longer dictates where a given airline will fly and which cities should have service. Rates and service are now determined through competitive forces. The impact on the industry has been tremendous. In 1991, alone, three carriers went through bankruptcy and liquidation, and in early 1992, TWA sought protection from its creditors. Very few airlines, such as Southwest, American, and Delta, have continued to grow into the 1990s.

In 1994, when industry earnings were only $100 million (on revenues of $54 billion), Southwest earned $179 million while spending an industry-low 7 cents a mile in operating costs. The following year, despite facing new competition from upstart low-cost airlines, Southwest had record earnings of nearly $183 million.

Both external factors, such as the price of jet fuel and the strength of the economy, and internal factors, including routing system designs, computerized reservation systems, and motivated, competent employees, help to determine success. The airline industry is capital intensive, with large expenditures for planes. In addition, carriers must provide superior customer service. Delayed flights, lost baggage, overbooked flights, cancellations, and unhelpful airline employees can quickly alienate an airline's passengers.

Southwest's corporate strategy

Herb Kelleher has been the primary force in developing and maintaining a vision and strategy which have enabled Southwest Airlines to grow and maintain profitability. Created in the late 1960s as a low-fare, high-frequency, short-haul, point-to-point, single-class, noninterlining, fun-loving airline, it expands by "doing the same old thing at each new airport," Kelleher reports.

"Taking a different approach" is the Southwest way, which has allowed the airline to maintain a 15 percent annual growth rate even during a period of drastic change. Although reservations and ticketing are done in advance of a flight, seating occurs on a first-come, first-served basis and is only one illustration of the company's noncomformist practices. Turnaround times are kept to an industry low of 15 minutes with the help of pilots and crew who clean and restock the planes.

Refreshments are limited to soft drinks and peanuts, except on longer flights when cookies and crackers are added to the menu. Southwest does not exchange tickets or baggage with other carriers. Kelleher has noted that if Southwest adopted an assigned seating and computerized, interlining reservation system, ground time would increase enough to necessitate the purchase of at least seven additional airplanes. At a cost of $25 million apiece, the impact on the fares customers pay would be high. Currently, Southwest charges significantly less than its competitors.

Corporate philosophy, culture, and management practices

How does Southwest maintain its unique, cost-effective position? In an industry in which atangonistic labor–management relations are common, how does Southwest build cooperation with a workforce that is 83 percent unionized? Led by Kelleher, the corporation has developed a culture that treats employees the same way it treats passengers—by paying attention, being responsive, and involving them in decisions.

According to Elizabeth Pedrick Sartain, vice-president of People (the company's top HRM person), Southwest's corporate culture makes the airline unique. "We feel this fun atmosphere builds a strong sense of community. It also counterbalances the stress of hard work and competition." As Kelleher has stated, "If you don't treat your own people well, they won't treat other people well." So, Southwest's focus is not only on the customer but on the employees, too.

At Southwest, the organizational culture includes a high value on flexibility of the workforce. Employees take pride in their ability to get a plane ready to go in only 20 minutes, less than half the industry average. A cultural refrain is "Can't make money with the airplane sitting on the ground." Ramp agents unload baggage, clean the lavatories, carry out trash, and stock the plane with ice, drinks and peanuts. Flight attendants prepare the cabin for the next flight, and pilots have been known to pitch in when they have time. Working hard is not just an obligation at Southwest; it is a source of pride. Ramp agent Mike Williams brags that in a conversation with an employee from another airline, the other man explained Southwest's fast turn-around by saying, in William's words, "The difference is that when one of [the other company's] planes lands, they work it, and when one of our planes lands, we *attack* it."

In addition to the high motivation and expectations for performance, evidence of the company culture can be seen in the recruitment and selection process. Southwest accepts applications for ground operations positions or as flight attendants all year round. Many of the applicants are Southwest customers who've seen recruitment ads like the one featuring Kelleher dressed as Elvis. In 1994, Southwest received more than 126,000 applicants for a variety of positions; the People Department interviewed more than 35,000 individuals for 4,500 positions. The expanding company was off to an even faster start the next year; in the first two months of 1995, it hired 1,200 new employees. This large labor pool allows the company to hire employees who most closely fit a culture in which they are asked to use their own judgment and to go beyond "the job description."

Kelleher's philosophy of "fun in the workplace" can be seen in a number of company practices. Company parties can be triggered by many events, including the CEO's birthday, when employees dress in black. The annual company chili cook-off, Southwest's annual awards dinner, and the every Friday "Fun Day," when employees wear casual clothes or even costumes to work, illustrate the company credo that a sense of humor is a must and that relaxed people are productive people. Kevin Krone, area manager of marketing in the Detroit office, described efforts by the Detroit area airport employees to set up get-togethers to foster both fun and the commitment to the Southwest family that supports the airline's culture.

Employee involvement in decision making is another key tenet of organizational culture at Southwest. An active, informal suggestion system and all types of incentives (cash, merchandise, and travel passes) serve to reward employees for their ideas. Both teams and individuals are expected, as part of their role at Southwest, to contribute to the development of customer service improvements and cost savings.

Corporate responses to difficult issues are consistently formulated around the company philosophy. As the cost of benefits has risen, cost-conscious Southwest redesigned the employee benefits program into a flexible plan. However, the company went a step further a few years ago, when Sartain was director of benefits and compensation. She believed that for the effort to succeed and satisfy employees, communication was critical. After seeking the advice of more than 700 employees in seven different cities, a promotional program that parodied newspapers and morning news shows was presented. Horoscopes, advice columns, and advertisements all promoted the new program, BenefitsPlus. Employees found this format more fun and less intimidating than the traditional benefits brochure. In fact, the effort won Southwest first place in the 1990 Business Insurance Employee Benefits Communication Awards competition. More importantly, employees understand their benefits options and appreciate the willingness of their organization to communicate openly.

Many management practices have been designed to support the company culture. Compensation programs are designed to increase the connections between Southwest and its employees, who enjoy the benefits of a profit-sharing program. Southwest employees own roughly 11 percent of the company's outstanding stock. The company's union contracts have avoided overly restrictive work rules in order to support the efficient operation of the company. Part of the company credo is that employees need to be able (and want to be able) to step in wherever they are needed, regardless of job title or classification. Southwest has not laid off an employee since its founding in 1971; annual employee turnover, at 7 percent, is the industry's lowest. A recently signed 10-year contract with the pilots includes stock options in lieu of guaranteed pay increases during the first five years, demonstrating the trust between the employees and the organization. Kelleher wanted a time frame that would give the pilots enough time to hold on to and exercise the stock options; the pilots' outside investment experts agreed. Also, in 1996 Kelleher voluntarily agreed to freeze his pay at its 1992 level through 1999 to match the pilots' freeze. Such shared sacrifice helps build morale and organizational commitment even further.

The combined focus on customers and employees has led to an increase in the diversity of Southwest's workforce. To serve passengers in the southwest United States even more effectively, the company has been recruiting Spanish-speaking employees as well as offering a Spanish Berlitz course at a discount to current employees.

The employees of Southwest are actively involved in numerous community-based service projects at Ronald McDonald house and the Junior Olympics, among others. This commitment to service is encourage and demostrated within the organization, too. A catastrophe fund, initiated by employees, supports individual employees during personal crises. Departments frequently show appreciation to other departments by giving awards and parties.

Kelleher claims that it is hard for Southwest to expand through the purchase of other airlines because the difficulty of merging two corporate cultures, particularly when one is so strong, is too great. In fact, the company's recent difficulties in the Pacific Northwest bear this out. Its expansion into that market was accomplished through the purchase of Morris Air. But Southwest continues to compete. In 1996 it expanded routes into Tampa, Houston, Las Vegas, and secondary routes in the Northeast.

"We tell our people that we value inconsistency," Kelleher explains. "By that I mean that . . . I can't foresee all of the situations that will arise at the stations across our system. So what we tell our people is, 'Hey, we can't anticipate all of these things, *you* handle them the best way possible. *You* make a judgment and use *your* discretion; we trust you'll do the right thing.' If we think you've done something erroneous, we'll let you know—without criticism, without backbiting."

Employees offer a large number of what they consider to be "everyday examples" of ways they provide high-qaulity service to their customers. When a California customer service agent was approached by a harried man who needed to catch a flight to meet his vacationing family, the man wanted to check his dog onto the flight. Because Southwest does not fly animals, this could have caused him to miss the flight and his family. The service agent involved volunteered to take the dog home, care for it, and bring the dog back to meet the man two weeks later, upon his return. A torn-up backyard and a very appreciative customer were the outcomes.

Critical Thinking

1. How has Southwest dealt with the competitive challenges in the airline industry today? Rank, in order of importance, the various management practices and business practices (such as low-price strategy) that Southwest Airlines has developed to successfully meet its competitive challenges.

2. Do you think that Southwest's success is more a result of business practices, human resource practices, or the interaction between the two? Can good management practices help a company be successful without good business practices?

3. How might a ground crew supervisor at Southwest describe her job, given the corporate culture and practices of this organization?

4. Which Southwest strategies directly support total quality management?

5. What aspects of work life at Southwest do you think you would most enjoy and least enjoy? Why?

6. Would the management practices used at Southwest Airlines work in other organizations? Why or why not?

Sources: Scott McCarthey, "Southwest Airlines Net Sets Record for 4th Quarter," *New York Times,* January 26, 1996, A4; Brenda Palk Sunoo, "How Fun Flies at Southwest Airlines," *Personnel Journal,* June 1995, 62–73; Scott McCartney, "Salary for Chief of Southwest Air Rises after Four Years," *The Wall Street Journal,* April 29, 1996, A24; "Southwest Air to Add Routes," *The Wall Street Journal,* April 4, 1996, C20; "Southwest Air to Add at Least One City before the Year Ends," *The Wall Street Journal,* May 17, 1996, C11; National Public Radio, "Morning Edition," June 30, 1994; J. Castelli, "Finding the Right Fit," *HRMagazine,* September 1990, 38–41; D. K. Henderson, "Southwest Luvs Passengers, Employees, Profits," *Air Transport World,* July 1991, 32–41; J. E. Hitchcock, "Southwest Airlines Renovates Benefits System," *HRMagazine,* July 1992, 54–56; C. A. Jaffe, "Moving Fast by Standing Still," *Nation's Business,* October 1991, 57–59; J. C. Quick, "Crafting an Organizational Culture: Herb's Hand at Southwest," *Organizational Dynamics,* 21 (1992): 45–56: R. S. Teitelbaum, "Southwest Airlines: Where Service Flies Right," *Fortune.* August 24, 1992, 115–116. For more information on Southwest Airlines, including the latest press releases, tour of a Boeing 737, or the most recent flight schedule, visit the Southwest Airlines home page on the World Wide Web at **http://www.iflyswa.com.**

No.2

Behavior within Organizations: The Individual

Chapter 4

Individual Behavior and Differences

Learning Objectives

Define

Perception and explain its role in understanding and coping with organizational life.

Describe

How self-efficacy can influence an employee's behavior.

Discuss

Why the increasing diversity of the workforce will require the adoption of a different approach/style of managing employees.

Compare

The meaning of the psychological contract from the employee perceptive and the employer perspective.

Identify

Why it's difficult to change a person's attitude.

Any attempt to learn why people behave as they do in organizations requires some understanding of individual

differences. Managers spend considerable time judging the fit between individuals, job tasks, and effectiveness. Both the manager's and the subordinate's characteristics typically influence such judgments. Without some understanding of behavior, decisions about who performs what tasks in a particular manner can lead to irreversible long-run problems.

Employees differ from one another in many respects. A manager needs to ask how such differences influence subordinates' behavior and performance. This chapter highlights individual differences and dispositions that can make one person a significantly better performer than another person. In addition, the chapter addresses several crucial individual differences that managers should consider.

We also talk about how the environment affects individual differences. It's incorrect to assume that individual differences have no connection at all with the environment (work, family, community, and society). They're inextricably intertwined.

The Basis for Understanding Behavior

The manager's observation and analysis of individual behavior and performance require consideration of variables that directly influence individual behavior, or what an employee does (e.g., produces output, sells cars, services machines). The individual variables include abilities and skills, background, and demographic variables. As Figure 4–1 shows, an employee's behavior is complex because it's affected by a number of environmental variables and many different individual factors, experiences, and events. Such individual variables as abilities/skills, personality, perceptions, and experiences affect behavior.

Whether any manager can modify, mold, or reconstruct behaviors is a much-debated issue among behavioral scientists and managerial practitioners. Although they usually agree that changing any individual psychological factor requires thorough diagnosis, skill,

Figure 4–1

Individual-Behavior Framework

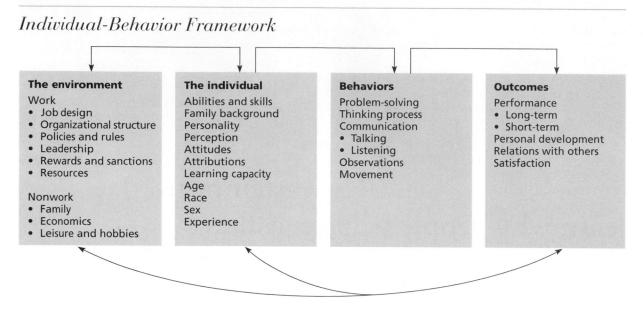

patience, and understanding on the part of a manager, there's no universally agreed-upon method managers can use to change personalities, attitudes, perceptions, or learning patterns. On the other hand, it is recognized that people's behavior patterns do change, albeit slightly, sometimes when managers would prefer that they remain stable. Managers must recognize the inherent difficulty in trying to get people to do and think about the things that are desirable to the organization.

Managers today face sweeping demographic changes in the workplace. There are more women and more African-American, Hispanic, and Asian applicants and employees. In the 21st century fewer people will be in the human resource pool, which means that more attention must be paid to improving the performance of the available people.[1]

Since many workers may lack needed skills, managers will probably have to devote more time to educating, training, and creating a positive motivational atmosphere for employees. Managers must determine how to make work better, more rewarding, and challenging. Unless they can accomplish this agenda, the outcomes associated with work—such as quality, quantity, and service—will suffer.[2]

Employees' behaviors lead to outcomes. They can result in positive long-term performance and personal growth or the opposite, poor long-term performance and a lack of growth. As Figure 4–1 also shows, behaviors and outcomes serve as feedback to the person and the environment.

Human behavior is too complex to be explained by one sweeping generalization. Figure 4–1 gives only a sampling of the relevant variables that influence human behavior. Since coverage of each of the variables in this figure is beyond the scope of this book, most of our attention is given to three major psychological variables: perception, attitudes, and personality. These three form the foundation for our discussion of motivation, group behavior, and leadership. Learning and motivation variables are discussed in Chapters 5 and 6; other chapters of the book present the organizational variables.

Figure 4–1 suggests that effective management requires that individual behavior differences be recognized and, when feasible, taken into consideration while managing organizational behavior. To understand **individual differences,** managers must (1) observe and recognize the differences, (2) study variables that influence individual behavior, and (3) discover relationships among the variables. For example, managers are in a better position to make optimal decisions if they know employees' attitudes, perceptions, and mental abilities as well as how these and other variables are related. It is also important to know how each variable influences performance. Being able to observe differences, understand relationships, and predict linkages facilitates managerial attempts to improve performance.

Behavior, as outlined in Figure 4–1, is anything that a person does. *Talking* to a manager, *listening* to a co-worker, *filing* a report, *inputting* a memo into a word processor, and *placing* a completed unit in inventory are behaviors. So are *daydreaming, reading* this book, and *learning* how to use a firm's accounting system. The general framework indicates that behavior depends on the types of variables shown in Figure 4–1. Thus, as Kurt Lewin originally proposed, B = f(I, E): an employee's behavior (B) is a function of individual (I) and environmental (E) variables.[3] The behavior that results on the job is unique to each individual, but the underlying process is basic to all people.

After years of theory building and research, it's generally agreed that

1. Behavior is caused.
2. Behavior is goal-directed.
3. Behavior that can be observed is measurable.
4. Behavior that's not directly observable (for example, thinking and perceiving) is also important in accomplishing goals.
5. Behavior is motivated.

To emphasize these points of agreement, consider the case of Jim, who usually has been an average performer but recently became a high performer. A manager's analysis (which may be totally incorrect) of this behavior change might be as follows: Jim recently increased his efforts to perform. He has shown more interest in his work and has expressed interest in a vacancy in another department. This suggests that the improved performance occurred because Jim became motivated to work harder to gain a possible promotion.

Another explanation of Jim's behavior change might be that personnel cutbacks have him worried. He doesn't want to lose his job, and fear of job loss motivates him to do more work.

The desired result of any employee's behavior is effective performance. In organizations, therefore, individual and environmental variables affect not only behavior but also performance. An important part of a manager's job is to define performance in advance—that is, to state what results are desired. Performance-related behaviors are directly associated with job tasks that need to be accomplished to achieve a job's objectives. For a manager, performance-related behavior would include such actions as identifying performance problems; planning, organizing, and controlling employees' work; and creating a motivational climate for subordinates.[4]

Focusing their attention on performance-related behaviors, managers search for ways to achieve optimal performance. If employees aren't performing well or consistently, managers must investigate the problem. These six questions can help managers focus on performance problems:

Individual Differences

Individuals are similar, but they are also unique. The study of individual differences such as attitudes, perceptions, and abilities helps a manager explain differences in performance levels.

1. Does the employee have the skills and abilities to perform the job?
2. Does the employee have the necessary resources to perform the job?
3. Is the employee aware of the performance problem?
4. When did the performance problem surface?
5. How do the employee's co-workers react to the performance problem?
6. What can I do as a manager to alleviate the performance problem?

These questions and their answers again call attention to the complexity of individual differences and performance. They also indicate that when performance problems are identified, some form of managerial action is required.[5]

Individual Differences

The individual variables in Figure 4–1 may be classified as abilities and skills, background, and demographic. Each of these classes of variables helps explain individual differences in behavior and performance.

Abilities and skills

Ability

A biological or learned trait that permits a person to do something mental or physical.

Skills

Task-related competencies.

Some employees, although highly motivated, simply don't have the abilities or skills to perform well. Abilities and skills play a major role in individual behavior and performance.[6] An **ability** is a trait (innate or learned) that permits a person to do something mental or physical. **Skills** are task-related competencies, such as the skill to operate a lathe or a computer, or the skill to clearly communicate a group's mission and goals. In this book, the terms are used interchangeably in most cases. Remember that B = f(I, E). Table 4–1 identifies 10 mental abilities that make up what's commonly referred to as intelligence.[7] Intelligence is often the best predictor of job success, but "best" does not mean "only" and many other factors play a role in performance.[8]

Thus managers must decide which mental abilities are required to successfully perform each job. For example, a language interpreter helping a manager put together a business deal with a Hungarian enterprise would especially need language fluency, number facility, and verbal comprehension in both English and Hungarian. The astute manager would search for an interpreter who had these abilities.

A secretary's job may especially require memory, perceptual speed, and verbal comprehension, as well as various physical skills (Table 4–2) to operate word-processing equipment. Managers attempt to match each person's abilities and skills with the job requirements. The matching process is important because no amount of leadership, motivation, or organizational resources can make up for deficiencies in abilities or skills. **Job analysis** is used to take some of the guesswork out of matching. It's the process of defining and studying a job in terms of tasks or behaviors and specifying the responsibilities, education, and training needed to perform the job successfully.[9]

Job Analysis

Process of defining and studying a job in terms of behavior and specifying education and training needed to perform the job.

Every job is made up of two things: people and job tasks. Matching people with jobs suited for their abilities and skills is often a problem.[10] Why do people end up in jobs in which they aren't productive, satisfied, or fulfilled? The effort to match jobs involves the following activities: employee selection, training and development, career planning, and counseling. To be successful in matching a person's abilities and skills to the job, a manager must examine *content, required behaviors,* and *preferred behaviors.* Content is the "what" of the job—the job

Table 4–1   Mental Abilities = Intelligence

MENTAL ABILITY	DESCRIPTION
1. Flexibility and speed of closure	The ability to hold in mind a particular visual configuration.
2. Fluency	The ability to produce words, ideas, and verbal expressions.
3. Inductive reasoning	The ability to form and test hypotheses directed at finding relationships.
4. Associative memory	The ability to remember bits of unrelated material and to recall.
5. Span memory	The ability to recall perfectly for immediate reproduction a series of items after only one presentation of the series.
6. Number facility	The ability to rapidly manipulate numbers in arithmetic operations.
7. Perceptual speed	Speed in finding figures, making comparisons, and carrying out simple tasks involving visual perceptions.
8. Deductive reasoning	The ability to reason from stated premises to their necessary conclusion.
9. Spatial orientation and visualization	The ability to perceive spatial patterns and to manipulate or transform the image of spatial patterns.
10. Verbal comprehension	Knowledge of words and their meaning as well as the application of this knowledge.

Source: Adapted from Marvin D. Dunnette, "Aptitudes, Abilities, and Skills," in *Handbook of Industrial and Organizational Psychology,* Marvin D. Dunnette, ed. (Skokie, IL.: Rand McNally, 1976), pp. 481–83.

Table 4–2   Samples of Physical Skills

PHYSICAL SKILL	DESCRIPTION
1. Dynamic strength	Muscular endurance in exerting force continuously or repeatedly.
2. Extent flexibility	The ability to flex or stretch trunk and back muscles.
3. Gross body coordination	The ability to coordinate the action of several parts of the body while the body is in motion.
4. Gross body equilibrium	The ability to maintain balance with nonvisual cues.
5. Stamina	The capacity to sustain maximum effort requiring cardiovascular exertion.

Source: Adapted from Edwin A. Fleishman, "On the Relation between Abilities, Learning, and Human Performance," *American Psychologist,* November 1972, pp. 1017–32.

description, responsibilities, goals and objectives, and specific tasks. Required behaviors are the "how" of the job—how it must be done in terms of quantity, quality, cost, and timing.

Preferred behaviors are often ignored in matching people and jobs. In order to be selected, some applicants don't honestly explain their preferences. Because they want the job so badly, they hold back or even mislead interviewers. Managers must attempt to determine a person's preference in terms of goals, style, career values, and achievement motives. An ideal job is one in which a person's skills and abilities can be applied to produce work that's satisfactory, fulfilling, and challenging. This is the goal of matching a person with the job.

Demographics

Among the most important demographic classifications are gender and race. Cultural diversity also can impact work situations.

GENDER DIFFERENCES   Are men and women different in terms of workplace behavior, job performance, leadership style, or commitment? Are the differences, if any, significant? It's generally accepted that, from the moment of birth, boys and girls are treated differently. Research has shown that men and women are equal in terms of learning ability, memory, reasoning ability, creativity, and intelligence.[11] Despite fairly conclusive research data to the contrary, some people still believe that there are creativity, reasoning, and learning ability differences between the sexes.

There have been debates about male and female differences in terms of job performance, absenteeism, and turnover rates. The job performance debate is inconclusive. There are no compelling data suggesting that men or women are better job performers. The only area in which a difference is found somewhat consistently is absenteeism. Women have a higher rate of absenteeism since they are usually the caregivers to children, elder parents, and ill spouses, which makes them absent more from the job.[12]

Whether or not changes in society will result in more similarity between men and women is difficult to gauge. When society emphasized the difference between the sexes and treated them differently, there were some differences in such areas as aggressiveness and social behavior. But as society places more emphasis on equal opportunity and treatment, many differences are likely to disappear.[13] Men and women are becoming more alike in terms of workplace behavior.

RACIAL AND CULTURAL DIVERSITY   Today's workforce doesn't look like the workforce of the past. The workforce is now much more diverse in terms of cultural background, values, language skills, and educational preparation. Diversity is a term used to describe the cultural, ethnic, and racial variations in a population. Many culturally diverse groups from around the world (e.g., Vietnam, South Korea, Mexico, Russia) are spread throughout the workforce. Whether significant differences in job performance across diverse groups exist isn't known. Studies haven't been conducted in sufficient numbers to reach a conclusion.[14]

Diversity

Used to describe human qualities such as race, gender, and ethnicity that are different from our own and outside the groups to which we belong.

As a more diverse workforce enters organizations, it will become mandatory to not base decisions, prescriptions, and techniques on white male research results.[15] Generalizing from a research dominant group (white males) to women, African-Americans, Hispanics, Asians, and other groups isn't sound. Faulty generalization can lead to making improper assumptions, presenting inadequate solutions, and implementing inaccurate reward, performance evaluation, and team-building programs. Similarly, minority-based study results are also unlikely to be generalizable to a majority group.

Managers aren't yet as diverse as the rest of the workforce. To manage the increasingly culturally diverse workforce will require flexibility, recognition of individual differences, and increased awareness of cultural background differences. There are a wide variety of Asian (Japanese, Chinese, Thai), European, Latin and Central American, and African workers. The ethnic minority share of the U.S. workforce is expected to be about 25 percent by the year 2000.

The proliferation of cultural and diverse backgrounds in the workplace brings onto center stage differences in values, work ethics, and norms of behavior. Communication issues, insensitivity, and ignorance are likely to become major managerial concerns. There are differences in how individuals from different cultures respond to a request to work harder or to correct a defective product.

Managers must learn how to deal with the differences they'll encounter with a diverse workforce. The increased proportion of people of color and immigrants combined with related educational and linguistic issues will cause managers to work hard to match people with jobs.[16] It will be important to fit the people with jobs appropriate for their abilities, skills, needs, values, and preferences. This isn't a new task for managers, but it will be more complex because of the diverse mix of workers. What seems right for the Russian immigrant may be incongruent for the Colombian immigrant. If managers can accurately assess and understand the values represented in their work units, they can produce the types of jobs, work atmospheres, and reward systems that result in excellent performance.

Individual Psychological Variables

Unraveling the complexity of psychological variables such as personality, perception, and attitudes is an immense task. Even psychologists have a difficult time agreeing on these variables' meaning and importance, so our goal is to provide meaningful information about them that managers can use in solving on-the-job behavior and performance problems. The manager must continually observe individuals because what goes on inside a person can be easily hidden.

Perception

Individuals use five senses to experience the environment: sight, touch, hearing, taste, and smell. Organizing the information from the environment so that it makes sense is called **perception.** Perception, as Figure 4–2 shows, is a cognitive process. Perception helps individuals select, organize, store, and interpret stimuli into a meaningful and coherent picture of the world. Because each person gives her own meaning to stimuli, different individuals "see" the same thing in different ways.[17] The way an employee sees a situation often has much greater meaning for understanding behavior than does the situation itself. Stated more thoroughly:

Perception

The process by which an individual gives meaning to the environment. It involves organizing and interpreting various stimuli into a psychological experience.

> *The cognitive map of the individual is not, then, a photographic representation of the physical world: it is, rather, a partial, personal construction in which certain objects, selected out by the individual for a major role, are perceived in an individual manner. Every perceiver is to some degree a nonrepresentational artist, as it were, painting a picture of the world that expresses his or her individual view of reality.[18]*

Figure 4–2

The Perceptual Process

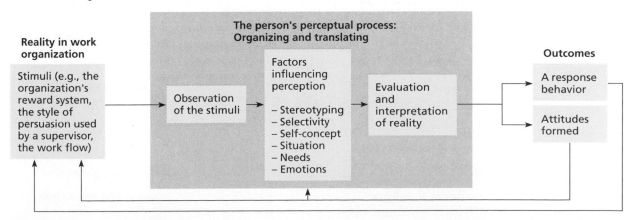

Because perception involves acquiring specific knowledge about objects or events at any particular moment, it occurs whenever stimuli activate the senses. Because perception involves cognition (knowledge), it includes the interpretation of objects, symbols, and people in the light of pertinent experiences. In other words, perception involves receiving stimuli, organizing them, and translating or interpreting the organized stimuli to influence behavior and form attitudes.

Each person selects various cues that influence his perceptions of people, objects, and symbols. Because of these factors and their potential imbalance, people often misperceive another person, group, or object. To a considerable extent, people interpret the behavior of others in the context of the setting in which they find themselves.

The following organizational examples point out how perception influences behavior:

1. A manager believes that an employee is given opportunities to use his judgment about how to do the job, while the employee feels that he has absolutely no freedom to make judgments.

2. A subordinate's response to a supervisor's request is based on what she thought she heard the supervisor say, not on what was actually requested.

3. The manager considers the product sold to be of high quality, but the customer making a complaint feels that it's poorly made.

4. An employee is viewed by one colleague as a hard worker who gives good effort and by another colleague as a poor worker who expends no effort.

5. The salesperson regards his pay increase as totally inequitable, while the sales manager considers it a fair raise.

6. One line operator views working conditions as miserable; a co-worker right across the line regards working conditions as pleasant.

These are a few of numerous daily examples of how perceptions can differ. Managers must recognize that perceptual differences exist. Figure 4–3 illustrates how perception works. Suppose the worker in this example has been told that he has the freedom to

Figure 4–3

Perceptual Differences and Behavior

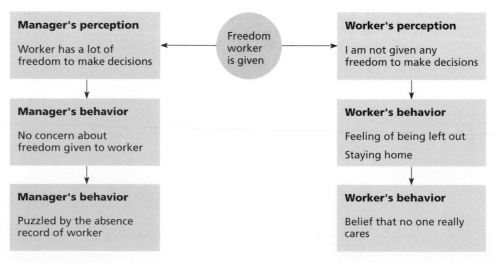

Manager's perception	Freedom worker is given	Worker's perception
Worker has a lot of freedom to make decisions		I am not given any freedom to make decisions
Manager's behavior		**Worker's behavior**
No concern about freedom given to worker		Feeling of being left out Staying home
Manager's behavior		**Worker's behavior**
Puzzled by the absence record of worker		Belief that no one really cares

make decisions about how the job is to be designed. Note that the manager and the employee perceive the job design freedom in different ways; they have different perceptions of the employee's amount of freedom.

Rensis Likert's classic research study clearly showed that managers and subordinates often have different perceptions. He examined the perceptions of superiors and subordinates to determine the amounts and types of recognition that subordinates received for good performance. Both supervisors and subordinates were asked how often superiors provided rewards for good work. The results (Table 4–3) show significant differences in what the two groups perceived. Each group viewed the type of recognition given at a different level. In most cases, subordinates reported that very little recognition was provided by their supervisors and that rewards were infrequent. The supervisors saw themselves as giving a wide variety of rewards for good performance. Likert's study illustrates how marked differences may exist between superiors' and subordinates' perceptions of the same events.

The manner in which managers categorize others often reflects a perceptual bias. The term **stereotype** is an overgeneralized, oversimplified, and self-perpetuating belief about people's personal characteristics. For example, many people stereotype used-car salespeople, men stereotype women executives, managers stereotype union stewards, and female workers stereotype male managers. Most people engage in some form of stereotyping, both of other people and of occupations.[19] Stereotypes are self-perpetuating because people tend to notice things that fit their stereotype and not notice things that don't.[20]

Stereotype

An overgeneralized, oversimplified, and self-perpetuating belief about people's personal characteristics.

Age has been the basis for stereotyping employees. Researchers have found that managerial actions against older workers are influenced by stereotyping.[21] An example of age-based stereotyping involved Richard Wilson, a former executive of Monarch Paper Company. Even after receiving good performance reviews, he was demoted to a warehouse job that required him to perform menial job tasks. The demotion occurred after he rejected a series of early retirement packages from Monarch. A jury awarded Wilson $3.2 million because of age bias in his demotion. The jury indicated that management attempted to intimidate Mr. Wilson as part of their plan to eliminate older workers who were considered less productive than younger employees.[22]

The inaccuracy of stereotyping can result in unfair programs for promotion, motivation, job design, or performance evaluation.[23] It can also result in not selecting the best person for a position. In an era of shortages of highly skilled job talent, organizations will suffer from stereotyping that results in the rejection of a limited pool of candidates. Age, race, gender, ethnicity, and lifestyle stereotyping can prove extremely costly in terms of lost talent, jury judgments against the firm, and the loss of goodwill and sales from customers in the stereotyped categories.

TYPE OF RECOGNITION	SUPERVISORS' PERCEPTIONS OF FREQUENCY	SUBORDINATES' PERCEPTIONS OF FREQUENCY	
Privileges	52%	14%	**Table 4–3**
More responsibility	48	10	The Perceptual Gap
A pat on the back	82	13	between
Sincere and thorough praise	80	14	Supervisors and
Training for better jobs	64	9	Subordinates
More interesting work	51	5	

Source: Adapted from Rensis Likert, *New Patterns in Management* (New York: McGraw-Hill, 1961), p. 91.

SELECTIVE PERCEPTION   The concept of selective perception is important to managers, who often receive large amounts of information and data and may tend to select information that supports their viewpoints. People ignore information or cues that might make them feel discomfort. For example, a skilled manager may be concerned primarily with an employee's final results or output. Since the employee is often cynical and negative when interacting with the manager, other managers may assume that the employee will receive a poor performance rating. However, this manager weeds out the negative features or cues and rates the subordinate on the basis of results. This is a form of selective perception.

THE MANAGER'S CHARACTERISTICS   People frequently use themselves as benchmarks in perceiving others. Research indicates that (1) knowing oneself makes it easier to see others accurately,[24] (2) one's own characteristics affect the characteristics identified in others,[25] and (3) persons who accept themselves are more likely to see favorable aspects of other people.[26] Basically these conclusions suggest that managers perceiving the behavior and individual differences of employees are influenced by their own traits. If they understand that their own traits and values influence perception, they can probably evaluate their subordinates more accurately. A manager who's a perfectionist tends to look for perfection in subordinates, just as a manager who's quick in responding to technical requirements looks for this ability in subordinates.

SITUATIONAL FACTORS   The press of time, the attitudes of the people a manager is working with, and other situational factors all influence perceptual accuracy. If a manager is pressed for time and has to fill an order immediately, his perceptions are influenced by time constraints. The press of time literally forces the manager to overlook some details, rush certain activities, and ignore certain stimuli, such as requests from other managers or from superiors.

NEEDS   Perceptions are significantly influenced by needs and desires. In other words, the employee, the manager, the vice president, and the director see what they want to see. Like the mirrors in the amusement park's fun house, needs and desires can distort the world the manager sees.

The influence of needs in shaping perceptions has been studied in laboratory settings. Subjects in various stages of hunger were asked to report what they saw in ambiguous drawings flashed before them. Researchers found that as hunger increased, up to a certain point, the subjects saw more and more of the ambiguous drawings as articles of food. Hungry subjects saw steaks, salads, and sandwiches, while subjects who had recently eaten saw nonfood images in the same drawings.[27]

EMOTIONS   A person's emotional state has a lot to do with perception. A strong emotion, such as total distaste for an organizational policy, can make a person perceive negative characteristics in most company policies and rules. Determining a person's emotional state is difficult. Because strong emotions often distort perceptions, managers need to discern which issues or practices trigger strong emotions within subordinates.

Attribution

The process of perceiving the causes of behavior and outcomes.

Dispositional Attributions

Emphasize some aspect of the individual, such as ability or skill, to explain behavior.

Attribution

Attribution theory provides insight into the process by which we assign causes or motives to people's behavior. By knowing how people decide among various explanations of behavior, we get a view of how causes of behavior are assessed. Observing behaviors and drawing conclusions is called *making an attribution.*

When causes of behavior are presented, they're usually explained in terms of individual or personality characteristics or in terms of the situation in which it occurred. **Dispositional attributions** emphasize some aspect of the individual such as ability, skill, or internal motivation. Explaining a behavior in terms of something "within" the person such as aggressiveness, shyness, arrogance, or intelligence indicates a dispositional attribution.

A **situational attribution** emphasizes the environment's effect on behavior. Explaining that a new worker's low performance was the result of a typical adjustment period in learning the ropes is an example of making a situational attribution. Tardiness at work can be explained by traffic jams or car trouble, which are examples of situational attributions.

Situational Attributions

Attributions that emphasize the environment's effect on behavior.

In attempting to decide whether a behavior should be attributed to the person or to the situation, Kelley proposed using three criteria:[28]

1. *Consensus.* Would most other people say or do the same thing in the situation? If so, we're less likely to attribute the behavior (e.g., low-quality production) to the person's unique qualities.

2. *Distinctiveness.* Is the behavior unusual or atypical for that person? If so (high distinctiveness), then we infer that some situational factor must be responsible. But, if the person behaves this way often, we tend to make a personal attribution.

3. *Consistency.* Does the person engage in the behavior consistently? When behavior occurs inconsistently, we tend to make situational attributions.

In many situations, managers have information about employee consensus, distinctiveness, and consistency. Suppose that a manager has three employees: Green, Brown, and Black. Making attributions about their performance is important. A quick review of the record is as follows:

1. *Green:* Currently a high performer. Co-workers are average performers. His record of achievements indicates a history of high performance.

2. *Brown:* Currently a high performer. Co-workers are high performers. His previous job record indicates some average to low performance.

3. *Black:* Currently a high performer. Co-workers are high performers. Her previous record is impeccable with only top performance ratings.

As a manager observing and reviewing these behaviors and records, what attributions can you make? Table 4–4 shows how the consensus, distinctiveness, and consistency criteria are applied. Green's performance is low in consensus, is not distinct because he was a good performer before, and is highly consistent for him. This combination would elicit a dispositioned explanation that Green is a self-initiator, highly motivated worker. Brown is inconsistent in terms of performance, is in line or has high consensus with co-workers, and is highly distinctive because on previous jobs Brown was only an average to low performer. Black's performance is constantly high, it's similar to co-workers' (so there's low distinctiveness), and there's high consensus.

ATTRIBUTION ERRORS   Despite guarding against attribution errors, most individuals have certain biases that can result in making inaccurate errors. An *attributional bias* is a tendency to prefer one type of behavior explanation over the other. The *fundamental*

Table 4–4   Criteria and Attributions

EMPLOYEE	CONSENSUS	DISTINCTIVENESS	CONSISTENCY	ATTRIBUTION
Green	Low	Low	High	Person (disposition)
Brown	High	High	Low	Situation
Black	High	Low	High	Mixed (more dispositional than situational)

attribution error is making a judgment with only limited information about the person or situation. Not making a judgment with incomplete information would often be the best action. There's a tendency to overattribute to the person or dispositional criteria. At the same time, people tend to minimize or ignore situational factors, even when the situation may completely explain the behavior of the individual.[29]

The fundamental attribution error can result in managers first attributing poor performance, excessive absence, or lack of skills to personal inadequacies and then trying to change the person. This error in judgment could result in corrective interventions such as training or reprimands that are totally ineffective.

The *actor-observer bias* results when a person attributes another person's behavior to personal traits, and attributes her own behavior to situational causes.[30] Consider the poor performance of an employee. The manager sees it as due to the employee's poor motivation, while the employee sees the problem as resulting from improper orientation to the job. The manager attributes the problem to dispositional causes and the employee attributes the problem to situational causes.

OTHER ATTRIBUTIONAL BIAS   Most people tend to make positive evaluations of others. This is referred to as a *general positivity* or *Pollyanna principle.* We generally have an inclination to be positive. Also, people have a tendency to take credit for successful work and deny responsibility for poor work. This is called a *self-serving bias.* Individuals tend to have egocentric recall, in which they keep in mind and recall the good things that were contributed on a project and ignore bad or failed contributions. The excuses people make generally are to blame problem behaviors on something in the environment instead of something within the individuals.[31] Making excuses for oneself often has positive effects since they lower anxiety and keep a person's self-esteem high.

Attitudes

Attitudes

Mental states of readiness for need arousal.

Attitudes are determinants of behavior because they're linked with perception, personality, and motivation. An **attitude** is a positive or negative feeling or mental state of readiness, learned and organized through experience, that exerts specific influence on a person's response to people, objects, and situations. Each of us has attitudes on numerous topics—unions, exercise, dieting, career goals, friends, and tax laws, for example. This definition of *attitude* has certain implications for managers. First, attitudes are learned. Second, attitudes define our predispositions toward given aspects of the world. Third, attitudes provide the emotional basis of our interpersonal relations and identification with others. And fourth, attitudes are organized and are close to the core of personality. Some attitudes are persistent and enduring; yet, like each of the psychological variables, attitudes are subject to change.[32]

Attitudes are intrinsic parts of a person's personality. Several theories attempt to account for the formation and change of attitudes. One such theory proposes that people "seek a congruence between their beliefs and feelings toward objects" and suggests that the modification of attitudes depends on changing either the feelings or the beliefs.[33] The theory further assumes that people have structured attitudes composed of various affective and cognitive components. These components' interrelatedness means that a change in one precipitates a change in the others. When these components are inconsistent or exceed the person's tolerance level, instability results. Instability can be corrected by (1) disavowal of a message designed to influence attitudes, (2) "fragmentation" or a breaking off into several attitudes, or (3) acceptance of the inconsistency so that a new attitude is formed. The theory proposes that affect, cognition, and behavior determine attitudes and that attitudes, in turn, determine affect, cognition, and behavior.

1. **Affect.** The emotional, or "feeling," component of an attitude is learned from parents, teachers, and peer group members. One study illustrates how the affective component can be measured. A questionnaire was used to survey the attitudes of a group of students toward the church. The students then listened to tape recordings that either praised or disparaged the church. As the tapes played, students' emotional responses were measured with a galvanic skin response (GSR) device. Both prochurch and antichurch students responded with greater emotion (displayed by GSR changes) to statements that contradicted their attitudes than to those that reflected their attitudes.[34]

Affect

The emotional segment of an attitude.

2. **Cognition.** The cognitive component of an attitude consists of the person's perceptions, opinions, and beliefs. It refers to the thought processes, with special emphasis on rationality and logic. An important element of cognition is the evaluative beliefs held by a person. Evaluative beliefs are manifested as the favorable or unfavorable impressions someone holds toward an object or person.

Cognition

The perception, opinion, or belief segment of an attitude.

3. **Behavior.** The behavioral component of an attitude refers to a person's intention to act toward someone or something in a certain way (friendly, warm, aggressive, hostile, or apathetic, for example). Such intentions could be measured or assessed to examine the behavioral component of attitudes.

Figure 4–4 presents the three components of attitudes in terms of work factors such as job design, company policies, and fringe benefits. These stimuli trigger affective (emotional), cognitive (thought), and behavioral intentions. In essence, the stimuli result in the formation of attitudes, which then lead to one or more responses (affective, cognitive, or behavioral).

The theory of affective, cognitive, and behavioral components as determinants of attitudes and attitude change has a significant implication for managers. They must be able to demonstrate that the positive aspects of contributing to the organization outweigh the negative aspects. Many managers achieve effectiveness by developing generally favorable attitudes in their employees toward the organization and the job.

Attitudes have many sources: family, peer groups, society, and previous job experiences. Early *family* experiences help shape individuals' attitudes. Young children's attitudes usually correspond to their parents'. As children reach their teens, they begin to be

Figure 4–4

The Three Components of Attitudes

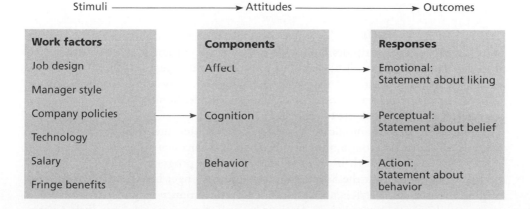

Stimuli ──────────→	Attitudes ──────────→	Outcomes
Work factors	**Components**	**Responses**
Job design	Affect	Emotional: Statement about liking
Manager style		
Company policies	Cognition	Perceptual: Statement about belief
Technology		
Salary	Behavior	Action: Statement about behavior
Fringe benefits		

more strongly influenced by *peers.* Peer groups influence attitudes because individuals want to be accepted by others. Teenagers seek approval by sharing similar attitudes or by modifying attitudes to comply with those of a group.

Culture, mores, and language influence attitudes. Attitudes of French Canadians toward France, of Americans toward people in Russia, and of Cubans toward capitalism are learned in *society.* Within the United States are subcultures—ethnic communities, ghetto communities, and religious groups—that help shape people's attitudes.

Through *job experiences,* employees develop attitudes about pay equity, performance review, managerial capabilities, job design, and work group affiliation. Previous experiences account for some individual differences in attitudes toward performance, loyalty, and commitment.

Individuals strive to maintain consistency among the components of attitudes. But contradictions and inconsistency often occur, resulting in a state of disequilibrium. The tension stemming from such a state is reduced only when some form of consistency is achieved.

Cognitive Dissonance

A mental state of anxiety that occurs when there's a conflict among an individual's various cognitions (for example, attitudes and beliefs) after a decision has been made.

The term **cognitive dissonance** describes a situation where there's a discrepancy between the cognitive and behavioral components of an attitude.[35] Any form of inconsistency is uncomfortable so individuals attempt to reduce dissonance. *Dissonance,* then, is viewed as a state within a person that, when aroused, elicits actions designed to return the person to a state of equilibrium.[36] For example, the chief executive officer of a cigarette company may experience cognitive dissonance if she believes that she's honest and hardworking but that cigarettes contribute to lung cancer. She may think, "I'm a good human being, but I'm in charge of a firm producing a cancer-contributing product." These thoughts create inconsistency. Instead of quitting and giving up her successful career, she's more likely to modify her thoughts or cognitions. She could state, "Our firm has manufactured a cigarette that's now very safe and free of cancer-producing products." Or she may think that cigarette smoking actually improves smokers' mental well-being, that it helps them reduce or cope with stress. When inconsistency in attitudes arises, the person can attempt to work the problem out cognitively or behaviorally. Here the CEO used a cognitive process to reduce her dissonance.

Cognitive dissonance has important organizational implications. First, it helps explain the choices made by an individual with attitude inconsistency. Second, it can help predict a person's propensity to change attitudes. If individuals are required, for example, by the design of their jobs or occupations to say or do things that contradict their personal attitudes, they may change those attitudes to make them more compatible with what they've said or done.

CHANGING ATTITUDES   Managers often face the task of changing employees' attitudes because existing attitudes hinder job performance. Although many variables affect attitude change, they can all be described in terms of three general factors: trust in the sender, the message itself, and the situation.[37] Employees who don't trust the manager won't accept the manager's message or change an attitude. Similarly, if the message isn't convincing, there's no pressure to change.

The greater the communicator's prestige, the greater the attitude change.[38] An example of how the communicator's prestige influences attitude is Mikhail Gorbachev's achievements with his *glasnost* and *perestroika* programs (1985–91). He convinced many people that the Soviet Union should no longer be referred to as the "evil empire." Gorbachev's style, message, and charisma produced significant changes in many people's attitude toward the Soviet Union.[39] A manager who has little prestige and isn't shown respect by peers and superiors is in a difficult position if the job requires changing subordinates' attitudes so that they work more effectively. Thus, managers need to be aware of their prestige rating among employees. If they have prestige, they should use it to change attitudes. If they don't have prestige, attitude change may be virtually impossible.

Liking the communicator produces attitude change because people try to identify with a liked communicator and tend to adopt attitudes and behaviors of the liked person.[40] Not all managers, however, are fortunate enough to be liked by each of their subordinates. Therefore, liking the manager is a condition for trusting the manager.

Even if a manager is trusted, presents a convincing message, and is liked, the problems of changing people's attitudes aren't solved. The strength of the employee's commitment to an attitude is important. A worker who has decided not to accept a promotion is committed to the belief that it's better to remain in his present position than to accept the promotion. Attitudes that have been expressed publicly are more difficult to change because the person has shown commitment, and changing is admitting a mistake.

How much people are affected by attempts to change their attitude depends in part on the situation. While listening to or reading a persuasive message, people are sometimes distracted by other thoughts, sounds, or activities. And studies indicate that people distracted while they listen to a message show more attitude change because the distraction interferes with silent counterarguing.[41]

Distraction is just one of many situational factors that can increase persuasion. Another factor that makes people more susceptible to attempts to change attitudes is pleasant surroundings. The pleasant surroundings may be associated with the attempt to change the attitude.

ATTITUDES AND VALUES Values are linked to attitudes in that a value serves as a way of organizing attitudes. **Values** are defined "as the constellation of likes, dislikes, viewpoints, shoulds, inner inclinations, rational and irrational judgments, prejudices, and association patterns that determine a person's view of the world."[42] Certainly, a person's work is an important aspect of his world. Moreover, the importance of a value constellation is that, once internalized, it becomes (consciously or subconsciously) a standard or criterion for guiding one's actions. The study of values, therefore, is fundamental to the study of managing. There's evidence that values are also extremely important for understanding effective managerial behavior.[43]

Values

The guidelines and beliefs that a person uses when confronted with a situation in which a choice must be made.

Are values in America's organizations changing? The Close-Up on pages 106–7 examines some new thinking about values.

Values affect the perceptions not only of appropriate ends but also of appropriate means to those ends. From the design and development of organizational structures and processes to the utilization of particular leadership styles and the evaluation of the performance of subordinates, value systems are persuasive. An influential theory of leadership is based on the argument that managers can't be expected to adopt a leadership style that's contrary to their "need structures" or value orientations.[44] Moreover, when managers evaluate subordinates' performance, the effects of the managers' values are noticeable. For example, one researcher reports that managers can be expected to evaluate subordinates with values similar to their own as more effective than subordinates with dissimilar values.[45] The impact of values is more pronounced in decisions involving little objective information and, consequently, a greater degree of subjectivity.

Another aspect of the importance of values occurs when the interpersonal activities of managers bring them into a confrontation with different, and potentially contradictory, values. Studies have shown that assembly-line workers, scientists, and persons in various professional occupations are characterized by particular, if not unique, value orientations.[46] Day-to-day activities create numerous situations in which managers must relate to others with different views of what's right or wrong. Conflicts between managers and workers, administrators and teachers, and line and staff personnel have been documented and discussed in the literature of management. The manner in which these conflicts are resolved is particularly crucial to the organization's effectiveness.[47]

Job Satisfaction

The attitude that workers have about their jobs. It results from their perception of the jobs.

ATTITUDES AND JOB SATISFACTION   Job satisfaction is an attitude that individuals have about their jobs. It results from their perceptions of their jobs, based on factors of the work environment, such as the supervisor's style, policies and procedures, work group affiliation, working conditions, and fringe benefits. While numerous dimensions have been associated with job satisfaction, five in particular have crucial characteristics:[48]

1. *Pay.* The amount received and the perceived equity of pay.
2. *Job.* The extent to which job tasks are considered interesting and provide opportunities for learning and for accepting responsibility.
3. *Promotion opportunities.* The availability of opportunities for advancement.
4. *Supervisor.* The supervisor's abilities to demonstrate interest in and concern about employees.
5. *Co-workers.* The extent to which co-workers are friendly, competent, and supportive.

In some studies, these five job satisfaction dimensions have been measured by the Job Descriptive Index (JDI). Employees are asked to respond yes, no, or ? (can't decide) as to whether a word or phrase describes their attitudes about their jobs. The JDI attempts to

---

C L O S E — U P

Changing Values in the Workplace

Corporate America has been undergoing a dramatic transformation in the past decade. Amid the chaos, researchers are finding renewed interest in values. For example, Jack Welch, chief executive officer of General Electric, has emphasized "soft values for a hard decade." Robert D. Haas of Levi Strauss has asserted that "values provide a common language for aligning a company's leadership and its people." Isadore Sharp of Four Seasons Hotels has described values as his company's "psychic core."

What's all this talk of values? Has the image of the stoic, tough-minded CEO given way to an image of a flowing robe and sandals? Over the past several decades, prudent executives managed by objectives, not values. Talking about shared values was regarded as too "soft" for the boardroom. Value talk was resurrected in the 1980s by management thinkers such as Tom Peters and Robert Waterman whose best-seller, *In Search of Excellence*, advocated a management revolution based on shared values in the workplace. They stated matter of factly, "Every excellent company takes the process of value shaping seriously, either buy into the company's values or get out." One current example is Hewlett-Packard, chosen by *Forbes* as its top corporate performer of 1995. H-P has found enormous success emphasizing to all employees such shared values as boundarylessness, innovation, growth, informality and flexibility. The maintenance of these values is so important to H-P that its CEO states that his primary activities focus on communicating and facilitating the achievement of these concepts.

How organizations attempt to develop and foster these shared values may vary considerably. Two types of values-management styles have been identified: make values and buy values. A make-value management style assumes that workers are malleable and assuming basic intellectual abilities, capable of being socialized to the corporate values. A buy-value management style, in contrast, assumes that one's values aren't changeable and looks to hire people who already share the organization's basic values.

measure a person's satisfaction with specific facets of the job. Other measures of job satisfaction, such as the Brayfield-Rothe measures, are more general. Figure 4–6 presents sample items from four scales measuring job satisfaction.

A major reason for studying job satisfaction is to provide managers with ideas about how to improve employee attitudes. Many organizations use attitude surveys to determine levels of employee job satisfaction. National surveys in the past have indicated that, in general, 75 to 80 percent of workers are satisfied with their jobs.[49] More recent assessments have suggested that this level may have decreased substantially, to the mid-60 percent range.[50] Of course, though they're interesting, national surveys may not reflect the degree of job satisfaction in a specific department or organization. Also, simply asking people how satisfied they are creates a problem; there's a bias toward giving a positive answer, since anything less indicates that the person is electing to stay in a dissatisfying job.

SATISFACTION AND JOB PERFORMANCE   One of the most debated and controversial issues in the study of job satisfaction is its relationship to job performance. For years, many managers believed that a satisfied worker was a high-performing employee. But most research studies find no clear link between satisfaction and performance. Some workers are satisfied with work and are poor performers. Of course, there are employees who aren't satisfied but are excellent performers.

The determination of which variable is affecting the other is difficult when performance and satisfaction are positively related, has resulted in three viewpoints: (1) satisfaction causes performance; (2) performance causes satisfaction; and (3) rewards intervene, and there's no inherent relationship.[51] (Figure 4–7 shows these three viewpoints.) The first two views are supported weakly by research. A review of 20 studies dealing with performance-satisfaction relationships found a low association between performance and

---

Figure 4–5 shows how a corporate vision can be analyzed into goals and values. This leads to the complementary outcomes of control and commitment and produces employee behavior that fulfills stakeholder needs.

Some critics contend that the new focus on values is just another passing fad. Research into the issue is difficult. No clear-cut framework has been developed to distinguish organizations with strong values from those without. Nonetheless, several studies have been conducted with managers in a variety of organizations to get their opinion on values' importance in the modern workplace.

In one study of 45 senior executives, the investigators found that, with one exception, each of the executives spoke with genuine interest and enthusiasm about shared values. Most said values were a very significant issue and that they spent a lot of time thinking about and discussing them. One executive in a multibusiness corporation referred to values as "the only glue we have."

In addition to these findings that demonstrate a concern among senior management over values, the highly educated worker of today also wants more out of work than a paycheck. A broad range of social factors have produced a modern workforce with expectations very different from a mere generation ago. At one time, the American dream consisted of a steady paycheck and a house in the suburbs. Today's workers want more—and this includes a sense of involvement and shared meaning. They expect to feel comfortable with the organization's values and culture. They want a sense of psychological attachment.

Sources: Adapted from Paul McDonald and Jeffrey Gandz, "Getting Value from Shared Values," *Organizational Dynamics,* Winter 1992, vol. 20, no. 3, pp. 64–77; Barry Z. Posner and Warren H. Schmidt, "Values and the American Manager," *California Management Review,* Spring 1992, vol. 34, pp. 80–94; Jean Doerge and Norma Hagenow, "Management Restructuring," *Nursing Management,* December 1995, pp. 32–38; Dana Wechsler Linden and Bruce Upbin, "Top Corporate Performance of 1995: Boy Scouts on a Rampage," *Forbes,* January 1, 1996, pp. 66–70; Martha M. Lauzen, "Public Relations Manager Involvement in Strategic Issue Diagnosis," *Public Relations Review,* Winter 1995, pp. 287–304.

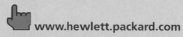 **www.hewlett.packard.com**

Figure 4–5

Integrating Vision and Values within a Strategic Framework

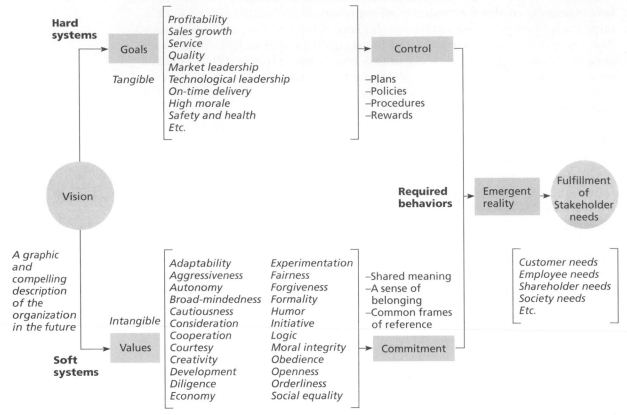

Source: Adapted from Paul McDonald and Jeffrey Gandz, "Getting Value from Shared Values," *Organizational Dynamics,* Winter 1992, vol. 20, no. 3, p. 75.

satisfaction.[52] Thus, evidence is rather convincing that a satisfied worker isn't necessarily a high performer: managerial attempts to satisfy everyone don't yield high levels of production. Likewise, the assumption that a high-performing employee is likely to be satisfied isn't supported. The third view, that factors such as rewards mediate the performance-satisfaction relationship, *is* supported by research findings. This means that performance isn't a consequence of satisfaction, or vice versa.

From a practical standpoint, however, most managers would like to have satisfied and productive workers (a goal requiring a lot of effort and sound decision making on the manager's part). So managers continue to be interested in job satisfaction despite evidence that satisfaction doesn't determine, in any significant way, the level of performance. But some theorists and researchers suggest performance has a broader meaning than simply units or quality of production.[53] Performance also covers a variety of citizenship behaviors, including showing untrained colleagues how to complete a job, helping a fellow worker complete a job when he's not feeling well, making positive comments in the community about the organization, working extra hard to deliver promised goods or services, and not complaining when management doesn't provide resources as promised. These behaviors are more prevalent among satisfied workers.[54]

Figure 4–6

Sample Items from Four Widely Used Job Satisfaction Scales

Brayfield-Rothe Satisfaction Scale (General Measure)

My job is like a hobby to me.
Strongly agree   Agree   Undecided   Disagree   Strongly disagree

I enjoy my work more than my leisure time.
Strongly agree   Agree   Undecided   Disagree   Strongly disagree

Job Descriptive Index (Facet Measure)

How well does each word describe your pay? Circle Y if it does describe your pay, N if it does not describe your pay, or ? if you cannot decide.

Less than I deserve Y N ?   Insecure Y N ?   Highly paid Y N ?

GM Faces Scale (General Measure)

Consider all aspects of your job. Circle the face which best describes your feelings about your job in general.

    7   6   5   4   3   2   1

Minnesota Satisfaction Questionnaire (Facet Measure)

On my present job, this is how I feel about...

1. Being able to keep busy all the time.
Very dissatisfied   Dissatisfied   Neutral   Satisfied   Very satisfied

2. The praise I get for doing a good job.
Very dissatisfied   Dissatisfied   Neutral   Satisfied   Very satisfied

Another reason for continued management interest is that research has found some indication of a modest correlation between satisfaction and turnover, but this is far from a strong linkage.[55] Evidence also exists of a moderate relationship between satisfaction and absenteeism. Dysfunctional turnover and absenteeism are expensive in terms of costs, lost opportunities, and overall morale. Some evidence shows a relationship between satisfaction and union activity. Dissatisfaction stemming from perceptions of pay inequities, poor supervisor-subordinate relationships, and inadequate working conditions initiate and sustain activities such as voting for union representation.[56]

Although job satisfaction doesn't influence quantity and quality of performance, it does influence citizenship behaviors, turnover, absenteeism, and preferences and opinions about unions. Because of these influences, managers continue to search for techniques and programs that improve employee job satisfaction. Many practicing managers have apparently concluded that performance means more than simply counting the quantity and quality of production.

Figure 4-7

Satisfaction-Performance Relationships: Three Views

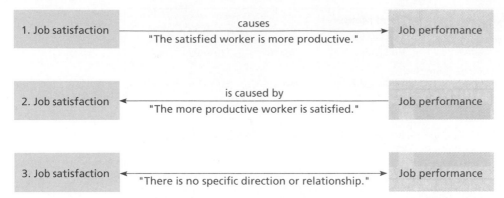

Personality
===========

Why are some people concerned about the quality of the job they do while others aren't? Why are some people passive and others very aggressive? The manner in which a person acts and interacts is a reflection of his personality. **Personality** is influenced by hereditary, cultural, and social factors. Regardless of how it's defined, however, psychologists generally accept certain principles:

Personality

Stable set of characteristics and tendencies that determine commonalities and differences in people's behavior.

1. Personality is an organized whole; otherwise, the individual would have no meaning.

2. Personality appears to be organized into patterns that are to some degree observable and measurable.

3. Although personality has a biological basis, its specific development is also a product of social and cultural environments.

4. Personality has superficial aspects (such as attitudes toward being a team leader) and a deeper core (such as sentiments about authority or the Protestant work ethic).

5. Personality involves both common and unique characteristics. Every person is different from every other person in some respects, while being similar to other persons in other respects.

These five ideas are included in this definition of personality:

An individual's personality is a relatively stable set of characteristics, tendencies, and temperaments that have been significantly formed by inheritance and by social, cultural, and environmental factors. This set of variables determines the commonalities and differences in the behavior of the individual.[57]

A review of the determinants shaping personality (Figure 4–8) indicates that managers have little control over them. But no manager should conclude that personality is an unimportant factor in workplace behavior simply because it's formed outside the organization. An employee's behavior can't be understood without considering the concept of personality. In fact, personality is so interrelated with perception, attitudes, learning, and motivation that any attempt to understand behavior is grossly incomplete unless personality is considered.

THEORIES OF PERSONALITY Three theoretical approaches to understanding personality are the trait approach, the psychodynamic approach, and the humanistic approach.

Figure 4–8

Some Major Forces Influencing Personality

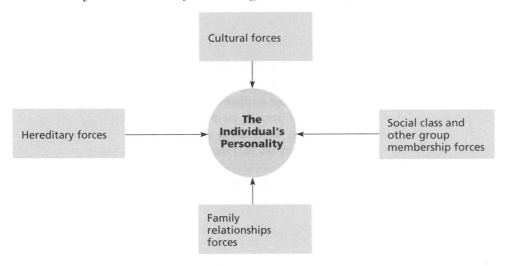

Trait Personality Theories   Just as the young child always seems to be searching for labels by which to classify the world, adults also label and classify people by their psychological or physical characteristics. Classification helps to organize diversity and reduce the many to a few.

Gordon Allport was the most influential of the trait theorists. In his view, traits are the building blocks of personality, the guideposts for action, the source of the individual's uniqueness. Traits are inferred predispositions that direct the behavior of an individual in consistent and characteristic ways. Furthermore, traits produce consistencies in behavior because they're enduring attributes, and they're general or broad in scope.[58]

For decades, psychologist Raymond B. Cattell has studied personality traits, gathering many measures of traits through behavioral observation, records of people's life histories, questionnaires, and objective tests.[59] On the basis of his research, Cattell has concluded that 16 basic traits underlie individual differences in behavior. The research resulted in the development of Cattell's 16PF (16 personality factors) questionnaire, which measures the degree to which people have these traits. Among the traits he identified are reserved-outgoing, practical-imaginative, relaxed-tense, and humble-assertive. All 16 of Cattell's traits are bipolar; that is, each trait has two extremes (e.g., relaxed-tense).

Trait theories have been criticized as not being real theories because they don't explain how behavior is caused. The mere identification of such traits as tough-minded, conservative, expedient, reserved, or outgoing doesn't offer insight into the development and dynamics of personality. Furthermore, trait approaches haven't been successful in predicting behavior across a spectrum of situations, due to the fact that situations (the job, the work activities) are largely ignored in trait theories.

Psychodynamic Personality Theories   The dynamic nature of personality wasn't addressed seriously until Sigmund Freud's work was published. Freud accounted for individual differences in personality by suggest-

Trait Personality Theories

Based on the premise that predispositions direct the behavior of an individual in a consistent pattern.

Psychodynamic Personality Theories

Freudian approach that discusses the id, superego, and ego. Special emphasis is placed on unconscious determinants of behavior.

ing that people deal with their fundamental drives differently. To highlight these differences, he pictured a continuing battle between two parts of personality, the id and the superego, moderated by the ego.[60]

The *id* is the primitive, unconscious part of the personality, the storehouse of fundamental drives. It operates irrationally and impulsively, without considering whether what's desired is possible or morally acceptable. The *superego* is the storehouse of an individual's values, including moral attitudes shaped by society. The superego, which corresponds roughly to conscience, is often in conflict with the id: the id wants to do what feels good, while the superego insists on doing what's "right." The *ego* acts as the arbitrator of the conflict. It represents the person's picture of physical and social reality, of what leads to what and of which things are possible in the perceived world. Part of the ego's job is to choose actions that gratify id impulses without having undesirable consequences. Often the ego has to compromise, to try and satisfy both id and superego. This sometimes involves using ego defense mechanisms—mental processes that resolve conflict among psychological states and external realities. Table 4–5 presents some of the ego defense mechanisms used by individuals.

Even Freud's critics admit that he contributed to the modern understanding of behavior. His emphasis on unconscious determinants of behavior is important. The significance he attributed to early-life origins of adult behavior encouraged the study of child development. In addition, his method of treating neurosis through psychoanalysis has added to our understanding of how to get people back on the right track toward effective functioning.[61]

Humanistic Personality Theories

Place emphasis on growth and self-actualization of people.

Humanistic Personality Theories   Humanistic approaches to understanding personality emphasize the individual's growth and self-actualization and the importance of how people perceive their world and all the forces influencing them. Carl Rogers' approach to understanding personality is humanistic (people-centered).[62] His advice is to listen to what people say about themselves and to attend to those views and their significance in the person's experiences. Rogers believes that the human organism's most basic drive is toward *self-actualization*—the constant striving to realize one's inherent potential.

It's hard to criticize theories that are so people-centered. Some critics complain, however, that the humanists never explain clearly the origin of the mechanism for attaining self-actualization. Other critics point out that people must operate in an environment largely ignored by the humanists; an overemphasis on self neglects the reality of having to function in a complex environment.

Each major theoretical approach improves our understanding of personality. Trait theories provide a catalog that *describes* the individual. Psychodynamic theories integrate the characteristics of people and *explain* the dynamic nature of personality development.

Table 4–5	Some Ego Defense Mechanisms

MECHANISM	HOW IT'S APPLIED IN AN ORGANIZATION
Rationalization	Attempting to justify one's behavior as being rational and justifiable. (I had to violate company policies to get the job finished.)
Identification	Increasing feelings of worth by identifying self with person or institution of illustrious standing. (I am working for Jim, who is really the best manager in the country.)
Compensation	Covering up weakness by emphasizing desirable traits or making up for frustration in one area by overgratification in another. (I may be a harsh manager, but I play no favorites.)
Denial of reality	Protecting self from unpleasant reality by refusing to perceive it. (There is no chance that this company will have to let people go because of the economy.)

Humanist theories emphasize the *person* and the importance of self-actualization to personality. Each approach attempts to highlight the unique qualities of an individual that influence her behavior patterns.

MEASURING PERSONALITY CHARACTERISTICS   Personality tests measure emotional, motivational, interpersonal, and attitudinal characteristics. Hundreds of such tests are available to organizations. One of the most widely used, the **Minnesota Multiphasic Personality Inventory (MMPI),** consists of statements to which a person responds: true, false, or cannot say. MMPI items cover such areas as health, psychosomatic symptoms, neurological disorders, and social attitudes, as well as many well-known neurotic or psychotic manifestations such as phobias, delusions, and sadistic tendencies.[63]

Managers in organizations aren't enthusiastic about using the MMPI. It's too psychologically oriented, is associated with psychologists and psychiatrists, and has a reputation of being used to help people with problems. A tool some managers find more comfortable is the **Myers-Briggs Type Indicator (MBTI),** briefly described in the accompanying Close-Up.

Projective tests, also used to assess personality, have people respond to a picture, an inkblot, or a story. To encourage free responses, only brief, general instructions are given; for the same reason, the test pictures or stories are vague. The underlying reason for this is that each individual perceives and interprets the test material in a manner that displays his personality. That is, the individual projects his attitudes, needs, anxieties, and conflicts.

A *behavioral measure* of personality involves observing the person in a particular situation. For example, an individual may be given a specific work situation problem to solve. The person's problem-solving ability is studied in terms of the steps taken, time required to reach a solution, and quality of the final decision.

Each of these measures of personality has drawbacks: self-report tests have an accuracy problem; projective tests require a subjective interpretation by a trained person, and behavioral measures rely on a small sample of a person's behavior.

PERSONALITY AND BEHAVIOR   An issue of interest to behavioral scientists and researchers is whether the personality factors measured by such inventories as the MBTI, the MMPI, and the 16PF questionnaire, by projective tests, or by behavioral measures collected in controlled settings can predict behavior or performance in organizations. Using a total inventory to examine whether personality is a factor in explaining behavior is rarely done in organizational behavior research. Typically, people try to gain a perspective on personality by measuring different facets of personality such as locus of control, creativity, or Machiavellianism.

 **www.mind spring.com**

Locus of Control   The **locus of control** of individuals determines the degree to which they believe that their behaviors influence what happens to them. Some people believe that they're autonomous—that they're masters of their own fate and bear personal responsibility for what happens to them. They see the control of their lives as coming from inside themselves. Rotter called these people *internals*.[64] Rotter also held that many people view themselves as helpless pawns of fate, controlled by outside forces over which they have little, if any, influence. Such people believe that the locus of control is external rather than internal. Rotter called them *externals*.

Personality Test

Test used to measure emotional, motivational, interpersonal, and attitude characteristics that make up a person's personality.

Minnesota Multiphasic Personality Inventory (MMPI)

A widely used survey for assessing personality.

Myers-Briggs Type Indicator (MBTI)

A scale that assesses personality or cognitive style. Respondents' answers are scored and interpreted to classify them as extroverted or introverted, sensory or intuitive, thinking or feeling, and perceiving or judging. Sixteen different personality types are possible.

Locus of Control

A personality characteristic that describes people who see the control of their lives as coming from inside themselves as *internalizers*. People who believe that their lives are controlled by external factors are *externalizers*.

A study of 900 employees in a public utility found that internally controlled employees were more content with their jobs, more likely to be in managerial positions, and more satisfied with a participative management style than were employees who perceived themselves to be externally controlled.[65]

An interesting study of 90 entrepreneurs examined locus of control, perceived stress, coping behaviors, and performance.[66] The study was done in a business district over a three and one-half year period following flooding by Hurricane Agnes. Internalizers were found to perceive less stress than did externalizers and to employ more task-centered coping behaviors and fewer emotion-centered coping behaviors. In addition, internalizers' task-oriented coping behaviors were associated with better performance. However, the available data have generally indicated that entrepreneurs in most fields, whether male or female, are likely to have an internal locus of control.[67]

In general, research results suggest that internals are more resistant to pressure to conform and are less likely to be persuaded to change their attitudes. Externals appear to be more receptive to structured jobs and seem more receptive to participation in job-related decision making.[68] Evidence suggests that people's behavior changes from one situation to another and that their belief in an internal or external locus of control varies depending on the culture that they have been socialized in[69] and the particular situation they face.[70] In regard to the latter, attempts are now being made to measure a person's specific internal or external locus of control concerning both work[71] and health issues.[72]

Self-Efficacy

The belief that one can perform adequately in a situation. Self-efficacy has three dimensions: magnitude, strength, and generality.

Self-Efficacy   When individuals acquire an internal control orientation that leads them to set goals and develop action plans to generally accomplish, they develop a sense of **self-efficacy.** Bandura discusses the self-efficacy concept as a part of social learning theory.[73] He contends that self-efficacy is a belief that we can perform adequately in a particular situation. People's sense of capability influences their perception, motivation, and performance. Most individuals don't even try to do things, such as accept a promotion or use a

CLOSE — UP

The Myers-Briggs Type Indicator (MBTI) Is Preferred by Managers

Apple, Exxon, and General Electric, as well as Murray Manufacturing and Douglas Electronics (small firms with about 800 employees each), are using the Myers-Briggs Type Indicator scale to learn about personality. In the 1920s, noted Swiss psychoanalyst Carl Jung developed a cognitive-style theory of personality, which the American mother-daughter team of Katherine Briggs and Isabel Briggs Myers later converted into the MBTI, a scale organizations like to use.

Jung had proposed that two dimensions (sensation and intuition) influence a person's perception. Also, two dimensions (thinking and feeling) affect individual judgment. He believed that an individual's cognitive style is determined by the pairing of a person's perception and judgment tendencies. Myers and Briggs developed a test (Samples: Which word appeals to you more: *build/invent*? In a large group, you more often introduce others or are introduced?) so that respondents can discover their personality or cognitive style type. The test identifies people as extroverted or introverted (E or I), sensing or intuitive (S or N), thinking or feeling (T or F), and perceiving or judging (P or J). A person's answers are divided and classified into 16 different personality types.

Four of the combinations and some typical occupations are cited in this Close-Up.

Can the MBTI be so good that over 2 million people a year use it to diagnose personality? Jim Talman, vice president of Bayson (a small firm that sells electrical parts in the Southwest and Mexico), believes that it is. It's one of a number of techniques Bayson uses to find the best sales personnel for a job in which language proficiency, cultural sensitivity, and openness in working with customers in computer, when they expect to be ineffectual. People avoid others and situations in which they feel inadequate.

Bandura believes that perceptions of one's abilities are best thought of as a host of specific evaluations.[74] Individuals evaluate their past and actual accomplishments, the performance of others, and their own emotional states. Besides influencing a person's choice of activities, tasks, and situations, these evaluations also influence how much effort is expended and how long the person continues to try to succeed.

Figure 4–9 displays a model of self-efficacy based on Bandura's work. The behaviors of a person with high self-efficacy are positive, success-driven, and goal-oriented. When they need assistance, they look for tangible aid and not reassurance or emotional support.[75] On the other hand, a person with low self-efficacy sees problems, worries, and thinks in terms of failing or not being able to do a high-quality job. Sam Walton, founder of Wal-Mart, was an example of a person with a high self-efficacy belief that he could beat Sears, Kmart, and Target. He selected opportunities, planned, visualized, and expressed how Wal-Mart would succeed. His speeches and behaviors reveal a person with high self-efficacy.[76]

www.sears.com

www.kmart.com

www.target.com

The organizational behavior implications of self-efficacy are numerous, relating to such diverse areas as seasickness among military recruits to job search activities among unemployed workers.[77] Self-efficacy's role in motivation and task performance is obvious. A person high in self-efficacy is more motivated to perform at high levels of achievement. Self-efficacy may be important in terms of training employees to improve skills they believe are inadequate to perform well.[78] Self-efficacy may also be a factor in feedback provided through performance evaluation programs.[79] Individuals with high self-efficacy may respond to the identification of problem areas in a more aggressive, corrective but sometimes self-serving way than those employees low in self-efficacy.[80] In addition, it has been suggested that self-efficacy is relevant to equal employment opportunity. Culture may have a significant effect on self-efficacy,[81] and as a more diverse workforce enters the mainstream, this could become an important issue. Individuals

Mexico are important. In addition, Bayson has found that the high-scoring sensation-feeling and extroverted salespeople have the best sales records in Mexico.

Bayson hasn't validated the MBTI, but management still believes that it helps them make better selections. Citicorp, 3M, and the U.S. armed forces, as well as thousands of other firms, also apparently find some value in the MBTI. Is it essentially sound, valid, and reliable? We aren't sure. But it seems to have appeal in the corporate community.

Sensation-Thinking: Thorough, logical, practical, and application-oriented.

Auditor of CPA firm, quality control supervisor, or safety engineer.

Intuitive-Thinking: Creative, independent, critical.

Lawyer, systems analyst, college professor.

Sensation-Feeling: Committed, responsible, conscientious.

Union negotiator, social worker, drug supervisor.

Intuitive-Feeling: Charismatic, people-oriented, and sociable.

Politician, public relations specialist, human resource director.

Source: Discussions with corporate executives in Juarez, Mexico, and Houston, El Paso, and San Antonio, Texas, in Summer and Fall 1989. See Don Hellriegal, John W. Slocum Sr., and Richard W. Woodman, *Organizational Behavior* (St. Paul, Minn.: West, 1989); Thomas More, "Personality Tests Are Back," *Fortune,* March 30, 1987, pp. 74–82; Carol Hildebrand, "I'm OK, You're Really Weird," *CIO,* October 1995, pp. 86–96; Bonnie G. Mani, "Progress on the Journey to Total Quality Management: Using the Myers-Briggs Type Indicator and the Adjective Check List in Management Development," *Public Personnel Management,* Fall 1995, pp. 365–98; Ruthann Fox-Hines and Roger B. Bowersock, "ISFJ, ENTP, MBTI: What's It All About?," *Business & Economic Review,* January-March 1995, pp. 3–7; Lance Lindon, "Linking an Intervention Model to the Myers-Briggs Type Indicator, Consultancy and Managerial Roles," *Journal of Managerial Psychology,* 1995, pp. 21–29; Gregory J. Boyle, "Myers-Briggs Type Indicator (MBTI): Some Psychometric Limitations," *Australian Psychologist,* March 1995, pp. 71–74.

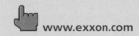

www.exxon.com

Figure 4–9

Bandura Self-Efficacy Workplace Application

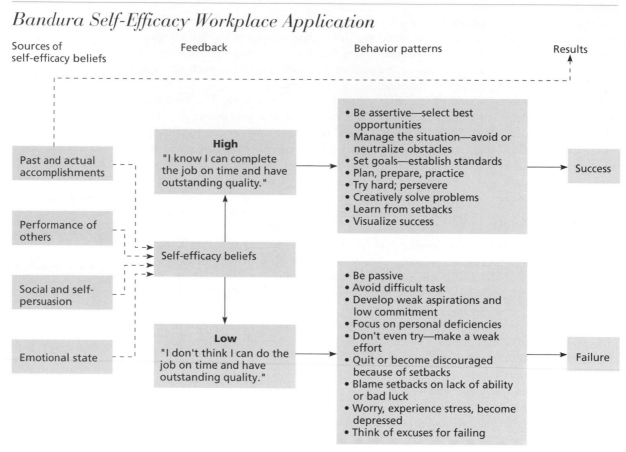

Sources: Adapted from Albert Bandura, "Regulation of Cognitive Processes through Perceived Self-Efficacy," *Developmental Psychology,* September 1989, pp. 729–35; Robert Wood and Albert Bandura, "Social Cognitive Theory of Organizational Management," *Academy of Management Review,* July 1989, pp. 361–84; and Robert Kreitner and Angelo Kinicki, *Organizational Behavior* (Homewood, Ill.: Richard D. Irwin, 1992), p. 90.

with low self-efficacy could preserve internal barriers to advancement and become passive. The shortage of successful role models among minorities could create self-doubts about advancement. Perhaps efficacy training could help minority group members minimize the self-doubt barrier to success.[82] Chapter 6 discusses self-efficacy in terms of motivation.

Machiavellianism   Imagine yourself in the following situation with two other people: Thirty new $1 bills are on the table to be distributed in any way the group decides. The game is over as soon as two of you agree to how it will be divided. Obviously, the fairest distribution would be $10 each. However, a selfish party could cut out the third person, and the remaining two would each end up with $15. Suppose that one person suggests this alternative to you, and before you can decide, the left-out person offers to give you $16, taking $14 as his or her share and cutting out the other person. What would you do?

Machiavellianism, a concept derived from the writings of Italian philosopher and statesman Niccolo Machiavelli (1469–1527), helps answer the question. Machiavelli was concerned with the manipulation of people and with the orientations and tactics used by manipulators versus

Machiavellianism

A term used to describe political maneuvers in an organization. Used to designate a person as a manipulator and power abuser.

nonmanipulators.[83] *Machiavellianism* (a term with negative connotations) is associated with being a political maneuverer and power manipulator.

From anecdotal descriptions of power tactics and the nature of influential people, various scales have been constructed to measure Machiavellianism. One scale organizes questions around a cluster of beliefs about tactics, people, and morality.

In the money allocation game discussed above, the individuals who get the lion's share are those who score high on this scale, the LOW MACH scorers get only slightly less than would be expected by a fair, one-third split. In a job situation, Machiavellianism does seem to have an effect on job performance.[84] HIGH MACH scorers would probably be suited for activities such as selling, negiotiating, and acquiring limited resources. LOW MACH scorers would seem to be better suited for structured, routine, and nonemotional situations. They would seem to be better suited for planning, conceptualizing, and working out details.[85]

Creativity   Many organizations feel that creativity and innovativeness are not only desirable but also should be core competencies and a consistent feature of their cultures.[86] Firms such as 3M, W. L. Gore, Canon, Intuit, and Hewlett-Packard demonstrate this very clearly by their support of creative activities by their employees.[87] But it is also the case that creativity may be viewed in many ways. First, you may consider the creative person as mad. The madness of creative artists such as Van Gogh and Nijinsky is often cited as proof of this view. But research evidence offers no support for it. Instead, creative people have been found to have superior ego strength and handle problems constructively. Second, you can see the creative person as being disconnected from the art of creativity. Creativity in this view is a mystical act. Third, you can conclude that to be creative, a person must be intelligent. However, research shows that some intelligent people are creative while others aren't.[88] Finally, you can view creativity as a possibility open to every person, as an expression of personality that can be developed.[89] This view and an increasing amount of research indicate that creativity can be taught. That is, individuals can learn to be creative.[90]

 www.wlgore.com

Many studies have examined creativity. Life histories, personality characteristics, and tests are often scrutinized to determine a person's degree of creativity. In a typical test, subjects might be asked to examine a group of drawings and then answer what the drawings represent. Figure 4–10 is a line drawing test used to determine young children's creativity.[91] Novel and unusual answers are rated as being creative.

Figure 4–10

Testing Creativity

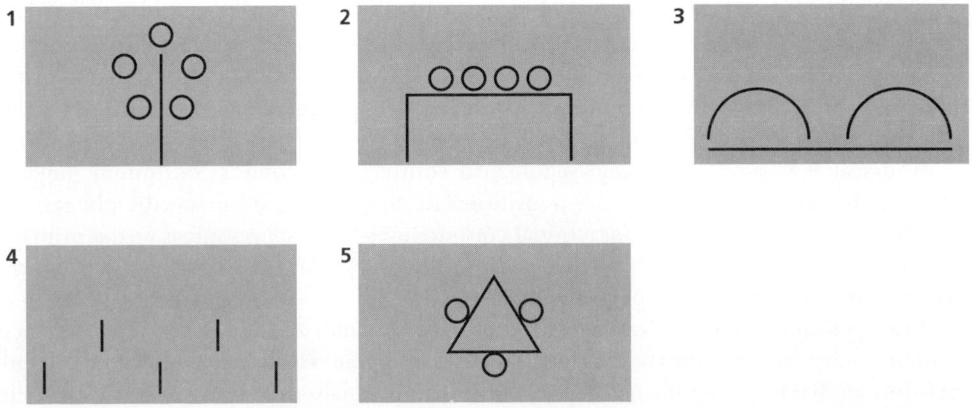

1	2	3
4	5	

Managers who adopt either of the first two views of creativity might attempt to keep creative people out of the organization. Adoption of the third view might result in the hiring of only highly intelligent people. But if management views creativity as a personality factor that can be developed, then it will initiate development procedures. A review of Japanese managers found a sample to be positive about allowing employees to be creative on the job. Japanese employees were "cheerful" about coming to work. A sample of 10 leading Japanese firms (e.g., Mazda, Fuji Electric, JVC) found in most companies an average of over 100 suggestions per employee. The typical U.S. firm receives about two suggestions per employee.[92] The Japanese firms in this study induced creative behavior. It appears that the Japanese encourage problem finding and problem solving.

www.mazda.com

www.jvcservice.com

Organizations can help develop creativity by[93]

1. *Buffering.* Managers can look for ways to absorb the risks of creative decisions made by their employees.

2. *Organizational time-outs.* Give people time off to work on a problem and allow them to think things through.

3. *Intuition.* Give half-baked or unsophisticated ideas a chance.

4. *Innovative attitudes.* Encourage everyone to think of ways to solve problems.

5. *Innovative organizational structures.* Let employees see and interact with many managers and mentors.

Managerial interest in developing creativity seems worthwhile. A review of research findings indicates that creative individuals share important characteristics. They are self-confident and motivated to succeed, they approach life enthusiastically, and they push on even when they must overcome obstacles.[94] The idea that an inexperienced person can look at a problem and immediately be creative is a myth. Mozart was a child genius because he could do what other children couldn't do. But he spent 10 years writing only average music before writing great music.[95]

The Psychological Contract

Psychological Contract

An implied understanding of mutual contributions between a person and his or her organization.

When a person accepts a job with an organization, an unwritten psychological contract is established. Because of differences in perception, attribution, attitudes, values, and general personality, individuals form a personal view of the expectations inherent in the psychological contract. The **psychological contract** is not a written document between a person and the organization, but it is an implied understanding of mutual contributions.[96] The individual has a perception of the reciprocal obligations he or she has with the organization. For example, employees may assume that if they work hard and display loyalty that the organization will provide good working conditions and job security. The psychological contract is a belief that promises have been made by the individual and the organization.

Rousseau has proposed that psychological contracts lie along a continuum ranging from transitional to relational.[97] A transitional contract is based on specific obligations and short time frames. The transactional contract uses financial resources as the primary means of exchange. They are focused on self-interest. A relational contract is characterized by long-term relationship development.

In organizations today a variety of trends such as plant relocation, increased reliance on temporary workers, downsizing and layoffs, demographic diversity, and foreign competition are having a significant impact on how individuals and organizations view their psychological contracts.[98] As environmental forces become more turbulent and the economy changes it is likely that individual perception and attitudes about the obligation of organizations will continue to be problematic and uncertain.

Psychological Contract Violations

A **psychological contract violation** is defined as the perception of the person that his or her organization has failed to fulfill or has reneged on one or more obligations. The perception has a cognitive portion and emotional or feeling portion as described by Morrison and Robinson.[99] A violation by an employer may effect not only the beliefs of the person but also what he or she feels obligated to provide or contribute to the organization. The majority of research on psychological contracts has not focused on violations of the perceived obligations among parties. Table 4–6 lists a number of possible organizational violations and offers quotes from the perspective of the employee. These types of violations of the psychological contract can seriously undermine the feelings of goodwill and trust held by employees toward the organization.

> **Psychological Contract Violation**
>
> The perception of the person that his or her firm has failed to fulfill or has reneged on one or more obligations.

The seven examples of violations indicates how trust is undermined, how the bond between an employer and employee can be weakened, and how perception plays a significant role in psychological contracts.[100] Rosseau believes that violation of a relational contract can produce intense feelings that can result in moral outrage.[101] Minor violations are not so intensely felt. However, a major violation could result from witholding good performance, sabotaging work, absenteeism, or quitting. A sequential pattern of responses to violations has been identified.[102] The first *voice;* the person voices concern about the violation and attempts to restore the psychological contract. If unsuccessful, voice is followed by *silence.* Silence connotes compliance with what the employer wants

Table 4–6   Psychological Contract Violations from Perceptions and Emotions of Individual Employees

VIOLATION	DEFINITION	EMPLOYEE STATEMENT
Job security	No such thing as security with good chance of layoff or downsizing.	"When I was recruited I heard on at least four occasions that we (the organization) had not laid off one person in fifteen years. What a shock when six of my friends were let go."
Child-care benefits	Failing to provide adequate care and services for child care during working hours on- or off-site.	"The firm has refused to improve their skimpy child-care benefits even though they brag about this every chance they have. I'm not sure they really care about children and working parents."
Job feedback	Poor attention and little effort to provide meaningful job feedback.	"My boss skips through the feedback session and makes me feel like I am infringing on his time and space."
Merit-based pay raises	No relationship between pay and actual performance.	"I see no effort to link what and how I do on the job to my pay raises (when I receive them, which is rare)."
Job autonomy	Failure to permit the employee to have the freedom to make job-related decisions about how to perform the job.	"I feel like I am constantly watched and checked."
Computer training	Failure to provide adequate training and coaching on the proper use of computers.	"I have been promised again and again the opportunity to undergo specific computer skills training. This is just not going to happen."
Promotion	Reneging on a specific promise to provide a promotion for excellent performance.	"Time after time I am informed about my superior preformance and promotion possibilities. This company just reneges and keeps on going like nothing has occurred."

or is doing, but with no commitment. Silence is followed by *retreat,* which is shown by negligence, shirking of responsibility, and passivity. *Destruction* can follow silence. In this stage the employee can retaliate through slowdown of work, sabotage, hiding papers or tools, theft, or even violence. Finally, of course the employee can exit or quit the firm.

The discussion has focused on the psychological contract from the employee's side. This is because most of the research and conjecture in the organizational behavior and management literature are from the employee's perspective. We need to increase our understanding and research from the employer's perspective. There is also the need to examine individual, group, and organizational effectiveness in situations, settings, and projects where both employees and employers believe and perceive that the expectations of the psychological contract have been met. Are there unique attributes, techniques, or methods that have a high probability of the psychological contract being achieved? Managers need to be aware of the importance of the psychological contract in committing the employer and employees to a trusting and development relationship over time.[103] As this chapter should illustrate, how each person views the relationship can significantly vary because of individual differences. Thus, there is no easy method or formula to provide managers for improving their ability to effectively manage the multiple psychological contracts of individuals.

Summary of Key Points

- Employees joining an organization must adjust to a new environment, new people, and new tasks. How people adjust to situations and other people depends largely on their psychological makeup and personal backgrounds.

- There's no compelling evidence that men or women perform better. Some women are better salespeople than some men. On the other hand, some men are better caregivers than some women. Searching for similarities and differences is likely to continue, since the majority of organizationally based research has been conducted with male samples.

- Individual perceptual processes help people face the realities of the world. People are influenced by other people and by situations, needs, and past experiences. While a manager is perceiving employees, they are also perceiving the manager.

- Attitudes are linked with behavioral patterns in a complex manner. They're organized, and they provide the emotional basis for most of a person's interpersonal relations. Changing attitudes is extremely difficult and requires, at the very least, trust in the communicator and strength of message.

- Job satisfaction is the attitude workers have about their jobs. Research findings suggest that a satisfied worker isn't necessarily a higher performer.

- Personality, developed long before a person joins an organization, is influenced by hereditary, cultural, and social determinants. To assume that personality can be modified easily can result in managerial frustration and ethical problems. Managers should try to cope with personality differences among people and not try to change personalities to fit their model of the ideal person.

- Personality variables, such as locus of control, self-efficacy, Machiavellianism, and creativity, are associated with behavior and performance. Although difficult to measure, these variables appear to be important personality facets in explaining and predicting individual behavior.

- When a person joins and remains a part of an organization, an implied psychological contract is formed between the employee and the employer.

- Violations of the psychological contract can create dramatic breaks in the relationship between employers and an employeee. Each person decides what is a minor or major violation of the psychological contract.

Discussion and Review Questions

1. Employee Joan Shirer opposes the introduction of a new financial control system. For 15 years she has worked with the old, manual system. Now the firm is introducing a new, computer-based system. How would you attempt to change Joan's attitude about the new system?

2. Some people believe that perception is a more important explanation of behavior than is reality. Why is this assumption about perception made?

3. "Ethnic diversity isn't a significant factor, since we're all Americans or Canadians, or Japanese." Comment on this type of thinking as it applies to the United States, Canada, and Japan.

4. The chapter focuses on the perspective of the employee in discussing the psychological contract. From the employer's perspective, what is generally expected from employees in terms of the contract?

5. Provide some examples of selective perception that could be used in purchasing a new car and in accepting a new position with an organization.

6. Some people state that being too concerned about dealing with individual differences can cause chaos in an organization. Do you agree? Why?

7. In the selection of job candidates, what should a manager know about the self-efficacy concept?

8. Why would a manager act differently in leading a subordinate who's an internal than in leading another subordinate who's an external?

9. It's generally agreed that value systems are largely developed before people begin to work for an organization. What are the managerial implications of this fact?

10. What's the meaning of the notion that, even when differences between the sexes exist, there's overlap between them? Explain this in terms of absenteeism rates and turnover rates.

CASE FOR ANALYSIS

A Potter's Wheel

Bill Strickland's life changed and began anew on a Wednesay afternoon in Pittsburgh in 1963. Strickland, then a 16-year-old African-American, was bored with high school and felt hemmed in by life in this decaying neighborhood. Looking through a classroom door, Strickland saw something he had never seen before: a rotating mound of clay being shaped into a vessel by a man absorbed in his work. He stated, "I saw a radiant and hopeful image of how the world ought to be. It opened up a portal that suggested that there might be a whole range of possibilities and experiences that I had not explored."

Strickland walked into the classroom, introduced himself to ceramics teacher Frank Ross, the man at the potter's wheel, and said, "I'd like to learn whatever that is." Ross became his mentor and Strickland took an entirely new path in life that led to earning a college degree.

Today Strickland applies his potter's hands and is involved in social change. People work with him and come to his programs at the Manchester Craftsmen Guild (MCG) and at the Bidwell Training Center, Inc. For nearly three decades, Strickland has worked at his craft back in the same Pittsburgh neighborhood he grew up in—creating a model for turning people with dead-end lives into productive workers. The source of Strickland's unique gift is, according to him, that Wednesday afternoon in 1963. "You start with the perception that the world is an unlimited opportunity. Then the question becomes, how are we going to rebuild the planet."

Strickland has brought all of his talents, aspirations, and thinking as an artist and applied them to make a change in the neighborhood where he lives. The use of art to change students' attitudes is at the heart of Strickland's vision of education. The goal is not to produce artists or potters. It's to find an individually tailored approach to learning that will redirect young people who are searching for goals and get them interested in education.

Strickland's story and life provide an example of how each person is unique. His background environment certainly had an impact on his individual characteristics. Strickland speaks with a moral authority that should ring true with struggling college students.

Discussion Questions

1. What environmental factors could Bill Strickland have changed in his life?

2. What moral authority does Bill Strickland speak from to struggling college students?

3. What impact did Strickland's mentor (Frank Ross) have on his goals, self-efficacy, and values?

Sources: Sara Terry, "Genius at Work," Fast Company, September 1998, pp. 171–183 and Michael Warsaw, "Have You Got the Right Stuff?" Fast Company, October 1998, pp. 219–225.

E X P E R I E N T I A L   E X E R C I S E

Applying Attribution Theory

Objectives

1. To examine the causes of a person's behavior.
2. To develop an approach that's best suited to improve unacceptable behavior.

Related Topics

The concept of perception plays a role in how each of us views other people. Making attributions in terms of dispositional or situational factors is based on how a person views the event, the behaviors of another person, and previous experience.

Starting the Exercise

Carefully read the situation facing a manager. If you were this manager, what would you conclude about causes and how would you proceed? Why?

The Loss of Quality

Don Dubose worked for Maybrooke Manufacturing since its beginning in 1964. He has won four top performer awards during his tenure in the firm. The last award he won was presented to him with a $5,000 bonus check about three years ago. But in the past 18 months, Don's relations with co-workers have become strained. He has never been talkative, but on occasion he has ordered co-workers out of his work area. Don has made it clear that tools have been missing, and he wants to protect his area. His work's quality has also suffered. Until about a year ago, Don's work producing generators was at the "zero-defect" level. Error-free, top-quality generators came from Don again and again. Today when random sample checks are made, Don occasionally produces generators that must be reworked less than 3 percent of the time. He has gone from zero defects to 3 out of 100 defects. His co-workers average about 1.5 defects out of 100 for reworking.

What could be causing Don's behavior changes? They could be caused by:

	1	2	3	4	5	6	7
	[						]

	Not very likely		Very likely				
1. Low motivation	1	2	3	4	5	6	7
2. Low self-efficacy	1	2	3	4	5	6	7

	1	2	3	4	5	6	7
3. Physical health problems	1	2	3	4	5	6	7
4. Family problems	1	2	3	4	5	6	7
5. Poor management	1	2	3	4	5	6	7
6. Lack of creativity	1	2	3	4	5	6	7

Comment on each of your ratings:

1. _____
2. _____
3. _____
4. _____
5. _____
6. _____

Don's behavior has become a topic of concern within the organization. An outstanding worker has become average. What actions would you take as the manager?

	Yes	No	Why?
Transfer Don to a new job.	___	___	_____
Fire Don.	___	___	_____
Call Don in to discuss your observation.	___	___	_____
Suspend Don after informing him about your concerns.	___	___	_____
Ask Don's co-workers why they believe his performance isn't up to previous norms.	___	___	_____
Leave the situation alone for another six months.	___	___	_____
Contact Don's wife to see if there's a personal reason for the performance problem.	___	___	_____
Examine your own behavior (as manager) in working with Don.	___	___	_____
Send Don to a human resource management counselor to discuss his attitudes about the job.	___	___	_____
Promote Don since he has been in the present job for over six years.	___	___	_____

Other courses of action:_____
_____
_____
_____
_____

In Class

After you've analyzed this situation, meet with class-mates to discuss their reactions. What did you learn about your attribution process? Are your reactions different from your classmates?

E X P E R I E N T I A L   E X E R C I S E

Who Controls Your Life? The Rotter Internal–External Scale

Objectives

1. To determine whether you believe you control your destiny or you believe that what happens in life is due to luck or chance.

2. To relate your internal–external attributes to other segments of your life: home, school, family, community.

Related Topics

Being self-aware helps people understand their own behavior better.

Starting the Exercise

Read the following statements and indicate whether you agree more with choice A or choice B. After you've completed the exercise, the instructor will share information with you on how others have completed this scale.

CHOICE A	CHOICE B
1. Making a lot of money is largely a matter of getting the right breaks.	1. Promotions are earned through hard work and persistence.
2. I have noticed that there is usually a direct connection between how hard I study and the grades I get.	2. Many times, the reactions of teachers seem haphazard to me.
3. The number of divorces indicates that more and more people are not trying to make their marriages work.	3. Marriage is largely a gamble.
4. It is silly to think that one can really change another person's basic attitudes.	4. When I am right, I can convince others.
5. Getting promoted is really a matter of being a little luckier than the next person.	5. In our society, a person's future earning power depends on her ability.
6. If one knows how to deal with people, they are really quite easily led.	6. I have little influence over the way other people behave.
7. The grades I make are the result of my own efforts; luck has little or nothing to do with it.	7. Sometimes, I feel that I have little to do with the grades I get.
8. People like me can change the course of world affairs if we make ourselves heard.	8. It is only wishful thinking to believe that one can readily influence what happens in our society at large.
9. Much of what happens to me is probably a matter of chance.	9. I am the master of my fate.
10. Getting along with people is a skill that must be practiced.	10. It is almost impossible to figure out how to please some people.

Source: Julian B. Rotter, "External Control and Internal Control," *Psychology Today,* June 1971, p. 42.; © 1971 by the American Psychological Association. Adapted with permission.

Chapter 5

Motivation: Content Theories and Applications

Learning Objectives

After completing Chapter 5, you should be able to:

Define
Motivation in terms that would be meaningful to managers.

Describe
The difference between Maslow's need hierarchy and Alderfer's ERG theory of motivation.

Discuss
McClelland's explanation of learned needs in terms of the economic achievement of a society (e.g., United States, Russia, and Japan).

Compare
Four content theories and how they explain motivation.

Identify
The reasons why an individual's needs change over the course of a work career.

Why some employees perform better than others is a continual and perplexing problem facing managers. To explain such differences, several interesting and important variables have been used—for example, ability, instinct, and aspiration levels, as well as demographic factors such as age, education, and family background. However, one issue that consistently captures the attention of managers and researchers alike is the motivation of people to perform their work. In fact, much of management's time is spent addressing the motivation of their employees.[1]

Despite its obvious importance, motivation is difficult to define and to analyze. By one definition, motivation has to do with (1) the direction of behavior, (2) the strength of the response (i.e., effort) once an employee chooses to follow a course of action, and (3) the persistence of the behavior, or how long the person continues to behave in a particular manner.[2] Another view suggests that the analysis of motivation should concentrate on the factors that incite and direct a person's activities.[3] One theorist emphasizes the goal-directedness aspect of motivation.[4] Another states that motivation is "concerned with how behavior gets started, is energized, is sustained, is directed, and is stopped, and what kind of subjective reaction is present in the organism while all this is going on."[5]

A careful examination of each of these views leads to several conclusions about motivation:

1. Theorists present slightly different interpretations and place emphasis on different factors.

2. It is related to behavior and performance.

3. Goal-directedness is involved.

4. It results from events and processes that are internal or external to the individual.

Motivating employees was an important topic as far back as 1789. Samuel Slater, a pioneer who introduced textile manufacturing to America, was concerned about creating a work setting where it was comfortable for workers to do their jobs. Other efforts to create a positive motivational work climate ranged from George M. Pullman's company town to Henry Ford's profit-sharing plan. The Edison Electric Illuminating Company of Boston provided tennis courts and bowling alleys. Other firms planted gardens for workers or constructed libraries and athletic facilities.

One reason for corporate generosity was fear of the trade union movement, but there were other motivators. One was greed, the desire to get employees to work harder for less money. Another was humanitarianism, the willingness to treat employees well. And some corporate leaders believed it was simply good business to satisfy workers' needs for good working conditions, a fair day's pay, and social interaction.

Two of the most radical experiments in creating a positive work environment occurred in the late 1800s. Disturbed by reports of worker resentment and sabotage, John H. Patterson, president of the National Cash Register (NCR) Company, investigated working conditions himself and found that there was little to motivate employees to achieve or even strive toward doing an adequate job. In response he increased wages, cleaned up the shop floor, improved safety, made company showers and dressing rooms available, and opened a company cafeteria that served hot lunches at reduced rates. NCR provided free medical care at its dispensary, gave additional food to those felt to be underweight, and redesigned the factory buildings to allow in natural light. Patterson also instituted industry's first paid "suggestion" system and provided opportunities for employees to take classes at a company-sponsored night school. These innovations helped to cut turnover and increase productivity and were a significant factor behind NCR's dominance in the cash register business for many years.[6]

Similarly, at the Pullman Company, George Pullman built a company town with houses to rent, stores, schools, a church, and a company plant.[7] He wanted to provide his employees with a feeling of community, a place of employment, and opportunities to practice religion and to educate their children. However, when the national economy slid into a depression, events in Pullman, Illinois, turned sour. Pullman cut his workers' wages without lowering rents or prices in the town. What started as an experiment to help workers satisfy various needs eventually spurred workers into attempting to organize a union. Pullman's workers went out on strike, riots occurred, and federal troops were called in to restore order.

Both of the above situations reflect efforts by management to influence the motivation of the workforce, with varying levels of success. Since that time, researchers have learned much about motivation, and managers need to consider these insights when attempting to create positive motivational atmospheres for their employees.

No matter what their nationality or cultural background, people are driven to fulfill needs and to achieve goals. But what are those needs, what goals are desired, and what can motivate people in different countries? This is the complex and difficult-to-answer question. For example, differences between motivational structures among Americans and Japanese need to take into consideration cultural differences that affect attitudes about money, work, incentives, teamwork, and performance reviews.[8] The Japanese tend to confer recognition for excellent performance with plaques, applause, and attention. Japanese employees are likely to be insulted by material incentives because this form of reward suggests they could work even harder. In Japanese firms bonuses are given because of seniority, gender, and marital status.

In examining each of the motivation theories, remember that cultural differences could be significant and need to be considered. Motivation is a universal concept that must be aligned with the setting and cultural background. What proves to be an extremely powerful motivator in one setting or country may be a miserable failure in another setting or nation.

What Is Motivation?

Imagine that you and a group of your friends like to go out together once a week to a club or a party. Over the past few weeks one of your friends has not gone along, saying that he was working overtime. You and your friends originally assumed that he needed the additional money, but then you remembered that he comes from a wealthy family and has never seemed to have any financial concerns. Based on this observation, you aren't sure that your assumption about your friend's motivation for working more hours is correct.

When you heard about your friend working overtime, you assumed that he was doing it for a specific purpose, namely that the need for money motivated his work schedule. **Motivation** is the concept we use when we describe the forces acting on or within an individual to initiate and direct behavior. We use the concept to explain differences in the intensity of behavior (regarding more intense behaviors as the result of higher levels of motivation) and also to indicate the direction of behavior (e.g., when you're tired or sleepy, you direct your behavior toward getting some sleep).

Motivation

Forces acting on an employee that initiate and direct behavior.

Motivation is an explanatory concept that we use to make sense out of the behaviors we observe. In other words, motivation is inferred. Instead of measuring it directly, we note what conditions exist and observe behavior, using this information as a basis for our understanding of the underlying motivation. You assumed that your friend worked overtime because he needed the additional pay. But your inference wasn't correct; your friend was actually doing the additional work to help out his boss and because he was fascinated by the specific project in which he was involved. The lesson is clear: we must always be cautious in making motivational inferences. As more and more information is accumulated, however, our inferences should become more accurate because we can eliminate alternative explanations.

One reason why our understanding of motivation is important is that high levels of motivation are significant contributors to exceptional performance. Managers prefer highly motivated employees because they strive to find the best way to perform their jobs. Motivated employees are interested in producing high-quality products or services; they're more likely to be productive than are nonmotivated or apathetic workers. They want to come to work and be part of a team; they're interested in helping, supporting, and encouraging co-workers. Self-confident and decisive employees display these and other desirable actions. However, finding a universal set of principles to motivate employees and managers isn't likely to occur, as there is no one approach that works best.

Harvard Business School publishes and circulates thousands of business cases worldwide. The most requested and purchased case is about Lincoln Electric Company of Cleveland. The firm produces industrial electric motors. The Lincoln Electric case is so popular because it illustrates how the company motivates workers. All of Lincoln's over 2,000 employees participate in the firm's pay incentive plan. This plan has been a success for decades because it clearly links pay and pay increases to performance.[9]

 www.lincoln-electric.com

Lincoln employees receive piece-rate (each piece or product produced results in payment) wages with no guaranteed minimum hourly wage. After two years of employment workers can participate in the year-end bonus plan (one-time lump-sum payment tied to performance). Determined by a formula that considers the firm's gross profits, the employees' base piece rate, and merit rating, Lincoln calculates a bonus system. The average bonus over five decades has been approximately 95 percent of the average wage.

Every six months, the chief executive officer personally reviews each employee's merit ratings. Everyone is rated on output, quality, dependability, and cooperation. Lincoln pays attention to performance, linking pay to performance and the quality of its products. The company has never faced a strike. It has no debt. It believes that success is based on individual accountability and the power of creating a positive motivational atmosphere. As each of the motivation theories in the next two chapters are presented, refer back to the simplicity and popularity of Lincoln Electric's approach to motivation.[10]

The Starting Point: The Individual

Managers are expected to understand the existing types and degrees of motivation in their employees and must also try to enhance the extent of motivation demonstrated in a diverse and in many respects unpredictable group of people. This diversity results in different behavioral patterns that in some manner are related to needs and goals.

Need

Deficiency that an individual experiences at a particular point in time.

A **need** is a deficiency or lack of something of value that an individual experiences at a particular point in time. Deficiencies may be physiological (e.g., a need for food), psychological (e.g., a need for self-esteem), or sociological (e.g., a need for social interaction). Needs are energizers or triggers of behavioral responses. The implication is that when needs (deficiencies) are present, the individual will seek to fulfill those needs and may be more susceptible to managers' motivational efforts.

In any discussion of motivation, the importance of goals is apparent. The motivational process, as interpreted by most theorists, is goal-directed. The goals, or outcomes, an employee seeks are viewed as forces that attract the person. Accomplishing desired goals can result in a significant reduction in need deficiencies.

As Figure 5–1 shows, people have need deficiencies, which trigger a search process for ways to reduce the tension they cause. A course of action is selected, and goal-directed behavior occurs. After a period of time, managers assess that behavior. Performance evaluation will result in rewards or punishments. Such outcomes are weighed by the person, and need deficiencies are reassessed. This in turn triggers the process, and the circular pattern begins again.

Motivation Theories: A Classification System

Each person is attracted to some set of goals. To predict behavior with any accuracy, a manager must know something about an employee's goals and about the actions that the employee has to take to achieve them. Numerous motivation theories and research findings attempt to explain this behavior–outcome relationship.

Content Motivation Theories

Theories that focus on factors within a person that energize, direct, sustain, and stop behavior.

Theories of motivation fall into two categories: content theories and process theories. **Content theories** focus on the factors *within* the person that energize, direct, sustain, and stop behavior. They attempt to determine the specific needs that motivate people. **Process theories** describe and analyze how behavior is energized, directed, sustained, and stopped by factors primarily *external* to the person. Both categories have important implications for managers, who by the nature of their jobs are involved with the motivational process. Table 5–1 summarizes the basic characteristics of content and process theories of motivation from a managerial perspective.

This chapter covers some of the most publicized content theories, while the next chapter discusses some process theories of motivation. The content theories focus on individual needs in explaining job satisfaction, worker behavior, and reward systems. The theories suggest that within a person, individual need deficiencies activate tensions that trigger a behavioral response. For managers to be effective, the content theories suggest that they must

Process Motivation Theories

Theories that describe and analyze how behavior is energized, directed, sustained, and stopped.

1. Determine what needs trigger desired performance, group, and personal behaviors.

2. Be able to offer meaningful rewards that help the employee satisfy needs.

Figure 5–1

The Motivational Process: An Initial Model

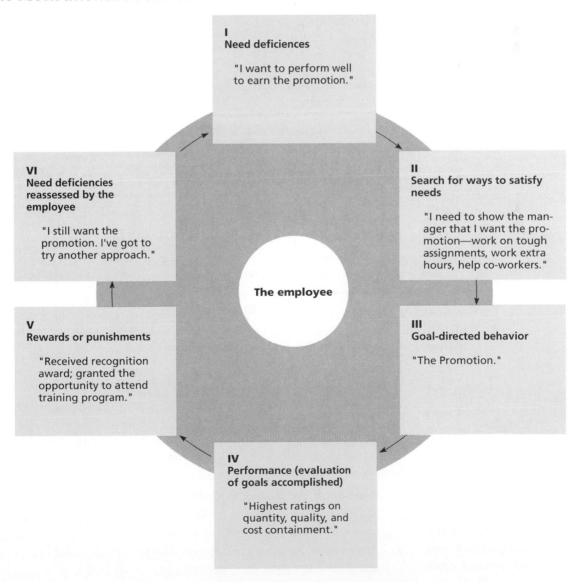

I
Need deficiencies

"I want to perform well to earn the promotion."

VI
Need deficiencies reassessed by the employee

"I still want the promotion. I've got to try another approach."

II
Search for ways to satisfy needs

"I need to show the manager that I want the promotion—work on tough assignments, work extra hours, help co-workers."

The employee

V
Rewards or punishments

"Received recognition award; granted the opportunity to attend training program."

III
Goal-directed behavior

"The Promotion."

IV
Performance (evaluation of goals accomplished)

"Highest ratings on quantity, quality, and cost containment."

Table 5–1	THEORETICAL BASE	THEORETICAL EXPLANATION	FOUNDERS OF THE THEORIES	MANAGERIAL APPLICATION
Managerial Perspective of Content and Process Theories of Motivation	Content	Focuses on factors within the person that energize, direct, sustain, and stop behavior. These factors can only be inferred.	**Maslow**—five-level need hierarchy. **Alderfer**—three-level hierarchy (ERG). **Herzberg**—two major factors called hygiene-motivators. **McClelland**—three learned needs acquired from the culture: achievement, affiliation, and power.	Managers need to be aware of differences in needs, desires, and goals because each individual is unique in many ways.
	Process	Describes, explains, and analyzes how behavior is energized, directed, sustained, and stopped.	**Vroom**—an expectancy theory of choices. **Skinner**—reinforcement theory concerned with the learning that occurs as a consequence of behavior. **Adams**—equity theory based on comparisons that individuals make. **Locke**—goal-setting theory that conscious goals and intentions are the determinants of behavior.	Managers need to understand the *process* of motivation and how individuals make choices based on preferences, rewards, and accomplishments.

3. Know when to offer appropriate rewards to optimize performance behavior.

4. Not assume that a person's need deficiencies will repeat themselves in a regular pattern. People change because of experiences, life events, aging, cultural and environmental changes, and other factors.

Maslow's need hierarchy, Alderfer's ERG theory, Herzberg's two-factor theory, and McClelland's learned needs theory are four important content theories of motivation. Each perspective can have an impact on managerial practices.

Maslow's Need Hierarchy

Need Hierarchy Model

Maslow's theory that assumes that people's needs depend on what they already have. In a sense, then, a satisfied need is not a motivator. Human needs, organized in a hierarchy of importance, are physiological, safety, belongingness, esteem, and self-actualization.

One of the most widely cited and discussed motivation theories is the **need hierarchy model** proposed by Abraham Maslow.[11] The lowest-level needs are the physiological needs, and the highest-level needs are for self-actualization. Maslow defined human needs as

1. *Physiological:* the need for food, drink, shelter, and relief from pain.

2. *Safety and security:* the need for freedom from threat; that is, the security from threatening events or surroundings.

3. *Belongingness, social, and love:* the need for friendship, affiliation, interaction, and love.

4. *Esteem:* the need for self-esteem and for respect from others.

5. *Self-actualization:* the need to fulfill oneself by maximizing the use of abilities, skills, and potential.

Maslow's theory assumes that a person attempts to satisfy the more basic needs (physiological) before directing behavior toward satisfying upper level needs (self-actualization). Lower order needs must be satisfied before a higher order need such as self-actualization begins to control a person's behavior. According to Maslow, a satisfied need ceases to motivate. When a person decides that she's earning enough pay for contributing to the organization, money loses its power to motivate.

One way in which this theory may be of use to managers is in suggesting strategies that the organization can implement to correct need deficiencies. These deficiencies can occur at all levels but are likely to be largest in the areas of self-actualization and esteem, needs that are often ignored in the reward structures of many organizations. Attempts to address these deficiencies may actually have a greater impact in initiating and directing behavior than focusing on lower level needs that may be closer to fulfillment.

In addition to dealing with individual differences in needs, managers face the issue that needs, work style, and work ethics may differ across cultures. It is the case that Americans are sometimes perceived by foreigners as lazy and not motivated. The problem often boils down not to laziness but to conflict between culturally different patterns of job behavior, management styles, and work's role in employees' lives.[12] For example, Americans are more job-oriented than company-oriented. Latin Americans work not for the job or company but for themselves. Australians say they're motivated to do a good job to earn a vacation. In China and some other cultures, a monetary bonus for outstanding performance could cause an employee embarrassment or even humiliation.[13]

Selected need hierarchy research

A number of research studies have tested the need hierarchy theory. The first reported field research that tested a modified version of Maslow's need hierarchy was by Lyman W. Porter.[14] Initially, he assumed that physiological needs were being adequately satisfied for managers, so he substituted a higher order need called *autonomy,* defined as the person's satisfaction with opportunities to make independent decisions, set goals, and work without close supervision.

Since the early Porter studies, other studies have reported:

1. Managers high in the organization chain of command place greater emphasis on self-actualization and autonomy.[15]

2. Managers at lower organizational levels in small firms with less than 500 employees are more satisfied than their counterparts in large firms with more than 5,000 employees. But managers at upper levels in large companies are more satisfied than their counterparts in small companies.[16]

3. American managers overseas are more satisfied with autonomy opportunities than are their counterparts working in the United States.[17]

In general, Maslow's theory hasn't been supported by field research.[18] Maslow himself stated that self-actualization theory in and of itself isn't enough, as the assumptions must be amplified into a more thorough formulation, taking into account such factors as the good of other people and the organization as a whole.[19] Therefore, we don't recommend using the theory to predict behavior. The hierarchy does explain aspects of human behavior in our society. But it's not accurate or thorough enough to explain individual-level behavior.

Alderfer's ERG Theory

Alderfer agrees with Maslow that individuals' needs are arranged in a hierarchy.[20] However, his proposed need hierarchy involves only three sets of needs:[21]

1. *Existence:* needs satisfied by such factors as food, air, water, pay, and working conditions.

2. *Relatedness:* needs satisfied by meaningful social and interpersonal relationships.

3. *Growth:* needs satisfied by an individual making creative or productive contributions.

Alderfer's three needs—existence (E), relatedness (R), and growth (G), or ERG—correspond to Maslow's in that the existence needs are similar to Maslow's physiological and safety categories; the relatedness needs are similar to the belongingness, social, and love category; and the growth needs are similar to the esteem and self-actualization categories.

ERG Theory of Motivation

Theory developed and tested by Alderfer that categorizes needs as existence, relatedness, and growth.

In addition to a difference in the number of categories, Alderfer's **ERG theory of motivation** and Maslow's need hierarchy differ on how people move through the different sets of needs. Maslow proposed that unfulfilled needs at one level are of most importance and that the needs on the next higher level aren't activated or triggered until the currently important needs are adequately satisfied. Thus, a person only progresses up the need hierarchy once his lower level needs have been effectively met. In contrast, Alderfer's ERG theory suggests that in addition to the satisfaction-progression process that Maslow proposed, a frustration-regression process is also at work. That is, if a person is continually frustrated in attempts to satisfy growth needs, relatedness needs reemerge as a major motivating force, causing the individual to redirect efforts toward exploring new ways to satisfy this lower-order need category. Figure 5–2 presents Alderfer's ERG theory.

Consider the case of Mary Higgins, a registered nurse in the pediatric unit in Methodist Hospital in Tampa, Florida. A single parent, Mary is concerned with job security, pay, and co-worker interaction and friendship. She must work to support her family and also enjoys the social aspect of work. Her performance is outstanding, and she has satisfied her existence and relatedness needs. A head nurse position becomes available in intensive care, a position that would help meet Mary's needs for growth and personal development. But two other candidates have more experience plus outstanding performance records in intensive care. Mary is dropped from further consideration for this job and becomes frustrated, disappointed, and concerned about her future.

Maria Herrera, her supervisor, explains to Mary why she's not being considered, assuring her that other opportunities will occur and that her value to other pediatric nurses is immeasurable. In fact, Maria and three co-workers take Mary to dinner to talk with her. This seems to help Mary refocus her attention on the positive aspects of work, and after a few days of feeling frustrated, she again seems to enjoy her work and her

Figure 5–2

ERG Theory Relationships among Frustration, Importance, and Satisfaction of Needs

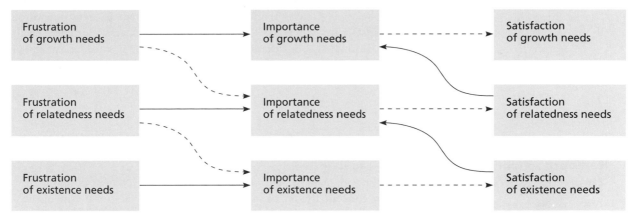

Source: F. J. Landy and D. A. Trumbo, *Psychology of Work Behavior,* rev. ed. (Homewood, Ill.: Dorsey Press, 1980).

colleagues. Mary has redirected her need for the promotion and the growth it would provide back to the relatedness category.

The ERG theory implies that individuals are motivated to engage in behavior to satisfy one of the three sets of needs. Alderfer's explanation of motivation provides an interesting suggestion to managers about behavior. If a subordinate's higher order needs (e.g., growth) are being blocked, perhaps because of a company policy or lack of resources, then it's in the manager's best interest to attempt to redirect the subordinate's efforts toward relatedness or existence needs.

ERG: Limited research base

The ERG theory hasn't stimulated many research studies. Thus, empirical verification is difficult to claim for the ERG explanation. Salancik and Pfeffer proposed that need models such as Maslow's and Alderfer's have become popular because they're consistent with other theories of rational choice and because they attribute freedom to individuals. The idea that individuals shape their actions to satisfy unfulfilled needs gives purpose and direction to individual activity. Furthermore, need explanations are also popular, despite little research verification, because they're simple, easily expressed views of human behavior.[22] Must need theories be verifiable to be of value to a manager?[23] Or are managers and practitioners less impressed by research-verified explanations than by simple, commonsense explanations?

Alderfer certainly didn't accept Salancik and Pfeffer's critique of need explanations of motivation.[24] He proposed that available research evidence supported at least the conceptualization of the ERG theory. Other evidence to support portions of the ERG theory has been added to the literature since his debate with Salancik and Pfeffer.

One study examined the ERG theory of motivation with regard to the human life cycle, using Levinson's theory of life-cycle development, which includes seven stages (e.g., early adult transition, 18–22 years old; midlife transition, 40–45 years old).[25] Some of the results indicated that (1) individuals whose parents achieved higher educational levels had significantly higher scores for strength of desire for growth, and (2) men had higher scores for strength of existence needs and lower scores for strength of relatedness than did women.

In another study of ERG theory, researchers collected data from 208 employees working in 13 different jobs in a telephone company.[26] In general, the ERG categories were supported. Relatively few individuals (17 out of 208) in this study reported high growth-need satisfaction when satisfaction of relatedness and existence needs was either moderate or low. Also, an examination of how pay can satisfy a variety of needs supported the three need categories proposed by Alderfer.[27] Much work would still need to be done, however, before the ERG theory's value in work settings could be confirmed.

Herzberg's Two-Factor Theory

Herzberg's Two-Factor Theory of Motivation

View that job satisfaction results from the presence of intrinsic motivators and that job dissatisfaction stems from not having extrinsic factors.

Psychologist and management consultant Frederick Herzberg developed the **two-factor content theory of motivation.**[28] The two factors are the dissatisfiers-satisfiers, the hygiene-motivators, or the extrinsic-intrinsic factors depending on who's discussing the theory. The original research testing this theory included a group of 200 accountants and engineers. Herzberg used interview responses to questions such as, "Can you describe, in detail, when you felt exceptionally good about your job?" and "Can you describe, in detail, when you felt exceptionally bad about your job?" Rarely were the same kinds of experiences categorized as both good and bad. This systematic procedure resulted in the development of two distinct kinds of experiences: satisfiers and dissatisfiers.

Herzberg's initial study resulted in two specific conclusions. First, there's a set of *extrinsic* conditions, the job context. They include: pay, status, and working conditions. The presence of these conditions to the satisfaction of the employee doesn't necessarily motivate him, but their absence results in dissatisfaction. Because they're needed to maintain at least a level of "no dissatisfaction," the extrinsic conditions are called the *dissatisfiers,* or *hygiene,* factors.

Second, a set of *intrinsic* conditions, the job content, is also present. These conditions include feelings of achievement, increased responsibility, and recognition. The absence of these conditions doesn't prove highly dissatisfying. But when present, they build strong levels of motivation that result in good job performance. Therefore, they're called the *satisfiers,* or *motivators.*

Prior to Herzberg's work, people studying motivation viewed job satisfaction as a unidimensional concept. That is, they placed job satisfaction at one end of a continuum and job dissatisfaction at the other end of the same continuum. If a job condition caused job satisfaction, removing it would cause dissatisfaction; similarly, if a job condition caused job dissatisfaction, removing it would cause job satisfaction. Herzberg's model basically assumes that job satisfaction isn't a unidimensional concept. His research leads to the conclusion that two continua are needed to interpret job satisfaction correctly. Figure 5–3 illustrates the two different views of job satisfaction.

Critique of Herzberg's theory

Of all the available content theories, we believe the most criticized is Herzberg's. Several reasons account for this. First, the theory was originally based on a sample of American accountants and engineers. Critics ask whether this limited sample can justify generalizing to other occupational groups and to other countries. The technology, environment,

Figure 5–3

Traditional and Herzberg Views of Satisfaction-Dissatisfaction

I. Traditional

High job dissatisfaction ●———————————————————● High job satisfaction

II. Herzberg's two-factor view

Low job satisfaction ●———————————————————● High job satisfaction

Motivators
• Feeling of achievement
• Meaningful work
• Opportunities for advancement
• Increased responsibility
• Recognition
• Opportunities for growth

Low job dissatisfaction ●———————————————————● High job dissatisfaction

Hygiene
• Pay
• Status
• Job Security
• Working conditions
• Fringe benefits
• Policies and procedures
• Interpersonal relations

and background of the two occupational groups are distinctly different from those of other groups, such as nurses, medical technologists, salespeople, computer programmers, clerks, and police officers.[29]

Second, some researchers believe that Herzberg's work oversimplifies the nature of job satisfaction, leading to the assumption that a manager can easily change hygiene factors or satisfiers and thus produce job satisfaction. This, of course, isn't an accurate view of how complex and difficult motivation and job satisfaction are in terms of workplace manipulation.

Other critics focus on Herzberg's methodology because it requires people to look at themselves retrospectively. Can people be aware of all that motivated or dissatisfied them? These critics believe subconscious factors aren't identified in Herzberg's analysis. Also, the "recency of events" bias of being able to recall one's most recent job conditions and feelings better than those occurring in the past is embedded in the methodology.[30]

Another criticism of Herzberg's work is that little attention is directed toward testing the theory's performance implications.[31] In the original study, only self-reports of performance were used, and in most cases, respondents were reporting on job activities that had occurred over a long time period. Herzberg has offered no explanation as to why the various extrinsic and intrinsic job factors should affect performance.

When the available evidence is reviewed, it's surprising that Herzberg's theory has withstood the test of time. The two-factor theory, not even mentioned by many academic researchers, remains popular with managers, who continue to discuss the theory and attempt to increase motivation by using Herzberg's identified motivators.[32] His theory spells out specific job factors that managers can work with to create a motivational atmosphere. (Job factors are discussed in more detail in Chapter 15 on job design.) Herzberg's theory brings out clearly the differences in perspectives held by practicing managers and academics. Instead of taking sides, we believe that Herzberg's explanation will continue to be cited and used by managers in the United States and around the world.[33] Of course, care must be utilized in applying this or any other theory in international settings, as one study suggests that Herzberg's theory may have applied to a British sample but not to one from Nigeria.[34] However, the general perception of this theory is that it warrants discussion and consideration as a potential applied approach to motivation.

McClelland's Learned Needs Theory

Learned Needs Theory

Theory that proposes that a person with a strong need will be motivated to use appropriate behaviors to satisfy the need. A person's needs are learned from the culture of a society.

Thematic Apperception Test (TAT)

Projective test that uses a person's analysis of pictures to evaluate such individual differences as need for achievement, need for power, and need for affiliation.

David C. McClelland has proposed a **learned needs theory** of motivation closely associated with learning concepts. He believes that many needs are acquired from the culture of a society.[35] Three of these *learned needs* are the need for achievement (n Ach), the need for affiliation (n Aff), and the need for power (n Pow). McClelland suggested that when a need is strong in a person, its effect is to motivate her to use behavior leading to its satisfaction. For example, a worker with a high n Ach would set challenging goals, work hard to achieve the goals, and use skills and abilities to achieve them.

How are these needs such as n Ach measured? It's not enough to assume that those who work hard and long have a need for achievement, while those who work slowly or in spurts don't. To assess individual differences in the three proposed needs, the **Thematic Apperception Test (TAT)** is used.[36] A person is shown pictures and asked to write a story about what he sees portrayed in them.

For example, the picture in Figure 5–4 would be presented to a person. What story does the picture illustrate? People tend to write stories that reflect their dominant needs. For example, individuals with a high or dominant achievement need typically write a story about Figure 5–4 that contains achievement factors. Evaluators reviewing a response to such a picture would search the written stories for recurring themes of hard work, extra effort, gratification received from success, and the setting of challenging goals as indications of a high need for achievement. McClelland believes that achievement, affiliation, and power needs can be inferred from the stories a person writes about a number of such pictures. He states,

> "If you want to understand motives behind . . . actions, find out what's on a person's mind. If you want to find out what's on a person's mind, don't ask him, because he can't always tell you accurately. Study his fantasies and dreams. If you do this over a period of time, you will discover the themes to which his mind returns again and again. And these themes can be used to explain his actions."[37]

McClelland proposes that a society's economic growth is based on the level of need achievement inherent in its population[38] and that economically backward nations can be dramatically improved by stimulating the need for achievement in the populace. If McClelland is correct (and some research supports his theory), his approach could have a significant impact on motivation in general, especially in Eastern European countries

Figure 5–4

Sample of Thematic Apperception Test (TAT) Picture

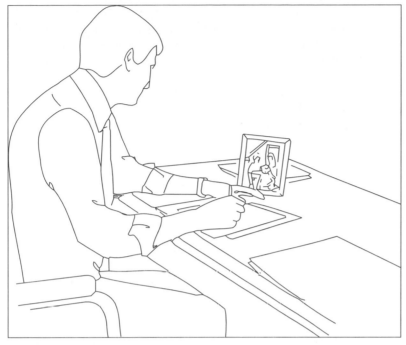

Source: Adapted with permission of the Tests and Scoring Division, McBer and Company, 137 Newbury St., Boston, Mass. 02116.

where free market economies are beginning to evolve. He also contends that motivation can be taught in organizational and nonorganizational settings.[39]

Research on learned needs

Most research evidence offered in support of McClelland's learned needs theory has been provided by McClelland or his associates. For example, a classic study suggested that better managers have a high need for power that is directed toward the benefit of the organization.[40] In general, research on the need for achievement has received the majority of attention from organizational behavior theorists and researchers. This research has provided a profile of the high achievers in society:

> High n Ach persons prefer to avoid easy and difficult performance goals. They actually prefer moderate goals that they think they can achieve.

> High n Ach persons prefer immediate and reliable feedback on how they are performing.

> The high n Ach person likes to be responsible for solving problems.

Research has pointed out the complexity of the achievement motive. High n Ach individuals who focus on attaining success differ from those who focus on avoiding failure.[41] Those who focus on attaining success tend to set more realistic goals and to choose moderately difficult tasks. Need for achievement has been also found to correlate highly with the need to attain status or wealth, especially for those involved in high-pay/high-status employment groups.[42]

In one ambitious project, researchers tried to raise the achievement motivation of business people in an entire village in India. This program, the Kakinada project, consisted of encouraging the business people to have high-achievement fantasies, to make plans that would help them realize the goals of a successful entrepreneur, and to communicate with one another about their goals and their methods of reaching them. The business people became more productive as entrepreneurs, started several industries, enlarged their businesses, and hired more than 5,000 of their neighbors. In a 10-year reassessment of the program, achievement motivation levels and results were still exceptional.[43] And recent work reported by McClelland suggests that at PepsiCo a high need for achievement was more associated with success than was a high need for power.[44]

Other studies have found that gender differences exist regarding competitiveness and money beliefs. Men are inclined to be more competitive and tend to focus their ambitions toward making money, as capital acquisition is highly desirable.[45] In total, men placed more value on salary, individual achievement, motivation, and directing others, whereas women emphasized good interpersonal relationships, interesting work, feelings of accomplishment, and professional growth.[46] Similarly, successful women may also fulfill their need for power in different ways than successful men.[47] As the Close-Up at the bottom of the page describes, women may be better suited to motivate employees than men.

Based on theory and research, McClelland has made specific suggestions about developing a positive high need for achievement (that is, a high n Ach where there's no fear of success). Using McClelland's prescriptions, a manager would be encouraged to

1. Arrange job tasks so that employees receive periodic feedback on performance, providing information that enables them to make modifications or corrections.

2. Point out models of achievement to employees. Identify and publicize the accomplishments of achievement heroes—the successful people, the winners—and use them as models.

C L O S E — U P

Women Managers: Better Motivators than Men?

Do women have a different management style than their male counterparts, and if so, do the consensus-building, participatory methods that are largely attributed to women work better than hierarchical, quasi-militaristic models? This subject has become increasingly controversial and leads to a deeper issue, namely whether women managers do a better job of motivating workers than men. Proponents of this theory argue that women are more likely to manage in an interactive style, encouraging participation, sharing information, and enhancing the self-worth of others. Women are thought to use "transformational" leadership, working well with people at all organizational levels, understanding how employees feel, and motivating others by transforming their self-interest into the organization's goals.

A successful example of this kinder, gentler style of management is that of Anita Roddick, owner of The Body Shop Skin and Hair Care stores. "It's just a family here," says Roddick. "We like to say, 'Partnerships, not power trips.' "

While advocates of these theories argue that women's strengths should be tapped, some critics counter that any type of stereotyping by gender is a form of sexism, one that will only shackle women to their traditional role as nurturer. Some women managers are worried that men are seen as being one way and women another. Others, including Dee Soder (president of the Endymion Company, which advises senior corporate executives on their managerial strengths and weaknesses), believe the distinctions are irrelevant. "I think there is a higher proportion of participative women managers than there is men," she says, "but the crossover is so high, it is a moot point."

But what does research say on this issue? In a recent major review in this area, male and female managers were

3. Work with employees to improve their self-image. High n Ach people like themselves and seek moderate challenges and responsibilities.

4. Introduce realism into all work-related topics: promotion, rewards, transfer, development opportunities, and team membership opportunities. Employees should think in realistic terms and think positively about how they can accomplish goals.

There are a number of criticisms of McClelland's work. First, use of the projective TAT to determine the three needs has been questioned. While projective techniques have some advantages over self-report questionnaires, the interpretation and weighing of a story are at best an art. Validation of such analysis is extremely important and often neglected, but a recent review of research has indicated that the TAT may be as effective in this area as questionnaire methods.[48] A critical-incident technique has been used to examine motivation in a developing country, but more research is needed to determine whether critical incidents or other methods can be used for assessing McClelland-type needs.[49]

Second, McClelland's claim that n Ach can be learned is in conflict with a large body of literature stating that motives are normally acquired in childhood and are difficult to alter in adulthood. McClelland acknowledges this problem but points to evidence in politics and religion to indicate that adult behaviors can be changed.[50]

Third, McClelland's notion of learned needs is questioned on the grounds of whether needs are permanently acquired. Research is needed to determine whether acquired needs last over a period of time. Can something learned in a training and development program be sustained on the job? This is an issue that McClelland and others have not been able to clarify.

A Synopsis of the Four Content Theories

Each of the four content theories explains behavior from a slightly different perspective. None of the theories can or should be used by managers as the sole basis for explaining

overall found to be equally effective. However, men were observed to be more effective than women in leadership roles that were defined in more masculine terms (e.g., in the military), while women were generally more effective in roles that were defined in less masculine terms (e.g., in educational or social service organizations). These are generalizations that have many exceptions, of course, such as Deborah Kent, the first woman to head a vehicle assembly plant for Ford Motor Company. Her position in this plant, the third largest Ford facility in the United States, is one that would typically be described as male in orientation, but while she has been described as tough, focused and hard-working, Ms. Kent has also been noted for her openness and her desire for input and feedback from her workers. Thus she may reflect the developing redefinition of both jobs and the people who inhabit them.

Whether it's a matter of gender or not, everyone involved in the debate agrees on one thing: it's time to expand the old management model. As we enter the 21st century, there is a greater need than ever to motivate workers. Managers who are nurturers and value-driven, be they male or female, will be well equipped for this challenging task.

Sources: Mary Billard, "Do Women Make Better Managers?" *Working Woman,* March 1992, pp. 68–107; Rose Mary Wentling, "Women in Middle Management: Their Career Development and Aspirations," *Business Horizons,* January–February 1992, pp. 47–54; Leslie Evelo, John Jessel, and Lawrence Beymer, "Sex-Typing of Occupational Preferences and Liberality," *Journal of Career Development,* Winter 1991, pp. 139–51; Alice H. Eagly, Steven J. Karau, and Mona G. Makhijani, "Gender and the Effectiveness of Leaders: A Meta-Analysis," *Psychological Bulletin,* January 1995, pp. 125–45; Lena Williams, "A Silk Blouse on the Assembly Line," *The New York Times,* February 5, 1995, p. 7.

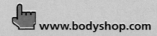 **www.bodyshop.com**

Figure 5–5

A Graphic Comparison of Four Content Theories of Motivation

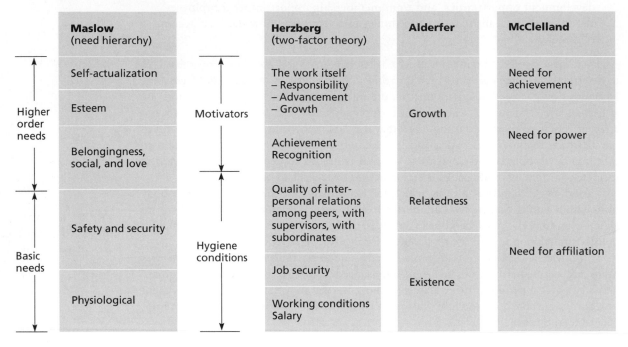

or inferring motivation. Although some critics are skeptical, it appears that people have innate and learned needs and that various job factors result in a degree of satisfaction. Thus, each theory provides managers with some understanding of behavior and performance.

Figure 5–5 compares the four theories. McClelland proposed no lower order needs. However, his needs for achievement and power aren't identical with Herzberg's motivators, Maslow's higher order needs, or Alderfer's growth needs, although there are some similarities. A major difference between the four content theories is McClelland's emphasis on socially acquired needs. Also, the Maslow theory offers a static need hierarchy system; Alderfer presents a flexible, three-need classification approach; and Herzberg discusses intrinsic and extrinsic job factors.

Each theory has strengths and limitations that practicing managers need to consider and be cautious about. Table 5–2 highlights each model's main characteristics. As is typically the case when competing theories exist, no one theory has clear-cut superiority.

Each of the content theories purports to present the clearest, most meaningful, and most accurate explanation of motivation. One concept that few of the content theories addresses explicitly, however, is the quality of work done by the employee. Do employees have a need to perform so that a high quality of product or service is the outcome? Or is it management's job, to a large degree, to get employees excited about and involved in making high-quality goods? At PepsiCo, parent company of Pepsi-Cola, Frito-Lay, Taco Bell, Kentucky Fried Chicken, Pizza Hut, and many others, managers feel that the answer to both questions is yes.[51]

www.pepsi
world.com

www.kfc.com

www.pizzahut
.com

Table 5–2   Comparison of Four Content Theories of Motivation

CONTENT MOTIVATION THEORIES	ASSUMPTIONS MADE	HOW MOTIVATION IS MEASURED	PRACTICAL APPLICATION VALUE	PROBLEMS AND LIMITATIONS
Maslow's need hierarchy	Individuals attempt to satisfy basic needs before directing behavior toward higher order needs.	Maslow, as a clinical psychologist, used his patients in asking questions and listening to answers. Organizational researchers have relied on self-report scales.	Makes sense to managers and gives many a feeling of knowing how motivation works for their employees.	Doesn't address the issue of individual differences; has received limited research support; and fails to caution about the dynamic nature of needs—needs change.
Alderfer's ERG theory	Individuals who fail to satisfy growth needs become frustrated, regress, and refocus attention on lower order needs.	Self-report scales are used to assess three need categories.	Calls attention to what happens when and if need satisfaction does not occur; frustrations can be a major reason why performance levels aren't attained or sustained.	Not enough research has been conducted; available research is self-report in nature, which raises the issue of how good the measurement is. Another issue is whether individuals really have only three need areas.
Herzberg's two-factor theory	Only some job features and characteristics can result in motivation. Some of the characteristics that managers have focused on may result in a comfortable work setting but don't motivate employees.	Ask employees in interviews to describe critical job incidents.	Talks in terms that managers understand. Identifies motivators that managers can develop, fine-tune, and use.	Assumes that every worker is similar in needs and preferences; fails to meet scientific measurement standards; hasn't been updated to reflect changes in society with regard to job security and pay needs.
McClelland's learned needs	A person's needs are learned from the culture (society); therefore, training and education can enhance and influence a person's need strength.	Thematic Apperception Test (TAT), a projective technique that encourages respondents to reveal their needs.	If a person's needs can be assessed, then management can intervene through training to develop needs that are compatible with organizational goals.	Interpreting the TAT is difficult; the effect that training has on changing needs hasn't been sufficiently tested.

PepsiCo attempts to do this by encouraging all of its half million employees worldwide to act as if they were the owner of a business, with the rationale that a sense of ownership and involvement in the company will generate the enthusiasm for producing the highest level of goods and services. SharePower is the name of the program at PepsiCo that enables all employees, not just upper level executives, to earn stock options in the company, each year totaling 10 percent of an employee's pay of the previous year. This program not only gives employees a greater stake in the survival of the company, it also has helped to create a culture where all employees have a sense of both greater responsibility and an opportunity to contribute to the success of their part of the larger organization. The Close-Up on page 142 further addresses the issue of when and why employees "go the extra mile" for their organizations.

SharePower is PepsiCo's answer to the question How can we best become a world class competitor? Any theory of motivation claiming to be complete in today's turbulent environment must directly address issues of quality and quality improvement as they are impacted by the strategies of today's organizations.

Summary of Key Points

- Any management attempt to improve individuals' job performance must utilize motivation theories. This results from the fact that motivation is concerned with behavior or, more specifically, goal-directed behavior.

- A major reason why employees' behaviors differ is that people's needs and goals vary. Social, cultural, hereditary, and job factors influence behaviors. To understand the nature of motivation, managers must learn about subordinates' needs.

- Theories of motivation can be classified as being either content theories or process theories. This chapter reviews four of the more widely cited content theories. These theories focus on factors within the person (e.g., needs, goals, motives) that energize, direct, sustain, and stop behavior.

- Maslow's theory assumes that people have a need to grow and develop. The implication is that motivational programs have a higher probability of success if need deficiencies are reduced. Although Maslow's need hierarchy hasn't met rigorous standards of scientific testing, it appears that an adequately fulfilled need doesn't provide a good target for managers in building motivators that can influence performance.

- Alderfer offers a three-level need hierarchy of existence, relatedness, and growth needs. In addition to the satisfaction-progression process proposed by Maslow, Alderfer states that there is also a frustration-regression process at work that plays a major role in motivating people.

- Herzberg's two-factor theory of motivation identifies two types of factors in the workplace: satisfiers and dissatisfiers. One apparent weakness of the theory is that its findings haven't been replicated by other researchers. Despite this and other shortcomings, it does focus on job-related factors in managerial terminology.

- McClelland has proposed a theory of learned needs. The behavior associated with the needs for achievement, affiliation, and power is instrumental in an individual's job performance. Managers should attempt to acquire an understanding of these needs.

C L O S E — U P

Organizational Citizenship Behavior: Going the Extra Mile

Much of the discussion of motivation focuses on getting employees to do the jobs they are assigned in an effective and efficient way. But what about the things that employees do that are beyond the call of duty, without consideration of rewards or bonuses? These "out-of-role" activities are called *organizational citizenship behaviors (OCBs),* and are intriguing because these are often the behaviors cited by customers when praising exemplary service. Why do empoyees engage in OCBs, and can anything be done to encourage them? While no clear relationships with most personality characteristics have been found, a higher frequency of OCBs has been found among those with a higher collectivist or group orientation than among those who have a more individualistic perspective.

Most of the research on this topic, however, has focused on situational factors that seem to be related to OCBs. One of these factors relates to what employees and managers define as part of the job and what is "out-of-role." Employees will often define their jobs quite broadly and will include activities as part of their duties that their managers perceive as "extra." These OCBs also are likely to influence managerial evaluations of employees, but sometimes they may be interpreted as attempts to influence those evaluations rather than efforts to do something good for the company and the customer.

Another major influence on OCBs is the leadership that employees receive from their managers. Specifically, trust between an employee and a manager and a management style that encourages the development of leadership skills among employees have been found to encourage the expression of OCBs. Given this, the obvious implication for organizations that want employees to go beyond minimal expectations is to define jobs to include those activities *and* to establish a climate of trust, encouragement and support for doing whatever must be done to achieve the highest quality. In other words, employees go the extra mile for organizations that go the extra mile for them.

Sources: Dennis W. Organ, "Personality and Organizational Citizenship Behavior," *Journal of Management,* Summer 1994, pp. 465–78; Mary A. Konovsky and S. Douglas Pugh, "Citizenship Behavior and Social Exchange," *Academy of Management Journal,* June 1994, pp. 656–69; Philip M. Posdakoff and Scott B. MacKenzie, "Organizational Citizenship Behaviors and Sales Unit Effectiveness," *Journal of Marketing Research,* August 1994, pp. 351–63; Kenneth K. Eastman, "In the Eyes of the Beholder: An Attributional Approach to Ingratiation and Organizational Citizenship Behavior," *Academy of Management Journal,* October 1994, pp. 1379–91; Ronald J. Deluga, "Supervisor Trust Building, Leader-Member Exchange and Organizational Citizenship Behaviour," *Journal of Occupational and Organizational Psychology,* December 1994, pp. 315–26; Elizabeth W. Morrison, "Role Definitions and Organizational Citizenship Behavior: The Importance of the Employee's Perspective," *Academy of Management Journal,* December 1994, pp. 1543–67; Jill W. Graham, "Leadership, Moral Development, and Citizenship Behavior," *Business Ethics Quarterly,* January 1995, pp. 43–54

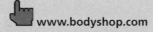 **www.bodyshop.com**

Discussion and Review Questions

1. Which content theory of motivation would have the most promise for explaining motivation and helping in the economic growth of developing Third World and Eastern European countries? Explain.

2. What motivational lessons could be learned from the Pullman Company's attempts to take care of workers' needs from "cradle to grave"?

3. Describe the major differences between Maslow's need hierarchy and Alderfer's ERG explanation of motivation.

4. What factors serve to make Maslow's hierarchy of needs theory so intuitively attractive to practicing managers despite its obvious flaws?

5. Why would it be interesting to examine and compare the needs, discussed by McClelland, in young, middle-aged, and older people in the United States, Japan, Germany, Poland, Egypt, Argentina, and Sweden?

6. How would Herzberg's motivation theory help to explain why two people, holding the same job in two different firms, might be motivated by different motivators?

7. Explain motivation in terms that a manager could apply on the job.

8. In your opinion, should managers attempt to motivate employees with different ethnic backgrounds all in the same manner? Why or why not?

9. Why is it important to understand that a manager must infer the motivation level of subordinates?

10. Describe how one of your professors could use McClelland's prescriptions to motivate students.

CASE FOR ANALYSIS

Entrepreneurs' Motivations: Do Theories Explain Them?

Thinking about starting or buying a business? If so, you've probably heard many times that most new business ventures fail within five years and that the two most common causes of failure are lack of financing and poor management. If you think this assessment sounds unduly pessimistic, we have good news for you. Most of what you've heard about the chances of succeeding in small business is more myth than reality, painting a far more dismal picture than actually exists.

Reflecting back on American business history, you shouldn't be surprised by this. Alfred P. Sloan, the guiding genius behind General Motors, graduated at the top of his class from Massachusetts Institute of Technology. On the other hand, Michael Dell, founder of Dell Computers, didn't graduate from college. We have similar difficulties predicting success using such other descriptive characteristics as age, sex, and prior work experience.

In a global economy where mergers, acquisitions, downsizing, and other accelerated changes disrupt every business sector, organizations view their executive leadership as a key factor in preserving their competitive edge. Human resources professionals have long recognized the implications of identifying the skills and characteristics that so distinctively set these executives apart. The growing sentiment among experts who study U.S. industry today is that competitiveness in the years ahead will be based increasingly on an organization's timing and flexibility.

The capacity to innovate, strengthen links with the consumer, and produce new generations of products and services at a rapid pace will be the major determinant of success. This type of competitive environment presents many opportunities for entrepreneurial executives of small growth companies. These companies are less hampered by systems and procedures than large corporations, so they can respond quickly.

But how realistic is the entrepreneurial dream? Does the potential to create a successful business lie within each of us? Is it the predominant need that drives us, or does it take some special combination of traits? Research into these questions is beginning to yield answers, but as yet there's nearly unanimous agreement on only one fact: the need for money isn't the driving force. Rather, says psychologist and management consultant Harry Levinson (president of the Levinson Institute in Belmont, Massachusetts), entrepreneurs work with such single-minded intensity because they're psychologically compelled to.

Other researchers argue that, regardless of gender, enterprise often proceeds from deep psychic disruption. As author George Gilder remarks, "It's really hard to be an entrepreneur. You have to commit yourself obsessively to a project that might well fail, and you have to forgo all kinds of gratifications and do all kinds of jobs that other people don't want to do." This may make some entrepreneurs hard to live with. John H. Patterson, described earlier in the chapter as the forward-looking president of NCR, also was known for firing management personnel for any reason that struck his fancy and was said to have trained and fired fully one-sixth of the nation's top executives between 1910 and 1930. This tendency on his part had its own entrepreneurial benefit, however, as one of his terminated managers was driven to build a bigger firm than Patterson and actually did so. He was Thomas J. Watson, founder of IBM.

John J. Kao, associate professor of business administration at Harvard Business School, highlights the importance of self-actualization. "This model posits entrepreneurship as a desire for personal growth and development," and "above all else the desire to create something, whether a new product or process, a new organization or new way of doing business." When Sandra Kurtzig describes how she created ASK Computer Systems, for example, she speaks fondly of "nurturing an idea, taking a seed and growing it into a baby." She also recalls the pleasure she took in hiring "good people and feeling responsible for them."

Other researchers also emphasize the entrepreneur's creative drive. David McClelland, author of the learned needs theory discussed in this chapter, found that entrepreneurs, like artists, tend to be strongly invested in their work. They have a great capacity for creative and innovative thoughts and behavior. They're motivated by the need for achievement, challenge, and the opportunity to be innovative. In addition, entrepreneurs have been found to work better under pressure than managers in larger firms.

Entrepreneurs have also been likened to juvenile delinquents. "It's not that they break the law or are dishonest," says psychoanalyst Abraham Zaleznik, a professor emeritus at Harvard Business School. "But they do have one thing in common: they don't have the normal fear or anxiety mechanisms." Often, in fact, they seem to act on impulse, to be reckless.

Fred Smith's story of tide bucking is well known. He researched and wrote the basic plan for Federal Express as a paper in college. His professor derided the very idea of a next-day air express company and flunked him on the paper. But Smith went ahead anyway and—after some very lean years—proved his vision to be spectacularly right.

Entrepreneurs have often been members of a religious or racial minority who've had to build their own innovative paths to achievement and recognition. It's no accident that Liz Claiborne, the first female Fortune 500 CEO who didn't inherit her position through family connections, took what *Working Woman* magazine dubbed "the outside route to the top" by starting her own firm.

In our time, the greatest source of entrepreneurial material has been politics, war, and the resulting international caravan of refugees. Gilder writes,

"In nearly every nation, many of the most notable entrepreneurs are immigrants. Immigration usually entails violation of ancestral ties and parental obligations. Dealing in their youths with convulsive change, thrown back on their own devices to create a productive existence . . . immigrants everywhere suffer the guilt of disconnection from their home and families and ally easily with the forces of the future against the claims of the past."

Perhaps the prototypical immigrant success story is Jack Tramiel, chairman of Atari, Inc. (the computer company), who came to America after surviving the horrors of Auschwitz in World War II. Polish-born Tramiel turned a former typewriter repair shop into the Commodore International computer corporation. He frankly regards the practice of business as a battle for survival, the equivalent of war. Characterized by *Forbes* magazine as "abrasive and autocratic" when he was forced out of Commodore in 1984, Tramiel rebuilt Atari into a force in the personal computer industry after it had been given up for dead by its previous owner.

Nonetheless, for every immigrant like Tramiel, schooled in the harshest adversity, there's a comfortable, middle-class American—Steve Jobs (Apple and NeXT computers) or Sandra Kurtzig—who simply felt compelled to realize a vision or an ambition. So is there, after all, a distinct entrepreneurial personality? Many experts have looked at the available evidence and aren't convinced the species is distinct.

But entrepreneurs' lives are observably different, and so are their achievements. As Joseph Schumpeter (one of the earliest economists to recognize and extol the place of the entrepreneur within capitalist society) once wrote, "To act with confidence beyond the range of familiar beacons and to overcome . . . resistance requires aptitudes that are present in only a small fraction of the population." And it's a simple fact that most of us choose lives that are less intense, less perilous, and not so filled with grand ambition.

Entrepreneurship is as varied as human ingenuity and enterprise, and so are the needs, goals, and motives that drive it. Its prevalence among those uprooted by political upheaval, victimized by discrimination, or oppressed by the daily grind suggest that the entrepreneur, like the artist or the intellectual, is simply looking for freedom—of expression and of the spirit.

Just as there's no one explanation of an entrepreneur's motivation (that internal drive), no specific set of principles found in motivational theories will help us understand entrepreneurship. But it's safe to predict that, whatever the next decade holds for the economies of Russia, Singapore, Ethiopia, Tanzania, Hungary, and Chile, their citizens' self-motivation will be important. For example, after years of being controlled and not

being able to express themselves freely, the people of the Eastern bloc are about to unleash a tremendous wave of self-motivation. Are there entrepreneurs lurking in these countries? We think so, and the content motivation theories will help us understand their behavior.

Discussion Questions

1. How can content theories be used to understand entire nations that are attempting to unleash entrepreneurial practices?

2. How would entrepreneurs' motivations differ from those of managers in larger firms?

3. How will entrepreneurs be able to compete effectively in the coming decade?

Sources: Donald M. Moretti, Carol L. Morken, and Jeanne M. Borkowski, "Profile of the American CEO: Comparing *Inc.* and *Fortune* Executives," *Journal of Business and Psychology,* Winter 1991, pp. 193–205; Henry H. Beam and Thomas Carey, "Could You Succeed in Small Business?" *Business Horizons,* September–October 1989, pp. 65–69; Diane Cole, "The Entrepreneurial Self," *Psychology Today,* June 1989, pp. 60–63; Mark Bernstein, "John Patterson Rang Up Success with the Incorruptible Cashier," *Smithsonian,* June 1989, pp. 150–166.

E X P E R I E N T I A L   E X E R C I S E

Applying Motivation Theory

Objectives

1. To evaluate the merits of different motivation theories.
2. To emphasize the decisions that must be made by managers in motivating people.
3. To apply motivation principles.

Related Topics

The manager's need to make decisions to succeed. The difficulty of diagnosing situations.

Starting the Exercise

Set up groups of five to eight students to read the facts and the situation facing Margo Williams.

The Facts

This chapter discussed several popular content theories. Major points included:

Maslow: motivation involves satisfying needs in a hierarchical order.

Herzberg: some job factors are intrinsically satisfying and motivate individuals.

McClelland: motives are acquired from a person's culture.

Alderfer: in addition to the satisfaction-progression process proposed by Maslow, a frustration-regression process is at work.

With these four theories in mind, review the work situation currently facing Margo Williams, project engineer director in a large construction company. She's responsible for scheduling projects, meeting customers, reporting progress on projects, controlling costs, and developing subordinates. A total of 20 men and 8 women report to Margo. All of them are college graduates with at least eight years of job experience. Margo has an engineering Ph.D. but only four years of project engineering experience.

Her biggest problems involve the lack of respect and response from her subordinates. Margo's supervisor has considered these problems and assumes that her moderate record of success could be improved if she could correct the situation. Margo is considering a course of action that could motivate her subordinates to show more respect and respond more favorably to her requests.

Completing the Exercise

1. Each discussion group should develop a motivation plan for Margo. The plan should use the content motivation principles discussed in this chapter.

2. After the group has worked together for about 30 minutes, a group leader should present the plan to the class.

3. Discuss each group's plan for the remainder of the class period.

Chapter 6

Motivation: Process Theories and Applications

Learning Objectives

After completing Chapter 6, you should be able to:

Define
Three types of learning useful to managers.

Describe
Why goal setting has become a popular motivation application in organizations.

Discuss
How self-managing can be useful in developing a motivation program in an organization setting.

Compare
The predictive power of equity, expectancy, and reinforcement theory in terms of productivity, absenteeism, and job satisfaction.

Identify
The three dimensions of self-efficacy.

In Chapter 5 we examined four *content* theories of motivation concerning what specific things motivate people.

While these issues are critical, it is also clear that most employees want to work and do a good job, and that management's role is to provide an environment that facilitates high levels of performance.[1] With that in mind, in this chapter we examine four process motivation theories, which attempt to explain and describe some of the factors, typically outside of the individual, that energize, direct, sustain, and stop behavior. The major process theories of motivation presented in this chapter are (1) reinforcement, (2) expectancy, (3) equity, and (4) goal setting. In discussing each, we will show how the motivation process works in organizational settings. However, since behavior and its influences are the focus of these theories, we must first examine the process by which workers acquire these behaviors, namely how they are learned.

Process Motivation Theories

Theories that describe and analyze the process by which behavior is energized, directed, sustained, and stopped.

Learning

Learning is one of the fundamental processes underlying behavior and, in turn, motivation. Most behavior within organizations is learned behavior. Perceptions, attitudes, goals, and emotional reactions are learned. Skills—for example, programming a computer or counseling a troubled employee—can be learned. The meanings and uses of language are learned.

Learning is the process by which a relatively enduring change in behavior occurs as a result of practice. The words *relatively enduring* signify that the change in behavior is more or less permanent. The term *practice* is intended to cover both formal training and uncontrolled experiences. The changes in behavior that characterize learning may be adaptive and promote effectiveness, or they may be nonadaptive and ineffective. A number of approaches have been proposed to explain the various ways in which this learning may occur.

Learning

Process by which relatively enduring change in behavior occurs as a result of practice.

Social learning

Social Learning

Albert Bandura's view that behavior is a function of continuous interaction between cognitive (person), behavioral, and environmental determinants.

Albert Bandura of Stanford University illustrated how people acquire new behavior by imitating role models (learning vicariously). **Social learning** refers to the fact that we acquire much of our behavior (e.g., hitting a golf ball, giving a speech, using a computer program) by observation and imitation of others in a social context.

The Bandura-inspired view of behavior is that it is a function of both personal characteristics and environmental conditions. According to Bandura, social learning theory explains behavior in terms of a continuous interaction between cognitive, behavioral, and environmental determinants.[2] Bandura stresses the point that cognitive functioning must not be ignored in explaining, understanding, and modifying individual behavior.[3] Figure 6–1 illustrates the relationships among cognition, behavior, and the environment.[4]

Social learning theory introduces vicarious learning (modeling), symbolism, and self-control. Parents, friends, heroes, and respected leaders are imitated because we identify with them. Each of us also uses symbolism as guides for our behavior. (We know not to pull the exit release handle on the airplane because of our mental picture of the consequences of a sudden loss in cabin pressure; we set personal goals to motivate ourselves; we use mental reminders to remember a customer's name.) We also attempt to exercise

Self-Efficacy

Belief that one can perform adequately in a situation. Has three dimensions: magnitude, strength, and generality.

self-control by not smoking, not drinking excessively, and not physically throwing out of the office the person who makes a personally disparaging remark about our family or ethnic background.

A central part of social learning theory which was introduced in Chapter 4 is the concept of **self-efficacy**, defined as the belief that one can perform adequately in a particular situation.[5] Self-efficacy has three dimensions: *magnitude*, the level of task difficulty a person believes she can attain; *strength*,

Figure 6–1

A Social Learning Theory Model

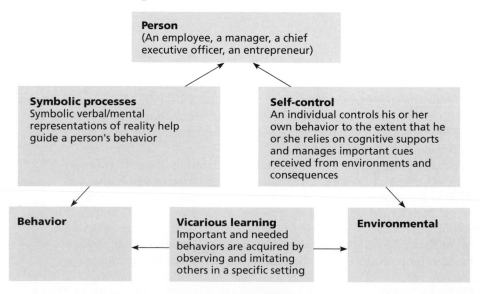

Source: Adapted from Robert Kreitner and Fred Luthans, "A Social Learning Approach to Behavioral Management: Radical Behaviorists 'Mellowing Out,' " *Organizational Dynamics,* Autumn 1984, p. 55. © American Management Association, New York. All rights reserved.

referring to the conviction regarding magnitude as strong or weak; and *generality,* the degree to which the expectation is generalized across situations. An employee's sense of capability (Can I do the job?) influences his perception, motivation, and performance.[6] We rarely try to do a job or task when we expect to be ineffective. How would you like to try to stop Grant Hill from scoring in a basketball game? How would you like to write a speech as emotion-packed as Abraham Lincoln's Gettysburg Address? We often avoid people, settings, and situations when we don't feel up to the required level of performance.

Self-efficacy judgments influence our choices of tasks, situations, and companions, how much effort we'll expend, and how long we'll try. How hard and long a student pursues a course or an area of study depends more on his sense of self-efficacy than on actual ability.

Self-efficacy has been related to other motivation concepts. Edwin Locke and associates suggested that self-efficacy provides an integrating mechanism between learning theory and goal-setting approaches.[7] Feedback is important in formulating efficacy perceptions that interact with goal setting to enhance performance motivation. Self-efficacy may also be related to effort-performance relationships in expectancy motivation theory. **Both goal setting and expectancy theories will be discussed below. The impact of culture** on self-efficacy is beginning to be realized.[8]

A concept that has a potential effect on self-efficacy is the **Pygmalion effect,** which refers to enhanced learning or performance that results from others having positive expectations of us. That is, the fact that others believe us capable of high levels of performance may lead us to perform at that level. Some believe that self-efficacy may be involved in the Pygmalion effect through the persuasive influence of others holding positive expectations.[9] A **leader's expectations about job performance might be viewed as an important input to the employees' perceptions of their own levels of efficacy. The strength of the persuasion** would be influenced by the leader's credibility, previous relationship with the employees, influence in the organization, and so on. It also may be related to the gender of the leader, as the Pygmalion effect has been found to have more impact among male than among female leaders.[10] However defined and whatever their impact, expectations play a major role influencing behavior.

Pygmalion Effect

The enhanced learning or performance that results from others having positive expectations of us.

Operant conditioning

In another perspective, learning often occurs as a *consequence of* behavior. This type of learning is called **operant conditioning.** The person most closely associated with operant conditioning is the late world-famous behaviorist B. F. Skinner. Behaviors that can be controlled by altering the consequences (reinforcers and punishments) that follow them are referred to as **operants.** An operant is strengthened (increased) or weakened (decreased) as a function of the events that follow it. Most workplace behaviors are operants. Examples of operant behaviors include performing job-related tasks, reading a budget report, pulling a defective part off a production line, listening to a customer's complaint about poor service, and coming to work on time. Operants are distinguished by virtue of being controlled by their consequences.

In operant conditioning, the desired response may not be present in the **subject. Teaching a subordinate to prepare an accurate weekly budget report is an exam-**ple of operant conditioning. The manager works with the subordinate and reinforces him as he successfully completes the various steps involved in preparing an accurate budget. Figure 6–2 illustrates the general form of the operant conditioning process. The relationships of $S_1 \rightarrow R_1 \rightarrow S_2 \rightarrow R_2$ are called the *contingencies of reinforcement.*[11]

Operant Conditioning

Learning that occurs as a consequence of behavior.

Operants

Behaviors that can be controlled by altering reinforcers and punishments that follow them.

Figure 6–2

An Example of Operant Conditioning

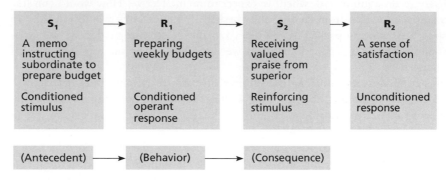

This sequence is also described as the *ABC* operant mode. *A* designates the antecedent or stimulus that precedes the behavior *B,* while *C* is the consequence, the result of the behavior. Skinner believed that such a sequence will be acted out in the future if it proves to be adaptive for the individual.[12]

The term more often used to describe operant conditioning principles applied to individuals is *behavior modification* (also called *B-mod* and *behavior mod*). Thus, **behavior modification** is individual learning by reinforcement. **Organizational behavior modification** or *OB Mod* (also indicated as *OBM*) is a more general term coined to designate "the systematic reinforcement of desirable organizational behavior and the nonreinforcement or punishment of unwanted organizational behavior."[13] Thus, OB Mod is an operant approach to organizational behavior. *Organizational* has been added to indicate that the operant approach is being used in work settings. In this discussion, the terms *behavior modification* and *organizational behavior modification* are used interchangeably.

Principles of Operant Conditioning

Several principles of operant conditioning can aid managers attempting to influence behavior. *Reinforcement* is an extremely important principle of learning. In a general sense, motivation is an internal cause of behavior, while reinforcement is an external cause. **Positive reinforcement** occurs when a positively valued consequence follows a response to a stimulus. Thus, positive reinforcement is anything that both increases the strength of response and induces repetitions of the behavior that preceded the reinforcement.[14] These positive reinforcers could include items such as raises, bonuses, or promotions or less tangible things such as praise or encouragement. Without reinforcement, no measurable modification of behavior is likely to take place.

Managers often use *positive reinforcers* to modify behavior. In some cases, reinforcers work as predicted; for example, positive reinforcement has been shown to be very effective in reducing accidents and producing safe behaviors at the workplace.[15] However, in other cases, they don't modify behavior in the desired direction because of competing reinforcement contingencies. When the receipt of reinforcers isn't made contingent or dependent on the behavior desired by the manager, desired behav-

Behavior Modification

Approach to motivation that uses principles of operant conditioning, achieving individual learning by reinforcement. In this text, used interchangeably with term *organizational behavior modification.*

Organizational Behavior Modification (OBM)

Operant approach to organizational behavior. In this text, used interchangeably with term *behavior modification.*

Positive Reinforcement

Action that increases the likelihood of a particular behavior.

iors don't occur. Also, giving reinforcers long after the occurrence of the desired behaviors decreases the probability of the recurrence of the behavior because the connection between the two is more difficult to make.

Increasingly, organizations are tying rewards and systems of positive reinforcement to corporate values.[16] For example, Conoco made environmental criteria a component of the incentive system. Likewise, Chemical Bank has set up programs to positively reinforce employee actions that lead to better customer service. Monetary rewards aren't the only type of positive reinforcers shown to be effective. Nonfinancial rewards (such as recognition programs, flexible hours, leaves of absence, time off, and merchandise incentives) can also be utilized.[17] Peer pressure, involvement, and pride have been shown to be as influential as money in producing desirable actions.[18] The dual powers of financial reinforcement and personal recognition are potent motivational forces.

👉 **www.conoco. com**

👉 **www.chemical bankmi.com**

Negative reinforcement refers to an increase in the frequency of a behavior following removal of something that is displeasing (e.g., an undesired situation) immediately after the response. An event is a *negative reinforcer* only if its removal after a response increases the performance of that response. A familiar example of negative reinforcement during the summer in Phoenix and Houston is turning on the car air conditioner on a stiflingly hot day. Turning on the air conditioner (the behavior) usually minimizes or terminates an aversive condition, namely being hot (negative reinforcer). This increases the probability of turning on the air conditioning when the car is hot. Similarly, exerting a high degree of effort to complete a job may be negatively reinforced by not having to listen to a nagging boss. By working hard, the employee can keep the nagging boss away. The unpleasant boss is removed because the employee works hard.

Negative Reinforcement

Negative reinforcement strengthens a behavior because the behavior removes some painful or unpleasant stimulus.

Punishment is an undesirable consequence of a particular behavior.[19] A professor who takes off 10 points for each day a paper is late is using punishment. A mechanic who doesn't hand in his report and is suspended for one day with a loss of pay is being punished. Punishment, when applied, is sending the message to not do something. Some people believe that punishment is the opposite of reward and is just as effective in changing behavior. Others consider punishment a poor approach to learning because:

Punishment

Undesirable consequence that results in the suppression (decrease in frequency) of the behavior that brought it about.

1. The results of punishment aren't as predictable as those of reward.
2. The effects of punishment are less permanent than those of reward.
3. Punishment is frequently accompanied by negative attitudes toward the administrator of the punishment, as well as toward the activity that led to the punishment.

Despite the potential costs of using punishment, it has been and will continue to be used as a method of altering behavior. In situations where the costs of not punishing outweigh the advantages of not punishing, punishment may be an appropriate method. For example, punishing a worker who deliberately and overtly slows down the flow of work may be an economically necessary way of altering behavior. (However, there might be ways of dealing with the problem other than punishment.) The point is that punishment and its use depend on the situation and on the manager's style of altering behavior. Punishment is discussed in more detail in the next chapter.

Extinction reduces the frequency of behavior because positive reinforcement is being withheld. When positive reinforcement for a learned response is withheld, individuals continue to practice that behavior for some period of time. If this nonreinforcement continues, the behavior decreases and eventually disappears. The decline in the response rate because of nonreinforcement is defined as **extinction.** For example, a member of a work team may have

Extinction

Decline in response rate because of nonreinforcement.

gotten into the habit of telling jokes at team meetings because people laughed at them (positive reinforcement). If the team began to feel that the jokes were not a desirable part of their activities and made an effort not to laugh, over time the team member's joke telling is likely to diminish. While extinction is a major form of behavior modification, it is less likely than the other approaches to be used in organizational settings because it is more passive (i.e., withholding of reinforcement) than the active styles preferred in the workplace.

An important base for these four important principles is Thorndike's classic *law of effect:*

> *Of several responses to the same situation, those that are accompanied or closely followed by satisfaction (reinforcement) . . . will be more likely to recur; those which are accompanied or closely followed by discomfort (punishment) . . . will be less likely to occur.*[20]

The idea that the consequences of behavior—reward or punishment—are critical in determining future behavior remains an important foundation for the use of operant conditioning in organizational settings.

Recall that positive reinforcement occurs when a positively valued consequence (e.g., a promotion) follows a response to a stimulus. Negative reinforcement occurs when a behavior causes an undesirable factor to be taken away (e.g., the nagging boss). Punishment occurs when an undesired behavior is followed by a negative consequence (e.g., loss of pay). In extinction, the behavior is weakened by the withdrawal of something positive.

Behavior Modification: A Managerial Perspective

Behavior modification is based on the assumption that behavior is more important than its "psychological causes," such as the needs, motives, and values held by individuals.[21] Thus, a behaviorist such as B. F. Skinner focuses on specific behaviors and not on such intangibles as esteem needs or personality structure. For example, a behaviorist, told that an employee isn't performing well, would probably ask, "What specific behaviors led to this observation?" Specific and distinguishable behaviors are the most important bases in developing any behavior modification plan to correct a performance problem.

In addition to the attention devoted to these behaviors, there's an emphasis on the consequences of behavior. For example, suppose that all new management trainees are given a two-day training program on preparing budget reports. Shortly after the training sessions, managers notice that few reports are prepared correctly. One explanation may be that the training program was ineffective. However, behaviorists might approach the problem from a different direction. First, they could determine whether the trainees understand the importance of correct reports. They might then find out which trainees are turning in correct reports and what consequences, if any, are being received by these trainees. It could be that turning in correct reports results in nothing, that there are no observable consequences. In the same manner, submitting an incorrect report may also result in no consequences, positive or negative. The behaviorists' findings might result in developing a program of positive and negative consequences (e.g., recognition, praise, a meeting with the boss to go over mistakes). Behaviorists believe people tend to repeat behaviors that lead to positive consequences. This principle could serve as a cornerstone in improving the report accuracy of trainees.

The proposed application of behavior modification in organizations follows a five-step problem-solving process similar to that in Figure 6–3 below.[22]

1. Managers must identify and define the specific behavior. A behavior is pinpointed when it can be accurately observed and reliably recorded. To be pinpointed as an important behavior, there must be positive answers to these questions: (1) Can it be seen? (2) Can it be measured?[23]

2. Managers must measure or count the occurrences of the pinpointed behavior. This count provides managers with a clear perspective of the strength of the behavior under the present, or before-change, situation. The count serves as the means of evaluating any later changes in behavior. Managers can graph these data to determine whether the behavior is increasing, decreasing, or remaining the same.

3. Managers conduct an analysis of the ABCs of the behavior,[24] also called *functionally analyzing the behavior.*[25] In **ABC analysis,** referred to earlier, the **A** designates analyzing the antecedents of **B,** the pinpointed critical behaviors; and the **C** indicates the associated consequence. Specific analyses of the ABCs attempt to determine where the problems lie. Thomas Connellan has developed a set of performance analysis questions to get at the problem source (Table 6–1).[26] The ABC analysis permits managers to consider performance analysis questions important in formulating any specific program. In analyzing absenteeism, for example, managers using a question format and the type of framework displayed in Table 6–2 are systematically viewing the problem of absenteeism in terms of antecedents, behaviors, and consequences.

ABC Analysis

Analysis of antecedents, behavior, and consequences when investigating work- or job-related issues.

4. The first three steps in an applied behavior modification program set the stage for the actual actions by the manager. The goal of operant conditioning is to strengthen desirable and observable critical performance behaviors and to weaken undesirable behaviors. The fourth step involves the strategies for accomplishing these goals, which are discussed earlier in this section. They are positive reinforcers, negative reinforcers, punishment, and extinction. Managers prefer to use positive reinforcement in most applied behavior modification programs. But identifying positive reinforcers isn't always easy. The most obvious approach for managers to take is to ask subordinates what's rewarding to them. Another identification method is to use attitude surveys asking about job reward preferences. Note also that punishment and extinction by themselves often do not give guidance to employees as to how they can improve their performance.

Figure 6–3

Applied Behavior Modification: A Manager's Step-by-Step Procedure

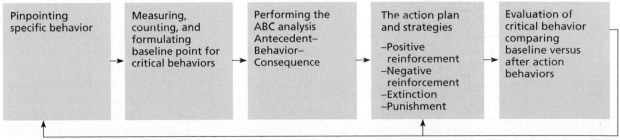

Table 6–1	
Performance Analysis Questions	**Antecedent**
	Does the employee know what is expected?
	Are the standards clear?
	Have they been communicated?
	Are they realistic?
	Behavior
	Can the behavior be performed?
	Could the employee do it if his or her life depended on it?
	Does something prevent its occurrence?
	Consequence
	Are the consequences weighted in favor of performance?
	Are improvements being reinforced?
	Do we note improvement even though the improvement may still leave the employee below company standards?
	Is reinforcement specific?

Source: Thomas K. Connellan, *How to Improve Human Performance: Behaviorism in Business and Industry* (New York: Harper & Row, 1978), p. 51.

Table 6–2

Using the ABC Analysis on an Absenteeism Problem

A ANTECEDENTS	B BEHAVIOR(S)	C CONSEQUENCE(S)
Family problems: spouse, children	Staying home	Public reprimand
Personal health	Shopping	Private reprimand
Illness	Oversleeping	Written record and reprimand
Jury duty	Getting up late	Reduction in pay
No transportation	Attending sporting event	Suspension
Company policies	Working at home	Firing
Group norm	Visiting	Social isolation from group
Friends visiting	Serving on jury	
Injured on way to work	In emergency room at hospital	
Hangover	At doctor's office	
No child care facilities		
Lack of proper tools or clothing		

Source: Adapted from Fred Luthans and Mark Martinko, "An Organizational Behavior Modification Analysis of Absenteeism," *Human Resource Management,* Fall 1976.

5. The fifth step involves evaluation. A major weakness in many applied motivational programs is that formal evaluations aren't conducted. The evaluation of an applied program permits the manager to trace and review changes in behavior before and after the implementation of an action program. Evaluation permits managers to measure performance on an ongoing basis.[27] Furthermore, evaluation can provide feedback to managers on the behaviors exhibited. This feedback enables managers to make necessary and timely corrections in the program.

Employees in the following Close-Up on pages 158–159 emphasizes how important it is to receive feedback.

Research on reinforcement theory

Research on reinforcement theory applications is often limited to small samples, single organizations, and brief periods of time. The list of organizational behavior modification users includes Michigan Bell Telephone, Ford Motor Co., American Can Company, United Air Lines, Warner-Lambert Company, Chase Manhattan Bank, Procter & Gamble, and Standard Oil of Ohio. A survey of empirical research on organizational behavior modification (OBM) examined research involving quantity of performance, quality of performance, absenteeism, employee safety, employee energy conservation and theft, and customer service.[28] The researchers found generally strong evidence that OBM is making

www.ual.com

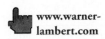
www.warner-lambert.com

and can make a positive contribution to organizational behavior. Absenteeism rates, quality of production, and employee safety behaviors appear to improve more often than not when organizations use OBM.

Criticisms of behavior modification

Critics have attacked behavior modification on a number of grounds. A frequent concern with the use of reinforcers is that there's no "real" change in behavior: the person is just being "bribed" to perform. Bribery refers to the illicit use of rewards to corrupt someone's conduct. In reinforcement, however, outcomes are typically delivered for behaviors designed to benefit the person and the organization. Thus, this criticism, although logical, really doesn't apply to the reinforcers usually used in organizations.

Another perspective is held by Locke, who believes that to view reinforcements as modifying responses automatically, independent of a person's beliefs, values, or mental processes, is simply a wrong way to view human behavior. He says that this theory is simple and appealing but that the facts don't support it. He claims that people can learn by seeing others get reinforcement and by imitating those who aren't reinforced (see social learning above). There's also self-reinforcement, which operant conditioning theorists ignore.[29]

Another criticism focuses on the point that individuals can become too dependent on extrinsic reinforcers (e.g., pay). Thus, behavior may become dependent on the reinforcer and never performed without the promise of the reinforcer. A last criticism, especially in the case of positive reinforcement, is that its utilization may be more perceived than actual.[30] Surveys on interpersonal relations find that while more than 80 percent of supervisors claim they frequently utilize forms of positive reinforcement (such as praise, recognition, and rewards), less than 20 percent of employees report that their supervisors express forms of appreciation more than occasionally. In light of these concerns, managers should remember three important principles when expressing appreciation and reinforcing good behavior. First, describe the desired behavior in specific terms, avoiding sweeping generalizations. Second, explain why the behavior was helpful to the organization. Third, regardless of the type of positive reinforcement given, it should always be accompanied by a personal expression of thanks.

When considering the above criticisms, we must keep in mind that the relevance and impact of any management approach may be greatly affected by the national culture where that approach is used. An excellent example of this is the study by Welsh, Luthans, and Sommer, in which they had managers in the largest textile plant in Russia use three different motivational styles toward their employees.[31] They found that while extrinsic rewards and behavioral management produced positive results, a strategy involving participation on the part of the workers (an approach endorsed and desired in the United States) not only did not increase performance but may have actually decreased production. Although more work is needed in this area, the significance of cultural and related factors on the appropriateness of managerial activities has to be carefully evaluated.

Behavioral Self-Management

Smoking cessation, dieting, personal growth and development, and an exercise regimen each involve the notion of self-control. The motivation of oneself has received some attention in the organizational literature in the past decade.[32] The concepts of self-motivation have evolved primarily from the social learning theory literature and related work in self-control. In the organization literature, this process has been referred to as **behavioral self-management (BSM).**

Behavioral Self-Management (BSM)

Process whereby person faces immediate response alternatives involving different consequences and selects or modifies behavior by managing cognitive processes, causes, or consequences.

Self-management, which is often called self-control, is defined as: "A person displays self-control when, in the relative absence of immediate external constraints, he engages in behavior whose previous probability has been less than that of alternatively available behaviors."[33]

In essence this suggests that there are times when individuals will choose behaviors that they have not chosen consistently in the past, and this selection may be based on the expectation of positive outcomes in the future from this course of action. Several features of self-management need to be noted. Self-management is a process whereby a person is faced with immediate response alternatives (e.g., to work moderately hard or to work very hard to complete the job) involving different consequences. Self-management behavior may include personal performance goals, self-instructions on how to achieve goals, self-administered consequences, a plan to behave in a particular manner, or a strategy for personally developing a set of skills.

In BSM, a person is assumed to have some control over her behavior, cognitive processes, and contingent consequences. Indeed, this control is the basis for the notion of empowerment, a broad movement toward providing workers with greater input into their jobs.[34] At the workplace or outside of it, everyone practices BSM to some degree,[35] and it appears to have an important impact on performance within various groups such as managers of joint ventures.[36] Usually we set certain behavior standards and reward or punish ourselves according to personal judgments we make about how our behavior relates to these standards.

C L O S E — U P

Feedback is Motivational

Employees are so hungry for guidance in today's pressure-filled workplace that many would prefer input from the manager over a hike in pay.

Sure, cash bonuses and raises are welcome rewards. But they're rarely enough. Scant feedback can lead to turnover, a concern that has employers increasing both the amount and quality of job critiques.

"I like to know there's something to the workplace that's more than just a paycheck," says Bob, 29, an investment advisor in Wauwatosa, Wis. "I'd rather be someplace I enjoy being, and feedback just goes along with it."

A survey for American Express looked at what workers most want from employers. It found the number one desire, at 46 percent, was personal feedback. That compares with the 32 percent who said they most wanted financial rewards.

Some trends behind the demand:

- **Worker autonomy.** Today's employees have more decision-making authority, but the increased responsibility also means many want to know where they stand.

  "You get uncomfortable day to day not knowing how you're doing," says Randolph, 58, a computer operations manager in Providence, RI "The feeling that someone cares far outweighs a money value."

- **Waning loyalty.** In an age of job-hopping and mass lay-offs, employees are looking for ways to quantify their worth to future employers. A history of promotions and enviable reviews can have more long-term value than pay.

- **Fewer guarantees.** Promotions and pay raises no longer are granted to workers solely based on years of service. Performance has become the catalyst for getting ahead.

"As employees see this, they naturally want to know how they're doing," says a mangement consultant in Princeton, N.J.

A self-regulation model

Since effective self-management appears to offer potential benefits to employees and organizations, a general framework could prove useful. Frederick Kanfer has proposed a three-stage model that has managerial application value. Figure 6–4 shows the Kanfer model of self-regulation as applied to a work situation.

According to the model, when a nonroutine event (e.g., new boss, unexpected equipment breakdown) disrupts the normal work pattern, a person begins to practice self-examination (what Kanfer designates as self-regulation).

A new boss taking over is a nonroutine occurrence. The event would initiate such thoughts as How am I performing? and How will I need to perform to project a good impression to the new boss? This is stage 1, self-monitoring. Self-evaluation (stage 2) would involve comparing the previous boss with the new boss and deciding whether previous performance will be sufficient to impress the new boss. In stage 3, self-reinforcement, the person would exercise his own reinforcement for performing at an acceptable level. Kanfer proposes that self-regulation occurs quickly and without much awareness by a person.[37]

BSM may appear to be simply another variant of organizational behavior modification. However, there's a distinct difference in terms of the importance of cognitive processes in BSM, as it combines the principles of learning with an emphasis on human interactions in a social setting. In contrast to OBM, which focuses specifically on antecedents, behavior, and consequences, the behavioral self-management approach places more stress on the uniquely human cognitive processes involved in acquiring and maintaining patterns of behavior without the input of other people.

The feedback can have an impact on productivity and boost morale. A survey by Menlo Park, Calif.–based staffing service OfficeTeam found 66 percent of respondents believe performance review sessions have a favorable impact on job motivation.

"There is a sense that employees aren't getting enough mentoring as organizations get flatter," says Peter Cappelli, author of *The New Deal at Work*, on managing a mobile workforce. "People are hungry for it."

Aware of the need, employers are turning to frequent job reviews, daily chats and performance appraisals that include input from co-workers, customers and subordinates.

Managers may be ranked on nontraditional goals such as fostering work–family balance and encouraging teamwork.

But getting stuck with bad managers can leave some wary of any feedback at all. Others argue that talk is cheap.

"I've been around long enough to know that you must put money where your mouth is," says Lisa, 40, a factory worker in Island Pond, Vt. "How many times have people said meaningless things? I want to take what somebody tells me to the bank."

That's not to say guidance doesn't last.

More than 20 years ago, Walter was a young chemical engineer toiling in a lab when his boss walked in. "You're doing a wonderful job," he remembers the supervisor saying, "I'm so glad you're part of the department."

It was just a few words, but the input was such a valuable motivator that Walker now 61 and retired, still talks of the lesson he learned: It takes more than cash to buy loyalty.

"Many other bosses have just taken my contributions for granted and felt that their response was more money," says Walter. The real motivator was genuinely realizing my successes and telling me so."

Sources: Stephanie Armour, "Cash or Critiques: Which Is Best?" *USA Today,* December 16, 1998, p. 6B, and Anne Faircloth, "How to Recover from a Firing, *Fortune,* December 7, 1998, pp. 239–240.

 www.americanexpress.com

Figure 6–4

Kanfer's Self-Regulation Methods

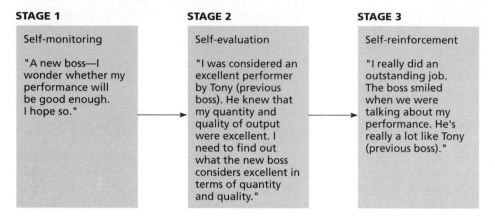

STAGE 1

Self-monitoring

"A new boss—I wonder whether my performance will be good enough. I hope so."

STAGE 2

Self-evaluation

"I was considered an excellent performer by Tony (previous boss). He knew that my quantity and quality of output were excellent. I need to find out what the new boss considers excellent in terms of quantity and quality."

STAGE 3

Self-reinforcement

"I really did an outstanding job. The boss smiled when we were talking about my performance. He's really a lot like Tony (previous boss)."

Expectancy Theory

A quite popular explanation of motivation, developed by Victor Vroom, is expectancy theory, rated as one of the most prominent motivation and leadership theories.[38] The majority of the early studies conducted (about 50) tested the accuracy of expectancy theory in predicting employee behavior.[39] Since then, additional studies have tested the theory itself.

Vroom defines *motivation* as a process governing choices among alternative forms of voluntary activity. In his view, most behaviors are under the voluntary control of the person and are consequently motivated.

Terminology

To understand the **expectancy theory of motivation,** we must define the terms in the theory and explain how they operate. The most important terms are discussed in this section.

FIRST- AND SECOND-LEVEL OUTCOMES   The first-level outcomes resulting from behavior are associated with doing the job itself. These outcomes include productivity, absenteeism, turnover, and quality of productivity. Second-level outcomes are those events (rewards or punishments) that the first-level outcomes are likely to produce, such as merit pay increase, group acceptance or rejection, and promotion.

INSTRUMENTALITY   This is an individual's perception that first-level outcomes are associated with second-level outcomes. Vroom suggests that **instrumentality** can take values ranging from -1, indicating a perception that attainment of the second level is certain without the first outcome and impossible with it, to $+1$, indicating that the first outcome is necessary and sufficient for the second outcome to occur. A value of 0 would indicate no relationship between first and second outcomes. This association between outcomes can thus be thought of in terms of correlation.

Expectancy Theory of Motivation

Theory in which an employee is faced with a set of first-level outcomes and selects an outcome based on how choice is related to second-level outcomes. The individual's preferences are based on strength (valence) of desire to achieve second-level state and perception of relationship between first- and second-level outcomes.

Instrumentality

Concept in expectancy theory of motivation in which a person's perception of association of first- and second-level outcomes is determined.

VALENCE   The preference for outcomes, as seen by the individual, is termed **valence.** For example, a person may prefer a 9 percent merit increase over a transfer to a new department, or the transfer over relocation to a new facility. An outcome is *positively* valent when it's preferred; it's *negatively* valent when it's not preferred or is avoided. An outcome has a valence of zero when the individual is indifferent to attaining or not attaining it. The valence concept applies to first- and second-level outcomes. For example, a person may prefer to be a high-performing (first-level outcome) employee because he believes that this will lead to a merit increase in pay (second-level outcome).[40]

Valence

Strength of a person's preference for particular outcome.

EXPECTANCY   This term refers to the individual's belief concerning the likelihood or subjective probability that a particular behavior will be followed by a particular outcome such as level of performance. That is, **expectancy** is the perceived chance of something occurring because of a behavior. Expectancy has a value ranging from 0, indicating no chance that an outcome will occur after the behavior or act, to $+1$, indicating certainty that a particular outcome will follow an act or a behavior. Expectancy is like a subjective probability.

Expectancy (probability)

Perceived likelihood that a particular act will be followed by a particular outcome.

In the work setting, individuals hold an *effort-performance expectancy.* This expectancy represents the individual's perception of how hard it is to achieve a particular behavior (say, completing the budget on time) and the probability of achieving that behavior. For example, Joan, who's preparing a budget, may have a high expectancy that if she works around the clock she can complete the budget on time; on the other hand, she may perceive that her chances of finishing on time are about 40 percent if she works only during the day. Given a number of alternative levels of behavior to finish the budget (working 8 hours, 10 hours, or around the clock), she'll choose the level of performance that has the greatest motivational force associated with it. In other words, when faced with *choices* about behavior, the person performing the task goes through a process of questioning: Can I perform at that level if I give it a try? If I perform at that level, what will happen? Do I prefer the things that will happen?

Two other terms are worth defining here as well. The term *force* is equated with motivation. The intent of expectancy theory is to assess the magnitude and direction of all the forces acting on the individual. The act associated with the greatest force is the one most likely to occur.

The term *ability* designates a person's potential for doing the job or work; it refers to the person's physical and mental abilities to do the job and not to what the person *will* do. That potential may or may not be utilized.

Principles of expectancy theory

Integration of the important expectancy theory concepts generates three major principles:[41]

1. $V_1 = \Sigma(V_2 \times I)$. The valence associated with various first-level outcomes is a sum of the multiplication of the valences (V_2) attached to all second-level outcomes with their respective instrumentalities (I).
2. $M = f(V_1 \times E)$. Motivation is a multiplicative function of the valence for each first-level outcome (V_1) and the perceived expectancy (E) that a given behavior will be followed by a particular first-level outcome. If expectancy is low, there will be little motivation. Similarly, if an outcome's valence is zero, neither the absolute value nor variations in the strength of the expectancies of accomplishing it will have any effect.

Figure 6–5

Application of Expectancy Theory: Joan's Situation

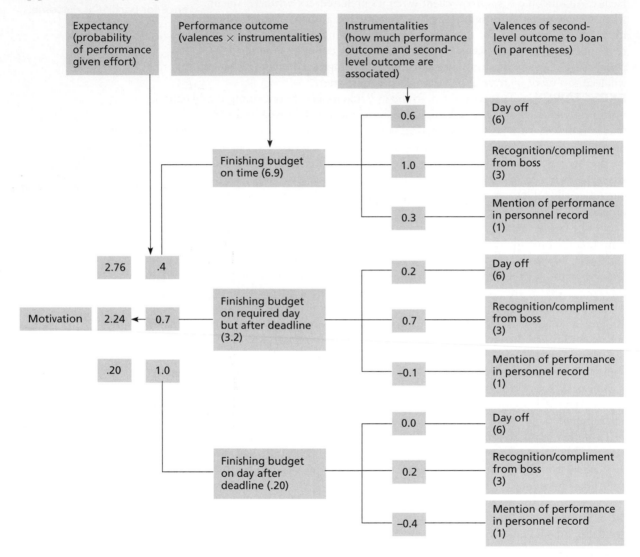

3. $P = f(M \times A)$. Performance is considered to be a multiplicative function of motivation (the force) and ability.

Figure 6–5 uses numerical values to illustrate how expectancy theory works conceptually. The situation portrayed involves Joan, a budget specialist, facing various performance (first- and second-level) outcomes. Starting at the second-level outcome point (the right side), the valence associated with finishing the budget on time is calculated by $V_1 = V_2 \times I$, or $VI = (6 \times 0.6) + (3 \times 1.0) + (1 \times 0.3)$, or 6.9.

We're assuming that Joan has indicated her preferences, or valence strength, for these three outcomes. She indicates a strength of preference of 6 for a day off, a 3 for recognition and compliments from the boss, and a 1 for a mention of performance in her personnel file. Her preference ratings indicate Joan values the day off much more than the two other outcomes. Her valences are multiplied by the instrumentalities, her perceptions of the association of performance outcomes, and each of the second-level outcomes. Remember the 6, 3, and 1 valance strengths are set for illustrative purposes. These values indicating strength are subjectively established. Thus, for the "finishing budget on time" performance, this would be 6(.6) + 3(1.0) + 1(.3) = 6.9.

The motivational force for the condition of finishing the budget on time is calculated by $M = f(V_1 \times E)$, or $M = 6.9 \times 0.4$, or 2.76. The motivational force for finishing the budget on the required day but after the deadline is 2.24, while finishing the budget the day after the deadline has a force of 0.20. Thus, the strongest force or motivation would be directed toward finishing the budget on time. Certainly, a manager would not engage in this type of mathematical calculation. However, he or she would attempt to determine how empoyees think in terms of expectancies, instrumentalities, and valences.

Management implications of expectancy theory

Managers can certainly use expectancy theory in developing their own motivation programs.[42] However, some managerial actions must be taken to improve the theory's value. First, managers need to focus on employee expectations for success. That is, do employees feel that they can attain the performance goals that are set for them, or do they perceive that the achievement of these goals and the resultant positive outcomes are beyond their capabilities? If this latter situation is the case, especially in group situations, then low productivity is often the result.[43] Managers need to realign assignments and rewards to facilitate the development of realistic challenge within jobs.

Second, managers must actively determine which second-level outcomes are important to employees. In our example, Joan valued a day off. Simply providing a notation in her personnel file commenting on her performance wasn't as valued as the day off. Managers who know what subordinates prefer can attempt to provide the highly valued outcomes. Because (as this kind of outcome preference information points out) individuals prefer different outcomes, motivation programs should be designed with enough flexibility to address such differences in individual preference.[44]

Third, managers should link desired second-level outcomes to the organization's performance goals. Showing through example that there's an actual association between performance goals and desired second-level outcomes increases employees' belief that hard work and good performance result in outcomes they prefer.

Expectancy theory assumes employees allocate their behavior according to anticipated consequences of actions. Workers weigh the information available to them and make decisions according to the value of the consequences and their own probabilities of achieving what they prefer. Expectancy theory thus views behavior as the product of what employees believe will happen in the future.

Research on expectancy

Each year brings more empirical research on expectancy theory. A few studies have used students in laboratory experiments. However, most research has been conducted in field settings. One interesting study, for example, examined performance-outcome instrumentality in a temporary organization.[45] The experiment used either an hourly rate of pay (low instrumentality or little link between immediate behavior and outcomes) or a piece rate (high instrumentality or payment based on each piece produced). After individuals worked for three four-hour days under one pay system, they were shifted to the other system and worked three more days. Immediately following the shift in pay systems and for all three subsequent days, the performance of the subjects shifted to the high-instrumentality system was higher than their own performance under the low-instrumentality system and higher than the performance of the subjects shifted to the low-instrumentality system.

Another research area focused on the model's valence and behavior factors. The results have been mixed.[46] However, three conditions apparently must hold for the valence of outcomes to be related to effort. Performance-outcome instrumentalities must be greater than zero; effort-performance expectancies must be greater than zero; and there must be some variability in the valence of outcomes.[47]

Criticisms of expectancy theory

Theorists, researchers, and practitioners (to a lesser extent) continue to work on defining, measuring, and applying expectancy concepts. Many difficulties are encountered when testing the model.[48] One problem involves the issue of effort, or motivation itself. The theory attempts to predict choice or effort. But without a clear specification of the meaning of effort, the variable can't be adequately measured. Typically, self, peer, or supervisor ratings of effort are used. Unfortunately, each study seems to have its own definition, measurement, and research design.

The issue of first-level performance outcomes presents another difficulty. Expectancy theory, as a process theory, doesn't specify which outcomes are relevant to a particular individual in a situation. Each researcher addresses this issue in a unique way. Consequently, no systematic approach is being used across investigations.

Furthermore, the expectancy approach contains an implicit assumption that all motivation is conscious. Individuals are assumed to consciously calculate the pleasure or pain they expect to attain or avoid; then a choice is made. Although it's generally accepted that individuals aren't always conscious of their motives, expectancies, and perceptual processes, expectancy theory says nothing about subconscious motivation. For the most part, this point has been neglected in the theory.

Most of the available field studies testing the model have relied on employees from a single organization who were doing the same or similar jobs. These studies seriously limit and restrict the range of expectancies and instrumentalities. This type of research also raises the issue of whether results from these studies can be generalized to other samples. Is it valid to make generalizations?

Equity Theory

Equity Theory of Motivation

Theory that examines discrepancies within Person after Person has compared his input/outcome ratio to that of reference person.

J. Stacey Adams, while working as a research psychologist with the General Electric Co. in Crotonville, New York, developed and tested an **equity theory of motivation.** The essence of equity theory is that employees compare their efforts and rewards with those of others in similar work situations. This theory of motivation is based on the assumption that individuals, who work in exchange for rewards from the organization, are motivated by a desire to be equitably treated at work. This is significant as authors such as Pfeffer believe that maintaining employee perceptions of equity is a critical aspect of the management role.[49] Four important terms in this theory are:

1. *Person:* the individual for whom equity or inequity is perceived.

2. *Comparison other:* any individual(s) or group used by Person as a referent regarding the ratio of inputs and outcomes.

Figure 6–6

The Equity Theory of Motivation

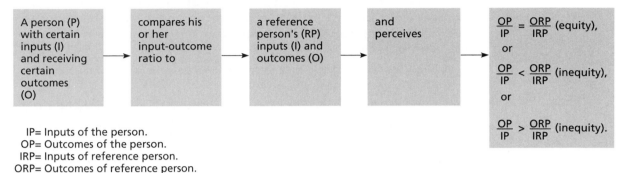

IP= Inputs of the person.
OP= Outcomes of the person.
IRP= Inputs of reference person.
ORP= Outcomes of reference person.

3. *Inputs:* the individual characteristics brought by Person to the job. These may be achieved (e.g., skills, experience, learning) or ascribed (e.g., age, sex, race).

4. *Outcomes:* what Person received from the job (e.g., recognition, fringe benefits, pay).

Equity exists when employees perceive that the ratios of their inputs (efforts) to their outcomes (rewards) are equivalent to the ratios of other similar employees. Inequity exists when these ratios aren't equivalent: an individual's own ratio of inputs to outcomes could be greater or less than that of others.[50] Figure 6–6 illustrates the equity theory of motivation in general; Table 6–3 gives an example. Note that Jeff has considered five points of comparison and has assigned hypothetical values (weights) to the importance of each point. Jeff is assessing his outcomes as 5 and inputs as 4, for a 1.25 index, while Jeff assesses Bob's situation as 6 outcomes and 2 inputs, or 3.0 (The two major differences in this case are Jeff's being paid $4,000 less than Bob and his 18 months more experience than Bob's.) Thus, Jeff concludes that he gets less out of the job than does Bob. In essence, he believes that he's being underpaid relative to Bob, he feels distressed or troubled by this unexplainable inequity, and he is motivated to resolve this situation.[51]

Table 6–3   Jeff's Concept of Equity Theory: An Application

OUTCOMES AND INPUTS	WEIGHTED VALUE OF OUTCOMES AND INPUTS	JEFF	BOB	WEIGHTED VALUE OF OUTCOMES AND INPUTS
College degree (input)	1	Yes	Yes	1
CPA (input)	1	Yes	Yes	1
Experience on job (input)	2	18 months	None	0
Executive dining room privileges (outcome)	1	Yes	Yes	1
Annual salary (outcome)	4	$27,000	$31,000	5

$$\frac{\text{Outcomes } (1 + 4)}{\text{Inputs } (1 + 1 + 2)} \qquad \frac{\text{Outcomes } (1 + 5)}{\text{Inputs } (1 + 1)}$$

$$\frac{5}{4} < \frac{6}{2}$$

(Jeff)   1.25 < 3.00   (Bob)

Alternatives to restore equity

Equity theory suggests alternative ways to restore a feeling or sense of equity. Some examples of restoring equity would be:

1. *Changing inputs.* Jeff may decide to put less time or effort into the job. Other inputs that could be changed are reliability, cooperation with others, initiative, and acceptance of responsibility.

2. *Changing outcomes.* Jeff may decide to confront his boss and ask for a raise, more time off, or better assignments.

3. *Changing the reference person.* The reference person (Bob) can be changed by making comparisons with the input/outcome ratios of some other person. This change can restore equity.

4. *Changing the inputs or outcomes of the reference person.* If the reference person is a coworker, it might be possible to attempt to change his inputs. Asking Bob to work harder or to take more responsibility on projects are examples of such an attempt.

5. *Changing the situation.* Jeff might quit the job to alter feeling of inequity. He could also transfer to get away from an inequitable situation.

Each of these methods is designed to reduce or change the feelings of discomfort and tension created by inequity. Equity theory proposes that when inequity exists, a person is motivated to take one or more of these five steps.

Research on equity

Most of the research on equity theory has focused on pay as the basic outcome.[52] One study incorporated workplace elements into an equity theory framework.[53] Employees reassigned to offices of workers two levels above them in the management hierarchy were expected to perform at a higher level than employees reassigned to offices of workers only one level above them. Similarly, employees reassigned to offices of workers two levels below them would be expected to perform at a lower level than employees reassigned to offices of workers only one level below them. The findings indicated that employees assigned to higher status offices increased their performance (a response to overpayment inequity) while those reassigned to lower status offices lowered their performance (a response to underpayment inequity). The study supported equity theory's predictions that the reaction to an inequity will be proportional to the magnitude of the inequity experienced. It's also important to note that the workplace environment—not pay inequity—was the focal point in the study. Indeed, a review of the research reveals that the pay is not always the outcome considered, as equity theory has shown predicted effects for both organizational citizenship behaviors[54] (going beyond the call of duty) and attitudes toward tasks and work groups.[55]

Several individuals have questioned the extent to which inequity that results from overpayment (rewards) leads to perceived inequity. Locke argues that employees are seldom told they're overpaid. He believes that individuals are likely to adjust their idea of what constitutes an equitable payment to justify their pay.[56] Because employer-employee exchange relationships are highly impersonal when compared to exchanges between friends, perceived overpayment inequity may be more likely when friends are involved. Thus, individuals probably react to overpayment inequity only when they believe that their actions have led to a friend's being treated unfairly. The individual receives few signals from the organization that it's being treated unfairly.

Most equity research focuses on short-term comparisons.[57] What is needed are longitudinal studies that examine inequity over a period of time. What happens over time as the inequity remains, or is increased, or is decreased? Are comparison others always within one's own organization, and do they change during a person's work career? These questions and research to answer them could provide insight into the dynamic character of equity theory and individual responses.[58]

Another interesting criticism of equity theory is that it ignores reactions to experienced inequities. Is it not likely that two people will react somewhat differently to the same magnitude of inequity if they believe different things caused the inequity? Folger has introduced the notion of *referent cognitions theory* to explore the role of the decision-making process in shaping perceptions of inequity.[59] In a work situation, suppose a manager allocates merit raises on the basis of a performance appraisal review. One employee may appreciate this strategy, while another may resent the manager, believing that another approach based on critical incidents and work on difficult assignments *should* have been used to allocate the merit raises. Thus the second employee is more likely to perceive inequity in the appraisal process.

Referent cognitions theory predicts resentment of unfair treatment when procedures yield poor outcomes for a person.[60] A study of manufacturing plant employees found that individual satisfaction with pay was highly related to the perceived fairness of the actual size of pay raises; however, the issues of commitment and trust in the organization were more affected by the *procedure* used to determine the raises. The researchers concluded that, in the allocation of pay increases, concerns other than the specific distribution of the money need to be seriously considered. They thus implied that an equity theory explanation of motivation is too restricted and incomplete.[61] However, since equity theory does seem to be applicable in other cultures such as China, and in a variety of occupations such as in the Close-Up on page 168, it must be taken seriously as an explanation of employee behavior.[62]

Goal-Setting Theory

Since 1968, when Edwin Locke presented what's now considered his classic paper,[63] there has been considerable and growing interest in applying goal setting to organizational problems and issues. Locke proposed that **goal setting** was a cognitive process of some practical utility. His view was that an individual's **conscious goals** and intentions are the primary determinants of behavior. That is, "one of the commonly observed characteristics of intentional behavior is that it tends to keep going until it reaches completion."[64] Once a person starts something (e.g., a job, a new project), she pushes on until a goal is achieved. Intent plays a prominent role in goal-setting theory.[65] Also, the theory places specific emphasis on the importance of conscious goals in explaining motivated behavior. Locke has used the notion of intentions and conscious goals to propose and provide research support for the thesis that harder conscious goals result in higher levels of performance if these goals are accepted by the individual.

The goal-setting process

A **goal** is the object of an action; it's what a person attempts to accomplish. For example, producing four units on a production line, or cutting direct costs by $3,000, or decreasing absenteeism in a department by 12 percent is a goal. Many examples could be given of the successful use of goal setting techniques in achieving important organizational outcomes, such as safety improvement.[66] Frederick W. Taylor has had a direct influence on the current thinking about goals and goal-setting practices.

Goal Setting

The process of establishing goals. In many cases, it involves superior and subordinate working together to set subordinate's goals for specified period of time.

Conscious Goals

Main goals that a person is striving for and is aware of when directing behavior.

Goal

Specific target that an individual is trying to achieve; the target (object) of an action.

Locke stated that Taylor used assigned goals as one of his key techniques of scientific management. Each employee was assigned a challenging but attainable goal based on the results of time and motion study. The individual's methods for achieving the assigned goal (e.g., the tools used, the work procedures followed, the pacing needed to do the job) were spelled out in detail.[67]

Thus, Locke pointed out the significant influence of Taylor in his formulation of goal setting. Locke also carefully described the attributes of the mental (cognitive) processes of goal setting. The attributes he highlighted are goal specificity, goal difficulty, and goal intensity.

Goal Specificity

Degree of quantitative precision of goal.

Goal Difficulty

Degree of proficiency or level of goal performance being sought.

Goal Commitment

Amount of effort actually used to achieve goal.

Goal specificity is the degree of quantitative precision (clarity) of the goal. **Goal difficulty** is the degree of proficiency or the level of performance sought. **Goal intensity** pertains to the process of setting the goal or of determining how to reach it.[68] To date, goal intensity hasn't been widely studied, although a related concept, **goal commitment,** has been considered in some studies. Goal commitment is the amount of effort used to achieve a goal.

Figure 6–7 portrays applied goal setting from a managerial perspective, showing the sequence of events for such a goal-setting program. The key steps in goal setting are (1) *diagnosing* whether the people, the organization, and the technology are suited for goal setting; (2) *preparing* employees via increased interpersonal interaction, communication, training, and action plans for goal setting; (3) *emphasizing* the attributes of goals that should be understood by a manager and subordinates; (4) *conducting* intermediate reviews to make necessary adjustments in established goals; and (5) *performing* a final review to check the goals set, modified, and accomplished. Each step needs to be care-

---

C L O S E — U P

Equity and Sports: The Game's Not the Only Thing?

Equity theory makes a plausible case that individuals may be motivated to change their behavior when they perceive that they are not being treated fairly in comparison to someone in similar circumstances to them. There are a number of problems when trying to conduct research on equity, however, such as finding out what workers' actual inputs and outcomes are, and who their reference persons might be. Some investigators have turned to the world of professional athletics, most frequently major league baseball, to explore the impact of inequity, because measures of input (i.e., performance) are religiously kept and publicized widely, players' salaries are often also a matter of public record, and thus comparisons with possible reference persons are made considerably simpler.

Generally speaking, the results in this area suggest that baseball players who are underrewarded for their performance will show decreases in their performance, as will those who go through salary arbitration (attempt to get a more substantial contract through the decision of a mediating party) and fail. Both of these findings support equity theory

and seem to be particularly relevant to comparisons made with players on one's own or other teams who have the same position. Also of interest is how inequity relates to behavior toward teammates. While baseball statistics are most reflective of individual accomplishments, basketball is a sport more dependent on interactions among those on the same team. Evidence from professional basketball suggests that underrewarded players act more selfishly and less cooperatively, again supporting an equity approach. While the world of professional athletics is obviously a special case, it demonstrates that a lack of equity can have a demonstrable effect on employee behavior.

Sources: Steve Werner and Neal P. Mero, "Fair or Foul?: The Effects of External, Internal and Employee Equity on Changes in Performance of Major League Baseball Players," paper presented at the Academy of Management Annual Meeting, Dallas, 1994; Larry W. Howard and Janis L. Miller, "Fair Pay for Fair Play: Estimating Pay Equity in Professional Baseball with Data Envelopment Analysis," *Academy of Management Journal,* August 1993, pp. 882–94; Robert D. Bretz and Steven L. Thomas, "Perceived Equity, Motivation, and Final-Offer Arbitration in Major League Baseball," *Journal of Applied Psychology,* June 1992, 280–87; Joseph W. Harder, "Play for Pay: Effects of Inequity in a Pay-for-Performance Context," *Administrative Science Quarterly,* June 1992, pp. 321–35; Joseph W. Harder, "Equity Theory versus Expectancy Theory: The Case of Major League Baseball Free Agents," *Journal of Applied Psychology,* June 1991, 458–64.

Figure 6–7

Goal Setting as Applied in Organizations

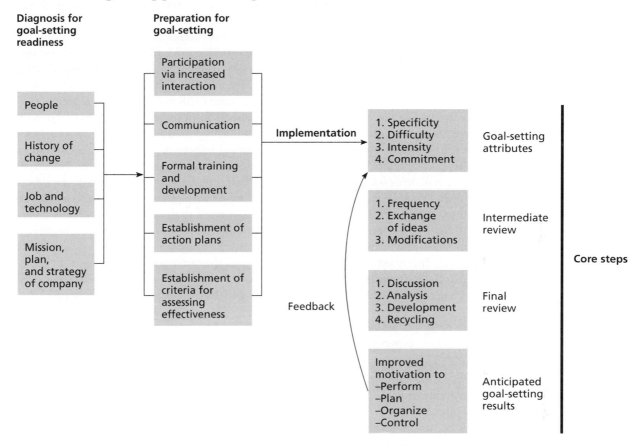

fully planned and implemented if goal setting is to be an effective motivational technique. In too many applications of goal setting, steps outlined in or issues suggested by Figure 6–7 are ignored.

Goal-setting research

Locke's 1968 paper contributed to a considerable increase in laboratory and field research on goal setting. Another force behind the increase in interest and research was the demand of managers for practical and specific techniques that they could apply in their organizations. Goal setting offered such a technique for some managers.[69] The degree of support for goal setting as a viable motivational technique is captured best by the authors of a review of the effects of goal setting on task performance. They stated,

> "If there is ever to be a viable candidate from the organizational sciences for elevation to the lofty status of a scientific law of nature, then the relationships between goal difficulty, specificity, commitment, and task performance are most worthy of serious consideration."[70]

Research has shown that specific goals lead to higher output than do vague goals such as "Do your best."[71] Field experiments using clerical workers, maintenance technicians, marketing personnel, truckers, engineers, typists, and manufacturing employees have compared specific versus do-your-best goal-setting conditions.[72] The vast majority of these studies support, partly or in total, the hypothesis that specific goals lead to better performance than do vague goals. In fact, in 99 out of 100 studies reviewed by Locke and his associates, specific goals produced better results.[73]

One study in particular highlights the practical significance of setting specific goals.[74] As part of a logging operation, truck drivers had to load logs and drive them to a mill for processing. Analysis of each trucker's performance showed that the truckers often weren't filling their trucks to the maximum allowable weight. For the three months in which underloading was being studied, trucks were seldom loaded in excess of 58 to 63 percent of capacity.

Researchers believed that underloading resulted from management's practice of simply instructing the truckers to do their best in loading the trucks. Researchers concluded that setting a specific goal could be the operational impetus needed to improve the situation. They assigned a specific goal of 94 percent of capacity to the drivers. No driver, however, was disciplined for failing to reach the assigned goal. No monetary rewards or fringe benefits other than praise from the supervisor were given for improvements in performance. No specific training or instruction was given to the managers or drivers.

Within the first month after the goal was assigned, performance increased to 80 percent of the truck's limit. After the second month, however, performance decreased to 70 percent. Interviews with drivers indicated that they were testing management's promise not to take disciplinary action if goals weren't met. After the third month, performance exceeded 90 percent of capacity. This performance was being maintained seven years after the original research.

The results of this field experiment are impressive. They suggest that setting specific goals can be a powerful force. The value of goal setting is reflected in a statement of the researchers:

> "The setting of a goal that is both specific and challenging leads to an increase in performance because it makes it clearer to the individual what he is supposed to do. This in turn may provide the worker with a sense of achievement, recognition, and commitment, in that he can compare how well he is doing now versus how well he has done in the past and, in some instances, how well he is doing in comparison to others."[75]

THE DIFFICULTY FACTOR   Generally, the more difficult the goal, the higher the level of performance. But a point of diminishing returns appears to be a real issue in goal difficulty. Although laboratory and field studies find that people with high (difficult) goals consistently perform better, there is a critical point.[76] If and when a goal is perceived as so difficult that it's virtually impossible to attain, the result is often frustration rather than achievement.

For example, an assessment of the difficulty level of the United Fund's fund-raising goals in one study points up the issue of frustration.[77] The more difficult the goal, the more money was raised. This was true, however, only when the goals were seen as attainable by the fund-raisers. When the goals were viewed as unreachable, fund-raisers' morale suffered. On the other hand, goals must be of a realistic difficulty so that they are not set too low.[78]

Goal acceptance is extremely important to any discussion of goal setting's effectiveness. One method to enhance goal acceptance is to permit individuals to participate in goal setting. Researchers suggest that when an individual faces a difficult goal, participative goal setting enhances goal acceptance more than assigned goal setting. In a two-part study, researchers found that participative and representative goal setting (group-elected members represented others in negotiating goals) significantly increased individual goal acceptance; consequently, individual goal acceptance significantly contributed to performance.[79]

Figure 6–8

The Goal Difficulty–Performance Relationship: Three Motivation Views

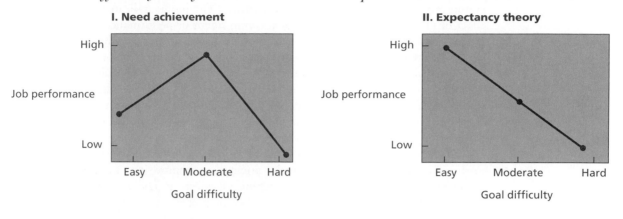

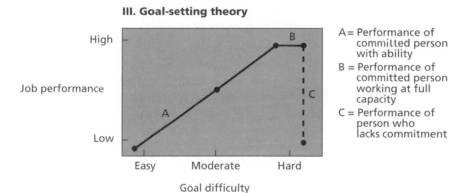

Locke has contrasted goal setting with the expectancy and need-for-achievement explanations of motivation.[80] Figure 6–8 highlights differences in the explanations of the goal difficulty–performance relationship proposed by these three theories.

Expectancy theory predicts increased performance will result from easier goals, since the probability of success (and also the probability of being rewarded) increases. The need-for-achievement prediction is that difficult goals improve performance up to a point but that when goals are too difficult, performance suffers.

One explanation of the goal difficulty–performance relationship is presented as graph III in Figure 6–8. Locke predicts that a person's performance (A) will increase as goal difficulty increases (assuming that the person is committed and has the ability to perform), until a ceiling of performance (B) is reached. Individuals who lack commitment to difficult goals have decreasing or poor performance (C).

ADDING THE PARTICIPATION FACTOR   In one of the more interesting studies of goal setting, a joint design of a series of experiments was conducted to study the effect of participation on goal commitment and performance.[81] Locke served as a third-party mediator of two views held by Latham and Erez. Latham proposed that when goal difficulty is held constant, there are virtually no differences in goal commitment or performance, regardless of whether the goal was assigned or set participatively. Erez believed that participation in goal setting is crucial to goal commitment; that is, if a person doesn't participate, there's little commitment to accomplish the goal.

A series of four experiments at the University of Maryland and University of Washington tested the two viewpoints of goal setting. The results indicated that there was no effect of value for participation on goal commitment or performance in any of the four experiments. The study is commendable for its completeness, the participation of researchers who disagreed with each other's previous findings, and the use of a third-party mediator. Each of these features contributes to improved public confidence in organizational research. But despite Locke's comments that the results of laboratory studies generalize well to the field, the laboratory setting is a weakness of the study.[82] Organizational practitioners would pay more attention to the results of such an innovative study if employees and work settings were used.

Can these results be confirmed in organizations in the United States and around the world? As Eastern European countries attempt to improve the performance of their economies and enterprises, will goal setting be effective? The economies of Hungary, Poland, and the former Soviet Union may not be prepared for participative goal setting. The past cultures of these and other countries may significantly moderate the effects, if any, of goal-setting programs. After years of having decisions handed down from top-level administrators and bureaucrats, when they were told what to do, many individuals aren't used to and prepared to participate in goal setting.

INDIVIDUAL DIFFERENCES   Scattered throughout the goal-setting literature are studies that examine the effects of individual differences on goal setting. Most of these studies have dealt with the effects of education, race, and job tenure on the goal-setting process. A study involving electronics technicians found that goal difficulty (challenge) was significantly related to performance only for those technicians with 12 or more years of education. For technicians with less education, goal clarity (i.e., having a clear understanding of the goal) and goal feedback (i.e., receiving feedback on how results matched the goal) were significantly related to performance.[83]

In a field experiment, loggers working under assigned, participative, and do-your-best conditions were compared. Researchers found that participative goal setting affected the performance of the less educated loggers but not of the more educated loggers.[84]

One study examined three explanations of why participation in goal setting may increase job performance: the social factor of group discussion, the motivational factor of being involved in the goal-setting process, and the cognitive factor of information sharing.[85] Results of this study of white-collar employees indicated that the social and motivational factors increased performance quantity, learning the task, goal acceptance, group commitment, and satisfaction.

Another recent study examined conflict as a goal-setting variable. Both a laboratory experiment and a field study of college professors suggested that conflicting goals can lead to decreases in performance.[86] These findings were not related to how committed subjects were to the goal, which goals were most important, or the strategies used to approach the task. This research points out the need to pay attention to the total situation experienced by employees who are faced with many (and sometimes contradictory) goals. It also suggests that consideration should be given to the kinds of goals that employees set for themselves.

Criticisms of goal setting

It is important to recognize that there are arguments against using goal setting or becoming too enthusiastic about it. Some managers and researchers have found that:

Goal setting is rather complex and difficult to sustain.

Goal setting works well for simple jobs (clerks, typists, loggers, and technicians), but not for complex jobs. Goal setting with jobs in which goals aren't easily measured (teaching, nursing, engineering, accounting) has posed some problems.

Goal setting encourages game playing. Setting low goals to look good later is one game played by subordinates who don't want to be caught short. Managers play the game of setting an initial goal that's generally not achievable and then finding out how subordinates react.

Goal setting is used as another check on employees. It's a control device to monitor performance.

Goal accomplishment can become an obsession. In some situations, goal setters have become so obsessed with achieving their goals that they neglect other important areas of their jobs.

Under the right conditions, goal setting can be a powerful technique for motivating employees. When used correctly, carefully monitored, and actively supported by managers, it can improve performance. (Goal difficulty and goal acceptance are two attributes that management must consider.) The clear implication for managers is that getting employees to set and strive to attain specific, relatively hard goals can generate a strong motivational force.

Reviewing Motivation

Chapters 5 and 6 portrayed a number of popular, empirically tested, and practical theories of motivation. That the theories are typically pitted against one another in the literature is unfortunate, since each theory can help managers better understand workplace motivation. Each theory attempts to organize, in a meaningful manner, major variables associated with explaining motivation in work settings.

The *content* theories concentrate on individuals, placing primary emphasis on people's characteristics. Each of the *process* theories has a specific orientation. Reinforcement theory focuses on the work environment, virtually ignoring the notion of individual needs and attitudes. Expectancy theory emphasizes individual, job, and environmental variables; it recognizes differences in needs, perceptions, and beliefs. Equity theory primarily addresses the relationship between attitudes toward inputs and outcomes and toward reward practices. Goal-setting theory emphasizes the cognitive processes and the role of intentional behavior in motivation.

Each of the theories we've presented has something to offer managers if used correctly, and various parts of the theories are complementary in many respects. The psychologists and social psychologists who formulated these theories were experts in explaining needs, motives, and values. They weren't, however, so astute at explaining what managers could do to motivate employees. And despite the abundance of theories, research, and complementarity, many managers still choose to ignore the academically generated theories of motivation.

But, if anything, Chapters 5 and 6 indicate that instead of ignoring motivation, managers must take an active role in motivating their employees. Nine specific conclusions are reached:

1. Managers can influence employees' motivation. If performance needs to be improved, then managers should intervene and help create an atmosphere that encourages, supports, and sustains improvement. Motivation can be managed.

2. Managers must remember that ability, competence, and opportunity all play a role in motivation. A person with little ability or few skills will have a difficult time being productive.

3. Managers need to be sensitive to variations in employees' needs, abilities, and goals. They must also consider differences in preferences (valences) for rewards.

4. Continual monitoring of employees' needs, abilities, goals, and preferences is each individual manager's responsibility.

5. Managers must attempt to channel self-motivated behavior into productive results. Some individuals practice a high degree of self-regulation and personal motivation.

6. Managers as role models can be influential in motivating employees. Social learning occurs on a regular basis, and managers must be aware that their style, techniques, and work behavior are being observed and can be easily imitated.

7. Managers need to provide incentives for their employees. When employees note that valued outcomes can be achieved through performance, a major part of the motivation strategy has succeeded.

8. Establishing moderately difficult goals to direct behavior is an important part of any motivational program.

9. Managers should try to provide employees with jobs that offer equity, task challenge, diversity, and a variety of opportunities for need satisfaction.

If motivation is to be energized, sustained, and directed, managers have to understand needs, intentions, preferences, goals, reinforcement, and comparison. Failure to learn about these concepts results in many missed opportunities to motivate employees in a positive manner.

Table 6–4 briefly summarizes how well the various themes and approaches predict productivity, absenteeism, and job satisfaction. Ratings are based on available empirical research conducted in organizations primarily in the United States and Canada. Ratings also use the judgments of researchers, anecdotal information, and managerial opinions.[87] While the data presented aren't scientifically validated in every instance, they're based on multiple sources of information.

Table 6–4   The Predictive Power of Selected Motivation Theories*

| | **Theories** | | | | | |
	NEED-BASED[†]	**REINFORCEMENT**	**BEHAVIORAL SELF-MANAGEMENT**	**EXPECTANCY**	**EQUITY**[‡]	**GOAL-SETTING**
Productivity	6[§]	6	6	7	7	9
Absenteeism		8	8[f]	8	8	
Job satisfaction	6				6	6[#]

* Ratings are based on a scale of 1 to 10 with 10 the highest.
†Includes theories of Maslow, Herzberg, Aldefer, and McClelland.
‡Based primarily on studies of pay issues.
§Primarily found for employees with a high need for achievement.
fLimited number of studies.
#Satisfaction levels are higher if goal program is considered fair, meaningful, and more than a control mechanism.

Summary of Key Points

- A central part of Bandura's social learning theory is the concept of self-efficacy; that is, the belief that a person knows that he can perform adequately in a particular situation.

- Reinforcement theory relies on applying the principles of operant conditioning to motivate people. A major assumption of operant conditioning is that behavior is influenced by its consequences.

- The nature of reinforcements and punishments and how they're employed influences behavior. Thus, reinforcement scheduling, or the timing of consequences, is an important feature of motivation.

- A concept that has evolved from social learning theory is called self-motivation. The concept of self-control is at the core of what's now called behavioral self-management in the organization literature.

- The expectancy theory of motivation is concerned with the expectations of a person and how they influence behavior. This theory provides managers with a means for pinpointing desirable and undesirable outcomes associated with task performance.

- Equity theory focuses on comparisons, tension, and tension reduction. To date, most research work on equity theory has involved pay. Equity theory is a more straightforward and understandable explanation of employee attitudes about pay than is expectancy theory. The manager should be aware that people compare their rewards, punishments, tasks, and other job-related dimensions to those of others.

- Goal-setting theory proposes that an individual's goals and intentions are the primary determinants of behavior. Perhaps the most empirically supported approach to motivation, goal setting continues to be refined and studied in laboratory and field settings.

- Despite impressive supportive studies, goal setting has been criticized as working primarily for easy jobs, encouraging game playing, and operating as another control check on employees.

Discussion and Review Questions

1. What are some similarities and differences between the reinforcement and expectancy explanations of motivation?

2. Could a manager who understands equity theory utilize this knowledge in developing pay programs? How?

3. How does self-control play a role in motivation?

4. Describe a situation you've previously encountered where reinforcement theory could have been successfully applied. What type of reinforcement schedule would you have utilized?

5. What ethical considerations should be considered before using a behavior modification program in a work setting?

6. The authors stressed that the Table 6–4 data weren't scientifically validated; that is, the data are subject to different interpretations. Why, after all the years of research, are the authors cautious in their statements about the data?

7. How could equity theory be used to explain a student's motivation level in a specific class she's taking?

8. How could goal setting for individual employees be disruptive for an organization as a whole?

9. Why is employee participation in goal-setting activities so important to an organization's eventual success in reaching its goals?

10. What is the major difference between a Skinner and a Bandura analysis of motivation?

CASE FOR ANALYSIS

Jack Welch of General Electric:
A Neutron Bomb or a Motivator?

Jack Welch, chairman of General Electric (GE), has been referred to as "Neutron Jack." (When he enters a GE facility, the building remains standing, but the workers are wiped out.) Welch picked up the nickname by cutting more than 100,000 workers from GE's payroll in his first five years. He eliminated the jobs through layoffs, attrition, and the sale of businesses. He has divested 289 lackluster businesses such as consumer electronics. He bought companies worth $19 billion. He sold companies worth $10 billion. When Welch took over at age 45 in 1981, he was GE's youngest chairman. Back then, GE was referred to as a "GNP company," one whose growth and prosperity never exceeded that of the overall economy.

Welch set out to create a company that could outpace the economy and thrive even in the toughest times. He utterly transformed GE, reshaping the corporate culture to reflect his relentless energy and informal but rigorous style. Welch sorted operations according to a simple criterion: to keep from being sold or shuttered, each had to be number 1 or number 2 in its market. He grouped businesses that he said met the test into a number of groups: services, such as GE Credit Corp. and a unit that maintains nuclear power plants; technology products in high-growth markets, such as jet engines and plastics; and what Welch calls the core businesses. These are the classic big players in such mature industries as lightbulbs and electric motors. Currently, GE is a global market leader in 12 large-scale businesses.

Welch is a sensitive but no-nonsense man who views the world as competitively tough. He sees global markets coming to be dominated by a few powerful steamrollers like Philips, Siemens, and Toshiba. To compete, a firm like GE must be bold, free of bureaucratic red tape, and staffed by self-motivated, proud, and quick-moving managers and employees. People who don't personally know Welch may fear his blunt, somewhat abrasive style. But those who spend time around him tend to like his intelligence, humor, and openness.

GE can be enormously exciting for those in the right places or attuned to the Welch mentality. By all accounts, Welch has transformed the company's bureaucratic culture to an astonishing degree. In eliminating managerial layers, Welch moved authority for most decisions down to the operating division level. He promotes a feeling of what he calls ownership, urging managers to act like entrepreneurs instead of hired help. Welch says he also promotes free communication: "We are out to get a feeling and a spirit of total openness. That's alien to a manager of 25 or 30 years who got ahead by knowing a little bit more than the employee who works for him." Welch says he wants to instill in managers "the confidence to lead and the confidence to share."

Welch's emphasis on communication and camaraderie is demonstrated by the long hours put in by GE's corporate officers commenting on drafts of a statement of corporate values that Welch titled, "What We Want to Be." These values—such as breaking down boundaries within the company, sharing good practices, emphasizing ownership—are more than just paperwork, however, as managers at GE are evaluated using the "Welch matrix"—namely assessing the attainment of bottom-line results and the level of commitment to these company values. Greater weight is given to the values dimension, as these are difficult to teach and will ultimately produce the numbers desired.

Welch is not shy about expressing his opinions on how to manage and motivate people. Here are a few of his thoughts:

On being a tough manager:

"I got a raw deal with all those things about tough-guy Jack—fear, intimidation, guns and sticks and whips and chains. If you're mean, you don't belong at General Electric. Let me tell you why the name Neutron Jack is wrong. Competitiveness means taking action. Nuking somebody means you kill him. We start a renewal process. When people leave our company, we provide a soft landing. People who have been removed for not performing may be angry, but not one will say he wasn't treated with dignity. I don't think anyone would say he was treated unfairly, other than that bad management might have messed up the strategy. We can look ourselves in the mirror every morning and say we did what we could."

On anxiety among employees left at GE:

"If you're a middle manager who's not going anywhere, not trained in tomorrow's technology, it's a tough issue, tough all across America. If you look at what we did as a nation and what companies like GE did over the last 25 years, a lot of people didn't stay current as we went from electro-mechanical to electronic technology. A lot of methods changed, and a lot of people didn't change with them. If you're a middle manager in General Electric who is pretty well plateaued out, do you like what's happening to you? Probably you're concerned."

On the role of GE's top management:

"[Vice Chairman] Larry Bossidy knows GE Credit. He built it. I know the plastics business. [Vice Chairman] Ed Hood knows jet engines. After that, we start to get into very shallow water. But we know people. We know how to spot good ones more often than we spot bad ones—we don't bat 1.000—and we know how to allocate resources."

On freedom in the American system:

Welch believes that the U.S. system of free enterprise is an advantage that Americans have over the Japanese.

"It allows people like me to become chairman of GE in one generation; it allows the talented young employees in our company to move up fast. . . . The idea of liberation and improvement for our workforce is not enlightenment—it's a competitive necessity."

The need for leaders:

"Call people managers and they are going to start managing things, getting in the way. The job of a leader is to take the available resources—human and financial—and allocate them rigorously. Not to

spread them out evenly, like butter on bread. That's what bureaucrats do." ". . . You clearly want somebody who can articulate a vision. They have to have enormous energy and the incredible ability to energize others. If you can't energize others, you can't be a leader."

On self-confidence:

"Self-confidence is the fuel of productivity and creativity, decisiveness and speed."

Welch has served as the chief executive for GE since 1981. It not only has survived under Welch's leadership but is looking youthfully exuberant. In the 1990s, Welch has infused the company with a sense of entrepreneurship, and in doing so has become one of the country's most admired CEOs. The quality Welch seems to value most in people is self-confidence, and he works hard to inspire it in others. He's a believer that people must control their own destinies or others will.

Discussion Questions

1. Welch practices a hard-nosed management style. How can such a no-nonsense approach create a motivational atmosphere? Does Jack Welch use negative reinforcement, goal setting, or behavioral self-management? Or does he use a combination of techniques?

2. Jack Welch has set goals to be number one in various markets. Assume that it's both a difficult and an assigned goal. What does goal-setting research say about the impact of such goals on performance?

3. Why does Jack Welch value self-confidence so highly? Does his style of management inspire it in others?

4. What actions does Jack Welch take to encourage employee self-management?

Sources: John Huey and Geoffrey Colvin, "The Jack and Herb Show," *Fortune,* January 11, 1999, pp. 163–166; Thomas A. Stewart, "Who Will Run GE?" *Fortune,* January 11, 1999, pp. 26–27; John A. Byrne, "Jack," *Business Week,* June 8, 1998, pp. 91–108; Thomas O' Boyle, *At Any Cost: Jack Welch, General Electric, and the Pursuit of Profit* (New York: Kropf, 1998); Ram Charan, "The Rules Have Changed," *Fortune,* March 16, 1998, pp. 159–162.

Chapter 7

Rewarding Organizational Behavior

Learning Objectives

After completing Chapter 7, you should be able to:

Define
Intrinsic and extrinsic rewards.

Describe
The key components of the reward process.

Discuss
The interaction of intrinsic and extrinsic rewards.

Compare
The various types of nontraditional reward systems.

Identify
Various types of intrinsic and extrinsic rewards.

In the previous two chapters we discussed a variety of approaches used to explain a subject which is very important to most managers, motivation. In this chapter, we examine reward systems managers use to motivate employees. It focuses on various systems (their uses, types, and applications) used to reward employees. We begin by presenting a model of individual rewards and discuss the different types of rewards, the relationship between rewards and some key organizational variables, and five notable innovative reward systems.

Organizational Reward Systems

Numerous changes are taking place in how performance is evaluated and rewards are being distributed. Requests to eliminate piece rate incentive systems,[1] convert all reward systems to group-based approaches, and legislate how much executives can earn are being presented as universally perfect ways to address rewards. Although parts of each suggestion have some validity, such radical proposals are unlikely to influence the majority of managers. Instead of radical changes and across-the-board debunking, progressive approaches are likely to draw more attention. Pay systems based on competencies and contributions made, team-based incentives, and rewards focusing on improved results are becoming more widely considered and implemented systems. As American firms become more involved in global transactions, business pay and rewards will be more closely limited to overall unit and total company results.[2]

Instead of eliminating individual reward systems and accepting group-based reward systems, it's better to examine the positive and negative features of various reward systems.

A model of individual rewards

The main objectives of reward programs are (1) to attract qualified people to *join* the organization, (2) to *keep* employees coming to work, and (3) to *motivate* employees to achieve high levels of performance. A model illustrating how rewards fit into an

Figure 7–1

The Reward Process

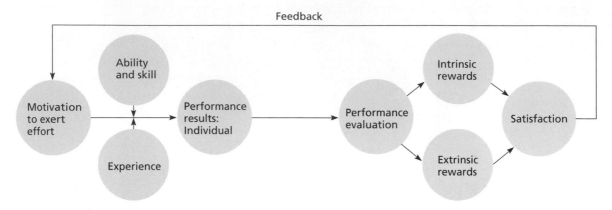

organization's overall policies and programs is useful to managers. Figure 7–1 presents a model that integrates motivation, performance, satisfaction, and rewards. It suggests that the motivation to exert effort isn't enough to cause acceptable performance. Performance results from a combination of the effort of an individual and that person's ability, skill, and experience. Management evaluates each individual's performance either formally or informally. As a result of the evaluation, it distributes extrinsic rewards. The rewards are evaluated by the individual. Individuals also receive or derive intrinsic rewards from the job. To the extent that rewards are adequate and equitable, the individual achieves a level of satisfaction.

A significant amount of research has been done on what determines whether individuals are satisfied with rewards. Edward Lawler has summarized five conclusions based on the behavioral science research literature:[3]

1. *Satisfaction with a reward is a function of both how much is received and how much the individual feels should be received.* This conclusion is based on the comparisons that people make. When individuals receive less than they feel they should, they're dissatisfied.

2. *An individual's feelings of satisfaction are influenced by comparisons with what happens to others.* People tend to compare their efforts, skills, seniority, and job performance with others'. They then attempt to compare rewards; that is, they compare their own inputs with others' inputs relative to the rewards received. Chapter 6 discussed this input–outcome comparison–when introducing the equity theory of motivation.

3. *Satisfaction is influenced by how satisfied employees are with both intrinsic and extrinsic rewards.* Intrinsic rewards are valued in and of themselves; they're related to performing the job. Examples would be feelings of accomplishment and achievement. Extrinsic rewards are external to the work itself; they are administered externally. Examples would be salary and wages, fringe benefits, and promotions. There's debate among researchers as to whether intrinsic or extrinsic rewards are more important in determining job satisfaction. Most studies suggest that both rewards are important.[4] One clear message from the research is that extrinsic and intrinsic rewards satisfy different needs.

4. *People differ in the rewards they desire and in the relative importance different rewards have for them.* In fact, preferred rewards vary at different points in a person's career, at different ages, and in various situations. The Close-Up "What Are Rewards in a Diverse Workforce?" points out that our cultural background may also influence how we respond to rewards.

5. *Some extrinsic rewards are satisfying because they lead to other rewards.* For example, a large office or an office that has carpeting or drapes is often considered a reward because it indicates the individual's status and power. Money is a reward that leads to such things as prestige, autonomy, security, and shelter.

The relationship between rewards and satisfaction isn't perfectly understood, nor is it static. It changes because people and the environment change. But there are important considerations that managers can use to develop and distribute rewards. First, rewards must be sufficient to satisfy basic human needs. Federal legislation, union contracts, and managerial fairness have provided at least minimal rewards in most work settings. Second, individuals tend to compare their rewards with those of others. People make comparisons regardless of the quantity of the rewards they receive. If inequities are perceived, dissatisfaction occurs. Finally, managers distributing rewards must recognize individual differences. Unless individual differences are considered, the reward process

---

C L O S E — U P

What Are Rewards in a Diverse Workforce?

With an increasingly diverse workforce, managers are finding that they may have to consider employees' cultural heritage when it is time to reward them. In fact, there are those who believe that many of our management and leadership models are culture-bound, that is, they do not consider the possibility that different personalities may flourish in different national cultures. But there are also those who believe that national cultural differences are overstated. Having said all of this, let us consider the following:

- Asians are often taught traditions such as enryo, which requires, among other things, modesty in the presence of one's superiors. Deference and reserved behavior are highly valued. As a result, they may feel reluctant to ask for rewards and may also be less likely to complain or ask questions. They may often not respond positively to recognition.

- The manager of a Native American was so impressed with his work that he honored him in a visible ceremony in front of his peers. The employee did not return to work for several days because he was very uncomfortable with public praise, especially in front of his Native American peers.

- Sales executives often accompany their praise of members of the sales force with well-intentioned touching

on the arms and pats on the back. Unfortunately, many Asian-Americans feel extremely uncomfortable with this behavior.

- A manager asked her primarily Filipino staff to let her know of any problems they were having with some new equipment that had recently been installed in the company's warehouse. The manager assumed that by delegating this responsibility to the group, positive feelings would result. Instead, the employees used every possible means including makeshift remedies to ensure that she never found out any problems existed. To the group, their inability to handle equipment problems meant losing face.

If managers consciously seek to learn about the cultural differences between groups, it seems that unintentional mistakes such as the above can be avoided. It is clear that managers have made mistakes in the past in their assumptions about males and females, minorities and whites, and old versus young. As our workforce continues to diversify, empathy and sensitivity to differences among people will be a critical managerial skill.

Sources: Martene Duchatelet, "Cultural Difference and Management/Leadership Models," *American Business Review,* June 1998, pp. 96–99; Livia Markoczy, "Us and Them," *Across the Board,* February 1998, pp. 96–99; Taylor Cos Jr., *Cultural Diversity in Organizations: Theory, Research, and Practice* (San Francisco: Berrett Koehler, 1993); and Kenneth N. Wexley and Stanley B. Silverman, *Working Scared: Achieving Success in Trying Times* (San Francisco: Jossey-Bass, 1993).

invariably is less effective than desired. Any reward package should (1) be sufficient to satisfy basic needs (e.g., food, shelter, clothing), (2) be considered equitable, and (3) be individually oriented.[5]

Extrinsic and Intrinsic Rewards

Extrinsic Rewards

Rewards external to the job, such as pay, promotion, or fringe benefits.

Intrinsic Rewards

Rewards that are part of the job itself: the responsibility, challenge, and feedback characteristics of the job.

Figure 7–1 classifies rewards into two broad categories: extrinsic and intrinsic. **Extrinsic rewards** are rewards external to the job, such as pay, promotion, or fringe benefits; **intrinsic rewards** are those that are part of the job itself, such as the responsibility, challenge, and feedback characteristics of the job. In either category, the first consideration is how the rewards are *valued* by employees. Individuals put forth little effort unless the reward has *value*. Both extrinsic and intrinsic rewards can have value.[6]

Extrinsic rewards

FINANCIAL REWARDS: SALARY AND WAGES   Money is a major extrinsic reward. It has been said that "although it is generally agreed that money is the major mechanism for rewarding and modifying behavior in industry . . . very little is known about how it works."[7] To really understand how money modifies behavior, the perceptions and preferences of the person being rewarded must be understood, which of course is a challenging task for managers. Success requires careful attention and observation of employees. In addition, managers must be trusted, so that workers freely communicate their feelings about financial rewards.

Unless employees see a connection between performance and merit increases, money isn't a powerful motivator. In some cases, a well-designed appraisal system can make the pay-performance connection clear to employees. This clarity doesn't just happen; managers must work hard at communicating the performance-financial reward connection.[8] Increasingly, critics charge that the pay-performance relationship should be strengthened for chief executives in large corporations and that *Fortune* 500 chief executive officers (CEOs) are grossly overpaid.

Executive compensation has become a controversial issue. Experts use different statistical techniques to illustrate which executive is the "best bargain" and who's the "worst buy."[9] Front-page stories contrasting million-dollar paychecks for executives and more layoffs for employees are painful and emotion laden.

Critics contend that American executives are paid too much and that their salaries aren't related to their companies' performance. This inequity is considered to be a reason why the United States is competitively being challenged. One study of corporate business units determined that a small difference in pay between lower level employees and upper echelon managers is associated with high product quality.[10] The researchers suggested that the smaller differential may have resulted in higher commitment to organizational goals.

The federal government is now reviewing laws to influence executives' pay.[11] The most controversial bills would limit the amount that an executive can be paid by capping it at some absolute level or at some multiple of what the lowest paid worker earns. The impact of legislation on executives' motivation to work hard, take risks, and even enter the profession needs to be considered by any politician introducing bills in Congress. Differences across jobs and industries also need to be cautiously considered before executive compensation becomes dictated by law.

FINANCIAL REWARDS: FRINGE BENEFITS   In the United States, organizations spend 35 to 40 percent of their total compensation amount on employee benefits. A recent Conference Board–Gallup Poll survey indicated that 74 percent of all workers in America say that employee benefits are crucial to job choice. If limited to only one benefit (beyond money), 64 percent say to provide them with health care.[12] In most cases, fringe benefits are primarily financial. But some (such as IBM's recreation program for employees and General Mills' picnic grounds) aren't entirely financial. A major financial fringe benefit in many organizations is the pension plan. Fringe benefits such as pension plans, health insurance, and vacations aren't usually contingent on employees' performance. In most cases, they're based on seniority or length of employment.

www.ibm.com

www.general-mills.com

INTERPERSONAL REWARDS   The manager has some power to distribute such **interpersonal rewards** as status and recognition. Managers and co-workers both play roles in granting job status. By assigning individuals to prestigious jobs, the manager can attempt to improve or remove a person's status. But if co-workers don't believe that an employee merits a particular job, status isn't likely to be enhanced. In some situations, by reviewing performance, managers can grant what they consider to be job changes that improve status.

Interpersonal Rewards

Extrinsic rewards such as receiving recognition or being able to interact socially on the job.

Much of what was just stated about status also applies to recognition. In a reward context, **recognition** refers to managerial acknowledgment of employee achievement that could result in improved status. Recognition from a manager could include public praise, expressions of a job well done, or special attention.[13] The extent to which recognition is motivating depends, as do most rewards, on its perceived value and on the connection that the individual sees between it and behavior. Examples of how performance is recognized at People's Bank, LifeScan, and Chrysler (Table 7–1) illustrate the vast array of recognition opportunities.

Recognition

Management's acknowledgment of work well done.

PROMOTIONS   For many employees, promotions don't happen often; some never experience even one in their careers. Managers making promotion reward decisions attempt to match the right persons with the jobs. Criteria often used to reach promotion decisions are performance and seniority. Performance, if it can be accurately assessed, is often given significant weight in promotion reward allocations.

www.lifescan.com

www.chrysler.com

Intrinsic rewards

COMPLETION   The ability to start and finish a project or job is important to some individuals. These people value *task completion*. The effect that completing a task has on them is a form of self-reward. Opportunities that allow such people to complete tasks can have a powerful motivating effect.

ACHIEVEMENT   Achievement is a self-administered reward derived from reaching a challenging goal. David C. McClelland has described individual differences in those striving for achievement.[14] Some seek challenging goals, while others seek moderate or low goals. In goal-setting programs, difficult goals may result in a higher level of individual performance than do moderate goals. Even in such programs, however, individual differences must be considered before reaching conclusions about the importance of achievement rewards.

AUTONOMY   Some people want jobs providing the right to make decisions; they want to operate without being closely supervised. A feeling of autonomy could result from the freedom to do what the employee considers best in a particular situation. In jobs that are highly structured and controlled by management, it's difficult to create tasks that lead to a feeling of autonomy.

Table 7–1

Recognition
Approaches

At People's Bank, Connecticut:
All award winners receive the following:

- Recognition gift.
- Newsletter announcement.
- Letter from the president.
- Managers' Meeting announcement.
- Letter for their personnel file.

In addition, Excellence and Quality Award winners get their photo and more detailed descriptions of their achievement in the employee newsletter.

At LifeScan, a Johnson & Johnson company:
What do I receive if I earn a Quality Excellence Award?
Achieving a significant improvement in quality is rewarding in itself—it means you've helped our products or services better meet our customers' requirements, and in the process made your job and your co-workers' more hassle-free.

In appreciation for your outstanding quality achievement, you'll receive a very special dinner for two at any of the Bay Area's finest restaurants, plus a sweater embroidered with the LifeScan quality logo. In addition, your photo will appear on *LifeScan's Quality Wall of Fame* along with photos of other award recipients.

Who will present the Quality Excellence Award? Where will it be presented?
Your Quality Excellence Award will be presented by one of LifeScan's officers at a Quarterly Employee Meeting. Your achievement will also be featured in a *LifeScan Monitor* article.

At Chrysler Corporation:
Chairman's Award
To recognize the *most outstanding* Divisional achievements, the Chairman's Award (trophy) will be presented to each recipient by the chairman of Chrysler Corporation.

- For achievements involving two or more people, the Chairman's Award will be granted in the name of the team, each team member and the associated organization(s) on a team version of the award. In the case of cross-functional teams, each organization will receive a copy of the team award. If selected, the team will be asked to designate a representative to accept the award at the ceremony. Chairman's Awards will be presented at a quarterly management meeting or other suitable occasion.

Other recognition for award recipients will include:

- A personal letter of congratulations, signed by the chairman of Chrysler Corporation, with a copy to the Division Quality Council chairman and/or operating unit head, and recipient's manager.
- When the Chairman's Award is granted in the name of a team, each team member will receive the personal letter of congratulations mounted on a special plaque, as a memento of their achievement.
- Recognition through publication of an article and recipient/group photograph in the *Chrysler Times*.
- Recognition sponsored by the recipient's local organization such as newsletters and displays featuring the recipient's photograph, nature of achievement, a copy of the chairman's congratulatory letter, and so on.

Source: Excerpted and adapted from company brochures.

PERSONAL GROWTH   The personal growth of any individual is unique. Individuals experiencing such growth can sense their development and see how their capabilities are being expanded. By expanding their capabilities, employees can maximize or at least satisfy skill potential. Some become dissatisfied with their jobs and organizations if not allowed or encouraged to develop their skills.

The rewards included in this section are distributed or created by managers, work groups, or individuals. Table 7–2 summarizes the rewards we've discussed. As the table indicates, managers can play either a direct or an indirect role in developing and administering rewards.

The interaction of intrinsic and extrinsic rewards

The general assumption has been that intrinsic and extrinsic rewards have an independent and additive influence on motivation. That is, motivation is determined by the sum of the person's intrinsic and extrinsic sources of motivation.[15] This straightforward assumption has been questioned by several researchers. Some have suggested that in situations in which individuals are experiencing a high level of intrinsic rewards, the addition of extrinsic rewards for good performance may cause a decrease in motivation.[16] Basically, the person receiving self-administered feelings of satisfaction is performing

TYPE	Source			Table 7–2
	MANAGER	**GROUP**	**INDIVIDUAL**	Types and Sources of Selected Extrinsic and Intrinsic Rewards
Extrinsic				
Financial				
Salary and wages	D			
Fringe benefits	D			
Interpersonal	D	D		
Promotion	D			
Intrinsic				
Completion	I		D	
Achievement	I		D	
Autonomy	I		D	
Personal growth	I		D	

Note: D = Direct source of the reward.
    I = Indirect source of the reward.

because of intrinsic rewards. Once extrinsic rewards are added, feelings of satisfaction change because performance is now thought to be due to the extrinsic rewards. The addition of extrinsic rewards tends to reduce the extent to which the individual experiences self-administered intrinsic rewards.[17]

The argument concerning extrinsic rewards' potential negative effects has stimulated a number of research studies. Unfortunately, these studies report contradictory results. Some researchers report a reduction in intrinsic rewards following the addition of extrinsic rewards for an activity;[18] others have failed to observe such an effect.[19] A review of the literature found that 14 of 24 studies supported the theory that extrinsic rewards reduce intrinsic motivation;[20] 10 didn't support it. Of the 24 studies reviewed, only two used actual employees as subjects. All of the other studies used college students or grade school students. In studies of telephone operators and clerical employees, the theory wasn't supported.[21] Managers need to be aware that no scientifically based and reported study substantiates that extrinsic rewards have a negative effect on intrinsic motivation.

Rewards, turnover, and absenteeism

Managers may assume that low turnover is a mark of an effective organization. However, some organizations would benefit if disruptive and low performers quit.[22] Thus, the issue of turnover needs to focus on *who* is leaving as well as on frequency.

Ideally, if managers could develop reward systems that retained the best performers and caused poor performers to leave, the overall effectiveness of an organization would improve.[23] To approach this ideal state, an equitable and favorably compared reward system must exist. The feelings of *equity* and *favorable comparison* have an external orientation. That is, the equity of rewards and favorableness involve comparisons with external parties. This orientation is used because quitting most often means that a person leaves one organization for an alternative elsewhere.

No perfect means exist for retaining high performers. A reward system based on **merit ratings** should encourage most better performers to remain with the organization. Also, the reward system needs some differential that discriminates between high and low performers. High performers must receive significantly more extrinsic and intrinsic rewards than low performers.[24]

Merit Rating

A formal rating system applied to employees.

Absenteeism, no matter for what reason, is a costly and disruptive problem facing managers.[25] It's costly because it reduces output and disruptive because it requires that schedules and programs be modified. Absenteeism in the United States is estimated to result in the loss of over 365 million workdays per year, costing over $40 billion per year.[26] Employees go to work because they're motivated to do so; the level of motivation remains high if an individual feels that attendance leads to more valued rewards and fewer negative consequences than alternative behaviors.

Managers appear to have some influence over attendance behavior. They have the ability to punish, establish bonus systems, and allow employee participation in developing plans. Whether these or other approaches reduce absenteeism is determined by the value of the rewards perceived by employees, the amount of the rewards, and whether employees perceive a relationship between attendance and rewards. These same characteristics appear every time we analyze the effects of rewards on organizational behavior.

Rewards and job performance

Researchers and managers agree that extrinsic and intrinsic rewards can be used to motivate job performance. It's also clear that certain conditions must exist if rewards are to actually motivate: the rewards must be *valued* by the person, and they must be related to a specific level of job performance.

Chapter 6 presented expectancy motivation theory. According to that theory, people associate every behavior with certain outcomes or rewards or punishments. In other words, an assembly-line worker may believe that by behaving in a certain way she'll get certain things. This is a description of the *performance-outcome expectancy.* On one hand, another worker may expect that a steady performance of 10 units a day will eventually result in a transfer to a more challenging job. On the other hand, a worker may expect that a steady performance of 10 units a day will result in his being considered a rate buster by co-workers.

Each outcome has a *valence,* or value, to the person. Because each person has different needs and perceptions, outcomes such as pay, a promotion, a reprimand, or a better job have different values for different people. Thus, in considering which rewards to use, a manager has to be astute in considering individual differences. If valued rewards are used to motivate, they can result in the exertion of effort to achieve high levels of performance.

Rewards and organizational commitment

Commitment

A sense of identification, loyalty, and involvement expressed by an employee toward the organization or unit of the organization.

There's little research on the relationship between rewards and organizational commitment.[27] **Commitment** to an organization involves three attitudes: (1) a sense of identification with the organization's goals, (2) a feeling of involvement in organizational duties, and (3) a feeling of loyalty for the organization.[28] Research evidence indicates that the absence of commitment can reduce organizational effectiveness.[29] Committed people are less likely to quit and accept other jobs. Thus, costs of high turnover aren't incurred. In addition, committed and highly skilled employees require less supervision. Close supervision and a rigid monitoring control process are time-consuming and costly. Furthermore, a committed employee perceives the value and importance of integrating individual and organizational goals. The employee thinks of his goals and the organization's goals in personal terms.

Intrinsic rewards are important for developing organizational commitment. Organizations able to meet employees' needs by providing achievement opportunities and by recognizing achievement when it occurs have a significant impact on commitment.[30]

Thus, managers need to develop intrinsic reward systems that focus on personal importance or self-esteem to integrate individual and organizational goals and to design challenging jobs.

Nontraditional Reward Systems

The typical list of rewards that managers can and do distribute in organizations has been discussed. We all know that pay, fringe benefits, and opportunities to achieve challenging goals are considered rewards by most people. It's also generally accepted that rewards are administered by managers through such processes as reinforcement, modeling, and expectancies. What are some newer and innovative, yet largely untested, reward programs that some managers are experimenting with? Four different reward approaches that aren't widely tested are cafeteria-style fringe benefits, banking time off, skill-based pay, and gainsharing. Table 7–3 summarizes their strengths and weaknesses.

Cafeteria-style fringe benefits

In a cafeteria-style plan, management establishes a menu and places an upper limit on how much the organization is willing to spend on fringe benefits. Employees then decide how they would like to receive the total fringe benefit amount. Employees develop individualized, personally attractive fringe benefit packages. Some employees take all of the fringes in cash; others purchase special medical protection plans. **Cafeteria-style fringe benefits** provide individuals with the benefits they prefer rather than the benefits that someone else establishes for them.

Cafeteria-Style Fringe Benefits

Each employee is allowed to develop and allocate a personally attractive fringe benefits package. The employee is informed of the total fringe benefits allowed and is allowed to distribute the benefits according to his preferences.

Table 7–3   Four Reward Approaches: A Summary and Comparison

REWARD APPROACH	MAJOR STRENGTHS	MAJOR WEAKNESSES	RESEARCH SUPPORT
Cafeteria-style fringe benefits	Since employees have different desires and needs, programs can be tailored to fit individuals.	Administration can become complex and costly. The more employees involved, the more difficult it is to efficiently operate the approach.	Limited, since only a few programs have been scientifically examined.
Banking time off	Can be integrated with performance in that time-off credits can be made contingent on performance achievements.	Organization needs a valid, reliable, and equitable performance appraisal program.	Extremely limited.
Skill-based pay	Employees must clearly demonstrate skill before receiving pay increases.	Training costs to upgrade employee skills are higher than under conventional pay systems. Labor costs increase if employees learn many skills. Employees may "top out."	Very limited, with no direct skill-based versus conventional pay compensation studies available.
Gainsharing	Can enhance teamwork. Employees focus on objectives, learn more about the organization, and may be more productive.	If plans focus only on productivity, employees may ignore other important objectives.	Limited, but a distinct increase in studies is being reported.

Using a cafeteria-style plan offers some distinct advantages. First, it allows employees to play an active rather than a passive role in deciding on the allocation of fringe benefits. Second, employees receive the benefits of greatest personal value to them. This provides many people with a psychologically uplifting feeling. Third, the cafeteria-style plan makes the economic value of fringe benefits obvious to each employee. In many situations, employees grossly underestimate the value of the fringe benefits their employers provide.

Some administrative problems are associated with cafeteria plans.[31] Because of employees' different preferences, records become more complicated. For a large organization with a cafeteria plan, a computer system is almost essential to do the record-keeping. Another problem involves group insurance premium rates. Most life and medical insurance premiums are based on the number of employees participating. It's difficult to predict the participation level under a cafeteria plan.

www.trw.com

TRW Corporation placed approximately 12,000 employees on a cafeteria plan. It allows employees to rearrange and redistribute their fringe benefit packages every year. Over 80 percent of the TRW participants have changed their benefit packages since the plan was initiated.[32]

Banking time off

Time off from work is attractive to most people. In essence, most companies have a time-off system built into their vacation programs. Employees receive different amounts of time off, based on the years they've worked for the organization. **Banking time off,** an extension of such a time-off reward, is the practice of granting time off for such behaviors as good performance or attendance. That is, a bank of time-off credits could be built up contingent on performance.

Banking Time Off

A reward practice of allowing employees to build up time-off credits for such behaviors as good performance or attendance.

Today, some organizations are selecting their best performers to attend educational and training programs. One company in Houston selects the best performers and provides them with an opportunity to attend a preferred executive educational program. There is excess demand to attend the program and having the time available allows the selected individuals to attend. Being eligible is largely contingent on the individual's performance record. Those finally selected are given two Fridays off a month to attend classes.

Skill-based pay

www.pg.com

www.polaroid .com

A study by the American Compensation Association found that 33 percent of respondents have skill-based pay systems. Procter & Gamble has implemented such plans in 30 plants, and Polaroid is attempting to become the first organization to pay virtually all employees through skill-based plans.[33]

Skill-Based Pay

Wages paid at a rate calculated and based on the skills employees possess, display, and develop in performing their jobs.

In traditional compensation systems, characteristics of the job performed (e.g., its difficulty and complexity) and local market rates determine an employee's pay rate and range. But in **skill-based pay** programs, the employee's pay depends not on the job, but on her level and number of job-related skills. The skill-based approach attempts to take into account efficiency, or the value added by the worker's performance.[34]

In skill-based programs, employees work as members of semiautonomous teams. When hired, an employee is paid a starting rate and receives pay increases as she learns new skills required by the team. Once an employee learns all of the team skills, opportunities are provided to learn skills outside the unit and throughout the organization. Pay increases accompany each new set of skills the employee masters. In skill-based programs that don't utilize teams, an employee moves up one pay grade for each job learned, and jobs can be learned in any sequence. Often, pay raises are the same size regardless of the content of jobs learned.[35]

Skill-based pay programs afford several benefits. The key advantage is a more highly skilled and flexible workforce. Productivity can increase, and supervisory costs are often reduced. Employees are more motivated to gain and use their skills; they often perceive their pay as being more equitable; and they have a better understanding of how their jobs fit into the organization.[36] The Close-Up on this page outlines some additional benefits of skill-based pay programs.

Pay levels and training costs, however, often increase. Employees can be frustrated when no openings are available in job areas for which they're newly trained. And a long-term problem may arise if employees have "topped out"—they've learned all the skills needed by the organization and so have nowhere to go. Dissatisfaction and turnover may result.[37] Overall, a careful cost-benefit analysis should be conducted before implementing a skill-based pay program.

Gainsharing

Gainsharing is a formula-based group incentive plan in which employees share in an organization's financial gain from its improved performance.[38] Traditional forms of gainsharing are the Scanlon Plan, Rucker Plan®, and Improshare®. These plans are differentiated by their measures as discussed in Table 7–4.

Gainsharing is the fastest growing incentive program in the United States, partly because of a widespread belief that gainsharing spurs motivation and teamwork. About 26 percent of U.S. companies utilize the program, with 75 percent of the plans installed since 1980.[39]

Carrier (the heating and air-conditioning equipment manufacturer and a subsidiary of United Technologies) provides an example of how gainsharing works. Carrier set as a benchmark the 1.8 hours that production employees take to make a finished product. When employees beat this benchmark with acceptable-quality products, the labor

Gainsharing

A formula-based group incentive plan in which employees share in an organization's financial gain from improved performance.

 **www.Carrier. com**

Skill-Based Pay Programs Can Increase Learning

As health care and other service industries realize the benefits and necessity of continuous learning, the challenge for much of the workforce is "how to bring it about." More and more of these types of organizations are finding that skill-based pay is an excellent way to challenge and motivate employees to increase their knowledge. In fact, some recent empirical research conducted in a plant found that over the three-year period of the study, greater productivity, lower labor costs, and favorable quality outcomes resulted from a skill-based pay program.

Many service industries rely heavily on relatively low-paid employees to provide customers, clients, and patients critical services. Hotels and health care, for example, rely heavily on these employees and they directly impact customer satisfaction and repeat business. Embassy Suites, a subsidiary of Holiday Corporation, uses a skill-based pay program that provides tremendous opportunities for advance-

ment. The program encourages employees to learn sequentially the 10 basic jobs of the hotel, from bartender to handling the front desk to cooking.

After three months in one of the jobs, an employee can take a written test and perform a work sample. If co-workers approve, the employee is "certified." A certified employee then receives a pay increase and the opportunity to train for another certification and another increase in pay.

It appears that management is satisfied with the results. The hotel chain continuously rates at or near the top in customer satisfaction, and more than half of the people in the organization's management training program began in the skill-based pay program.

Sources: Genevieve Capowski, "HR View Online," *HR Focus,* June 1998, pp. 2; Brian Murry and Barry Gerhart, "An Empirical Analysis of a Skill-Based Pay Program and Plant Performance Outcomes," *Academy of Management Journal,* February 1998, pp. 68–78; and J. T. Rich, "Focus on the Customer," *Boardroom Reports,* January 15, 1993, p. 9.

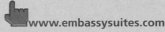 **www.embassysuites.com**

Table 7–4 Gainsharing Models	$\dfrac{(\$)(\text{Labor costs})}{(\$)(\text{Revenue})}$	**Scanlon Plan.** Scanlon formulas measure the labor costs required to produce services in a given base period; that is, labor costs are compared with sales volume. Assume, for example, that it requires \$500,000 in labor costs to generate \$1 million in sales. This .50 ratio (500,000/1,000,000) becomes the standard for determining incentive awards. In future periods, if labor costs are less than 50% of sales, savings are allocated among employees and the organization on the basis of a preestablished formula.
	$\dfrac{(\$)(\text{Labor Costs})}{(\$)(\text{Adj. revenue})}$	**Rucker Plan®.** Rucker plans also use labor costs as the numerator. The Rucker Plan, however, attempts to adjust for the effects of inflation by subtracting from sales the costs associated with materials and supplies. The assumption is that in this way inflationary effects are roughly accounted for because increased sales value of goods is offset by the increased material and supply costs. As with the Scanlon plan, any improvements in the ratio are subsequently used to calculate the incentive award.
	$\dfrac{(\text{Earned hours})}{(\text{Available hours})}$	**Improshare®.** This approach establishes a standard that identifies the expected hours required to produce an acceptable level of output. The standard is derived either from a time and motion study and/or from an analysis of the group's historical experience. Any savings resulting from an increase in output in fewer than expected hours are shared between the organization and the employee group on the basis of a preestablished formula. **Profit sharing.** A profit-sharing plan allows employees to participate in the organization's profits. A qualified plan must provide a definite predetermined formula for allocating the contributions made to the plan among the participants and for distributing the funds accumulated under the plan after a fixed number of years, after the attainment of a stated age, or upon the prior occurrence of some event, such as layoff, disability, retirement, or severance of employment.

Source: Adapted from David Beck, "Implementing a Gainsharing Plan: What Companies Need to Know," *Compensation & Benefits Review,* January–February 1992, p. 22.

savings are split 50-50 between the subsidiary and every employee in the plant, from machinists to secretaries to managers. To keep employees informed, plant productivity information is posted daily on the plant bulletin boards, and employees are encouraged to provide timesaving ideas. In 1988, Carrier's 2,500 employees received over \$3 million in bonus pay for being over 25 percent more productive than the 1986 benchmark.[40]

Although many observers believe that an effective gainsharing program can boost productivity, cut absenteeism and turnover, and improve product quality, some critics assert that these effects aren't long lasting and that research on results is still limited. But most agree that gainsharing is most effective in business units with fewer than 500 employees and when rewards are based on results that employees can directly affect.[41]

The increased interest and attention paid to group incentive plans is likely to continue. Team performance, evaluation, and reward systems will grow in importance as a shifting away from predominately individually based rewards to a mix of individual and group reward systems gains momentum.[42] Since people are being encouraged, directed, and motivated to work more closely together, reward systems must keep pace.[43] The strict individual-based systems don't encourage teamwork.

At Johnsonville Foods in Sheboygan Falls, Wisconsin, the 600-member workforce is divided into 14 cross-functional teams. Employees receive base pay according to the market value of their jobs. When a team member believes she's ready to receive a salary increase, a request to peers is made. Peers decide whether an employee has mastered the skills needed to contribute more. If peers answer yes, a raise is received. In addition to base pay, employees are eligible for individual and/or team bonuses based on performance. Only if the entire team is profitable and adds value will its members receive a bonus.

At Eaton Corporation, team members study daily sales results. Money saved for Eaton is shared by all team members.[44] Understanding sales, costs, and profitability helps Eaton team members earn more pay. The team bonus approach has caught on as teams look for bottlenecks and ways to become more efficient and attack waste. A sharing of financial data with management helps each Eaton team study its performance. Individuals can also earn bonuses for perfect attendance and skill improvement.

The link between the performance evaluation system and reward distribution was shown in Figure 7–1. The discussion of this and other linkages in the reward process suggests the complexity of using rewards to motivate better performance. Managers need to use judgment, diagnosis, and the resources available to reward their subordinates individually or as part of a team. Administering rewards is perhaps one of the most challenging and frustrating tasks that managers around the world must perform.

Summary of Key Points

* Reward systems seek to attract people to join the organization, to keep them coming to work, and to motivate them to perform at high levels.

* Organizations typically provide two types of rewards. *Extrinsic* rewards are those external to the job, such as promotions, fringe benefits, and pay. *Intrinsic* rewards are associated with doing the job. They include responsibility, challenge, and meaningful work.

* An individual's satisfaction with a reward is influenced by: how much is received and how much the person feels should be received; comparisons with what happens to

others; how satisfied the person is with both intrinsic and extrinsic rewards; the relative importance of different rewards; and whether the reward leads to other rewards.

* If effectively used, rewards can affect such individual behaviors as turnover, absenteeism, performance, and commitment. Research evidence showing how rewards influence these behaviors is becoming increasingly available.

* Nontraditional reward strategies include cafeteria-style fringe benefits, banking time off, skill-based pay, and gainsharing. These nontraditional reward systems each have strengths and weaknesses and are currently being used in many organizations.

Discussion and Review Questions

1. Explain why it would be difficult to conclude that perfectly acceptable skill-based pay systems can be developed for engineers, teachers, and machinists.

2. Why is it exceptionally difficult to distribute rewards based on merit?

3. Discuss the grade you receive in this class in terms of the model of the reward process presented in Figure 7–1.

4. Are there any intrinsic rewards for students? Discuss any that you believe apply to you.

5. If equity and favorable comparisons are so important in reward systems, how can an organization develop a program generally viewed as equitable and favorable?

6. What is your opinion about the financial rewards received by professional athletes?

7. Of the four nontraditional reward systems described in the chapter, which system in your opinion would be the most challenging to successfully implement and maintain? Explain.

8. What problems or concerns, if any, do you have about legislation that would cap the amount executives could earn?

C A S E   F O R   A N A L Y S I S

The Windsor Account

Sarah Curtis had just finished addressing the executive committee of Windsor Bank concerning the Windsor Account, a major new product that has caused the bank a great deal of trouble since it was introduced in 1994. Sarah had called the meeting this morning to discuss with the group something she had learned yesterday. By now all of the members of the committee had returned to their offices to think about what she had asked them to do for their next meeting. She leaned back in her chair and began to review the short and troubled history of the product.

Background

Sarah Curtis is Executive Vice President of Retail Banking for Windsor Bank. She is in charge of all of the retail banking branch offices and all activities directed at the retail customer. The Windsor Account is the bank's first attempt at what is known as *service packaging*. A package product combines several products (checking account, debit card, credit card, traveler's checks, etc.) into one product which is sold to the customer for a single fee per month. An advantage for the customer is that it combines several widely used products together for a single fee with a single statement. An advantage for the bank is that it allows them to bundle several services under one convenient brand name, in this case the Windsor Account, and hopefully discourages customers from splintering their business among various suppliers. A brief history of the Windsor Account begins with its launch in 1994.

The launch of 1994

The Windsor Account was developed during 1992 and 1993. The bank's executive committee was extremely careful to ensure that all the steps were taken to increase the probability of success. Customer research was undertaken before decisions were made regarding what specific services should be included in the account and the appropriate price and name for the account.

All decisions regarding the Windsor Account were made by the middle of 1993. To ensure sound implementation of the strategy, Sarah Curtis wanted to be sure that all of the bank's customer service representatives were properly trained and motivated to sell the account to bank customers. Thus, the last six months of 1993 were devoted to an intensive sales training program and the design of an incentive program for the bank's 125 customer service representatives.

The Windsor Account was launched with great expectations during the first quarter of 1994. After three months, results were dismal. The bank's executive committee was stumped as to what might have gone wrong. In mid-year 1994, a consulting firm was retained to salvage the Windsor Account.

The relaunch of 1995

After studying the problem for several weeks, the consultants reported to the bank's executive committee that the problem appeared to be in the pricing of the account. The consultants believed that price-conscious customers saw little advantage in purchasing the service bundle. They recommended that management either unbundle the account which would, in effect, mean eliminating the Windsor Account from the bank's product line, or reprice the product to appeal to the price-conscious shopper. After some deliberation, management elected to reprice the product. Believing that the product had been poorly priced, they relaunched the Windsor Account during the first quarter of 1995 with an extensive and expensive advertising and direct mail campaign. Results were worse this time.

The aftermath

Yesterday afternoon Sarah Curtis sat in her office thinking about the Windsor Account. It appeared that all the time and money that had been devoted to the product would be lost. She did not know what to do. She decided to leave the office early and spend the remainder of the afternoon with her family.

On the way out of the bank, she passed through the main lobby and saw Debbie Sherman, the customer service representative for the main office. Sarah decided to stop and chat with her about the Windsor Account. Perhaps she could provide some insight into where the product needed to be fixed, if that was even possible. She asked Debbie, "What do you think is the biggest problem with selling the Windsor Account? Is it the name, the price, the components of the package?" Debbie thought for a moment and said, "Mrs. Curtis, I really think the Windsor Account is a great product. It is an easy sell because customers see value in the product. In fact, the original higher price was not, in my opinion, a barrier to purchase. The problem as I see it has nothing to do with the product. It has to do with the incentive system. I believe there are a large number of customer service representatives who view the incentive program as making no sense. As you know, we receive more money for opening a new account than for converting an existing customer to the Windsor Account. Now I'm sure the emphasis on getting new customers is a good one, but selling a new customer is much easier than the work involved in converting an existing customer. Account conversions are a great deal of paperwork. So I believe since the incentive is higher to do what is easier, most customer service representatives are concentrating all of their sales efforts on new customers, which was what was stressed in all of our sales training, and not bothering with account conversions."

Curtis was stunned. She returned to her office and phoned Steve Wiley, the bank's marketing director. She asked him to check the numbers. Within five minutes Wiley phoned with the bad news. Since the Windsor Account has been launched in 1994, almost four of every five sales were to customers new to the bank. Only one in five was an account conversion by an existing customer. Sarah called an executive committee meeting for this morning to discuss the Windsor Account.

At the meeting this morning Sarah concluded her remarks by saying, "I just don't understand how we let this happen. All of the money we have invested and time we have lost to our competition. And it turns out that we could have fixed the problem at no cost and no loss of time. In fact, we could have avoided the entire mess in the first place. But the truth is, in hindsight, how could we have known? I would like us to learn a lesson from this ordeal, but I can't figure out what it is. By our regular meeting on Friday, let's each come up with a lesson we can share with the rest of the group."

Discussion Questions

1. List as many management lessons as you can think of that you would provide to the executive committee at Windsor Bank.

2. Review the case using the model presented in Figure 7–1. How could it be used to help the executive committee at Windsor Bank?

EXPERIENTIAL EXERCISE

Making Choices about Rewards

Objectives

1. To illustrate individual differences in reward preferences.

2. To emphasize that both extrinsic and intrinsic rewards are considered important.

3. To enable people to explore the reasons for the reward preferences of others.

Related Topics

Since rewards are so pervasive in organizational settings, they tend to be linked to merit, seniority, and attendance. In fact, they're so related to organizational behavior that few issues of work life can be discussed without mentioning rewards.

Starting the Exercise

After reviewing Exhibit 1, individuals should work alone to establish their own lists of reward preferences. The instructor should set up groups of four to six students to examine individual preferences and complete the exercise.

The Facts

It's possible to develop an endless list of on-the-job rewards. Exhibit 1 identifies some rewards that could be available to employees.

Completing the Exercise

Phase I: 25 minutes.

1. Using Exhibit 1, each individual should make lists of extrinsic and intrinsic rewards.

2. Each person should then rank the items on her list from the most important to least important.

3. From the two lists, rank the eight most important rewards. How many are extrinsic, and how many are intrinsic?

Phase II: 30 minutes.

1. The instructor sets up groups of four to six individuals.

2. The individual lists in which the extrinsic and intrinsic categories were developed should be discussed within the groups.

3. The final rank orders of the eight most important rewards decided on within the groups should be placed on a board or chart at the front of the room.

4. Rankings should be discussed within the groups. Which major differences between individual-generated and group-generated lists were found?

Exhibit 1   Some Possible Rewards for Employees

Company picnics	Smile from manager	Participation in decisions
Watches	Feedback on performance	Stock options
Trophies	Feedback on career progress	Vacation trips for excellent performance
Piped-in music	Larger office	Manager asking for advice
Job challenge	Most prestigious job	Informal leader asking for advice
Achievement opportunity	More job involvement	Office with a window
Vacation	Use of company recreational facilities	The privilege of completing a job from start to finish
Autonomy	Bonus	Paid sabbatical
Pay increase	Paid health insurance	Financial counseling
Recognition	Health club membership	College tuition grants
Company car	Day care services	
Entertainment expense account		

E X P E R I E N T I A L   E X E R C I S E

Valuing Diversity

The modern workplace is fast becoming a microcosm of the American population. Minority groups that previously have not had access to management and leadership positions in organizations are now a significant proportion of the overall workforce. Organizations must be able to take advantage of this broader talent pool, ensuring that all people have the opportunity to contribute to the extent of their potential.

Not all organizations have evolved to the point where they are able to see beyond a person's gender or ethnic status and to appreciate people for what they are able to contribute. Eliminating barriers to merit-based advancement is a central part of valuing diversity in the modern workplace.

Purposes

To heighten your awareness of the issues that companies are facing as the workplace becomes more diverse and to help you understand the issues faced by individuals who work there.

Procedure

In this exercise, you will identify and interview a corporate diversity officer, and you will identify and interview a person employed in a business or nonprofit organization whose ethnic or gender status differs from your own to learn about the issues he or she faces in the workplace.

1. *Identify and interview a corporate diversity officer:* Many organizations today have designated a staff position to handle diversity issues for the firm. You should identify a person who serves this function in a medium to large organization. Contact this person and arrange a one-hour information interview. Besides developing your own set of questions for the diversity officer, your interview should cover the following issues:
   - What type of diversity training program does the company have?
   - What are the major diversity issues the company faces?
   - What are the major problems faced by women and minorities in the organization?
   - Does the company recruit in a way that increases its diversity?
   - Does the company have an active affirmative action program?

2. *Identify and interview a person of different gender or ethnicity.* Identify and interview a person of managerial rank or better in a medium to large company who is different in gender or ethnicity from you. This person should *not* be directly involved in the organization's diversity function and preferably should be in a line position. Arrange a one-hour information interview with this person to learn more about the challenges he

or she perceives as directly related to his or her gender or ethnicity. This could be a sensitive issue for some people, so you may have to guarantee anonymity to the person you are interviewing. What you want to learn from this interview is how the individual believes her or his career has been affected because of gender or ethnicity. Several issues to explore include:

- Has the person ever been passed up for career advancement based on gender or ethnic status?
- Has the person ever felt that he or she has been given special consideration based on gender or ethnic status?
- What kinds of organizational barriers does the person feel as a function of her or his gender or ethnic status?

- What strategies does the person use to overcome these barriers?

3. *Report your findings to the class:* After conducting your two informal interviews, be prepared to discuss your findings with the class. You should be able to summarize the types of diversity training programs the organization you identified is using, and describe the effect of this training on the organization. You should also be able to summarize your interview with the individual of different gender or ethnic status. What are the key issues as this person sees them? Has this person benefited from or been harmed by corporate diversity programs?

Tellabs, Inc.: Motivating the Organization

It's important to understand the reasons why effective managers must be concerned with employee motivation. After identifying some of the factors contributing to motivation, this video looks at how Tellabs, Inc., has successfully applied motivation theory.

Tellabs is based in the Chicago area, but is internationally known for its telecommunications products and services. However, recently the company gained fame when its stock increased 1,683 percent over a five-year period, making Tellabs the best performing stock at that time on the New York Stock Exchange, the American Stock Exchange and Nasdaq. Tellabs was founded in 1975 by a group of engineers brainstorming at a kitchen table, and grew from 20 employees with annual sales of $312,000 to 2,600 employees with annual sales of $494 million in 1994. Tellabs currently designs, manufactures, markets, and services voice and data transport and network access systems.

One of the principal reasons for Tellabs' remarkable success has been its ability to motivate its workforce. In simple terms, employee motivation refers to an employee's willingness to perform in his or her job. Effective managers must be concerned with motivating employees toward common goals that will improve the success of the company. At Tellabs, a motivated workforce has enhanced the quality of its products and services.

Tellabs' manager of quality, Joe Taylor, explains what's behind the company's motivated workers: "In the past 10 years we've found that to improve our quality we had to invest in our employees through training programs. Specifically, they have the tools and the resources now to make a difference within our processes in the factory and provide us with process improvements."

A motivated workforce contributes to increased quality in goods and services, greater efficiency in work processes, and improved customer service. Grace Pastiak said, "When I look at the improvements that Tellabs has made since implementing just-in-time and Total Quality Commitment, by far the biggest gain has been exciting employees to do their best and giving them the opportunity to implement their own ideas."

At its core, motivation results from an individual's desire to satisfy personal needs or goals. Every person has a set of needs or goals that influences his or her behavior. Abraham Maslow postulated that needs can be placed in a hierarchy and that as each need level in the hierarchy is satisfied, the person will concentrate on meeting needs at the next level.

Frederick Herzberg, conducted a study in the 1960s that concluded that factors pertaining to the work itself, such as achievement, recognition, and responsibility, tended to actually motivate employees. Other factors, such as supervision, pay, and company policies, might increase job satisfaction, but not necessarily employee motivation.

A third approach to motivation, developed by Douglas McGregor, involves two opposing theories about the nature of human behavior. Theory X holds that some employees are lazy or unwilling to work unless motivated by negative factors such as threats and constant supervision. Theory Y holds that employees want to work and do a good job and are motivated best by incentives, responsibility, and ownership of their work.

Maslow's hierarchy, Herzberg's factors, and McGregor's theories suggest that it's in a company's best interest to offer employees adequate rewards and to appeal to their pride of workmanship. At Tellabs, many employees say that the entrepreneurial atmosphere nurtured by managers makes them feel good about themselves. So Tellabs clearly takes a Theory Y approach.

Effective managers help create a work environment that encourages, supports, and sustains improvement in work performance. At Tellabs, managers have implemented job rotation systems and a cadre of high performance teams to help enrich jobs and create an innovative working environment. Another innovation at Tellabs to ensure a high level of employee motivation is high performance teams.

Some companies may use a combination of motivation theories. In 1992, Tellabs presented its corporate goals, known as Strategic Initiatives, to its employees.

The corporate mission statement emphasized the company's goals of quality, customer satisfaction, profits, and growth, its people, and its corporate integrity.

Tellabs' total compensation plan includes an Employee Stock Option Plan and retirement investments, such as 401(k). Also, employees receive an annual bonus based on the company's productivity.

At Tellabs, employee motivation and performance are enhanced by an atmosphere in which employees are openly told they are valued and trusted. Managers encourage calculated risk-taking and innovation. They empower workers through cross-functional teams so that they are able to identify problems and develop effective solutions.

Tellabs' Career Development System trains internal candidates for key management positions, while its competitive compensation plan shares the wealth, contributes to employee satisfaction, and encourages peak performance.

Critical Thinking Questions

1. McGregor's Theory X and Theory Y have totally different views of the typical worker. Which of the two theories do you think managers should adopt? Explain. Describe how adopting Theory X would affect a manager's behavior toward employees. Do the same for Theory Y.

2. What are some of the potential pitfalls of using employee empowerment as a motivational device in the workplace?

3. Herzberg's theory says workplace factors lead to employee motivation. What are some workplace factors not mentioned in the video that could affect employee motivation?

**www.tellabs.com**

No.3

Behavior within Organizations: Groups and Interpersonal Influence

Chapter 8

Group Behavior and Teamwork

Learning Objectives

After completing Chapter 8, you should be able to:

Define
The terms *group* and *team*.

Describe
Various groups and teams that exist in organizations.

Discuss
Why people form groups and managers form teams.

Compare
The various stages of group development.

Identify
The major characteristics of groups and requirements for effective teams in organizations.

This chapter examines groups and teams in organizations. Groups in organizations can alter the individual's motivations or needs and can influence the behavior of individuals in an organizational setting. Organizational behavior is more than the logical composite of the behavior of individuals. It is also the behavior of groups that interact and the activities within groups. This chapter provides a model for understanding the nature of groups in organizations. The chapter begins by defining the various types of groups, reasons for their formation, and characteristics of groups. Next, a particular type of task group, a team, is defined and reasons why managers form teams are given, as are requirements for forming effective teams. Finally the concepts of roles and role conflict are discussed.

The Meaning of a Group

In this textbook, a group is defined as

> two or more employees who interact with each other in such a manner that the behavior and/or performance of a member is influenced by the behavior and/or performance of other members.[1]

Types of Groups

An organization has technical requirements that arise from its stated goals. Accomplishment of these goals requires that certain tasks be performed and that employees be assigned to perform these tasks.[2] As a result, most employees are members of a group based on their positions in the organization; these

Organizational Behavior

The field of study that draws on theory, methods, and principles from various disciplines to learn about individual perceptions, values, learning capacities, and actions while working in groups and within the total organization; analyzing the external environment's effect on the organization and its human resources, missions, objectives, and strategies.

Group

Collection of individuals in which behavior and/or performance of one member is influenced by behavior and/or performance of other members.

Formal Groups

Groups created by managerial decision to accomplish stated goals of organization.

Informal Groups

Groups that arise from individual efforts and develop around common interests and friendships rather than deliberate design.

are **formal groups.** In addition, whenever individuals associate on a fairly continuous basis, groups tend to form whose activities may be different from those required by the organization; these are **informal groups.** Both formal groups and informal groups exhibit common characteristics.

Formal groups

The demands and processes of the organization lead to the formation of two types of formal groups: command and task.

COMMAND GROUP   The command group, which is specified by the organization chart, comprises the subordinates who report directly to a given supervisor. The authority relationship between a department manager and the supervisors or between a senior nurse and her subordinates exemplifies a command group.

TASK GROUP   A task group comprises the employees who work together to complete a particular task or project. For example, activities of clerks in an insurance company are required tasks. When an accident claim is filed, several clerks must communicate and coordinate with one another if the claim is to be handled properly. These required tasks and interactions facilitate the formation of a task group.[3] Nurses assigned to duty in the emergency room of a hospital usually constitute a task group, because certain activities are required when a patient is treated. A special type of task group is called a *team.* Team performance is affected by all the factors that influence groups; but teams are also affected by additional factors that do not affect the productivity of other sorts of groups. For this reason, the concept of teams will be discussed separately later in the chapter.

Informal groups

Informal groups are natural groupings of people in the work situation, who come together in response to social needs. In other words, informal groups do not arise as a result of deliberate design but rather evolve naturally. Two specific informal groups exist: interest and friendship.

INTEREST GROUPS   Individuals who may not be members of the same command or task group may affiliate to achieve some mutual objective. The objectives of such groups are not related to those of the organization but are specific to each group. Employees banding together to present a unified front to management for more benefits and waiters pooling their tips are examples of interest groups.

FRIENDSHIP GROUPS   Many groups form because members have something in common, such as age, political beliefs, or ethnic background. These friendship groups often extend their interaction and communication to off-the-job activities.

If employees' affiliation patterns were documented, it would become readily apparent that they belong to numerous and often overlapping groups. A distinction has been made between two broad classifications of groups: formal and informal. The major difference between them is that formal command and task groups are designated by the formal organization as a means to an end. Informal interest and friendship groups are important for their own sake. They satisfy a basic human need for association.[4]

Even though friendship groups are informal, managers should make efforts to become aware of and, if possible, positively influence such groups, directing efforts toward organizational goals.[5] Indeed, in some organizations, the associations that individuals form through friendship groups are more powerful than formal affiliations.[6] Some suggested ways to influence these groups are through building good relations with the informal group's leader, providing group behavior and human relations training for the leader, and supporting members' efforts in sustaining the group relationship.

Why People Form Groups

Formal and informal groups form for various reasons.[7] Some reasons involve needs, proximity, attraction, goals, and economics.

The satisfaction of needs

The desire for need satisfaction can be a strong motivating force leading to group formation.[8] Specifically, some employees' security, social, esteem, and self-actualization needs can be satisfied to a degree by their affiliation with groups.

SECURITY   Without the group to lean on when various management demands are made, certain employees may feel they are standing alone, facing management and the entire organizational system. This "aloneness" leads to a degree of insecurity. By being a member of a group, the employee can become involved in group activities and discuss management demands with other employees who hold supportive views. In situations solely affecting the individual employee, the member can still count on the group to support her actions.[9] Interaction and communication among the group's members serve as a buffer to management demands. The need for a buffer may be especially strong in two cases. First, a new employee may depend heavily on the group for aid in correctly performing his job. Second, as a result of many corporate downsizing efforts, individuals depend on group support as a means to adjust to new demands and overcome feelings of insecurity.[10]

SOCIAL   The gregariousness of people stimulates their need for affiliation; a desire to be part of a group points up the intensity of social needs. The need to socialize exists not only on the job but away from the workplace, as evidenced by the vast array of social, political, civic, and fraternal organizations we can join.

ESTEEM   For a variety of reasons, a certain group in a particular work environment may be viewed by employees as having a high level of prestige (technical competence, outside activities, etc.). Consequently, membership in this group carries with it a certain status not enjoyed by nonmembers. For employees with high esteem needs, membership in such a group can provide much-needed satisfaction.[11]

Proximity and attraction

Interpersonal interaction can result in group formation. Two important facets of interpersonal interaction are proximity and attraction. Proximity involves the physical distance between employees performing a job. Attraction designates the degree to which people are drawn to each other because of perceptual, attitudinal, performance, or motivational similarity.[12]

Individuals who work in close proximity have numerous opportunities to exchange ideas, thoughts, and attitudes about various on- and off-the-job activities. These exchanges often result in some type of group formation. Proximity also makes it possible for individuals to learn about the characteristics of other people. To sustain the interaction and interest, a group is often formed.

For example, space station crews need to be trained in interpersonal, emotional support, and group interaction skills.[13] Because of proximity and attraction due to the nature of the work task, group formation is inevitable. Whole-crew training is indispensable for crew productivity and well-being. Such training circumvents many problems faced by long-duration space flights, where reliance on ground-based professionals is impractical.

Group goals

A group's goals, if clearly understood, can be reasons why an individual is attracted to it. For example, an individual may join a group that meets after work to become familiar with new production methods to be implemented in the organization over the next year. The person who voluntarily joins the after-hours group believes that learning the new system is a necessary and important goal for employees. The Close-Up "Teams Go Global" describes several situations where work teams have proven to be very effective.

Identifying group goals is not always possible. The assumption that formal organizational groups have clear goals must be tempered by the understanding that perception, attitudes, personality, and learning can distort goals.[14] For example, a new employee may never be formally told the goals of the unit that he's joined. By observing the behavior and attitudes of others, individuals may conclude what they believe the goals to be. These perceptions may or may not be accurate.

C L O S E — U P

Teams Go Global

During the 1990s, hundreds of American companies have reorganized around teams in order to leverage the knowledge of all employees. Now it appears that the concept is going global. Recent research conducted in Western Europe has supported the wisdom of teams.

In America, Cummins Engine, Ford Motor Co., and LTV among others, have found that allowing employees to make key decisions—not just following the boss's orders—has spurred productivity and quality. At Motorla, a basic belief in participative management has grown into a focus on teams made up of individuals from all levels of management. What follows are some examples of where the effective use of teams made the difference between success and failure for the organization. However, whether operating domestically or globally, it is also important to note that while teams can improve quality, efficiency, creativity, and satisfaction, it takes time and money to develop high-performing teams. And the time and money must be invested on the front end of the team-building effort. In other words, it must be viewed as an investment. This is the case in the following accounts.

The Ritz-Carlton Hotel Co. has created "self-directed work teams" that increase the amount of decision-making capability for nonmanagement staff. The goal is to improve quality and lower costs. One of the high-cost areas was associated with employee turnover. In the hotel's Tysons Corner, Virginia, facility, a "pilot" site for the company's program, the use of these teams has led to a decrease in turnover from 56 percent to 35 percent. At a cost of $4,000 to $5,000 to train each new employee, the savings was significant.

The service industry is not alone in gaining the benefits of the teams. At Air Products, a chemical manufacturer,

one cross-functional team, working with suppliers, saved $2.5 million in one year. At Olin, in order to meet customer expectations, the company also uses cross-functional teams instead of the traditional functional department structure. Customer satisfaction has increased significantly.

Finally, Osh-Kosh B'Gosh has combined the use of work teams and advanced equipment. The company has been able to increase productivity, speed, and flexibility at its U.S. manufacturing locations, which enabled the company to maintain 13 of its 14 facilities in the United States, making it one of the few children's garment makers able to do so.

There is no doubt that teams work. As we mentioned, the front end costs of time and money cannot be avoided. Finally, work teams cannot be forced on employees. By allowing employees to take the lead in team formation, an atmosphere of effective collaboration to promote everyone's interest can be developed.

Sources: Vegt Vander Gerber, Ben Emans, and Evert van de Vlient, "Motivating Effects of Task and Outcome Interdependence in Work Teams," *Group and Organization Management,* June 1998, pp. 124–143; Laurel Coppersmith and Arlene Grubbs, "Team-Building: The Whole May Be Less Than the Sum of Its Parts," *Human Resource Professional,* May/June 1998, pp. 10–14; Cheryl Rosen, "Ritz Staff Gets Authority: Work Teams to Start Making Line Decisions," *Business Travel News,* July 31, 1995, pp. 1–2; and Barbara Kanegsberg, "Cultural Revolution," *Chemical Marketing Reporter,* April 10, 1995, pp. SR3–5.

www.cummins.com, www.ford.com, www.ltvsteel.com, www.mot.com

www.ritzcarlton.com

www.airproducts.com, www.olin.com

www.oshkoshbgosh.com

Economics

In many cases, groups form because individuals believe that they can derive greater economic benefits from their jobs if they organize. Indeed, group pay incentives can be extremely valuable in supporting the way management wants to run the company.[15] For example, individuals working at different points on an assembly line may be paid on a group incentive basis, where the group's production determines each member's wages. By working and cooperating as a group, the individuals may obtain higher economic benefits. Conversely, by paying for individual performance, the structure may get in the way of group productivity by stressing self-, versus group, dependencies.[16] By matching incentive plans with a company's work culture and the type of group being used, the group's processes can be better aligned with those of the organization.[17]

Stages of Group Development

Groups learn, just as individuals do. Group performance depends both on individual learning and on how well members learn to work with one another.[18] For example, a new product committee formed to develop a response to a competitor may evolve into an effective team, with the interests of the company being most important; however, it may be ineffective if its members are more concerned about their individual departmental goals than about developing a response to a competitor. This section describes some general stages through which groups evolve, and it points out the sequential developmental process involved.

One model of group development assumes that groups proceed through four stages of development: (1) mutual acceptance, (2) communication and decision making, (3) motivation and productivity, and (4) control and organization. Although competing models of group development exist, we believe that the model presented here is the most useful for students of organizational behavior.[19]

Mutual acceptance

In the early stages of group formation, members are generally reluctant to communicate with one another. Typically, they aren't willing to express opinions, attitudes, and beliefs. This is similar to the situation facing a faculty member at the start of a new semester. Until class members accept and trust one another, little interaction or class discussion is likely to occur.

Communication and decision making

After a group reaches the point of mutual acceptance, its members begin to communicate openly with one another. This communication results in increased confidence and even more interaction within the group. Discussions begin to focus more specifically on problem-solving tasks and on developing alternative strategies to accomplish the tasks.[20] All groups will still have occasional communication breakdowns. However, effective groups work through such periods, and in the process, build stronger relationships.[21]

Motivation and productivity

In this stage of development, effort is expended to accomplish the group's goals. The group works as a cooperative rather than competitive unit. As experience in working together increases, so does the effectiveness of the group's decisions and actions.[22] This, in turn, positively reinforces favorable attitudes on group formation.[23]

Control and organization

At this point, group affiliation is valued, and members are regulated by group norms. Group goals take precedence over individual goals, and the norms are complied with— or sanctions are exercised. The ultimate sanction is ostracism for not complying with the group goals or norms. Other forms of control include temporary isolation from the group or harassment by the other members.

Characteristics of Groups

As groups evolve through their various stages of development, they begin to exhibit certain characteristics: structure, status hierarchy, roles, norms, leadership, cohesiveness, and conflict. Conflict in groups is such an important topic that it will be the subject of the next chapter. This section examines the other characteristics of groups. Understanding group behavior requires an awareness of these general characteristics.[24]

Structure

Within any group, some type of structure evolves over a period of time. Group members are differentiated on the basis of such factors as expertise, aggressiveness, power, and status; each member occupies a position in the group. The pattern of relationships among the positions constitutes a group structure.[25] Members of the group evaluate each position's prestige, status, and importance to the group. In most cases, status differences among positions create a hierarchical group structure.

Status in formal groups is usually based on position in the formal organization, while status in informal groups can be based on anything relevant to the group (e.g. golf scores, ability to communicate with management). Other members expect the occupant of each position to enact certain behaviors. The set of expected behaviors associated with a position in the structure constitutes the role of that position's occupant.

Status hierarchy

Status and position are so similar that the terms are often interchangeable. The status assigned to a particular position is typically a consequence of certain characteristics that differentiate one position from other positions. In some cases, a person is assigned status because of such factors as job seniority, age, or ability. For example, the oldest worker may be perceived as being more technically proficient and is therefore attributed status by a group of technicians. Thus, assigned status may have nothing to do with the formal status hierarchy.

Roles

Each person in the group structure has an associated role that consists of the expected behaviors of the occupant of that position.[26] The director of nursing services in a hospital is expected to organize and control the department of nursing and to assist in preparing and administering its budget. A nursing supervisor, on the other hand, is expected to supervise the activities of nursing personnel engaged in specific nursing services, such as obstetrics, pediatrics, and surgery. These expected behaviors generally are agreed to not only by the occupants but also by members of the nursing group and other hospital personnel.

In addition to the *expected role,* there are a perceived role and an enacted role. The *perceived role* is the set of behaviors that a person in a position believes he should enact. (In some cases, the perceived role may correspond to the expected role.) The *enacted role,* in contrast, is the behavior that a person actually carries out. Fairly stable or permanent groups typically foster good agreement between expected and perceived roles. But conflict and frustration may result from differences in the three roles. When the enacted role deviates too much from the expected role, the person can either become more like the expected role or leave the group.

Norms

Norms are the standards shared by the members of a group.[27] They have certain characteristics that are important to group members. First, norms are formed only with respect to things that have significance for the group. They may be written, but they're often verbally communicated to members. In many cases, they are never formally stated but somehow are known by group members. Second, norms are accepted in various degrees by group members. Some are accepted completely, others only partially. And third, norms may apply to every group member or to only some group members.

Both formal and informal groups may have a variety of norms. For example, most groups have loyalty norms fostering the development of a strong degree of loyalty and commitment from their members. Members are expected to do certain things (e.g., work late, accept transfers, help out other members) to prove they are loyal. Other groups have formal or informal dress norms. Company sales force members may all dress similarly to present the company's desired image to customers; people working in the operations center of a bank away from customers, however, may come to work in very casual clothing. Finally, groups have resource allocation norms and performance norms. Resource allocation norms of a formal organization relate to how status symbols, pay, and promotions should be allocated. Informal groups may also have allocation norms regarding such informal rewards as who works with whom or who gets helped and who does the helping. Performance norms relate to evaluating satisfactory performance. In formal groups, this may be made relatively clear by management; but as we shall see, performance norms may not be accepted by the informal group. In fact, informal groups may have performance norms of their own. Table 8–1 contains examples of some positive and negative norms, as expressed in one study.[28] Managers must take into account both formal and informal norms when they try to assemble high-performance groups.[29]

Leadership

The leadership role in groups is a crucial group characteristic as the leader plays an important role in determining group success.[30] The leader of a group exerts some influence over group members. In the formal group, the leader can exercise legitimately

Norms

Generally agreed-upon standards of individual and group behavior developed as a result of member interaction over time.

POSITIVE NORMS	NEGATIVE NORMS	**Table 8–1**
1. It's a tradition around here for people to stand up for the company when others criticize it unfairly.	1. In our company, they are always trying to take advantage of us.	Examples of Positive and Negative Norms
2. In our company, people always try to improve, even when they are doing well.	2. Around here, there's no point in trying harder; nobody else does.	
3. Around here, people are good listeners and actively seek out the ideas and opinions of others.	3. Around here, its dog-eat-dog and save your own skin.	
4. Around here, managers and supervisors really care about the people they supervise.	4. In our company, it's best to hide your problems and avoid your supervisor.	

sanctioned power. That is, the leader can reward or punish members who don't comply with directives, orders, or rules.

The leadership role is also a significant factor in an informal group. The person who becomes an informal group leader is generally a respected, high-status member who

1. Contributes to the group in accomplishing its goals.

2. Enables members to satisfy needs.

3. Embodies the values of the group. In essence, the leader is a personification of the values, motives, and aspirations of the members.

4. Is the choice of the group members to represent their viewpoint when interacting with other group leaders.

5. Is a facilitator of group conflict, is an initiator of group actions, and is concerned with maintaining the group as a functioning unit.

Leaders are rare. Often, members of a group look for someone to follow.[31] Becoming an effective group leader doesn't necessarily require charm or a library of theories waiting to be applied. It does, however, require vision, creativity, clear goals, a willingness to work horizontally and vertically, and good communication skills.[32] A good leader focuses on engaging in conversations that create, take care of, and initiate new commitments toward actions leading to common goals—especially on conversations that secure effective cooperative action within an organization.[33]

Whether in charge of a formal or informal group, the leader must be both open (encouraging members to participate) and authoritarian (intervening when necessary to accomplish group goals).[34] Indeed, the good leader must play social, spanning, and organizing roles.[35]

Cohesiveness

Cohesiveness

Strength of group members' desires to remain in the group and their commitment to the group.

Formal and informal groups seem to possess a closeness or commonness of attitude, behavior, and performance. This closeness, referred to as **cohesiveness,** is generally regarded as a force acting on the members to remain in a group that is greater than the forces pulling the member away from the group. Joining a group allows an individual to have a sense of belonging and feelings of morale.[36] A cohesive group, then, involves individuals who are attracted to one another. A group that is low in cohesiveness doesn't possess interpersonal attractiveness for the members.

There are, of course, numerous sources of attraction to a group. A group may be attractive to an individual because[37]

1. The goals of the group and the members are compatible and clearly specified.

2. The group has a charismatic leader.

3. The reputation of the group indicates that the group successfully accomplishes its tasks.

4. The group is small enough to permit members to have their opinions heard and evaluated by others.

5. The members are attractive in that they support one another and help each other overcome obstacles and barriers to personal growth and development.

Since highly cohesive groups consist of individuals who are motivated to be together, there's a tendency to expect effective group performance. This logic isn't supported conclusively by research evidence. In general, as the cohesiveness of a work group increases, the level of conformity to group norms also increases. But the group norms may be inconsistent with those of the organization.

COHESIVENESS AND PERFORMANCE   The concept of cohesiveness is important for understanding groups in organizations. A group's degree of cohesiveness can have positive or negative effects, depending on how well group goals match those of the formal organization. Four distinct relationships are possible, as Table 8–2 shows.

The table indicates that if cohesiveness is high and the group accepts and agrees with formal organization goals, then group behavior will be positive from the formal organization's standpoint. However, if the group is highly cohesive but its goals aren't congruent with those of the formal organization, then group behavior will be negative from the formal organization's standpoint.

Table 8–2 also indicates that if a group is low in cohesiveness and members have goals not in agreement with those of management, then the results probably are negative from the organization's standpoint. Behavior is more on an individual basis than on a group basis because of the low cohesiveness. A group can be low in cohesiveness and yet have members' goals agree with those of the formal organization. Here, the results are probably positive, although again more on an individual basis than on a group basis.

GROUPTHINK   Highly cohesive groups are important forces in organizational behavior. In other words, the organization should place people with many similarities in an isolated setting, give them a common goal, and reward them for performance. On the surface, this may look like a good idea. However, one author has provided a provocative analysis of highly cohesive groups.[38] Irving Janis studied foreign policy decisions made by several presidential administrations and concluded that these groups were highly cohesive and close-knit. He labeled their decision-making process *groupthink*. Janis defines groupthink as the "deterioration of mental efficiency, reality testing, and moral judgment" in the interest of group solidarity. In his book, he described the following characteristics associated with groupthink:

1. *Illusion of invulnerability.* Members of groups believe that they are invincible.

2. *Tendency to moralize.* Any opposition to group views is characterized by members as weak, evil, or unintelligent.

3. *Feeling of unanimity.* Each member of the group supports the leader's decisions. Members may have reservations about decisions but do not share their views. Rather than appearing weak, members keep views to themselves. This indicates how pressure toward group solidarity can distort individual members' judgments.

Groupthink

A cohesive group's desire for agreement interferes with the group's consideration of alternative solutions.

		Agreement with Organization Goals	
		LOW	**HIGH**
Degree of Group Cohesiveness	**Low**	Performance probably oriented away from organizational goals.	Performance probably oriented toward achievement of organizational goals.
	High	Performance oriented away from organizational goals.	Performance oriented toward achievement of organizational goals.

Table 8–2

Relationship between Group Cohesiveness and Agreement with Organizational Goals

4. *Pressure to conform.* Formal and informal attempts are made to discourage discussion of divergent views. Groups exert great pressure on individual members to conform.

5. *Opposing ideas dismissed.* Any individual or outside group that criticizes or opposes a decision receives little or no attention from the group. Group members tend to show strong favoritism toward their own ideas in the manner by which information is processed and evaluated, thus guaranteeing that their ideas will win out.

Certainly, some level of group cohesiveness is necessary for a group to tackle a problem. If seven individuals from seven different organizational units are assigned a task, the task may never be completed effectively. The point, however, is that when it comes to cohesiveness, more may not necessarily be better. While members of task groups may redefine solving a problem to mean reaching agreement rather than making the best decision, members of cohesive groups may redefine it to mean preserving relations among group members and preserving the image of the group. Groupthink illustrates the impact of group dynamics and cohesiveness on group performance.

A recent study examined effects of group loyalty and distortion tendencies in management teams.[39] Results showed that once groups have worked together on a few successful group activities, the resultant group cohesion manifests itself in the form of in-group loyalty, whereby members related their best ideas to a measure of their group's value and status. Loyalty to the group decision overwhelmed logic and denied the existence of value in ideas from other sources.

The groupthink phenomenon could even explain such events as Watergate, the Iran-Contra affair, and ethically questionable decisions in many large organizations. Indeed, one researcher reviewing the situation surrounding the decision to launch the space shuttle Challenger blames groupthink for the disaster.[40] Leaders had a preferred solution and engaged in behaviors designed to promote the launch rather than critically appraise other alternatives.

The Nature and Types of Teams

So far, the chapter's discussion has focused on issues related to all types of groups. Now, attention is turned to one special type of group, a team.[41] The use of teams has become an increasingly popular work design in all types of organizations, both on a domestic and foreign basis.[42] As discussed earlier, teams are a special type of task group, consisting of two or more individuals responsible for the achievement of a goal or objective. Teams tend to fall into one of three categories based on their duration and objectives. The three categories of teams are: problem-solving, cross-functional, and self-directed work teams.

Problem-solving teams

Problem-solving teams are formed on a temporary basis to address a specific problem that is confronting the organization. For example, a manufacturing manager may form a team to study space and equipment requirements needed to reconfigure production space to accommodate a new product. Likewise, a marketing manager may assemble a team to evaluate the effects a competitor's new advertising campaign may have on company sales. As seen by the examples, the duration of a problem-solving team's existence is usually short in nature. For the most part, problem-solving teams are composed of individuals from the same department or area of an organization who meet together to address and solve a specific problem. Once the problem is solved, the team disbands.

Cross-functional teams

Recently, a growing number of organizations have begun utilizing teams that are composed of individuals from different departments or work areas who come together on a task or project basis. These groups, called *cross-functional teams,* monitor, standardize, and improve work processes that cut across different parts of the organization. For example, a computer company may form a cross-functional team made up of members from marketing, sales, research and development, engineering, and human resources to design and develop marketing plans for a new product. In a similar vein, some innovative colleges of business are bringing together professors from various departments such as marketing, finance, management, and operations to plan and teach integrated principles of business courses. Cross-functional teams can have a life span of indeterminate length. A general rule associated with the use of cross-functional teams is that the longer the duration, the more the team members rotate in and out.

An effective cross-functional team can reduce the amount of time a project might otherwise take to complete if it consists of representatives of departments critical to the project's completion. Many cross-functional teams run best without an established boss, as the team itself provides a basis for various individuals to exhibit leadership skills.[43] When establishing a cross-functional team, management should be concerned with more than just getting representation from all relevant departments. Rather, a focus should be placed on recruiting open-minded individuals, who can take the long view of situations and who are not afraid of confrontation and change. It should be realized that cross-functional teams can take a longer time to develop than problem-solving teams due to the fact that initially there may be feelings of mistrust between members from differing departments. In fact, the early stages of most cross-functional team building efforts emphasize the building of trust and teamwork.

Self-directed work teams

The third type of team, self-directed work teams, usually comprise 10 to 15 individuals who take on the long-term responsibilities of their former supervisors as well as retain their prior responsibilities. It's important to note that teams of this type should not be considered unmanaged teams; rather, they should be viewed as differently managed teams—those run by the workers themselves. Typically, the self-directed work team holds control over the determination and assignment of work to be performed, choice of operating procedures, and allocation of resources. Some self-directed teams even select individuals who will serve on the teams and have members evaluate each other's performance in order to assign rewards or pay incentives. Many major companies, including Boeing, Caterpillar, Cummins Engine, Digital Equipment, Ford, General Electric, LTV Steel, and Tektronix, have begun using self-directed work teams. It is estimated that by the end of the century, up to 50 percent of all companies, both large and small, will be utilizing some form of self-directed work teams.

It should be noted that self-directed work teams are not appropriate for every organization. Before designing these teams and establishing expectations for them, the organization should conduct an environmental analysis to determine if self-directed work teams are consistent with: (1) the organization's business requirements; (2) the organization's values and goals; and (3) the organization's competencies. Success in implementing and using self-directed work teams is usually contingent on whether the organization is ready for such teams.[44]

www.boeing.com

www.cat.com

www.cummins.com

www.dec.com

www2.ford.com

www.ge.com

www.ltvsteel.com

Why Teams Are Formed

There is no simple explanation for the increased usage of teams in organizations, especially those that are self-directed. The authors believe there are a number of reasons why managers of organizations form teams, including enhanced productivity, flattening of organizations, need for flexibility and quicker decisions, workforce diversity, improved quality, and increased customer satisfaction.

Enhanced productivity

In a nutshell, the single most important reason why teams are formed is to enhance organizational productivity. Organizations throughout the world have realized that team performance leads to higher productivity levels than what would be achieved by many individuals working individually. This is primarily due to the fact that teams bring together complementary skills that can fall into one of three categories: technical or functional expertise, problem-solving and decision-making skills; and interpersonal skills.

TECHNICAL OR FUNCTIONAL SKILLS It would make little sense for a marketer to design technical specifications for a new type of cellular phone. Likewise, it would make little sense for an engineer to try to guess what features consumers find most important in making decisions as to which type cellular phone to purchase. However, teams of engineers and marketing personnel often work together to identify and design cellular phones that are widely accepted by the buying public. In this case, product development groups that consist of marketers only or engineers only are less likely to succeed than those with the complementary skills of both.

PROBLEM-SOLVING AND DECISION-MAKING SKILLS Teams must possess the ability to identify problems and opportunities their organization faces, to identify feasible decision alternatives and trade-offs, as well as to make necessary decisions leading to optimum results. Most individuals do not possess the necessary skills needed to perform all these tasks effectively. However, among a well-chosen team, it is likely that taken together, the requisite skills are present and can be utilized in the organization's best interests.

INTERPERSONAL SKILLS Common understanding and knowledge of problems faced and decisions needed cannot arise without effective communication and constructive conflict, which greatly depends on interpersonal skills. These include risk-taking, helpful criticism, objectivity, active listening, giving the benefit of the doubt, support, and recognizing the interests and achievement of others. An effective team is made up of members who, in total, possess each of these skills. Individual members, at various times, will be called on to utilize their unique skill to lead the team forward. Thus, it is critical that team members are chosen based on skills and skill potential, not solely on personality.

www.xerox.com

www.gm.com

www.fedex.com

www.home depot.com

The effective use of the complementary skills teams possess can lead to extraordinary results for organizations. For example, Xerox Corporation plants using work teams are over 25 percent more productive than conventionally organized plants. Likewise, General Motors reports more than 20 percent productivity gains in plants that use team-based manufacturing systems. Examples of this type are cropping up in news stories on a weekly basis as more and more organizations realize the power unleashed by teams. Indeed, organizations as diverse as the U.S. Government, Federal Express, Home Depot, and Fresh Choice restaurants have all seen their productivity benefit from the use of teams.

Flattening organizations

Businesses around the world are restructuring, reorganizing, and downsizing their companies in order to eliminate waste and to better serve their constituencies. As a result, there has been a continual flattening of organizations wherein whole levels of management have been eliminated. As a result, front-line teams of workers are assuming many of the tasks formerly performed by supervisors, midlevel managers, and support staff. Work teams provide the flexibility to trim unneeded forms of redundant bureaucracy. In fact, some companies believe that any function that does not support the efforts of front-line work teams can be considered an option for elimination.

Need for flexibility and quicker decisions

To thrive in today's increasingly competitive markets, organizations must be capable of producing small runs of tailored products on a tight schedule to meet growing demands in emerging markets. This ability calls for innovative technical procedures and bright workers who are flexible and can move from assignment to assignment. Self-directed work teams have the skills, the knowledge, and the motivation to quickly adapt to change. As a result, managers who traditionally spent a large portion of their time supervising workers and fighting mini-crises can be freed up to perform more strategic-type thinking. In total, the use of teams provides the best of both worlds: long-term vision coupled with greater flexibility for quicker short-term decisions.

Workforce diversity

An individual will bring to his/her job experiences based largely on a lifestyle lived among individuals sharing similar experiences. A major advantage associated with teams is that they are made up of members from different backgrounds and with differing life experiences. As a result, the use of teams composed of individuals with varied backgrounds may lead to more innovative forms of thought and superior decision making than would be the case if individuals alone made decisions. For example, marketing teams made up of individuals with differing ethnic backgrounds would be in a much better position than a single individual to determine whether or not a market for a specific product should be segmented along a particular dimension. The Close-Up "Diversity and Group Dynamics" focuses on what some organizations are doing to assist employees with changing group dynamics.

Improved quality

Individuals can and will only assume responsibility for the distinct component or part of a project or product they work on. On the other hand, teams assume responsibility for entire projects or products. When teams assume responsibility, they develop an appreciation of the nuances associated with all aspects of their work. As a result, it becomes a matter of professional pride for team members to search out and act on opportunities for quality improvements. In addition, since team members perform both technical and administrative functions, they gain the commitment, experience, and skills requisite to improve the interface between the two functions.

Increased customer satisfaction

Customer satisfaction is the key to organizational success for it is the satisfied customer who accounts for the repeat business that organizations need to survive and thrive. The energy, commitment, and flexibility associated with work teams promote customer satisfaction through quick response and improved quality.

Requirements for Effective Teams

Teams are incapable of performing miracles on their own. Much like individuals, teams need the nurturing and support of management. Toward this end, there are several requirements for effective teams. These requirements include top-level commitment and provision of clear goals; management–employee trust; willingness to take risks and share information; and time, resources, and a commitment to training.

Top-level commitment and provision of clear goals

Top-performing organizations have leaders who are deeply committed to the team concept. Through their time, attention, and other behavior, leaders continually express and reinforce the notion that the use of teams is the only means to succeed. Truly committed leaders inspire confidence that team performance is the single best path to economic and personal fulfillment. As a result, high performance teams have a clear understanding of the goals the organization seeks to achieve through the use of teams, and the importance of these goals encourages individuals to defer their own concerns to team goals.

Management–employee trust

Top management must trust that, given time, workers will actively support the massive changes in responsibility and authority bestowed on them as team members. Conversely, employees need to know and believe that management is serious about wanting people

---

CLOSE—UP

Diversity and Group Dynamics

Although the definition of diversity may vary from company to company, the main idea is consistent—to increase the hiring and promoting of women and minorities. As programs are designed to increase diversity, the number of different cultures and personalities in the workforce increases. Consequently, the group dynamics in many organizations are changing and will continue to change.

Corporate diversity training attempts to promote harmony and understanding within the workforce and assists employees in adapting to the resulting change in group dynamics. It is safe to say that more than half of U.S. companies offer diversity training. For some geographically disbursed organizations, offering diversity training can be quite a challenge. For example, U.S. West Dex, a division of U.S. West, operates in 14 states with 3,500 employees. However, by 1998 the company had trained 60 percent of its employees in three-day diversity awareness workshops.

Many other organizations, such as Home Depot, provide their employees with special training in the areas of cultural orientation and multicultural sensitivity training. The goals of these programs include the desire to understand each other's differences and thereby work more effectively as a group.

Many organizations seem to be doing quite well in increasing the diversity of their workforce. J.C. Penney, for example, moved from having only a few minority employees in any management levels and women in mainly entry- and middle-level management positions to a point where 76 percent of entry-level managers are women and minorities and 42 percent of middle managers and 20 percent of senior managers are women and minorities.

However, does success in diversity lead to overall corporate success? Lucio A. Noto, chairman of the board and CEO of Mobil Corporation, recently commented, "At Mobil, we are increasing using a team approach to decision making, and our teams reflect our diversity in gender, race, and professional background. This should help us break free of traditional solutions to find creative and innovative ways to solve business problems." This statement captures the necessity for organizations to leverage all of the talent that exists in all of its employees. It also means that it is time to begin measuring how successful organizations are in achieving the goals of diversity training.

Sources: "The Diversity Initiative at U.S. West Dex," *Successful Meetings,* March 1998, pp. 55–57; Michael L. Wheeler, "Measuring Diversity: A Strategy for Organizational Effectiveness," *Employment Relations Today,* Spring 1998, pp. 66–68; "Focus Shifts in Diversity Training Needs to Prove That It Improves the Corporate Bottom Line in Order to Survive," *The Wall Street Journal,* Eastern ed., June 16, 1995, p. B5A.

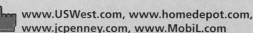 **www.USWest.com, www.homedepot.com, www.jcpenney.com, www.MobiL.com**

(as team members) to take risks and express their opinions and that the formation of teams is not just a new mechanism to gain additional work from employees.

On a team level, there must exist a high level of trust among members. Members must believe in the integrity, character, and abilities of one another. As we are all well aware, trust takes a long time to build and can be jeopardized by a single careless action. The climate of trust within a team seems to be highly dependent on members' perceptions of management's trust of the group as a whole, and therefore the level of management trust can serve to enhance or detract from members' trust. Organizations that value employee honesty, openness, and collaborative processes with high employee involvement are more likely to stimulate trusting cultures than those who do not.

Willingness to take risks and share information

Teams, by acknowledging their existence, must accept the willingness to take risks, while simultaneously being held accountable for their actions. Toward this end, the risk of self-direction is personal. Workers and supervisors must be willing to trade their safer, traditional jobs for ones that are less clear-cut and more demanding, time consuming, and challenging. Management must accept the notion that their daily routines and activities will probably be changed forever as teams begin to assume more responsibility for the running of the organization. In other words, change, once started, is difficult to reverse.

Likewise, if teams are to take responsibility and assume risk in making decisions, they will need detailed information about the organization's overall operations, including financial information concerning individual members and departments. To manage themselves, teams need information that was once the exclusive domain of management. Armed with information, it is inevitable that teams will begin asking questions of management which, in turn, will lead to the revealing of more sensitive, detailed information. As teams evolve, the point is eventually reached where team knowledge of certain facets of operations is as great or greater than management's. For teams to succeed, management must be willing to accept and actively encourage this knowledge equality.

Time, resources, and a commitment to training

Successful work teams can take months, even years, to mature to a level commensurate with the responsibilities they must take on. Management needs to recognize that the rewards of self-direction and self-management depend on massive planning, intense and prompt access to resources (financial and other), and often the physical redesigning of plants and offices. Internally, the team needs to be provided with a sound and understandable measurement system with which team members can evaluate their performance, an incentive system that rewards team activities, and supportive management which encourages team-building exercises.

In addition, self-directed work teams can either succeed or fail based on the amount, intensity, and duration of training they receive. In working as a team, individuals have to put aside personal privileges and contribute to the group well-being. For many individuals, this represents a massive change from either just giving or receiving orders. Team members therefore need proper, long-term training in the interpersonal, administrative, and technical skills that may counteract habits, attitudes, and work styles left over from years of employment in a more traditionally run organization.

Intergroup Behavior and Conflict

Few trends have so affected organizations as that of the movement toward group-based systems. The successful transition from a time where employees worked alone to one where individuals are dependent on others requires employees to share information, cooperate with each other, address personal differences, and share a desire to work for the greater good of the entire organization. The emphasis in this chapter has been on intra-group behavior.

An equally important characteristic of groups is that they frequently conflict with other groups in the organization. Groups conflict with others for many reasons, and the resulting outcomes can either be good or negative for the organization. What happens between groups (intergroup behavior) is the subject of the next chapter.

The Role Concept

Role

Organized set of behaviors expected of an individual in a specific position.

The concept of role is vital to understanding group behavior. **Role** refers to the expected behavior patterns attributed to a particular position in an organization. The roles of physician and patient are familiar to everyone. Those roles are culturally defined expectations associated with particular positions.

A role may include attitudes and values as well as specific kinds of behavior. It is what an individual must do to validate her occupancy of a particular position. In other words, what kind of physician or patient an individual is depends a great deal on how he performs the culturally defined role associated with the position. Consider your own perceptions of the roles associated with law enforcement officers, military officers, politicians, college professors, and business executives.

In the formal organization, every position has certain activities that are expected. These activities constitute the role for that position from the standpoint of the organization. The organization develops job descriptions that define the activities of each particular position and how it relates to other positions in the organization. However, for both formal (task and command) and informal (interest and friendship) groups, roles may not be set forth explicitly and yet are clearly understood by group members. For example, members of the marketing department in a bank may know that only the director of marketing represents the bank at national conventions and that they have no chance of attending, even though this has never been explicitly stated. Thus, whether they are formally or informally established, status hierarchies and accompanying roles are integral parts of every organization.

Multiple Roles

Roles performed simultaneously because the individual holds many positions in a variety of organizations and groups.

Multiple roles and role sets

Most of us perform **multiple roles.** We occupy many different positions in a variety of organizations (home, work, church, civic groups, and so forth). Within each of these organizations, we occupy and perform certain roles. We may simultaneously be playing the role of parent, mate, supervisor, and subordinate. Each position involves different role relationships. For example, the position of college professor involves not only the role of teacher in relation to students but also numerous other roles relating the position to administrators, peers, the community, and alumni. Each group may expect different things: students may expect good classroom performance, research, and publication; the college community may expect community service; and alumni may expect help in recruiting students and athletes. This we term the **role set.** A

Role Set

Individuals' expectations for behavior of a person in a particular role, because most groups have their own role expectations.

role set refers to others' expectations for the behavior of the individual in the particular role. The more expectations, the more complex is the role set.

Multiple roles refer to different roles, while role set refers to the different expectations associated with one role. Therefore, an individual involved in many different roles, each with a complex role set, faces the ultimate in complexity of individual behavior. Multiple roles and role sets are important concepts because of possible complications that make defining specific roles extremely difficult, especially in organizational settings. This can often result in *role conflict* for the individual.

Role perception

Different individuals have different perceptions of the behavior associated with a given role. In an organizational setting, accuracy in role perception can have a definite impact on performance. This matter is further complicated because within the organization there may be three different perceptions of the same role: the formal organization's, the group's, and the individual's. For example, a college dean, the students, and the professors themselves have perceptions of the role of professor. But as we saw in the preceding discussion of role sets, students' perceptions of the role of a professor may be very different from college administrators' perceptions. These differences in perception increase even further the possibility of role conflict.

Role conflict

Because of the multiplicity of roles and role sets, an individual may face a complex situation of simultaneous role requirements where performance of one role precludes the performance of the others. As a group member, the individual faces tremendous pressures to give up his self-identity and accountability in exchange for in-group loyalty.[45] When this occurs, the individual faces a situation known as role conflict. Several forms of this conflict can occur in organizations.

Role Conflict

Conflict that arises when a person in an organization receives incompatible messages regarding appropriate role behavior.

PERSON-ROLE CONFLICT   Person-role conflict occurs when role requirements violate the basic values, attitudes, and needs of the individual occupying the position. A supervisor who finds it difficult to dismiss a subordinate with a family and an executive who resigns rather than engage in some unethical activity reflect person-role conflict.[46]

INTRAROLE CONFLICT   Intrarole conflict occurs when different individuals define a role according to different sets of expectations, making it impossible for the person occupying the role to satisfy all of them. This is more likely to occur when a given role has a complex role set (many different role relationships). The supervisor in an industrial situation has a rather complex role set and thus may face intrarole conflict. On the one hand, top management has a set of expectations that stresses the supervisor's role in the management hierarchy. On the other hand, the supervisor may have close friendship ties with members of the command group who may be former working peers. This is why supervisors are often described as being "stuck in the middle."

INTERROLE CONFLICT   Interrole conflict can result from facing multiple roles.[47] It occurs because individuals simultaneously perform many roles, some with conflicting expectations. A scientist in a chemical plant who's also a member of a management group might experience role conflict of this kind. In such a situation, the scientist may be expected to behave in accordance with the expectations of management as well as the expectations of professional chemists. The next chapter describes how this type of role conflict often causes conflict between groups in many organizations.

Results of role conflict

An individual confronted with role conflict experiences psychological stress that may result in emotional problems and indecision.[48] Research has shown that role conflict occurs frequently and with negative effects on performance over a wide spectrum of occupations.[49]

While managers can do little to avoid certain kinds of role conflict, many kinds can be minimized. For example, some role conflict (especially intrarole conflict) can result from violations of the classical principles of chain of command and unity of command. In other words, when individuals are faced with conflicting expectations or demands from two or more sources, the likely result is a decline in performance.

In addition, interrole conflict can be generated by conflicting expectations of formal or informal groups, with results similar to those of intrarole conflict. Thus, a highly cohesive group whose goals are not consistent with those of the formal organization can cause a great deal of interrole conflict for its members.

Summary of Key Points

- A group consists of employees who interact in such a manner that the behavior or performance of one group member is influenced by the behavior or performance of other group members.

- By being aware of group characteristics and behaviors, managers can be prepared for the potential positive and negative results of group activities. A manager can proactively intervene to modify the perceptions, attitudes, and motivations that influence the results.

- People are attracted to groups because of their potential for satisfying needs, their physical proximity and attraction, and the appeal of group goals and activities. In essence, people are attracted to one another; that is a natural process.

- Groups develop at different rates and with unique patterns that depend on the task, the setting, the members' individual characteristics and behavioral patterns, and the manager's style of managing.

- Characteristics of groups include structure, status hierarchy, roles, norms, leadership, cohesiveness, and intergroup conflict. These characteristics pervade all groups. In an informal group, they emerge from within the unit; in a formal group, they are established by the managerial process.

- Group characteristics provide a degree of predictability for the members that is important to the group and to the outside (e.g., management, other groups). An unstable or unpredictable group is a problem for its members and for others who interact with it.

- Each group possesses some degree of cohesiveness. This attractiveness of the group can be a powerful force in influencing individual behavior and performance.

- Research studies indicate that cohesive groups can formulate goals and norms that may not agree with those of management. When a group's goals and norms are incongruent with the organization's, some form of managerial intervention is necessary.

- Teams are a special type of task group. Three common categories of teams exist in organizations: (1) problem-solving teams, (2) cross-functional teams, and (3) self-directed work teams.

- Managers form teams predominately to enhance productivity. Teams also form due to flattening organizations, need for flexibility and quick decisions, workforce diversity, improved quality, and increased customer satisfaction.

- The requirements for effective teams include top-level commitment and provision of clear goals; management–employee trust; willingness to take risks and share information; and time, resources, and a commitment to training.

- The concept of role is vital to an understanding of group behavior. A role consists of the expected behavior patterns attributed to a particular position. Most individuals perform multiple roles, each with its own role set (others' expectations for the role). An individual involved in many different roles, each having a complex role set, faces the ultimate in complexity of individual behavior.

- In organizations, there may be as many as three perceptions of the same role: the organization's, the group's, and the individual's. When an individual faces two or more simultaneous role requirements for which the performance of one precludes performance of the other(s), she experiences role conflict.

- Three different types of role conflict—person-role, intrarole, and interrole—can occur in organizational settings. Research has shown that consequences of role conflict to the individual include increased psychological stress and other emotional reactions. Management can minimize certain types of role conflicts and should be continually aware that the consequences of conflict to the organization can include ineffective performance by individuals and groups.

Discussion and Review Questions

1. Imagine you are the manager of a factory and you want your maintenance employees to develop a schedule whereby they each take a specific role in finishing the required daily tasks. Which type of group would you form and why?

2. Have you ever been in a friendship group that was influenced by an outside party to accomplish his/her own goals? If so, discuss how this person influenced your group and if he/she was successful. If not, give an example of how someone could do so.

3. Think of a formal group you belong or belonged to. Did your expected, perceived, and enacted role behaviors differ? Describe each one and any differences that existed.

4. Think of a group project you were involved in for a particular class. Describe how the group evolved or did not evolve.

5. Describe a team of which you are or have been a member. What type of team was it and why was the team formed?

6. Regarding the team you discussed above, were the requirements for effective teams fulfilled? Why or why not?

7. Give an example of when you have experienced person-role conflict, intrarole conflict, and interrole conflict.

8. Why should a manager be familiar with concepts of group behavior?

9. From your own experience, give an example of a group leader you thought was effective and one that was ineffective. What was the difference between the two?

10. You are a manager, and a member of one of your task groups comes to you and says that his group is engaging in groupthink and he is being pressured to conform to their rules. You can't disclose this information to anyone, yet you want to discourage this group's cohesiveness. What would you do?

CASE FOR ANALYSIS

The "No Martini" Lunch

Jim Lyons had just completed his second month as manager of an important office of a nationwide sales organization. He believed that he had made the right choice in leaving his old company. This new position offered a great challenge, excellent pay and benefits, and tremendous opportunity for advancement. In addition, his family seemed to be adjusting well to the new community. However, in Jim's mind there was one serious problem that he believed must be confronted immediately, or it could threaten his satisfaction in the long run.

After taking the job, Jim found out that the man he replaced had made an institution of the hard-drinking business lunch. He and a group of other key executives had virtually a standing appointment at various local restaurants. Even when clients were not present, they would have several drinks before ordering their lunches. When they returned, it was usually well into the afternoon, and they were in no condition to make decisions or take the actions that were often the pretext of the lunch in the first place. This practice had also spread to the subordinates of the various executives; it wasn't uncommon to see various groups of salespeople doing the same thing a few days each week.

Jim decided to end the practice, at least for himself and the members of his group. He knew that this wouldn't be easy. The drinking had become institutionalized with a great deal of psychological pressure from a central figure—the man he had replaced. Jim decided to plan his approach and then discuss the problem and his approach for solving it with his superior, Norm Landy.

Norm listened intently as Jim explained the drinking problem but showed no surprise at learning about it. Jim then explained his plan.

"Norm, I'm making two assumptions on the front end. First, I don't believe it would do any good to state strong new policies about drinking at lunch or to lecture my people about the evils of the liquid lunch. About all I'd accomplish would be to raise a lot of latent guilt that would only result in resentment and resistance. Second, I'm assuming that the boss is often a role model for his subordinates. Unfortunately, the man I replaced made a practice of the drinking lunch. The subordinates close to him then conformed to his drinking habits and exerted pressure on other members of the group. Before you know it, everyone is a drinking buddy, and the practice becomes institutionalized even when one member is no longer there.

"Here's what I intend to do about it. First, when I go to lunch with the other managers, I'll do no drinking. More important, however, for the members of my group, I'm going to establish a new role model. For example, at least once a week, we have a legitimate reason to work through lunch. In the past, everyone has gone out anyway. I intend to hold a business lunch and have sandwiches and soft drinks sent in. In addition, I intend to make it a regular practice to take different groups of my people to lunch at a no-alcohol coffee shop.

"My goal, Norm, is simply to let my subordinates know that alcohol isn't a necessary part of the workday and that drinking will not win my approval. By not drinking with the other managers, I hope sooner or later to make the point with them also. As you can see, I intend to get the message across by my behavior. There will be no words of censure. What do you think, Norm?"

Norm Landy pushed himself away from his desk, came around, and seated himself beside Jim. He then looked at Jim and whispered, "Are you crazy? I guarantee you, Jim, that you're going to accomplish nothing but cause a lot of trouble—trouble between your group and other groups if you succeed, trouble between you and your group, and trouble between you and the other managers. Believe me, Jim, I see the problem, and I agree with you that it's a problem. But the cure might kill the patient. Will all that conflict and trouble be worth it?

Jim thought for a moment and said, "I think it will be good for the organization in the long run."

Discussion Questions

1. Do you agree with Norm Landy or with Jim Lyons? Why?

2. Do you think that anything can be done about this situation? Why? What's your opinion of Jim's plan?

3. What would you do in Jim's situation? Be specific.

EXPERIENTIAL EXERCISE

Participation in and Observations of Group Processes

Objectives

1. To provide experience in participating in and observing groups undertaking a specific task.

2. To generate data that can be the focus of class discussion and analysis.

Starting the Exercise

The situation: You're appointed to a personnel committee in charge of selecting a manager for the department that provides administrative services to other departments. Before you begin interviewing candidates, you're asked to develop a list of the personal and professional qualifications the manager needs. The list will be used as the selection criteria.

Completing the Exercise

1. Select five to seven members to serve on the committee.

2. Ask the committee to rank the items in the following list in their order of importance in selecting the department head.

3. The students not on the committee should observe the group process. Some should observe the whole group; others should observe individual members. The observers can use observation guides A and B.

4. The observers should provide feedback to the participants.

5. The class should discuss how the committee might improve its performance.

Selection Criteria

- Strong institutional loyalty
- Ability to give clear instructions
- Ability to discipline subordinates
- Ability to make decisions under pressure
- Ability to communicate
- Stable personality
- High intelligence
- Ability to grasp the overall picture
- Ability to get along well with people
- Familiarity with office procedures
- Professional achievement
- Ability to develop subordinates

A. Group Process Observation Guide

Instructions: Observe the group behavior in the following dimensions. Prepare notes for feedback.

GROUP BEHAVIORS	DESCRIPTION	IMPACT
Group goal: Are group goals clearly defined?		
Decision procedure: Is the decision procedure clearly defined?		
Communication network: What kind of communication network is used? Is it appropriate?		
Decision making: What kind of decision process is used? Is it appropriate?		
Group norm: Observe the degrees of cohesiveness, compatibility, and conformity.		
Group composition: What kind of group is it?		
Other behavior: Is there any behavior that influences the group process?		

B. Individual Role Observation Guide

Instructions: Observe one committee member. Tabulate (or note) his behaviors as the group works.

Initiating ideas: Initiates or clarifies ideas and issues.	**Confusing issues:** Confuses others by bringing up irrelevant issues or by jumping to other issues.
Managing conflicts: Explores, clarifies, and resolves conflicts and differences.	**Mismanaging conflicts:** Avoids or suppresses conflicts, or creates "win-or-lose" situations.
Influencing others: Appeases, reasons with, or persuades others.	**Forcing others:** Gives orders or forces others to agree.
Supporting others: Reinforces or helps others to express their opinions.	**Rejecting others:** Deflates or antagonizes others.
Listening attentively: Listens and responds to others' ideas and opinions.	**Showing indifference:** Does not listen to or brushes off others.
Showing empathy: Shows the ability to see things from other people's viewpoint.	**Self-serving behavior:** Exhibits self-serving behavior.
Exhibiting positive nonverbal behaviors: Pays attention to others, maintains eye contact, composure, and other signs.	**Exhibiting negative nonverbal behaviors:** Tense facial expression, yawning, little eye contact, and other behaviors.

Source: Kae H. Chung and Leon C. Megginson, *Organizational Behavior* (New York: Harper & Row, 1981), pp. 241–44. Used by permission.

Chapter 9

Intergroup Behavior, Negotiation, and Team Building

For any organization to perform effectively, interdependent individuals and groups must establish working

relationships across organizational boundaries, between individuals, and among groups. Individuals or groups may depend on one another for information, assistance, and coordinated action. This interdependence may foster either cooperation or conflict.

For example, a firm's production and marketing executives may meet to discuss ways to deal with foreign competition. Such a meeting may be reasonably free of conflict. Decisions get made, strategies are developed, and the executives return to work. Thus, there is intergroup cooperation to achieve a goal. However, this may not be the case if sales decline because the firm is not offering enough variety in its product line. The marketing department desires broad product lines to offer more variety to customers, while the production department desires narrow product lines to keep production costs manageable and to increase productivity. Conflict is likely to occur at this point because each function has its own goals, which in this case conflict. Thus, groups may cooperate on one point and conflict on another.

Intergroup problems aren't the only conflicts that can exist in organizations.[1] That interpersonal conflict is a pervasive and fundamental aspect of organizational life has been well-documented.[2] Conflict between individuals, however, can usually be more easily resolved through existing mechanisms. For example, troublesome employees can be fired, transferred, or given new work schedules.

This chapter focuses on conflict between groups in organizations. We begin by examining attitudes toward conflict. Reasons for intergroup conflict and its consequences are also presented. Finally, we outline techniques for successfully managing intergroup conflict.

A Realistic View of Intergroup Conflict

Conflict is inevitable in organizations. However, because it can be both a positive and a negative force, management should not strive to eliminate all conflict, only that which has disruptive effects on the organization's efforts to achieve its goals. Some type or degree of conflict may prove beneficial if it is used as an instrument for change or innovation. Thus, the critical issue appears to be not conflict itself but rather how it's managed. Using this approach, we can define conflict in terms of the *effect it has on the organization*. In this respect, we discuss both functional and dysfunctional conflict.[3]

Functional conflict

Functional Conflict

From the organization's standpoint, confrontation between groups that results in benefits to the organization.

A **functional conflict** is a confrontation between groups that enhances and benefits the organization's performance. For example, two departments in a hospital may conflict over the most efficient method of delivering health care to low-income rural families. The two departments agree on the goal but not on the means to achieve it. Whatever the outcome, low-income rural families will probably end up with better medical care once the conflict is settled. Without such conflict in organizations, there would be little commitment to change; most groups would probably become stagnant. Thus, functional conflict can be thought of as a type of creative tension.

Dysfunctional conflict

Dysfunctional Conflict

From the organization's standpoint, confrontation between groups that hinders organizational performance.

A **dysfunctional conflict** is any confrontation or interaction between groups that harms the organization or hinders the achievement of organizational goals. Management must seek to eliminate dysfunctional conflicts.

Beneficial conflicts can often turn into harmful ones. In most cases, the point at which functional conflict becomes dysfunctional is impossible to identify precisely. The very same level of stress and conflict that creates a healthy and positive movement toward goals in one group may prove extremely disruptive and dysfunctional in another group (or at a different time for the same group). A group's tolerance for stress and conflict can also depend on the type of organization it serves. Auto manufacturers, professional sports teams, and crisis organizations such as police and fire departments would have points at which functional conflict becomes dysfunctional that differ from those of universities, research and development firms, and movie production firms.

Conflict and organizational performance

Conflict may have either a positive or a negative impact on organizational performance, depending on the nature of the conflict and how it is managed. For every organization, an optimal level of conflict exists that can be considered highly functional; it helps generate positive performance. On one hand, when the conflict level is *too low,* performance can suffer. Innovation and change are difficult, and the organization may have difficulty in adapting to change in its environment. If this low conflict level continues, the organization's very survival can be threatened. On the other hand, if the conflict level becomes *too high,* the resulting chaos can also threaten its survival. An example is dissension in labor unions and its impact on performance. Fighting between rival factions in the union that becomes too great can render the union less effective in pursuing its mission of furthering its members' interests. The proposed relationship between level of intergroup conflict and organizational performance is presented in Figure 9–1 and explained for three hypothetical situations.

Views on intergroup conflict in practice

Some organizational researchers contend that dysfunctional conflict should be eliminated and functional conflict encouraged. But this isn't what actually happens in most organizations. In practice, most managers attempt to eliminate all types of conflict, whether dysfunctional or functional. But why? Some reasons are:

Figure 9–1

Proposed Relationship between Intergroup Conflict and Organizational Performance

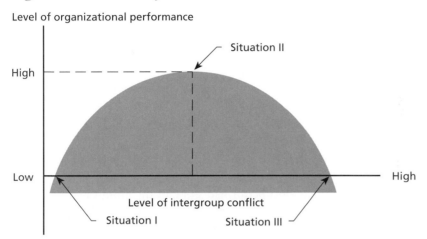

	LEVEL OF INTERGROUP CONFLICT	PROBABLE IMPACT ON ORGANIZATION	ORGANIZATION CHARACTERIZED BY	LEVEL OF ORGANIZATIONAL PERFORMANCE
SITUATION I	Low or none	Dysfunctional	Slow adaptation to environmental changes Few changes Little stimulation of ideas Apathy Stagnation	Low
SITUATION II	Optimal	Functional	Positive movement toward goals Innovation and change Search for problem solutions Creativity and quick adaptation to environmental changes	High
SITUATION III	High	Dysfunctional	Disruption Interference with activities Coordination difficult Chaos	Low

1. Anticonflict values have historically been reinforced in the home, school, and church. Traditionally, conflict between children or between children and parents has mostly been discouraged. In school systems, conflict was discouraged; teachers had all the answers, and both teachers and children were rewarded for orderly class-rooms. Finally, most religious doctrines stress peace, tranquillity, and acceptance without questioning.

2. Managers are often evaluated on and rewarded for the lack of conflict in their areas of responsibility. Anticonflict values, in fact, become part of the culture of the organization. Harmony and satisfaction are viewed positively, while conflicts and dissatisfaction are viewed negatively. Under such conditions, managers seek to avoid conflicts—functional or dysfunctional—that could disturb the status quo.

Why Intergroup Conflict Occurs

Every group comes into at least partial conflict with every other group with which it interacts. In this section, we examine four factors that contribute to group conflict: work interdependence, differences in goals, differences in perceptions, and the increased demand for specialists.

Work interdependence

Work interdependence occurs when two or more organizational groups depend on one another to complete their tasks. Conflict potential in such situations is high. Three distinct types of interdependence among groups have been identified.[4]

Pooled Interdependence

Interdependence that requires no interaction among groups except through the total organization.

www.ibm.com

POOLED INTERDEPENDENCE   Pooled interdependence requires no interaction among groups because each group, in effect, performs separately. However, the pooled performances of all the groups determine how successful the organization is. For example, the staff of an IBM sales office in one region may have no interaction with their peers in another region; similarly, two bank branches may have little or no interaction. In both cases, however, the groups are interdependent because the performance of each must be adequate if the total organization is to thrive. The conflict potential in pooled interdependence is relatively low, and management can rely on standard rules and procedures developed at the main office for coordination.

Sequential Interdependence

Interdependence that requires one group's output to serve as another group's input, thereby providing basis for great potential conflict.

SEQUENTIAL INTERDEPENDENCE   Sequential interdependence requires one group to complete its task before another group can complete its task. Tasks are performed in a sequential fashion. In a manufacturing plant, for example, the product must be assembled before it can be painted. Thus, the assembling department must complete its task before the painting department can begin painting.

Under circumstances in which one group's output serves as the input for another, conflict between groups is more likely to occur. Coordinating sequential interdependence involves effective planning by management.[5]

Reciprocal Interdependence

Interdependence that requires each group's output to serve as input to other groups in the organization.

RECIPROCAL INTERDEPENDENCE   Reciprocal interdependence requires each group's output to serve as input to other groups in the organization. Consider the relationships among the anesthesiology staff, nursing staff, technicians, and surgeons in a hospital operating room; such relationships create a high degree of reciprocal interdependence. The same interdependence exists among groups involved in space launchings. Another example is the interdependence between airport control towers, flight crews, ground operations, and maintenance crews. Clearly, the potential for conflict is great in any of these situations. Effective coordination involves management's skillful use of the organizational processes of communication and decision making.

All organizations have pooled interdependence among groups. Complex organizations also have sequential interdependence. The most complicated organizations experience pooled, sequential, and reciprocal interdependence among groups. The more complex the organization, the greater is the potential for conflict and the more difficult is the task facing management. The Close-Up on the next page illustrates the concept of interdependence in team sports.

Differences in goals

As the subunits of organization become specialized, they often develop dissimilar goals. A goal of a production unit may include low production costs and few defective products. A goal of the research and development unit may be innovative ideas that can be converted into commercially successful new products. These different goals can lead to different expectations among the members of each unit: production engineers may expect close supervision, while research scientists may expect a great deal of participation in decision making. Because of the different goals, conflict can result when these two groups interact. Finally, marketing departments usually have a goal of maximum gross income; in contrast, credit departments seek to minimize credit losses. Depending on which department prevails, different customers might be selected. Here again, conflict can occur because each department has a different goal. Because of differences in goals, certain conditions (such as resource availability and reward structures) foster intergroup conflict.

Limited resources

When limited resources must be allocated, mutual dependencies increase, and any differences in group goals become more apparent. If money, space, labor, and materials were unlimited, each group could pursue (at least to a relative degree) its own

---

CLOSE—UP

Interdependence in Sports

Sports teams are good examples of organizations where members must depend on one another if the entire group is to succeed. Examples of work interdependence in three team sports are shown in the table.

	BASEBALL TEAM	FOOTBALL TEAM	BASKETBALL TEAM
1. What is the nature (and degree) of tasks-based interaction among unit members?	Pooled (low).	Sequential (moderate).	Reciprocal (high).
2. What is the geographical distribution of unit members?	Widely dispersed.	Somewhat clustered.	Highly concentrated.
3. Given team objectives and constraints, where does autonomy reside?	Within each unit member.	Above the unit (that is, within unit management).	Among unit members (that is, within the unit as a whole).
4. How is coordination achieved?	Through unit design in which the sum of individual unit members' objectives approximates unit objectives.	Through complex protocols that clearly and tightly specify the roles and responsibilities of each unit member.	Through continuous self-regulation and responsibility sharing among unit members.
5. What sports expression metaphorically sums up the operating management task?	Fill out (revise) the lineup card.	Prepare (execute) the game plan.	Influence the game's flow.

Source: Robert W. Keidel, *Seeing Organizational Patterns: A New Theory and Language of Organizational Design. (San Francisco: Berett-Koehler Publishers), 1995. Adapted from Robert W. Keidel, "Baseball, Football and Basketball: Models for Business," Organizational Dynamics,* Winter 1984, pp. 12–14.

goals. But resources must be allocated and shared. Groups seek to lower pressure on themselves by gaining control over critical resource supplies, thus reducing the uncertainty of gaining these supplies.[6] What often occurs in limited-resource situations is a win–lose competition that can easily result in dysfunctional conflict if groups refuse to collaborate.

Reward structures

Intergroup conflict is more likely to occur when the reward system is related to individual group performance rather than to overall organizational performance. This potential for conflict escalates even further when one group has primary responsibility for distributing rewards. The group will tend to show strong partiality toward its own members in allocating favorable outcomes and strong partiality toward the out group in distributing negative outcomes.[7]

When rewards are aimed at individual groups, performances are viewed as an independent variable even while the group's performance is in reality very interdependent. For example, in the marketing versus credit situation just described, suppose that the marketing group is rewarded for sales produced and that the credit group is also rewarded for minimizing credit losses. In such a situation, competition is directly reinforced and dysfunctional conflict is inadvertently rewarded.

Intergroup conflict arising from differences in goals may be not only dysfunctional to the organization as a whole, but also dysfunctional to third-party groups—usually the organization's clients. An example is conflict in many teaching hospitals between meeting the goals of quality health care for patients and meeting future physicians' learning needs.

Differences in perceptions

Differences in goals can be accompanied by differing perceptions of reality; disagreements over what constitutes reality can lead to conflict. For instance, a problem in a hospital may be viewed in one way by the administrative staff and in another way by the medical staff; or alumni and faculty may have different perceptions concerning the importance of a winning football program. Many factors cause groups in organizations to form differing perceptions of reality.[8] Major factors include different goals, different time horizons, status incongruency, and inaccurate perceptions.

Different goals

Differences in group goals are an obvious contributor to differing perceptions. For instance, if the goal of marketing is to increase market shares and sales throughout the world, that department's personnel would not appreciate a reorganization task force goal to reduce expansion of the company's products to the Pacific Rim. Marketing perceives the Pacific Rim as important, and the task force perceives the Pacific Rim as too far from the home office to control and manage.

Different time horizons

Time perspectives influence how a group perceives reality. Deadlines influence the priorities and importance that groups assign to their various activities. Research scientists working for a chemical manufacturer may have a time perspective of several years, while the same firm's manufacturing engineers may work within time frames of less than a year. A bank president might focus on 5- and 10-year time spans, while middle managers might concentrate on much shorter spans. With such differences in time horizons, problems and issues deemed critical by one group may be dismissed as unimportant by another, setting the stage for conflict.

Status incongruency

Usually, many different status standards, rather than an absolute one, are found in an organization. The result is many status hierarchies. Conflicts concerning the relative status of different groups are common and influence perceptions. For example, status conflicts are often created by work patterns—which group initiates the work and which group responds. A production department may perceive a change as an affront to its status because it must accept a salesperson's initiation of work. This status conflict may be aggravated deliberately by salespeople. Another example involves the academic snobbery that's certainly a fact of campus life at many colleges: members of a particular academic discipline perceive themselves, for one reason or another, as having higher status than others.

Inaccurate perceptions

Inaccurate perceptions often cause one group to develop stereotypes about other groups. While the differences between groups may actually be small, each group tends to exaggerate them. Thus, you hear that "all women executives are aggressive" or "all bank officers behave alike." When differences between the groups are emphasized, stereotypes are reinforced, relations deteriorate, and conflict develops.

Increased demand for specialists

Conflicts between staff specialists and line generalists are probably the most common intergroup conflict. Line and staff persons simply view one another and their roles in the organization from different perspectives. With the growing necessity for technical expertise in all areas of organizations, staff roles might be expected to expand, and line and staff conflicts might be expected to increase. Table 9–1 summarizes some causes of conflict between staff specialists and generalists.[9] The increased sophistication, specialization, and complexity in most organizations make line–staff conflicts a major concern in managing of organizational behavior.

Consequences of Dysfunctional Intergroup Conflict

Researchers have spent more than four decades researching and analyzing how dysfunctional intergroup conflict affects those who experience it.[10] They have found that groups placed in a conflict situation tend to react in fairly predictable ways, in changes that occur within groups and between groups as a result of dysfunctional intergroup conflict.

Changes within groups

Many changes are likely to occur within groups involved in intergroup conflict. Unfortunately, these changes generally result in either continuance or escalation of the conflict.

individual groups involved in the conflict.[17] For example, in recent years several unions in the auto and airline industries have agreed to forgo pay increases and in some cases to accept pay reductions, because the survival of their firm or industry was threatened. When the crisis was over, demands for higher wages were again made.

Expansion of resources

As noted earlier, a major cause of intergroup conflict is limited resources. Whatever one group succeeds in obtaining is gained at the expense of another group. The scarce resource may be a particular position (e.g., presidency of the firm), money, or space. Expansion of resources may be one way of solving such problems. For example, when one major publishing firm decided to expand by establishing a subsidiary firm, most observers believed that the major reason for the expansion was to allow the firm to become involved in other segments of the market. While this was partially correct, a stronger reason was to enable the firm to stem the exit of valued personnel. By establishing the subsidiary, the firm was able to double its executive positions because the subsidiary needed a president, various vice presidents, and other executives. Expanding resources is potentially a successful technique for solving conflicts in many cases, since this technique may enable almost everyone to be satisfied. But in reality, resources usually aren't expanded.

Avoidance

Frequently, managers can find some way to avoid conflict. While avoidance may not bring any long-term benefit, it can certainly work as a short-run solution. However, avoiding a conflict could be misinterpreted as agreement with group actions or lack of fortitude on the manager's part.[18] Avoiding a conflict neither effectively resolves it nor eliminates it. Eventually, the conflict has to be faced. But in some circumstances, avoidance may be the best temporary alternative.

Smoothing

The technique known as *smoothing* emphasizes the common interests of the conflicting groups and de-emphasizes their differences. The basic belief behind smoothing is that stressing shared viewpoints on certain issues facilitates movement toward a common goal. The manager must explain to the conflicting groups that the organization's work will be jeopardized if the groups won't cooperate with each other.[19] As long as both groups see that the manager isn't taking sides, they may rise to the occasion and agree, at least, to a limited truce. But if differences between groups are serious, smoothing—like avoidance—is at best a short-run solution.

Compromise

Compromise is a traditional method for resolving intergroup conflicts. With compromise, there's no distinct winner or loser, and the decision reached is probably not ideal for either group. Compromise can be used effectively when the goal sought (e.g., money) can be divided equitably. If this isn't possible, one group must give up something of value as a concession.

Managers who endorse compromise as a conflict resolution tactic send out a message that they're sympathetic to both groups' demands. If used effectively, the manager can simultaneously take an aggressive approach to conflict resolution while exhibiting concern for those involved.[20]

Compromise may also involve third-party interventions, as well as total group or representative negotiating and voting.[21] The process of negotiation will be examined in detail later in the chapter.

Authoritative command

The use of authority may be the oldest, most frequently used method for resolving inter-group conflict. Using this method, management simply resolves the conflict as it sees fit and communicates its desires to the groups involved. Subordinates usually abide by a superior's decision, whether or not they agree with it. Thus, authoritative command usu-ally works in the short run. As with avoidance, smoothing, and compromise, however, it doesn't focus on the cause of the conflict but rather on its results. If the causes remain, conflict will probably recur.

Altering the human variable

Altering the human variable involves trying to change group members' behavior. This method focuses on the cause or causes of the conflict and on the attitudes of the people involved. While the method is certainly difficult, it does center on the cause of the con-flict. Part 6 of this book focuses specifically on changing behavior. In it, we show that, although slower than other methods and often costly, altering the human variable can have significant long-run results.

Altering the structural variables

Another way to resolve intergroup disputes is to alter the structural variables. This involves changing the formal structure of the organization. Structure refers to the fixed relationships among the jobs of the organization and includes the design of jobs and departments. Alter-ing the structure of the organization to resolve intergroup conflict involves such things as transferring, exchanging, or rotating members of the groups or having a coordinator, liai-son, or go-between who keeps groups communicating with one another.

Identifying a common enemy

In some respects, identifying a common enemy is the negative side of superordinate goals. Groups in conflict may temporarily resolve their differences and unite to combat a common enemy. The common enemy may be a competitor that has just introduced a clearly superior product. Conflicting groups in a bank may suddenly work in close har-mony when government bank examiners make a visit. The common-enemy phenome-non is very evident in domestic conflicts. Most police officers prefer not to become involved in heated domestic conflicts because, in far too many cases, combatants close ranks and turn on the police officer.

   The most commonly used methods for managing intergroup conflict each have strengths and weaknesses and are effective or ineffective in different situations. What this chapter has said thus far about intergroup conflict is summarized in Figure 9–2. The fig-ure illustrates the relationship between causes and types of intergroup conflict, the conse-quences of intergroup conflict, and techniques for resolution.

   Whatever the techniques utilized to deal with intergroup conflict (and there undoubt-edly are others not in the table), managers must learn how to recognize the existence and causes of intergroup conflict. They must also develop skills to effectively deal with it.

Managing Intergroup Conflict through Negotiation

A widely used yet often less recognized method of managing intergroup conflict is the process of negotiation. Despite its importance, the process is often misunderstood and badly carried out.[22] If done effectively, the negotiation process can be called a collabora-

Figure 9–2

An Overview of Intergroup Conflict

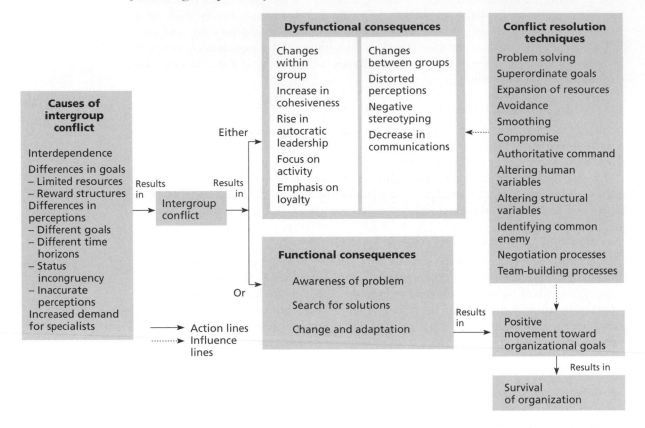

tive pursuit of joint gains and a collaborative effort to create value where none previously existed.[23] If done poorly, the process can be described as a street fight.

Negotiation entails having two sides with differing or conflicting interests come together to forge an agreement. Usually, each side will bring to the process a series of proposals that then are discussed and acted on. Everyone is familiar with the importance of bargaining to settle union disputes, formulate trade pacts, handle hostage situations, and reach arms agreements. Managers in organizations perform the same function on a continuing basis, negotiating with subordinates, superiors, vendors, and customers daily.

Group negotiations

Group negotiations take place whenever one group's work depends on the cooperation and actions of another group over which the first group's manager has no control.[24] Negotiations between marketing and production functions regarding order deliveries, between finance and engineering over research and development funding, and between maintenance and manufacturing over machine maintenance are all examples of the group process.

Negotiation differs from compromise in that the only really successful negotiations are those in which all the affected parties walk away feeling like they've won.[25] Several tasks and tactics can be undertaken by managers prior to and during the negotiation process to increase the probability of achieving mutually beneficial results.

Prenegotiation tasks

UNDERSTANDING THE OTHER SIDE   Prior to sitting down and negotiating with managers and/or representatives of other groups, managers must thoroughly understand the other side's needs and positions regarding the issues to be resolved.[26] A product manager who desperately wants a customer order filled by manufacturing within the next two weeks should be aware of other obligations currently being placed on manufacturing. Likewise, a sales group negotiating with a customer over a major purchase should know how the customer uses the product/service, how important it is to the customer's business, what elements of the purchase (e.g., delivery date, training, warranty, price) are critical to the customer, and what other alternatives are available to the customer. Regardless of whether the customer is internal (a more frequent occurrence as a result of divisionalization and decentralization efforts undertaken by organizations) or external to the organization, the same procedures apply.

To gain this information, the manager must ask questions. Although positions are usually up-front, underlying interests or problems often aren't.[27] A manager's goal should be to come to the negotiations with a full appreciation of the values, beliefs, and wants that drive the other side's actions. By freely exchanging information with the other group and performing as much outside or third-party research as possible, the manager can come prepared for the process. The element of surprise, which can prove to be of value in many business tactics, only serves to delay and hinder the negotiation process.

KNOWING ALL THE OPTIONS   Perhaps more important than the accumulation of information is its use in developing, understanding, and evaluating options available to resolve the conflict. Although the same issue may be negotiated over and over again, the outcomes may differ, depending on the parties involved or the timing of the negotiations.[28] One instance of a negotiation between two groups in an organization would be funding a capital investment. For example, discussions between finance and manufacturing may lead to the funds becoming available immediately, contingent on manufacturing's formulation of a detailed spending plan. A second outcome may consist of the funds being allocated over time, with the capital investment project being completed on a piecemeal basis. A third possible outcome would be the allocation of a certain percentage of the funding, with the remainder coming from the sale of the assets being replaced. The important point is that the greater the number of options that can be identified, the greater is the likelihood that both groups can benefit from the negotiation process.

Negotiation tactics

A countless number of specific negotiation tactics can be employed by managers involved in the process.[29] Several of the most often used ones will be discussed.

1. *Good-guy/bad-guy team.* Anyone who has read a detective story or seen a TV police show is familiar with this tactic. The bad-guy member of the negotiating group advocates positions so much out of line that whatever the good guy says sounds reasonable.

2. *The nibble.* This tactic involves getting an additional concession or perk after an agreement has been reached. An example would be the request for an additional staff position by a marketing manager after an agreement was reached between her group and another marketing group regarding division of market research duties.

3. *Joint problem solving.* A manager should never assume that the more one side wins, the more the other loses. Feasible alternatives not yet considered may exist. For instance, can manufacturing provide earlier completion dates on products if the sales department increases the order size and reduces the order frequency?

4. *Power of competition.* Tough negotiators use competition to make opponents think they don't need them. A line manager may use this tactic by threatening that his group will procure computer services outside the organization if the headquarters computer staff doesn't comply with demands. The most effective defense against this tactic is for a manager to remain objective. Don't commit quickly to unfavorable terms because of the fear of quick action on the other group's part.

5. *Splitting the difference.* This can be a useful technique when two groups come to an impasse. Managers should be careful, however, when the other group offers to split the difference too early. It may mean the other group has already gotten more than it thinks it deserves.

6. *Low-balling.* Ridiculously low offers and/or concessions are often used to lower the other group's expectations. A manager shouldn't let this type of offer lower her expectations or goals; nor should the manager walk out assuming the other group's position is inflexible. The communications process should continue.

Different situations call for different tactics. A manager should be aware of the options available and strive to understand the rationale behind the options.

The impact of personalities on the negotiation process

The process of negotiating is a very people-oriented experience. In addition to understanding the goals, needs, and wants of the other side, the successful negotiator tries to understand the relevant personality traits of the other individual(s) negotiating.[30] Negotiators come to the bargaining session from quite varied backgrounds; their experiences, like their perspectives, differ. Their propensities to take risk vary, and their personalities and attitudes are diverse. All this affects behavioral actions.[31] Managers must stop and look beneath the roles the other party to a negotiation is playing and ask what really motivates the individual(s).[32] Knowing these traits allows the manager to "read" and understand the opposing side, a valuable tool in negotiations.

Four of the most common types of personalities a manager will face at the negotiation table are:[33]

1. *The power seeker*—task- and results-oriented, seeking challenges and opportunities, and potentially confrontational. A good decision maker.

2. *The persuader*—outgoing, socially oriented, ambitious, and tough under a cloak of amiability, likability, and affability. A dangerous opponent at the negotiating table.

3. *The reliable performer*—solid, dependable, comfortable in supportive surroundings, and resistant to sudden change. Dependent on past precedents for confidence in decision making.

4. *The limited performer*—lacking in self-confidence, in need of a sheltered environment, nondecisive, and introverted. Likely to crack under pressure.

The degree of a manager's ability to successfully understand and handle people will ultimately determine his or her success at negotiating.

The role of trust

This chapter has defined *functional conflict* as a confrontation between groups that enhances and benefits the organization's effectiveness. In the negotiation process, there will be a greater likelihood of a beneficial outcome for the organization if a high degree of trust exists between the conflicting groups. Negotiators tend to regard making statements about their group's needs, wants, and priorities as risky and therefore are only willing to make them if there's mutual trust (i.e., they believe that the other side is also cooperatively motivated).[34] A high level of trust between the two conflicting parties will lead to greater openness and sharing of information.

Managers tend to expect a little chicanery when they're negotiating.[35] Even relatively cooperative bargainers often inject straw issues or exaggerate minor problems' importance to gain concessions on what really matters.[36] In nearly all bargaining encounters, a negotiator's key skill is the ability to communicate that she's firm on positions when, in fact, the negotiator is flexible—in short, bluffing about one's intentions. But bluffing doesn't constitute lying or fraud—managers should be well aware of the difference.

In addition, a good negotiator will never place the other party in a position from which he can't move without losing face.[37] By offering choices between alternatives (sometimes done by following mild demands with stronger ones), the other side will be more likely to view the process as cooperative and thus be more willing to reach an agreement.

Alternatives to direct negotiations

Occasionally, groups are unable to resolve their differences through direct negotiations. Likely candidates are groups that conflict often or are led by managers of equal rank. Groups can reach a point where they feel stuck in disagreement. Rather than letting the conflict evolve into a long, nasty battle, the two sides should seek outside help. A third party, often a CEO or other top executive, can be called in to mediate the dispute.[38] Use of a mediator allows an impartial person to work with the two sides to reach an agreement that benefits both sides and the organization as a whole. Bringing in a mediator early enough in the process allows conflicts to be resolved before group hostilities set in, which could lead to dysfunctional results.

An option to mediation is arbitration, in which groups are bound by the arbitrator's decision. Some companies set up formal committees of high-ranking executives whose sole purpose is to resolve disputes between groups.[39] These committees have the authority either to render a clear-cut decision in favor of one group, to provide for a mutually agreeable resolution, or to ask the involved parties to collect more information before a decision is reached. A benefit of this approach is that disagreeing parties don't have to compromise themselves in order to settle an issue. Once a decision is reached, both groups are able to return to a cooperative status.

Resolving Group Conflict through Team Building

In the previous chapter we focused a great deal of attention on teams as groups. We discussed the rationale for teams and various types of teams such as cross-functional teams and self-managed teams. Obviously one of the rationales for developing teams is to enable the work of the organization to be accomplished more effectively. We saw the many claimed benefits associated with teams such as improved productivity, streamlining, flexibility, quality, increased employee commitment, and improved customer satisfaction. The causes of intergroup conflict discussed in this chapter indicate that the potential for this type of conflict is present in every type of organization. Thus, there is great interest in team building as a means to reduce intergroup conflict. In fact, many people believe that the development of teams is the wave of the future for American organizations.[40] In fact, its widespread acceptance in the United States is also being accompanied by similar acceptance in Europe.[41]

Team Building

Encouraging people who work together to meet as a group in order to identify common goals, improve communications, and resolve conflicts.

The purpose of **team building** is to enable work groups to more effectively get their work done, to improve their performance.[42] It involves people who work together meeting as a group in order to examine such issues as:

- Is there an understanding of and commitment to common goals?
- Are we utilizing all of the skills and abilities of group members?
- Is there trust and communication among group members?
- Are we continually improving our performance as a group?

The group may be an existing or relatively new command or task group. Global organizations have found team building particularly useful when management groups consist of individuals from various national and cultural backgrounds.[43] Multinational groups reflect not only cultural diversity, but also the diversity due to their technical/functional expertise in one aspect of the business. Table 9–2 presents some conditions under which team building may be successful.

The specific aims of team building include setting goals and priorities, analyzing how the group does its work, examining the group's norms and processes for communicating and decision making, and assessing the interpersonal relationships within the group. As each of these aims is undertaken, the group is placed in the position of having to recognize explicitly the contributions, positive and negative, of each group member.[44]

Team building as a process

Team building is not a short-term strategy to reduce intergroup conflict. It requires a long-term commitment because it is an ongoing process that is really never completed. Ordinarily, the process begins with a series of *diagnostic* meetings. These meetings, which may last an entire day, allow all of the members of the groups to share their perceptions of problems and causes of conflict with all other members. If the groups are large, subgroups can be formed to discuss the issues and report their ideas to the larger group. Clearly, the purpose of these sessions is to obtain the views of all members and to make these views public. Thus, the ultimate purpose of the diagnostic phase is to openly confront issues and problems that previously were talked about in relative secrecy. Organizations such as DuPont have used the diagnostic step in their successful implementation of team building.[45]

 **www.dupont**
.com

Identifying problems and causes of conflict and reaching consensus as to their priority are important initial steps in the process of team building. Then a *plan of action* must be agreed on. The action plan should require each group member or members to

---

Table 9–2

Where Team Building Might Work in Reducing Intergroup Conflict

1. The work is extremely complex. One individual cannot be expected to make every decision.

2. Group members who do the work have the knowledge and expertise about how it should be done.

3. Working as individuals or separate groups has not been productive.

4. External demands or other circumstances often require quick responses and decisions.

5. Group members want to assume responsibility for the processes and product of their efforts.

6. The work requires people in different parts of the organization to interact frequently and often one group does not know what the other is doing.

7. External demands from competition and technology require a more flexible and responsive organization.

Sources: Adapted from M. D. Maginn, *Effective Teamwork,* (Burr Ridge, Ill.: Irwin Professional Publishing, 1994), pp. 5–7, and J. D. Orsburn, L. Moran, E. Musselwhite, J. Zenger, and C. Perrin, *Self-Directed Work Teams,* (Burr Ridge, Ill.: Irwin Professional Publishing, 1990), Chapter 2.

undertake a specific action to alleviate one or more of the problems. If, for example an executive committee agrees that a major cause of conflict is a lack of understanding and commitment to a set of goals, a subgroup can be appointed to recommend goals to the total group at a subsequent meeting. Other group members can work on other problems. For example, if causes of conflict are identified in the relationships among the members, another subgroup can initiate a process for examining the roles of each member. However, team-building activities do not always require a complex process of diagnostic and plan of action meetings as is illustrated in the Close-Up. It features a relatively simple as well as successful application of team building in a small manufacturing firm.

Management's role in building teams

In the previous chapter we saw the benefits that can occur from the successful implementation of teams. It should be clear that major changes are required in most organizations if teams are to succeed. Teams require resources and authority if they are to gain the flexibility and commitment from members. If team building is to succeed the following elements are critical to its success:[46]

- *Management commitment.* Team building cannot be "this year's thrust." It requires the commitment of management to understand the early-stage problems that often occur in any transition, such as resistance to change, as well as to ensure the availability of the necessary resources. Team building will fail without a committed management group with a long-term focus.

- *Trust.* Mutual trust between management and employees is a prerequisite for success in team building. Managers must trust that, given sufficient time, employees

CLOSE—UP

Resolving Conflict through Team Building in a Small Organization

The chief executive officer of a small manufacturing firm recognized that conflict within his executive group was creating tension between the functional departments. He also realized that his practice of dealing on a one-to-one basis with each of the executive group members (each of whom headed a functional department) contributed to the tension and conflict. Rather than viewing themselves as team members having a stake in the organization, the functional heads viewed each other as competition. The chief executive's practice of dealing with them individually confirmed their beliefs that they managed relatively independent units.

To counteract the situation, the chief executive decided to require the top group to meet twice weekly. One meeting focused on operating problems, the other on personal problems. The ground rule for these meetings was that the group must reach consensus on decisions. After one year

of such meetings, the executive group routinely made company-oriented decisions and the spirit of cooperation replaced the climate of interdepartmental conflict.

The chief executive believes that the team-building efforts were a success and overcame certain problems, including

1. Confusion as to roles and relationships within the team.

2. Members having a fairly clear understanding of short-term functional goals but vague understanding of long-term organizational goals.

3. Individuals having technical skills, which puts them on the team, but lacking interpersonal skills, which prevents them from contributing to the team.

4. Members often paying more attention to the tasks of the team than to the relationships among the team members.

The CEO believes that had he not initiated team-building meetings, the group would have continued to focus on task problems, but ignored the relationship issues.

will support the changes necessary to effectively implement team building. Employees must trust that management really wants to know their opinion. Where there is a great deal of mistrust of management, employees may cynically look at the team-building effort as just another management ploy to get more work done with fewer people.

• *Sharing information.* Obviously, if teams are to support the goals of the organization, they will require information about overall results, including financial information. Here again, mutual trust is critical. Secrecy in many organizations has done little to nurture an environment in which information is willingly shared by management with employees and by managers with other managers. A willingness to share information is critical to successful team building.

• *Training.* Most teams cannot manifest on their own. They usually require training because individuals are being asked to put aside personal concerns and contribute to a group effort. Members therefore usually need training in team building, listening, communication, that will counteract habits and attitudes left over from the previous work environment.

• *Union partnership.* If the organization is unionized, the union must be an active participant and partner in the team-building effort. Here again, trust and the sharing of information will be critical.

Managing Intergroup Conflict through Stimulation

Throughout this chapter, we have stressed that some conflict is beneficial. This point is made again in Figure 9–2 on page 236, which includes functional consequences of intergroup conflict. The figure indicates that, out of conflict, change can develop from an awareness of problems and from a creative search for alternative solutions. We've already examined a situation where conflict is dysfunctional because it's too high and requires resolution. But it's also possible that intergroup conflict may be too low and require stimulation to generate action.

While lack of conflict may prove beneficial in the short run, it could lead to situations where one group holds tremendous influence over another. For example, observers of the Japanese style of participative management question whether the lack of conflict between managers and employees in Japanese firms is healthy.[47] This section provides techniques that have stimulated conflict to a functional level, where it contributes positively to organizational performance.[48]

Communication

By intelligent use of the organization's communication channels, a manager can stimulate beneficial conflict. Information can be placed carefully into formal channels to create ambiguity, reevaluation, or confrontation. Information that's threatening (e.g., a proposed budget cut) can stimulate functional conflict in a department and improve performance. Carefully planted rumors can also serve a useful purpose. For example, a hospital administrator may start a rumor about a proposed reorganization of the hospital. The purpose is twofold: (1) to stimulate new ideas on how to more effectively carry out the mission of the hospital and (2) to reduce apathy among the staff.

Bringing outside individuals into the group

A technique widely used to bring a stagnant organization or subunit of an organization "back to life" is to hire or transfer in individuals whose attitudes, values, and backgrounds differ from those of the group's present members. Many college faculties consciously seek new members with different backgrounds, often discouraging the hiring of graduates of their own programs. This is to ensure a diversity of viewpoints on the faculty. The technique of bringing in outsiders is also widely used in government and business. Recently, a bank president decided not to promote from within for a newly created position of marketing vice president. Instead, he hired a highly successful executive from the very competitive consumer products field. The bank president felt that while the outsider knew little about marketing financial services, her approach to and knowledge of marketing were what the bank needed to become a strong competitor.

Altering the organization's structure

Changing the structure of the organization not only helps resolve intergroup conflict; it also *creates* conflict. For example, suppose a school of business has one large department. The Department of Business Administration includes all faculty members who teach courses in management, marketing, finance, and production management. Accordingly, the department is rather large, with 32 members under one department chairperson, who reports to the dean. A new dean has recently been hired, and he's considering dividing the business administration unit into several separate departments (e.g., marketing, finance, management), each with five or six members and a chairperson. The reasoning is that reorganizing in this manner will create competition among the groups for resources, students, faculty, and so forth, where none existed before because there was only one group. The dilemma is whether this restructuring will improve performance.

Stimulating competition

Many managers utilize various techniques to stimulate competition among groups. Incentives, such as awards and bonuses for outstanding performance, often stimulate competition. If properly utilized, such incentives help maintain a healthy atmosphere of competition that may result in a functional level of conflict. Incentives can be given for least defective parts, highest sales, best teacher, or most new customers as well as in any area where increased conflict is likely to lead to more effective performance.

Managing intergroup conflict through stimulation is a difficult challenge for a manager. It can easily backfire and quickly become dysfunctional conflict.

Summary of Key Points

- Conflict between groups is inevitable in organizations. This conflict may be positive or negative, depending on its impact on the organization's goal achievement.

- Functional conflict represents a confrontation between groups that enhances and benefits the organization's performance.

- Dysfunctional conflict results from a confrontation or interaction between groups that hinders the achievement of organizational goals.

- While most managers try to eliminate conflict, evidence indicates that for most organizations an optimal level of conflict can positively influence organizational performance.

- Intergroup conflict results from such factors as work interdependence, differences in goals, differences in perceptions, and the increasing demand for specialists.

- Dysfunctional conflict causes changes to take place within and between the groups involved. Within the group, there may be an increase in group cohesiveness, a rise in autocratic leadership, a focus on the task, and an emphasis on loyalty. Changes occurring between the groups include distorted perceptions, negative stereotyping, and a decrease in communication.

- One difficult task a manager must confront is diagnosing and managing intergroup conflict. Techniques for resolving intergroup conflict include problem solving, superordinate goals, expansion of resources, avoidance, smoothing, compromise, authority, changing either the people or the organization's structure, and identifying a common enemy. The processes of negotiation and team building are also valuable conflict management techniques. Each of these techniques is useful in specific situations and circumstances and both are becoming increasingly popular among managers.

• Conflict management techniques also exist for situations where the manager diagnoses a level of conflict that's dysfunctional because it's too low. Conflict stimulation techniques include using the communication channels, hiring or transferring in differently oriented individuals, changing the organization's structure, and stimulating competition. The important point is that effective conflict management involves both resolution and stimulation.

Discussion and Review Questions

1. Should the process of negotiation such as the one described in this chapter be implemented to resolve student–faculty conflicts? Why?

2. Discuss a situation in which your group was involved in a conflict with another group. Describe any changes that took place within your group and between the two groups.

3. Some individuals believe that compromise isn't a good conflict resolution technique because there's no distinct winner and the decision reached is probably not ideal for either group. What are your beliefs about compromise as a conflict resolution technique?

4. Describe how the three types of work interdependence could each lead to conflict between two groups within a specific student organization you're familiar with.

5. Why is trust such an important aspect of the negotiation process?

6. Is competition for grades among students functional or dysfunctional? Why?

7. Some individuals believe that conflict is necessary for change to take place. Comment.

8. Identify a situation at your school where higher levels of conflict could be beneficial. Describe how you would stimulate such conflict.

9. The president of your school asks you to recommend strategies for eliminating student apathy. What do you suggest?

10. What is meant when it's said that a manager must be able to diagnose intergroup conflict situations? How can a manager obtain these diagnostic skills?

C A S E   F O R   A N A L Y S I S

A Successful Partnership at Ford-Mazda

While international joint ventures among auto manufacturers make great sense, often they don't make great profits. After years of arguments, General Motors is selling its half-ownership in Korea's Daewoo Motor Co. The auto giant must also bail out loss-plagued Isuzu, in which it owns a 37.5 percent stake. The list of cross-cultural disappointments goes on: Chrysler-Mitsubishi, Chrysler-Masserati, and Fiat-Nissan have all produced as much rancor as rewards. With U.S.–Japan ties frayed, especially over auto trade, links between American and Japanese carmakers are under extra strain.

Ford-Mazda is the exception. Their marriage has weathered disagreements over specific projects, trade disputes between Japan and the United States, and even allegations by the Big Three that Mazda and other Japanese rivals were dumping minivans in the United States. The alliance, founded when Ford stepped in to rescue the struggling Japanese carmaker in 1979, stands strong. The two companies cooperate on new vehicles and exchange valuable expertise— Ford in international marketing and finance. Mazda in manufacturing and product development.

Ford and Mazda work jointly on 10 current auto models, usually with Ford doing most styling and Mazda making key engineering contributions. Jointly worked cars included the Ford Escort and Mercury Tracer models, the subcompact Festiva, the sporty Ford Probe and Mercury Capri, and the off-road Explorer. The Ford-aided Mazdas are the MX-6, 323, Protege, and Navajo. In all, approximately one of every four Ford cars sold in the United States benefits from some degree of Mazda involvement—everything from manufacturing methods to steering designs—while two of every five Mazdas has some Ford influence.

Ford and Mazda can call on some hard-learned principles for managing a successful strategic alliance, many of which would apply to ties in any industry. The secrets to the Ford-Mazda success are:

Keep top management involved. The boss must set a tone for the relationship. Otherwise, middle managers will resist ceding partial control of a project to a partner.

Meet often, and often informally. Meetings should be at all levels and should include time for socializing. Trust can't be built solely around a boardroom table.

Use a matchmaker. A third party can mediate disputes, suggest new ways of approaching the partner, and offer an independent sounding board.

Maintain your independence. Independence helps both parties hone the areas of expertise that made them desirable partners in the first place.

Allow no "sacrifice deals." Every project must be viable for each partner. Senior management must see that an overall balance is maintained.

Appoint a monitor. Someone must take primary responsibility for monitoring all aspects of the alliance.

Anticipate cultural differences. They may be corporate or national. Stay flexible and try to place culturally sensitive executives in key posts.

Underlying these principles is the idea that benign neglect is no basis for a partnership. Or, as Ford President Phillip E. Benton Jr. stated, "There's a lot of hard work in making it work."

Discussion Questions

1. Why might there be high potential for conflict in relationships such as the one enjoyed by Ford-Mazda?

2. What means of managing group conflicts, as discussed in Chapter 9, are utilized in the Ford-Mazda partnership?

3. Why do you think the Ford-Mazda partnership has been so successful, while many others (including those listed at the beginning of the case) haven't been?

Sources: "The Partners," *Business Week,* February 10, 1992, pp. 102–7; Stratford Shersan, "Are Strategic Alliances Working?" *Fortune,* September 21, 1992, pp. 77–78; Arvind Parkhe, "Interfirm Diversity, Organizational Learning, and Longevity in Global Strategic Alliances," *Journal of International Business Studies,* Winter 1991, pp. 579–602.

 **www2.ford.com, www.Mazda.com**

E X P E R I E N T I A L   E X E R C I S E

The Old Stack Problem

Objectives

1. To closely examine the dynamics of intergroup competition.

2. To illustrate a group's effectiveness in solving a problem.

Starting the Exercise

Step 1: Group problem solving (30 minutes). Divide into groups of four to six persons each. Each group member should read "The Problem" below. The best procedure is for each person to develop a solution independently and for the group to spend a period of time discussing these solutions without evaluating them. Then solutions should be evaluated and the best solution adopted.

The problem may be assigned in advance of class to give students more time to develop solutions. However, the final discussion and selection process should be done as a group in the classroom.

Step 2: Select judges and spokespeople (5 minutes). Each group should select one member to serve on a panel of judges to select the best solution. A spokesperson must also be selected to present the solution to the panel of judges.

Step 3: Present solutions (15 minutes). Spokespeople for each group will present their group's solution to the judges and the remainder of the class. A chalkboard or flip chart should be used to illustrate the solution along with the spokesperson's explanation. The explanation should be brief and concise, and spokespeople may not criticize other solutions. Spokespeople should provide quality arguments in support of their solutions.

Step 4: Straw vote (5 minutes). After all group solutions have been presented, the judges may think about the solutions for one or two minutes. Then judges will state in turn which solution they prefer. *Judges must make their judgments independently, without discussion among themselves.* Judges are asked simply to state the solution they prefer. They don't explain their reasons for voting. The instructor should record the number of votes given for each solution on the chalkboard or flip chart next to that solution.

Step 5: Modified problem solving (10 minutes). Student groups re-form and discuss their approach. Judges and spokespeople return to their original groups. At this time, the groups may not change the basic strategy of their solution, but they may provide refinements. Groups are encouraged to compare their solution to other solutions at this point and may instruct the spokesperson to present weaknesses in other solutions as well as strengths of their own. The group also has the freedom to nominate a new spokesperson or judge at this time.

Step 6: Restate solutions (10 minutes). The group spokespeople briefly restate the solutions using the earlier illustration. Minor modifications can be made. Spokespeople are encouraged to point out the strengths of their group's solutions and to criticize other solutions. Spokespeople's goal is to persuade the judges that their group's solution is best.

Step 7: Final vote. The judges are given one or two minutes to individually decide which solution to vote for. Judges may not discuss the solutions among themselves, and they must state their vote out loud. The instructor will indicate the number of votes next to each solution's illustration. The solution that receives the most votes is the winner.

Step 8: Discussion (15 minutes). The class as a whole should reflect on their experience and discuss what happened. Students are encouraged to be self-reflective about their feelings toward their own group's solution, toward the judges, and so on. Judges are encouraged to express their feelings about any pressures they felt from the group to vote in a certain way. The instructor or student may also wish to compare their observations to theories of intergroup behavior as illustrated in lectures or readings. The following questions may help guide that discussion.

1. Did any examples of scapegoating occur? Did losing groups express dissatisfaction or unfairness with the judges or the evaluation process?

2. Did any groups pressure the judges to act as a representative of their group rather than to vote in an unbiased fashion? Did judges feel pressure to represent their group even if pressure was not overtly expressed?

3. Did any groups develop a superiority complex, wherein they truly believed that their own group solution was best although from an objective perspective the solution may not have been best?

4. What were the reactions of the winning group and losing groups? Did winners seem happy and satisfied while losers seemed discontented with one another or with the exercise?

5. During the second round of presentations, were certain solutions singled out for more criticism? Were these solutions the ones that received the most votes in the straw ballot, as if people were trying to tear down the strongest contender?

6. How does this group exercise compare to functioning of groups in the real world? These groups existed temporarily, while groups in the real world engage in real competitions and have strong and lasting commitments. Would representatives of real-world groups tend to reflect group wishes or to reach unbiased decisions? How might intergroup difficulties be overcome in organizations?

Exhibit 1

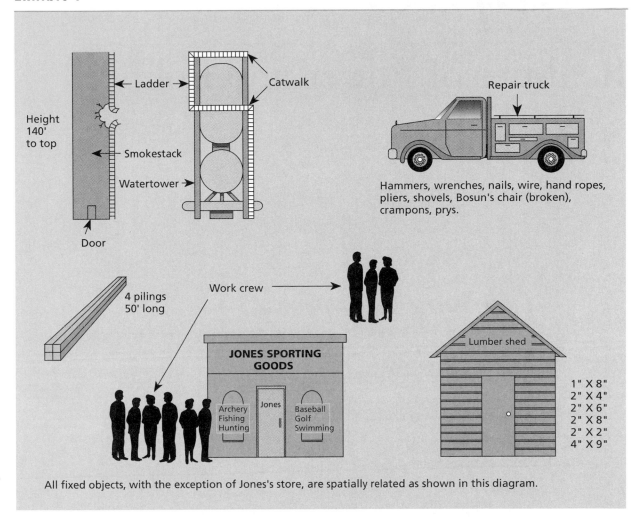

All fixed objects, with the exception of Jones's store, are spatially related as shown in this diagram.

The Problem

An explosion has ripped a hole in a brick smokestack. The stack appears to be perfectly safe, but a portion of the access ladder has been ripped away and the remainder loosened. Your engineers need to inspect the damage immediately to determine whether the stack may collapse. How do you get one of your engineers up to inspect the hole safely and efficiently?

The smokestack is 140 feet high. The structure next to the smokestack is a water tower. Your solution should use only those materials in Exhibit 1, including what you assume to be in the truck and sporting goods store.

Source: The original source for this exercise couldn't be identified.

Chapter 10

Realities of Power and Politics

Learning Objectives

After completing Chapter 10, you should be able to:

Define
What is meant by the expression "two faces of power."

Describe
The five interpersonal power bases.

Discuss
How subunits within an organization acquire and use power.

Compare
The tactics used in the insurgency and counterinsurgency political games.

Identify
The reasons why an illusion of power can influence a person's behavior.

P

ower is a pervasive part of the fabric of organizational life.[1] Getting things done requires power.[2] Every day, managers in public and private organizations acquire and use power to accomplish goals and, in many cases, to strengthen their own position. A person's success or failure at using or reacting to power is largely determined by understanding power, knowing how and when to use it, and being able to anticipate its probable effects.

This chapter explains power and its uses in organizational settings. We also examine the bases of power, the need for power, and the relationship between power and organizational politics. The chapter indicates that power is not a dirty secret but is actually a mechanism used continually to achieve organizational, group, and individual goals.

Power and Authority

The study of power and its effects is important to understanding how organizations operate. Every interaction and every social relationship in an organization involves an exercise of power.[3] How organizational subunits and individuals are controlled is related to the issue of power. In an organizational setting, **power** is simply the ability to get others to do what one wants them to do.

Power involves a relationship between two or more people. Robert Dahl, a political scientist, captures this important relational focus when he defines power as "A has power over B to the extent that he can get B to do something B would not otherwise do."[4] A person or group cannot have power in isolation; power has to be exercised or have the potential for being exercised in relation to some other person or group.

Some feel that power is best used in isolation by one person over other people. Conversely, the power-sharing argument asserts that unless some power is shared, productivity, quality, and customer satisfaction will never reach their highest potential levels. However, this raises the problem of determining how to implement power sharing.

Power

Ability to get others to do what one wants them to do.

Power sharing requires time to develop within an organization's culture. It cannot be forced on people, and proper leadership and vision are needed to implement the process.[5] Time is needed to develop (1) better lines of communication, (2) more trust, and (3) openness between the power sharers—managers and subordinates or subunits. Since organizations have for many years relied on authority hierarchies to accomplish goals, it is unreasonable to expect managers simply to begin sharing their power with others without some resistance.

The literature distinguishes between power and authority. Max Weber was the first to call attention to differences between these two concepts.[6] He believed that power involves force and coercion. Authority, however, is a subset of power. Much narrower in scope, authority does not carry the implication of force. Rather, it involves a "suspension of judgment" on the part of its recipients. **Authority** is the formal power that a person has because of his position in the organization. Directives or orders from a manager in an authority position are followed because they must be followed. That is, persons in higher positions have legal authority over subordinates in lower positions. In the authority hierarchy, the chief executive officer (CEO) is above the district manager, who is above the salesperson. Authority has the following characteristics:

Authority

Formal power a person holds because of her position in the organizational hierarchy.

1.   It is vested in a person's position. An individual has authority because of the position that he holds, not because of any specific personal characteristics.

2.   It is accepted by subordinates. The individual in a legal authority position exercises authority and can gain compliance because she has a legitimate right.

3.   Authority is used vertically and flows from the top down in the hierarchy of an organization.

Influence is a word we often come across when studying power. We agree with Henry Mintzberg and others that making a distinction between *influence* and *power* adds little to understanding.[7] Therefore, we use the terms *influence* and *power* interchangeably throughout this chapter.

Power can be derived from many sources. How it's obtained in an organization depends to a large extent on the type of power being sought. Power can be derived from interpersonal, structural, and situational bases.

Interpersonal Power

John French and Bertram Raven suggested five interpersonal bases of power: legitimate, reward, coercive, expert, and referent.[8]

Legitimate power

Legitimate Power

A person's ability to influence others by being in a more powerful position.

Legitimate power is a person's ability to influence because of position. A person at a higher level has power over people below. In theory, organizational equals (e.g., all first-line supervisors) have equal legitimate power. However, each person with legitimate power uses it with a personal flair. Legitimate power is similar to the concept of authority.

Subordinates play a major role in the exercise of legitimate power. If subordinates view the use of power as legitimate, they comply. However, the culture, customs, and value systems of an organization determine the limits of legitimate power. A company president who suggests that all employees should vote for a particular political candidate may find that only some people comply with the suggestion.

Reward power

A person derives power from the ability to reward compliance. **Reward power** is often used to back up the use of legitimate power. If followers value the rewards or potential rewards that the person can provide (recognition, a good job assignment, a pay raise, additional resources to complete a job), they may respond to orders, requests, and directions. For example, a sales manager who can reward salespeople with cash bonuses, expanded client lists, or additional entertainment funds can exert reward power. Reward power works best when employees understand how they can achieve rewards and are kept abreast of their status toward earning the reward.[9] A type of reward becoming more prevalent is the granting of ownership through issuing stock shares to employees when they reach certain milestones. In this way, employees are further encouraged to work harder and smarter as the value of their ultimate reward is dependent on organization results.[10]

Reward Power

A person's ability to reward the behavior of others.

Coercive power

The opposite of reward power is **coercive power,** the power to punish. Followers may comply because of fear. A manager may block a promotion or transfer a subordinate for poor performance. These practices, and the fear that they'll be used, are coercive power. Although punishment may result in some unexpected side effects, it's a form of coercive power that's still used to bring about compliance or to correct nonproductive behavior in organizations. For example, when he was CEO of Scott Paper, Albert Dunlap fired 11,125 employees and 9 of 11 members of his executive committee in his first year in office due to his discontent with their job performance.[11] For this and similar actions with other organizations, Dunlap has earned the name "Chainsaw Al". Managers tend to use coercive power in situations where large numbers of employees are being supervised.[12]

Coercive Power

Capability to punish noncompliance of followers.

Expert power

A person with special expertise that's highly valued has **expert power.** Experts have power even when their rank is low. An individual may possess expertise on technical, administrative, or personal matters. The more difficult it is to replace the expert, the greater the expert power she possesses.

Expert power is a personal characteristic, while legitimate, reward, and coercive power are largely prescribed by the organization. A secretary who has a relatively low-level organizational position may have high expert power because she knows the details of operating the business—where everything is or how to handle difficult situations.

Expert Power

The power to influence others based on special expertise.

Referent power

Many individuals identify with and are influenced by a person because of the latter's personality or behavioral style. The charisma of the person is the basis of **referent power.** A person with charisma is admired because of her personality and the means she uses to speak from her heart.[13] The strength of a person's charisma is an indication of her referent power. *Charisma* is a term often used to describe the magnetic personalities of some politicians, entertainers, or sports figures. Some managers are also regarded by their subordinates as charismatic.

The five bases of interpersonal power can be divided into two major categories: organizational and personal. Legitimate, reward, and coercive power are primarily prescribed by the organization, the position, formal groups, or specific interaction patterns.

Referent Power

Power based on charisma due to personality or style of behavior.

A person's legitimate power can be changed by transferring the person, rewriting the job description, or reducing the person's power by restructuring the organization. In contrast, expert and referent power are very personal. A person has expertise, or he develops a set of credentials or the image characteristics of an expert. A person has or does not have charisma. It can't be tampered with, modified, or developed through training programs. It's a personal style that's quite individualized.

The five types of interpersonal power aren't independent. On the contrary, managers can use these power bases effectively in various combinations in differing circumstances. Several studies have examined issues related to contextual uses of power. One study of organizations found that legitimate, expert, and referent power were the three most important reasons employees reported for doing what a peer or boss requested.[14] Two other studies' findings determined a strong correlation between managers' levels and use of expert and referent power and employees' emotional involvement and commitment to their jobs.[15] Legitimate power was found to be highly associated with compliance but negatively associated with employee satisfaction.

An interesting study conducted in three organizations investigated whether gender differences existed in subordinates' perceptions of managers' power.[16] Results indicated that male and female managers did not show significant differences in reward, coercive, legitimate, and referent bases of power. However, subordinates rated female managers higher than male managers on expert power. Male managers with female subordinates were rated lower on expert power than other gender combinations. Thus, sex-role stereotypes appear not to bias perceptions of power possession. Rather, it appears that an individual manager's level in the organizational power structure has a greater effect on employee perceptions of power than does the manager's gender.[17]

One must also realize that regardless of the organization, an individual's power cannot last forever. For some, loss of power is an expected evolutionary process. For others, it is a more sudden, dramatic loss. There are some who believe that organizations are changing in ways that may result in fewer all-powerful executives. The Close-Up "Is the All-Powerful Executive Becoming Extinct?" examines this issue.

Need for Power

Throughout history, human beings have been fascinated by power. In ancient Chinese writings, concern about power is clearly expressed—the taming power of the great, the power of light, the power of the dark. Early religious writings contain numerous references to persons who possess or acquire power. Historical records show differences in the extent to which individuals have pursued, feared, enjoyed, and misused power. The image of those who seek power is, for the most part, quite negative. For example, power seekers have been portrayed as:[18]

Neurotics covering up feelings of inferiority, anxiety, or hatred.

Persons substituting power for lack of affection, being alone, or being deprived of friendship.

Those attempting to compensate for some childhood deprivation.

Need for Power (n pow)

Desire to influence others.

David McClelland proposes that power can be responsibly sought and used.[19] The **need for power** (or **n Pow** as he refers to it) is defined by McClelland as the desire to have an impact on others. This impact may be shown basically in three ways: (1) by strong action, by giving help or advice, by controlling someone, (2) by action that produces emotion in others, and (3) by a concern for reputation.

Research has attempted to determine how people high in n Pow behave as contrasted with people low in n Pow. In general, individuals high in n Pow are competitive and aggressive, are interested in prestige possessions (e.g., an expensive car), prefer action situations, and join a number of groups. In an organizational setting, results of a recent study somewhat surprisingly found that the degree of a manager's need for power is correlated with success.[20] The most effective managers disciplined and controlled their desire for power so that it was directed toward the organization as a whole—not toward their own personal aggrandizement. These individuals tended not to display personal insecurity; rather, they possessed great emotional maturity and a democratic, coaching managerial style.[21]

CLOSE — UP

Is The All-Powerful Executive Becoming Extinct?

In the last decade, several powerful executives fell from power. William Agee's career began after completing his MBA from Harvard, and by the early age of 31, he was chief financial officer of Boise Cascade. After a position as CEO of an auto-parts maker, he became chairman and CEO of Morrison Knudsen in 1988. His decline followed shortly thereafter after he was accused of having "delusions of grandeur" and misusing company assets. He was fired. He now lives in exile far away from the corporate world.

Robert Buckely, former chairman of Allegheny International, was fired after seven years with the organization and filed for personal bankruptcy in 1995. Unfortunately for Buckely, the company is asking him to repay a $2.9 million low-interest loan he took from the company while he was CEO.

There were others in the 1990s as well. Ivan Boesky, a powerful and "successful inside trader," found his reward in $100 million in fines and two years in jail. William Aramony, former head of United Way, quickly fell from power after being accussed of misusing funds.

As the decade of the '90s ends, there are some who believe that organizations are changing in ways that might result in fewer all-powerful executives. First, knowledge organizations with highly educated and trained employees often rely on project teams. To be effective, these teams require cross-functional cooperation, which often cannot exist in an environment of strict obedience to authority and formal hierarchy. In such an environment, executives often are forced to share power.

Second, megamergers often result in two or more powerful executives sharing power. In fact, these types of power-sharing arrangements are increasing in such numbers that there have been recommendations suggested on how to make power-sharing work. One set recommends: (1) agree on a definition of success; (2) acknowledge each other's strengths and define roles accordingly; (3) make communications a priority; (4) build trust; and (5) get to know the other guy's people.

Although there can be no denying the rise to an all-powerful executive can be an exciting ride, it can also come to an unhappy end. While it may be premature to declare the all-powerful executive to be extinct, perhaps as we have seen here, circumstances in the new millenium will be such that there will be a new power game in many organizations, namely the sharing of power.

Adapted from: Thomas A. Steward, "Get with the New Power Game," *Fortune*, June 13, 1997, pp. 58–62; Ram Charan, "Two on Top," *Fortune*, May 25, 1998, pp. 193–196; Brian O'Reilly, "Agee in Exile," *Fortune*, May 29, 1995, pp. 50–74; Patricia Sellers, "So You Fail, Now Bounce Back," *Fortune*, May 1, 1995, pp. 48–66; and Stephen Baker, "A Hard Look at an Ex-CEO's Hard Luck," *Business Week*, April 10, 1995, p. 8.

 **www.bcop.com**

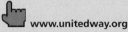 **www.unitedway.org**

Structural and Situational Power

Power is primarily prescribed by the structure of the organization.[22] The organization's structural arrangements allocate decision-making discretion to various positions. Structure also establishes patterns of communication and the flow of information. Thus, organizational structure creates formal power and authority by specifying certain individuals to perform specific jobs and make certain decisions.

We've already discussed how formal position is associated with power and authority. Certain rights, responsibilities, and privileges accrue from a person's position. Other forms of structural power exist because of resources, decision making, and information.[23]

Resources

Rosabeth Kanter argues convincingly that power stems from access to resources, information, and support and from the ability to get cooperation in doing necessary work.[24] Power occurs when a person has open channels to resources (money, workers, technology, materials, and customers). In organizations, vital resources are allocated downward along the lines of the hierarchy.[25] The top-level manager has more power to allocate resources than do managers further down in the managerial hierarchy. The lower-level manager receives resources granted by top-level managers. To ensure compliance with goals, top-level managers (e.g., presidents, vice presidents, directors) allocate resources on the basis of performance and compliance. Thus, a top-level manager usually has power over a lower-level manager, who must receive resources from above to accomplish goals.

The *dependency* relationship exists because of limited resources and division of labor.[26] The division of labor (e.g., positions in the hierarchy) grants upper management, by position, the privilege of allocating limited resources.[27] Without adequate compliance with top management's goals and requests, a lower level manager cannot receive the necessary resources to do the job. On the other hand, a wise top management team knows that to improve performance, lower level managers must be given adequate power and resources to control their destinies.[28]

Decision-making power

The degree to which individuals or subunits (e.g., a department or a special project group) can affect decision making determines their level of power. A person or subunit with power can influence how the decision-making process occurs, what alternatives are considered, and when a decision is made. For example, shrewd employees can help their bosses avoid making hasty decisions—first by describing the issue in full and then by explaining why the decision needs to be made carefully.[29] Conversely, managers need to provide employees with parameters for making decisions, thereby simultaneously delegating power and guiding the use of it toward organizational objectives.[30]

Information power

Having access to relevant and important information gives power. Information is the basis for making effective decisions. Thus, those who possess information needed to make optimal decisions have power. The accountant's position in the organization structure may not accurately portray the power she wields. Accountants do not generally have a particularly strong or apparent interpersonal power base in an organization; they have power because they control important information. Likewise, a person's power may be weakened by sharing too much information, for it reduces his relative share of this valuable commodity.[31] A true picture of a person's power is provided not only by the person's position but also by the person's access to relevant information.

POSITION	SYMPTOMS	SOURCES	
First-line supervisors (e.g., line supervisor)	Supervise too closely.	Routine, rule-minded jobs.	**Table 10–1**
	Fail to train subordinates.	Limited lines of communication.	Symptoms and Sources of Powerlessness
	Not sufficiently oriented to the management team.	Limited advancement opportunities for themselves and their subordinates.	
	Inclined to do the job themselves.		
Staff professionals (e.g., corporate lawyer, personnel/human resources specialists)	Create islands and set themselves up as experts.	Routine tasks are only adjuncts to real line job.	
	Use professional standards as basis for judging work that distinguishes them from others.	Blocked career advancement. Replaced by outside consultants for nonroutine work.	
	Resist change and become conservative risk-takers.		
Top-level managers (e.g., chief executive officer, vice president)	Have short-term time horizon. Emphasize top-down communication systems.	Uncontrollable lines of supply.	
	Reward followers to think like the manager; do not welcome bearers of bad news.	Limited or blocked lines of information about lower managerial levels.	
		Diminished lines of support because of challenges to legitimacy.	

Source: This classic table is reprinted by permission of the *Harvard Business Review.* Adapted from "Power Failures in Management Circuits," by Rosabeth Moss Kanter (July–August 1979). p. 73. Copyright © 1979 by the President and Fellows of Harvard College; all rights reserved.

Many organizational situations illustrate how different sources can create powerful and powerless managers. Powerful managers exist because they allocate required resources, make crucial decisions, and have access to important information. Powerful managers also seek out and use information from all their employees.[32] They are likely to make things happen. Powerless managers, however, lack the resources, information, and decision-making prerogatives needed to be productive. Table 10–1 presents common symptoms and sources of powerlessness of first-line supervisors, staff professionals, and top-level managers. The table indicates that a first-line manager may display a number of symptoms of powerlessness, such as supervising very closely and not showing much concern about training or developing subordinates. If these symptoms persist, the individual is probably powerless.

Upward Flow of Power

Most people think of power as being exerted in a downward direction. It's true that individuals in positions at the lower end of the power hierarchy generally have less power than do individuals in higher level positions. However, power can also be exercised up the organization.[33] In sociological terms, a person exerting power upward has personal power but no authority.

The discussion of legitimate authority suggests that individuals in higher level positions (supervisors) can exert only as much power as individuals in lower level positions (subordinates) accept. The concept of subordinate power can be linked to expertise, location, and information. Significant upward power or influence can sometimes be exerted by a relatively low-ranking secretary, computer programmer, or clerk who possesses expertise, is in a position to interact with important individuals, or has access to and control of important information.[34] Expertise, location, and information control are important determinants of the power potential of employees at lower levels of the hierarchy.

Two important sources of upward influence have been referred to as manipulative persuasion and manipulation.[35] *Manipulative persuasion* is a person's direct attempt to disguise the true persuasion objective. This is the hidden-agenda ploy. Through persuasive skills, the individual accumulates power to gain an objective. For example, a manager trying to have a poor worker transferred may present only the strengths of the worker to a project manager looking for people for a new assignment. Although the manager's true objective is to unload the worker on someone else, that objective is hidden within the manager's persuasive presentation of the employee's strengths.

Manipulation refers to the form of influence in which both the objective and the attempt are concealed. For example, instead of providing customer complaints to a manager as they're received, the clerk receiving the complaints may arrange them in such a way as to place other employees or a department in a more or less favorable light.[36] If the clerk arranges the incoming complaints so that the manager in charge reprimands a departmental supervisor whom the clerk doesn't like, the clerk's action would be considered manipulation in the upward direction.

Organizational level has been found to be inversely related to a manager's propensity to use upward influence appeals.[37] This makes sense as managers at higher levels would likely feel they have enough authority to exercise influence, while managers and other employees lower down in an organizational hierarchy may feel less confident about exercising influence without the backing of higher authority.

Interdepartmental Power

To this point, the primary focus has been on individual power and how it's obtained. However, interdepartmental power is also important. Even though all vice presidents of departments at the same level in the managerial hierarchy are supposed to have the same amount of power, this isn't usually the case. Some vice presidents have more power than others by virtue of being in a particular unit or department. For example, in some companies, marketing may wield the most power. In others, production or engineering might have the upper hand.

Strategic Contingency

Event or activity of crucial importance to completing a project or accomplishing a goal.

The strategic contingency theory focuses on subunit power. A **strategic contingency** is an event or activity that's extremely important for accomplishing organizational goals.[38] Hinnings and associates studied the strategic contingency explanation of power in 28 subunits of seven manufacturing organizations in Canada and the United States.[39] Engineering, marketing, production, and accounting departments were studied. Each subunit interacted with the three others. The researchers examined various indicators of power, such as substitutability (ability of the subunit to obtain alternative performance for its activities), work flow pervasiveness (the degree to which the work flows of a subunit were linked to the work flows of other subunits), uncertainty (the lack of information about future events), and work flow immediacy (the speed and severity with which the work flow of a subunit affected the final outputs of the organization). Researchers found that only a combination of high values on all the power indicators gave a subunit dominant, first-rank power. Thus, being able to deal with uncertainty alone or possessing substitutability power alone does not provide a subunit with dominant power over other subunits. The model in Figure 10–1 suggests that subunit power, the power differential between subunits, is influenced by (1) the ability to cope with uncertainty, (2) the centrality of the subunit, and (3) the substitutability of the subunit.

Figure 10–1

A Strategic Contingency Model of Subunit Power

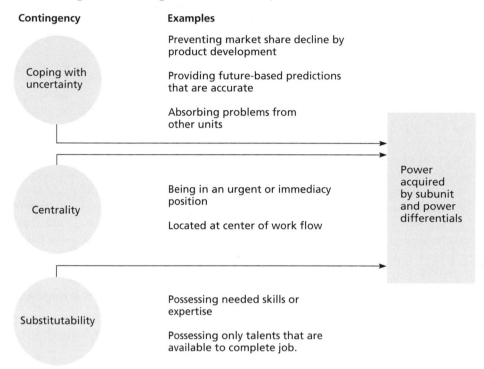

Contingency

Coping with uncertainty

Examples

Preventing market share decline by product development

Providing future-based predictions that are accurate

Absorbing problems from other units

Centrality

Being in an urgent or immediacy position

Located at center of work flow

Substitutability

Possessing needed skills or expertise

Possessing only talents that are available to complete job.

Power acquired by subunit and power differentials

Sources: This figure is based on the early research work conducted by D. J. Hickson, C. R. Hinnings, C. A. Lee, R. E. Schneck, and J. M. Pennings. See Hickson et al., "A Strategic Contingency Theory of Intraorganizational Power," *Administrative Science Quarterly*, June 1971, pp. 216–29; C. R. Hinnings, D. J. Hickson, J. M. Pennings, and R. E. Schneck, "Structural Conditions of Intraorganizational Power," *Administrative Science Quarterly*, March 1974, pp. 22–44.

Coping with uncertainty

Unanticipated events can create problems for any organization or subunit. Therefore, the subunits most capable of coping with uncertainty typically acquire power.

> *Uncertainty itself does not give power; coping gives power. If organizations allocate to their various subunits task areas that vary in uncertainty, then those subunits that cope most effectively with the most uncertainty should have the most power within the organization.*[40]

Coping activities comprise three types. In *coping by prevention*, a subunit works at reducing the probability that some difficulty will arise. For example, designing a new product to prevent lost sales because of new competition in the marketplace is a coping technique. Another example would be to hire two individuals when only one is actually needed, because of expected turnover.

Coping by information is another type. The use of forecasting is an example. Possessing timely forecasting information enables a subunit to deal with such events as competition, strikes, shortages of materials, and consumer demand shifts. Planning departments conducting forecasting studies acquire power when their forecasts prove accurate.

Coping by absorption, the third type, involves dealing with uncertainty as it impacts the subunit. For example, one subunit might take a problem employee from another subunit and then attempt to retrain and redirect that employee. This is done as a favor, so that the other subunit does not have to go through the pain of terminating or continuing to put up with the employee. The subunit that takes in the problem employee gains the respect of other subunits, which results in an increase in power. Regarding the relation of coping with uncertainty to power, the more a subunit copes with uncertainty, the greater its power within the organization.[41]

Centrality

The subunits most central to the flow of work in an organization typically acquire power. No subunit has zero centrality since all are somehow interlinked with other subunits. A measure of centrality is the degree to which the work of the subunit contributes to the final output of the organization.[42] A subunit in a position to affect other subunits has some degree of centrality and, therefore, power.

A subunit also possesses power if its activities have a more immediate or urgent impact than that of other subunits. For example, Ben Taub is a major public hospital in Houston. The emergency and trauma treatment subunit is crucial. Because failures in this subunit could result in the death of emergency victims, it possesses significant power within the hospital. The psychiatric subunit does important work that's not as crucial and immediate. Therefore, it has significantly less subunit power than the emergency and trauma treatment subunit. This leads to two main centrality propositions:

1. The higher the pervasiveness of the work flows of a subunit, the greater is its power within the organization; and

2. The higher the immediacy of the work flows of a subunit, the greater is its power within the organization.[43]

Substitutability

Substitutability

Extent to which other subunits can perform the job or task of a subunit.

Substitutability refers to other subunits' ability to perform activities of a particular subunit. If an organization has or can obtain alternative sources of skill, information, and resources to perform the job done by a subunit, the subunit's power is diminished. On one hand, training subunits lose power if training work can be done by line managers or outside consultants. On the other hand, a subunit with unique skills and competencies is hard to duplicate or replace; this increases the subunit's power over other subunits.

Changes in the labor market may result in changes in a subunit's power. Today, there's a shortage of robotic technical specialists. Since robotic technicians are difficult to replace, train, and substitute for, the robotic subunit of an organization possesses inordinate power. Of course, other reasons exist for the emergence of powerful robotics subunits, such as their access to technical information, their centrality, and the productivity improvements that they bring about.

Hinnings and associates captured the importance of substitutability power when they proposed that the lower the substitutability of the activities of a subunit, the greater is its power within the organization.[44]

In summary, the first step a subunit may take to increase its power is to assume responsibility for activities critical to the organization.[45] The subunit may then seek to increase its pervasiveness, ability to cope with uncertainty, and/or nonsubstitutability. Eventually, the subunit will possess enormous levels of power in relation to other subunits in the organization.

The Illusion of Power

Admittedly, some individuals and subunits have vast amounts of power to get others to do things the way they want them done. However, there are also illusions of power. Imagine that one afternoon your supervisor says, "You know we're really losing money using that Beal stamping machine. I'd like you to do a job for the company. I want you to destroy the machine and make it look like an accident." Would you comply with this request? After all, this is your supervisor, and he's in charge of everything: your pay, your promotion opportunities, your job assignments. You might ask, "Does my supervisor have this much power over me?"

Where a person's or a subunit's power starts and stops is difficult to pinpoint. One might assume that the supervisor in the hypothetical example has the specific power to get someone to do this unethical and illegal "dirty work." However, even individuals who seemingly possess only a little power can influence others. A series of classic studies by Stanley Milgram focused on the illusion of power.

Milgram conducted highly controversial experiments on "obedience to authority."[46] Subjects in the experiments were adult men from a variety of occupations and social positions in the New Haven, Connecticut, area. Upon arriving at the laboratory, each subject was introduced to his supposed cosubject, a man of about 50 who was actually working with Milgram. The two were asked to draw lots to determine who would be the "teacher" and who the "learner." The drawing was rigged. The real subject always became the teacher.

The experiment was ostensibly designed to find out about the effects of punishment on learning. Whenever the learner made a mistake, he was to be punished with an electric shock. A shock-generating machine was used. It had 30 switches on it, the first delivering 15 volts, the second 30, and so on up to 450 volts, where the switch was labeled, "Danger—Severe Shock—XXX."

The teacher (the real subject) then took his place at the shock-generating machine, where he could not see the learner (Milgram's confederate). The plan was for the learner to make many mistakes in repeating words given to him by the teacher. With each mistake, the teacher was told to increase the shocks. At 75 volts, the teacher could hear grunts coming from the learner, who was actually faking as instructed by Milgram. At 150 volts, the learner shouted, "Let me out," and said his heart couldn't stand the pain. He began to yell. He let out an agonizing scream at 285 volts and refused to go on, but seemingly kept trying and made even more mistakes.

Most teachers became very upset. Some asked the experimenter whether it was proper to continue. No matter what the teacher asked or how he protested, the experimenter only said, "The experiment requires that we go on." The subjects were also told, "You have no other choice; you must go on." Milgram wanted to know how many subjects would defy the orders to go on and how many would continue. Before these experiments were conducted, 40 psychiatrists were asked their opinions about whether the subjects would quit. Only 4 percent of the subjects, the psychiatrists predicted, would continue to shock learners who failed to respond. But look at Figure 10–2 to see what actually happened.

Out of a total of 40 subjects, 26 (65 percent) obeyed the experimenter all the way to the very highest voltage level on the shock generator (XXX). These men weren't abnormal. In fact, most showed extreme signs of emotional strain and psychological conflict during the experiment. They trembled, bit their lips, and dug their fingernails into the

Figure 10–2

Results of Milgram's Classic Experiment on Obedience

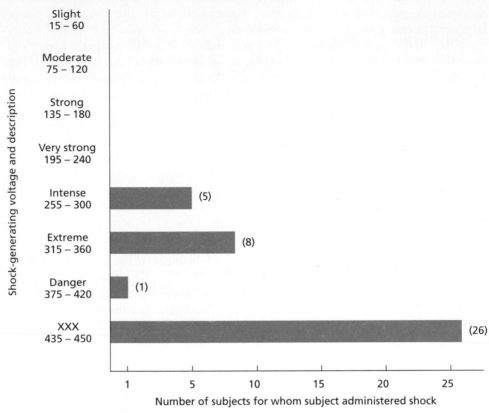

Source: Based on descriptions and data presented by Stanley Milgram.

palms of their hands. They repeatedly asked for the experimenter's permission to stop. Yet, they continued increasing the voltage. Milgram stated:

> "I observed a mature and initially poised businessman enter the laboratory, smiling and confident; within 20 minutes he was reduced to a twitching, stuttering wreck, who was rapidly approaching a point of nervous collapse . . . yet he continued to respond to every word of the experimenter and obeyed to the end."[47]

Why did the subjects obey the experimenter? Although he possessed no specific power over the subjects, he appeared to be a powerful person. The experimenter created an illusion of power: he dressed in a white lab coat, was addressed by others as "doctor," and was very stern. The subjects perceived him as possessing legitimacy to conduct the study. The experimenter apparently did an excellent job of projecting the illusion of having power.

The Milgram experiments indicate that exercising power in an authoritative way isn't the only way that power can be exerted. Power is often exerted by individuals who have only minimum or no actual power. An individual may be able to significantly influence others simply because she's perceived to have power. The "eye of the beholder" plays an important role in the exercise of power.[48]

Political Strategies and Tactics

Individuals and subunits continually engage in **political behavior.** By political behavior, we mean:

1. Behavior that is usually outside the legitimate, recognized power system.

2. Behavior that is designed to benefit an individual or subunit, often at the expense of the organization in general.

3. Behavior that is intentional and is designed to acquire and maintain power.

Political Behavior

Behavior outside the normal power system, designed to benefit an individual or a subunit.

As a result of political behavior, the formal power that exists in an organization is often sidetracked or blocked. The Close-Up, "Some Realities of Politics," outlines some of the negative effects of political behavior.

Research on Politics

A number of studies have explored political behavior and perceptions in organizations.[49] An early study of 142 purchasing agents examined their political behavior.[50] Their job objective was to negotiate and fill orders in a timely manner. However, the purchasing agents also viewed their jobs as being a crucial link with the environment—competition, price changes, market shifts. Thus, they considered themselves information processors. This vital link between each purchasing agent and the external environment placed them in conflict with the engineering department. As a result of the conflict, attempts to influence the engineering subunit were a regular occurrence.

C L O S E — U P

Some Realities of Politics

Politics has long been a force in organizations. And it would probably be naive to assume that the situation is going to change. Rarely a month goes by that an executive resignation or reorganization is not blamed on politics. It also causes many other problems.

While it certainly is a reality of organizational life, *politics can often drive away valuable employees.* When Roger Farah left R. H. Macy and Company, he was offered high-level executive jobs with many top retail companies. He turned them all down because, as he stated, "He had already been burned by corporate politics—at Macy's and Federated—and decided to run his own show."

Politics can also influence who gets what in the organization. Some believe that certain political games exclude women from climbing the corporate ladder. They believe some unwritten "political" ways in which organizations balance power in favor of men are: (1) encouraging workers to spend long days at the office, thereby making it difficult for women who have family commitments; (2) scheduling meetings at inaccessible times; (3) talking about matters that women cannot easily share in; and (4) having inadequate or no child-care facilities.

Politics can also negatively influence productivity. With so many organizations implementing self-directed work teams and cross-functional teams into their culture, it should not be surprising that one of the most frequent causes of failure of the team concept is that the team has raised or allowed company politics to interfere with team goals.

What can we do about politics? Probably just live with it. Here are some recent suggestions for influencing your manager on an internal political issue: (1) seek advice from a mentor and another neutral party; (2) gather and mentally rehearse the arguments; (3) pick the right time; and, (4) keep an open mind throughout the exchange.

Sources: "Office Politics," *Office Systems,* March 1998, pp. 8–9; Steven Titch, "No. 1 with the Bullet," *Telephony,* July 21, 1997, p. 5; and Sandi Mann, "Politics and Power in Organizations: Why Women Lose Out," *Leadership and Organizational Development Journal,* 16, no. 2 (1995), pp. 9–15.

This study found a variety of political tactics used by purchasing agents:

1. *Rule evasion*   evading the organization's formal purchasing procedures.
2. *Personal-political*   using friendships to facilitate or inhibit the processing of an order.
3. *Educational*   attempting to persuade engineering to think in purchasing terms.
4. *Organizational*   attempting to change the formal or informal interaction patterns between engineering and purchasing.

These four political tactics were outside the legitimate power system, occasionally benefited the purchasing agent at the expense of the rest of the organization, and were intentionally developed so that more power was acquired by the purchasing agent.

Another classic study of political behavior was conducted in the electronics industry in southern California.[51] A total of 87 managers (30 chief executive officers, 28 higher level staff managers, 29 supervisors) were interviewed and asked about political behavior. Table 10–2 summarizes the eight categories of political tactics (behavior) mentioned most frequently by the three managerial groups. Managers were also asked to describe personal characteristics of the individuals who used political behavior effectively. Thirteen personal characteristics were identified as important (see Table 10–3).

A recent study developed a profile of individuals active in office politics, based on a survey completed by 225 managers.[52] The results indicated that managerial level, job function, and sex were unrelated to managers' levels of political activity. However, certain personality traits corresponded highly with the individual manager's propensity to engage in office politics. The profile that emerged characterized the "political player" as a highly self-monitoring man who viewed the world as difficult and as posing complex (possibly unsolvable) problems, or as a woman with high need for power.

A more recent study in the 1990s focused on forms of defensive political behaviors exhibited by managers.[53] Defensive behaviors included avoiding action via overconforming, passing the buck, playing dumb, and stalling; avoiding blame via bluffing, justifying, scapegoating, and misrepresenting; and avoiding change via resisting change and protecting one's turf. Personality traits of managers who exhibited defensive behavior included insecurity and anxiety, emotional exhaustion, work alienation, self-monitoring, and low self-efficacy.

Table 10–2

Managerial Perceptions of Organizational Political Behavior

TACTIC	COMBINED GROUPS	CHIEF EXECUTIVE OFFICERS	STAFF MANAGERS	SUPERVISORS
Attacking or blaming others	54.0%	60.0%	50.0%	51.7%
Use of information	54.0	56.7	57.1	48.3
Image building/impression management	52.9	43.3	46.4	69.0
Developing base of support	36.8	46.7	39.3	24.1
Praising others, ingratiation	25.3	16.7	25.0	34.5
Power coalitions, strong allies	25.3	26.7	17.9	31.0
Associating with the influential	24.1	16.7	35.7	20.7
Creating obligations/reciprocity	12.6	3.3	14.3	30.7

Source: R. W. Allen, D. L. Madison, L. W. Porter, P. A. Renwick, and B. T. Mayes, "Organizational Politics: Tactics and Characteristics of Its Actors." Copyright 1979 by the Regents of the University of California. Reprinted from *California Management Review*, December 1979, p. 79, by permission of the Regents.

PERSONAL CHARACTERISTICS	COMBINED GROUPS	CHIEF EXECUTIVE OFFICERS	STAFF MANAGERS	SUPERVISORS
Articulate	29.9%	36.7%	39.3%	12.8%
Sensitive	29.9	50.0	21.4	17.2
Socially adept	19.5	10.0	32.1	17.2
Competent	17.2	10.0	21.4	20.7
Popular	17.2	16.7	10.7	24.1
Extroverted	16.1	16.7	14.3	17.2
Self-confident	16.1	10.0	21.4	17.2
Aggressive	16.1	10.0	14.3	24.1
Ambitious	16.1	20.0	25.0	3.4
Devious	16.1	13.3	14.3	20.7
"Organization person"	12.6	20.0	3.6	13.8
Highly intelligent	11.5	20.0	10.7	3.4
Logical	10.3	3.3	21.4	6.9

Table 10–3

Personal Characteristics of Effective Politicians

Source: R. W. Allen, D. L. Madison, L. W. Porter, P. A. Renwick, and B. T. Mayes, "Organizational Politics: Tactics and Characteristics of Its Actors." Copyright 1979 by the Regents of the University of California. Reprinted from *California Management Review*, December 1979, p. 79, by permission of the Regents.

Playing politics

If anything, the available research indicates that politics exists in organizations and that some individuals are very adept at political behavior. Mintzberg and others describe these adept politicians as playing games.[54] The games that managers and nonmanagers engage in are intended to resist authority (e.g., the insurgency game); counter the resistance to authority (e.g., the counterinsurgency game); build power bases (e.g., the sponsorship game and coalition-building game); defeat rivals (e.g., the line versus staff game); and affect organizational change (e.g., the whistle-blowing game). In all, Mintzberg describes and discusses 13 political games. Six are briefly presented here.

INSURGENCY GAME This game is played to resist authority. For example, suppose that a plant supervisor is instructed to reprimand a particular worker for violating company policies. The reprimand can be delivered according to the supervisor's feelings and opinions about its worth and legitimacy. A reprimand delivered in a halfhearted manner will probably have no noticeable effect. However, if delivered aggressively, it may be effective. Insurgency in the form of not delivering the reprimand as expected by a higher level authority would be difficult to detect and correct. Insurgency as a game to resist authority is practiced in organizations at all levels.

COUNTERINSURGENCY GAME Often, a person in an authority position fights back when faced with insurgency. The supervisor's superior may have to carefully monitor whether policies concerning the reprimand are being followed. One tactic is to occasionally follow up requests given to subordinates with a detailed checking system. For example, the person with ultimate authority could ask the supervisor on occasion whether the reprimand had been given, when it was given, what the person's reaction was, and how the supervisor would make presentation improvements in the future. The superior could also check with the person reprimanded to determine when and how the reprimand was given. The purpose of periodic monitoring is to encourage the supervisor to deliver the reprimand according to company procedures.

SPONSORSHIP GAME In this rather straightforward game, a person attaches herself to someone with power. The sponsor is typically the person's boss or someone else with higher power and status. Typically, individuals attach themselves to someone who is on the move up in the organization. A few rules are involved in playing this game. First, the person must be able to show commitment and loyalty to the sponsor. Second, the person must follow each sponsor-initiated request or order. Third, the person must stay in the background and give the sponsor credit for everything. Finally, the person must be thankful and display gratitude to the sponsor. The sponsor is not only a teacher and trainer but also a power base. Some of the sponsor's power tends to rub off on the person through association.

COALITION-BUILDING GAME A subunit such as a personnel/human resources department or a research and development department may be able to increase its power by forming an alliance, or coalition, with other subunits. The strength-in-numbers idea is encouraged by coalition building.[55] When such alliances are formed within the organization, common goals and common interests are emphasized. However, forming coalitions with groups outside the organization can also enhance the power of a subunit.

LINE VERSUS STAFF GAME The line manager versus the staff advisor game has existed for years in organizations. In essence, this game pits line authority to make operating decisions against staff advisors' expertise. There are also value differences and personality clashes. On the one hand, line managers are typically more experienced; more oriented to the bottom line; and more intuitive in reaching decisions. Conversely, staff advisors tend to be younger, better educated, and more analytical decision makers. These differences result in the two groups viewing the organizational world from different perspectives.

Withholding information, having access to powerful authority figures, creating favorable impressions, and identifying with organizational goals are tactics used by line and staff personnel. The line versus staff clash must be controlled in organizations before it reaches the point at which, because of the disruption, organizational goals aren't being achieved.

WHISTLE-BLOWING GAME This game is played to bring about organizational change. It takes place when a person in an organization identifies a behavior that violates his sense of fairness, morals, ethics, or law and then blows the whistle. Whistle-blowing means that the person informs someone—a newspaper reporter, a government representative, a competitor—about an assumed injustice, irresponsible action, or violation of the law.

Whistle–Blowing

Informing someone about an organizational practice or behavior that violates the law or conflicts with a personal value or belief.

The whistle-blower, who may come from any level in the organization, attempts to correct the behavior or practice by bypassing the authority system within the organization. This is viewed in a negative light by managers with position power. For example, when a pilot complained to management first and then to the public about defects in his plane's automatic pilot mechanisms, his complaints were attacked by management as being groundless. An engineer complained about the O-rings of the Challenger booster rockets—which later cracked, leading to the death of seven astronauts. The engineer's complaints weren't given a high priority to be checked out. In another example, a biologist reported to the Environmental Protection Agency that his consulting firm had submitted false data to the agency on behalf of an electric utility company. As a result, he was fired.

Although federal law protects whistle-blowers' rights and some innovative organizations encourage valid internal whistle-blowing, most organizations continue to retaliate against an informant.[56] In fact, a recent study found that identified whistle-blowers were as likely to experience retaliation after the passage of the federal law protecting them as they were prior to passage.[57] As a result, whistle-blowing is often done secretly to avoid retribution by the authority system.

Ethics, Power, and Politics

Issues of power and politics often involve ethical issues as well. For example, if power is used within the formal boundaries of a manager's authority and within the framework of organizational policies, job descriptions, procedures, and goals, it's really nonpolitical power and most likely doesn't involve ethical issues. But use of power outside the bounds of formal authority, politics, procedures, job descriptions, and organizational goals is political in nature. When this occurs, ethical issues are likely to be present. Some examples might include bribing government officials, lying to employees and customers, polluting the environment, and a general "ends justify the means" mentality.

Managers confront ethical dilemmas in their jobs because they frequently use power and politics to accomplish their goals. Each manager, therefore, has an ethical responsibility. Recently researchers have developed a framework that allows a manager to integrate ethics into political behavior. Researchers recommend that a manager's behavior must satisfy certain criteria to be considered ethical.[58]

1. *Utilitarian outcomes.*   The manager's behavior results in the optimal satisfaction of people both inside and outside the organization. In other words, it results in the greatest good for the greatest number of people.

2. *Individual rights.*   The manager's behavior respects the rights of all affected parties. In other words, it respects basic human rights of free consent, free speech, freedom of conscience, privacy, and due process.

3. *Distributive justice.*   The manager's behavior respects the rules of justice. It treats people equitably and fairly, not arbitrarily.

What does a manager do when a potential behavior cannot pass the three criteria? Researchers suggest that it may still be considered ethical in the particular situation if it passes the criterion of *overwhelming factors.* To be justified, the behavior must be based on tremendously overwhelming factors in the nature of the situation, such as conflicts among criteria (e.g., the manager's behavior results in both positive and negative results), conflicts within the criteria (e.g., a manager uses questionable means to achieve a positive result), and/or an incapacity to employ the first three criteria (e.g., the manager acts with incomplete or inaccurate information).

Summary of Key Points

- *Power* is defined as the ability to get things done in the way that one wants them done.

- Authority is a much narrower concept than power. Authority is a form of power that is made legitimate because it is accepted by subordinates or followers.

- There are five interpersonal power bases: legitimate (position-based), reward, coercive (punishment-based), expert, and referent (charismatic). These five bases can be divided into two major categories: organizational and personal. Legitimate, reward, and coercive power are primarily prescribed by an organization, while expert and charismatic power are based on personal qualities.

- Structural and situational power bases also exist. An organization's structural arrangement establishes patterns of communication and information flow that play an important role in power formation and use.

- Many managers with a high need for power are effective, use their power to accomplish organizational goals, and are involved heavily in coaching subordinates.

- Power and influence can flow from the bottom to the top in an organization. Lower level employees can have significant power because of expertise, location, and access and control of information. Some lower level employees acquire power through persuasion and manipulation skills.

- Subunits within organizations acquire and use power. The strategic contingency approach addresses subunit power. A strategic contingency is an event or activity that is important for accomplishing organizational goals.

- Individuals can sometimes exercise power because of illusion.

- Politics is present in all organizations. Politics comprises those activities used to acquire, develop, and use power and other resources to obtain one's preferred outcome when there is uncertainty or disagreement about choices.

- Mintzberg introduced the notion of political game playing. Examples of political games are the insurgency and counter-insurgency games, the sponsorship game, the coalition-building game, the line versus staff game, and the whistle-blowing game.

- Issues of power and politics often involve ethical issues, especially when the use of power is political in nature.

Discussion and Review Questions

1. If you could only have one type of interpersonal power, which would it be and why?
2. Give an example of how a college professor could exhibit each of the five interpersonal bases of power.
3. Some cynics comment that the golden rule is "Those who have the gold make the rules." Discuss this statement in light of your understanding of the various power bases.
4. Give an example of where resource power would be critical in getting the job done.
5. With the creation of the "information highway," do you think information power will be easier to obtain. Why or why not?
6. If you were in charge of an organization with various subunits, would you design substitutable subunits? Why or why not?
7. Why is it unrealistic to assume that little or no political game playing exists in an organization such as McDonald's or Chrysler?
8. The sponsorship game has also been referred to, in a more negative tone, as "riding someone's coattails." Why do you think some view this game in a negative way?
9. If someone blows the whistle on his company's actions because the actions endanger lives, do you believe he should be fired? If not, what do you think should happen to this employee.
10. Do you believe there is any type of organization that frequently operates *without* ethical standards in order to maintain success and profitability? Why or why not?

C A S E   F O R   A N A L Y S I S

A Powerful Ending at Armstrong

All companies go through hard times, and the Armstrong Co., unfortunately, was no exception. In 1992, for the first time since the Depression, CEO David Armstrong decided drastic actions were necessary to keep the company afloat. He instituted a wage freeze to help the company get through what looked to be a very difficult year. The freeze took effect immediately and the normal raise given to employees at the beginning of each new year was forgone.

Employees' reaction was amazing. They accepted the freeze with few complaints. "The company has always been fair with me. Now it's my turn to be fair to the company," seemed to be the prevailing attitude.

A few months into the new year, it looked like 1992 was going to be much better than projected. Armstrong decided that not only could the company give everybody raises, but it could also afford to make them retroactive. Back pay came to about $400 per employee.

The company didn't give the employees that $400 by check. Instead, all employees were called into the recreation building. There, standing behind a large table covered with a white sheet, Armstrong explained that since the company was doing better than anticipated, it wanted to share its good fortune.

With that, he lifted the sheet, and every employee saw that the table was covered with $10 bills—some 12,500 of them—stacked two feet high. One by one, each employee came up, shook hands with Armstrong and the company's managers, and was told, "Thank you for your understanding." Each employee then walked away with 40 crisp, new $10 bills.

Discussion Questions

1. What forms of interpersonal power did David Armstrong rely on in making his decisions?

2. Do you think Armstrong possesses a high need for power? Why?

3. How did Armstrong cope with uncertainty? Do you agree with his actions?

4. What power, if any, did Armstrong employees possess? How could they have used this power in a negative sense?

Source: Adapted from David M. Armstrong, "Management by Story-telling," *Executive Female*, May–June 1992, pp. 38–41.

 **www.armstrong.com**

E X P E R I E N T I A L   E X E R C I S E

Office Diplomacy: The Dos and Don'ts

Objectives

1. To examine situations where power and office politics impact social decisions.
2. To illustrate the difficulties of office etiquette.

Starting the Exercise

Phase I (20 minutes). Here are four tricky situations dealing with office diplomacy that managers commonly encounter. Read through each scenario and the alternative answers. Choose the answer that most closely matches the response you feel a manager should make. Write down why you chose this particular response and not the others, supporting your choice with material contained in this chapter.

Scenario 1. At a meeting with your boss and others, you're asked your opinion concerning a problem. You offer your ideas but see right away that your boss is upset and surprised. After the meeting, you should:

1. Tell your boss that you made a mistake, and you'll be sure to discuss your ideas with her before a meeting.

2. Elaborate on your ideas in a report that you personally deliver to the committee.

3. Say nothing. These things happen.

Scenario 2. The newly appointed manager of another department has adopted an aggressive attitude toward you. Your department and the new manager's department work together closely, and you realize that your department's success is in jeopardy unless you can resolve the problem. Each time you try to communicate directly with the other manager, all you get is hostility. You should:

1. Confront the manager head-on. Explain that like it or not, you two will be working together.

2. Work around the other manager. Avoid talking to him directly whenever possible.

3. Make your relationship more personal. Invite him to lunch, but avoid trying to talk business.

Scenario 3. Having been hired from the outside, you've just started your new job as manager, when one employee in your department comes to you and states that she should have been promoted to your position. You should:

1. Help her to transfer to another department where her abilities will be better appreciated.

2. Tell her that, like it or not, you hold the postition and she had better get used to it.

3. Give her more responsibility by putting her in charge of a major project.

Scenario 4. An employee asks you, his manager, to lunch to discuss a work-related issue. Which one of you should pick up the tab?

1. The employee should pay since he arranged the lunch.

2. You, as the manager who was invited, should pay.

3. The tab should be split evenly.

Scenario 5. You and one of your employees are in the middle of a meeting in your office when the telephone rings. You don't have an assistant to pick up your calls. You should:

1. Ignore the phone. Eventually it will stop ringing.

2. Answer the phone, excuse yourself to your employee, and then give the call your full attention.

3. Answer the call. Say you're in a meeting and can't talk, but will call back as soon as possible.

Phase II (15 minutes). The instructor will form small groups of 4, 6, or 8 students to discuss their choices and the rationale behind their choices.

Phase III (15 minutes). The instructor will wrap the session up and discuss the various alternatives.

Source: Michael C. Thomsett, "How's Your Office Diplomacy?" *Executive Female*, March–April 1992, pp. 68–69.

Chapter 11

Leaders: Born, Made, or Responsive to the Situation?

Learning Objectives

After completing Chapter 11, you should be able to:

Define
The term *leadership*.

Describe
Why many managers appear to prefer the Hersey-Blanchard situational leadership theory.

Discuss
Whether leaders are really needed in work settings.

Compare
The situational factors used in discussions of the contingency and path–goal approaches to leadership.

Identify
The assumptions made about followers of the path–goal and the leader–member exchange theories.

E

very group to which you've belonged—family, sports, social, study, work— doubtlessly included one person

you considered to be more influential than others. When this person spoke, others listened; when this person suggested or directed action to be taken, others took that action. You thought of and perhaps referred to this person as a leader. Perhaps you yourself have been such a person—a leader. Maybe you enjoyed the experience of being a leader. Maybe you didn't. In any event you recognize the circumstance. You also recognize the importance of leaders in groups, organizations, institutions, nations, and alliances of nations.

We take for granted the importance of leaders for the well-being and effectiveness of efforts undertaken by groups of individuals who alone could not accomplish their intended purposes. Because of the importance of leaders in society, they have been the subjects of countless studies, novels, stories, and vignettes, all attempting to say something about what leaders do, what leadership is, and even how to be a leader. Certainly a text that seeks to prepare students for careers in organizations would have to include considerable attention to leaders and leadership. As the title of this chapter asks: Are individuals born to be leaders? Can individuals learn how to apply leadership behavior? Or does the question of who will become a leader depend entirely upon the situation?

This and the next chapter will present the main contemporary ideas about leadership from the perspective of behavioral science theory and research. We will be keenly interested in arriving at well-founded understandings of leadership not only from the perspective of science but also from the perspective of practice and application. Yet we will have to deal with considerable ambiguity because even though scientists have studied leadership for decades, it remains something of a mystery. Even after thousands of studies, the experts still lack consensus on exactly what leadership is and how it should be analyzed.

Generally speaking however, we can say that leaders are individuals who influence other individuals to do what they might not do in the absence of the leader's influence. We will examine somewhat more complete ideas about leaders in the following pages, but we can certainly appreciate at this point the difficulty of understanding how and why certain individuals become leaders and what they do to exercise their influence. What personal characteristics distinguish leaders from nonleaders? What personal characteristics distinguish effective leaders from ineffective leaders? How do they behave as leaders and what distinguishes the behavior of effective from ineffective leaders? What role do followers play in leadership? Is each leader better suited to influence some types of individuals over others? What can we say about the context, or situation, within which leadership occurs? For that matter, do all situations involving group effort require leadership? These questions present some of the ideas that we will be discussing in the following pages.

The discussion will begin with a definition of leadership as we will use the term. The reader should be alert to the ambiguity of the terms, *leader* and *leadership*, and recognize that discussions of them often result in confusion because of differing definitions. We will then direct our attention to the studies of leaders and leadership beginning with those studies that attempt to identify the particular *traits* that leaders share that distinguish them from nonleaders. Next we will discuss the ideas associated with leader *behavior*, specifically the behaviors associated with effective leaders. The discussion concludes with an introduction to the idea that effective leadership depends on the interaction between the leader's traits, behavior, and the *situation* in which the leadership occurs.

Leadership Defined

Leadership

An attempt to use influence to motivate individuals to accomplish some goal.

The authoritative source of leadership theory and research, the *Handbook of Leadership* defines **leadership** as "an interaction between members of a group. Leaders are agents of change, persons whose acts affect other people more than other people's acts affect them. Leadership occurs when one group member modifies the motivation or competencies of others in the group."[1] The leadership definition implies that it involves the use of influence and that all interpersonal relationships can involve leadership. A second element in the definition involves the importance of being a change agent—being able to affect followers' behavior and performance. Last, the definition focuses on accomplishing goals. The effective leader may have to deal with individual, group, and organizational goals.

Leader effectiveness is typically measured by the accomplishment of one or a combination of these goals. Individuals may view the leader as effective or ineffective according to the satisfactions they derive from the total work experience. In fact, acceptance of a leader's directives or requests rests largely on the followers' expectations that a favorable response can lead to an attractive outcome.

The central interest of this textbook is to prepare individuals to manage in organizations. Thus we should here distinguish between managing and leading. Leadership is a narrower concept than management. A manager in a formal organization is responsible for and entrusted with such functions as planning, organizing, and controlling, but not necessarily leading. A manager may or may not engage in leadership. For example if the manager does not have to interact in any way with other individuals and thus does not have to influence their behavior, that manager would not be a leader in the sense of our definition.

A useful framework for organizing ideas and theories about leadership is presented in Figure 11–1. This figure indicates many of the terms and concepts of leadership ideas

Figure 11–1

A Framework for Studying Leadership

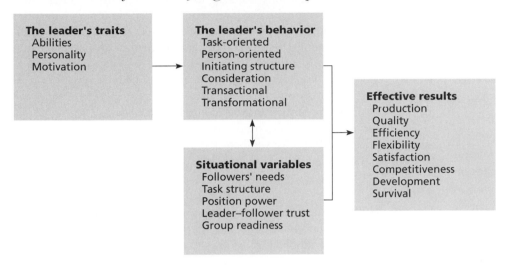

and theory. It includes the various traits, behavioral styles, and situational variables that one finds in the leadership literature. This and the following chapter will rely heavily on Figure 11–1 for our discussion.

As Figure 11–1 suggests, a leader can make a difference in measures of organizational effectiveness: production, efficiency, quality, flexibility, satisfaction, competitiveness, and development. However, scholars and practitioners of leadership have a long way to go before they will be able to measure the exact degree of difference that leaders can and do make in any organization. First, organizations tend to select their leaders from those with similar backgrounds, experiences, and qualifications. The similarity across selected individuals reduces the range of characteristics exhibited by leaders. The similarity of leaders also can produce a self-selection bias: leaders select individuals similar to themselves. Second, leaders at even the highest levels do not have unilateral control over resources. Major decisions require approval, review, and suggested modification by others. Third, leaders cannot control or modify many important factors in a situation. Labor markets, environmental factors, and policies are often outside a leader's direct control. External factors may be overwhelming and uncontrollable, no matter how astute, insightful, and influential a leader may be in a job situation.[2]

Despite some studies that dispute the claim that leadership makes a difference, there's plenty of evidence that leadership can impact performance.[3] Leaders don't always make a difference, but they can and do in enough cases. Did Sam Walton make a difference at Wal-Mart? Did Harry Truman make a difference as president? Did Anwar Sadat make a difference in Egypt? In these and similar cases, there's no clear-cut answer. However, a majority of people would probably conclude that Walton, Truman, and Sadat were leaders who made a difference.

www.wal-mart
.com

Thus we can safely conclude that leaders and leadership are important and that we should be interested in what sets apart those individuals who become leaders from those who do not. We should be interested in the distinctive traits of leaders.

Traits That Appear to Identify Leaders

Much early discussion and research on leadership focused on identifying intellectual, emotional, physical, and other personal traits of effective leaders. This approach assumed that a finite number of individual traits of effective leaders could be found. To a significant extent, the personnel testing component of scientific management supported the **trait theory of leadership**. In addition to being studied by personnel testing, the traits of leaders have been studied by observation of behavior in group situations, by choice of associates (voting), by nomination or rating by observers, and by analysis of biographical data.

Trait Theory of Leadership

Theory that attempts to identify specific characteristics (physical, mental, personality) associated with leadership success. Relies on research that relates various traits to certain success criteria.

Those who study these traits have correlated nearly every measurable characteristic of leaders.[4] We will here review some of the findings associated with the most often studied characteristics.

Abilities

Effective leaders share certain abilities and skills that enable them to do their job, although the exact importance of a particular ability cannot be known with certainty. For example, early studies of the relationship between intelligence (as measured on intelligence tests) and leadership have resulted in some mixed results. One early review of these studies found that leaders were more intelligent than followers.[5] One significant finding was that extreme intelligence differences between leaders and followers might be dysfunctional. For example, a leader with a relatively high IQ attempting to influence a group whose members have average IQs may be unable to understand why the members don't comprehend the problem. In addition, such a leader may have difficulty in communicating ideas and policies. Intelligence in the larger sense of the term involves judgment, knowledge, and fluency of speech.

Some of the more important abilities associated with leadership effectiveness include the ability to get along with people. This interpersonal skill includes persuasiveness, tact, and diplomacy. The effective leader must demonstrate more than passing technical knowledge relevant to the task undertaken by the followers. These abilities no doubt vary in importance from situation to situation, but research confirms their importance in most leader–follower situations.

Since organizations exist to get work done, we should expect that the most effective leaders exhibit the ability to cause their followers to accomplish the desired work. This ability, termed *supervisory ability*, involves setting objectives, planning work, assigning people to do the work, and following up on the results of the work. Citing the research of Ghiselli, we can state with some assurance that leaders exhibit this ability. Ghiselli reports that this ability becomes more pronounced as one moves up the organizational hierarchy, although the nature of the work becomes more abstract and distant from the individual. First-line managers see daily the work their subordinates perform, whereas CEOs rarely see the actual work they initiate.[6]

Personality traits

Some research results suggest that such personality traits as alertness, energy level, tolerance for stress, emotional maturity, originality, personal integrity, and self-confidence are associated with effective leadership.[7] Edwin Ghiselli reported several personality traits associated with leader effectiveness.[8] Ghiselli studied leaders in organizations and was particularly interested in differences among leaders at different levels in organizations. He contrasted supervisors, middle managers, and CEOs and found some differences in certain personality traits. For example, he found that the ability to initiate action decisively was related to the individual's level in the organization. The higher the person went in the organization, the more important this trait became; CEOs were more decisive than middle managers, who were more decisive than supervisors. Ghiselli also found that self-assurance was related to hierarchical position in the organization.

A more recent review of the trait theory literature concludes that achievement, motivation, ambition, tenacity, initiative, and self-confidence are associated with leadership.[9] Although these traits do not identify actual or potential leaders in every instance, they do appear to have sufficient validity as predictors to warrant continued study. Certainly the testing activity of human resource departments in major organizations continues to use measures of these personality traits to identify employees with leadership potential.

Motivation

Leaders seem to exhibit a relatively high need for power, but they act on that need in socially acceptable ways. Effective leaders work within the system to accomplish socially desirable outcomes. This particular orientation to use power for constructive purposes, termed *socialized power orientation,* has been well established as one of the motivations of leaders. Another motivation that sets leaders apart is a relatively high need for achievement, particularly as reflected in the field of their interests. Thus Iacocca would certainly rate very high on his need for achievement in the field of automobile design and production. In addition, effective leaders have relatively weak need for affiliation, suggesting that they would be more motivated by getting a task completed than by interacting with other people. However, the weak need for affiliation does not preclude the effective leader from the application of interpersonal skills.

Table 11–1 summarizes a number of the most researched traits of leaders (traits found most likely to characterize successful leaders). Some studies have reported that these traits contribute to leadership success. However, leadership success is neither primarily nor completely a function of these or other traits.[10]

Synopsis of trait theory

Although some studies conclude that traits such as those in Table 11–1 differentiate effective from ineffective leaders, research findings are still contradictory for a number of possible reasons. First, the list of potentially important traits is endless. Every year, new traits, such as the sign under which a person is born, handwriting style, and order of birth, are added to personality, physical characteristics, and intelligence. This continual "adding on" results in more confusion among those interested in identifying leadership traits. Second, trait test scores aren't consistently predictive of leader effectiveness. Leadership traits don't operate singly to influence followers, but act in combination. This interaction influences the leader–follower relationship. Third, patterns of effective behavior depend largely on the situation: leadership behavior that's effective in a bank

PERSONALITY	MOTIVATION	ABILITY	**Table 11–1**
Energy level	Socialized power orientation	Interpersonal skill	Traits Associated
Stress tolerance	Strong need for achievement	Cognitive skill	with Leadership
Self-confidence	Weak need for affiliation	Technical skill	Effectiveness
Emotional maturity		Persuasiveness	
Integrity			

Source: Gary Yukl, *Leadership in Organizations* (Englewood Cliffs, N.J.: Prentice-Hall, 1994), pp. 251–80.

may be ineffective in a laboratory. Finally, the trait approach fails to provide insight into what the effective leader does on the job. Observations are needed that describe the behavior of effective and ineffective leaders.

Despite its shortcomings, the trait approach is not completely invalid. Kirkpatrick and Locke find evidence that effective leaders are different from other people.[11] Their studies show that leaders don't have to be great intellects to succeed. However, leaders need to have the "right stuff" or traits to have a good chance to be effective. Simply put, leaders are not like all people, but the ways in which they differ are not altogether known or understood. The appeal of the trait theory of leadership has global implications as the Close-Up regarding Russian managers suggests.

Stogdill concisely captures the value of the trait approach:

"The view that leadership is entirely situational in origin and that no personal characteristics are predictive of leadership . . . seems to overemphasize the situational and underemphasize the personal nature of leadership."[12]

Thus our view of leadership must include the ideas that leaders differ from non-leaders and that effective leaders differ from ineffective leaders.

The Behaviors of Effective Leaders

In the late 1940s, researchers began to explore the idea that how a person acts determines that person's leadership effectiveness. Instead of searching for traits, these researchers examined behaviors and their impact on measures of effectiveness such as production and satisfaction of followers. The preponderance of theory and research

CLOSE—UP

Russian Business Leaders in the Global Economy

Since 1991 the Russian nation has been making the painful transition from a planned economy and controlled market to a competitive economy and a free market. At the same time the focus of all business throughout the world has turned to global competition. At no time in the histories of these organizations have we seen greater emphasis on business leadership development. The strains of this transition have been felt throughout the country and the world. At the personal level the strain has been felt keenly by those Russians in leadership positions who must practice leadership in different ways than in their past. In particular they are being encouraged to learn the ways of leadership that have proved effective in the Western economies that they seek to emulate.

Trait theory of leadership has produced considerable understanding about the correlation between traits such as use of power, acceptance of responsibility, achievement motivation, ambition, initiative, energy, tenacity, integrity, and self-confidence. Western leaders have learned through socialization the appropriate ways to channel the behaviors that result from the application of these traits. Russian

managers have to unlearn and then relearn the ways they used to lead. For example, during the days before the Berlin wall fell and signaled the end of the USSR as the world had known it since 1917, Russian leaders practiced power by centralizing it and stifling local initiative. Now, however, they must share power with subordinates. Previously they were discouraged from acting on initiative except on behalf of the party and the collective; now, however, they are encouraged to "get on with it."

The experiences of Russian leaders have caused westerners to rethink the relationship between leadership traits and leadership behavior. We now see rather clearly that the manner in which leadership traits manifest in a particular culture or society may be quite different depending upon the needs of that culture. When the needs of the culture change, its needs for leadership behavior also change. Russian leaders are presently experiencing the pains of making the necessary changes.

Sources: Sheila M. Puller, "Understanding the Bear: A Portrait of Russian Business Leaders, *The Executive,* February, 1994, pp. 41–54; Loizos Heracleous, "Getting Europe Fit for Global Competition: The Leadership and Human Resources Challenges," *Long Range Planning,* April 1997, pp. 299–304, reports the proceedings of an international conference on the issues addressed in this Close-Up.

along these lines has depended upon the idea that leaders must cope with two separate but interrelated aspects of their situations: they must accomplish the task, and they must do so through the efforts of those they lead. Thus, even though a variety of different terms have been used to identify these two facts of leadership, all can be understood as relating to task and people. Leadership behavior can be studied by analyzing what leaders do in relation to accomplishing the task and to maintaining the effort of people doing the task. As we will see, researchers and theorists (and leaders) use several different terms to refer to these two important foci of leadership behaviors.

Job-centered and employee-centered leadership

In 1947, Rensis Likert began studying how best to manage the efforts of individuals to achieve desired production and satisfaction objectives.[13] The purpose of most leadership research of the Likert-inspired team at the University of Michigan (UM) was to discover the principles and methods of effective leadership. The effectiveness criteria used in many of the studies included

 www.umich.edu

1. Productivity per work hour, or other similar measures of the organization's success in achieving its production goals.
2. Job satisfaction of members of the organization.
3. Turnover, absenteeism, and grievance rates.
4. Costs.
5. Scrap loss.
6. Employee and managerial motivation.

Studies were conducted in a wide variety of organizations: chemical, electronics, food, heavy machinery, insurance, petroleum, public utilities, hospitals, banks, and government agencies. Data were obtained from thousands of employees doing different job tasks, ranging from unskilled work to highly skilled research and development work.

Through interviewing leaders and followers, researchers identified two distinct styles of leadership, referred to as *job-centered* and *employee-centered*. The **job-centered leader** focuses on completing the task and uses close supervision so that subordinates perform their tasks using specified procedures. This leader relies on coercion, reward, and legitimate power to influence the behavior and performance of followers. Leaders exhibiting this leadership style seemed to view concern for people an important luxury that they couldn't always afford.

The **employee-centered leader** focuses on the people doing the work and believes in delegating decision making and aiding followers in satisfying their needs by creating a supportive work environment. Employee-centered leaders concerned themselves with followers' personal advancement, growth, and achievement. Such leaders emphasized individual and group development with the expectation that effective work performance would naturally follow.

Although the findings of this extensive research effort are quite complex, we can credit it with making a very strong case for the relative advantage of employee-centered over job-centered leadership. However the studies suggest that a leader must be either one or the other; an individual cannot be both job- and employee-centered. The seeming inability to be both job-centered and person-centered and be an effective leader stimulated other studies to test that conclusion.

Job-Centered Leader

A person who closely supervises and observes the work of others.

Employee-Centered Leader

A person who only generally supervises the work of others. He attempts to permit others to sense autonomy and support.

Initiating structure and consideration leadership

www.psy.ohio-
state.edu

Initiating Structure

Leadership acts that imply the structuring of job tasks and responsibilities for followers.

Consideration

Acts of the leader that show supportive concern for the followers in a group.

Among the several large leadership research programs that developed after World War II, one of the most significant was undertaken at Ohio State University (OSU). This program resulted in the development of a two-factor theory of leadership and indicated that leaders could be both job- and employee-centered.[14] A series of studies isolated two leadership behaviors, referred to as *initiating structure* and *consideration*. **Initiating structure** (or job-centered in Likert's terms) involves behavior in which the leader organizes and defines the relationships in the group, tends to establish well-defined patterns and channels of communication, and spells out ways of getting the job done. The leader with a high initiating structure tendency focuses on goals and results. **Consideration** (or employee-centered in Likert's terms) involves behavior indicating friendship, mutual trust, respect, warmth, and rapport between the leader and the followers. The leader with a high consideration tendency supports open communication and participation.

The Ohio State researchers measured leaders' tendencies to practice these two leadership behaviors and were able to depict them graphically. Figure 11–2 shows behaviors of five different leaders. Individual 1 is high on both initiating structure and consideration; individual 4 is low on both dimensions.

The original premise was that a high degree of consideration and a high degree of initiating structure (High-High) was the most effective of the four possible combinations. Since the original research undertaken to develop the questionnaire, there have been numerous studies of the relationship between these two leadership dimensions and various effectiveness criteria. In a study at International Harvester, researchers began to find some more complicated interactions of the two dimensions. Supervisors who scored high on initiating structure not only had high proficiency ratings from superiors but also had more employee grievances. A high consideration score was related to lower proficiency ratings and lower absences.[15]

Figure 11–2

Scores of Five Leaders: Initiating Structure and Consideration

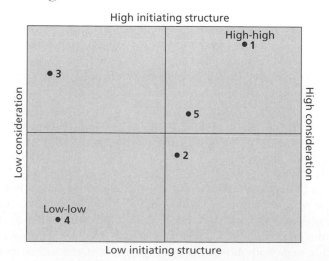

Other studies have examined how male and female leaders utilize initiating structure and consideration. A review of the literature reporting the results of such studies found that male and female leaders exhibit equal amounts of initiating structure and consideration and have equally satisfied followers.[16]

The OSU theory has been criticized for simplicity (e.g., only two dimensions of leadership), lack of generalizability, and reliance on questionnaire responses to measure leadership effectiveness. Despite these limitations, these studies made considerable headway in our understanding of effective leadership behavior. In particular, they broke from the traditional thinking that a leader must focus either on task or people. The researchers found that leaders could behave in ways that gave equal attention to both factors in any and all leadership situations—the task to be done and the people to do the task.

The search for answers regarding the most effective leadership behavior has known no national boundaries. The following Close-Up reports studies of leadership in Japan and China.

Comparisons of effective leadership behavior theories

The two theories of leadership behavior are compared and contrasted in Table 11–2. These two theories have provided practitioners with information on what behaviors leaders should possess. This knowledge has resulted in the establishment of training programs for individuals who perform leadership tasks. Each approach is also associated with highly respected theorists, researchers, or consultants, and each has been studied in different organizational settings. Yet, the linkage between leadership and such important performance indicators as production, efficiency, and satisfaction hasn't been conclusively resolved by either of the two personal-behavioral theories.

CLOSE—UP

Studies of Leadership in Japan and China

The relationship between leadership effectiveness and leadership behavior has international implications. In particular, researchers have been interested in the leadership sytles of managers in Japan and China, the great Asian economic powers. In recent years a considerable body of thought has emerged around the reports of a Japanese study of the effective behaviors of leaders. Interestingly, the two principal behaviors studied in these Japanese studies are identical to those of American studies, namely task versus people.

The Japanese studies used the term *performance* to refer to a leader's emphasis on subordinate performance and *maintenance* to refer to the leader's emphasis on interpersonal harmony. Consequently, the study authors coined the term PM leadership theory to denote their ideas. Similar terms in American leadership theory are job-centered and employee-centered. Although the terms and populations of subjects differ, the findings are generally consistent.

Recent studies of Chinese leaders found a strong relationship between the way Chinese leaders handled work-related issues and who they were working with to resolve the issues. If the leader was paired with another Chinese, the issue resolved rather quickly due to shared beliefs between the partners about how to solve the problem. But if the Chinese leader had to work with Japanese or westerners to solve the issue, the process of reaching agreement was considerably more difficult.

Thus, although we can identify certain leadership behaviors that cross cultural and national boundaries, differences remain in underlying beliefs and values. Western leaders doing business in Japan and China would be well-served by acknowledging both the similarities and the differences in leadership behavior around the world.

Sources: Peter B. Smith, Zhong Ming Wang, and Kwok Leung, "Leadership, Decision-Making, and Cultural Context: Event Management within Chinese Joint Ventures," *Leadership Quarterly,* Winter 1997, pp. 413–31; Mark F. Peterson, Jyuji Misumi, and Charlene Herreid, "Adapting Japanese PM Leadership Field Research for Use in Western Organizations," *Applied Psychology: An International Review,* January, 1994, pp. 49–74.

Table 11–2   A Review of Two Theories of Effective Leadership Behavior

LEADERSHIP FACTORS	PRIME INITIATOR(S) OF THE THEORY	METHOD OF MEASUREMENT	SUBJECTS	PRINCIPAL CONCLUSIONS
Employee-centered and job-centered.	Likert.	Interview and questionnaire responses of groups of followers.	Formal leaders and followers in public utilities, banks, hospitals, manufacturing, food, government agencies.	Employee-centered and job-centered styles result in production improvements. However, after a brief period of time, the job-centered style creates pressure that is resisted through absenteeism, turnover, grievance, and poor attitudes. The best style is *employee-centered*.
Initiating structure and consideration.	Fleishman, Stogdill, and Shartle.	Questionnaire responses of groups of followers, peers, the immediate superior, and the leader.	Formal leaders and followers in military, education, public utilities, manufacturing, and government agencies.	The combination of initiating structure and consideration behavior that achieves individual, group, and organizational effectiveness depends largely on the situation.

The simplicity of the initiating structure and consideration view of leadership is appealing. However, most researchers believe that environmental variables play some role in leadership effectiveness. For example, when successful initiating structure behavior is found, what other variables in the environment are at work? A worker who prefers to have a structured job and needs to have a job is likely to perform effectively under high initiating structure. What situational variables need to be considered? Neither the Ohio State nor the University of Michigan approach points out situational factors.

The Effects of Situational Differences

Situational Theories of Leadership

An approach to leadership that advocates that leaders understand their own behavior, the behavior of their subordinates, and the situation before utilizing a particular leadership style. This approach requires the leader to have diagnostic skills in human behavior.

The search for the "best" set of traits or behavior has failed to discover an effective leadership mix and style for all situations. Thus, **situational theories of leadership** evolved that suggest leadership effectiveness depends on the fit between personality, task, power, attitudes, and perceptions.[17] A number of situation-oriented leadership approaches have been publicized and researched. Two of the earlier ones are the Fiedler contingency model and the path–goal theory. In this section we will discuss these two theories as well as two other prominent situational theories: Hersey and Blanchard's SLT theory and leader–member exchange (LMX) theory.

Only after inconclusive and contradictory results evolved from much of the early trait and personal-behavioral research was the importance of the situation studied more closely by those interested in leadership. Eventually, researchers recognized that the leadership behavior needed to enhance performance depends largely on the situation: what's effective leadership in one situation may be disorganized incompetence in another. The situational theme of leadership, while appealing, is certainly a challenging orientation to implement.[18] Its basic foundation suggests that an effective leader must be flexible enough to adapt to the differences among subordinates and situations.

Deciding how to lead other individuals is difficult and requires an analysis of the leader, the group, and the situation.[19] Managers who are aware of the forces they face are able to modify their styles to cope with changes in the work environment. Three factors of particular importance are: (1) forces within the managers: (2) forces in the subordinates, and: (3) forces in the situation.[20] Tannenbaum and Schmidt state the situational theme in this way:

> *Thus, the successful manager of men can be primarily characterized neither as a strong leader nor as a permissive one. Rather, he is one who maintains a high batting average in accurately assessing the forces that determine what his most appropriate behavior at any given time should be and in actually being able to behave accordingly.*[21]

As the importance of situational factors and leader assessment of forces became more recognized, leadership research became more systematic, and contingency models of leadership began to appear in the organizational behavior and management literature. Each model has its advocates, and each attempts to identify the leader behaviors most appropriate for a series of leadership situations. Also, each model attempts to identify the leader-situation patterns important for effective leadership.

Contingency leadership model

Developed by Fiedler,[22] the contingency model of leadership effectiveness postulates that the performance of groups is dependent on the interaction between leadership style and situational favorableness.

LEADER'S STYLE   Fiedler's studies led him to believe that leaders practiced one or the other of two styles: *task-oriented leadership* or *relationship-oriented leadership*. He and his colleagues spent many years developing a way to measure an individual's tendency to practice these two styles, eventually settling on a method that relies on psychological reasoning. According to Fiedler, individuals whose personality favors task completion and a sense of accomplishment would more likely practice task-oriented leadership. An individual whose personality values warm, supportive relationships with others would likely practice relationship-oriented leadership.

Moreover, Fiedler's studies convinced him that individuals cannot be both task- and relationship-oriented. Individuals in leadership positions will be more comfortable, sincere, and effective practicing the leadership behavior that supports their own underlying personality. Thus the most important leadership issue is to match leaders' personalities and styles to the situation in which they will be effective.

SITUATIONAL FACTORS   Fiedler proposes three situational factors that determine whether a task- or relationship-oriented style is more likely to be effective: leader–member relations, task structure, and position power. From theoretical as well as intuitive points of view, interpersonal leader–follower relationships are likely to be the most important variable in a situation.

The **leader–member relations** factor refers to the degree of confidence, trust, and respect that followers have in the leader. This situational variable reflects acceptance of the leader. The leader's influence depends in part on acceptance by followers. If others are willing to follow because of charisma, expertise, or mutual respect, the leader has little need to rely on task-oriented behavior; the followers willingly follow the leader. If, however, the leader isn't trusted and is viewed negatively by followers, the situation would likely, but not necessarily, call for task-oriented behavior.

Leader–Member Relations

A factor in the Fiedler contingency model that refers to the degree of confidence, trust, and respect that the leader obtains from the followers.

Task Structure

Factor in Fiedler contingency model that refers to how structured a job is with regard to requirements, problem-solving alternatives, and feedback on job success.

The second most important situational factor is referred to as **task structure**. This factor refers specifically to the characteristics of the work to be done. Some of the important work characteristics include:

1. The degree to which the job's tasks and duties are clearly stated and known to the people performing the job.

2. The degree to which problems encountered in the job can be solved by a variety of procedures. An assembly line worker solves problems within a systematic framework, while a scientist has many different ways to solve a problem.

3. The degree to which the "correctness" of the solutions or decisions typically encountered in a job can be demonstrated by appeal to authority, by logical procedures, or by feedback. A quality control inspector can show defective parts and clearly indicate why a part is sent back for reworking.

4. The degree to which there's generally more than one correct solution. An accountant preparing a balance sheet has few choices, while a research scientist may have numerous potentially correct alternatives to choose from.

If we think of combining these four characteristics to describe any job, task, or assignment, we can conclude that they do indeed vary from high structure (those clearly known and understood, with relatively few solutions to any encountered problem, whose correctness can be demonstrated) to low task structure (those vaguely known and understood, with many possible solutions to encountered problems, whose correctness cannot be demonstrated). Thus the second most important situational variable refers to the nature of the task assigned to the leader and the group.

Position Power

A factor in the Fiedler contingency model that refers to the power inherent in the leadership position.

Position power in the contingency model refers to the power inherent in the leadership position. This situational characteristic takes into account that leadership occurs in a variety of different organizations and groups differentiated according to how much formal authority the leader has to make decisions and to exact obedience from subordinates. To determine leader position power, we ask questions such as:[23]

1. Can the supervisor recommend subordinate rewards and punishments to the boss?

2. Can the supervisor punish or reward subordinates on her own?

3. Can the supervisor recommend promotion or demotion of subordinates?

Fiedler contends that such questions provide a profile of strong or weak position power.

FAVORABLENESS OF THE SITUATION   The three situational factors can now be combined to describe different situations. These situations will differ in the degree to which they are favorable to the leader's influence attempts. Ask yourself this question: Would you rather be a leader in a situation where leader–member relations are good, the task is relatively structured, and your position power is relatively strong or in the opposite situation with poor leader–member relations, an unstructured task, and weak position power? Chances are you selected the first situation because it would be more *favorable* to your leadership efforts. Figure 11–3 combines the three situational factors such that we now have eight different situations ranging from Situation 1, which is very favorable to the leader, to Situation 8, which is very unfavorable to the leader.

WHICH LEADER FOR WHICH SITUATION?   We can use the figure to classify any particular situation if we know anything about leader–member relations, task structure, and position power. And as we have also seen, leaders have a preference for either task-oriented or relationship-oriented behavior. With this information, research can be

Figure 11–3

Summary of Fiedler's Situational Variables and Their Preferred Leadership Styles

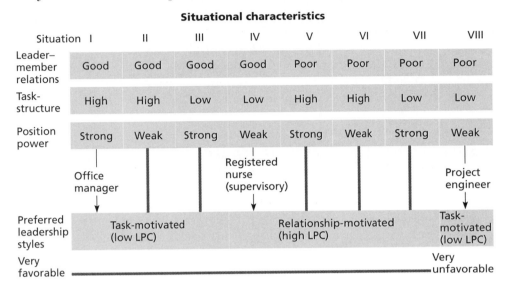

undertaken that identifies situations as one of the eight possibilities, and with sufficient samples of different situations and leaders, we could determine whether a particular style of leadership is more effective leadership.

Over the past three decades, Fiedler and advocates of the contingency model have studied military, educational, and industrial leaders. In a summary of 63 studies based on 454 separate groups, Fiedler suggests the kind of leadership that's most appropriate for the situational conditions.[24] Figure 11–3 summarizes these studies. As noted in the figure, task-oriented leaders perform better than relationship-oriented leaders in relatively favorable situations (1, 2, and 3) and in relatively unfavorable (8). Second, relationship-oriented leaders perform better than task-oriented leaders in intermediately favorable situations (4, 5, 6, and 7). These findings support the notion that each type of leader is effective in certain situations.

Consider the following situations:

Office manager. This individual has eight subordinates who like her. She structures the job by making work assignments and by setting goals for required outputs. She is also responsible for reviewing the work of subordinates and is the main spokesperson for and evaluator of the employees at merit review time.

Project engineer. This individual was appointed as the leader of a five-person project study group. None of the assigned members really want to serve in the group; they have other, more pressing jobs. As the appointed leader, the project engineer was actually given no power. His calls for meetings are generally unanswered. And when he gets the assigned members together, they're rather hostile, negative, and discourteous.

Registered nurse (supervisor). This individual is well liked by her subordinates, but the physicians have almost total control of the work. They won't permit the registered nurse to perform what she feels are nursing activities. This nurse is in a constant battle with the physicians to let her do the job and to stop interfering.

Figure 11–3 classifies these three individuals based on what we know about the situation in which they lead. The office manager is in situation 1, in which she is liked, has a structured task, and has position power. The project engineer is in situation 8, with poor leader–member relations, low task structure, and weak position power. The registered nurse is in situation 4. She's well liked, but she has no task-structure opportunities and no position power because of the physicians. The situation is more favorable for the situation 1 leader than for the situation 8 leader.

When the situation is highly favorable or highly unfavorable, a task-oriented approach generally produces the desired performance. The well-liked office manager, who has power and has clearly identified the performance goals, is operating in a highly favorable situation. The project engineer, who faces a group of suspicious and hostile subordinates and has little power and vague task responsibilities, needs to be task-oriented in this highly unfavorable situation.

CHANGING SITUATIONS TO FIT THE LEADER   Fiedler recommends that organizations should concentrate on changing situations to fit their leaders, rather than changing (training) leaders to fit their situations. Thus individuals who prefer task-oriented behavior will not benefit from training in human relations skills. The reverse also holds; relationship-oriented leaders will not respond to training to make them more task-oriented. He also suggests that leaders can make changes that result in more favorable situations. Table 11–3 presents some of his suggestions for changing particular situational factors.

A practical application of Fiedler's contingency approach is the training program LEADER MATCH.[25] Most training programs try to change the leader's personality to fit the situation; but this programmed learning system trains leaders to modify their leadership situation to fit their personalities. In LEADER MATCH training, participants read a workbook, assess their preferred leadership style, discuss and analyze leadership situations, and evaluate their performance in analyzing the situations. To date, LEADER MATCH has been used with managers, military personnel, and students. In the majority of studies, leaders trained with LEADER MATCH were rated more highly by their supervisors than untrained leaders were rated by their supervisors.

CRITIQUE OF FIEDLER'S CONTINGENCY MODEL   Fiedler's model and research have elicited pointed criticisms and concerns. First, Graen and associates present evidence that research support for the model is weak, especially if studies conducted by researchers not associated with Fiedler are examined.[26] The earlier support and enthusiasm for the model came from Fiedler and his students, who conducted numerous studies of leaders. Second, researchers have called attention to the questionable measurement of preferred leadership style; these researchers claim that the reliability and validity of the questionnaire measure are low.[27] Third, the meaning of the variables presented by Fiedler isn't clear. For example, at what point does a *structured* task become an *unstructured* task? Who can define or display this point? Finally, critics claim that Fiedler's theory can accommodate nonsupportive results. This point is specifically made by one critic who states, "Fiedler has revealed his genius twice; first, in devising the model, which stands like calculus to arithmetic compared with previous leadership models, and second, in his ability to integrate new findings into his models."[28]

Despite supporters and detractors, Fiedler's contingency model has made significant contributions to the study and application of leadership principles. Fiedler called direct attention to the situational nature of leadership. His view of leadership stimulated numerous research studies and much-needed debate about the dynamics of leader behavior. Certainly, Fiedler has played one of the most prominent roles in encouraging the scientific study of leadership in work settings. He pointed the way and made others uncomfortably aware of the complexities of the leadership process.

Modifying Leader–Member Relations

1. Spend more—or less—informal time (lunch, leisure activities, etc.) with your subordinates.
2. Request particular people for work in your group.
3. Volunteer to direct difficult or troublesome subordinates.
4. Suggest or effect transfers of particular subordinates into or out of your unit.
5. Raise morale by obtaining positive outcomes (e.g., special bonuses, time off, attractive jobs) for subordinates.

Modifying Task Structure

If you wish to work with less structured tasks:

1. Ask your boss, whenever possible, to give you the new or unusual problems and let you figure out how to get them done.
2. Bring the problems and tasks to your group members and invite them to work with you on the planning and decision-making phases of the tasks.

If you wish to work with more highly structured tasks:

1. Ask your superior to give you, whenever possible, the tasks that are more structured or to give you more detailed instructions.
2. Break the job down into smaller subtasks that can be more highly structured.

Modifying Position Power

To raise your position power:

1. Show your subordinates who's boss by exercising fully the powers that the organization provides.
2. Make sure that information to your group gets channeled through you.

To lower your position power:

1. Call on members of your group to participate in planning and decision-making functions.
2. Let your assistants exercise relatively more power.

Table 11–3

Leadership Actions to Change Situations

Path–goal model

Like the other situational or contingency leadership approaches, the **path–goal leadership model** attempts to predict leadership effectiveness in different situations. According to this model, developed by Robert J. House, leaders are effective because of their positive impact on followers' motivation, ability to perform, and satisfaction. The theory is designated *path–goal* because it focuses on how the leader influences the followers' perceptions of work goals, self-development goals, and paths to goal attainment.[29]

The foundation of path–goal theory is the expectancy motivation theory discussed in Chapter 6. Some early work on the path–goal theory asserts that leaders become effective by making rewards available to subordinates and by making those rewards contingent on subordinates' accomplishment of specific goals.[30] It is argued that an important part of the leader's job is to clarify for subordinates the behavior most likely to result in goal accomplishment. This activity is referred to as *path clarification*.

LEADERSHIP BEHAVIOR   The early path–goal work led to the development of a complex theory involving four specific leader behaviors (directive, supportive, participative, and achievement) and three subordinate attitudes (job satisfaction, acceptance of the leader, and expectations about effort-performance-reward relationships).[31] The *directive leader* tends to let subordinates know what's expected of them. The *supportive leader* treats subordinates as equals. The *participative leader* consults with subordinates and considers their suggestions and ideas before reaching a decision. The *achievement-oriented* leader sets challenging goals, expects subordinates to perform at the highest level, and continually seeks improvement in performance. As is evident, these four behaviors are more refined conceptualizations of the two general behaviors we have been discussing throughout the chapter: directive and achievement-oriented behaviors are but two distinct dimensions of task-oriented behavior; supportive and participative behaviors are two distinct dimensions of person-oriented behavior.

Path–Goal Leadership Model

Theory that suggests a leader needs to influence followers' perceptions of work goals, self-development goals, and paths to goal attainment.

A study of professional employees from research and development organizations examined the path-goal model.[32] The results indicated that need for clarity moderated the relationship between a leader's path clarification and employees' satisfaction. The higher the need for clarity among subordinates, the stronger the relationship between the leader's initiating structure and job satisfaction.

Research studies also suggest that these four behaviors can be practiced by the same leader in various situations. These findings are contrary to the Fiedler notion concerning the difficulty of altering style. The path–goal approach suggests more flexibility than the Fiedler contingency model.

THE MAIN PATH–GOAL PROPOSITIONS   The path–goal theory has led to the development of two important propositions:[33]

1. Leader behavior is effective to the extent that subordinates perceive such behavior as a source of immediate satisfaction or as instrumental to future satisfaction.

2. Leader behavior is motivational to the extent that it makes satisfaction of subordinates' needs contingent on effective performance and that it complements the environment of subordinates by providing the guidance, clarity of direction, and rewards necessary for effective performance.

According to the path–goal theory, leaders should increase the number and kinds of rewards available to subordinates. In addition, the leader should provide guidance and counsel to clarify the manner in which these rewards can be obtained. This means that the leader should help subordinates clarify realistic expectancies and reduce the barriers to the accomplishment of valued goals. For example, counseling employees on their chances for promotion and helping them eliminate skill deficiencies so that a promotion becomes a more realistic possibility are appropriate leadership behaviors. The leader works at making the path to goals as clear as possible for subordinates. The style best suited to accomplish this is selected and applied. Thus, the path–goal approach requires flexibility from the leader to use whichever style is appropriate in a particular situation.

SITUATIONAL FACTORS   Two situational, or contingency, variables are considered in the path–goal theory: *personal characteristics of subordinates* and *environmental pressures and demands* with which subordinates must cope to accomplish work goals and derive satisfaction.

An important personal characteristic is subordinates' *perceptions of their ability*. The higher the degree of perceived ability relative to the task demands, the less likely the subordinate is to accept a directive leader style. This directive style of leadership would be viewed as unnecessarily close. In addition, a person's *locus of control* also affects responses. Individuals with an internal locus of control (they believe that rewards are contingent upon their efforts) are generally more satisfied with a participative style, while individuals who have an external locus of control (they believe that rewards are beyond their personal control) are generally more satisfied with a directive style.

Environmental variables include factors that aren't within the control of the subordinate but are important to satisfaction or to the ability to perform effectively. These include the tasks, the formal authority system of the organization, and the work group. Any of these environmental factors can motivate or constrain the subordinate. Environmental forces may also serve as rewards for acceptable levels of performance. For example, the subordinate could be motivated by the work group and receive satisfaction from co-workers' acceptance for doing a job according to group norms.

The path–goal theory proposes that leader behavior is motivational to the extent that it helps subordinates cope with environmental uncertainties. A leader who reduces the uncertainties of the job is considered to be a motivator because he increases subordinates' expectations that their efforts lead to desirable rewards.

Figure 11–4 presents the path–goal approach. The total path–goal approach has not been subjected to a complete test. Parts of the model, however, have been examined in field settings. One study found that when task structure (the repetitiveness or routineness of the job) was high, directive leader behavior was negatively related to satisfaction; when task structure was low, directive leader behavior was positively related to satisfaction. Also, when task structure was high, supportive leadership was positively related to satisfaction; under low task structure, there was no relationship between supportive leader behavior and satisfaction.[34]

CRITIQUE OF THE PATH–GOAL MODEL   There is some question about the predictive power of the path–goal model. One researcher suggested that subordinate performance might be the cause of changes in leader behavior instead of, as predicted by the model, the other way around.[35] A review of the path–goal approach suggested that the model had resulted in development of only a few hypotheses. These reviewers also point to the record of inconsistent research results associated with the model. They agree that research has consistently shown that the higher the task structure of subordinate jobs, the higher the relationship between supportive leader behavior and subordinate satisfaction. However, they maintain that the second main hypothesis of the path–goal model hasn't received consistent support. This hypothesis—the higher the task structure, the lower the relationship between directive leader behavior and subordinate satisfaction—has received only some support.[36]

On the positive side, one must admit that the path–goal model is an improvement over the trait and personal-behavioral theories. It attempts to indicate which factors affect motivation to perform. In addition, the path–goal approach introduces both situational factors and individual differences when examining leader behavior and outcomes such as satisfaction and performance. The approach makes an effort to explain why a particular style of leadership works best in a given situation. As more research accumulates, this type of explanation will have practical utility for those interested in the leadership process in work settings.

Figure 11–4

The Path–Goal Model

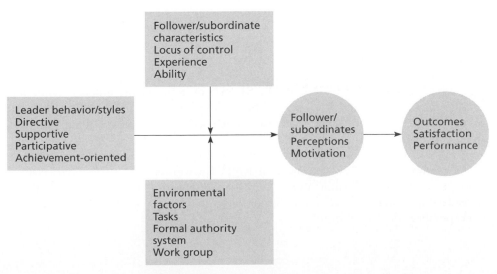

Hersey-Blanchard situational leadership theory (SLT)

Managers often complain that esoteric theories don't help them do a better job on the production line, in the office, or in a research and development lab. They request something they can apply and use. Hersey and Blanchard developed a situational leadership theory that has appealed to many managers.[37] Large firms and small businesses have used the situational leadership theory (SLT) and enthusiastically endorse its value.

SLT's emphasis is on followers and their level of maturity. The leader must properly judge or intuitively know followers' maturity level and then use a leadership style that fits the level. **Readiness** is defined as the ability and willingness of people (followers) to take responsibility for directing their own behavior. It's important to consider two types of readiness: job and psychological. A person high in job readiness has the knowledge and abilities to perform the job without a manager structuring or directing the work. A person high in psychological readiness has the self-motivation and desire to do high-quality work. Again, this person has little need for direct supervision.

Readiness

The followers' skills and willingness to do a job.

LEADERSHIP BEHAVIOR   Hersey and Blanchard used the Ohio State studies to further develop four leadership styles available to managers:

1. *Telling*. The leader defines the roles needed to do the job and tells followers what, where, how, and when to do the tasks.

2. *Selling*. The leader provides followers with structured instructions, but is also supportive.

3. *Participating*. The leader and followers share in decisions about how best to complete a high-quality job.

4. *Delegating*. The leader provides little specific, close direction or personal support to followers.

By determining followers' readiness level, a manager can choose from among the four leadership styles. Figure 11–5 depicts the important elements of the SLT.

SITUATIONAL FACTORS   Application of the model works as follows. Suppose that a manager determines that his recently hired followers are unable to do the work and unwilling to take the risk associated with learning to do it. The followers are at the (R1) readiness state. By moving vertically from R1 to the leadership behavior appropriate for this state, we see that telling is the appropriate style. That is, an R1 follower requires a leader who is high on task orientation, gives direct instructions, and is low in support behavior. Task behavior is more needed than supportive behavior. In fact, research is available to support the S1 style over any of the others.[38] Some may assume that a participative (S3) style is best. However, asking an insecure follower to participate may result in more insecurity about making a mistake or saying something that's considered dumb.

A follower will be more ready to take on more responsibility as other leadership styles become more effective. For example, an R&D lab with expert, experienced scientists who are totally able and willing to do the job would flourish under a delegative (S4) style of leadership. Using the readiness indicator with the four-style model helps the manager conceptualize what's best for followers.

Figure 11–5

The Hersey-Blanchard Situational Leadership Theory

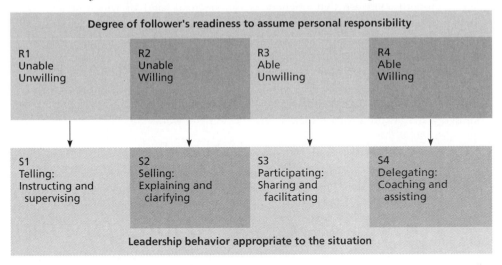

Degree of follower's readiness to assume personal responsibility

R1 Unable Unwilling	R2 Unable Willing	R3 Able Unwilling	R4 Able Willing

S1 Telling: Instructing and supervising	S2 Selling: Explaining and clarifying	S3 Participating: Sharing and facilitating	S4 Delegating: Coaching and assisting

Leadership behavior appropriate to the situation

Blanchard has responded to some critics of the SLT by revising the original model.[39] He retitled various terms, calling task behavior *directive behavior* and relationship behavior *supportive behavior*. The four leadership styles are now called S1-directing, S2-coaching, S3-supporting, and S4-delegating. Readiness is now called the *development level of followers*. The development level is defined in terms of followers' current competence and commitment to do the job.

In training programs Hersey and Blanchard use the Leader Behavior Analysis[40] survey scale to assess participants' attitudes about leadership. It consists of 20 questions that have training participants judge what leadership style is best suited. Here's one question:

Recently, you have begun to have trouble with one of the people you supervise. He has become lackadaisical, and only your constant prodding has brought about task completion. Because of past experience with him, you suspect he may not have all the expertise needed to complete the high-priority task you have given him. You would:

a. *Continue to direct and follow up on his efforts to complete the task.*

b. *Continue to supervise his work and try to draw out his attitudes and feelings concerning the task assignment.*

c. *Involve him in problem solving with his task, offer support, and use his ideas in the task completion.*

d. *Let him know that this is an important task and ask him to contact you if he has any questions or problems.*

The experts state that a selling leadership style is best. This is reflected in the (b) response. The follower has a motivation problem. He also isn't knowledgeable about how best to do the job. The worst style to use would be a delegation approach (d). The person isn't ready to be given responsibility to complete this important task. By analyzing and critiquing trainees' responses to this type of questions, trainers attempt to improve managers' judgments about which leadership style is best.

Although managers are attracted to the SLT, there are some serious unanswered questions. The most important may be, does it really work? Testing of the model, over 20 years after its inception, is still limited. Even the originators, Hersey and Blanchard, have failed to provide evidence that predictions can be made and of which style is best. Another issue revolves around the notion that a leader can change or adapt his style to fit a follower or group. Are people in leadership positions this adaptable? Again, research is needed to validate the flexibility possibility among leaders.[41]

Despite the words of caution about limited research and flexibility, many managers like the SLT. It's thought to be practical, meaningful, and visible in training settings. As leadership continues to command attention in organizations, the SLT appears to remain a popular way to express what leaders should be doing at work.

Leader–member exchange (LMX) theory

Personal-behavioral explanations of leadership suggest that the leader's behavior is the same across all followers.[42] This thinking is similar to assuming that a parent treats or interacts with each of her children the same. Graen has proposed the leader–member exchange (LMX) theory of leadership, which proposes that there's no such thing as consistent leader behavior across subordinates. A leader may be very considerate toward one subordinate and very rigid and structured with another. Each relationship has a uniqueness, and it's the one-on-one relationships that determine subordinates' behaviors.

The LMX approach suggests that leaders classify subordinates into *in-group members* and *out-group members*. In-group members share a common bond and value system, and interact with the leader. Out-group members have less in common with the leader and don't share much with her. The Leader–Member Exchange Questionnaire partially presented in Table 11–4 measures in-group versus out-group status.[43]

The LMX explanation suggests that in-group members are likely to receive more challenging assignments and more meaningful rewards. Research indicates that in-group members are more positive about the organization culture and have higher job performance and satisfaction than employees in the out-group.[44] An out-group member isn't considered to be the type of person the leader prefers to work with, and this attitude is likely to become a self-fulfilled prophecy. Out-group members receive less challenging assignments, receive little positive reinforcement, become bored with the job, and often quit. They experience a lower quality relationship with their leader.[45]

Table 11–4

Items that Assess Leader–Member Exchange

1. How flexible do you believe your supervisor is about evolving change in *your* job? 4 = Supervisor is enthused about change; 3 = Supervisor is lukewarm to change; 2 = Supervisor sees little need to change; 1 = Supervisor sees no need for change.

2. Regardless of how much formal organizational authority your supervisor has built into his position, what are the chances that he would be personally inclined to use his power to help you solve problems in your work? 4 = He certainly would; 3 = Probably would; 2 = Might or might not; 1 = No.

3. To what extent can *you* count on your supervisor to "bail you out," at her expense, when *you* really need her? 4 = Certainly would; 3 = Probably; 2 = Might or might not; 1 = No.

4. How often do you take suggestions regarding your work to your supervisor? 4 = Almost always; 3 = Usually; 2 = Seldom; 1 = Never.

5. How would *you* characterize *your* working relationship with your supervisor? 4 = Extremely effective; 3 = Better than average; 2 = About average; 1 = Less than average.

The five items are summed for each participant, resulting in a possible range of scores from 5 to 20.

The LMX approach rests on the assumption that the leader's perception of followers influences the leader's behavior, which then influences the follower's behavior. This exchange or mutual influence explanation is also found in the equity theory explanation of motivation.[46]

Comparing the situational approaches

The four models for examining situation leadership have some similarities and some differences. They are similar in that they (1) focus on the dynamics of leadership, (2) have stimulated research on leadership, and (3) remain controversial because of measurement problems, limited research testing, or contradictory research results.

The themes of each model are summarized in Table 11–5. Fiedler's model, the most tested, is perhaps the most controversial. His view of leader behavior centers on task- and relationship-oriented tendencies and how these interact with task and position power. The path–goal approach emphasizes the instrumental actions of leaders and four styles for conducting these actions (directive, supportive, participative, and achievement-oriented).

The situational variables discussed in each approach differ somewhat. There is also a different view of outcome criteria for assessing how successful the leader behavior has been: Fiedler discusses leader effectiveness, and the path–goal approach focuses on satisfaction and performance.

Table 11–5   Summary Comparison of Four Important Situational Models of Leadership

	FIEDLER'S CONTINGENCY MODEL	HOUSE'S PATH–GOAL MODEL	HERSEY-BLANCHARD SITUATIONAL LEADERSHIP THEORY	LEADER–MEMBER EXCHANGE (LMX) APPROACH
Leadership qualities	Leaders are task- or relationship-oriented. The job should be engineered to fit the leader's style.	Leaders can increase follower's effectiveness by applying proper motivational techniques.	Leader must adapt style in terms of task and relationship behavior on the basis of followers.	Leader must be adaptive since there is no such thing as consistent leader behavior across subordinates.
Assumptions about followers	Followers prefer different leadership styles, depending on task structure, leader–member relations, and position power.	Followers have different needs that must be fulfilled with the help of a leader.	Followers' maturity (readiness) to take responsibility and ability influences the leadership style that is adopted.	Followers are categorized as in-groups (which share a common bond and value system, and interact with the leader) and out-groups (which have less in common with the leader).
Leader effectiveness	Effectiveness of the leader is determined by the interaction of environment and personality factors.	Effective leaders are those who clarify for followers the paths or behaviors that are best suited.	Effective leaders are able to adapt directing, coaching, supporting, and delegating style to fit the followers' levels of maturity.	The perceptive leader is able to adapt her style to fit followers' needs.
History of research: problems	If investigations not affiliated with Fiedler are used, the evidence is contradictory on the accuracy of the model.	Model has generated very little research interest in past two decades.	Not enough research is available to reach a definitive conclusion about the predictive power of the theory.	Approach has generated a limited amount of research to support its assumptions and predictions.

Summary of Key Points

- As the ability to influence followers, leadership involves the use of power and the acceptance of the leader by the followers. This ability to influence followers is related to the followers' need satisfaction.

- The trait approach has resulted in attempts to predict leadership effectiveness from physical, sociological, and psychological traits. The search for traits has led to studies involving effectiveness and such factors as height, weight, intelligence, and personality.

- There continues to be a great deal of semantic confusion and overlap in the definition of leadership behavior. Such terms as *employee-centered, job-centered, initiating structure,* and *consideration* are classified as descriptions of what the leader does.

- The *situational approach* emphasizes the importance of forces within the leader, the subordinates, and the organiza-

tion. These forces interact and must be properly diagnosed if effectiveness is to be achieved.

- The *contingency model* proposes that groups' performance is dependent on the interaction of leadership style and situational favorableness. The three crucial situational factors are leader–member relations, task structure, and position power.

- The *path–goal model* deals with specific leader behaviors and how they might impact employee satisfaction.

- The *Hersey-Blanchard situational leadership theory* is popular among managers. It proposes that by determining followers' readiness level, a manager can choose the best leadership style. It assumes that a manager can readily learn to adapt his style to each follower.

- The *leader–member exchange theory (LMX)* approach suggests that each superior–subordinate relationship is unique. The theory assumes that a leader can behave in different ways with different followers.

Discussion and Review Questions

1. Compare the trait, behavioral, and situational approaches to leadership in terms of practical value to organizations seeking to identify and develop present and future leaders.

2. In your experience, can leaders relate to followers both as members of the group and as individuals? What are the implications for leadership theory and practice if you decide that leadership is essentially a one-on-one interaction?

3. Explain the path–goal theory of leadership. Now apply the main ideas of this theory to a different setting, perhaps the case of a parent attempting to help her daughter improve her college study habits and grades.

4. Why is measurement of important variables such a crucial issue in the development of practically useful leadership theories of the kinds discussed in this chapter?

5. How useful are university courses on management or on organizational behavior for purposes of developing future leaders? Explain.

6. Why has the trait approach failed to present a universally acceptable set of effective leadership traits?

7. According to the contingency theory, an alternative to modifying the style of leadership through training is changing the favorableness of the situation. What's meant by changing the favorableness of the situation?

8. Would a leader (on an assembly line) from Eastern Europe (Poland or Romania) be able to lead French workers on an assembly line in France? Explain.

9. In your experience, are leaders flexible enough to adapt leadership styles to the situation or followers? Explain.

10. Would it be difficult for a manager to accurately determine a follower's readiness level? Explain.

C A S E   F O R   A N A L Y S I S

A New Leadership Position

At Dancey Electronics Company in a suburb of Dallas, management forecasts have indicated that the company should enjoy moderate growth during the next 10 years. This growth rate would require the promotion of three employees into newly created general manager positions. These individuals would then be required to spend most of their time working with

departmental managers and less time on production, output, and cost issues.

A majority of the candidates for the three new positions have been with company for at least 15 years. They're all skilled in the production aspects of operations. Company vice president Don Kelly believed, however, that none of the candidates has the training

Exhibit 1

Morris Profile of Leadership

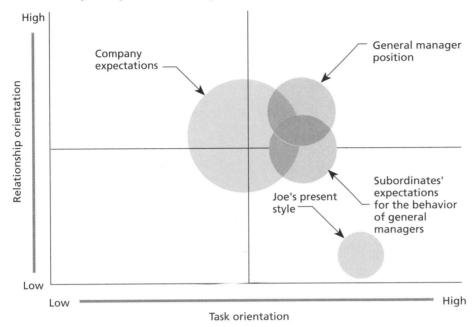

or overall insight into company problems to move smoothly into the general manager positions. Despite these anticipated problems, the board of directors decided that the three new general managers would be recruited from within Dancey.

In attempting to find the best candidates for the new positions, Dancey hired a consulting firm, Management Analysis Corporation (MAC), to perform an internal search for qualified individuals. Through interviews, testing, and a review of company records, the consulting firm generated a list of six candidates.

One candidate was Joe Morris. The analysis used to assess Joe involved the study of environmental variables and his current style of leadership. Exhibit 1 profiles Joe's leadership style and various environmental factors that have some impact on this style.

Joe's present leadership style, which is high in task orientation and low in relationship orientation, is similar to the leadership styles of the other five general manager candidates. The expectations of the company, the potential subordinates of the general manager, and the new position of general manager aren't consistent with any of the candidates' present

leadership styles. The intersecting area indicates where the expectations of the company, the new position, and the subordinates would be consistent. According to MAC, this is the ideal leadership style for candidates to use as the general managers. If Joe or any other candidate were to accept the general manager job, he would have to significantly increase his relationship orientation. If he didn't change his orientation, the probability of failure, according to the consulting firm, would be high.

Don Kelly was adamant about not going outside Dancey to find three potentially successful new general managers. He and the entire board of directors wanted to utilize a recruitment-from-within policy to secure the three best general managers. It was Don's belief that a leader could modify his style of leadership to meet new situational demands. This belief and the internal recruitment plan led Don to call a meeting to discuss a program to improve the compatibility between the three general managers finally selected (Joe Morris, Randy Santiago, and Ann Shumate) and the environmental factors (the company, the subordinates, and the requirements of the new position).

Discussion Questions

1. Do you believe that the diagnosis and resulting profile prepared by Management Analysis Corporation were a necessary step in the process of finding a potentially successful group of general managers? Explain.

2. What alternatives are available to modify Joe Morris's potential effectiveness in the new general manager position?

3. Why will it be difficult for Joe Morris to modify his style of leadership?

EXPERIENTIAL EXERCISE

Adapting Leadership Skills to People Problems

Objectives

1. To determine if a particular style of leadership could be used to solve the problem.

2. To identify how a leader must proceed in a delicate situation involving employees, organization culture, and work performance.

Related Topics

Motivation, work rules, and organization etiquette are all issues covered in this exercise.

Starting the Exercise

Each class member is to read the case involving Bob and Nancy.

Case: What to Do with Bob and Nancy?

Dave Lopresti was sitting at his desk, wondering how the devil to handle this situation. In engineering school, they don't tell you what to do when you think two of your key subordinates are having an affair! Dave knew a lot about the relative conducting properties of metals, but what about the properties of people?

Dave was engineering manager of a division in a large corporation on the East Coast. The division comprised 3 engineering supervisors, 6 lead engineers, and approximately 42 engineers (Exhibit 2). The past two years had seen several reductions in workforce due to a temporary decline in the business base. The remaining staff were cream of the crop, all hard workers with a professional attitude about their jobs; any deadwood was long gone. The division had just won a large contract that would provide for long-term growth but would also require a heavy workload until new people could be hired and trained.

The firm's work was highly technical and required considerable sharing of ideas within and between individual groups. This need for internal cooperation and support had been amplified because the organization was still understaffed.

Dave's previous secretary had transferred to an out-plant location just before the new contract award, and it had taken a long time to find a suitable replacement. Because of a general shortage within the company, Dave had been forced to hire temporary help from a secretarial service. After several months, he found Nancy and felt very fortunate to have located an experienced secretary from within the company. She was in her mid-30s, was attractive, had a pleasant disposition, and was very competent.

In the electronic design group was an enthusiastic, highly respected lead engineer named Bob. Bob and Dave had been close friends for several years, having started with the company at the same time. They shared several common interests, which had led to spending a fair amount of time together away from work.

Bob was struggling to get into management, and Dave's more rapid advancement had put a strain on the friendship. Dave had moved up from coworker to being his boss and finally to being his boss's boss. Dave felt they could still be good friends at work, but he couldn't show Bob any favoritism. Bob understood the situation.

From Nancy's first day on the job, Bob began to hang around her desk. He would go out of his way to start conversations and draw her attention. This was no surprise, since Nancy was attractive and Bob had gained a reputation over the years as being a bit of a

Exhibit 2

Table of Organization

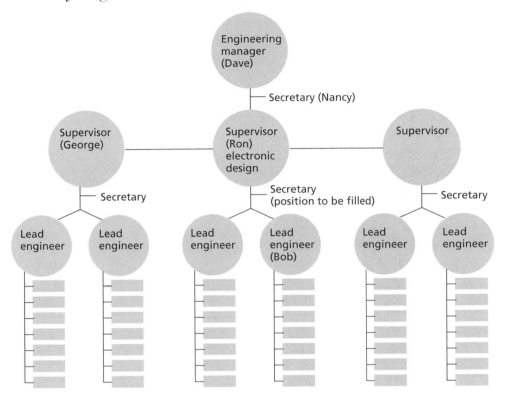

wolf. He was always the first on the scene when an attractive new female joined the program.

Before long, Bob and Nancy began eating lunch together. As time passed, the lunch dates became a regular routine, as did their trips together to the coffee machine. Their conversations during the working day also became more frequent. Dave felt slightly concerned about the wasted time, but since the quality and quantity of their work was not suffering in any measurable way, he did not say anything to either person. Furthermore, it was not unreasonable for Bob to be having numerous conversations with her since she had been instructed to provide typing and clerical support to the engineers whenever she had idle time. (Bob's section was temporarily looking for a secretary, and the engineers were developing several new documents.)

After a few months, Bob and Nancy introduced their spouses to each other, and the two couples began to get together for an increasing number of social gatherings. Bob and Nancy continued their frequent

lunch dates, now leaving the plant for lunch and occasionally returning late. This was not considered a major rule infraction if the lateness was infrequent and if the time was made up in the long run. This tolerance policy was generally respected by all, including Bob and Nancy. On balance, the company seemed to be receiving at least a full week's work from both of them, since they often worked late.

What was also going on (but Dave didn't learn about until later) was that Bob and Nancy were calling each other on the phone during the workday even though they worked in the same general area, just desks apart. They would wait until Dave had left the office and then chat on the phone. However, Nancy's work performance was not visibly affected.

Of course, the internal grapevine was at work, and occasionally Dave would be asked about the situation between Bob and Nancy. "Do you know they've been seen having cocktails together in the evening?" "Did you know Nancy was having marital problems?" "Does Bob's wife know what's going on?"

It was apparent that Bob and Nancy were starting to have an affair, but how serious it was, and how long it would last, wasn't known. They were being very careful around Dave, and almost all of what Dave knew was based upon second- and third-hand information and rumors. At this point, about four months after Nancy had started work, Dave did speak to Ron, Bob's supervisor, about it; but Ron was anxious to downplay the whole thing. He was willing to talk to Bob about the late lunches but unwilling to discuss anything else. This seemed appropriate since, from the company's standpoint, employees' private lives were their own business. Ron was new to the organization, and this factor contributed to his reluctance to discuss a delicate issue.

Dave decided not to confront Bob directly. If their relationship had been as close as it had been in years past, he might have spoken to Bob about the rumors going around, but during this period the friendship had further deteriorated. They were talking on a less personal level, and Bob was spending less off-hours time with old friends. Furthermore, Dave knew from previous discussions that Bob was particularly sensitive about private matters. He probably wouldn't welcome my advice, thought Dave.

Dave had spoken to Nancy about the need to be back in the office at the end of the lunch hour, but he hadn't made an issue out of it. Even though it was a definite annoyance when she wasn't there to answer the phone or type a memo, her performance hadn't declined. Dave certainly didn't want to bring up the issue of an affair to Nancy. He imagined what might arise: tears, defensive denial (much of what Dave thought was going on would be difficult to substantiate if Nancy were to challenge his assessment), and even potential legal ramifications if the situation were handled improperly. Bob and Nancy could claim that their reputations or careers had been damaged. (Dave also didn't want to raise this issue with Personnel; it might permanently tarnish both of their records.)

During this time frame, there was a dramatic change in Bob's personal appearance. Instead of his usual coat-and-tie attire, he started wearing open-front shirts and a beaded necklace in an attempt to acquire the current "macho" look. Although perhaps acceptable in a southern California business office, it certainly was out of place in the Northeast with the more conservative environment of the company. As a lead engineer, Bob directed, and often presented to management, the work of 12 other engineers. The custom was for all engineers and managers to wear a coat and tie, especially since they might be called upon, with little notice, to meet with a customer or higher management. Even though Bob's attire was considered unprofessional, there was nothing in the company's written dress code requirement to forbid it.

Up to this point, there had been no serious violation of company rules by either Bob or Nancy, although rules were being bent and tolerance policies abused.

Then the situation took a turn for the worse while Dave was on a two-week company trip with Ron. Bob and Nancy used the opportunity to go out for a very long lunch. When they returned just before quitting time, George, one of the other supervisors, called Bob into his office and suggested that he clean up his act. George told Bob that he was being foolish in chasing Nancy and that, among other things he was jeopardizing his career opportunities with the company. Bob denied being anything more than friends with Nancy and politely told George to stay out of his private affairs.

When Dave returned from his trip and heard of the incident, he told Ron to reprimand Bob and make it clear to him that "his actions are unacceptable and that further long lunch periods will not be tolerated." Bob apologized, said he would make up the time, and that it wouldn't happen again.

Dave spoke to Nancy, and she also promised that there would be no more long lunches. But this was not the end of their noontime, outplant lunch dates, and before long, Nancy's husband Ted got involved. Ted was a salesman for the company and worked in the same building. He began to drop by at lunchtime to question the engineers about Nancy's whereabouts. In addition, he started calling Dave after work, wanting to know when Nancy had left and expressing concern that she had not yet arrived home. This questioning was an unpleasant experience for everybody.

By now, the entire organization was well aware of the irregular relationship and was growing disrespectful of both Bob and Nancy. This was a difficult situation for the engineers. The attitudes of the organization had always been very professional, and the success of each group depended upon teamwork and strong leadership from its lead engineer. Bob had been highly respected for his technical competence and ability to direct. In addition, the members of his group knew Bob's family and had always considered him to be a good family man. Now this image had been destroyed.

From a technical standpoint, Bob was still an excellent engineer and a vital resource on the new contract. But with the group's declining respect, Bob was becoming less effective as a leader. Bob's own engineers felt very uncomfortable about the situation. They believed that Bob's real intersts at work were more with Nancy than with them.

The situation had now deteriorated to the point where total organization effectiveness was being measurably affected. Something had to be done to remedy this situation. But what to do?

Completing the Exercise

After individually reviewing the case, the class will divide into groups of four to eight members. In a 20- to 30-minute period, the group will discuss what actions Dave should take and why. Each group will then report its proposal strategies to the entire class.

Source: Reprinted with permission of Stanford University Graduate School of Business. © 1983, by the Board of Trustees of the Leland Stanford Junior University.

Chapter 12

Leadership: Emerging Concepts and Approaches

Learning Objectives

After completing Chapter 12, you should be able to:

Define
What is meant by a normative model of leadership.

Describe
The type of research needed to further develop an explanation of charismatic leadership.

Discuss
Why transformational leadership is a difficult concept to use in developing a leadership training program.

Compare
Internal and external causes of performance attribution.

Identify
Situations and settings in which self-managed groups and self-leadership would be useful and effective.

As Chapters 11 and 12 illustrate, the topic of leadership doesn't lack theories, models, or prescriptions. What, if any, value do all of the theories provide to practicing managers? The most academically criticized theory of all is the Hersey-Blanchard situational leadership theory. On the other hand, it is the one theory that many managers embrace. It is straightforward, it offers suggestions, and it discusses the need for flexibility or the ability to modify leadership behaviors and style to fit the followers and situation.

Examination of the host of theories discloses concerns about tasks, people, and situations. The terms used are often stated in complex language, but the themes are similar across theories. The issue of flexibility is not accepted by all theories. Can a person really be as flexible as the Hersey-Blanchard theory requires? It seems that some individuals can be flexible, but others are dry, rigid, and inflexible. Determining a leader's flexibility would seem like a worthwhile endeavor for an organization. How can this be done? In work settings, it must be done by observation, discussion, and actual behavior monitoring.

Leadership appears to play a role in helping individuals and groups attain performance goals. Some leaders are better at performance enhancement than others. Efficient leaders provide a coordination and control function that seems to bring people together, to chart the direction, and to provide verbal encouragement and recognition. Certainly, there are many factors outside a leader's control.[1] For example, a department manager must work with the pool of employees available to complete projects. If the pool is self-motivated, achievement-oriented, and positively inclined toward accomplishing organizational goals, the leader's job will be easier than if faced with a lethargic, antagonistic, and negatively oriented group.

Even in situations involving self-managed groups, signs of leadership are present. Self-managed groups have a responsibility to complete a whole task. The members possess the skills to do the whole job and have the power to schedule work, evaluate performance, and sanction nonperformers. Someone in the group may take the lead in sanctioning nonperformers. That person may ask nonperformers to try to do better or may express the group's displeasure with the nonperformance. A little bit of leadership is creeping in even in the self-managed situation.

www.wlgore.com

The concept of self-leadership involves workers motivating themselves to perform tasks.[2] Is this the wave of the future? In some situations, yes. Some individuals don't like authority and control systems imposed on them. They prefer to manage their own work and build rewards into completing a high-quality job. W. L. Gore & Associates (makers of Gore-Tex and medical products) uses a self-leadership approach. Everyone in the firm has a sponsor responsible for seeing that Gore's four guiding principles are followed: fairness, freedom, commitment, and discretion. The sponsors guide new employees, help them find answers to questions, and show them how goals can be accomplished. The sponsor certainly has characteristics of a leader but is not the traditionally discussed leader. At Gore & Associates, the message is that self-leadership is important, encouraged, and recognized.[3]

Self-managed groups, self-leadership, situational approaches, transformational leaders, contingency leadership, and no leadership at all are all possible in a changing world. In our opinion, the least likely occurrence is that no leaders at all will exist in work settings in the 21st century. We believe that leaders will be important, will be constantly trained, and will have to experiment with how to best lead followers. There simply is no one best prescription or set of guidelines.[4] Although unnecessarily isolating effective leadership traits or behaviors seems impossible, it's likely that sets of characteristics do, in fact, fit with situations and followers. Chapters 11 and 12 encourage identifying and experimenting with the set. As the environment, competition, technology, and demographics of the workforce change, we'll need experimentation. Understanding and applying these two chapters should aid such experimentation.

A frequently heard complaint about the study of leadership is that it's simply a list of traits, behaviors, and situational concepts. Chapter 12 presents theories and research that have stimulated the criticisms. The scarcity and ambiguities of leadership have fueled the problem. There is a scarcity when we compare our present-day leaders to world class figures, executives, and social leaders of yesterday: Abraham Lincoln, Winston Churchill, Gandhi, Susan B. Anthony, and Alfred Sloan.

To develop more precision about leadership as we know it today, a number of approaches have been proposed. They do not answer the past-versus-today leadership comparisons. However, the approaches are informative, meaningful, and realistic in that they often use job-related or task-oriented settings and examples. This chapter examines what we refer to as emerging leadership models, research, and applications. Are these approaches the final answer, the most refined, or the most rigorously studied views of leadership? No. They are, however, interesting, progressive, and integrative explanations of leadership.

As this chapter illustrates, leaders can command respect, transform organizations from also-rans to successful units, and find the best combination of persuasion and authority to complete the job. As you review each of the approaches in this chapter, think about the role that diagnosis and listening play. A leader who doesn't encourage communication is at a disadvantage. In using the Vroom-Yetton, attribution, or transformational approach, the effective leader must be skilled in diagnosis and communication. Do you possess these skills?

Vroom-Jago Revised Leadership Model

Vroom and Yetton initially developed a leadership and decision-making model that indicates the situations in which various degrees of participative decision making are appropriate.[5] In contrast to Fred Fiedler, Vroom and Yetton attempted to provide a *normative model* (prescriptive) that a leader can use in making decisions. Their approach assumes that no one particular leadership style is appropriate for each situation. Unlike Fiedler, they assume that leaders must be flexible enough to change their leadership styles to fit situations. It was Fiedler's contention that the situation must be altered to fit an individual's leadership style.

In developing their model, Vroom and Yetton made these assumptions:

1. The model should be of value to leaders or managers in determining which leadership styles they should use in various situations.

2. No single leadership style is applicable to all situations.

3. The main focus should be the problem to be solved and the situation in which the problem occurs.

4. The leadership style used in one situation should not constrain the styles used in other situations.

5. Several social processes influence the amount of participation by subordinates in problem solving.

Applying these assumptions resulted in the initial model that was concerned with leadership and decision making. The **Vroom-Yetton leadership model** generated interest among researchers, practitioners, and trainers. However, to improve the accuracy and predictability of the initial model, Vroom and Jago have developed a modified model.[6]

Nature of the Vroom-Jago model

The new model shares two key features with its predecessor. First, it employs the same decision processes as those of the original Vroom-Yetton model. The terms for describing decision processes—AI, AII, CI, CII, and GII, with the addition of GI and DI for individual problems—are carried over intact from the previous model. These are presented in Table 12–1.

Second, the new model also retains the criteria against which the effects of participation are evaluated. Like the earlier model, the new model concerns evaluating the effects of participation on decision quality, decision acceptance, subordinate development, and time.

DECISION EFFECTIVENESS   The new model retains the concept of decision effectiveness (D_{Eff}). As shown in the following equation, D_{Eff} is dependent on decision quality (D_{Qual}) and decision commitment (D_{Comm}). **Decision quality** refers to the technical aspects of a decision. A decision is considered to be of high quality to the extent that it's consistent with the organizational goals to be attained and with potentially available information. **Decision commitment** refers to the acceptance of decisions by subordinates. Participation in decisions by subordinates tends to produce feelings of commitment and joint ownership.

$$D_{Eff} = DQ_{ual} + DC_{omm} - DTP$$

However, there is a third term in the equation, DTP (*decision time penalty*). This term acknowledges that having sound thinking and a committed group to implement the decision is often not all that is needed to produce effective decisions. Decisions must also be made in a timely manner. Many decisions are made under severe time constraints. For example, an air traffic controller has limited time to place airplanes in various zones before increasing the risk of an accident. DTP takes on a value of zero whenever no stringent time constraints limit the process chosen.

Vroom-Yetton Model

Leadership model that specifies leadership decision-making procedures most effective in each of several different situations: two autocratic (AI, AII); two consultative (CI, CII); one oriented toward joint decisions of the leader and group (GII).

Decision Quality

An important criterion in the Vroom-Yetton model that refers to objective aspects of a decision that influence subordinates' performance, aside from any direct impact on motivation.

Decision Commitment

The degree to which subordinates accept a particular decision. Participation in decisions often tends to increase the commitment of subordinates.

Table 12–1	**INDIVIDUAL LEVEL**	**GROUP LEVEL**
Decision Styles for Leadership: *Individuals and Groups*	AI. You solve the problem or make the decision yourself, using information available to you at that time.	AI. You solve the problem or make the decision yourself, using information available to you at that time.
	AII. You obtain any necessary information from the subordinate, then decide on the solution to the problem yourself. You may or may not tell the subordinate what the problem is while getting the information. The role played by your subordinate in making the decisions is clearly one of providing specific information that you request, rather than generating or evaluating alternative solutions.	AII. You obtain any necessary information from subordinates, then decide on the solution to the problem yourself. You may or may not tell subordinates what the problem is in getting the information from them. The role played by your subordinates in making the decision is clearly one of providing specific information that you request, rather than generating or evaluating solutions.
	CI. You share the problem with the relevant subordinate, getting ideas and suggestions. Then *you* make the decision. This decision may or may not reflect your subordinate's influence.	CI. You share the problem with the relevant subordinates individually, getting their ideas and suggestions without bringing them together as a group. Then *you* make the decision. This decision may or may not reflect your subordinates' influence.
	GI. You share the problem with one of your subordinates, and together you analyze the problem and arrive at a mutually satisfactory solution in an atmosphere of free and open exchange of information and ideas. You both contribute to the resolution of the problem, with the relative contribution of each being dependent on knowledge rather than formal authority.	CII. You share the problem with your subordinates in a group meeting. In this meeting, you obtain their ideas and suggestions. Then *you* make the decision, which may or may not reflect your subordinates' influence.
	DI. You delegate the problem to one of your subordinates, providing him with any relevant information that you possess, but giving him responsibility for solving the problem alone. Any solution the person reaches receives your support.	GII. You share the problem with your subordinates as a group. Together, you generate and evaluate alternatives and attempt to reach a consensus on a solution. Your role is much like that of chairperson, coordinating the discussion, keeping it focused on the problem, and making sure that the critical issues are discussed. You do not try to influence the group to adopt "your" solution, and you are willing to accept and implement any solution that has the support of the entire group.

Decision effectiveness is the criterion to use if there are no values attached to either time or development or if those values are completely unknown. However, a more comprehensive criterion called *overall effectiveness* (O_{Eff}) is introduced. O_{Eff} is greatly influenced by decision effectiveness, but as shown in the following equation, its values reflect the remaining two criteria affected by degree of participation. Both consequences pertain to effects of the decision process on available "human capital." Independent of the effectiveness of the decisions produced, a decision process can have effects, either positive or negative or both, on the energy and talent available for subsequent work.

$$O_{Eff} = D_{Eff} - \text{Cost} + \text{Development}$$

Negative effects on human capital occur because decision processes use time and energy, even in the absence of a time constraint. An executive group meeting including a senior executive and five subordinates and lasting two hours would consume 12 work hours. The value of that time is certainly not zero, although its precise cost varies with the opportunity costs of the meeting. Which other activities did each manager forsake to participate in that meeting? When critically important activities are not carried out because of time spent in meetings, costs are incurred that must, at the very least, be "traded off" against the benefits of the meeting. In the preceding equation, cost represents the value of time lost through use of a given decision process.

On the other hand, participation can *contribute* to human capital. Participation in decision making can build teamwork, strengthen commitment to organizational goals, and contribute to the development of participants' technical and managerial skills. In the O_{Eff} equation, development is intended to represent organizational benefits that extend beyond the individual decision under consideration. The extent to which these gains from participative leadership can be realized depends on the leader's ability to facilitate team work. The following Close-Up describes one approach to team leadership.

SITUATIONAL VARIABLES One of the biggest differences between the traditional Vroom-Yetton model and the new one lies in the problem attributes. Vroom-Yetton used seven problem attributes; the new model continues the use of these seven and adds five.

The most important additional problem attribute takes into consideration the information and expertise possessed by subordinates. This additional attribute pertaining to information was included because the original Vroom-Yetton model performed somewhat better in accounting for differences in the acceptance of decisions than it did in predicting decision quality. Incorporating information possessed by subordinates and that possessed by the leader is expected to improve predictions about the quality of decisions and to further enhance the validity, or batting average, of the model.[7]

A second new problem attribute pertains to the existence of stringent time constraints that could restrict opportunities to involve subordinates. The third involves geographical restrictions on interactions among subordinates. The original Vroom-Yetton model envisioned managers and subordinates located, if not in adjacent offices, at least sufficiently proximate to one another so that interaction could take place relatively easily. Thus, the Vroom-Yetton model prescribed group meetings of managers separated by thousands of miles. Without denigrating the usefulness of such meetings, the benefits that the Vroom-Yetton model predicted from joint decision making may not outweigh the costs of assembling far-flung managers in one central location. The revised model addresses this issue by ascertaining not only the existence of geographical constraints but also whether the expected benefits might outweigh the costs.

CLOSE—UP

The Roles of Leaders in Self-Managed Teams

The roles of leaders in self-managed teams has not been well-understood either in theory or in practice. Those organizations undertaking the change to self-managed teams have found the change somewhat difficult as leaders held to their historical roles. One organization, Metropolitan Life Insurance Company (Met Life), has undertaken the change and the experience of this organization provides some insights. Met Life begins by defining a team as a group of people with specific roles and responsibilities organized to work together toward common goals or objectives in which each member depends on others to carry out responsibilities to reach those goals and objectives. Met Life managers say the key word in the definition is *depends*. A team must be able to depend on its members to carry out their tasks, to communicate effectively, to put team needs first, and to help each other. Good teams also depend on good team leadership.

Met Life's managers recommend that team leadership be divided into two roles: client and facilitator. The client is the team leader who asks for help to solve a problem. This person is responsible for what team meetings are supposed to address. The facilitator is responsible for how the meeting goes. Facilitators have four basic responsibilities: helping other team members keep time commitments, keeping group members on track, remaining neutral about the meeting's content, and clarifying group members' ideas and making sure other members' ideas are protected from attack.

These two roles bear a sharp relationship to the behaviors of participative and considerate leaders, as noted in many leadership theories. The problem seems not so much with the existence of ideas on how leaders should act generally; rather the problem seems to be how they should act in a particular situation—as self-managed work teams.

Sources: Milan Moravec, Jan Johannessen, and Thor A. Hjelmas, "The Well-Managed Self-Managed Team," *Management Review,* June 1998, pp. 56–59; Evan Lembke and Marie G. Wilson, "Putting the 'Team' into Teamwork: Alternative Theoretical Contributions for Contemporary Management Practice," *Human Relations,* July 1998, pp. 927–45; and Yvette DeBow, "Met's IT Set for Continuous Improvement," *Insurance and Technology,* December 1994, p. 48.

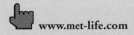 **www.met-life.com**

Finally, the other two new attributes concern the importance of time and development. In the new model, these are not either-or judgments introduced after the fact to guide the choice among equally feasible alternatives. Instead, they are independent judgments obtained simultaneously with judgments of other problem attributes; taken together, they affect the benefits and costs of employing participative methods.

CONTINUOUS SCALES   The original Vroom-Yetton model utilized dichotomous (yes-no) judgments in generating the prescriptions of the model: Do you have enough information to make a high-quality decision? Of the 12 problem attributes in the new model, 10 have been designed to be expressed as five-point scales. The four attributes dealing with importance (quality, commitment, time, and development) are answered on scales ranging from "no importance" to "critical importance." Another six attributes (leader information, problem structure, commitment probability, goal congruence, conflict, and subordinate information) are expressed as probability estimates. For example, the question "Do you have sufficient information to make a high-quality decision?" can now be answered no, probably no, maybe, probably yes, or yes. Table 12–2 shows 1 of the 12 attributes, an example of the questions used to measure them, and the permissible responses for each.

Application of the new model

Using the manager's analysis of the situation represented by that manager's responses to the diagnostic questions, the formulas predict the most appropriate way of handling the situation, the second-best way, and so forth. However, the equations' complexity precludes their pencil-and-paper application.

Vroom and Jago offer two alternatives for the application of their new model to actual managerial problems. The first is a computer program that guides the manager through the analysis of the situation and, with speed and accuracy, solves the relevant equations. The second method, more familiar to users of the original Vroom-Yetton model, employs decision trees that represent the operation of the complex equations if certain simplifying assumptions are made.[8]

Figure 12–1 shows one of these decision trees. The first simplifying assumption is that each problem attribute can be given a clear yes or no (or high or low) response. This restricts the application of the model to relatively unambiguous situations. The second simplifying assumption is that 4 of the 12 problem attributes are held constant. Severe time constraints and the geographical dispersion of subordinates (relatively infrequent occurrences) are assumed not to exist. Additionally, it's assumed that the manager's motivation to conserve time and to develop subordinates doesn't change. Figure 12–1 depicts what Vroom and Jago label the "time-driven" decision tree. It's designed for the manager who places maximum weight on saving time and minimum weight on developing subordinates.

Validity of the Vroom-Jago model

As was the case with the original Vroom-Yetton model when it was first introduced, the revised model currently lacks complete empirical evidence establishing its validity. Certainly, the model is thought to be consistent with what we now know about the

Table 12–2	How important is the technical quality of this decision?				
QR: *Quality Requirement*	(1)	(2)	(3)	(4)	(5)
	No import	Low import	Average Import	High import	Critical import

Figure 12–1

Time-Driven Decision Tree

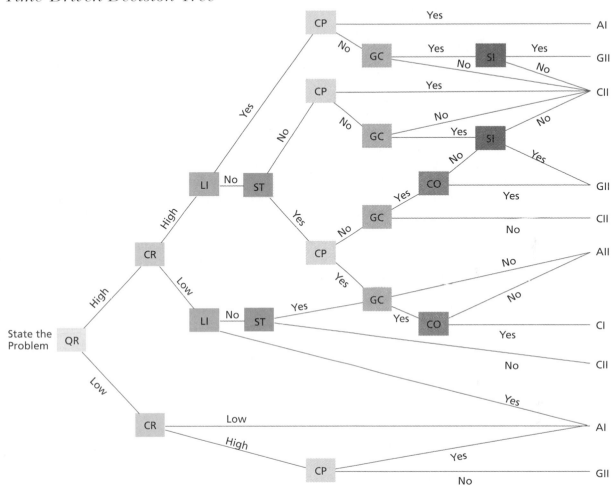

Quality requirement

QR   How important is the technical quality of this decision?

Commitment requirement

CR   How important is subordinate commitment to the decision?

Leader's information

LI   Do you have sufficient information to make a high-quality decision?

Problem structure

ST   Is the problem well structured?

Commitment probability

CP   If you were to make the decision by yourself, is it reasonably certain that your subordinate(s) would be committed to the decision?

Goal congruence

GC   Do subordinates share the organizational goals to be attained in solving this problem?

Subordinate conflict

CO   Is conflict among subordinates over preferred solutions likely?

Subordinate information

SI   Do subordinates have sufficient information to make a high-quality decision?

benefits and costs of participation and represents a direct extension of the original 1973 model. Nonetheless, without extensive evidence that use of the new model can improve decision effectiveness—and, by extension, leadership success—its value as a theoretical contribution and as a practical tool remains open to question.

International research

A valuable aspect of the Vroom-Yetton and Vroom-Jago approaches to leadership is that research has been conducted both in and outside of the United States. In an increasingly interdependent world, it's increasingly important not to reach conclusions about a theory or an approach based solely on domestic samples of leaders.

One study of Austrian managers used real decisions made by the participants.[9] Small discussion groups of managers reviewed each situation and provided the decision process used by the manager and an analysis of the problem attributes present in the situation. The study results indicated that small-group judgments were more accurate than a single person's judgments in analyzing written descriptions of the situations.

Another study looked at owner-operated cleaning franchises in the United States and Canada.[10] Leadership behavior of American and Canadian owner-managers was assessed through problem sets. The results indicated that U.S. and Canadian managers who had above-average conformity to what the model prescribes had significantly more profitable businesses and more satisfied employees.

Limitations of the model

After a thorough review of leadership theories, models, and concepts, one behavioral scientist concluded that the Vroom-Yetton approach is unsurpassed in terms of scientific validity and practical usefulness.[11] Nevertheless, the model has limitations.

The model forces a person to make a definite response. Because it fails to permit a "probably yes" or a "probably no," a yes or no response must be made. Work situations aren't that easy to categorize; in many situations, neither yes nor no is accurate. The model is also criticized for being too complex. It includes decision trees, ratings, and problem sets. Although the model is complex, we believe this criticism is not warranted. The model is precise and specific, which means that some complexity is likely to be needed. Instead of discussing complexity, we might better state that the model, like most leadership explanations, simplifies how managers think and process stimuli.

Finally, organizational life is complex, and the way individual managers think is complex. The model, according to some critics, fails to deal with the realities today's managers face in terms of change, technological advancement, and international competition. Can any model deal with every contingency of leading and remain understandable and useful? Perhaps critics are expecting too much.

Attribution Theory of Leadership

Chapter 4 used attribution theory to explain how managers assign causes or motives to people's behavior. Attribution theory also has application value as an explanation and analysis of leadership. Attribution theory mainly concerns the cognitive process by which a person interprets behavior as being caused by (attributed to) certain cues in the relevant environment.[12]

Since most causes of subordinate, or follower, behaviors are not directly observable, determining causes requires reliance on perception. In attribution theory, individuals are assumed to be rational and to be concerned about the causal linkages in their environments.

The attributional approach starts with the position that the leader is essentially an *information processor*.[13] In other words, the leader searches for informational cues as to "why" something is happening and then attempts to construct causal explanations that guide her leadership behavior. The process in simple terms appears to be follower behavior → leader attributions → leader behavior.

Leader's attributions

The leader's primary attributional task is to categorize the causes of follower, or subordinate, behavior into one of three source dimensions: person, entity, or context. That is, for any given behavior, such as poor quality of output, the leader's job is to determine whether the poor quality was caused by the person (e.g., inadequate ability), the task (entity), or some unique set of circumstances surrounding the event (context).

The leader seeks three types of information when forming attributions about a follower's behavior: distinctiveness, consistency, and consensus. For any behavior, the leader first attempts to determine whether the behavior is *distinctive* to a task—that is, whether the behavior occurs on this task but not on other tasks. Next, the leader is concerned about *consistency*, or how frequently the behavior occurs. Finally, the leader estimates *consensus*, the extent to which others behave in the same way. A behavior unique to one follower has low consensus; if it is common to other followers, this reflects high consensus.

Leader's perception of responsibility

The judgment of responsibility moderates the leader's response to an attribution. Clearly, the more a behavior is seen as caused by some characteristic of the follower (i.e., an internal cause) and the more the follower is judged to be responsible for the behavior, the more likely the leader is to take some action toward the follower.

Attributional leadership model

Attribution theory offers a framework for explaining leader behavior more insightfully than either trait or personal-behavioral theories. **Attribution leadership theory** attempts to explain why behaviors are happening; trait and personal-behavioral theories are more descriptive and don't focus on the why issue.[14] Furthermore, attribution theory can offer some predictions about a leader's response to a follower's behavior. Attributions are more likely to be made when failures or problems occur.[15] However, successful outcomes also can trigger the question, "Why did this success occur?"

Figure 12–2 presents an attributional leadership model that emphasizes two important linkages. At the first linkage point, the leader attempts to make attributions about poor performance. These attributions are moderated by the three information types: distinctiveness, consistency, and consensus. The second linkage point suggests that the leader's behavior, or response, is determined by the attributions that he makes. This relationship between attribution and leader behavior is moderated by the leader's perception of responsibility. Is the responsibility internal or external?

As discussed previously, distinctiveness, consistency, and consensus influence a leader's attributions. For example, a study of nursing supervisors found that leaders who made attributions of internal causes (e.g., lack of effort) tended to use more punitive behaviors, and leaders tended to make more internal attributions and to respond more harshly when the problems were serious.[16]

An interesting research approach has been to include sex effects in the attributional model of leadership. Research regarding the sex of the leader and the sex of the subordinate has been largely neglected. A study of college students examined whether

Attribution Leadership Theory

A theory of the relationship between individual perception and interpersonal behavior. The theory suggests that understanding of and the ability to predict how people will react to events are enhanced by knowing those events' causal explanations.

Figure 12–2

An Attributional Leadership Model

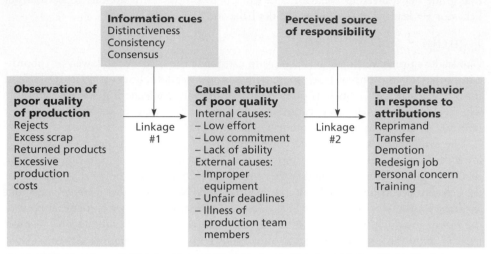

Source: Adapted from Terence R. Mitchell and Robert E. Wood, "An Empirical Test of an Attributional Model of Leader's Responses to Poor Performance," *Academy of Management Proceedings*, ed. Richard C. Huseman, 1979, p. 94.

sex of the leader, sex of the subordinate, and the interaction between these two factors would affect both the attributions made for employees' poor performance and the corrective action taken by leaders.[17] The researchers concluded that the sex composition of the leader–subordinate dyad was a critical and neglected variable in attributional research.

Research support for the attributional theory of leadership is limited. There is a need to test the theory in more organizational settings.[18] Understanding the causes of leader behavior or at least searching for these causes seems more promising for managerial use than does simply adding another trait or descriptive theory to the leadership literature.[19]

Leader behavior: cause or effect?

We have implied that leader behavior has an effect on the follower's performance and job satisfaction. However, a sound basis exists for proposing that follower performance and satisfaction cause the leader to vary his leadership style. It has been argued that people develop positive attitudes toward objects that are instrumental in satisfying their needs. This argument can be extended to leader–follower relationships. For example, organizations reward leaders (managers) based on the performance of followers (subordinates). Leaders might then be expected to develop positive attitudes toward high-performing followers.[20] Let us say that employee Joe's outstanding performance enables his boss, Mary, to receive the $1,000 supervisory excellence award. The expectation then is that Mary would think highly of Joe and reward him with a better work schedule or job assignment. In this case, Joe's behavior leads to Mary's being rewarded, and she in turn rewards Joe.

In a field study, data were collected from first-line managers and from two of each manager's first-line supervisors. The purpose of this research was to assess the direction of causal influence in relationships between leader and follower variables. The results strongly suggested that leader consideration behavior caused subordinate satisfaction and that follower performance caused changes in the leader's emphasis on both consideration and the structuring of behavior-performance relationships.[21]

Research on the cause-effect issue is still quite limited. To conclude that all leader behavior or even a significant portion of such behavior is a response to follower behavior would be premature. However, an examination of the leader–follower relationship in terms of **reciprocal causation** is needed. In reciprocal causation, leader behavior causes follower behavior, and follower behavior causes leader behavior. Japanese management techniques suggest that the reciprocal causation view has some validity. Leaders and followers are emphasized in the Japanese consensus approach to managing.

Reciprocal Causation

Argument that follower behavior impacts leader behavior and leader behavior influences follower behavior.

Charismatic Leadership

Individuals such as John F. Kennedy, Winston Churchill, Mikhail Gorbachev, and Walt Disney possessed an attractiveness that enabled them to make a difference with citizens, employees, or followers. Their leadership approach is referred to as *charismatic leadership*. Max Weber suggested that some leaders have a gift of exceptional qualities—a charisma—that enables them to motivate followers to achieve outstanding performance.[22] Such a charismatic leader is depicted as being able to play a vital role in creating change.

Sam Walton is considered by many to have possessed charismatic qualities. He worked hard to explain his vision of retailing and serving the customer. He would visit Wal-Mart stores to continually inform his associates (the employees) that customer service is the first, second, and third priorities that must be accomplished so that the firm can be recognized as the top retailer. As people responded to his vision and goals, Walton kept up a fast pace to meet other people and express his viewpoint. He paid attention to his employees and his customers—the human assets of business. Walton had a "gift" for making other people feel good about working for him and buying his products and service.

Steven Jobs, cofounder of Apple Computer, provides another example of how charisma inspires others. Jobs's impact, attraction, and inspiration when he was with the firm were described as follows:

👉 **www.Apple.com**

> "When I walked through the Macintosh building with Steve, it became clear that he wasn't just another general manager bringing a visitor along to meet another group of employees. He and many of Apple's leaders weren't managers at all; they were impresarios . . . . Not unlike the director of an opera company, the impresario must cleverly deal with the creative temperaments of artists . . . . His gift is to merge powerful ideas with the performance of his artists."[23]

Defining charismatic leadership

Charisma is a Greek word meaning gift. Powers that couldn't be clearly explained by logical means were called **charismatic**. Presently, no definitive answer has been given on what constitutes **charismatic leadership** behavior.[24] House suggests that charismatic leaders are those who have charismatic effects on their followers to an unusually high degree.[25]

Conger's model

Jay Conger has proposed a model that illustrates how charisma evolves.[26] Figure 12–3 presents his four-stage model of charismatic leadership. In stage one, the leader continuously assesses the environment, adapts, and formulates

Charismatic Leadership

The ability to influence followers based on a supernatural gift and attractive powers. Followers enjoy being with the charismatic leader because they feel inspired, correct, and important.

Figure 12–3

Stages in Charismatic Leadership

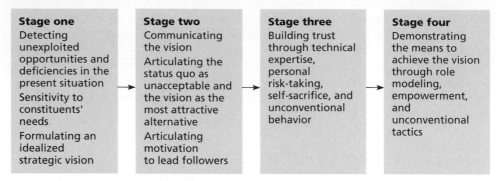

Source: Adapted from Jay A. Conger and Rabindra N. Kanungo, "Behavioral Dimensions of Charismatic Leadership," in *Charismatic Leadership,* ed. Jay A. Conger, Rabindra N. Kanungo, and associates (San Francisco: Jossey-Bass, 1988), p. 27.

a vision of what must be done. The leader's goals are established. In stage two, the leader communicates his vision to followers, using whatever means are necessary. Stage three is highlighted by working on trust and commitment. Doing the unexpected, taking risk, and being technically proficient are important in this stage. In stage four, the charismatic leader serves as a role model and motivator. The charismatic leader uses praise and recognition to instill within followers the belief that they can achieve the vision.

What constitutes charismatic leadership behavior?

What behavioral dimensions distinguish charismatic leaders from noncharismatic leaders? A criticism of the early work on charismatic leadership is that explanations of it lacked specificity. Limited attempts have been made to develop and test specific charismatic qualities such as vision, acts of heroism, and the ability to inspire.[27] However, in most cases, clarifying what specifically constitutes charismatic behavior has been generally ignored.

A number of empirical studies have examined behavior and attributes of charismatic leaders, such as articulation ability, affection from followers, ability to inspire, dominating personality, and need for influence.[28] However, no specific set of behaviors and attributes is universally accepted by theorists, researchers, and practitioners. A descriptive behavioral framework that builds on empirical work has been offered. The framework, presented in Table 12–3, assumes that charisma must be viewed as an attribution made by followers within the work context.

Two types of charismatic leaders

Discussions of charismatic leadership identify two types based on the leader's emphasis on the future: *visionary charismatic leaders* focus on the long term; *crisis-based charismatic leaders* focus on the short term. Through communication ability, the visionary, charismatic leader links followers' needs and goals to job or organizational long-term goals and possibilities. Through the exercise of communications skill, the visionary leader links followers needs and goals with those of the organization. Linking followers' goals with the organization's is easier if the followers are dissatisfied or not challenged by the current situation.

COMPONENT	CHARISMATIC LEADER	NONCHARISMATIC LEADER
Relation to status quo	Essentially opposed to status quo and strives to change it (Steve Jobs at Apple).	Essentially agrees with status quo and strives to maintain it.
Future goal	Idealized vision highly discrepant from status quo (Tom Monaghan with the Domino's Pizza concept).	Goal not too discrepant from status quo.
Likableness	Shared perspective and idealized vision makes him a likable and honorable hero worthy of identification and imitation (Lee Iacocca in first three years at Chrysler).	Shared perspective makes her likable.
Expertise	Expert in using unconventional means to transcend the existing order (Al Davis, owner of the Los Angeles Raiders).	Expert in using available means to achieve goals within the framework of the existing order.
Environmental sensitivity	High need for environmental sensitivity for changing the status quo (Edgar Woolard at Du Pont).	Low need for environmental sensitivity to maintain status quo.
Articulation	Strong articulation of future vision and motivation to lead (Ross Perot at EDS).	Weak articulation of goals and motivation to lead.
Power base	Personal power, based on expertise, respect, and admiration for a unique hero (Jan Carlzon at Scandinavian Airlines System—SAS).	Position power and personal power (based on reward, expertise, and liking for a friend who is a similar other).
Leader–follower relationship	Elitist, entrepreneur, an exemplary (Mary Kay Ash of Mary Kay Cosmetics). Transforms people to share the radical changes advocated (Edward Land, inventor of Polaroid camera).	Egalitarian, consensus-seeking, or directive. Nudges or orders people to share her views.

Table 12–3

Behavioral Components of Charismatic and Noncharismatic Leaders

Source: Adapted from Jay A. Conger and Rabindra Kanungo, "Toward a Behavioral Theory of Charismatic Leadership in Organizational Settings," *Academy of Management Review,* October 1987, pp. 637–47.

Crisis-based charismatic leaders have an impact when the system must handle a situation for which existing knowledge, resources, and procedures are not adequate.[29] The crisis-produced charismatic leader communicates clearly what actions need to be taken and what their consequences will be.

Crisis management is a growing field of study and inquiry.[30] The crises managers face enable charismatic leadership to emerge. First, under conditions of stress, ambiguity, and chaos, followers give power to individuals who have the potential to correct the crisis situation. The leader is empowered to do what's necessary to correct the situation or solve the problem. In many cases, the leader is unconstrained and is allowed to use whatever she thinks is needed.[31] This relatively high degree of freedom to act without constraints raises important ethical issues related to charismatic leadership as discussed in the Close-Up at the bottom of page 312.

A crisis also permits the leader to promote nontraditional actions by followers. The crisis-based charismatic leader has greater freedom to encourage followers to search for ways to correct the crisis. Some methods, procedures, and tactics adopted by followers may be disorderly, chaotic, and outside the normal boundary of actions. However, the charismatic leader in a crisis situation encourages, supports, and usually receives action from followers.[32]

Our knowledge about charismatic leadership is still relatively abstract and ambiguous. Despite Weber's concept of charismatic authority, Conger's framework of how charismatic leadership evolves, House's definition and propositions about the characteristics of charismatic leaders, and some limited research results, much more theoretical and research work needs to be done. There is a void in understanding about whether charismatic leaders can be harmful in expressing visions that are unrealistic or inaccurate or in the way they attack a crisis problem. Management scholar and writer Peter Drucker claims that "charisma becomes the undoing of leaders." How accurate is Drucker? No one knows at this time. However, evidence suggests that charismatic leaders (e.g., Hitler, Stalin, Jim Jones) can secure greater commitment to failing, personally demeaning, and tragic goals than can the average leader.[33] In the business world, John DeLorean was able to raise hundreds of millions of dollars for his failed automobile venture because of his powers of persuasion and impression management. He promoted himself as an innovative genius.

Transactional and Transformational Leadership

Each of the leadership theories discussed emphasizes that leadership is an exchange process. Followers are rewarded by the leader when they accomplish agreed-upon objectives. The leader helps followers accomplish the objectives.

CLOSE—UP

Ethical Responsibilities and Charismatic Leaders

As we have seen, some individuals have the power to motivate others to undertake great effort on their behalf. These individuals wield enormous power for good and for evil by virtue of their personal magnetism, or charisma. Charismatic leaders are often cited as heroes, individuals able to communicate a compelling vision that inspires extraordinary performance in followers while at the same time building faith in the leader. While charismatic leaders' virtues are often extolled in the popular media, their potential dark side is often ignored.

Charismatic leaders can be very effective, yet differ greatly in their ethical standards. The label "charismatic" has been applied to diverse leaders in politics (Adolf Hitler and Franklin Delano Roosevelt), religious circles (Jim Jones and Billy Graham), social movement organizations (Mahatma Gandhi and Malcolm X), and business (Lee Iacocca and Mary Kay Ash). This list highlights the fact that

application of the term charismatic is value-neutral—it doesn't distinguish between moral, immoral, and amoral intentions.

Charisma can lead to blind fanaticism in the service of megalomaniacs and dangerous values, or to heroic self-sacrifice in the service of a beneficial cause. Organizations aware of the dangers inherent in charismatic leadership can use that knowledge in selecting and training future leaders.

Most charismatic leaders possess some sort of vision. That vision can incorporate the hopes and values of followers, or it can be a personal vision. The latter type of charismatic leader motivates followers through manipulation, promoting what is best for himself rather than the larger group.

Sources: Ali Gini, "Moral Leadership: An Overview," Journal of Business Ethics, February 1997, pp. 323–30; Willard C. Butcher, "The Need for Ethical Leadership," Executive Speeches, April/May 1997, pp. 83–86; and Jane M. Howell and Bruce J. Avolio, "The Ethics of Charismatic Leadership: Submission or Liberation?" Academy of Management Executive, May 1992, pp. 43–54.

Transactional leadership

The exchange role of the leader has been referred to as *transactional*. Figure 12–4 presents the **transactional leadership** roles. The leader helps the follower identify what must be done to accomplish the desired results: better quality output, more sales or services, reduced cost of production. In helping the follower identify what must be done, the leader takes into consideration the person's self-concept and esteem needs. The transactional approach uses the path–goal concepts as its framework.

In using the transaction style, the leader relies on contingent reward and on management by exception. Research shows that when contingent reinforcement is used, followers exhibit an increase in performance and satisfaction; followers believe that accomplishing objectives will result in their receiving desired rewards.[34] Using management by exception, the leader won't be involved unless objectives aren't being accomplished.

Transactional leadership is not often found in organizational settings. One national sample of U.S. workers showed that only 22 percent of the participants perceived a direct relationship between how hard they worked and how much pay they received.[35] That is, the majority of workers believed that good pay was not contingent on good performance. Although workers prefer a closer link between pay and performance, it was not present in their jobs. Why? There are probably a number of reasons, such as unreliable performance appraisal systems, subjectively administered rewards, poor managerial

Transactional Leadership

Leader identifies what followers want or prefer and helps them achieve level of performance that results in rewards that satisfy them.

Figure 12–4

Transactional Leadership

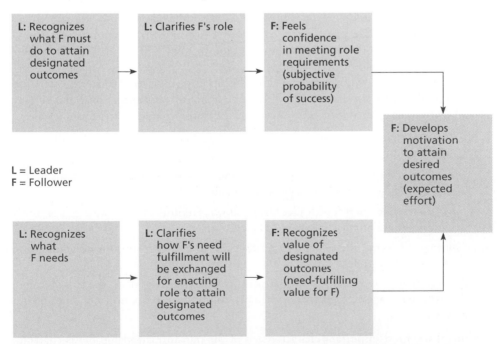

Source: Bernard M. Bass, *Leadership and Performance beyond Expectations* (New York: Free Press, 1985), p. 12.

skills in showing employees the pay-performance link, and conditions outside the manager's control. Also, managers often provide rewards that aren't perceived by followers to be meaningful or important.

A small pay increase, a personal letter from the boss, or a job transfer may not be what employees want in the form of a contingent reward. Until managers understand what the employee wants, administer rewards in a timely manner, and emphasize the pay-performance link, there's likely to be confusion, uncertainty, and minimal transactional impact in leader–follower relationships.

Transformational leadership

An exciting new kind of leader, referred to as the transformational leader,[36] motivates followers to work for transcendental goals instead of short-term self-interest and for achievement and self-actualization instead of security.[37] In **transformational leadership,** viewed as a special case of transactional leadership, the employee's reward is internal. By expressing a vision, the transformational leader persuades followers to work hard to achieve the goals envisioned. The leader's vision provides the follower with motivation for hard work that is self-rewarding (internal).

Transformational Leadership

Ability to inspire and motivate followers to achieve results greater than originally planned and for internal rewards.

Transactional leaders will adjust goals, direction, and mission for practical reasons. Transformational leaders, on the other hand, make major changes in the firm's or unit's mission, way of doing business, and human resource management to achieve their vision. The transformational leader will overhaul the entire philosophy, system, and culture of an organization.

www.disney.com

www.GE.com

www.microsoft. com

Names that come to mind when we think about transformational leaders are Michael Eisner at Walt Disney, Jack Welch at General Electric, and Bill Gates at Microsoft Corporation. Under Eisner's leadership, for example, Disney has moved into live action movies (some R-rated), syndicated a business show for television, introduced a TV channel, developed new cartoon characters, and licensed new apparel products.[38] Eisner took risks and pushed the company along a path that was unheard of for 40 years. He transformed Walt Disney Company from a conservative firm into an assertive, proactive one. Eisner brought in a work ethic, a style, and a vision that has helped put Disney back into the forefront of entertainment.[39]

The development of transformational leadership factors has evolved from research by Bass.[40] He identified five factors (the first three apply to transformational and the last two apply to transactional leadership) that describe transformational leaders. They are:

1. *Charisma.* The leader is able to instill a sense of value, respect, and pride and to articulate a vision.

2. *Individual attention.* The leader pays attention to followers' needs and assigns meaningful projects so that followers grow personally.

3. *Intellectual stimulation.* The leader helps followers rethink rational ways to examine a situation. He encourages followers to be creative.

4. *Contingent reward.* The leader informs followers about what must be done to receive the rewards they prefer.

5. *Management by exception.* The leader permits followers to work on the task and doesn't intervene unless goals aren't being accomplished in a reasonable time and at a reasonable cost.

One of the most important characteristics of the transformational leader is charisma. However, charisma by itself isn't enough for successful transformational leadership, as Bass clearly states:

"The deep emotional attachment which characterizes the relationship of the charismatic leader to followers may be present when transformational leadership occurs, but we can distinguish a class of charismatics who are not at all transformational in their influence. Celebrities may be identified as charismatic by a large segment of the public. Celebrities are held in awe and reverence by the masses who are developed by them. People will be emotionally aroused in the presence of celebrities and identify with them in their fantasy, but the celebrities may not be involved at all in any transformation of their public. On the other hand, with charisma, transformational leaders can play the role of teacher, mentor, coach, reformer, or revolutionary. Charisma is a necessary ingredient of transformational leadership, but by itself it is not sufficient to account for the transformational process."[41]

In addition to charisma, transformational leaders need assessment skills, communication abilities, and a sensitivity to others. They must be able to articulate their vision, and they must be sensitive to the skill deficiencies of followers.

Substitutes for Leadership

We have seen throughout the discussion in Chapters 11 and 12 a very strong case made for leadership that encourages followers to take on self-direction. For example Situational Leadership Theory suggests that the appropriate leadership behavior for followers able and willing to assume responsibility is coaching and assisting them. Thus when individuals are fully able to direct themselves they do not need a leader in the usual sense of the term. In addition to characteristics of followers that reduce the need for leadership, other task and organizational characteristics may have a similar effect. In addition we should think of instances which neutralize the effects of leadership.[42]

Researchers have identified a wide variety of individual, task, environmental, and organizational characteristics as leadership substitute factors that influence relationships between leader behavior and follower satisfaction and performance. Some of these variables (e.g., follower expectations of leader behavior) appear to influence which leadership style will enable the leader to motivate and direct followers. Others, however, function as *substitutes for leadership*. Substitute variables tend to negate the leader's ability to either increase or decrease follower satisfaction or performance.[43]

Substitutes for leadership are claimed to be prominent in many organizational settings. However, the dominant leadership approaches fail to include substitutes for leadership in discussing the leader behavior–follower satisfaction and performance relationship.

Table 12–4, based on previously conducted research, provides substitutes for only two of the more popular leader behavior styles: relationship-oriented and task-oriented. For each of these styles, Kerr and Jermier present substitutes (characteristics of the subordinate, the task, or the organization) that neutralize the style.[44] For example, an experienced, well-trained, knowledgeable employee doesn't need a leader to structure the task (e.g., a task-oriented leader). Likewise, a job (task) that provides its own feedback doesn't require a task-oriented leader to inform the employee how he's doing. Also, an employee in a close-knit, cohesive group doesn't need a supportive, relationship-oriented leader. The group substitutes for this leader.[45]

Table 12–4

Substitutes for
Leadership

| | Neutralizes | |
CHARACTERISTIC	RELATIONSHIP-ORIENTED LEADERSHIP	TASK-ORIENTED LEADERSHIP
Of the subordinate:		
1. Ability, experience, training, knowledge		X
2. Need for independence	X	X
3. "Professional" orientation	X	X
4. Indifference toward organizational rewards	X	X
Of the task:		
5. Unambiguous and routine		X
6. Methodologically invariant		X
7. Provides its own feedback concerning accomplishment		X
8. Intrinsically satisfying	X	
Of the organization:		
9. Formalization (explicit plans, goals, and areas of responsibility)		X
10. Inflexibility (rigid, unbending rules and procedures)		X
11. Highly specified and active advisory and staff functions		X
12. Close-knit, cohesive work groups	X	X
13. Organizational rewards not within the leader's control	X	X
14. Spacial distance between superior and subordinates	X	X

Source: Adapted from Steven Kerr and John M. Jermier, "Substitutes for Leadership: Their Meaning and Measurement," *Organizational Behavior and Human Performance*, December 1978, p. 378.

Summary of Key Points

- Vroom and Yetton originally, and Vroom and Jago more recently, have developed a leadership model to select the amount of group decision-making participation needed in a variety of problem situations. The model suggests that the amount of subordinate participation depends on the leader's skill and knowledge, whether a quality decision is needed, the extent to which the problem is structured, and whether acceptance by subordinates is needed to implement the decision.

- The Vroom-Yetton-Jago explanations are criticized for being too complex. Because leadership is a complex process, a more accurate criticism perhaps is that the explanation is too simplistic with regard to managerial cognition about how to lead and the consequences of leadership behaviors.

- The attribution theory of leadership suggests that a leader's ability to predict how followers will react is enhanced by knowing how followers explain their behavior and performance.

- Leaders attribute followers' behaviors to the person, the task, or a unique set of circumstances called the *context.*

- The word *charisma* comes from a Greek word meaning gift. The ability to influence people that can't be clearly explained by logical means is called charisma.

- Charisma evolves over a period of time. By assessing, adapting, and formulating goals and actions, articulating a vision, and building and reinforcing commitment, the leader builds his charismatic profile.

- Two types of charismatic leaders have been suggested: one who articulates a vision and one who exercises leadership in a crisis situation.

- Transactional leadership involves engaging in an exchange role in which the leader helps followers accomplish meaningful objectives to achieve satisfactory rewards.

- To achieve a vision, the transformational leader makes major changes in mission, the way of doing business, and how human resources are managed.

- The transactional approach is involved in the more expansive transformational leadership framework. Three main characteristics of transformational leadership are charisma, individual attention to followers, and intellectual stimulation of followers.

- There's insufficient research evidence to promote charismatic, transactional, or transformational practices in organizations. The romantic aspects of being charismatic or transformational haven't been supported with research evidence. Explanations are interesting but not yet sufficiently supported with scientific facts.

- Despite the seeming necessity for leadership as a factor in achieving organizational effectiveness, we can identify circumstances that neutralize the effects of leadership. Follower initiative, structured tasks, and work group cohesiveness can reduce the necessity for leadership.

Discussion and Review Questions

1. Identify individuals in your college or university whom you believe to be charismatic leaders. Compare your list with your classmates and note the reasons why the lists will contain both identical *and* different individuals.

2. Compare the available research on the Vroom-Yetton-Jago model of leadership to the transactional explanation. What research is needed in both theories of leadership?

3. Under what circumstances would leadership effects be neutralized in an organization?

4. If you were able to study and document leadership behavior in politics, business, military, and street gangs, what do you believe would be the most prevalent styles in each of these settings?

5. As you progress in this course, what attributions do you make about what you are learning?

6. How could a leader use attribution theory to explain the poor performance of a group of followers?

7. Collect information on Michael Eisner's work at the Walt Disney Studio. After reviewing your sources, write a brief report indicating which type of leader he is in the company: task-oriented, person-oriented, or charismatic. Why?

8. Which of the theories in Chapters 11 and 12 would be most useful in explaining to someone from Hungary what leadership approaches will be needed to make Hungary more competitive in the international marketplace?

9. What women are examples of transformational leaders? Would you include Liz Claiborne, Debbie Fields (Mrs. Fields' Cookies), and Hillary Rodham Clinton? Why?

10. Why is communication such an important skill in charismatic, transactional, and transformational explanations of leadership?

C A S E   F O R   A N A L Y S I S

Six Sigma at Motorola: All about Being the Best in International Markets

Who is Robert W. Galvin? And why do the Japanese respect his views on management, quality control, and marketing?

Galvin, as chief executive officer of Motorola, Inc., is the main leader in one of the world's leading high tech companies. He's a charismatic leader who hasn't been afraid to take on the Japanese or anyone else competing in the international marketplace.

Galvin has instilled a competitive spirit throughout Motorola. The company intends to become the best manufacturer of electronic hardware in the world. Wristwatch pagers, cellular phones, and other electronic devices are some of the products with which Motorola intends to beat everyone in the marketplace. Under the guidance of Galvin, the company has upgraded quality, improved manufacturing processes to cut costs, and aggressively pursued specific markets. It has also supported research and development consortiums and working with other firms to gain new footholds in foreign markets. Motorola is becoming a major force in Japan's home markets by offering high-quality products and forcefully marketing the company.

Galvin travels to Washington, D.C., regularly to brief legislators on the realities of international competition.

the foreign competition is no longer free from Galvin's lobbying, comments, and observations. He wants to compete fairly, which is the message he constantly delivers.

Like the Japanese, Motorola has discovered that better quality pays for itself. High quality costs less because floor space, equipment, and people used for nothing cost money. Motorola attempts to stay lean and to keep its eye on the hidden cost of poor quality.

Promotions, bonuses, and raises at Motorola are as important as at any other firm. Each, however, is tied to quality improvement. Workers now see and believe that better quality means more rewards. They're convinced that they can be number 1 in any market Motorola enters. They're convinced that teamwork, vision, and rewards are important to that goal.

Can one man make a difference? Can leaders be trained to be Galvin-like? There are no empirical studies to support the idea that one man's ideas, vision, and passion can inspire, motivate, and direct people. However, the Motorola approach seems to be working. The firm is a major competitor and a world leader in markets from Scandinavia to Japan to South America.

Of course, Motorola's competitors aren't sitting around. Not willing to settle for second best, Motorola is committed to compete. The goals of a tenfold reduction in defects, teamwork, and the Six Sigma quality plan have provided Motorola employees with a cause, a mission. (Six Sigma is statistical jargon for near-perfect manufacturing—a rate of just 3.4 defects per million products.)

Motorola is not satisfied with any defects. All employees have wallet-size cards stating Motorola's Six Sigma goals in 11 languages. At officers' meetings, Six Sigma and quality are the first topics discussed. Motorola, at the direction of Galvin, has increased its spending on employee training: about 40 percent, or $40 million, is spent on developing skills to sustain and improve on the Six Sigma goals.

Galvin believes that Motorola can produce products that are virtually perfect. His vision of perfection has resulted in attention, awards, and international respect for Motorola and its 105,000 employees.

Discussion Questions

1. What charismatic qualities does Robert W. Galvin project?

2. What behaviors and skills of Galvin's suggest that he's not only a manager but also a leader?

3. Can it be concluded that Galvin is a transformational leader at Motorola? Why?

Sources: Fred R. McFadden, "Six Sigma Quality Programs," *Quality Progress,* June 1993, pp. 37–42. Based on Thomas A. Stewart, "How to Manage in the New Era," *Fortune,* January 15, 1990, pp. 58–72; Lois Therrien, "The Rival Japan Respects," *Business Week,* November 13, 1989, pp. 108–18; John Hillkerk, "Top Quality Is Behind Comeback," *USA Today,* March 28, 1989, pp. 1–2B.

www.mot.com

E X P E R I E N T I A L   E X E R C I S E

Leadership Style Analysis

Objectives

1. To learn how to diagnose different leadership situations.

2. To learn how to apply a systematic procedure for analyzing situations.

3. To improve understanding of how to reach a decision.

Related Topics

Decision making and problem solving when given facts about a situation.

Starting the Exercise

Review the decision tree in Figure 12–1. The instructor will then form groups of four to five people to analyze the following cases. Try to reach a group consensus on which decision style is best for the particular case. Select the best style, based on use of the modified model, available decision styles, and decision rules. Each case should take 30 to 45 minutes to analyze.

Case I: R&D Director

You're head of a research and development (R&D) lab in the nuclear reactor division of a large corporation. Often, whether a particular piece of research has potential commercial interest or is merely of academic interest to the researchers isn't clear. In your judgment, one major area of research has advanced well beyond the level at which operating divisions pertinent to the area could possibly assimilate or use the data being generated.

Recently, two new areas with potentially high returns for commercial development have been promised by one of the operating divisions. The team working in the area referred to in the previous paragraph is ideally qualified to research these new areas. Unfortunately, both new areas are relatively devoid of scientific interest, while the project on which the team is currently engaged is of great scientific interest to all members.

At the moment, this team is, or is close to being, your best research team. It's cohesive, has a high level of morale, and has been productive. You're concerned not only that team members wouldn't want to switch their effort to these new areas but also that forcing them to concentrate on these two new projects could adversely affect their morale, their good intragroup working relations, and their future productivity both as individuals and as a team.

You have to respond to the operating division within the next two weeks, indicating which resources, if any, can be devoted to working on these projects. It would be possible for the team to work on more than one project, but each project would need the combined skills of all the members of the team, so fragmenting of the team isn't technically feasible. This fact, coupled with the fact that the team is cohesive, means that a solution that satisfies any team member would probably go a long way to satisfying everyone on the team.

Case II: U.S. Coast Guard Cutter Captain

You're captain of a 210-foot, medium-endurance U.S. Coast Guard cutter, with a crew of 9 officers and 65 enlisted personnel. Your mission is general at-sea law enforcement and search and rescue. At 2 A.M. this morning, while en route to your home port after a routine two-week patrol, you received word from the New York Rescue Coordination Center that a small plane had ditched 70 miles offshore. You obtained all available information concerning the location of the crash, informed your crew of the mission, and set a new course at maximum speed for the scene.

You've now been searching for survivors and wreckage for 20 hours. Your search operation has been increasingly impaired by rough seas, and a severe storm is building to the southwest. Communication

ATTRIBUTE	ANALYSIS	RATINGS ON SCALES
Quality requirement	High importance	(QR = 4)
Commitment requirement	High importance	(CR = 4)
Leader information	Probably yes	(LI = 4)
Problem structure	Yes	(ST = 5)
Commitment probability	No	(CP = 1)
Goal congruence	Probably no	(GC = 2)
Subordinate conflict	Probably no	(CO = 2)
Subordinate information	No	(SI = 1)
Time constraints	No	(TC = 1)
Geographical dispersion	No	(GD = 1)
Motivation—time	No importance	(MT = 1)
Motivation—development	Critical importance	(MD = 5)
Highest overall effectiveness (leadership style choice): _____		

with the New York Rescue Center is impossible. A decision must be made shortly about whether to abandon the search and place your vessel on a northeasterly course to ride out the storm (thereby protecting the vessel and your crew but relegating any possible survivors to almost certain death from exposure) or continuing a potentially risky search.

You've contacted the weather bureau for up-to-date information on the severity and duration of the storm. While your crew is extremely conscientious about its responsibility, you believe that the members would be divided on the decision of leaving or staying.

Completing the Exercise

Phase I: 10–15 minutes. Individually read each case and select the proper decision style using the Vroom-Jago model.

Phase II: 30–45 minutes. Join a group appointed by the instructor and reach group consensus.

ATTRIBUTE	ANALYSIS	RATINGS ON SCALES
Quality requirement	Critical importance	(QR = 5)
Commitment requirement	High importance	(CR = 4)
Leader information	Yes	(LI = 4)
Problem structure	Yes	(ST = 5)
Commitment probability	Yes	(CP = 5)
Goal congruence	Yes	(GC = 5)
Subordinate conflict	Yes	(CO = 5)
Subordinate information	Maybe	(SI = 3)
Time constraints	No	(TC = 1)
Geographical dispersion	No	(GD = 1)
Motivation—time	High importance	(MT = 4)
Motivation—development	No importance	(MD = 1)
Highest overall effectiveness (leadership style choice): _____		

Lou Gerstner: Leading the Organization

To compete in today's dynamic markets, an organization has to have leadership and management that are in tune with the needs of customers and other stakeholders. Lou Gerstner of IBM is one of those managers. IBM was a lumbering giant whose markets were being taken by smaller, more flexible, customer-oriented firms, but Gerstner brought a new vision to the firm and used the four functions of management to implement that vision and make the firm more responsive.

The four functions of management are: (1) planning; (2) organizing, including staffing; (3) leading; and (4) controlling. At the planning stage, Gerstner had a vision of a company that made computers more user friendly. Emphasis was placed on problem solving, not just building bigger and faster computers. More emphasis was placed on software and what it could do to make life easier. For example, IBM is developing programs that will link all your home appliances; your refrigerator will have an Internet address and will e-mail the service department if it needs repair. A large part of his vision was the development of the Internet and the company's own intranet. Now, all employees are linked electronically and have access to company data.

Gerstner knew that long-term success would rely on bringing in the right people. Technically, that is called staffing, and it is part of the organizing function. Gerstner reached outside the firm to find managers who were not steeped in the IBM tradition, but were more attuned to customers and their wants and needs. Richard Thoman, for example, had worked with Gerstner at American Express and other companies. He became the senior vice president for the IBM PC company. Thoman's strong sense of values and ethics led them through a difficult time when a flawed chip showed up in their PCs. He halted sale of the PCs and worked with other firms to develop a better one. In the long run, this decision proved to be the right one.

The real test of an executive's worth, however, is in his or her success at leadership. Gerstner is a man with strong moral values. Leadership means that everyone in the organization buys into your vision and works together to make it happen. To develop the communication necessary to build internal relationships, Gerstner focused on building the company's intranet so that communication flows were free and easy. All employees have access to him via e-mail, and Gerstner reads and responds to those messages.

Finally, a leader must have control over the organization. But how do you measure success in an organization that is trying new things? The answer is to focus on the customer and customer satisfaction. However, IBM also needed to raise its profits to keep its stockholders happy. Also, employee morale was low because so many had been dismissed from the company because of declining profits and slow growth. By 1996, IBM was reporting a profit for the first time in three years. Morale at IBM is now higher, stockholders are happy with the rapid increase of the stock price, and customers are pleased with the new goods and services IBM is providing.

Lou Gerstner is just one of the many new corporate leaders who have led U.S. businesses successfully into a new era of global competition. They still apply the same functions, but they have a different vision, a vision that includes empowering employees, building internal and external communications, and leading the organization to closer and better relationships with customers.

Critical Thinking

1. What specific management and management skills did Gerstner use to make IBM a more responsive organization? Explain.

2. Is the job of a manager of a small business different from a manager of a large corporation like IBM? What are the similarities and differences?

3. What are some of the ways Gerstner is making use of technology in his job as a top manager? How will managers of the future use technology to make their companies world-class competitors?

No.4

The Structure and Design of Organizations

Chapter 13

Organization Structure

Learning Objectives

After completing Chapter 13, you should be able to:

Define
The term *organization structure.*

Describe
The relationships among the four managerial decisions and the three dimensions of organization structure.

Discuss
The relative advantages and disadvantages of centralization and decentralization of authority.

Compare
The alternative bases for departmentalization.

Identify
The circumstances that would cause management to consider the matrix organization structure.

he subject
of this section of the book is
organization structure. It,
behavior, and process are the three

major subjects of the entire book. The discussion of organization structure reflects the ideas in Figure 13–1. Organization structure results from managerial decisions about four important attributes of all organizations: division of labor, bases for departmentalization, size of departments, and delegation of authority. The decisions managers make are influenced by job design factors and organization design factors such as individual differences, task competence, technology, environmental uncertainty, strategy, and certain characteristics of managers themselves. The attributes of the structure determine the extent to which the organization reflects the dimensions of formalism, complexity, and centralization. The structure of the organization contributes to organizational effectiveness and that relationship justifies our interest. In this chapter we focus on the four decisions and their relationships with the three dimensions. Chapter 14 analyzes issues associated with job design; Chapter 15 analyzes organizational design issues.

The Concept of Organization Structure

Organization structure is an abstract concept. No one has ever actually seen one. What we see is the evidence of structure. Then from that evidence we infer the presence of structure. We therefore need to identify what we mean when we discuss structure in this and subsequent chapters.

Structure as an influence on behavior

In Chapter 1, we noted the importance of organization structure as an influence on the behavior of individuals and groups who make up the organization. The importance of structure as a source of influence is so widely accepted that some experts define the concept as those features of the organization that serve to control or distinguish its parts. The key word in this definition is *control*. All of us have worked in

Organization Structure

Pattern of jobs and groups of jobs in an organization. An important cause of individual and group behavior.

Figure 13–1

Organizational Structure

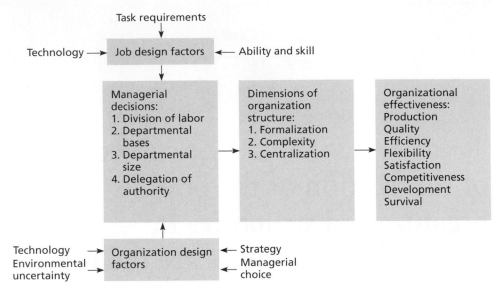

organizations (we were one of its parts) and we have experienced the way our behavior was controlled. We didn't simply go to work and do what we wanted to do; we did what the organizations wanted and paid us to do. We gave up free choice when we undertook the work necessitated by the jobs we held. Jobs are important features of any organization.

All organizations have a structure of jobs. In fact, the existence of structure distinguishes organizations. While the most visible evidence of structure is the familiar organizational chart, charts are not always necessary to describe the structure. In fact, small organizations can get along very well without them as long as everyone understands what they are to do and who they are to do it with.

But jobs are not the only features of an organization. Again from experience we know that organizations consist of departments, divisions, units, or any of a number of terms denoting groups of jobs. No doubt, your college is made up of a number of academic departments: management, accounting, economics if you are in a business school. Each of these departments contains individuals performing different jobs that combine to produce a larger outcome than is possible from the efforts of any single job or department. When you graduate, your education will have been made possible by the combined efforts of individual departments. But the point is not that these departments combine the effects of many different jobs; rather we're noting here the effect of the departments on the behavior of the individuals in them. As members of departments, individuals necessarily must abide by commonly held agreements, policies, and rules and thereby give up the freedom to act independently.

Structure as recurring activities

A second perspective focuses on activities performed as consequences of the structure. According to this perspective, the dominant feature of organizational structure is its patterned regularity. This definition emphasizes persistence and regularity of activities. Note that this definition states nothing about the reason for the patterned regularity, only that it exists. This definition points out that within organizations, certain activities can be counted on to occur routinely. For example, people come to work each morning at 8 A.M., clock in, go to their work stations, and begin doing the same work they did the day before. They talk to the same people, they receive information from the same people, they are periodically (but predictably) evaluated for promotion and raises. Without these predictable activities, the work of the organization could not be achieved.

Definitions that focus on regularly occurring organizational activities emphasize the importance of what in this book we term *organizational processes*. The subsequent section of the book discusses the processes of communication, decision making, performance evaluation, career, and socialization. These processes occur with considerable regularity, and it is certainly possible and even useful to analyze the patterns of communication, decision making, and other processes. But it's also useful to distinguish between activity (or processes) and the causes of that activity. Thus, when we discuss structure in the following pages, we refer to a relatively stable framework of jobs and departments that influences the behavior of individuals and groups toward organizational goals.

Structure as purposeful and goal-oriented behavior

Organizations are purposeful and goal-oriented. It follows that the structure of the organization is likewise purposeful and goal-oriented. Our concept of organization structure will take into account the existence of purposes and goals, and it will be our attitude that management should think of structure in terms of its contribution to organizational effectiveness.

The statement that organization structures facilitate the achievement of organizational goals assumes that managers know how to match organization structures and goals and that they desire to do so. It is entirely reasonable to acknowledge that in many instances, organization structures do not contribute positively to organizational performance because managers are unable by training or intellect to design a structure that guides the behavior of individuals and groups to achieve high levels of production, efficiency, satisfaction, quality, flexibility, and development. It is also reasonable to acknowledge that, in some instances, organization structures reflect and contribute to managers' personal goals at the expense of the goals of the organization. Thus, to say that organization structures contribute positively to organizational effectiveness requires assumptions about the abilities and motivations of those who have power to design them. The structure of an organization is without doubt related to the achievement of organizational effectiveness, even though the exact nature of the relationship is inherently difficult to know.[1]

The Effects of Structure on Individual and Group Behavior

We need to study the structure of organizations because we are interested in individual and group behavior in organizations. As suggested in the discussion above, individuals and groups respond in significant ways to the jobs they perform, to the groups they work with, to the leaders who influence them. The job itself provides powerful stimuli for individual behavior. The demands on, and expectations of, individuals can result in high levels of personal satisfaction or stress, anxiety, and physiological difficulties.[2] People's jobs require them to perform activities in combination with other people in the organization. Activities can be routine or nonroutine; they can require high or low levels of skill; they can be perceived as challenging or as trivial. The required relationships can be with co-workers, managers, clients, suppliers, or buyers. These relationships can result in feelings of friendship, competition, cooperativeness, and satisfaction, or they can be causes of stress and anxiety.[3]

Structure also affects the behavior and functioning of groups in organizations. Depending upon the specific configuration of jobs and departments, groups can be either more or less cohesive and more or less communicative. For example, a department in a firm containing 10 individuals performing the same job will act quite differently from one containing 10 individuals each performing a different job. Studies of organization structure indicate that the group containing people doing the same job will be less cohesive, less open to new ideas, and less communicative than the group of people doing different jobs.

The importance of organization structure as a factor in organization effectiveness does not go unnoticed in corporate America. For example, IBM Corporation has been undergoing dramatic changes in its organization structure since the mid-1980s in response to the company's declining status as a computer manufacturer. The effort began January 28, 1986, when IBM CEO John F. Akers (since replaced) announced the initial steps of a massive reorganization which some analysts describe as nothing less than reinventing IBM. After three years of slumping sales and profit, Akers decided that the situation required what he termed a drastic change. IBM's organization could best be described as a centralized structure in which central headquarters made major decisions. Local managers were unable to act on market and technological developments because they did not have the authority to do so. The centralized way that IBM was organized restricted its ability to take advantage of local opportunities. The first step in getting IBM back on track was to delegate authority for products and markets to managers of autonomous lines of business (LOBs) who are closer to the action than corporate headquarters.

Akers' decision affected more than 20,000 people as they moved into new jobs in new locations. Individual jobs changed and many jobs were eliminated. IBM permitted early retirements and job transfers to dampen the effects of job eliminations. The most visible evidence of the reorganization is autonomous LOBs such as personal computer systems, midrange systems, mainframes, communications, and chip technology. These LOBs have nearly complete authority to develop and market products and services within their sphere of activity. The creation of LOBs is the initial point of departure for the reorganization. Other groups could emerge as market and technology forces dictate the necessity for change. [4]

Designing an Organization Structure

Managers who set out to design an organization structure face difficult decisions. They must choose among a myriad of alternative frameworks of jobs and departments. The process by which they make these choices is termed **organizational design** and it means quite simply the decisions and actions that result in an organization structure.[5] This process may be explicit or implicit, it may be "one-shot" or developmental, it may be done by a single manager or by a team of managers.[6] However the actual decisions come about, the content of the decisions is always the same. The first decision focuses on individual jobs, the next two decisions focus on departments or groups of jobs, the fourth decision considers the issue of delegation of authority throughout the structure.

Organizational Design

Management decisions and actions that result in a specific organization structure.

1. Managers decide how to divide the overall task into successively smaller jobs. Managers divide the total activities of the task into smaller sets of related activities. The effect of this decision is to define jobs in terms of specialized activities and responsibilities. Although jobs have many characteristics, the most important one is their degree of specialization.

2. Managers decide the bases by which to group the individual jobs. This decision is much like any other classification decision and it can result in groups containing jobs that are relatively homogeneous (alike) or heterogeneous (different).

3. Managers decide the appropriate size of the group reporting to each superior. As we have already noted, this decision involves determining whether spans of control are relatively narrow or wide.

4. Managers distribute authority among the jobs. Authority is the right to make decisions without approval by a higher manager and to exact obedience from designated other people. All jobs contain some degree of the right to make decisions within prescribed limits. But not all jobs contain the right to exact obedience from others. The latter aspect of authority distinguishes managerial jobs from nonmanagerial jobs. Managers can exact obedience; nonmanagers can't.

Thus, organization structures vary depending upon the choices that managers make. If we consider each of the four design decisions to be a continuum of possible choices, the alternative structures can be depicted as in Figure 13–2.

Generally speaking, organization structures tend toward one extreme or the other along each continuum. Structures tending to the left are characterized by a number of terms including *classical, formalistic, structured, bureaucratic, System 1*, and *mechanistic*. Structures tending to the right are termed *neoclassical, informalistic, unstructured, nonbureaucratic, System 4*, and *organic*. Exactly where along the continuum an organization finds itself has implications for its performance as well as for individual and group behavior.[7]

Division of Labor

Division of labor concerns the extent to which jobs are specialized. Managers divide the total task of the organization into specific jobs having specified activities. The activities define what the person performing the job is to do. For example, activities of the job "accounting clerk" can be defined in terms of the methods and procedures required to process a certain quantity of transactions during a period of time. Other accounting clerks could use the

Division of Labor

Process of dividing work into relatively specialized jobs to achieve advantages of specialization.

Figure 13–2

The Four Key Design Decisions

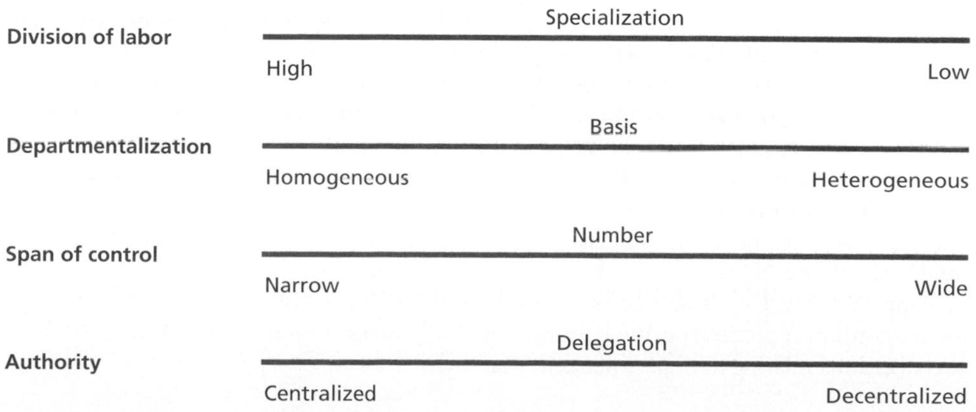

Division of labor	Specialization	
	High	Low

Departmentalization	Basis	
	Homogeneous	Heterogeneous

Span of control	Number	
	Narrow	Wide

Authority	Delegation	
	Centralized	Decentralized

same methods and procedures to process different types of transactions. One could be processing accounts receivable, while the others process accounts payable. Thus, jobs can be specialized both by method and by application of the method.

The economic advantages of dividing work into specialized jobs are the principal historical reasons for the creation of organizations.[8] As societies became more and more industrialized and urbanized, craft production gave way to mass production. Mass production depends on the ability to obtain the economic benefits of specialized labor, and the most effective means for obtaining specialized labor is through organizations. Although managers are concerned with more than the economic implications of jobs, they seldom lose sight of specialization as the rationale for dividing work among jobs.

Division of labor in organizations can occur in three different ways:[9]

1. Work can be divided into different *personal* specialties. Most people think of specialization in the sense of occupational and professional specialties. Thus, we think of accountants, engineers, scientists, physicians, and the myriad of other specialties that exist in organizations and everyday life.

2. Work can be divided into different activities necessitated by the natural sequence of the work the organization does. For example, manufacturing plants often divide work into fabricating and assembly, and individuals will be assigned to do the work of one of these two activities. This particular manifestation of division of work is termed *horizontal specialization.*

3. Finally, work can be divided along the *vertical plane* of an organization. All organizations have a hierarchy of authority from the lowest level manager to the highest level manager. The CEO's work is different from the shift supervisor's.

Determining what each job in the organization should do is a key managerial decision. We'll discuss the decision more fully in the next chapter. The important point to keep in mind for now is that jobs vary along a general dimension of specialization with some jobs being more highly specialized than others. Managers can change an organization's structure by changing the degree of specialization of jobs. For example, Procter & Gamble (P&G) CEO Edwin Artzt changed the degree of specialization of the company's sales reps. Artzt believes that sales reps interested in developing strong ties with customers lose their competitive instinct. He believes that team members devote too much energy to building relationships within the team and with the customers and too little attention to building volume and profit. He reversed P&G's team approach in favor of sales representatives who represent narrow sectors such as soap and food products. One organizational effect of Artzt's decision has been a move to create separate sales groups within each sector. In terms of specialization of labor, sales representatives now have more specialized jobs (they sell fewer different products) and the organization has more specialized units (the sales units in each of the sectors).[10]

www.pg.com

One dramatic effect of the trend toward downsizing organizations during the 1980s has been to despecialize managerial jobs, particularly middle managers' jobs. General Electric aggressively pursued a policy of reducing the number of managers in the hierarchy. The result is that managers have more to do and their jobs are less specialized as their spans of control have increased.

www.ge.com

The process of defining the activities and authority of jobs is analytical; that is, the total task of the organization is broken down into successively smaller ones. But then management must use some basis to combine the divided tasks into groups or departments containing some specified number of individuals or jobs. We will discuss these two decisions relating to departments in that order.

Departmental Bases

The rationale for grouping jobs rests on the necessity for coordinating them. The specialized jobs are separate, interrelated parts of the total task, whose accomplishment requires the accomplishment of each of the jobs. But the jobs must be performed in the specific manner and sequence intended by management when they were defined. As the number of specialized jobs in an organization increases, there comes a point when they can no longer be effectively coordinated by a single manager. Thus, to create manageable numbers of jobs, they are combined into smaller groups and a new job is defined—manager of the group.

The crucial managerial consideration when creating departments is determining the basis for grouping jobs. Of particular importance is the determination for the bases for departments that report to the top management position. In fact, numerous bases are used throughout the organization, but the basis used at the highest level determines critical dimensions of the organization. Some of the more widely used **departmentalization** bases are described in the following sections.

Departmentalization

Process in which an organization is structurally divided by combining jobs in departments according to some shared characteristic or basis.

Functional departmentalization

Managers can combine jobs according to the functions of the organization. Every organization must undertake certain activities to do its work. These necessary activities are the organization's functions. The necessary functions of a manufacturing firm include production, marketing, finance, accounting, and personnel. These activities are necessary to create, produce, and sell a product. Necessary functions of a commercial bank include taking deposits, making loans, and investing the bank's funds. The functions of a hospital include surgery, psychiatry, housekeeping, pharmacy, nursing, and personnel. Each of these functions can be a specific department and jobs can be combined according to them. The functional basis is often found in relatively small organizations providing a narrow range of products and services. It is also widely used as the basis in divisions of large multiproduct organizations.

Manufacturing organizations are typically structured on a functional basis (Figure 13–3). The functions are engineering, manufacturing, reliability, distribution, finance, personnel, public relations, and purchasing. Organization charts for a commercial bank and a hospital structured along functional lines are also depicted in Figure 13–3. The functional basis has wide application in both service and manufacturing organizations. The specific configuration of functions that appear as separate departments varies from organization to organization.

The principal advantage of the basis is its efficiency. That is, it seems logical to have a department that consists of experts in a particular field such as production or accounting. By having departments of specialists, management creates efficient units. An accountant is generally more efficient when working with other accountants and other individuals who have similar backgrounds and interests. They can share expertise to get the work done. General Motors (GM) attracted considerable attention when it combined traditional product divisions into two functional departments: production and sales. Now under the direction of a new chief operations officer (COO), GM has accelerated consolidation of its auto divisions into one functionally organized entity.[11] The driving force behind GM's reorganization was a desire to reduce the cost of developing and marketing cars by realizing the efficiencies of function-based organization structure.

 www.gm.com

Figure 13–3

Functional-Base Organization in Three Settings

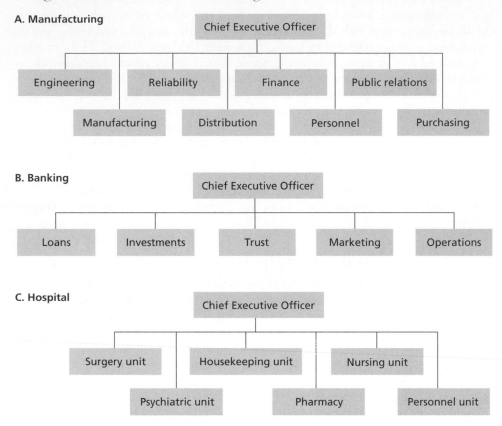

A major disadvantage of this departmental basis is that because specialists are working with and encouraging each other in their areas of expertise and interest, organizational goals may be sacrificed in favor of departmental goals. Accountants may see only their problems and not those of production or marketing or the total organization. In other words, the culture of, and identification with, the department are often stronger than identification with the organization and its culture.

Territorial departmentalization

Another basis for departmentalizing is to establish groups according to geographic area. The logic is that all activities in a given region should be assigned to a manager. This individual would be in charge of all operations in that particular geographic area.

In large organizations, territorial arrangements are advantageous because physical separation of activities makes centralized coordination difficult. For example, it is extremely difficult for someone in New York to manage salespeople in Kansas City. It makes sense to assign the managerial job to someone in Kansas City.

Large multi-unit retail stores are often organized along territorial lines. Specific retail outlets in a geographic area will constitute units, often termed divisions, which report to a regional manager who in turn may report to a corporate manager. For example, the manager of the Lexington, Kentucky, retail store of a national chain reports to the president, Midwest Division. The Midwest Division reports to the headquarters unit.

Territorial departmentalization provides a training ground for managerial personnel. The company is able to place managers in territories and then assess their progress in that geographic region. The experience that managers acquire in a territory away from headquarters provides valuable insights about how products and/or services are accepted in the field.

Product departmentalization

Managers of many large diversified companies group jobs on the basis of product. All jobs associated with producing and selling a product or product line will be placed under the direction of one manager. Product becomes the preferred basis as a firm grows by increasing the number of products it markets. As a firm grows, it's difficult to coordinate the various functional departments and it becomes advantageous to establish product units. This form of organization allows personnel to develop total expertise in researching, manufacturing, and distributing a product line. Concentrating authority, responsibility, and accountability in a specific product department allows top management to coordinate actions.

The organization structure using products as the basis for departments has been a key development in modern capitalism. The term *divisional organization* refers to this form of organization structure. Most of the major and large firms of developed countries use it to some degree. The product-based divisions are often freestanding units that can design, produce, and market their own products, even in competition with other divisions of the same firm.[12] General Motors pioneered the divisional structure when it evolved into the five separate auto divisions: Chevrolet, Pontiac, Oldsmobile, Buick, and Cadillac. As we noted in our discussion of the functional form, General Motors has begun a process of moving away from the purely product-based, divisional form.

The Consumer Products Division of Kimberly-Clark reflects product departmentalization. The specific product groups shown in Figure 13–4 include feminine hygiene, household, and commercial products. Within each of these units we find production and marketing personnel. Since managers of product divisions coordinate sales, manufacturing, and distribution of a product, they become the overseers of a profit center. In this manner, profit responsibility is implemented in product-based organizations. Managers are often asked to establish profit goals at the beginning of a time period and then to compare actual profit with planned profit.

www.kimberly-clark.com

Product-based organizations foster initiative and autonomy by providing division managers with the resources necessary to carry out their profit plans. But such organizations face the difficult issue of deciding how much redundancy is necessary. Divisional structures contain some degree of redundancy because each division wants its own research, engineering, marketing, production, and all other functions necessary to do business. Thus, technical and professional personnel are found throughout the organization at the division levels. The cost of this arrangement can be exorbitant.

Customer departmentalization

Customers and clients can be a basis for grouping jobs.[13] Examples of customer-oriented departments are the organization structures of educational institutions. Some institutions have regular (day and night) courses and extension divisions. In some instances, a professor will be affiliated solely with the regular division or extension division. In fact, titles of some faculty positions specifically mention the extension division.

Another form of customer departmentalization is the loan department in a commercial bank. Loan officers are often associated with industrial, commercial, or agricultural loans. The customer will be served by one of these three loan officers.

Figure 13–4

Consumer Products Division, Kimberly-Clark Corporation: Organizational Structure

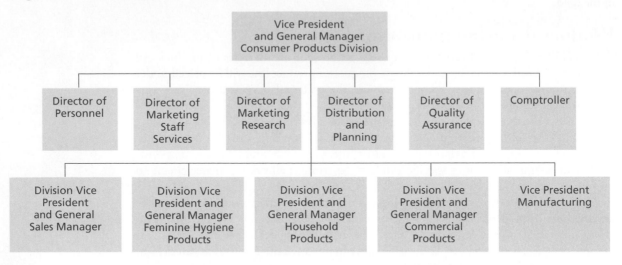

The chart shows the Vice President and General Manager Consumer Products Division at the top, reporting to six positions: Director of Personnel; Director of Marketing Staff Services; Director of Marketing Research; Director of Distribution and Planning; Director of Quality Assurance; Comptroller. Below are five Division positions: Division Vice President and General Sales Manager; Division Vice President and General Manager Feminine Hygiene Products; Division Vice President and General Manager Household Products; Division Vice President and General Manager Commercial Products; Vice President Manufacturing.

 www.att.com

 www.avco.com

www.caterpillar .com

www.hughes .com

www.itt.com

www.monsanto .com

The importance of customer satisfaction has stimulated firms to search for creative ways to serve people better. Since the Bell System broke up, competition for customers has forced AT&T to organize into customer-based units that identify with the needs of specific customers. Prior to the breakup, the firm was organized around functions. The move toward customer-based departments at Bell Labs was accompanied by efforts to implement total quality management (TQM), a customer-focused management practice that is reinforced in the customer-based structure.[14]

Some department stores are departmentalized to some degree on a customer basis. They have groupings such as university shops, men's clothing, and boys' clothing. They have bargain floors that carry a lower quality of university, men's, and boys' clothing. Organizations with customer-based departments are better able to satisfy customer-identified needs than organizations that base departments on noncustomer factors.[15]

Combined bases for departmentalization: The matrix organization

Matrix Organization

Organizational design that superimposes product- or project-based design on existing function-based design.

 www.ncr.com

www.prudential .com

www.trw.com

www.ti.com

An organization design, termed **matrix organization,** attempts to maximize the strengths and minimize the weaknesses of both the functional and product bases. In practical terms, the matrix design combines functional and product departmental bases.[16] Companies such as American Cyanamid, Avco, Carborundum, Caterpillar Tractor, Hughes Aircraft, ITT, Monsanto Chemical, National Cash Register, Prudential Insurance, TWR, and Texas Instruments are only a few of the users of matrix organization. Public sector users include public health and social service agencies. Although the exact meaning of matrix organization varies in practice, it's typically seen as a balanced compromise between functional and product organization, between departmentalization by function and by product.

Matrix organizations achieve the desired balance by superimposing, or overlaying, a horizontal structure of authority, influence, and communication on the vertical structure. In the arrangement shown in Figure 13–5, personnel assigned in each cell belong not only to the functional department but also to a particular product or project. For example, manufacturing, marketing, engineering, and finance specialists are assigned to work on one or more projects or products A, B, C, D, and E. As a consequence, personnel report to two managers: one in their functional department and one in the project or product unit. The existence of a *dual authority system* is a distinguishing characteristic of matrix organization. The potential conflict between allegiance to one's functional manager and one's project manager must be recognized and dealt with in matrix organizations.[17]

Matrix structures are found in organizations that (1) require responses to rapid change in two or more environments, such as technology and markets; (2) face uncertainties that generate high information processing requirements; and (3) must deal with financial and human resources constraints. Managers confronting these circumstances must obtain certain advantages that are most likely to be realized with matrix organization.[18]

Matrix organization facilitates the utilization of highly specialized staff and equipment. Each project or product unit can share the specialized resource with other units, rather than duplicating it to provide independent coverage for each. This is a particular advantage when projects don't require the specialist's full-time efforts. For example, a project may require only half a computer scientist's time. Rather than having several underutilized computer scientists assigned to each project, the organization can keep fewer of them fully utilized by shifting them from project to project.

Such flexibility speeds response to competitive conditions, technological breakthroughs, and other environmental changes. Also, these interactions encourage crossfertilization of ideas, such as when a computer scientist must discuss the pros and cons of electronic data processing with a financial accounting expert. Each specialist must be able to listen, understand, and respond to the other's views. At the same time, specialists maintain ongoing contact with members of their own discipline because they are also members of a functional department. An important UK car manufacturer, the Rover Group, has found the matrix structure to be useful, as noted in the Close-Up.

A fully developed matrix organization has product management departments along with the usual functional departments. Figure 13–6 depicts an organization that has product managers reporting to top management and with subproduct managers for each family cereal product line. In some instances, subproduct managers are selected from

Figure 13–5

Matrix Organizations

Projects, Products	Functions			
	Manufacturing	Marketing	Engineering	Finance
Project or product A				
Project or product B				
Project or product C				
Project or product D				
Project or product E				

specific functional departments and continue to report directly to their functional managers. In other instances, product managers are permanently assigned to the product management department. There is considerable diversity in the application of matrix organization, yet the essential features are the creation of overlapping authority and the existence of dual authority.

Departmentalization in multinational corporations (MNCs)

Corporations that cross national boundaries must decide how to include foreign activity in the organization. How should international activities be coordinated? In fact, foreign activities are but extensions of the domestic businesses, and how they're coordinated to achieve strategic outcomes involves issues not much different from those of local activities.[19] Japanese corporations' outstanding success in international markets has initiated great interest in the ways firms can and should organize if they're to compete with the Japanese. At the heart of the discussion is which departmental basis is appropriate under which circumstances.[20]

The most prevalent departmental basis is *territory*. This arrangement has national and regional managers reporting to a headquarters in the same national or regional area. Territorial-based organizations for MNCs have the same characteristics as those for domestic organizations. Each national or regional office has all the resources necessary to produce and market the product or service. This organizational form is suitable for organizations with limited product lines such as ITT and Charles Pfizer Corporation.

www.pfizer.com

Rover Group Uses Matrix Organization to Great Advantage

The Rover Group (UK) has been developing innovative management practices that incorporate teamwork, total quality management (TQM), and corporate reorganization. Among its most successful achievements is the development of the K series engine, Rover's first volume car engine in 30 years. The K series engine development effort began in 1986. To spur along the process, Rover used a project management approach. This management approach combines the time and talents of individuals from throughout the organization from all functional departments. The company selected members for the K series project team on the basis of their ability and willingness to adapt to constant change. The 18 members of the team were trained to work with other people from different functions and with different educational and technical expertise. Although team members were a part of the K series project, they continued to report to the managers of their home functional departments.

As the cross-functional project approach proved successful, management created project groups to deal with quality

problems and to launch the Land Rover Discovery four-wheel-drive vehicle. Each project group contains functional experts with demonstrated technical and interpersonal skills. Rover has found that these project groups integrate from the beginning all the concerns of the functional groups that must eventually bring the car to the market, from product design to production to marketing to sales. In traditional auto-manufacturing plants, functional departments work in isolation and only after they've received information and specifications from the preceding department in the developmental process.

Thus, Rover's initial positive experience with project management has led it to integrate the practice throughout the organization. Nearly every employee has an assignment in a functional department and one or more product or project groups.

Sources: Mohammed K. El-Najdawi and Matthew J. Liberatore, "Matrix Management Effectiveness: An Update for Research and Engineering Organizations," *Project Management Journal*, March 1997, pp. 25–31; Frank Muller, "A New Engine of Change in Industrial Relations," *Personnel Management* (UK), July 1991, pp. 30–33; and Ralph Bertodo, "Implementing a Strategic Vision," *Long Range Planning*, October 1990, pp. 22–30.

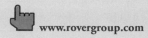
www.rovergroup.com

Figure 13–6

Fully Evolved Matrix Organization

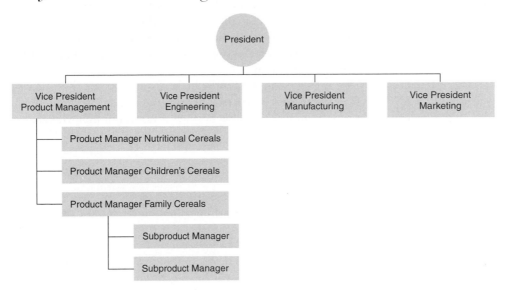

MNCs having a diversified product line will find certain advantages in the *product-based* organization structure. This structure assigns worldwide responsibility for a product or product line to a single corporate office, and all foreign and domestic units associated with that product report to the corporate product office. Eastman Kodak uses the product-based structure to assign responsibility for worldwide research and development, manufacturing, marketing, and distribution of its products. The basic product unit, termed a *line of business (LOB),* makes its own decisions and succeeds or fails accordingly. Eastman Kodak believes this structure enables managers to respond more quickly to market conditions.[21]

www.kodak.com

MNCs with very restrictive product lines such as firms in the mining industry will use the *function* approach. According to this structure, a corporate office for each business function such as production, marketing, and finance has authority over those functions wherever they take place throughout the world. Thus, production personnel in Europe and South America as well as North America will report to corporate officials in charge of production. Although MNCs share certain common managerial and organizational problems, how they deal with them will reflect their own national culture as well as the local, host country culture.

We can summarize our discussion of how MNCs organize by describing how many Japanese firms go about it. Typically they concentrate on a relatively narrow set of business activities, unlike their typical Western counterparts that enter several lines of business. One effect of this difference is that Japanese employees perform relatively fewer specialized jobs with relatively more homogeneous skills and experiences due to the fewer business specialties to be performed. The typical Japanese manufacturing job has less range than the typical Western manufacturing job. The authority associated with each job is relatively less in Japanese firms, although the Japanese practice of participative management enables individual workers to have a say in matters that immediately affect their own jobs. Middle managers in Japanese firms are expected to initiate opportunities for workers to be involved, and they are evaluated on this criterion as well as on economic and performance criteria.

Departments in Japanese firms are more often based on function and process than on product, customer, or location. The preference for the internal-oriented bases reflects again Japanese firms' preference to do business in fewer industries such that more complex divisional firms aren't as likely to develop. There are, of course, many diversified organizations in Japan, but these firms typically follow holding company patterns of organization. The Japanese have developed the practice of creating close ties with supplier organizations and thus have avoided the necessity of vertical integration as is the case of many Western business organizations.

The differences between organization structures in Japan and in the West can be accounted for by differences in business practices. These business practices are no doubt due to national and cultural developments in how business is done, not in how organizations are structured.[22]

Span of Control

Span of Control

Number of individuals who report to specific manager.

The determination of appropriate bases for departmentalization establishes the kinds of jobs that will be grouped together. But that determination doesn't establish the number of jobs to be included in a specific group, the issue of **span of control.** Generally, the issue comes down to the decision of how many people a manager can oversee; that is, will the organization be more effective if the span of control is relatively wide or narrow? The question is basically concerned with determining the volume of interpersonal relationships that the department's manager is able to handle. Moreover, the span of control must be defined to include not only formally assigned subordinates, but also those who have access to the manager. Not only may a manager be placed in a position of being responsible for immediate subordinates, she may also be chairperson of several committees and task groups.[23]

The number of potential interpersonal relationships between a manager and subordinates increases geometrically as the number of subordinates increases arithmetically. This relationship holds because managers potentially contend with three types of interpersonal relationships: direct single, direct group, and cross. Direct single relationships occur between the manager and each subordinate individually (that is, in a one-on-one setting). Direct group relationships occur between the manager and each possible permutation of subordinates. Finally, cross relationships occur when subordinates interact with one another.

The critical consideration in determining the manager's span of control is not the number of potential relationships. Rather it's the frequency and intensity of the actual relationships that are important. Not all relationships will occur, and those that do will vary in importance. If we shift our attention from potential to actual relationships as the bases for determining optimum span of control, at least three factors appear to be important: required contact, degree of specialization, and ability to communicate.

Required contact

In research and development as well as medical and production work, there's a need for frequent contact and a high degree of coordination between a superior and subordinates. Conferences and other forms of consultation often aid in attaining goals within a constrained time period. For example, the research and development team leader may have to consult frequently with team members so that a project is completed within a time period that will allow the organization to place a product on the market. Thus, instead of relying on memos and reports, it is in the best interest of the organization to have as many in-depth contacts with the team as possible. A large span of control would preclude contacting subordinates so frequently, which could impede the project. In general, the greater the inherent ambiguity in an individual's job, the greater the need for supervision to avoid conflict and stress.[24]

Degree of specialization

The degree to which employees are specialized is a critical consideration in establishing the span of control at all levels of management. It is generally accepted that a manager at the lower organizational level can oversee more subordinates because work at the lower level is more specialized and less complicated than at higher levels of management. Management can combine highly specialized and similar jobs into relatively large departments because the employees may not need close supervision.

Ability to communicate

Instructions, guidelines, and policies must be communicated verbally to subordinates in most work situations. The need to discuss job-related factors influences the span of control. The individual who can clearly and concisely communicate with subordinates is able to manage more people than one who can't.

The widespread practice of downsizing and "flattening" organizations of all kinds has direct implications for the span of control decision. Downsizing reduces the number of all employees, but relatively more managers (usually middle managers) than nonmanagers.[25] This increases the number of nonmanagers per manager; consequently, the average span of control of each manager increases. Whether the factors of required contact, degree of specialization, and ability to communicate have any bearing on the resultant spans of control can be debated. In fact, many middle managers whose spans of control have been widened believe that top management made the decision without regard to these factors. The Close-Up describes experiences with downsizing in American firms.

Even though we can identify some specific factors that relate to optimal spans of control, the search for the full answer continues.[26]

Delegation of Authority

Managers decide how much authority should be delegated to each job and each jobholder. As we have noted, authority refers to individuals' right to make decisions without approval by higher management and to exact obedience from others. **Delegation of authority** refers specifically to making decisions, not to doing work. A sales manager can be delegated the right to hire salespeople (a decision) and the right to assign them to specific territories (obedience). Another sales manager may not have the right to hire but may have the right to assign territories. Thus, the degree of delegated authority can be relatively high or relatively low with respect to both aspects of authority. Any particular job involves a range of alternative configurations of authority delegation.[27] Managers must balance the relative gains and losses of alternatives.

Delegation of Authority

Process of distributing authority downward in an organization.

Reasons to decentralize authority

Relatively high delegation of authority encourages the development of professional managers. Organizations that decentralize (delegate) authority enable managers to make significant decisions, to gain skills, and to advance in the company. By virtue of their right to make decisions on a broad range of issues, managers develop expertise that enables them to cope with problems of higher management. Managers with broad decision-making power often make difficult decisions. Consequentially, they are trained for promotion into positions of even greater authority and responsibility.[28] Upper management can readily compare managers on the basis of actual decision-making performance. Advancement of managers on the basis of demonstrated performance can eliminate favoritism and minimize personality in the promotion process.

Second, high delegation of authority can lead to a competitive climate within the organization. Managers are motivated to contribute in this competitive atmosphere because they're compared with their peers on various performance measures. A competitive environment in which managers compete on sales, cost reduction, and employee development targets can be a positive factor in overall organizational performance. Competitive environments can also produce destructive behavior if one manager's success occurs at the expense of another's. But regardless of whether it's positive or destructive, significant competition exists only when individuals have authority to do those things that enable them to win.

Finally, managers who have relatively high authority can exercise more autonomy, and thus satisfy their desires to participate in problem solving. This autonomy can lead to managerial creativity and ingenuity which contribute to the adaptiveness and development of the organization and managers. As we've seen in earlier chapters, opportunities to participate in setting goals can be positive motivators. But a necessary condition for goal setting is authority to make decisions. Many organizations, large and small, choose to follow the policy of decentralization of authority.

 **www.hp.com**

Decisions to decentralize often follow experiences with centralization. For example, in 1991, Hewlett-Packard (HP) began to rethink decisions it had made in the 1980s. Those 1980s decisions had centralized operations at the expense of product managers' autonomy. The impetus for the decision to centralize was the increasing cost of duplication at

---

CLOSE—UP

The Effects of Downsizing on the Spans of Control of Managers

Nearly every firm in the global economy either has downsized or has considered the implications of doing so. Some giants in the basic industries, such as IBM, GM, Ford, Hewlett-Packard, and Chrysler as well as many of the 21 winners to date of the prestigious Baldridge Award, have already reduced the number of middle managers and increased the spans of control of all managers. This decision is based on the idea that highly trained individuals throughout the organization, empowered with authority and competence, can manage themselves. The idea isn't new, but widespread application of the idea is new. Many firms, large and small, have reported their experiences with wider spans of control—some positive, others negative. Positive experiences stress the renewed commitment of employees who have the benefits of empowerment; negative experiences stress the additional pressures placed on managers to be responsible for the work performance of more employees.

One observer points out that for flattening to reach its full potential, managers and employees must exercise initiative to "add value" to the directives they receive. The idea of adding value implies that individuals take the directive and evaluate its full potential for adding to the organization's well-being and effectiveness. Another observer of flattening in the U.S. banking industry states that whether the practice works depends upon the wilingness and ability of employees at the local level to provide quality service and high performance, even peak performance, of their assigned duties. But perhaps the most important factor bearing on the practice's success is the manager's ability to comprehend the new relationship between managers and nonmanagers: No longer can managers set themselves apart from those they manage; they must develop helping and coaching relationships with their subordinates.

Sources: Karen E. Mishra, Gretchen M. Spreitzer, and Aneil K. Mishra, "Preserving Employee Morale during Downsizing," *Sloan Management Review,* Winter 1998, pp. 83–95; Aaron Bernstein, "Oops, That's Too Much Downsizing," *Business Week,* June 8, 1989, p. 38; and Kim S. Cameron, "Strategies for Successful Downsizing," *Human Resource Management,* Summer 1994, pp. 189–211.

the local level. For example, each HP unit once manufactured its own circuit boards for its own products, even though the circuit boards were interchangeable. This arrangement enabled local managers to have control and flexibility over volume and quality. But the cost of duplication became intolerable as competition forced down the prices of HP products. Circuit board production was consolidated in a few manufacturing sites under the direction of a single manager.

The downside of the decision was the creation of committees and procedures, a seemingly impenetrable maze of bureaucracy. The company reversed its earlier decision to centralize when it announced a major reorganization. John Young, HP's CEO, decided to go the way of many competitors, including IBM, by reducing the number of managerial levels in the organization structure and decentralizing decisions to managers of more or less independent operating units. Each unit has its own sales force concentrating on selling the unit's product. No doubt, the reorganization will be worked out over a long time and with mixed results, but HP's way of the future seems to rest on decentralization rather than centralization.[29]

Decentralization of authority has its benefits, but these benefits aren't without costs. Organizations that are unable or unwilling to bear these costs will find reasons to centralize authority.

Reasons to centralize authority

Managers must be trained to make the decisions that go with delegated authority. Formal training programs can be quite expensive, which can more than offset the benefits.

Second, many managers are accustomed to making decisions and resist delegating authority to their subordinates. Consequently, they may perform at lower levels of effectiveness because they believe that delegation of authority involves losing control.

Third, administrative costs are incurred because new or altered accounting and performance systems must be developed to provide top management with information about the effects of their subordinates' decisions. When lower levels of management have authority, top management must have some means of reviewing the use of that authority. Consequently, they typically create reporting systems that inform them of the outcomes of decisions made at lower levels in the organization.

The fourth and perhaps most pragmatic reason to centralize is that decentralization means duplication of functions. Each autonomous unit must be truly self-supporting to be independent. But that involves a potentially high cost of duplication. Some organizations find that the cost of decentralization outweighs the benefits.[30]

Decision guidelines

Like most managerial issues, whether authority should be delegated in high or low degree cannot be resolved simply. Managers faced with the issue should answer the following four questions:

1. How routine and straightforward are the job's or unit's required decisions? The authority for routine decisions can be centralized. For example, fast-food restaurants such as Kentucky Fried Chicken centralize the decision of food preparation so as to ensure consistent quality at all stores. However, the local store manager makes the decisions to hire and dismiss employees. This question points out the importance of the distinction between deciding and doing. The local store prepares the food, but the headquarters staff decides how to prepare it.

 **www.kfc.com**

2.   Are individuals competent to make the decision? Even if the decision is nonroutine (as in the case of hiring employees), if the local manager is not competent to recruit and select employees, then employment decisions must be centralized. This question implies that delegation of authority can differ among individuals depending upon each one's ability to make the decision.

3.   Are individuals motivated to make the decision? Capable individuals aren't always motivated individuals. We discussed motivation and individual differences in earlier chapters. Decision making can be difficult and stressful, thus discouraging some individuals from accepting authority. It can also involve a level of commitment to the organization that an individual isn't willing to make. Motivation must accompany competency to create conducive conditions for decentralization.

4.   Finally, to return to the points we made earlier, do the benefits of decentralization outweigh its costs? This question is perhaps the most difficult to answer because many benefits and costs are assessed in subjective terms. Nevertheless, managers should at least attempt to make benefit–cost analysis.

Like most managerial issues, whether authority should be delegated in high or low degree cannot be resolved simply. As usual, in managerial decision making, whether to centralize or decentralize authority can only be guided by general questions.

Dimensions of Structure

The four design decisions (division of labor, delegation of authority, departmentalization, and span of control) result in a structure of organizations. Researchers and practitioners of management have attempted to develop their understanding of relationships between structures and performance, attitudes, effectiveness, and other variables thought to be important. This development of understanding has been hampered not only by the complexity of the relationships themselves, but also by the difficulty of defining and measuring the concept of organizational structure.

Although universal agreement on a common set of dimensions that measure differences in structure is neither possible nor desirable, some suggestions can be made. Three dimensions are often used in research and practice to describe structure: formalization, centralization, and complexity.

Formalization

Formalization

Extent to which an organization relies on written rules and procedures to predetermine actions of employees.

The dimension of **formalization** refers to the extent to which expectations regarding the means and ends of work are specified, written, and enforced. An organization structure described as highly formalized would be one with rules and procedures to prescribe what each individual should be doing.[31] Such organizations have written standard operating procedures, specified directives, and explicit policy. In terms of the four design decisions, formalization is the result of high specialization of labor, high delegation of authority, the use of functional departments, and wide spans of control.

1.   High specialization of labor (as in the auto industry) is amenable to the development of written work rules and procedures. Jobs are so specialized as to leave little to the discretion of the job holder.

2.   High delegation of authority creates the need for checks on its use. Consequently, the organization writes guidelines for decision making and insists upon reports describing the use of authority.

3. Functional departments are made up of jobs with great similarities. This basis brings together jobs that make up an occupation such as accountants, engineers, and machinists. Because of the similarity of the jobs and the rather straightforward nature of the department's activities, management can develop written documents to govern those activities.

4. Wide spans of control discourage one-on-one supervision. There are simply too many subordinates for managers to keep up with on a one-to-one basis. Consequently, managers require written reports to inform them. Although formalization is defined in terms of written rules and procedures, we must understand how they're viewed by the employees. Some organizations have all the appearances of formalization, complete with thick manuals of rules, procedures, and policies, yet employees don't perceive them as affecting their behavior. Thus, where rules and procedures exist, they must be enforced if they're to affect behavior.

Centralization

Centralization
Degree to which top management delegates authority to make decisions.

Centralization refers to the location of decision-making authority in the hierarchy of the organization. More specifically, the concept refers to delegation of authority among the jobs in the organization. Typically, researchers and practitioners think of centralization in terms of decision making and control. But despite the apparent simplicity of the concept, it can be difficult to apply.

The difficulty derives from three sources. First, people at the same level can have different decision-making authority. Second, not all decisions are of equal importance in organizations. For example, a typical management practice is to delegate authority to make routine operating decisions (i.e., decentralization), but to retain authority to make strategic decisions (i.e., centralization). Third, individuals may not perceive that they really have authority even though their job descriptions include it. Thus, objectively they have authority, but subjectively they don't.

The relationships between centralization and the four design decisions are generally as follows:

1. The higher the specialization of labor, the greater the centralization. This relationship holds because highly specialized jobs do not require the discretion that authority provides.

2. The less authority is delegated, the greater the centralization. By definition of the terms, centralization involves retaining authority in the top management jobs, rather than delegating it to lower levels in the organization.

3. The greater the use of functional departments, the greater the centralization. The use of functional departments requires that activities of the several interrelated departments be coordinated. Consequently, authority to coordinate them will be retained in top management.

4. The wider the spans of control, the greater the centralization. Wide spans of control are associated with relatively specialized jobs which, as we've seen, have little need for authority.

Complexity

Complexity
Number of different job titles and authority levels in an organization.

Complexity is the direct outgrowth of dividing work and creating departments. Specifically, the concept refers to the number of distinctly different job titles, or occupational groupings, and the number of distinctly different units, or departments. The fundamental idea is that organizations with many different kinds of jobs and units create more complicated managerial and organizational problems than those with fewer jobs and departments.[32]

Complexity, then, relates to differences among jobs and units. Therefore, it's not surprising that differentiation is often used synonymously with complexity. Moreover, it has become standard practice to use the term *horizontal differentiation* to refer to the number of different units at the same level; *vertical differentiation* to refer to the number of levels in the organization. The relationships between complexity (horizontal and vertical differentiation) and the four design decisions are generally as follows:

1. The greater the specialization of labor, the greater the complexity. Specialization is the process of creating different jobs and thus more complexity. Specialization of labor contributes primarily to horizontal differentiation.

2. The greater the delegation of authority, the greater the complexity of the organization. Delegation of authority is typically associated with a lengthy chain of command (i.e., with a relatively large number of managerial levels). Thus, delegation of authority contributes to vertical differentiation.

3. The greater the use of territorial, customer, and product bases, the greater the complexity. These bases involve creating self-sustaining units that operate much like free-standing organizations. Consequently, there must be considerable delegation of authority and thus considerable complexity.

4. Narrow spans of control are associated with high complexity. This relationship holds because narrow spans are necessary when the jobs to be supervised are quite different one from another. A supervisor can manage more people in a simple organization than in a complex organization. The apparently simple matter of span of control can have profound effects on organizational and individual behavior. Hence, we should expect the controversy that surrounds it.

Relationships between dimensions of organizational structure and the four design decisions are summarized in Table 13–1. It notes only the causes of high formalization, centralization, and complexity. However, the relationships are symmetrical—the causes of low formalization, centralization, and complexity are the opposite of those in the table.

Table 13–1   Organization Dimensions in Relation to Organizational Decisions

DIMENSIONS	DECISIONS
High formalization	1. High specialization 2. Functional departments 3. Wide spans of control 4. Delegated authority
High centralization	1. High specialization 2. Functional departments 3. Wide spans of control 4. Centralized authority
High complexity	1. High specialization 2. Territorial, customer, and product departments 3. Narrow spans of control 4. Delegated authority

Summary of Key Points

- The structure of an organization consists of relatively fixed and stable relationships among jobs and groups of jobs. The primary purpose of organization structure is to influence the behavior of individuals and groups to achieve effective performance.

- Four key managerial decisions determine organization structures. These decisions are dividing work, delegating authority, departmentalizing jobs into groups, and determining spans of control.

- The four key decisions are interrelated and interdependent, although each has certain specific problems that can be considered apart from the others.

- Dividing the overall task into smaller related tasks depends initially on the technical and economic advantages of specialization of labor.

- Delegating authority enables an individual to make decisions and to exact obedience without approval by higher management. Similar to other organizing issues, delegated authority is a relative, not absolute, concept. All individuals, whether managers or nonmanagers, in an organization have some authority. The question is whether they have enough to do their jobs.

- Grouping jobs into departments requires the selection of common bases such as function, territory, product, and customer. Each basis has advantages and disadvantages that must be evaluated in terms of overall effectiveness.

- The matrix form of organization provides some opportunities to realize the advantages of function and product as bases for departments in combination. The principal disadvantage is the creation of dual reporting channels for members of product departments and groups.

- The optimal span of control is no one specific number of subordinates. Although the number of potential relationships increases geometrically as the number of subordinates increases arithmetically, the important considerations are the frequency and intensity of the actual relationships.

- The current practice of downsizing has important implications for the spans of control of managers. As a consequence of the reduced number of managers relative to nonmanagers, the average span of control will necessarily increase.

- Organization structures differ as a consequence of the four management decisions. To measure these differences, we must identify measurable attributes, or dimensions, of structure. Three often-used dimensions are complexity, centralization, and formalization.

- Complexity refers to the extent to which jobs in the organization are relatively specialized; centralization refers to the extent to which authority is retained in the jobs of top management; and formalization refers to the extent to which policies, rules, and procedures exist in written form.

Discussion and Review Questions

1. Explain how you would go about determining the organization structure for a small retail firm that has no organization chart.

2. Compare functional and product departmentalization in terms of relative efficiency, production, satisfaction, flexibility, quality, competitiveness, and development. Consider particularly the possibility that one basis may be superior in achieving one aspect of effectiveness, yet inferior in achieving another.

3. Explain why an organization must use various departmental bases at different levels of the structure.

4. Discuss the statement that to manage effectively, a person must have the authority to hire subordinates, assign them to specific jobs, and reward them on the basis of performance. Interview the chairperson of an academic department and determine whether he has this authority.

5. The terms *responsibility*, *authority*, and *accountability* appear in the management and organization literature. What is your understanding of these terms? Are they different? Do they refer to fundamental questions of organizational design?

6. What implications for managerial spans of control can be expected in organizations that downsize? What additional demands will be placed on remaining managers after downsizing?

7. Discuss the relationship between delegation of authority and bases for departmentalization. In particular, is it desirable to create product-based divisions without delegating considerable authority to managers of those divisions? Explain.

8. Explain how you could use the three dimensions of structure to compare two organizations.

9. Describe managerial skills and behaviors that would be required to manage effectively in a functional department. Are these skills and behaviors different from those required in a product department? Explain.

10. What circumstances would cause managers of an organization to consider a matrix organization structure? What would cause them to consider abandoning a matrix organization?

C A S E   F O R   A N A L Y S I S

Restructuring at Motorola

Competitive pressures from home and abroad have forced many firms to consider ways to cut costs and eliminate waste. At the same time firms sought ways to cut costs, they also looked for ways to increase the flow of innovative ideas. Many companies responded to these twin challenges in the 1980s by reducing the levels of management and increasing the spans of control. These flatter structures had the advantages of reducing costs by eliminating managerial jobs (and salaries) and increasing the flow of ideas by giving individuals more authority to make decisions. Reports of the positive results of these restructuring efforts filled the popular press.

Notable success stories include Ford Motor's acknowledgment that its 12 layers of management should be reduced and brought more in line with Toyota's 7 and Xerox Corporation's reduction in middle management. Even those firms with records of efficient operations announced that they were attempting to do better by reducing the managers in their organizations. For example, Dana Corporation (an acknowledged efficiency leader) announced its intention to reduce its five levels of management to four. These success stories came to the attention of Motorola's top management, who instructed the company's human resource professionals to evaluate potential gains through flattening the structure.

Motorola's top management was particularly concerned with how many efforts to reduce managerial personnel would affect the company's long-standing commitment to certain values. The company enjoyed the reputation of treating employees with respect and dignity, including protecting employees who had served the company well in the past. Any restructuring effort to eliminate managerial jobs would have to be consistent with the company's reputation. Top management was also concerned with how managers themselves would respond to efforts to reduce managerial jobs. Would they see such efforts as threats, particularly if it meant reducing personnel in their own departments?

Aware of these issues, human resource professionals devised the following strategy for dealing with the necessity to cut costs and, at the same time, to adhere to people-first values. The process consisted of five steps involving the managers and human resource professionals in joint activities:

Step 1: Data gathering. Each top manager drew an organization chart showing every reporting relationship down to the direct-labor level. These hand-drawn charts showed what really went on in the unit, as distinct from what was supposed to go on.

Step 2: Analysis. Human resource professionals analyzed the charts and identified issues for discussion with the managers. The analysis indicated instances of too many managerial levels, too narrow spans of control, and overlapping responsibilities.

Step 3: Discussion. The analyses of the human resource professionals were presented to the managers for discussion. Managers were given opportunities to explain and clarify relationships shown on the charts.

Step 4: Goals negotiation. As discussions between managers and the human resources staff revealed problems, managers were asked to propose solutions. When managers disagreed with the staff, they were challenged to present their own analyses and solutions.

Step 5: Implementation and tracking. As managers implemented the changes in organizational structure, they documented the resultant cost savings. The sources of these savings were salaries of managers not replaced on retirement or transfer. A second source of savings was the replacement of a manager with a nonmanager at a lower salary.

Thus, through elimination of some jobs and redefinition of others, Motorola succeeded in its efforts to reduce costs by restructuring its organization. The restructuring has caused Motorola's managers to constantly ask themselves whether they each can effectively direct one more employee. They ask, "If I manage five, why not six?" Results of restructuring have been impressive in economic terms, with savings in excess of $4.3 million in the first year. Other results include improved vertical communications, more effective managerial selection and training, and greater participation in decision making by all employees.

Discussion Questions

1. Evaluate Motorola's decision to restructure from a tall to a flat organization.

2. If Motorola had not been pressured by competition, would it have restructured its organization? Explain your answer.

3. Based on the experience of Motorola, can you make the case for flat organizations being rela-

tively more effective than tall organizations in dealing with competitive pressures? Explain your answer.

Source: Based on Phil Nienstedt and Richard Wintermantel, "Motorola Restructures to Improve Productivity," *Management Review,* January 1987, pp. 47–49.

www.mot.com

E X P E R I E N T I A L   E X E R C I S E

Designing the New Venture

Objective

To provide students with firsthand experience in organizing a new business venture.

Related Topics

Organizational design necessitates making assumptions about the market, competition, labor resources, scheduling, and profit margins, to name just a few areas. There is no one best design that should be regarded as a final answer.

Starting the Exercise

Read the scenario presented. Then the instructor will set up teams of five to eight students to serve as organizational design experts who will provide the Gammons brothers with the best structure for their new venture.

Scenario

Some years ago, George Ballas got so frustrated trying to keep his lawn neatly trimmed around the roots of oak trees that he developed what's now called the Weed Eater. The original Weed Eater was made from a popcorn can that had holes in it and was threaded with nylon fishing line. Weed Eater sales in 1972 totaled $568,000; by 1978, sales were in excess of $100 million. Twenty or so similar devices are now on the market.

Two brothers from Pittsburgh, George and Jim Gammons, are starting a new venture called Lawn Trimmers, Inc. Their competition (the Weed Eater and similar products) often have breaks in the nylon lines that require the user to turn off the trimmer and readjust the line. The Gammons have developed a new type of cutting fabric that's not physically harmful and cuts for over 2,000 applications.

To sell the Lawn Trimmers, the Gammons brothers must market their products through retail establishments. They will make the products in their shop in Pittsburgh and ship them to retailers. Profits will come entirely from sales of Lawn Trimmers to retailers. The price of the product is already set. It appears that there will be sufficient market demand to sell at least 6,000 Lawn Trimmers annually.

Completing the Exercise

Each group should:

1. Establish a design that would be feasible for the Gammons at this stage in their venture.
2. Select a spokesperson to make a short presentation of the group's organizational design for the Gammons.

The class should compare the various designs and discuss why there are similarities and differences in what is presented.

Chapter 14

Designing Productive and Motivating Jobs

Learning Objectives

After completing Chapter 14, you should be able to:

Define
Job design.

Describe
Alternative job design approaches that organizations use to improve job performance.

Discuss
The various factors and relationships that link job design and job performance.

Compare
Job enrichment and job enlargement design strategies.

Identify
Specific individual differences that account for different perceptions of job content.

The jobs that people perform in organizations are the building blocks of all organization structures. In fact, organizations exist to enable people to do work in assigned jobs. The phrase *Let's get organized!* usually means that we need to clarify what job each individual should be doing. But we are also interested in performing jobs effectively and we need to understand the causes of effective and ineffective job performance.

A major cause of effective job performance is job design—what we get when we clarify what each employee should be doing. In a more technical sense, job design refers to the process by which managers decide individual job tasks and authority. Apart from the very practical issues associated with job design (i.e., issues that relate to effectiveness in economic, political, and monetary terms), we can appreciate its importance in social and psychological terms. Jobs can be sources of psychological stress and even mental and physical impairment. On a more positive note, jobs can provide income, meaningful life experiences, self-esteem, esteem from others, regulation of our lives, and association with others. Thus, the well-being of organizations and people relates to how well management designs jobs.

Job Design

The process by which managers decide individual job tasks and authority.

This chapter describes some of the many theories and practices that deal with job design and redesign. We must understand the implication of the term job redesign in the context of our discussion. It means that management has decided that it's worthwhile to reconsider what employees are expected to do on the job. In some instances, the redesign effort may be nothing more than requiring the individual to use a computer rather than a calculator to do clerical work. In other instances, the redesign effort may require the individual to work with other employees in a team effort rather than to work alone on the task. The contemporary trend in organizations is to redesign jobs that require individuals to work together in groups. Whether Americans can work effectively in groups is the controversial issue.

Job Redesign

The process by which managers reconsider what employees are expected to do.

In contrast to job redesign, job design refers to the first instance in which management creates a job by specifying its duties and responsibilities. But with the passage of time and the development of new tools and processes, management's expectations for that job will change (i.e., it will be redesigned). We should understand job design to be an ongoing, dynamic process. Thus we will use the term *job design* to refer to any and all managerial efforts to create jobs whether initially or subsequently.

We begin the discussion of job design by introducing the issue of quality of work life. As is apparent to anyone who has ever worked, what we do on the job plays a major role in our social, health, and psychological statuses as well as in our economic standing. After introducing the relationships between job design and quality of work life, we'll address the more technical aspects of job design.

Designing Jobs to Enhance Quality of Work Life

Quality of Work Life (QWL)

Management philosophy that enhances employee dignity, introduces cultural change, and provides opportunities for growth and development.

In recent years, the issue of designing jobs has gone beyond the determination of the most efficient way to perform tasks. The concept of **quality of work life (QWL)** is now widely used to refer to "a philosophy of management that enhances the dignity of all workers; introduces changes in an organization's culture; and improves the physical and emotional well-being of employees (e.g., providing opportunities for growth and development)."[1] Indicators of quality of work life include accident rates, sick leave usage, employee turnover, and number of grievances filed.[2] In some organizations, QWL programs are intended to increase employee trust, involvement, and problem solving so as to increase both worker satisfaction and organizational effectiveness.[3] Thus, the concept and application of QWL are broad and involve more than jobs, but the jobs that people do are important sources of satisfaction. It is not surprising to find that the quality of work life concept embodies theories and ideas of the human relations movement of the 1950s and the job enrichment efforts of the '60s and '70s.

The continuing challenge to management is to provide for quality of work life and to improve production, quality, and efficiency through revitalization of business and industry. At present, the trade-offs between the gains in human terms from improved quality of work life and the gains in economic terms from revitalization aren't fully known. Some believe that we must defer quality of work life efforts so as to make the American economy more productive and efficient.[4] Others observe that the sense of urgency to become more competitive in domestic and overseas trade presents opportunities to combine quality of life and reindustrialization efforts.[5] To those ends, job design can play a vital role.

Job design attempts to identify the most important needs of employees and the organization and to remove obstacles in the workplace that frustrate those needs. Managers hope that the results are jobs that fulfill important individual needs and contribute to individual, group, and organizational effectiveness. Managers are, in fact, designing jobs for teams and groups. Some studies have reported that employees who participate in teams get greater satisfaction from their jobs.[6] But other studies report contrary results.[7] So we're left with the uncomfortable but realistic conclusion that quality of work life improvements through job design cannot be assured in specific instances. Obviously, designing jobs is complex. This chapter reviews the important theories, research, and practices of job design. As will be seen, contemporary management has at its disposal a wide range of techniques that facilitate the achievement of personal and organizational performance.

The Important Concepts of Job Design

The conceptual model in Figure 14–1 is based on the extensive research literature appearing since the 1970s. The model includes the various terms and concepts appearing in the current literature. When linked together, these concepts describe the important determinants of job performance and organizational effectiveness. The model takes into account a number of sources of complexity. It recognizes that individuals react differently to jobs. While one person may derive positive satisfaction from a job, another may not. It also recognizes the difficult trade-offs between organizational and individual needs. For example, the technology of manufacturing (an environmental difference) may dictate that management adopt assembly-line mass production methods and low-skilled jobs to achieve optimal efficiency. Such jobs, however, may result in great unrest and worker discontent. Perhaps these costs could be avoided by carefully balancing organizational and individual needs.

The ideas reflected in Figure 14–1 are the bases for this chapter. We'll present each important cause or effect of job design, beginning with the end result of job design, **job performance.**

Job Performance

The outcome of jobs which relate to the purposes of the organization such as quality, efficiency, and other criteria of effectiveness.

Job Performance Outcomes

Job performance includes a number of outcomes. In this section we'll discuss performance outcomes that have value to the organization and to the individual.

Figure 14–1

Conceptual Model of Job Design and Job Performance

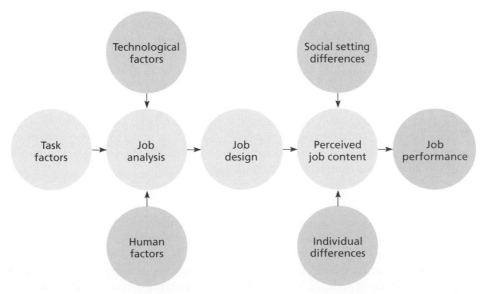

Objective outcomes

Quantity and quality of output, absenteeism, tardiness, and turnover are objective outcomes that can be measured in quantitative terms. For each job, implicit or explicit standards exist for each of these objective outcomes. Industrial engineering studies establish standards for daily quantity, and quality control specialists establish tolerance limits for acceptable quality. These aspects of job performance account for characteristics of the product, client, or service for which the jobholder is responsible. But job performance includes other outcomes.

Personal behavior outcomes

The jobholder reacts to the work itself. She reacts by either attending regularly or being absent, by staying with the job or by quitting. Moreover, physiological and health-related problems can ensue as a consequence of job performance. Stress related to job performance can contribute to physical and mental impairment; accidents and occupation-related disease can also result.

Intrinsic and extrinsic outcomes

Job outcomes include intrinsic and extrinsic work outcomes. The distinction between intrinsic and extrinsic outcomes is important for understanding people's reactions to their jobs. In a general sense, an intrinsic outcome is an object or event that follows from the worker's own efforts and doesn't require the involvement of any other person. More simply, it's an outcome clearly related to action on the worker's part. Contemporary job design theory defines intrinsic motivation in terms of the employee's "empowerment" to achieve outcomes from the application of individual ability and talent.[8] Such outcomes typically are thought to be solely in the province of professional and technical jobs; yet all jobs potentially have opportunities for intrinsic outcomes. Such outcomes involve feelings of responsibility, challenge, and recognition; they result from such job characteristics as variety, autonomy, identity, and significance.[9]

Extrinsic outcomes, however, are objects or events that follow from the workers' own efforts in conjunction with other factors or persons not directly involved in the job itself. Pay, working conditions, co-workers, and even supervision are objects in the workplace that are potentially job outcomes but aren't a fundamental part of the work. Dealing with others and friendship interactions are sources of extrinsic outcomes.

Most jobs provide opportunities for both intrinsic and extrinsic outcomes so we must understand the relationship between the two. It's generally held that extrinsic rewards reinforce intrinsic rewards in a positive direction when the individual can attribute the source of the extrinsic reward to his own efforts. For example, a pay raise (extrinsic reward) increases feeling good about oneself if the cause of the raise is thought to be one's own efforts and competence and not favoritism by the boss. This line of reasoning explains why some individuals get no satisfaction out of sharing in the gains derived from group effort rather than individual effort.

Job satisfaction outcomes

Job Satisfaction

An individual's expression of personal well-being associated with doing the job assigned.

Job satisfaction depends on the levels of intrinsic and extrinsic outcomes and how the jobholder views those outcomes. These outcomes have different values for different people. For some people, responsible and challenging work may have neutral or even negative value depending on their education and prior experience with work providing intrinsic outcomes.[10] For other people, such work outcomes may have high positive values. People differ in the importance they attach to job outcomes. Those differences alone would account for different levels of job satisfaction for essentially the same job tasks. For example, one company that has initiated management systems intended to provide employees with a great deal of opportunity for exercising judgment and making decisions has found many individuals unable or unwilling to work for it. The company, W. L. Gore & Associates, has been the subject of considerable interest among those who advocate employee empowerment.[11]

Other important individual differences include job involvement and commitment to the organization.[12] People differ in the extent that (1) work is a central life interest, (2) they actively participate in work, (3) they perceive work as central to self-esteem, and (4) they perceive work as consistent with self-concept. Persons who are not involved in their work or the organizations that employ them cannot be expected to realize the same satisfaction as those who are. This variable accounts for the fact that two workers could report different levels of satisfaction for the same performance levels.

A final individual difference is the perceived equity of the outcome in terms of what the jobholder considers a fair reward.[13] If outcomes are perceived to be unfair in relation to those of others in similar jobs requiring similar effort, the jobholder will experience dissatisfaction and seek means to restore the equity, either by seeking greater rewards (primarily extrinsic) or by reducing effort.

Thus, we see that job performance includes many potential outcomes. Some are of primary value to the organization—the objective outcomes, for example. Other outcomes, such as job satisfaction, are of primary importance to the individual. Job performance is without doubt a complex variable that depends on the interplay of numerous factors. Managers can make some sense of the issue by understanding the motivational implications of jobs through the application of job analysis.[14]

Describing Jobs through Job Analysis

The purpose of **job analysis** is to provide an objective description of the job itself.[15] Individuals who perform job analysis gather information about three aspects of all jobs: job content, job requirements, and job context. Many different job analysis methods help managers identify content, requirements, and context.

Job content

Job content refers to the activities required of the job. Depending upon the specific job analysis used, this description can be broad or narrow in scope. The description can vary from general statements of job activities down to highly detailed statements of each and every hand and body motion required to do the job. One widely used method, **functional job analysis (FJA)**, describes jobs in terms of:

1. What the worker does in relation to data, people, and jobs.
2. What methods and techniques the worker uses.
3. What machines, tools, and equipment the worker uses.
4. What materials, products, subject matter, or services the worker produces.

The first three aspects relate to job activities. The fourth aspect relates to job performance. FJA provides descriptions of jobs that can be the bases for classifying jobs according to any one of the four dimensions. In addition to defining what activities,

Job Analysis

Providing a description of how one job differs from another in terms of demands, activities, and skills required.

Job Content

Specific activities required in a job.

Functional Job Analysis (FJA)

Method of job analysis that focuses on specific activities, machines, methods, and required output.

methods, and machines make up the job, FJA also defines what the individual doing the job should produce. FJA can, therefore, be the basis for defining standards of performance.

FJA is the most popular and widely used of the job analysis methods.[16] In addition, it's the basis for the most extensive available list of occupational titles.[17]

Job requirements

Job Requirements

The education, experience, licenses, and other personal characteristics needed by an individual to perform the job content.

Position Analysis Questionnaire (PAQ)

A method of job analysis that takes into account human characteristics as well as task and technological factors of job and job classes.

Job requirements refer to education, experience, licenses, and other personal characteristics that are expected of an individual if he's to perform the job content. In recent years, the idea has emerged that job requirements should also identify skills, abilities, knowledge, and other personal characteristics required to perform the job content in the particular setting. One widely used method, **position analysis questionnaire (PAQ)**, takes into account these human factors through analysis of the following job aspects:

1. Information sources critical to job performance.
2. Information processing and decision making critical to job performance.
3. Physical activity and dexterity required of the job.
4. Interpersonal relationships required of the job.
5. Reactions of individuals to working conditions.[18]

The position analysis questionnaire can be adapted to jobs of all types, including managerial jobs.

Job context

Job Context

Physical environment and other working conditions, along with other factors considered to be extrinsic to a job.

Job context refers to factors such as the physical demands and working conditions of the job, the degree of accountability and responsibility, the extent of supervision required or exercised, and the consequences of error. Job context describes the environment within which the job is to be performed.

Numerous methods exist to perform job analysis. Different methods can give different answers to important questions such as "How much is the job worth?" Thus, selecting the method for performing job analysis isn't trivial—it's one of the most important decisions in job design. Recent surveys of expert job analysts' opinions bear out the popularity of PAQ and FJA.[19]

Job analysis in different settings

People perform their jobs in a variety of settings—too many to discuss them all. We'll instead discuss two significant job settings: the factory and the office. One has historical significance, the other has future significance.

JOBS IN THE FACTORY   Job analysis began in the factory. Industrialization created the setting in which individuals perform many hundreds of specialized jobs. The earliest attempts to do job analysis followed the ideas advanced by the proponents of scientific management. They were industrial engineers who, at the turn of the 20th century, began to devise ways to analyze industrial jobs. The major theme of scientific management is that objective analyses of facts and data collected in the workplace could provide the bases for determining the one best way to design work.[20] F. W. Taylor stated the essence of scientific management as follows:

First: Develop a science for each element of a man's work that replaces the old rule-of-thumb method.

Second: Scientifically select and then train, teach, and develop the workman, whereas in the past he chose his own work and trained himself as best he could.

Third: Heartily cooperate with the men so as to ensure that all of the work is done in accordance with the principles of the science that has been developed.

Fourth: There is almost an equal division of the work and the responsibility between management and workmen. Management takes over all work for which it's better fitted than workmen, while in the past, almost all of the work and the greater part of the responsibility were thrown upon workmen.[21]

These four principles express the theme of scientific management methods. Management should take into account task and technology to determine the best way for each job and then train people to do the job that way.

Scientific management produced many techniques in current use. Motion and time study, work simplification, and standard methods are at the core of job analysis in factory settings. Although the mechanistic approach to job analysis is widespread, many service organizations as well as manufacturers are discovering some of the negative consequences of jobs that are overly routine as the Close-Up suggests.[22]

Consequently, many organizations are turning away from the idea of one person doing one specialized job. As we'll learn later in the chapter, many manufacturing firms are now analyzing jobs to determine the extent to which content and requirements can be increased to tap a larger portion of the individual's talents and abilities.

JOBS IN THE OFFICE   In the short space of time since the advent of scientific management, the American economy has shifted from factory-oriented to office-oriented work. The fastest growing segment of jobs is secretarial, clerical, and information workers. The growth of these jobs is due to technological breakthroughs in both factory and office settings.

Technological breakthroughs in automation, robotics, and computer-assisted manufacturing have reduced the need for industrial jobs. But that same technology has increased the need for office jobs. Still, the modern office isn't a mere extension of the traditional factory. The modern office reflects the new computer technology. Its most striking feature is the replacement of paper with some electronic medium, usually a visual display terminal (VDT). One individual interacts with the VDT to do a variety of tasks that in earlier times would have required many individuals. A significant aspect of job analysis in modern offices is the creation of work modules, interrelated tasks that can be assigned to a single individual.

In recent times, managers and researchers have found that human factors must be given special attention when analyzing jobs in the electronic office. VDT operators report that they suffer visual and postural problems such as headaches, burning eyes, and shoulder and backaches.[23] The sources of these problems seem to be in the design of the workplace, particularly the interaction between the individual and the VDT.

Job analysis in the office must pay particular attention to human factors. The tendency is to overemphasize the technological factor—in this case, the computer—and to analyze jobs only as extensions of the technology. As was true of job analysis in factories, it's simply easier to deal with the relatively fixed nature of tasks and technology than to deal with the variable of human nature.[24]

Job Designs: The Results of Job Analysis

Job designs are the results of job analysis. They specify three characteristics of jobs: range, depth, and relationships.

Range and depth

Job Range

Number of tasks a person is expected to perform while doing a job. The more tasks required, the greater the job range.

Job Depth

Degree of influence or discretion that an individual possesses to choose how a job will be performed.

Job range refers to the number of tasks a jobholder performs. The individual who performs eight tasks to complete a job has a wider job range than a person performing four tasks. In most instances, the greater the number of tasks performed, the longer it takes to complete the job.

A second characteristic is **job depth,** the amount of discretion an individual has to decide job activities and job outcomes. In many instances, job depth relates to personal influence as well as delegated authority. Thus, an employee with the same job title who's at the same organizational level as another employee may possess more, less, or the same amount of job depth because of the personal influence.

Job range and depth distinguish one job from another not only within the same organization, but also among different organizations. To illustrate how jobs differ in range and depth, Figure 14–2 depicts the differences for selected jobs of firms, hospitals, and universities. For example, business research scientists, hospital chiefs of surgery, and university presidents generally have high job range and significant depth. Research scientists perform a large num-

Total Quality Management and Flexible Jobs in Contemporary Management Practice

Many organizations in all sectors of society have moved away from traditional methods of designing jobs to a more contemporary method that acknowledges inevitable change. One of the leaders in this trend, Motorola, Inc., learned in the mid-1980s that its products weren't competitive in the global market and that the primary cause for this poor quality was the way the company had traditionally designed jobs. Motorola's search for quality was triggered by its winning an antidumping suit against Japanese manufacturers of cellular phones. But that suit did not solve Motorola's underlying problem of poor quality. The company's product was simply not up to standards of competition, so product-quality improvement became the most important management problem to solve. Management responded by shifting responsibility for quality control from inspectors at the end of the assembly line to individual production workers. Then, to encourage individual workers to learn to understand and do all the jobs on the line so as to recognize potential and actual sources of

quality failures, Motorola revised its compensation plan to reward individuals who learned a variety of jobs. The effect was to increase the content and requirements of the production workers' jobs and to decrease the rate of product failure by 77 percent.

These developments were the early evidence of Motorola's commitment to quality and to the ideas of total quality management. Subsequently Motorola has invested heavily in employee training and education and has been a national leader in pushing for greater appreciation of TQM. Although Motorola uses modern technology and sophisticated computer applications in its production departments, it maintains that the primary source of its gains is employees who have taken on the responsibility for bigger jobs with greater responsibility.

Sources: Clinton O. Longenecker, Timothy C. Stansfield, and Deborah J. Dwyer, "The Human Side of Manufacturing Improvement," *Business Horizons,* March/April 1997; Greg L. Stewart and Kenneth P. Carson, "Moving Beyond the Mechanistic Model," *Human Resource Management,* Summer 1997, pp. 157–84; and Ralph Barra, "Motorola's Approach to Quality," *Journal for Quality and Participation,* March 1989, pp. 46–50.

 **www.mot.com**

ber of tasks and are usually not closely supervised. Chiefs of surgery have significant job range in that they oversee and counsel on many diverse surgical matters. In addition, they aren't supervised closely and they have the authority to influence hospital surgery policies and procedures.

University presidents have a large number of tasks to perform. They speak to alumni groups, politicians, community representatives, and students. They develop, with the consultation of others, policies on admissions, fund raising, and adult education. They can alter the faculty recruitment philosophy and thus alter the course of the entire institution. For example, a university president may want to build an institution that's noted for high-quality classroom instruction and for providing excellent services to the community. This thrust may lead to recruiting and selecting professors who want to concentrate on these two specific goals. In contrast, another president may want to foster outstanding research and high-quality classroom instruction. Of course, yet another president may attempt to develop an institution that's noted for instruction, research, and service. The critical point is that university presidents have sufficient depth to alter the course of a university's direction.

Examples of jobs with high depth and low range are packaging machine mechanics, anesthesiologists, and faculty members. Mechanics perform the limited tasks that pertain to repairing and maintaining packaging machines, but they can decide how breakdowns on the packaging machine are to be repaired. The discretion means that the mechanics have relatively high job depth.

Anesthesiologists also perform a limited number of tasks. They are concerned with the rather restricted task of administering anesthetics to patients. However, they can decide the type of anesthetic to be administered in a particular situation, a decision indicative of high job depth. University professors specifically engaged in classroom instruction have relatively low job range. Teaching involves comparatively more tasks than the work of the anesthesiologist, yet fewer tasks than that of the business research scientist. However, professors' job depth is greater than graduate student instructors' since professors determine how they'll conduct the class, what materials will be presented, and the standards to be used in evaluating students. Graduate students typically don't have complete freedom in the choice of class materials and procedures. Professors decide these matters for them.

Figure 14–2

Job Depth and Range: Differences in Selected Jobs

	Low ← Job range → High	
High	College professors	College presidents
	Hospital anesthesiologists	Hospital chiefs of surgery
Job depth	Business packaging machine mechanics	Business research scientists
	College instructors	College department chairpersons
	Hospital bookkeepers	Hospital nurses
Low	Business assembly-line workers	Business maintenance repair workers

Highly specialized jobs are those having few tasks to accomplish by prescribed means. Such jobs are quite routine; they also tend to be controlled by specified rules and procedures (low depth). A highly despecialized job (high range) has many tasks to accomplish within the framework of discretion over means and ends (high depth). Within an organization, there typically are great differences among jobs in both range and depth. Although there are no precise equations that managers can use to decide job range and depth, they can follow this guideline: Given the economic and technical requirements of the organization's mission, goals, and objectives, what is the optimal point along the continuum of range and depth for each job?

Job relationships

Job Relationships

Interpersonal relationships required or made possible on the job.

Job relationships are determined by managers' decisions regarding departmentalization bases and spans of control. The resulting groups become the responsibility of a manager to coordinate toward organization purposes. These decisions also determine the nature and extent of jobholders' interpersonal relationships, individually and within groups. As we already have seen in the discussion of groups in organizations, group performance is affected in part by group cohesiveness. And the degree of group cohesiveness depends on the quality and kind of interpersonal relationships of jobholders assigned to a task or command group.

The wider the span of control, the larger the group and, consequently, the more difficult the establishment of friendship and interest relationships. Simply, people in larger groups are less likely to communicate and interact sufficiently to form interpersonal ties than people in smaller groups. Without the opportunity to communicate, people will be unable to establish cohesive work groups. Thus, an important source of satisfaction may be lost for individuals who seek to fulfill social and esteem needs through relationships with co-workers.

The basis for departmentalization that management selects also has important implications for job relationships. The functional basis places jobs with similar depth and range in the same groups, while product, territory, and customer bases place jobs with dissimilar depth and range. Thus, in functional departments, people will be doing much the same specialty. Product, territory, and customer departments, however, comprise jobs that are quite different and heterogeneous. Individuals who work in heterogeneous departments experience feelings of dissatisfaction, stress, and involvement more intensely than those in homogeneous, functional departments. People with homogeneous backgrounds, skills, and training have more common interests than those with heterogeneous ones. Thus, it's easier for them to establish satisfying social relationships with less stress, but also with less involvement in the department's activities.

Job designs describe the *objective* characteristics of jobs. That is, through job analysis techniques managers can design jobs in terms of required activities to produce a specified outcome. But yet another factor—perceived job content—must be considered before we can understand the relationship between jobs and performance.

The Way People Perceive Their Jobs

The way people do their jobs depends in part on how they perceive and think of their jobs. Even though Taylor proposed that the way to improve work (i.e., to make it more efficient) is to determine the "best way" to do a task (motion study) and the standard time for completion of the task (time study), the actual performance of jobs goes beyond its technical description.

The belief that job design can be based solely on technical data ignores the very large role played by the individual who performs the job. Individuals differ profoundly, as we noted in the chapter on individual differences. They come to work with different backgrounds, needs, and motivations. Once on the job, they experience the social setting in which the work is performed in unique ways. It's not surprising to find that different individuals perceive jobs differently.

Perceived job content refers to characteristics of a job that define its general nature as perceived by the jobholder. We must distinguish between a job's *objective properties* and its *subjective properties* as reflected in the perceptions of people who perform it.[25] Managers can't understand the causes of job performance without considering individual differences such as personality, needs, and span of attention.[26] Nor can managers understand the causes of job performance without considering the social setting in which the job is performed. According to Figure 14–1, perceived job content precedes job performance. Thus, if managers desire to increase job performance by changing perceived job content, they can change job design, individual perceptions, or social settings—the causes of perceived job content.

If management is to understand perceived job content, some method for measuring it must exist. In response to this need, organization behavior researchers have attempted to measure perceived job content in a variety of work settings. The methods that researchers use rely on questionnaires that jobholders complete and that measure their perceptions of certain job characteristics.

Perceived Job Content

Specific job activities and general job characteristics as perceived by individual performing the job. Two individuals doing the same job may have the same or different perceptions of job content.

Job characteristics

The pioneering effort to measure perceived job content through employee responses to a questionnaire resulted in the identification of six characteristics: variety, autonomy, required interaction, optional interaction, knowledge and skill required, and responsibility.[27] The index of these six characteristics is termed the Requisite Task Attribute Index (RTAI). The original RTAI has been extensively reviewed and analyzed. One important development was the review by Hackman and Lawler, who revised the index to include the six characteristics shown in Table 14–1.[28]

Variety, task identity, and feedback are perceptions of job range. Autonomy is the perception of job depth; and dealing with others and friendship opportunities reflect

CHARACTERISTIC	DESCRIPTION
Variety	Degree to which a job requires employees to perform a wide range of operations in their work, and/or degree to which employees must use a variety of equipment and procedures in their work.
Autonomy	Extent to which employees have a major say in scheduling their work, selecting the equipment they use, and deciding on procedures to be followed.
Task identity	Extent to which employees do an entire or whole piece of work and can clearly identify with the results of their efforts.
Feedback	Degree to which employees, as they are working, receive information that reveals how well they are performing on the job.
Dealing with others	Degree to which a job requires employees to deal with other people to complete their work.
Friendship opportunities	Degree to which a job allows employees to talk with one another on the job and to establish informal relationships with other employees at work.

Table 14–1

Six Characteristics of Perceived Job Content

Source: Henry P. Sims Jr., Andrew D. Szilagyi, and Robert T. Keller, "The Measurement of Job Characteristics," *Academy of Management Journal,* June 1976, p. 197.

perceptions of job relationships. Employees sharing similar perceptions, job designs, and social settings should report similar job characteristics. Employees with different perceptions, however, report different job characteristics of the same job. For example, an individual with a high need for social belonging would perceive "friendship opportunities" differently than another individual with a low need for social belonging.

Individual differences

Individual differences in need strength, particularly the strength of growth needs, have been shown to influence the perception of task variety.[29] Employees with relatively weak higher order needs are less concerned with performing a variety of tasks than are employees with relatively strong growth needs. Thus, managers expecting higher performance to result from increased task variety would be disappointed if the jobholders did not have strong growth needs. Even individuals with strong growth needs cannot respond continuously to the opportunity to perform more and more tasks. At some point, performance turns down as these individuals reach the limits imposed by their abilities and time.

Social setting differences

Differences in social settings of work also affect perceptions of job content. Examples of social setting differences include leadership style and what other people say about the job. As more than one research study has pointed out, how one perceives a job is greatly affected by what other people say about it. Thus, if one's friends state their jobs are boring, one is likely to state that his job is also boring. If the individual perceives the job as boring, job performance will no doubt suffer. Job content, then, results from the interaction of many factors in the work situation.

The field of organization behavior has advanced a number of suggestions for improving the motivational properties of jobs. Invariably, the suggestions, termed *job design strategies,* attempt to improve job performance through changes in actual job characteristics. The next section reviews the more significant of these strategies.

Designing Job Range: Job Rotation and Job Enlargement

www.western
electric.com

www.Ford.com

www.TRW.com

www.Grey
hound.com

The earliest attempts to design jobs date to the scientific management era. Efforts at that time emphasized efficiency criteria. With that emphasis, the individual tasks that constitute a job are limited, uniform, and repetitive. This practice leads to narrow job range and, consequently, reported high levels of job discontent, turnover, absenteeism, and dissatisfaction. Accordingly, strategies were devised that resulted in wider job range through increasing the requisite activities of jobs. Two of these approaches are job rotation and job enlargement.

Job rotation

Job Rotation

Practice of moving individuals from job to job to reduce potential boredom and increase potential motivation and performance.

Managers of organizations such as Western Electric, Ford, Bethlehem Steel, TRW Systems, and Greyhound Financial Corporation have utilized different forms of the **job rotation** strategy.[30] This practice involves rotating managers and nonmanagers alike from one job to another. In so doing, the individual is expected to complete more job activities because each job includes different tasks.[31] Job rotation involves increasing the range of jobs and the perception of variety in the job content. Increasing task variety should, according to recent studies, increase employee satisfaction, reduce mental overload, decrease the number of errors due to fatigue, improve production and efficiency,[32] and reduce on-the-job injuries.[33] However, job rotation doesn't change the basic characteristics of the assigned jobs. Some relatively small firms have successfully used job rotation.

One relatively small manufacturer, Rohm & Haas Bayport, was founded in 1981 to produce specialty chemicals. The plant is located in LaPorte, Texas, and its 67 employees play active roles in management because their jobs are designed with that activity in mind. The company's philosophy is to provide autonomy and responsibility in each individual's job and, consequently, to enable employees to feel a sense of "ownership" of key decisions and actions. Every person in the organization is trained to be and to act like a manager. The 46 process technicians and 15 engineers and chemists report to one of the two manufacturing unit managers who in turn report to the executive team.

The technicians make operating decisions among themselves while working in teams of four to seven people. The company has no shift foremen or line supervisors in the usual sense of these positions. Rather, technicians are expected to be self-managed. Team members rotate jobs with other team members every 4 to 12 weeks to provide task variety and cross-training. They're also trained to do routine maintenance and repairs of their equipment and not to depend on a separate maintenance team for that support. The company's idea is to give individuals near complete control of the conditions that govern work pace and quality. They evaluate each other's performance and interview applicants for positions. Job designs at Rohm & Haas Bayport contribute to individual performance according to company spokespersons.[34]

Critics state that job rotation often involves nothing more than having people perform several boring and monotonous jobs rather than one. An alternative strategy is job enlargement.

Job enlargement

The pioneering Walker and Guest study[35] was concerned with the social and psychological problems associated with mass production jobs in automobile assembly plants. They found that many workers were dissatisfied with their highly specialized jobs. In particular, they disliked mechanical pacing, repetitiveness of operations, and a lack of a sense of accomplishment. Walker and Guest also found a positive relationship between job range and job satisfaction. Findings of this research gave early support for motivation theories that predict that increases in job range will increase job satisfaction and other objective job outcomes. **Job enlargement** strategies focus upon the opposite of dividing work—they're a form of despecialization or increasing the number of tasks that an employee performs. For example, a job is designed such that the individual performs six tasks instead of three.

Job Enlargement

Practice of increasing the number of tasks for which an individual is responsible. Increases job range, but not depth.

Although, in many instances, an enlarged job requires a longer training period, job satisfaction usually increases because boredom is reduced. The implication, of course, is that job enlargement will lead to improvement in other performance outcomes.

The concept and practice of job enlargement have become considerably more sophisticated. In recent years, effective job enlargement involves more than simply increasing task variety. In addition, it's necessary to design certain other aspects of job range, including providing worker-paced (rather than machine-paced) control. Each of these changes involves balancing the gains and losses of varying degrees of division of labor. Contemporary applications of job enlargement involve training individuals to perform several different jobs, each requiring considerable skill, whether in manufacturing or service organizations.

Some employees can't cope with enlarged jobs because they can't comprehend complexity; moreover, they may not have a sufficiently long attention span to complete an enlarged set of tasks. However, if employees are amenable to job enlargement and have the requisite ability, then job enlargement should increase satisfaction and product quality and decrease absenteeism and turnover. These gains aren't without costs, including the likelihood that employees will demand larger salaries in exchange for performing enlarged jobs. Yet these costs must be borne if management desires to implement the design strategy—job enrichment—that enlarges job depth. Job enlargement is a necessary precondition for job enrichment.

Designing Job Depth: Job Enrichment

The impetus for designing job depth was provided by Herzberg's two-factor theory of motivation. The basis of his theory is that factors that meet individuals' need for psychological growth (especially responsibility, job challenge, and achievement) must be characteristic of their jobs. The application of his theory is termed **job enrichment.**

Job Enrichment

Practice of increasing discretion individual can use to select activities and outcomes. Increases job depth and accordingly fulfills growth and autonomy needs.

The implementation of job enrichment is realized through direct changes in job depth. Managers can provide employees with greater opportunities to exercise discretion by making the following changes:

1. Direct feedback; the evaluation of performance should be timely and direct.
2. New learning; a good job enables people to feel that they are growing. All jobs should provide opportunities to learn.
3. Scheduling; people should be able to schedule some part of their own work.
4. Uniqueness; each job should have some unique qualities or features.
5. Control over resources; individuals should have some control over their job tasks.
6. Personal accountability; people should be provided with an opportunity to be accountable for the job.

The process as implemented in TI is continuous and pervades the entire organization. Every job in TI is viewed as subject to analysis to determine if it can be enriched to include managerial activities. Moreover, as the jobs of nonmanagerial personnel are designed to include greater depth, the jobs of managers must emphasize training and counseling of subordinates and de-emphasize control and direction.

As the theory and practice of job enrichment have evolved, managers have become aware that successful applications require numerous changes in how work is done. Important changes include giving workers greater authority to participate in decisions, to set their own goals, and to evaluate their (and their work group's) performance. Job enrichment also involves changing the nature and style of managers' behavior. Managers must be willing and able to delegate authority. Given employees' ability to carry out enriched jobs and managers' willingness to delegate authority, gains in performance can be expected. These positive outcomes are the result of increasing employees' expectations that efforts lead to performance, that performance leads to intrinsic and extrinsic rewards, and that these rewards have power to satisfy needs. These significant changes in managerial jobs when coupled with changes in nonmanagerial jobs suggest that a supportive work environment is a prerequisite for successful job enrichment efforts.

Job enrichment and job enlargement aren't competing strategies. Job enlargement may be compatible with the needs, values, and abilities of some individuals, while job enrichment may not. Yet job enrichment, when appropriate, necessarily involves job enlargement. A promising new approach to job design that attempts to integrate the two approaches is the job characteristic model. Hackman, Oldham, Janson, and Purdy devised the approach, basing it on the *Job Diagnostic Survey.*[36]

The model attempts to account for the interrelationships among (1) certain job characteristics, (2) psychological states associated with motivation, satisfaction, and performance, (3) job outcomes, and (4) growth need strength. Figure 14–3 describes the relationships among these variables. Although variety, identity, significance, autonomy, and feedback don't completely describe perceived job content, according to this model they sufficiently describe those aspects that management can manipulate to bring about gains in productivity.

Steps that management can take to increase the core dimensions include

1. Combining task elements.
2. Assigning whole pieces of work (i.e., **work modules**).
3. Allowing discretion in selection of work methods.
4. Permitting self-paced control.
5. Opening feedback channels.

Work Modules

Whole pieces of work assigned to individuals.

These actions increase task variety, identity, and significance; consequently, the "experienced meaningfulness of work" psychological state is increased. By permitting employee participation and self-evaluation and by creating autonomous work groups, the feedback and autonomy dimensions are increased along with the psychological states "experienced responsibility" and "knowledge of actual results."

Implementing the job characteristics in a particular situation begins with a study of existing job perceptions by means of the Job Description Survey. Hackman and Oldham have reported numerous applications of the model in a variety of organizations.[37] They

Figure 14–3

The Job Characteristics Model

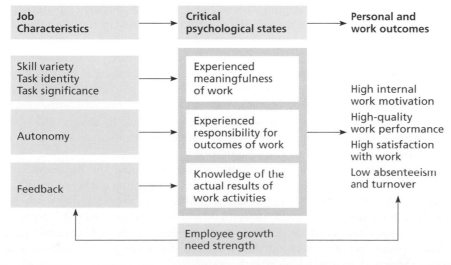

Source: J. Richard Hackman and Greg R. Oldham, "Development of the Job Diagnostic Survey," *Journal of Applied Psychology,* 1975, pp. 159–70.

have also compiled normative data for a variety of job categories so that managers and practitioners can compare the responses of their own employees to those of a larger population.[38] Although the track record of job design efforts is generally positive, some caveats are warranted.

The positive benefits of these efforts are moderated by individual differences in the strength of employees' growth needs. That is, employees with strong need for accomplishment, learning, and challenge will respond more positively than those with relatively weak growth needs. In more familiar terms, employees with high need for self-esteem and self-actualization are the more likely candidates for job design. Employees who are forced to participate in job design programs but who lack either the need strength or the ability to perform designed jobs may experience stress, anxiety, adjustment problems, erratic performance, turnover, and absenteeism.

The available research on the interrelationships between perceived job content and performance is meager. It's apparent, however, that managers must cope with significant problems in matching employee needs and differences and organizational needs.[39]

Problems associated with job design include:

1. The program is time-consuming and costly.

2. Unless lower-level needs are satisfied, people will not respond to opportunities to satisfy upper-level needs. And even though our society has been rather successful in providing food and shelter, these needs regain importance when the economy moves through periods of recession and high inflation.

3. Job design programs are intended to satisfy needs typically not satisfied in the workplace. As workers are told to expect higher order need satisfaction, they may raise their expectations beyond what's possible. Dissatisfaction with the program's unachievable aim may displace dissatisfaction with the jobs.

4. Job design may be resisted by labor unions who see the effort as an attempt to get more work for the same pay.

5. Job design efforts may not produce tangible performance improvements for some time after the beginning of the effort. One study indicated that significant improvements in effectiveness couldn't be seen until four years after the beginning of the job design program.[40]

www.volvo.com

Practical efforts to improve productivity and satisfaction through job design have emphasized autonomy and feedback as described in the Close-Up featuring the experience of Volvo. Relatively less emphasis has been placed on identity, significance, and variety. Apparently, it's easier to provide individuals with greater responsibility for the total task and increased feedback than to change the essential nature of the task itself. To provide identity, significance, and variety often requires enlarging the task to the point of losing the benefits of work simplification and standardization. But within the economic constraints imposed by the logic of specialization, it's possible to design work so as to give individuals complete responsibility for its completion to the end and at the same time to provide supportive managerial monitoring.

In general, one reaches two conclusions when considering the experience of job design approaches. First, they're relatively successful in increasing quality of output. This conclusion pertains, however, only if the reward system already satisfies lower-level needs. If it presently doesn't satisfy lower-level needs, employees can't be expected to experience upper-level need satisfaction (intrinsic rewards) through enriched jobs. In particular, managers can't expect individuals with relatively low growth needs to respond as would those with relatively high growth needs.[41]

Successful efforts are the result of the circumstances that initiate the effort and the process undertaken to manage the effort. Organizations under external pressure to change have a better chance of successfully implementing job design than those not under such pressure. Moreover, successful efforts are accompanied by broad-scale participation of managers and employees alike. Since a primary source of organizational effectiveness is job performance, managers should design jobs according to the best available knowledge.[42]

Total Quality Management and Job Design

TQM, according to those who espouse and practice it, combines technical knowledge and human knowledge. To deal with the inherent complexity and variability of production and service delivery technology, people must be empowered with authority to make necessary decisions and must be enabled with knowledge to know when to exercise that authority. Aspects of TQM job designs have appeared throughout this discussion. We've discussed job enrichment including provision of autonomy, creation of work modules, and development of trust and collaboration. We've seen these attributes of jobs in the practices of organizations discussed throughout this chapter. But even as we close this chapter, we must raise a fundamental question: Can American workers adjust to the requirements for working together in teams and in collaboration with management? Are the ideas of TQM totally applicable to the

CLOSE—UP

Job Redesign through Applications of Modular Tasks

A cardinal principle of task redesign theory as well as sociotechnical theory requires combining technical and social attributes of tasks. Volvo and other European organizations have lead the way in this endeavor. A leading proponent of job redesign, Pehr Gyllenhammar, joined Volvo in 1971 as managing director when performance indicators such as productivity, absenteeism, and turnover were unsatisfactory. Gyllenhammar took a keen interest in the experiments of Ingvar Barrby, head of the upholstery department, in job rotation (termed job alternation in Volvo). The reduction in turnover from 35 percent to 15 percent encouraged the new managing director to adopt other aspects of job redesign. For example, group management and work modules are used at the Torslanda car assembly plant. Employees, in groups, follow the same auto body for seven or eight workstations along the line for a total period of 20 minutes.

Job redesign at Volvo reached a major milestone when the Kalmar, Sweden, assembly plant opened. Gyllenhammar had been personally and visibly behind the design and construction phases of the new plant to assure that opportunities to provide job enrichment were part of the physical and technological layout. The plant incorporates a technology of assembly in which overhead carriers move the auto body, chassis, and subassemblies to assembly team areas. There, work teams of 20 to 25 employees complete major segments of auto assembly: electrical systems, instrumentation, finishing, and so on. Each group is responsible for a whole piece of work; it functions as an autonomous unit much as those at the truck assembly plant.

Sources: Melissa Larson, "Knowing More Earlier: Profiles in Quality," *Quality*, April 1998, pp. 48–52; Gerben Van der Vegt, Ben Emans, and Evert Van de Vliert, "Motivating Effects of Task and Outcome Interdependence on Work Teams," *Group and Organization Management*, June 1998, 124–43; and Tomas Engstrom and Lars Medbo, "Intra-Group Work Patterns in Final Assembly of Motor Vehicles," *International Journal of Operations and Production Management* vol. 14, no. 3 (1994), pp. 101–113.

American worker? Is TQM the wave of the future? Do American managers have the ability and commitment to implement the necessary changes in jobs required by new technologies and new global realities?[43] Many contemporary observers warn us that the answers to all these questions must be yes because no other choice exists.[44]

Job design strategy focuses on jobs in the context of individuals' needs for economic well-being and personal growth. But let's put the issue in a broader framework and include the issue of the sociotechnical system. Sociotechnical theory focuses on interactions between technical demands of jobs and social demands of people doing the jobs. The theory emphasizes that too great an emphasis on the technical system in the manner of scientific management or too great an emphasis on the social system in the manner of human relations will lead to poor job design. Rather, job design should take into account both the technology and the people who use the technology.

Sociotechnical theory and application of job design developed from studies undertaken in English coal mines from 1948 to 1958.[45] The studies became widely publicized for demonstrating the interrelationship between the social system and the technical system of organizations. The interrelationship was revealed when economic circumstances forced management to change how coal was mined (the technical system). Historically, the technical system consisted of small groups of miners (the social system) working together on "short faces" (seams of coal). But technological advancement improved roof control and safety and made longwall mining possible. The new technical system required a change in the social system. The groups would be disbanded in favor of one-person, one-task jobs. Despite the efforts of management and even the union, miners eventually devised a social system that restored many characteristics of the group system. This experience has been completely described in organizational behavior literature and has stimulated a great deal of research and application.

There's no contradiction between sociotechnical theory and total quality management. In fact, the two approaches are quite compatible. The compatibility relates to the demands of modern technology for self-directed and self-motivated job behavior. Such job behavior is made possible in jobs designed to provide autonomy and variety. As worked out in practice, such jobs are parts of self-regulating work teams responsible for completing whole tasks. The work module concept pervades applications of sociotechnical theory.[46] One of the most publicized applications of sociotechnical design theory has been ongoing in Volvo Corporation, as the Close-Up on page 365 relates.

www.sherwin-williams.com

www.quakeroats.com

Numerous applications of sociotechnical design and total quality management are reported in the literature.[47] Some notable American examples include the Sherwin-Williams Paint factory in Richmond, Kentucky, and the Quaker Oats pet food factory in Topeka, Kansas. Both factories were constructed from the ground up to include and allow for specific types of jobs embodying basic elements of autonomy and empowerment. Firms that don't have the luxury of building the plant from scratch must find ways to renovate both their technology and their job designs to utilize the best technology and people. Some of the most influential industrial and service organizations have confronted the necessity to design jobs to take advantage of the rapid pace of technological advance. In the contemporary global environment, sociotechnical system design has been incorporated in the total quality management approach to management.

Summary of Key Points

- Job design involves managerial decisions and actions that specify objective job depth, range, and relationships to satisfy organizational requirements as well as the social and personal requirements of jobholders.

- Contemporary managers must consider the issue of quality of work life when designing jobs. This issue reflects society's concern for work experiences that contribute to employees' personal growth and development.

- Strategies for increasing jobs' potential to satisfy the social and personal requirements of jobholders have gone through an evolutionary process. Initial efforts were directed toward job rotation and job enlargement. These strategies produced some gains in job satisfaction but didn't change primary motivators such as responsibility, achievement, and autonomy.

- During the 1960s, job enrichment became a widely recognized strategy for improving quality of work life factors. This strategy is based upon Herzberg's motivation theory and involves increasing jobs' depth through greater delegation of authority to jobholders. Despite some major successes, job enrichment isn't universally applicable because it doesn't consider individual differences.

- Individual differences are now recognized as crucial variables to consider when designing jobs. Experience, cognitive complexity, needs, values, valences, and perceptions of equity are some of the individual differences influencing jobholders' reactions to the scope and relationships of their jobs. When individual differences are combined with environmental, situational, and managerial differences, job design decisions become increasingly complex.

- The most recently developed strategy of job design emphasizes the importance of core job characteristics as perceived by jobholders. Although measurements of individual differences remain a problem, managers should be encouraged to examine ways to increase positive perceptions of variety, identity, significance, autonomy, and feedback. By doing so, the potential for high-quality work performance and high job satisfaction is increased given that jobholders possess relatively high growth need strength.

- Many organizations including Volvo, Citibank, General Motors, and General Foods have attempted job design with varying degrees of success. The current state of research knowledge is inadequate for making broad generalizations regarding exact causes of success and failure in applications of job design. Managers must diagnose their own situations to determine the applicability of job design in their organizations.

- Sociotechnical theory combines technological and social issues in job design practice. Sociotechnical theory is compatible with job design strategy and in fact emphasizes the practical necessity to design jobs that provide autonomy, feedback, significance, identity, and variety.

- Total quality management (TQM) combines the ideas of job enrichment and sociotechnical theory. Managers who implement TQM design jobs that empower individuals to make important decisions about product/service quality. The empowerment process encourages participative management, team-oriented task modules, and autonomy.

Discussion and Review Questions

1. Do you believe that American workers will accept the idea that they must work together in groups and receive group-based rewards rather than working as individuals and receiving individual-based rewards? Explain your reasoning.

2. Explain the differences between job rotation and job enrichment and analyze the relative advantages of these two approaches in organizations you have worked for.

3. What is the significance of the idea of quality of work life (QWL)? In particular what would seem to be the trade-offs between meaningful jobs and productive jobs during periods of declining economic activity and unemployment?

4. What in your experience are the fundamental differences between factory jobs and office jobs and how do these differences relate to the application of job design practices?

5. What characteristics of jobs can't be enriched? Do you believe that management should ever consider any job to be incapable of enrichment?

6. Explain the relationships between feedback as a job content factor and personal goal setting. Is personal goal setting possible without feedback? Explain.

7. This chapter has described job designs in various service and manufacturing organizations. In which type of organization is job enrichment likely to be more effective as a strategy of increasing motivation and performance? Explain.

8. Explain which core dimension you now value most highly. Rank their order of importance to you.

9. Is it possible for American auto assembly plants to adopt job design strategies similar to those adopted in the Volvo plants? Explain.

10. As you understand the idea and practice of total quality management, do you believe that it's the wave of the future in American organizations? Explain.

Work Redesign in an Insurance Company

The executive staff of a relatively small life insurance company is considering a proposal to install an electronic data processing system. The proposal is being presented by the assistant to the president, John Skully. He has been studying the feasibility of the equipment after a management consultant recommended a complete overhaul of jobs within the company.

The management consultant had been engaged by the company to diagnose the causes of high turnover and absenteeism. After reviewing the situation and speaking with groups of employees, the consultant recommended that the organization structure be changed from a functional to a client basis. The change in departmental basis would enable management to redesign jobs to reduce the human costs associated with highly specialized tasks.

The present organization includes separate departments to issue policies, collect premiums, change beneficiaries, and process loan applications. Employees in these departments complained that their jobs were boring, insignificant, and monotonous. They had stated that the only reason they stayed with the company was because they liked the small-company atmosphere. They felt that management had a genuine interest in their welfare but that the trivial nature of their jobs contradicted that feeling. As one employee said, "This company is small enough to know almost everybody. But the job I do is so boring that I wonder why they even need me to do it." This and similar comments had led the consultant to believe that the jobs must be altered to provide greater motivation. Recognizing that work redesign opportunities were limited by the organization structure, he recommended that the company change to a client basis. In such a structure, each employee would handle every transaction related to a particular policyholder.

When the consultant presented his views to the members of the executive staff, they were very much interested in his recommendation. In fact, they agreed that his recommendation was well founded. They noted, however, that a small company must pay particular attention to deficiency in handling transactions. The functional basis enabled the organization to achieve the degree of specialization necessary for efficient operations. The manager of internal operations stated, "If we move away from specialization, the rate of efficiency must go down because we'll

lose the benefit of specialized effort. The only way we can justify redesigning the jobs as suggested by the consultant is to maintain our efficiency; otherwise, there won't be any jobs to redesign because we'll be out of business."

The internal operations manager explained to the executive staff that despite excessive absenteeism and turnover, he was able to maintain acceptable productivity. The narrow range and depth of the jobs reduced training time to a minimum. It was also possible to hire temporary help to meet peak loads and to fill in for absent employees. "Moreover," he said, "changing the jobs our people do means that we must change the jobs our managers do. They're experts in their own functional areas, but we've never attempted to train them to oversee more than two operations."

A majority of the executive staff believed that the consultant's recommendations should be seriously considered. At that point, the group directed John Skully to evaluate the potential of electronic data processing (EDP) as a means of obtaining efficient operations in combination with the redesigned jobs. He has completed the study and is presenting his report to the executive staff.

"The bottom line," Skully says, "is that EDP will enable us to maintain our present efficiency, but with the redesigned jobs we won't obtain any greater gains. If my analysis is correct, we'll have to absorb the cost of the equipment out of earnings, because there will be no cost savings. So it comes down to what price we're willing and able to pay for improving the satisfaction of our employees."

Discussion Questions

1. Explain which core characteristics of employees' jobs will be changed if the consultant's recommendations are accepted.

2. Which alternative redesign strategies should be considered? For example, job rotation and job enlargement are possible alternatives. What are the relevant considerations for these and other designs in the context of this company?

3. What would be your decision in this case? What should management be willing to pay for employees' satisfaction? Defend your answer.

E X P E R I E N T I A L   E X E R C I S E

Personal Preferences

Objectives

1. To illustrate individual differences in preferences about various job design characteristics.

2. To illustrate how your preferences may differ from those of others.

3. To examine the most important and least impor-tant job design characteristics and how managers cope with them.

Related Topics

This exercise is related to intrinsic and extrinsic rewards. The job design characteristics considered could be viewed as either intrinsic or extrinsic job issues.

JOB DESIGN PREFERENCES

A.   Your Job Design Preferences

Decide which of the following characteristics is most important to you. Place a *1* in front of the most important characteristic. Then decide which characteristic is the second most important to you and place a *2* in front of it. Continue numbering the items in order of importance until the least important is ranked *10*. There are no right answers, since individuals differ in the job design preferences. Do not discuss your individual rankings until the instructor forms groups.

_____ Variety in tasks
_____ Feedback on performance from doing the job
_____ Autonomy
_____ Working as a team
_____ Responsibility
_____ Developing friendships on the job
_____ Task identity
_____ Task significance
_____ Having the resources to perform well
_____ Feedback on performance from others (e.g., the manager, co-workers)

B.   Others' Job Design Preferences

In the A section, you provided your job design preferences. Now number the items as you think others would rank them. Consider others who are in your course or program—that is, who are also completing this exercise. Rank the factors from *1* (most important) to *10* (least important).

_____ Variety in tasks
_____ Feedback on performance from doing the job
_____ Autonomy
_____ Working as a team
_____ Responsibility
_____ Developing friendships on the job
_____ Task identity
_____ Task significance
_____ Having the resources to perform well
_____ Feedback on performance from others (e.g., the manager, co-workers)

Starting the Exercise

First, you'll respond to a questionnaire asking about your job design preferences and how you view the preferences of others. After you've worked through the questionnaire *individually*, small groups will be formed. In the groups, discussion will focus on the individual differences in preferences expressed by group members.

The Facts

Job design is concerned with a number of attributes of a job. Among them are the job itself, the requirements of the job, the interpersonal interaction opportunities on the job, and performance outcomes. Individuals prefer certain attributes: some prefer job autonomy, while others prefer to be challenged by different tasks. Obviously, individual differences in preferences would be an important consideration for managers. An exciting job for one person may be a demeaning and boring job for another person. Managers could use this information in attempting to create job design conditions that match organizational goals with individual goals and preferences.

Read and complete the accompanying Job Design Preferences form after considering each of the characteristics listed. Due to space limitations, not all job design characteristics are included for your consideration. Use only those included on the form.

Completing the Exercise

Phase I: 15 minutes. Individually complete the A and B portions of the Job Design Preferences form.

Phase II: 30 minutes.

1. The instructor will form groups of four to six students.

2. Discuss the differences in the ranking individuals made on the A and B parts of the form.

3. Present each of the A rank orders of group members on a flip chart or the blackboard. Analyze areas of agreement and disagreement.

4. Discuss what implications the A and B rankings would have to a *manager* who would have to supervise a group such as the one you're in. What could a manager do to cope with the individual differences displayed in the preceding steps?

Chapter 15

Designing Effective Organizations

Learning Objectives

Define

Organizational design.

Describe

The ways organizations can respond to the need to process information about their environments.

Discuss

The important conclusions from studies of the relationship among structure and technology, environmental uncertainty, and information processing demands.

Compare

The mechanistic and organic models of organization design.

Identify

The circumstances that would cause management to design an organization according to mechanistic or organic principles.

M anagers
must design effective organizations.
This critical responsibility refers to
the decisions they make that

determine the structure and processes that coordinate and control the jobs of the organization. The outcome of organizational design decisions is a system of jobs and work groups including processes that link them. These linking processes include authority relationships and communication networks in addition to specific planning and controlling techniques. In effect, *organizational design implies the creation of a superstructure within which the organization's work takes place.*

Organizational design has been at the core of managerial work since the earliest efforts to develop management theory. The importance of design decisions has stimulated a great deal of interest in the issue. Managers and organizational behavior theorists and researchers have contributed to what is now a considerable body of literature. The manager who faces the necessity of designing an organizational structure is at no loss for ideas. Quite the contrary, the literature of organizational design holds forth numerous conflicting ideas as to how an organization should be designed to optimize effectiveness.

Managers can design organizations to be more or less specialized, formalized, and centralized. As we will see throughout this chapter, the way management designs organizations must take into account these dimensions of organization structure. How they're combined has great impact on the effectiveness of individuals, groups, and the organization itself. Managers must consider numerous factors when designing the organization. Among the most important ones are technology, the nature of the work itself, the characteristics of people who'll do the work, the demands of the organization's environment, the necessity to receive and process information from that environment, and the overall strategy the organization chooses to relate to its environment.

To make some sense of this apparent complexity, the flow of the discussion is as follows. We'll first describe two general models of organization design: the mechanistic and the organic models. Next, we'll examine three important factors that managers must take into account when designing the structure: technology, environmental uncertainty, and information processing requirements. Finally, we'll integrate this and the previous two chapters' discussions in a model of organizational design.

Mechanistic and Organic Models of Organization Design

The two models of organizational design described in this section are important ideas in management theory and practice. Because of their importance, they receive considerable theoretical and practical attention. Despite this importance and attention, there's little uniformity in the use of terms that designate the two models. The two terms we use here, *mechanistic* and *organic,* are relatively descriptive of the important features of the models.[1]

The mechanistic model

A body of literature emerging during the early 20th century considered the problem of designing the structure of an organization as but one of a number of managerial tasks, including planning and controlling. These writers' objective was to define *principles* that could guide managers in performing their tasks. An early writer, Henri Fayol, proposed a number of principles that he had found useful in managing a large coal mining company in France.[2] Some of Fayol's principles dealt with the management function of organizing; four of these are relevant for understanding the mechanistic model.

1. *The principle of specialization.* Fayol stated that specialization is the best means for making use of individuals and groups of individuals. At the time of Fayol's writings, the limit of specialization (that is, the optimal point) had not been definitively determined. As the previous chapter showed, scientific management popularized a number of methods for implementing specialization of labor. These methods, such as work standards and motion and time study, emphasized technical (not behavioral) dimensions of work.

2. *The principle of unity of direction.* According to this principle, jobs should be grouped according to specialty. Engineers should be grouped with engineers, salespeople with salespeople, accountants with accountants. The departmentalization basis that most nearly implements this principle is the functional basis.

3. *The principle of authority and responsibility.* Fayol believed that a manager should be delegated sufficient authority to carry out her assigned responsibilities. Because the assigned responsibilities of top managers are considerably more important to the future of the organization than those of lower management, applying the principle inevitably leads to centralized authority. Centralized authority is a logical outcome not only because of top managements' larger responsibilities but also because work at this level is more complex, the number of workers involved is greater, and the relationship between actions and results is remote.

4. *The scalar chain principle.* The natural result of implementing the preceding three principles is a graded chain of managers from the ultimate authority to the lowest ranks. The scalar chain is the route for all vertical communications in an organization. Accordingly, all communications from the lowest level must pass through each superior in the chain of command. Correspondingly, communication from the top must pass through each subordinate until it reaches the appropriate level.

Fayol's writings became part of a literature that, although each contributor made unique contributions, had a common thrust. Writers such as Mooney and Reiley,[3] Follet,[4] and Urwick[5] all shared the common objective of defining the principles that should guide the design and management of organizations. A complete review of their individual contributions won't be attempted here. However, we'll review the ideas of one individual, Max Weber, who made important contributions to the mechanistic model. He described applications of the mechanistic model and coined the term *bureaucracy.*

BUREAUCRACY   *Bureaucracy* has various meanings. The traditional usage is the political science concept of government by bureaus but without participation by the governed. In laymen's terms, bureaucracy refers to the negative consequences of large organizations, such as excessive red tape, procedural delays, and general frustration.[6] But in Max Weber's writings, bureaucracy refers to a particular way to organize collective activities.[7] Weber's interest in bureaucracy reflected his concern for the ways society develops hierarchies of control so that one group can, in effect, dominate other groups. Organizational design involves domination in the sense that authority involves the legitimate right to exact obedience from others. His search for the forms of domination that evolve in society led him to the study of bureaucratic structure.

According to Weber, the bureaucratic structure is

"superior to any other form in precision, in stability, in the stringency of its discipline and its reliability. It thus makes possible a high degree of calculability of results for the heads of the organization and for those acting in relation to it."[8]

The bureaucracy compares to other organizations "as does the machine with nonmechanical modes of production."[9] These words capture the essence of the mechanistic model of organizational design.

To achieve the maximum benefits of the bureaucratic design, Weber believed that an organization must have the following characteristics.

1. All tasks will be divided into highly specialized jobs. Through specialization, jobholders become expert in their jobs, and management can hold them responsible for the effective performance of their duties.

2. Each task is performed according to a system of abstract rules to ensure uniformity and coordination of different tasks. The rationale for this practice is that the manager can eliminate uncertainty in task performance due to individual differences.

3. Each member or office of the organization is accountable for job performance to one, and only one, manager. Managers hold their authority because of their expert knowledge and because it's delegated from the top of the hierarchy. An unbroken chain of command exists.

4. Each employee of the organization relates to other employees and clients in an impersonal, formal manner, maintaining a social distance with subordinates and clients. The purpose of this practice is to assure that personalities and favoritism do not interfere with efficient accomplishment of the organization's objectives.

5. Employment in the bureaucratic organization is based on technical qualifications and is protected against arbitrary dismissal. Similarly, promotions are based on seniority and achievement. Employment in the organization is viewed as a lifelong career, and a high degree of loyalty is engendered.

These five characteristics of bureaucracy describe the kind of organizations Fayol believed to be most effective. Both Fayol and Weber described the same type of organization, one that functions in a machinelike manner to accomplish the organization's goals in a highly efficient manner. Thus, the term **mechanistic** aptly describes such organizations.

Mechanistic Model

Organizational design empasizing importance of achieving high levels of production and efficiency through extensive use of rules and procedures, centralized authority, and high specialization of labor.

The mechanistic model achieves high levels of production and efficiency due to its structural characteristics:

1. It's highly complex because of its emphasis on specialization of labor.
2. It's highly centralized because of its emphasis on authority and accountability.
3. It's highly formalized because of its emphasis on function as the basis for departments.

www.ups.com

These organizational characteristics and practices underlie a widely used organizational model. One of the more successful practitioners of the mechanistic model has been United Parcel Service (UPS).[10] This profitable delivery firm competes directly with the U.S. Post Office in the delivery of small packages. Even though the Post Office is subsidized and pays no taxes, UPS has been able to compete successfully by stressing efficiency of operations. It apparently achieves great efficiencies through a combination of automation and organization design. Specialization and formalization are highly visible characteristics of UPS structure. UPS uses clearly defined jobs and an explicit chain of command. The tasks range from truck washers and maintenance personnel to top management and are arranged in a hierarchy of authority consisting of eight managerial levels. The high degree of specialization enables management to use many forms of written reports such as daily worksheets that record each employee's work quotas and performance. Company policies and practices are in written form and routinely consulted in hiring and promotion decisions. Apparently, UPS has found the mechanistic form of organization to be well suited for its purposes.

UPS has more than 1,000 industrial engineers on its payroll. Their job is to design jobs and to set the standards that specify the way UPS employees do their jobs. For example, engineers instruct drivers to walk to the customer's door at the rate of three feet per second and to knock on the door. Company management believes that the standards aren't just a way to obtain efficiency and production but also are a means to provide the employee with important feedback on how he's doing the job. All in all, the company's efficiency bears testimony to its use of mechanistic design principles.

The organic model

Organic Model

Organizational design emphasizing importance of achieving high levels of flexibility and development through limited use of rules and procedures, decentralized authority, and relatively low degrees of specializaton.

The **organic model** of organizational design stands in sharp contrast to the mechanistic model due to their different organizational characteristics and practices. The most distinct differences between the two models are a consequence of the different effectiveness criteria each seeks to maximize. While the mechanistic model seeks to maximize efficiency and production, the organic model seeks to maximize satisfaction, flexibility, and development.

The organic organization is flexible to changing environmental demands because its design encourages greater utilization of the human potential. Managers are encouraged to adopt practices that tap the full range of human motivations through job design that stresses personal growth and responsibility. Decision making, control, and goal-setting processes are decentralized and shared at all levels of the organization. Communications flow throughout the organization, not simply down the chain of command. These practices are intended to implement a basic assumption of the organic model that states that an organization will be effective to the extent that its structure is

"such as to ensure a maximum probability that in all interactions and in all relationships with the organization, each member, in the light of his background, values, desires, and expectations, will view the experience as supportive and one which builds and maintains a sense of personal worth and importance."[11]

An organizational design that provides individuals with this sense of personal worth and motivation and that facilitates satisfaction, flexibility, and development would have the following characteristics:

1. It's relatively simple because of its de-emphasis of specialization and its emphasis on increasing job range.
2. It's relatively decentralized because of its emphasis on delegation of authority and increasing job depth.
3. It's relatively informal because of its emphasis on product and customer as bases for departments.

A leading spokesperson and developer of ideas supporting applications of the organic model is Rensis Likert. His studies at the University of Michigan have led him to argue that organic organizations (Likert uses the term *System-4*) differ markedly from mechanistic organizations (Likert uses the term *System-1*) along a number of structural dimensions. The important differences are shown in Table 15–1.

The literature is filled with reports of efforts to implement organic designs in actual organizations.[12] Likert himself reports many of these studies. One organization has received considerable attention for its efforts to implement organic principles. Aid Association for Lutherans (AAL) operates a huge insurance business. It has transformed its organization from a mechanistic to an organic structure in an effort to take advantage of benefits of the *self-directed team* concept. Prior to reorganization, AAL was organized

 www.aal.org

PROCESS	MECHANISTIC STRUCTURE	ORGANIC STRUCTURE	
1. Leadership	Includes no perceived confidence and trust. Subordinates do not feel free to discuss job problems with their superiors, who in turn do not solicit their ideas and opinions.	Includes perceived confidence and trust between superiors and subordinates in all matters. Subordinates feel free to discuss job problems with their superiors, who in turn solicit their ideas and opinions.	**Table 15–1** Comparison of Mechanistic and Organic Structures
2. Motivation	Taps only physical, security, and economic motives, through the use of fear and sanctions. Unfavorable attitudes toward the organization prevail among employees.	Taps a full range of motives through participatory methods. Attitudes are favorable toward the organization and its goals.	
3. Communication	Information flows downward and tends to be distorted, inaccurate, and viewed with suspicion by subordinates.	Information flows freely throughout the organization: upward, downward, and laterally. The information is accurate and undistorted.	
4. Interaction	Closed and restricted. Subordinates have little effect on departmental goals, methods, and activities.	Open and extensive. Both superiors and subordinates are able to affect departmental goals, methods, and activities.	
5. Decision	Relatively centralized. Occurs only at the top of the organization.	Relatively decentralized. Occurs at all levels through group process.	
6. Goal setting	Located at the top of the organization, discouraging group participation.	Encourages group participation in setting high, realistic objectives.	
7. Control	Centralized. Emphasizes fixing of blame for mistakes.	Dispersed throughout the organization. Emphasizes self-control and problem solving.	
8. Performance goals	Low and passively sought by managers, who make no commitment to developing the organization's human resources.	High and actively sought by superiors, who recognize the need for full commitment to developing, through training, the organization's human resources.	

Source: Adapted from Rensis Likert, *The Human Organization* (New York: McGraw-Hill, 1967), pp. 197–211.

mechanistically according to the traditional functions of the insurance industry, and employees were highly trained to deal with processing, underwriting, valuations, and premium services functions. Specialization resulted in considerable efficiency dealing with customers requiring the attention of one of the functions. But when multiple functions were involved, the organization became bogged down.

AAL's management explored potential benefits of establishing teams of employees that could handle all details of any customer transaction, whether health, life, or casualty insurance. The teams consist of individuals who once were responsible for functions; now they're responsible for customers and take initiative that once required management prodding. As a result of teams' assumption of responsibility for their own management, three levels of management have been eliminated from the organization. The organization is now simpler and more decentralized than before and, therefore, more organic and less mechanistic.

AAL also implemented a form of employee compensation termed pay for knowledge to encourage employees to adopt the new work system. It provides individuals with pay increases for obtaining additional knowledge that enables them to improve their job performance. In the context of AAL's organic organization, employees needed to learn not only new technical knowledge but also new interpersonal knowledge because working with other individuals in teams is critical to the success of the new organizational design.[13]

There is, likewise, no question that proponents of the organic organization believe it is universally applicable; that is, the theory is proposed as the "one best way" to design an organization. In this regard, proponents of both the mechanistic and organic models are equally zealous in their advocacy.

Contingency Design Theories

The demands of a situation are termed *contingencies*. Accordingly, neither the mechanistic nor the organic is necessarily the more effective organization design; either can be better depending on the situation. The contingency point of view provides opportunity to get away from the dilemma of choosing between mechanistic and organic models. As such, it's an evolution of ideas whose bases are found in the work of earlier writers.

Contingency Design Theory

Organizational design approach that emphasizes the importance of fitting a design to demands of a situation, including technology, environmental uncertainty, and management choice.

The essence of the **contingency design theory** approach is expressed by the question: Under what circumstances and in what situations is either the mechanistic or the organic design relatively more effective? The answer requires the manager to specify the contingencies in a situation that influence a particular design's relative effectiveness. Obviously, the contingency approach is quite complicated because of the necessity to consider so many contingencies, technology being one of the more important ones.

Technology and Organizational Design

Technology

Physical and mental actions by an individual to change the form or content of an object or idea.

The effects of **technology** on organization structure can be readily understood at an abstract level of analysis. Although various definitions of technology exist, it's generally understood as "the *actions* that an individual performs upon an object with or without the aid of tools or mechanical devices, in order to make *some change* in that object."[14] Thus, organization structures reflect technology in the ways that jobs are designed (the division of labor) and grouped (departmentalization). In this sense, the current state of knowledge regarding the appropriate actions to change an object acts as a constraint on management.

In recent years, the state of technological knowledge has increased exponentially as computers and robots have entered the workplace. One effect of this new knowledge has been to increase managers' interest in the relationship between organization structure and technology.

The organization theory literature includes a number of studies that examine the relationship between technology and organization structure. We can't possibly survey all these studies here—it would take considerable space and would go beyond the intent of our discussion. Rather, we'll briefly review the classic study that stimulated a number of follow-up studies and has become important in the literature of organizational design.

The classic study of technology and organizational design

Joan Woodward gained considerable notoriety when she released the findings of analyses of 100 manufacturing firms' organization structures in southern England.[15] While she and her colleagues had sought to answer a number of questions regarding contributions of organization structure to organizational effectiveness, it was their conclusions regarding technology and structure that are widely acclaimed.

She and her team of researchers had set out to determine if there were structural differences between the more and less effective firms. They used a number of measures of effectiveness to classify firms into three categories: above average, average, and below average. But when they compared organization structures within each category, no consistent pattern emerged. It was then that the team began analyzing the information relating to technology, "the methods and processes of manufacture."[16] The team measured technology in terms of three related variables:

(1) stages in the historical development of production processes, (2) the interrelationship between the items of equipment used for these processes, and (3) the extent to which the operations performed in the processes were repetitive or comparable from one production cycle or sequence to the next."[17]

Applying the measure to information about the firm's manufacturing methods resulted in a continuum of technology with job-order manufacturing and process manufacturing methods at the extremes, separated by mass-production manufacturing.

The research team classified firms according to the three categories of technology. It then discovered that the organizational structures of firms within each category were different in comparison to other categories. The important differences were:[18]

1. Organizations at each end of the continuum were more flexible; that is, they resembled the organic model with job duties and responsibilities being less clearly defined. Organizations in the middle of the continuum were more specialized and formalized; that is, they resembled the mechanistic model.

2. Organizations at each end of the continuum made greater use of verbal than written communications; organizations in the middle made greater use of written communications and were more formalized. This pattern is also consistent with distinctions between organic and mechanistic models of design.

3. Managerial positions were more highly specialized in mass production than in either job order or process manufacturing. First-level supervisors engaged primarily in direct supervision, leaving technical decisions to staff personnel. In contrast, managers in job order firms were expected to have greater technical expertise, while managers in process manufacturing were expected to have greater scientific expertise.

4. Consistent with the preceding point, actual control of production in the form of schedule making and routing was separated from supervision of production in mass production firms. The two managerial functions were more highly integrated in the role of the first-level supervisor in organizations at the extremes of the continuum.

Thus, the data indicated sharp organizational differences due to technological differences.

Understanding the relationship between technology and structure

The relationship between technology and organizations can be understood with reference to the natural business functions: product development, production, and marketing. The job order firm produces according to customer specifications; the firm must secure the order, develop the product, and manufacture it. The cycle begins with marketing and ends with production.

This sequence requires the firm to be especially adept at sensing market changes and adjusting to them. But more importantly, the product development function holds the key to the firm's success. This function must convert customer specifications into products that are acceptable to both the customer and the production personnel. Various approaches exist to facilitate the kinds of interactions and communication patterns required to meet the market and product development problems associated with job order or unit production. The more complicated ones involve interactions better managed in organic-type structures.

At the other extreme of the technological continuum is the process manufacturer. In these firms, the cycle begins with product development. The key to success is the ability to discover a new product through scientific research—a new chemical, gasoline additive, or fabric—that can be produced by already existing facilities or by new facilities once a market is established. The development, marketing, and production functions in process manufacturing all tend to demand scientific personnel and specialized competence at the highest levels in the organization. Since these firms' success depends upon adjustment to new scientific knowledge, the organic design is more effective than the mechanistic design.

The mechanistic design is effective for firms that use mass production technology. The market exists for a more or less standardized product—autos, foods, clothing—and the task is to manufacture the product through fairly routine means, efficiently and economically. Workers tend machines designed and paced by engineering standards. Actual control of the work flow is separated from supervision of the workforce. In such organizations, the ideas of scientific management and mechanistic design are applicable.

This explanation of the relationship between technology and structure rests on traditional views of manufacturing technology. Recent advances in computers and robots have initiated new understanding of manufacturing possibilities and organization structures that are compatible with those advances.

Flexible Manufacturing Technology (FMT)

Modern manufacturing methods that combine computer and robotics to achieve high levels of production and flexibility

Flexible manufacturing technology and organizational design

Flexible manufacturing technology (FMT) enables management to use the computer to integrate marketing, design, manufacturing, inventory control, materials handling, and quality control into a continuous operation.[19] The effect of this technology is to increase the flexibility of manufacturing through the ability to transfer information, material, and other resources throughout the organization, to design products quickly in consultation with customers, manufacturing personnel, and marketing personnel, and to set up machines to manufacture only the needed quantity of parts and components, thus reducing the need for inventory.

Flexible manufacturing technology makes it possible to combine the positive attributes of job order, mass production, and process technology in ways that weren't previously contemplated. FMT's major effect on organization structure is to challenge the case for mechanistic designs in mass production firms. FMT in mass production settings creates managerial problems similar to those in job order and process manufacturing settings. The principal managerial problem is to manage interdependent activities that must respond to rapidly changing conditions. But the possibilities are unlimited including the ability to be more responsive to changing customer needs and preferences.[20] Organic structures begin to emerge as the preferred structure among mass producers that have moved into the flexible manufacturing era. A notable example of the successful implementation of FMT and reorganization to achieve startling increases in effectiveness has been Ford Motor Company. The Close-Up summarizes this firm's experience.

The paradox of FMT and other evolutionary developments in manufacturing is that it enables parts of the company to become more independent of one another even as they become more dependent.[21] This paradox emphasizes the importance of integrating the activities of these interdependent, yet independent, units. Integration is a key element in the relationship between environmental uncertainty and organizational design.

CLOSE — UP

Organizing for Innovative Product Development at Ford Motor Company

Ford Motor Company has attracted international attention as it turned from traditional mechanistic organization design toward a more organic one. To make this transformation Ford had to undertake significant changes in the way it manages its employees as well as in how it builds its cars to attain this respect. But even with this hard-earned respect, as the company moved into the 1990s it had reason to be concerned.

One of the biggest changes has been in the way employees perform their jobs. Jobs at Ford have become less specialized with greater depth and range. Nonmanagerial personnel now perform tasks once reserved for managers, such as scheduling production and ensuring quality. They work in teams under the general supervision of managers who've been trained in the development of teamwork. The training of Ford managers has focused on their becoming more flexible and adaptable to change. The corporation has acknowledged that change has become commonplace for the business, so change must also become

commonplace for its employees. The recognition of change as routine meant that managers and employees would have to be trained in managing change within an organic organization structure that differed markedly from the mechanistic structure of the past.

Although Ford has responded to many different factors that required change in its basic management practices, one of the most important stimulants has been flexible manufacturing technology. Ford can now combine the advantages of job order, assembly line, and process manufacturing without suffering the disadvantages of either of the technologies. Manufacturing facilities can change, add, and custom-make autos for specific customers within time frames unheard of only a few years ago. FMT has necessitated the development of organic organization design features throughout Ford Motor Company.

Sources: Laurel Coppersmith and Arlene Grubbs, "Team-Building: The Whole May Be Less Than the Sum of the Parts," *Human Resources Professional,* May/June 1998, pp. 10–14; Jean V. Owen, "High Velocity at Dearborn Engine," *Manufacturing Engineering,* May 1997, pp. 72–82; and Thomas L. Zeller, Darin M. Gillis, "Achieving Market Excellence through Quality: The Case of Ford Motor Company," *Business Horizons,* May/June 1995, pp. 23–31.

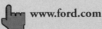 **www.ford.com**

Environment and Organizational Design

The relationship between technology and effective organizational design is firmly established. Yet, as we see, interpreting these relationships requires that the organizations' environment be taken into account. Thus, the more basic explanation for differences in organization is differences in the environment. This line of reasoning has been pursued by a number of researchers. We'll review one of the classic studies in this section.

The classic study of the relationship between environment and organizational design

Lawrence and Lorsch base their findings on detailed case studies of firms in the plastics, food, and container industries.[22] An initial exploratory study consisted of case studies of six firms operating in the plastics industry. Lawrence and Lorsch analyzed these studies to answer the following questions:[23]

1. How are the environmental demands facing various organizations different and how do environmental demands relate to the design of effective organizations?

2. Is it true that organizations in certain or stable environments make more exclusive use of centralized authority to make key decisions, and, if so, why? Is it because fewer key decisions are required, or because these decisions can be made more effectively at higher organization levels or by fewer people?

3. Is the same degree of specialization and differences in orientation among individuals and groups found in organizations in different industrial environments?

4. If greater specialization and differences among individuals and groups are found in different industries, do these differences influence problems of coordinating the organization's parts? Does it influence the organization's means of achieving integration?

To answer these four questions, Lawrence and Lorsch studied structure in the three industries. During their investigation, they coined three terms that have become widely used in the theory and practice of organizational design: *differentiation, integration,* and *environment.*

DIFFERENTIATION   The "state of segmentation of the organizational system into subsystems, each of which tends to develop particular attributes in relation to the requirements posed by its relevant external environment," is termed

Differentiation

Degree of differences among units of an organization due to individual and structural differences.

differentiation.[24] This concept refers in part to the idea of specialization of labor, specifically to the degree of departmentalization. But it's broader and also includes behavioral attributes of employees of these subsystems, or departments. The researchers were interested in three behavioral attributes:

1. They believed that employees of some departments would be more or less task-oriented or person-oriented than employees in other departments. This belief reflects ideas in Fiedler's situational theory of leadership.

2. They proposed that employees of some departments would have longer or shorter time horizons than members of other departments. They believed these differences could be explained by different environmental attributes, specifically the length of time between action and the feedback of results.

3. They expected to find some employees more concerned with goals of their department than with goals of the total organization.

The organization of each department in the six firms was classified along a continuum from mechanistic to organic.

Employees in mechanistically organized departments were expected to be more oriented toward tasks and have shorter time horizons than employees in organic departments.

INTEGRATION   The "process of achieving unity of effort among the various subsystems in the accomplishment of the organization's task" is labeled **integration,** and it can be achieved in a variety of ways. Proponents of the mechanistic model argued for integration through the creation of rules and procedures to govern subsystem members' behavior. But this method of integration can be effective only in relatively stable and predictable situations.[25] Rules and procedures lose their effectiveness as the environment becomes more unstable; thus, integration by *plans* takes on greater significance. But as we approach the highly unstable environment, integration is achieved by mutual adjustment. Mutual adjustment requires a great deal of communication through open channels throughout the organization, a characteristic of organically designed organizations. In terms of the Lawrence and Lorsch research, the type of integrative devices that managers use should be related to the degree of differentiation. Highly differentiated organizations would tend to use mutual adjustment as a means of achieving integration.

Integration

Achieving unity of effort among different organizational units and individuals through rules, planning, and leadership.

ENVIRONMENT   The independent variable, environment, was conceptualized from the perspective of the organization members as they looked outward. Consequently, the researchers assumed that a basic reason for differentiating into subsystems is to deal more effectively with subenvironments. Lawrence and Lorsch identified three main subenvironments: the market subenvironment, the technical-economic subenvironment, and the scientific subenvironment. These three subenvironments correspond to the sales, production, and research and development functions within organizations. Most organizations create separate departments for sales, production, and research and development. These departments represent parts of the total organization or, in researchers' terms, subsystems of the total system.

The researchers believed that the degree of differentiation within each subsystem would vary depending on specific attributes of the relevant subenvironment. Specifically, the subenvironment could vary along three dimensions: (1) the rate of change of conditions over time, (2) the certainty of information about conditions at any particular time, and (3) the time span of feedback on the results of employee decisions.[26]

Figure 15–1 depicts the idea that an organization consists of separate parts, usually departments, which must deal with different aspects of the total environment. Lawrence and Lorsch identify the organizational parts, or subsystems, as marketing, production, and research. They identify the environmental parts, or subenvironments, as market, technical-economic, and science. Subsystems must be organized so as to deal effectively with their relevant subenvironments. The greater the differences among the three subenvironments in terms of rate of change, certainty of information, and time span of feedback, the greater will be the differences among the three subsystems in terms of organization structure and behavioral attributes. The greater these differences (i.e., the more differentiated are the three subsystems), the more important is the task of integrating the three subsystems.

Other evidence of the importance of environmental uncertainty

Other studies have established the relationship between environmental factors and organization structure.[27] But there are inconsistencies and contradictions in these studies. The causes of these inconsistencies are much like those associated with studies of technology. For example, some studies use qualitative measures of environmental uncertainty; others use quantitative measures. Still other studies use questionnaire responses

Figure 15–1

Conceptualization of the Lawrence and Lorsch Model

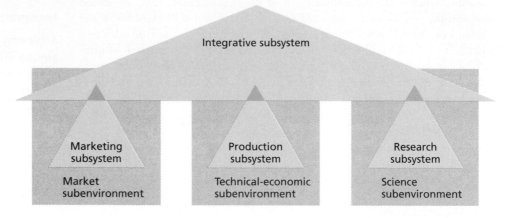

completed by participants in the organization, while others use objective indexes of uncertainty.[28] We must evaluate critically the studies reporting environmental effects before drawing any final conclusions. We must also consider environmental uncertainty's precise effects on the organization and distinguish between the kinds of environments different kinds of organizations face. For example, the service delivery organization deals with a particular kind of environment compared to the manufacturing organization.

Environmental uncertainty and organizational design in the service sector

The growing importance of the service sector of the economy has stimulated much interest in understanding how to design service firms for optimal performance.[29] An increasingly promising approach is to use the concept of environmental uncertainty to identify the optimal design. One variation of this approach focuses on the relative uncertainty of two customer attributes: diversity of customer demand for services and variation in customer disposition to participate in the delivery of the service.[30] According to this perspective, a service firm should organize in relatively mechanistic or organic forms depending upon the degree of uncertainty in these two attributes.

Service organizations whose customers demand relatively homogeneous services and have little disposition to participate in the delivery of those services can be managed according to mechanistic principles. Examples of such organizations include banks, insurance firms, and airlines. Mechanistic designs provide appropriate mechanisms for integrating activities of relatively undifferentiated functions.

At the far extreme of these types of service firms are those whose customers demand a diverse array of services and are predisposed to participating in the service delivery. Such organizations include medical care, legal advice, and higher education. These organizations are better able to integrate the activities of highly differentiated activities through organic organizations. This is because the organic structure provides the flexibility required to deal with the highly uncertain environment that is characteristic of customers demanding quite different services and desiring to play an active part in their delivery.

In between these two extremes are intermediate levels of uncertainty. The appropriate organizational designs would be less mechanistic and organic than the extremes and would be tailored to deal with different degrees of services demanded and participation expected.

The idea that an organization's structure should enable customers to access its services can be applied at the subunit level as well as at the overall organizational level. For example, we note that banks are examples of organizations whose customers demand relatively homogeneous services and who aren't disposed to participate in delivery of those services. At the overall organizational level of thinking, the typical bank customer may well be so characterized. But within the bank, there may be different units whose customers require more or less diverse services and who desire more or less participation in the delivery of those services. The trust unit of a bank that serves affluent customers with diverse financial and personal needs is quite different from the installment loan unit that only serves short-term credit customers whose sole participation in the delivery of the service is to provide credit-scoring information. The implication for organizational design is that the trust division should reflect relatively more organic characteristics than the installment loan unit.

Understanding the relationship between environmental uncertainty and structure

The differentiation-integration approach is based on the fundamental viewpoint that organizations must be designed to cope with environmental demands. But this approach goes further to show that different organization designs can and often do exist within a single large organization. A manufacturing firm may find it necessary to design its production department quite differently from its research and development department. In some instances (for example, in mass production), the production department must be designed according to the mechanistic model, but the research and development department may be designed according to the organic model. Differences in the designs are due to differences in the environmental uncertainty each department confronts. Because the production environment is relatively certain, there's no need to stress adaptability and the department can be designed to achieve high levels of efficiency. But the research and development environment is likely to be highly uncertain with considerable need to cope flexibly with unforeseen changes.

The process of departmentalizing creates the necessity for integrating activities of the departments. Integration of separate, yet interdependent, activities is a familiar problem in managing organizations. Mechanistic design proponents believe that integration can be achieved through the creation of rules, procedures, plans, and a hierarchical chain of command that places managers in the position of integrators. The solutions of organic design proponents, however, differ. They believe that committees, task groups, cross-functional teams, integrators, and group-centered decision making are better approaches. In fact, either approach is appropriate depending upon the situation, according to Lawrence and Lorsch.

Environmental uncertainty, information processing, and adaptive design strategies

The relationships among environment, technology, and organization structure can be synthesized. The key concept is *information* and the key idea is that organizations must effectively receive, process, and act on information to achieve performance.[31] Information flows into the organization from the subenvironments. The information enables the organization to respond to market, technological, and resource changes. The more rapid the changes, the greater the necessity for, and availability of, information.[32]

Organizations in relatively certain and unchanging environments rely on hierarchical control, rules and procedures, and planning to integrate the behavior of subunits. These integrative methods are fundamental features of classical organization designs and are effective as long as the environment remains stable and predictable. Information processing requirements are relatively modest in such environments. For example, firms manufacturing and selling paper containers can plan production schedules with relative assurance that sudden shifts in demand, resource supply, or technology will not disrupt the schedule. Information requirements consist almost solely of projections from historical sales, cost, and engineering data.

Organizations in dynamic and complex environments, however, are unable to rely on traditional information processing and control techniques. Changes in market demand, resource supplies, and technology disrupt plans and require adjustments *during* task performance. On-the-spot adjustments to production schedules and task performance disrupt the organization.

From a managerial perspective, the effect of environmental uncertainty and increased flow of information is to overload the organization with exceptional cases. As a greater number of nonroutine, consequential events occur in the organization's environment, managers are more and more drawn into day-to-day operating matters. Problems develop as plans become obsolete and as the various functions' coordinating efforts break down.[33] Some organizations are designed from their inception to deal with information processing demands; most, however, must confront the problem subsequent to their creation. For these organizations that discover that their present design is incapable of dealing with the demands of changing environments, the problem becomes one of selecting an appropriate adaptive strategy. The two general approaches are to (1) reduce the need for information and (2) increase capacity to process information.

Strategies to reduce the need for information

Managers can reduce the need for information by reducing the number of exceptions that occur and the number of factors to be considered when exceptions do occur. These two ends can be achieved by creating slack resources or by creating self-contained units.

CREATING SLACK RESOURCES   Slack resources include stockpiles of materials, manpower, and other capabilities that enable the organization to respond to uncertainty. Other examples include lengthening planning periods, production schedules, and lead times. These practices limit the number of exceptional cases by increasing the time span within which a response is necessary. For example, job order manufacturers can intentionally overestimate time required to complete a customized product, thus allowing time to deal with any difficulties that arise.[34]

An additional effect of slack resources is to reduce the interdependence between units within the organization. If inventory is available to meet unexpected sales, no interaction is required between production and sales units. If inventory isn't available, production and sales units must necessarily interact and coordinate their activities. Obviously, creating slack resources has cost implications. Excess inventory (safety stocks, buffer stocks) represents money that can be invested; thus, carrying costs will increase. Extended planning, budgeting, and scheduling time horizons lower expected performance. Whether the strategy of creating slack resources is optimal depends upon careful balancing of the relevant costs and benefits.[35]

CREATING SELF-CONTAINED UNITS   Creating slack resources can be undertaken within the present organization structure. Creating self-contained units involves a complete reorganization away from a functional basis toward product, customer, or territorial bases. Each unit is provided its own resources: manufacturing, personnel, marketing, and engineering. Ordinarily, accounting, finance, and legal functions would remain centralized and made available to the new units on an "as-needed" basis. Reorganization around products, customers, or territories enables the organization to achieve desired flexibility, but at the cost of lost efficiency.

In terms of information processing, self-contained units inherently face less environmental uncertainty than the larger whole. They deal with a complementary grouping of products or customers and don't have to coordinate activities with other units. With reduced required coordination, the units don't have to process as much information as before the reorganization. An additional benefit of self-contained units is that they can be the bases for product innovation in environments that demand such innovation. The strategy of creating self-contained units to initiate innovation has considerable application as the experience of 3M in the Close-Up illustrates.

CREATING VIRTUAL ORGANIZATIONS   One of the fastest developing practices in business throughout the world involves firms in cooperative relationships with their suppliers, distributors, and even competitors. These networks of relationships enable organizations to achieve both efficiency and flexibility to exploit advantages of the mechanistic and organic organization designs. These "virtual organizations" have become so pervasive that some experts refer to them as the models for 21st century organizations. Cooperative relationships enable the principal organization to rely upon the smaller, closer-to-the-market partner to sense impending changes in the environment and to respond at the local level, thus relieving the parent organization of that necessity.

The exact form of the virtual organization varies. Some organizations develop relationships only with key suppliers. Other organizations develop relationships with marketers and distributors. In the extreme case, the parent organization functions much like a broker and deals independently with product designers, producers, suppliers, and markets. The critical managerial and organizational decisions involve which of the

CLOSE—UP

Self-Contained Units in the 3M Company

Minnesota Mining and Minerals (3M) has been a leader in product innovation. 3M's success has inspired others to emulate its management practices and organizational structure. Although 3M relies on many strategies to stimulate and reward innovation behavior throughout the firm, a cornerstone is its policy of keeping divisions small, with average sales of about $200 million each. The norm within these small divisions is to share information and resources. Informal information-sharing and brainstorming sessions can crop up any time, any place within the divisions, and often include customers.

Innovation occurs when individuals have information and encouragement, and 3M provides both ingredients. Employees can spend up to 15 percent of their time on ideas that promise to result in new products. And the firm has the policy that each division's sales revenue must be generated by products developed within the past five years. Other innovative firms such as Rubbermaid, Hewlett-Packard, and General Electric have similar policies. At the core, however, is the practice of maintaining relatively small, self-contained units that can deal effectively with information relevant to their success.

Sources: Wayne Burkan, "Giving New Meaning to the Competitive Edge," *Journal of Quality and Participation,* March/April 1998, pp. 14–19; Karen A. Zien and Sheldon A. Buckler, "Dreams to Market: Creating a Culture of Innovation," *Journal of Product Innovation Management,* July 1997, pp. 74–87; and James J. Thompson, "Quality and Innovation at 3M: A Partnership for Customer Satisfaction," *Tapping the Network Journal,* Winter 1993/1994, pp. 2–5.

   **www.mmm.com**

functions to buy and which to produce and how to manage the relationships with their partners. Managers in these organizations have less environmental uncertainty to deal with because they have, in a sense, subcontracted that responsibility to their counterparts in the network. Such organization structures are, in a sense, boundaryless organizations.[36]

Virtual organizations originated in Japan where firms create alliances with other firms. These alliances take the form of cooperative agreements, consortia, and equity ownerships to establish networks of businesses. In Japan, this form of doing business is termed *keiretsu* and involves a very large financial institution, a very large industrial conglomerate, and smaller firms in a network of relationships that enable the large firm to produce the product and the smaller firms to supply components, do research and design, and perhaps distribute and market. The participating bank provides the financial requirements to support the network of cooperative relationships. This form of interorganizational network has enabled Japanese industry to grow without bottlenecks of supply and damaging competition from domestic firms.

How these relationships should be organized and managed has just begun to be examined. Although the Japanese experience provides some guidelines, much is left to be learned and put into practice. Studies at the Aston Business School in Great Britain suggest that development of these cooperative relationships represents but yet another reaction from organizations that must maintain flexibility to deal with the dynamic changes of the global economy.[37]

Strategies to increase capacity to process information

Instead of reducing the amount of information needed, managers may choose to increase the organization's capacity to process it. Two strategies to accomplish this objective are: (1) invest in vertical information systems and (2) create lateral relationships.

INVESTING IN VERTICAL INFORMATION SYSTEMS   The result of increased environmental uncertainty is information overload. Managers are simply inundated with information requiring action of some kind. A strategic response to the problem is to invest in information processing systems, such as computers, clerks, and executive assistants. These resources process information quickly and format the data in efficient language. The increasingly sophisticated personal computer now available to nearly every individual in an organization enables information to be assembled, condensed, and distributed to appropriate decision-makers without great difficulty.

CREATING LATERAL RELATIONSHIPS   As the necessity for increased coordination among functional units intensifies, decisions must be made that cross authority lines. Introducing lateral relationships facilitates joint decision making among the functional units, but without the loss of efficiency due to specialization. The cost of the strategy is an increase in the number of managers who deal with the environment. The roles of managers in boundary-spanning roles are particularly demanding; the success of this strategy depends on how effectively role occupants perform.

Boundary-Spanning Roles

Jobs that require employees to relate to people in different units, both inside and outside an organization.

Boundary-spanning roles perform two functions: to gather information and to represent the organization. Sales personnel, purchasing agents, salespeople, lobbyists, public relations personnel, market researchers, and personnel recruiters are a few of the staff who gather information and represent the organization. Roles of this type exist at the interface between the organization and its environments, including other organizations that are networked; they can be termed *external boundary roles*.

In contrast, *internal boundary roles* exist within the organization at the interface between subunits such as functional and product departments. Product managers, expediters, integrators, and liaison personnel are examples of roles between subunits. As we've seen, organizations cope with environmental uncertainty and increase information by establishing such roles. They perform tasks similar to those performed by external boundary roles, except that they gather information that facilitates joint decision making.

The demands on those who perform boundary-spanning positions are qualitatively different from others in the organization. These unique demands result from the fact that individuals who do these jobs must deal with other people who have conflicting expectations, but without the authority to settle the disagreement.[38]

Organizations' adaptation to increasing uncertainty combined with the need for information requires some changes in organization structure. Managers can choose to cope with information processing demands either by reducing the need or by increasing the organization's capability to process it. These adaptations are effective when the environmental pressure is episodic or temporary. If environmental pressure is persistent and permanent, more complete solutions are called for. In particular, management will begin to develop matrix and virtual organizations. Both of these variations on the basic hierarchical organization are effective structures for adapting to and coping with environmental uncertainty, regardless of organizational type or national boundaries. Figure 15–2 depicts the relationships among environmental uncertainty, information requirements, and managerial responses.

An Integrated Framework of Organization Design

Many complex factors and variables go into the design of an optimal organization structure. The most important considerations are shown in Figure 15–3. Chapters 13, 14, and 15 reflect the current state of knowledge regarding organizational design. As we've seen, the key decisions are division of labor, departmentalization, spans of control, and delegation of authority. These decisions, which reflect *environmental* and

Figure 15–2

Management's Responses to Environmental Demands for Increased Information Processing

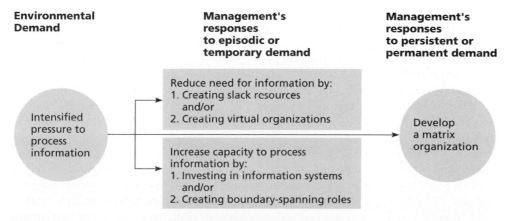

Figure 15–3

Integrative Framework for Organizational Design

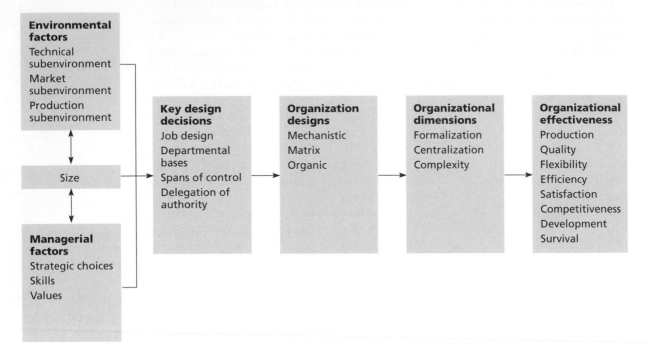

Environmental factors
Technical subenvironment
Market subenvironment
Production subenvironment

Size

Managerial factors
Strategic choices
Skills
Values

Key design decisions
Job design
Departmental bases
Spans of control
Delegation of authority

Organization designs
Mechanistic
Matrix
Organic

Organizational dimensions
Formalization
Centralization
Complexity

Organizational effectiveness
Production
Quality
Flexibility
Efficiency
Satisfaction
Competitiveness
Development
Survival

managerial interactions, are complex; managers don't have the luxury of designing a one-best-way structure. Instead, optimal design is determined by the interaction of size, environmental, and managerial factors. Matching the appropriate structure to these factors is the essence of *contingency design* theory and practice.

The overall structure of tasks and authority resulting from the key decisions is a specific *organizational design.* The alternative designs range along a continuum with mechanistic design at one extreme and organic design at the other. The matrix design, at the midpoint, represents a balance between the two extremes.

Organization structures differ on many dimensions, the more important being shown in Figure 15–3. In general, mechanistic organizations are more formalized, centralized, and specialized than organic organizations. They're also less differentiated and achieve integration through hierarchy, rules and procedures, and planning. Organic organizations, however, must achieve integration through more complex methods including boundary-spanning roles, task groups, committees, and other forms of mutual adjustment.[39] Regardless of the specific configuration of organization dimensions and integration strategies, the overriding purpose of organizational design is to channel behavior of individuals and groups into patterns that contribute to effective organization performance.

Thus, managerial decision making plays a key role in organizational design.[40] In fact, much of this section can be summarized in the idea that structure follows strategy[41] and that maximum performance is achieved when there's congruence between strategy and structure.[42] Managerial strategy involves the choice of what products and services the organization will supply to specific customers and markets. Thus, managers who decide to supply a single product to a specific set of customers can be expected to design a far simpler organizational structure than a manager of a highly diversified company serving multiple markets with multiple products and services.[43] Moreover, the strategic choice affects not only organizational design, but also job design and, apparently, leadership behavior as well.

Organizational design remains an important issue in the management of organizational behavior and effectiveness. As the 1990s progress, organizational design is becoming even more important. As is apparent, organizational designs that were successful in the past will prove ineffectual in the face of new international competition, technological change, and the shifting patterns of industrial development.[44] As organizations experiment with new strategies, they will be forced to experiment with new organizational designs. These designs will bear close resemblance to organic designs and virtual organizations.[45]

Summary of Key Points

- Task and authority relationships among jobs and groups of jobs must be defined and structured according to rational bases. Practitioners and theorists have recommended two specific yet contradictory theories for designing organizational structures.

- One theory, termed *mechanistic design*, is based on the assumption that the more effective organizational structure is characterized by highly specialized jobs, homogeneous departments, narrow spans of control, and relatively centralized authority. The bases for these assumptions are found in the historical circumstances within which this theory developed. It was a time of fairly rapid industrialization that encouraged public and private organizations to emphasize the production and efficiency criteria of effectiveness. To achieve these ends, classical design theory proposes a single best way to structure an organization.

- Beginning with the human relations era of the 1930s and sustained by behavioral scientists' growing interest in the study of management and organization, an alternative to mechanistic design theory developed. This alternative theory, termed *organic design*, proposes that the more effective organization has relatively despecialized jobs, heterogeneous departments, wide spans of control, and decentralized authority. Such organization structures, it's argued, achieve not only high levels of production and efficiency but also satisfaction, adaptiveness, and development.

- The design of an effective organization structure can't be guided by a "one-best-way" theory. Rather, the manager

must adopt the point of view that either the mechanistic or the organic design is more effective for the total organization or for subunits within its organization.

- The manager must identify and describe the relevant subenvironments of the organization. These subenvironments determine the relationships within units, among units, and between units and their subenvironments.

- The manager must evaluate each subenvironment in terms of its rate of change, relative certainty, and time span of feedback. These conditions are the key variables for determining the formal structure of tasks and authority.

- Each subunit structure is designed along the mechanistic-organic continuum in a manner consistent with the state of environmental conditions. Specifically, slower rates of change, greater certainty, and shorter time spans of feedback are compatible with the mechanistic design; the converse is true for the organic design.

- Concurrent with the design of subunit structures is the design of integrative techniques. The appropriate techniques, whether rules, plans, or mutual adjustment, depend on the degree of subunit differentiation. The greater the differentiation, the greater is the need for mutual adjustment techniques. The smaller the differentiation, the greater is the need for rules and plans.

- Information processing is required for all organizations, given their size, technology, and environments. Thus, information processing, as a concept, summarizes the contingency theory of organizational design.

Discussion and Review Questions

1. Describe the alternative ways that an organization can respond to the necessity to process vast amounts of information.

2. Distinguish between an organization, an organization design, and an organization structure. Apply these concepts to the college you attend to describe your experience as a student.

3. Would it be easier to change an organization from mechanistic to organic or from organic to mechanistic? Explain.

4. What are the forces in the environment that appear to be driving firms to adopt matrix and virtual organization designs? Will these forces increase or decrease in

importance as we move into the next millennium? Explain.

5. What in your experience has been the dominant contingency factor in the design of the organizations in which you have worked? Technology? Environmental uncertainty? Strategy?

6. Use the characteristics of mechanistic and organic organizations to describe two different organizations that you know about. After determining the organizational differences, see if you can relate the differences to technological and environmental differences.

7. What are the counterparts to the market, technical-economic, and scientific subenvironments of a university? A hospital? A pro football team?

8. Which organizational design discussed in this chapter do you see most often discussed in articles appearing in daily newspapers and other news sources? What seems to be the everyday usage of the idea of organization design?

9. Discuss how technology and environmental certainty interact to determine the most effective organization.

10. Based upon whatever information is at your disposal, rank from high to low the environmental uncertainty of a college of arts and sciences, a college of engineering, a college of business, and a college of education. What does your ranking suggest about the integration techniques that would be appropriate in each college?

CASE FOR ANALYSIS

Defining the Role of a Liaison Officer

Recently, the governor of a southeastern state created a Department for Human Resources. It combined many formerly distinct state agencies that carried out health and welfare programs. The department's organization chart is shown in Exhibit 1. The functions of each of the bureaus were described in the governor's press release:

> The Bureau for Social Insurance *will operate all income maintenance and all income supplementation programs of the Department for Human Resources. That is, it will issue financial support to the poor, unemployed, and needy, and it will issue food stamps and pay for medical assistance.*

The Bureau for Social Services *will provide child welfare services, foster care, adoptions, family services, and all other general counseling in support of families and individuals who require assistance for successful and adequate human development.*

The Bureau for Health Services *will operate all departmental programs that provide health service, including all physical and mental health programs. This bureau will take over the functions of the Department of Health, the Department of Mental Health, and the Commission for Handicapped Children.*

Exhibit 1

Department for Human Resources: Organization Chart

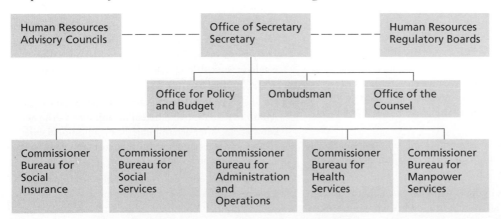

The Bureau for Manpower Services *will operate all labor force development and job placement programs of the department, including all job recruitments and business liaison functions, job training, worker readiness functions, and job counseling and placement.*

The Bureau for Administration and Operations *will consolidate numerous support services, such as preaudits, accounting, data processing, purchasing, and duplicating, now furnished by 19 separate units.*

Soon after the department began to operate in its reorganized form, major problems arose that were traceable to the Bureau for Administration and Operations (BAO). Prior to reorganization, each department had had its own support staff for data processing, accounting, personnel, and budgeting. Those staffs and equipment had all been relocated and brought under the direction of the BAO commissioner. Employees who had once specialized in the work of one area, such as mental health, were now expected to perform work for all the bureaus. In addition, they had to revise forms, procedures, computer programs, accounts, and records to conform to the new department's policies.

Consequently, the department began to experience administrative problems. Payrolls were late and inaccurate; payments to vendors and clients were delayed; and personnel actions got lost in the paperwork. Eventually, the integrity of the department's service programs was in jeopardy.

The executive staff of the department, consisting of the secretary, commissioner, and administrator of the Office for Policy and Budget, soon found itself spending more time dealing with these administrative problems than with policy formulation. Apparently, the department's effectiveness would depend on its ability to integrate the functions of BAO with the needs of the program bureaus. Also, the executive staff was not the appropriate body to deal with these issues. Aside from the inordinate amount of time spent on the administrative problems, a great deal of interpersonal conflict was generated among the commissioners.

The BAO commissioner was instructed by the secretary to give his full-time attention to devising a means for integrating the administrative functions. After consultation with his staff, the idea of an administrative liaison officer was formulated. The BAO commissioner presented the staff paper that described this new job (Exhibit 2) to the executive staff for discussion and adoption. According to the commissioner, there was simply no procedural or planning means for integrating the administrative functions. Rather, it would continue to be a conflict-laden process requiring the undivided attention of an individual assigned to each of the four bureaus.

Discussion Questions

1. Evaluate the concept of "administrative liaison officer" as a strategy for achieving integration. Is this an example of the mutual adjustment strategy?

2. How will the officers achieve integration when they will have no authority over either the administrative functions or the programs to be integrated?

3. What would be the most important personal characteristics to look for in an applicant for these positions?

Exhibit 2

Description of Responsibilities, Administrative Liaison Officer

Introduction

Executive Order 86-777 abolished the former human resources agencies and merged their functions into a new, single department. A prime element in the organizational concept of the new department is the centralization of administrative and support activities into a Bureau of Administration and Operations, which supports the four program bureaus of the department. While the centralization of these administrative and support activities only included those functions that were located in centralized administrative units in the former human resources agencies, the size of the Department for Human Resources dictates that extra levels of effort be applied to ensure close coordination and cooperation between the four program bureaus and the Bureau for Administration and Operations.

As one element in the comprehensive range of efforts now being applied to ensure a high level of responsiveness and cooperation between the Bureau for Administration and Operations and each program bureau, there will be created within the office of the Commissioner for Administration and Operations four positions for administrative liaison officers, one of which will be assigned responsibility for liaison with each program bureau.

Responsibilities

1. Each administrative liaison officer will provide, to the program bureau commissioner and other officials of the program bureau to which assigned, assistance in the following areas:
   a. Identification and definition of the administrative and operational support needs of that program bureau.
   b. Determination of the relative priorities of those needs for services.
   c. Identification of programmatic and operational requirements of the program bureau that may be assisted by the enforcement of administrative regulations by the Bureau for Administration and Operations.
   d. Identification of resources available within the Bureau for Administration and Operations that may be of value to the program bureau.
   e. Coordination of the delivery of services by the various divisions of the Bureau for Administration and Operations to the program bureau.
   f. Interpretation of data and information provided by the Bureau for Administration and Operations.
   g. Interpretation and distribution of administrative regulations and procedures issued by the Bureau for Administration and Operations with respect to its responsibilities under policies delineated by the secretary and the commissioners of the Department for Human Resources.

2. Each administrative liaison officer will provide assistance to the Commissioner for Administration and Operations and other officials of the Bureau for Administration and Operations in the following areas:
   a. Development of strategies for providing the maximum possible quality and quantity of support services that can be made available to the officer's particular program bureau within budgetary and policy constraints.
   b. Understanding of special needs and problems of respective program bureaus.
   c. Identification of new procedures and systems whereby services rendered to the program bureau can result in improved coordination between all organizational units of the Department for Human Resources.
   d. Identification of inadequacies or gaps in presently available services provided by the Bureau for Administration and Operations.
   e. Direction and/or coordination of task forces and other temporary organizational units created within the Bureau for Administration and Operations assigned to provide resources specific to the program bureau.
   f. Supervision of all personnel of the Bureau for Administration and Operations that may be on a temporary duty assignment to the program bureau to which the officer is assigned.

Operational Arrangement

1. The administrative liaison officer will be appointed to a position within the Office of the Commissioner for Administration and Operations.
2. The assignment of an administrative liaison officer to a program bureau will require the concurrence of the commissioner of that program bureau.
3. The Office of the Administrative Liaison Officer will be physically located within the suite of offices of the program bureau commissioner to whom the officer is assigned.
4. The administrative liaison officer will attend all staff meetings of the commissioner of the program bureau to which assigned and all staff meetings of the Commissioner for Administration and Operations.

EXPERIENTIAL EXERCISE

Identifying and Changing Organization Design

Objectives

To increase the reader's understanding of different organization designs.

Related Topics

Chapters 13, 14, and 15 provide the reader with sufficient information to complete the analysis.

Starting the Exercise

The instructor will form groups of five to eight individuals toward the end of a class meeting. Each group will meet for 5 to 10 minutes and select a specific organizational unit within your college that will be the focus of the group's analysis. The unit can be an academic department, division, or college or a nonacademic unit such as the athletic department, business affairs office, student housing, or any other formally recognized campus unit.

Before the next class meeting, each group will complete the six steps of the exercise and prepare a report to present to the class.

Completing the Exercise

1. What is the primary purpose of the unit? What functions must be performed to accomplish the mission? What customers does the unit serve with what products or services? What are the primary environments that influence the unit's performance?

2. Describe the unit's primary technology, the relative uncertainty of the primary environments, and the primary information that must be processed.

3. Describe the existing organization structure in terms of the characteristics that distinguish between mechanistic and organic designs.

4. Which organization design more accurately describes the existing organization structure?

5. If the organization structure were changed to be more mechanistic or organic, what would be the effects on jobs, departmental bases, and delegation of authority?

6. Is the existing organization design appropriate for the mission of the unit, given its mission, functions, customers, products/services, and environment? Justify your answer.

V I D E O   C A S E

The World Wide Web: Advancing the Organization

The World Wide Web is a fast-flowing river of information. Internet surfers have found that navigating the Web takes them to a wide range of sites from homemade personal sites to multimedia corporate sites. Why are businesses willing to invest $200,000 to $1 million to create an impressive Web site? Some want to bolster their corporate image; others want to sell their products on-line.

How companies choose to reach out and hold their audiences' attention depends upon what they intend their sites to accomplish. Some Web sites function as general promotion and brand identity tools. For example, General Mills doesn't use its Web site to sell Betty Crocker cake mix, rather it uses the site to present menu plans and household tips. The goal is to link the brand's image with the information the Web site provides.

Another function of some business Web sites is to conduct on-line business (sometimes called on-line commerce, e-commerce, or transactional sites). For example, you can book airline tickets on Sabre Group's Travelocity site; buy a computer on the Gateway 2000, Dell, and Micron sites; or buy stock from e.Schwab, Datek, and Quick & Reilly.

Unlike e-commerce sites, some broad-based corporate sites don't sell—they give things away. The aim of these sites is to give surfers easy access to huge banks of free information—particularly information about the companies' products. Microsoft is most likely the largest broad-based corporate site on the Web. The information about Microsoft products is so vast that the site changes about eight times a day as new information is added. Web designers have found that the better the Web site's organization, the more faith visitors have in the site's information and in the company. Corporate Web sites might contain information found in a brochure: description of products, phone numbers, addresses, e-mail address, and so forth. They can also contain information that might be found in an annual report: shareholder information, corporate mission statements, company history, and press releases.

How companies use the Web, then, depends upon the type of company and on what the company wants their Web site to accomplish. One thing is certain, though, communication remains the main function of this new medium. People want answers to their questions and the Web can be the most efficient way to get them.

Discussion Questions

1. How could your college use a Web site to improve its services to students and the community?

2. The purpose of on-line commerce Web sites is to sell the company's products on-line. Would you feel comfortable buying on-line? What are the advantages and disadvantages of on-line commerce?

3. Suppose you were to design a Web site for our hypothetical product, Fiberiffic. Which of the Web site functions described in this case would you choose (general promotion/brand identity, on-line business, or broadbased corporate site)? Describe your proposed Web site. What content would you include? Justify using funds to develop this Web site rather than on more traditional promotional/sale tools.

No. 5

The Processes of Organizations

Chapter 16

Managing Effective Communication Processes

Learning Objectives

After completing Chapter 16, you should be able to:

Define
The term *communication*.

Describe
The major elements in the process of communication.

Discuss
How nonverbal cues influence communication effectiveness.

Compare
The different styles of interpersonal communication.

Identify
The major barriers to effective communication and the means to overcome these barriers.

Communication

Communication pervades organizational activity; it's the process by which things get done in organizations. Every employee is continually involved in and affected by the communications process. For managers, effective communicating is a critical skill because the manager's planning, organizing, and controlling functions become operationalized only through communicative activity. Because of its importance in organizations, we devote a chapter to providing an understanding of the communication process and to the task of understanding how to become a better communicator.

The Importance of Communication

"You said to get to it as soon as I could. How did I know you meant now?" "How did I know she was really serious about resigning?" In these and similar situations, someone usually ends up saying, "What we have here is a failure to communicate." This statement has meaning for everyone because each of us has faced situations in which the basic problem was communication. Whether on a person-to-person or nation-to-nation basis, in organizations, or in small groups, breakdowns in communication are pervasive.

Finding an aspect of a manager's job that does not involve communication would be extremely difficult. Serious problems arise when directives are misunderstood, when casual kidding in a work group leads to anger, or when informal remarks by a top-level manager are distorted. Each of these situations results from a breakdown somewhere in the process of communication.

Accordingly, the pertinent question is not whether managers engage in communication because communication is inherent to the functioning of an organization. Rather, the real issue is whether managers communicate well or poorly. In other words, communication itself is unavoidable in an organization's functioning; but *effective* communication is avoidable. *Every manager must be a communicator.* In fact, everything a manager does communicates something in some way to somebody or some group. The only question is, "With what effect?" While this may appear an overstatement at this point, it will become apparent as you proceed through the chapter.

Despite the tremendous advances in communication and information technology, communication among people in organizations leaves much to be desired.[1] Communication among people depends not on technology but rather on forces in people and their surroundings. It is a *process* that occurs within people. Recognizing the ever-growing importance of communication, more and more organizations are implementing programs designed to assess managerial communication skills and to provide follow-up training to overcome any deficiencies. Managers who have participated in such programs have been found to possess significantly higher interpersonal skills and problem-solving abilities—leading to higher productivity levels—than those who have not.[2] The following Close-Up presents some examples of the benefits of effective communication between management and the rest of the organization.

The Communication Process

The general process of communication contains five elements: the communicator, the message, the medium, the receiver, and feedback (Figure 16–1). It can be simply summarized as: Who . . . says what, . . . in which way, . . . to whom, . . . with what effect?[3] To appreciate each element in the process, we must examine how communication works.

CLOSE—UP

Communication Can Make the Difference

It is not surprising that at management meetings and conferences across the country, a common theme usually emerges: Good communication is the common thread that ties people, plans, strategies, and commitment—in other words, the entire organizational fabric—together. In times of rapid change, organizations need fast adaptation to change. Accomplishing this requires high levels of management and employee trust and cooperation. Effective communication can help to foster trust and cooperation. Let's examine some instances where it appears to be happening.

Emerson Electronics is a world-class competitor. It believes one of the reasons is its plan to utilize effective communication to outline corporate economic goals for employees and to explain why those goals affect jobs, salaries, and survival. This is no small feat for Emerson considering that it has over 70,000 employees at some 250 plants around the world.

At Martin Marietta Government Electronic Systems, a union facility, a method of communicating change within 48 hours has been instituted. This speeded-up information-sharing process has cut plant grievances from 281 per year to just 12. Management believes this improvement happened because everyone knows what is going on at all times. Thus, there are no surprises.

Some organizations are using communication to help employees manage their careers. To do this, management must be willing to share their vision and create an environment of trust, respect, and nurturing for employees. General Electric and Colgate-Palmolive are two organizations that provide employees with information so they can manage their careers. In these kinds of programs, managers often meet frequently with employees in goal-setting sessions where there is dialogue about the path the employee is on or hopes to be on.

One management consultant, Karen Greenbaum, defines organizational communication as consisting of four activities: leading, informing, listening, and involving. She believes that it is in the last two elements—llistening and involving—that most organizational communication efforts fall short. She appears to be correct. Note that in the efforts outlined above, each of the organizations are trying to listen to and involve their employees.

Sources: Amanda J. S. Kaufman, "Helping to Build Careers," *Infoworld,* July 13, 1998, pp. 99–100; Peter Lilienthal, "Help Management Really Communicate," *Communication World,* February/March 1995, pp. 19–22; and George Taninecz, "Preaching Winning Practices: America's Best Plants Deliver Secrets of Success," *Industry Week,* June 5, 1995, p. 24.

 **www.emersoncumingmp.com, www.martin-marietta.com, www.ge.com, www.colgate.com**

Figure 16–1

The Communication Process

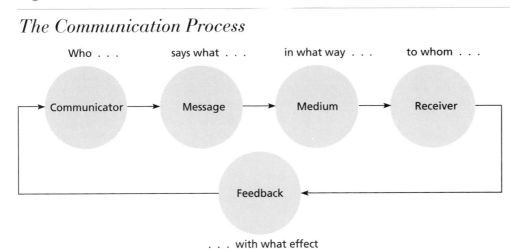

Experts tell us that effective communication is the result of a common understanding between the communicator and the receiver. Communication is successful only if the communicator transmits that understanding to the receiver. In fact, the word **communication** is derived from the Latin *communis,* meaning "common"— the communicator seeks to establish a "commonness" with a receiver. Hence, we can define communication as the transmission of information and understanding through the use of common symbols. The common symbols may be verbal or nonverbal. We'll see later that in the context of an organizational structure, information can flow up and down (vertically), across (horizontally), and down and across (diagonally).

Communication

Transmitting information and understanding, using verbal or nonverbal symbols.

A contemporary model

The most widely used contemporary model of the process of communication has evolved mainly from the early work of Shannon and Weaver, and Schramm.[4] These researchers were concerned with describing the general process of communication in a way that could be useful in all situations. The model that evolved from their work aids our understanding of communication. The basic elements include a communicator, an encoder, a message, a medium, a decoder, a receiver, feedback, and noise (Figure 16–2). Each element in the model can be examined in the context of an organization.

COMMUNICATOR   In an organizational framework, the communicator is an employee with ideas, intentions, information, and a purpose for communicating.

ENCODING   Given the communicator, an encoding process must take place that translates the communicator's ideas into a systematic set of symbols—into a language expressing the communicator's purpose. The major form of encoding is language. For example, a manager often takes accounting information, sales reports, and computer data and translates them into one message. The function of encoding, then, is to provide a form in which ideas and purposes can be expressed as a message.

MESSAGE   The result of the encoding process is the message. The purpose of the communicator is expressed in the form of the message—either *verbal* or *nonverbal.* Managers have numerous purposes for communicating, such as to have others understand their ideas, to understand the ideas of others, to gain acceptance of themselves or their ideas, or to produce action.

Figure 16–2

A Communication Model

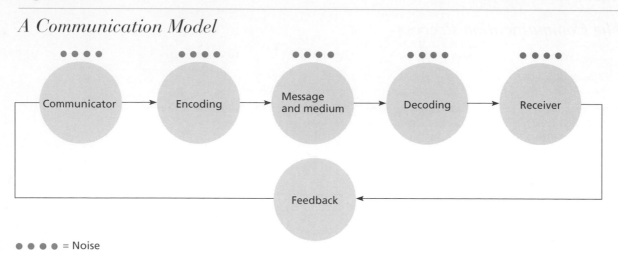

● ● ● ● = Noise

Not as obvious, however, are *unintended messages* that can be sent by silence or inaction on a particular issue as well as decisions on which goals and objectives not to pursue and which methods not to utilize. For example, a decision to utilize one performance evaluation method rather than another may send a message to certain people that an instructor's decision not to give a final exam may send an unintended message to certain students that the course is easy. This is what we meant earlier when we said that everything a manager does communicates.

The message, then, is what the individual hopes to communicate to the intended receiver. The exact form it takes depends to a great extent on the medium used to carry the message. Decisions relating to the two are inseparable.

MEDIUM   The medium is the carrier of the message—the means by which the message is sent. Organizations provide information to members in a variety of ways, including face-to-face communication, telephone conversations, group meetings, fax messages, memos, policy statements, reward systems, production schedules, and video teleconferences. The medium is sometimes a neglected element of the communication process. Often, managers don't adequately consider the impact of the choice of medium on a communication's effectiveness. However, selecting the appropriate medium can have a major impact on communication effectiveness and even managerial performance.

DECODING/RECEIVER   For the process of communication to be completed, the message must be decoded so it's relevant to the receiver. *Decoding,* a technical term for the receiver's thought processes, involves interpretation. Receivers interpret (decode) the message in light of their own previous experiences and frames of reference. Thus, a salesperson will probably decode a memo from the company president differently than a production manager will. A nursing supervisor may decode a memo from the hospital administrator differently than the chief of surgery does. The closer the decoded message comes to the intent desired by the communicator, the more effective is the communication. This underscores the importance of the communicator being "receiver-oriented."

FEEDBACK   *One-way* communication processes do not allow receiver-to-communicator feedback, increasing the potential for distortion between the intended message and the received message. Provision for feedback in the communication process is desirable.[5] A feedback loop provides a channel for receiver response that enables the communicator to determine whether the message has been received and has produced the intended response. *Two-way* communication processes provide for this important receiver-to-communicator feedback.

For the manager, communication feedback may come in many ways. In face-to-face situations, *direct* feedback through verbal exchanges is possible, as are such subtle means of communication as facial expressions of discontent or misunderstanding. In addition, *indirect* means of feedback (such as declines in productivity, poor production quality, increased absenteeism or turnover, and poor coordination and/or conflict between units) may indicate communication breakdowns.

NOISE   In the framework of human communication, noise can be thought of as all factors that distort the intended message. Noise may occur in each of the elements of communication. For example, a manager under a severe time constraint may be forced to act without communication or may communicate hastily with incomplete information. Or a subordinate may attach a different meaning to a word or phrase than was intended by the manager. These are examples of noise in the communication process.

The elements discussed in this section are essential for communication to occur. They should not, however, be viewed as separate. They are, rather, descriptive of the acts that must be performed for any communication to occur. The communication may be vertical (superior–subordinate, subordinate–superior) or horizontal (peer–peer), or it may involve one individual and a group, but the elements discussed here must be present.

Nonverbal messages

The information a communicator sends that is unrelated to the verbal information—that is, nonverbal messages, or **nonverbal communication**—is an area of growing research interest among behavioral scientists.[6] One of the most interesting aspects of nonverbal communication is that it's irrepressibly impactful.[7] Try as they might, people cannot refrain from behaving nonverbally. If, for example, a person tries to act as passive as possible, she's likely to be perceived as inexpressive, inhibited, withdrawn, and uptight.

A recent study examined the relationship between nonverbal behavior and speaker persuasiveness in a public speaking context.[8] Speakers with greater vocal pleasantness, facial pleasantness, and facial expressiveness were judged by audiences to have greater perceived competence and composure than speakers exhibiting less appealing nonverbal behavior. As a result, these speakers were found to be more persuasive, even though message content for all speakers was identical.

Vocal inflection refers to how a message is transmitted: loudly or softly, quickly or slowly, with controlled or uncontrolled inflection, or with a high or low pitch. The method of transmission adds meaning to the receiver, who assesses these cues. Body expressions are another important source of nonverbal communication. Ekman and Friesen have classified body language into five types of expression: emblems, illustrators, regulators, adaptors, and affect displays.[9]

Emblems are gestures much like sign language (the hitchhiker's thumb, the OK sign with thumb and forefinger, the V sign for victory, and the high-five for significant achievement). These movements quickly convey an understood word or phrase. *Illustrators* are gestures that give a picture of what is being said (a raised forefinger to indicate the first point of a sender's position, extended hands to illustrate the size of an object). *Regulators* are movements that regulate a conversation. For example, an upraised palm from the receiver tells a sender to slow down, an arched eyebrow can convey a request for the sender to clarify what has been said, and a nod of the head indicates understanding. Emblems, illustrators, and regulators are consciously used by individuals.

Nonverbal Communication

Messages sent with body posture, facial expressions, and hand and eye movements; as important as verbal communication.

Adaptors and affect displays, on the other hand, are often subconsciously communicated and can reveal much about both the sender's and receiver's feelings and attitudes. *Adaptors* are expressions used to adjust psychologically to the interpersonal climate of a particular situation.[10] Usually learned early in life, adaptors are frequently used to deal with stress in an interpersonal situation. Drumming fingers on a table, tugging a strand of hair, or jiggling a leg or foot are all ways of releasing some degree of stress. *Affect displays,* usually subconscious, directly communicate an individual's emotions. Most affect displays are facial expressions, which are particularly important communicators of a person's feelings. There is a long-held assumption that a person's emotions are mirrored in the face and that these emotions can be "read" with a great deal of accuracy. Affect displays are also expressed in body positions. For example, a "closed posture" (arms folded across the chest, legs crossed) communicates defensiveness and often dislike.

Reading an individual's body language can be a challenging exercise because it involves subjectively evaluating nonverbal communication. The task becomes more difficult for American employees who work in international environments, where meanings of nonverbal cues often differ strikingly from those back home. Consider, for example, a nod of the head, which means yes in the United States but no in Bulgaria. The OK sign with thumb and forefinger means "money" in France, "worthless" in Japan, and something very obscene in Brazil. Waving, a greeting or farewell in the United States, is a grave insult in Greece and Nigeria.[11]

An interesting study was conducted to determine whether differences existed between how American and Japanese individuals recognized facial expressions.[12] The subjects were 41 American and 44 Japanese college undergraduates. Each group was given 48 posed pictures of six universal emotions (eight each of anger, disgust, fear, happiness, sadness, and surprise) to evaluate. For each emotion, there were two males and two females of both Japanese and American descent pictured.

The study's findings revealed that several differences do indeed exist between the two cultures. First, Americans were more accurate than the Japanese at recognizing four of the six emotions (anger, disgust, fear, and sadness), regardless of the culture or sex of the poser being judged. Second, neither the culture nor sex of the poser affected Americans' judgments of the photos, whereas female emotions were more easily identified than male emotions by the Japanese. Third, both Americans and Japanese agreed that happiness was the easiest emotion to identify and that fear was the hardest.

Communicating within Organizations

Directions of communication

The design of an organization should provide for communication in four distinct directions: downward, upward, horizontal, and diagonal. These four directions establish the framework within which communication in an organization takes place. Briefly examining each one will enable us to better appreciate the barriers to effective organizational communication and the means to overcome these barriers.

Downward communication flows from individuals in higher levels of the hierarchy to those in lower levels. The most common forms of downward communication are job instructions, official memos, policy statements, procedures, manuals, and company publications. In many organizations, downward communication often is both inadequate and inaccurate, as reflected in the often heard statement among organization members that "we have

Downward Communication

Communication that flows from higher to lower levels in an organization; includes management policies, instructions, and official memos.

absolutely no idea what's happening." Such complaints indicate inadequate downward communication and individuals' needs for information relevant to their jobs. Absence of job-related information can create unnecessary stress among organization members.[13] A similar situation is faced by a student who hasn't been told an instructor's requirements and expectations.

Many times, the theme of the narrative portion of downward communication is a direct consequence of corporate communication decisions. A study evaluated the message content in the president's letter to stockholders, which is contained in most organizations' annual reports.[14] The purpose of the study was to determine if differences existed between high-performing and low-performing organizations in terms of the themes in presidents' letters. Results of the study indicate that within annual reports, poorly performing firms tend to dwell more on future opportunities than on past financial performance while the opposite is true for the more successful organizations. Another recent study on annual reports found that candor and clear writing, not flashy design or multilayered financial data, are critical in making reports more understandable and effective.[15]

An effective organization needs **upward communication** as much as it needs downward communication. Indeed, a recent study found that, in organizations where upward communication programs were effectively implemented, a majority of managers improved their performance.[16] However, achieving effective upward communication—getting open and honest messages from employees to management—is an especially difficult task, particularly in larger organizations.[17] Some studies suggest that of the four formal communication channels, upward communication is the most ineffective. Upper-level managers often don't respond to messages sent from lower-level employees, and lower-level employees often are reluctant to communicate upward, especially if the message contains bad news.[18] However, upward communication is often necessary for sound decision making.

Some of the most common upward communication devices are suggestion boxes, group meetings, and appeal or grievance procedures. In their absence, people somehow find ways to adapt to nonexistent or inadequate upward communication channels. One such strategy is the emergence of "underground" employee publications in many large organizations.[19]

Varying forms of upward communication play a key role in the successful operation of many Japanese businesses.[20] The Japanese place a strong emphasis on face-to-face communication between top-level managers and rank-and-file employees. It is common practice for nonmanagerial levels to talk directly to top-level executives on work-related matters. Often, top-level managers participate in orientation and training programs to enable employees to access them. In addition, there are frequently both formal and informal mechanisms to actively solicit suggestions from employees, with rewards given for implemented ideas.

Often overlooked in the design of organizations is the provision for **horizontal communication**. In a college of business administration, when the chairperson of the accounting department communicates with the chairperson of the marketing department concerning the course offerings, the flow of communication is horizontal. Although vertical (upward and downward) communication flows are the primary considerations in organizational design, effective organizations also need horizontal communication. Horizontal communication—for example, communication between production and sales in a business organization and among the different departments or colleges within a university—is necessary for the coordination and integration of diverse organizational functions.

Upward Communication

Communication flowing from lower to higher levels in an organization; includes suggestion boxes, group meetings, and grievance procedures.

Horizontal Communication

Communication that flows across functions in an organization; necessary for coordinating and integrating diverse organizational functions.

Since mechanisms for assuring horizontal communication ordinarily do not exist in an organization's design, its facilitation is left to individual managers. Peer-to-peer communication is often necessary for coordination and can also provide social need satisfaction.

Diagonal Communication

Communication that cuts across functions and levels in an organization; important when members cannot communicate through upward, downward, or horizontal channels.

Diagonal communication, while probably the least used channel of communication in organizations, is important in situations where members cannot communicate effectively through other channels. For example, the comptroller of a large organization may wish to conduct a distribution cost analysis. One part of that task may involve having the sales force send a special report directly to the comptroller rather than going through traditional channels in the marketing department. Thus, the flow of communication would be diagonal as opposed to vertical (upward) and horizontal. In this case, a diagonal channel is most efficient in terms of time and effort for the organization.

The grapevine: an informal communication channel

The grapevine is a powerful means of communication that cuts across formal channels of communication. Despite the efforts of many companies to limit or disapprove of the grapevine's use, it is still extremely prevalent.[21] Though the nature of its impact on organizational effectiveness is debatable, there's no denying that its impact is real. Many if not most of an organization's employees listen to the assortment of facts, opinions, suspicions, and rumors the grapevine provides. This is information that normally does not travel through the organization's formal channels. According to research, an organization has several grapevine systems. Further, information traveling in a grapevine does not follow an orderly path and the grapevine is at least 75 percent accurate.[22]

Managers must recognize that a grapevine that serves as a constant source of rumors can be troublesome. Rumors are an everyday part of business and management. In fact, an estimated 33 million-plus rumors are generated in U.S. businesses every day.[23] The best that managers can hope for is that they can manage rumors—keeping them from disrupting organizational activities—rather than eliminate them.[24]

A rumor is an unverified belief that is in general circulation inside the organization (an internal rumor) or in the organization's external environment (an external rumor).[25] A rumor has three components. The *target* is the object of the rumor. The *allegation* is the rumor's point about the target. The rumor has a *source,* the original communicator of the rumor. Often, individuals will attribute a rumor to a prestigious or authoritative source to give the rumor more credibility.[26]

Some grapevine rumors are true; some are not. Rumors can be divided into four categories.[27]

1. *Pipe dreams or wish fulfillment.* These express the wishes and hopes of those who circulate rumors. These are the most positive rumors, helping to stimulate the creativity of others. Often solutions to work problems are a result of employees verbally expressing desire for change. These improvements sometimes increase efficiency for certain departments within the organization. Even though the tone is positive, they still represent employee concerns.

2. *The Bogie rumor.* This type of rumor comes from employees' fears and anxieties, causing general uneasiness among employees, such as during budget crunches. In this case, employees verbally express their fears to others. These rumors are sometimes damaging (such as a rumor about possible layoffs) and need a formal rebuttal from management.

3.   *Wedge drivers*. This is the most aggressive and damaging type of rumor. It divides groups and destroys loyalties. These rumors are motivated by aggression or even hatred. They are divisive and negative rumors. They tend to be demeaning to a company or individual and can cause damage to the reputation of others. A wedge driver rumor may involve someone at X Company saying that V Company's corporate logo represents the sign of the devil; an employee telling co-workers that another employee has AIDS or some other tale such as "Louise, the office manager, was seen the other day alone with that new accountant. They were in a car together leaving Motel Six." Or someone may spread the word that "Mary got the promotion because she's sleeping with the boss." Women are more likely to be attacked with the sexual type of rumor.

4.   *Home-stretchers*. These are anticipatory rumors. They occur after employees have been waiting a long time for an announcement. There may be just one final thing necessary to complete the puzzle and this, in effect, enhances the ambiguity of the situation.

Grapevines, rumors, and gossip are deeply ingrained in organizational life, so managers must be tuned in to what's being said. Managers must also seek to keep employees informed about what's going on.[28] A formal company newsletter can help. Falsified facts traveling through the rumor mill can be corrected by managers acting promptly, feeding accurate information to primary communicators or liaison individuals. Rumors are more difficult to correct over time because they "harden"—the details become consistent and the information becomes publicly accepted. Informal communications systems, such as the grapevine itself, can provide yet another, albeit weak, communication vehicle to keep the workforce informed about job-related matters. Finally, the organization can conduct training programs for employees on the disruptive nature of damaging rumors.

Interpersonal Communications

Within an organization, communication flows from individual to individual in face-to-face and group settings. Such flows, termed **interpersonal communications**, can vary from direct orders to casual expressions. Interpersonal communication is the primary means of managerial communication; on a typical day, over three-fourths of a manager's communications occur in face-to-face interactions.[29]

The problems that arise when managers attempt to communicate with other people can be traced to *perceptual differences* and *interpersonal style differences*. We know that each manager perceives the world according to his background, experiences, personality, frame of reference, and attitude. Managers relate to and learn from the environment (including the people in that environment) primarily through information received and transmitted. And how managers receive and transmit information depends in part on how they relate to two very important *senders* of information: *themselves* and *others*.

Interpersonal styles

Interpersonal style refers to *how an individual prefers to relate to others*. The fact that much of any interpersonal relationship involves communication indicates the importance of interpersonal style.

Let's begin by recognizing that information is held by oneself and by others but that no one of us fully has or knows that information. The different combinations of knowing and not knowing relevant information

Interpersonal Communications

Communications that flow between individuals in face-to-face and group situations.

Interpersonal Style

Manner in which we relate to other persons.

are shown in Figure 16–3. The figure, popularly known as the Johari Window, identifies four combinations, or regions, of information known and unknown by the self and others.[30]

1.   *The arena.* The region most conducive to effective interpersonal relationships and communication is termed the *arena.* In this setting, both the communicator (self) and the receivers (others) know all of the information necessary to carry on effective communication. For a communication attempt to be in the arena region, the parties involved must share identical feelings, data, assumptions, and skills. Since the arena is the area of common understanding, the larger it becomes, the more effective communication is.

2.   *The blind spot.* When relevant information is known to others but not to the self, a *blind spot* results. This constitutes a handicap for the self, since one can hardly understand the behaviors, decisions, and potentials of others without having the information on which these are based. Others have the advantage of knowing their own reactions, feelings, perceptions, and so forth, while the self is unaware of these. Consequently, interpersonal relationships and communications suffer.

3.   *The facade.* When information is known to the self but unknown to others, a person (self) may resort to superficial communications—that is, present a "false front," or facade. Information that we perceive as potentially prejudicial to a relationship or that we keep to ourselves out of fear, desire for power, or whatever, makes up the *facade.* This protective front, in turn, serves a defensive function for the self. Such a situation is particularly damaging when a subordinate "knows" and an immediate supervisor "does not know." The facade, like the blind spot, diminishes the arena and reduces the possibility of effective communication.

4.   *The unknown.* This region constitutes that portion of the relationship where relevant information is known by neither the self nor other parties. As is often stated, "I don't understand them, and they don't understand me." It is easy to see that interpersonal communication is poor under such circumstances. Circumstances of this kind often occur in organizations when individuals in different specialties must communicate to coordinate what they do.

Figure 16–3

The Johari Window: Interpersonal Styles and Communications

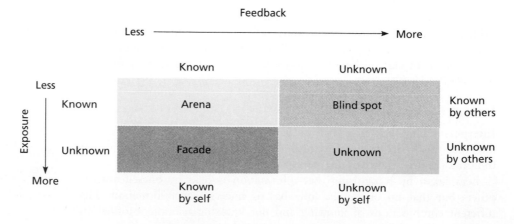

Interpersonal strategies

Figure 16–3 indicates that an individual can improve interpersonal communications by utilizing two strategies: exposure and feedback.

1. *Exposure.* Increasing the arena area by reducing the facade area requires that the individual be open and honest in sharing information with others. The process that the self uses to increase the information known to others is termed *exposure* because it sometimes leaves the self in a vulnerable position. Exposing one's true feelings by "telling it like it is" often involves risk.

2. *Feedback.* When the self doesn't know or understand, more effective communications can be developed through feedback from those who do know. Thus, the blind spot can be reduced, with a corresponding increase in the arena. Of course, whether feedback can be used depends on the individual's willingness to "hear" it and on the willingness of others to give it. Thus, the individual has less control over the provision of feedback than over the provision of exposure. Obtaining feedback is dependent on the active cooperation of others, while exposure requires the active behavior of the communicator and the passive listening of others.

Managerial styles

The day-to-day activities of managers are closely tied to effective interpersonal communications. Managers provide *information* (which must be *understood*), they give *commands* and *instructions* (which must be *obeyed* and *learned*), and they make *efforts to influence* and *persuade* (which must be *accepted* and *acted on*). Thus, how managers communicate, both as senders and receivers, is crucial to effective performance.

Theoretically, managers who desire to communicate effectively can use both exposure and feedback to enlarge the area of common understanding, the arena. As a practical matter, such is not the case. Managers differ in their ability and willingness to use exposure and feedback. At least four different managerial styles can be identified.

TYPE A   Managers who use neither exposure nor feedback are said to have a Type A style. The unknown region predominates in this style because such managers are unwilling to enlarge the area of their own knowledge or the knowledge of others. Type A managers exhibit anxiety and hostility and give the appearance of aloofness and coldness toward others. In an organization with a large number of such managers in key positions, expect to find poor and ineffective interpersonal communications and a loss of individual creativity. Type A managers often display characteristics of autocratic leaders.

TYPE B   Some managers desire some degree of satisfying relationships with their subordinates. Because of their personalities and attitudes, however, these managers are unable to open up and express their feelings and sentiments. Since they cannot use exposure, they must rely on feedback. The facade is the predominant feature of interpersonal relationships when managers overuse feedback to the exclusion of exposure. Subordinates probably distrust such managers, realizing these managers are holding back their own ideas and opinions. Type B behavior is often displayed by managers who desire to practice some form of permissive leadership.

TYPE C   Managers who value their own ideas and opinions but not the ideas and opinions of others use exposure at the expense of feedback. The consequence of this style is the perpetuation and enlargement of the blind spot.

Type A

Managers who are autocratic leaders, typically aloof and cold; often poor interpersonal communicators.

Type B

Managers who seek good relationships with subordinates but are unable to openly express feelings; often ineffective interpersonal communicators.

Type C

Managers interested only in their own ideas, not ideas and opinions of others; usually not effective communicators.

Type D

Managers who feel free to express feelings to others and to have others express feelings; most effective interpersonal communicators.

Subordinates soon realize that such managers are not particularly interested in communicating, only in telling, and are mainly interested in maintaining their own sense of importance and prestige. Consequently, Type C managers usually have subordinates who are hostile, insecure, and resentful.

TYPE D   The most effective interpersonal communication style balances exposure and feedback. Managers who are secure in their positions feel free to expose their own feelings and to obtain feedback from others. To the extent that a manager practices Type D behavior successfully, the arena region becomes larger, and communication becomes more effective.

To summarize, the importance of interpersonal styles in determining the effectiveness of interpersonal communication cannot be overemphasized. The primary determinant of effectiveness of interpersonal communication is the manager's attitude toward exposure and feedback. The most effective approach is that of the Type D manager. Type A, B, and C managers resort to behaviors that are detrimental to the effectiveness of communication and to organizational performance.

Barriers to Effective Communication

A manager has no greater responsibility than to develop effective communications.[31] Why then does communication break down? On the surface, the answer is relatively easy. We have identified the elements of communication as the communicator, the encoding, the message, the medium, the decoding, the receiver, and the feedback. If noise exists in these elements *in any way,* complete clarity of meaning and understanding do not occur. In this section, we discuss the following barriers to effective communications: frame of reference, selective listening, value judgments, source credibility, semantic problems, filtering, in-group language, status differences, proxemic behavior, time pressures, and communication overload. These sources of noise can exist in both organizational and interpersonal communications.

Frame of reference

Different individuals can interpret the same communication differently, depending on previous experiences that result in variations in the encoding and decoding processes. Communication specialists agree that this is the most important factor that breaks down the "commonness" in communications. When the encoding and decoding processes aren't alike, communication tends to break down. Thus, while the communicator actually speaks the "same language" as the receiver, the message conflicts with how the receiver "catalogs" the world. This problem is depicted in Figure 16–4. The interior areas in this diagram represent the accumulated experiences of the participants in the communication process. If they share a large area, effective communication is facilitated. If a large area is not shared—if there has been no common experience—then communication becomes impossible or, at best, highly distorted. Communicators can encode and receivers can decode only in terms of their experiences.

Distortion often occurs because of participants' differing frames of reference. Teenagers perceive things differently than do their parents; college deans perceive problems differently than do faculty members. People in various organizational *functions* can also interpret the same situation differently. A business problem may be viewed differently by the marketing manager than by the production manager. Different *levels* in the organization also have different frames of reference. First-line supervisors' frames of

Figure 16–4

Overlapping Fields of Experience

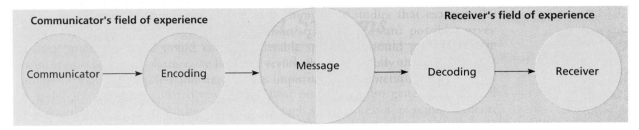

reference differ in many respects from those of vice presidents. Their different positions in the organization structure influence their frames of reference.[32] As a result, their needs, values, attitudes, and expectations differ, often resulting in unintentional distortion of communication.

Effective managerial problem solving depends on the manager adopting the appropriate frame of reference to guide the search for solutions. If the problem is mislabeled or the wrong frame of reference is used, chances for success are lowered.[33] Many other barriers examined in this section also result from variations in encoding and decoding.

Selective listening

In this form of selective perception, the individual tends to block out new information, especially if it conflicts with existing beliefs. Thus, in a directive from management, the receiver notices only things that reaffirm his beliefs. Things that conflict with preconceived notions are either ignored or distorted to confirm those preconceptions.

For example, a notice may be sent to all operating departments that costs must be reduced if the organization is to earn a profit. The communication may not achieve its desired effect because it conflicts with the perceived "reality" of the receivers. Thus, operating employees may ignore or be amused by such information in light of the large salaries, travel allowances, and expense accounts of some executives. Whether such preconceptions are justified is irrelevant; what's important is that they result in breakdowns in communication. In other words, if we only hear what we want to hear, our "reality" can't be disturbed.

Value judgments

In every communication situation, the receiver makes value judgments. This basically involves assigning an overall worth to a message prior to receiving the entire communication. Value judgments may be based on the receiver's evaluation of the communicator, previous experiences with the communicator, or on the message's anticipated meaning. For example, a college professor, perceiving the department chairperson as not being concerned enough about teaching quality, may consider a merit evaluation meeting with the chairperson as "going through the motions." A cohesive work group may form negative value judgments concerning all actions by management.

Source credibility

Source credibility is the trust, confidence, and faith that the receiver has in the words and actions of the communicator. The level of credibility that the receiver assigns to the communicator in turn directly affects how the receiver views and reacts to the communicator's words, ideas, and actions. Thus, subordinates' evaluation of their manager affects how they view a communication from her. This, of course, is heavily influenced by previous experiences with the manager. Again, we see that everything done by a manager communicates. Union leaders who view management as exploiters and managers who view union leaders as political animals are likely to engage in little real communication.

Semantic problems

Communication has been defined as the transmission of *information* and *understanding* through the use of *common symbols*. Actually, we cannot transmit understanding. We can merely transmit information in the form of words, which are the common symbols. Unfortunately, the same words may mean entirely different things to different people. The understanding is in the receiver, not in the words.

Because different groups use words differently, communication can often be impeded. This is especially true with abstract or technical terms or phrases. "Cost-benefit study" would have meaning to those involved in the administration of the hospital but might mean very little to some staff physicians. In fact, it might even carry a negative meaning. Such concepts as *trusts, profits,* and *Treasury bills* may have concrete meaning to bank executives but little or no meaning to bank tellers. Thus, because words mean different things to different people, a communicator may speak the same language as a receiver but still not transmit understanding.

Filtering

Filtering, a common occurrence in upward communication in organizations, refers to the manipulation of information so that the receiver perceives it as positive. For example, subordinates "cover up" unfavorable information in messages to their superiors. The reason for such filtering should be clear; this is the direction (upward) that carries control information to management. Management makes merit evaluations, grants salary increases, and promotes individuals based on what it receives by way of the upward channel. The temptation to filter is likely to be strong at every level in the organization.

In-group language

Each of us at some time has undoubtedly been subjected to highly technical jargon, only to learn that the unfamiliar words or phrases described simple procedures or familiar objects. For example, students may be asked by researchers to "complete an instrument as part of an experimental treatment." The student soon learns that this involves nothing more than filling out a paper-and-pencil questionnaire.

Occupational, professional, and social groups often develop words or phrases that have meaning only to members. Such special language can serve many useful purposes. It can provide members with feelings of belongingness, cohesiveness, and (in many cases) self-esteem; it can also facilitate effective communication *within* the group. The use of in-group language can, however, result in severe communication breakdowns when outsiders or other groups are involved. Management, in this case, should provide communication skills training to affected individuals to facilitate effective communication between involved parties.[34]

Status differences

Organizations often express hierarchical rank through a variety of symbols (titles, offices, carpets, etc.). Such status differences can be perceived as threats by persons lower in the hierarchy, and this can prevent or distort communication. Not wanting to look incompetent, a nurse may remain quiet instead of expressing an opinion or asking a question of the nursing supervisor.

In an effort to utilize their time efficiently, supervisors many times make status barriers more difficult to surmount. The government administrator or bank vice president may be accessible only by appointment or by passing the careful quizzing of a secretary. This widens the communication gap between superiors and subordinates.

Isolation from accurate feedback is particularly pervasive at top levels of an organization. There, an executive of a company of 20,000 employees may have direct relationships with only 10 or 15 individuals. The personality of the highly successful executive may discourage honest feedback: an executive demeanor of total confidence and command doesn't easily invite criticism from subordinates; an abrasive style with subordinates has the same effect.[35] Upper-level executives also often take on an exaggerated importance. For example, one executive once casually wondered aloud how a proposed law would affect the company, knowing that the bill stood little chance of being passed. Later, he discovered that his subordinates had responded to the casual remark with a thorough, costly—and ultimately useless—analysis of the bill's impact. From then on, the executive was cautious with his comments.[36]

Some organizations are de-emphasizing status and power differences to encourage more open supervisor–subordinate communication. Others are actively encouraging employees to ask questions not only about objective facts but also about the reasons and motives behind those facts.[37] At Honda Motors in Marysville, Ohio, for example, visible differences in status and power have been intentionally avoided. The plant has no executive cafeteria or washroom and no special parking spaces, and executives work in open offices with no frills. Management believes that these actions reduce communication barriers between managers of all levels and their subordinates.

www.Honda.com

Proxemic behavior

An important but often overlooked element of nonverbal communication is *proxemics*, defined as an individual's use of space when interpersonally communicating with others. According to Edward Hall, a prominent researcher of proxemics, people have four zones of informal space—spatial distances they maintain when interacting with others: the intimate zone (from physical contact to 18 inches), the personal zone (from 18 inches to 4 feet), the social zone (from over 4 to 12 feet), and the public zone (more than 12 feet).[38] For Americans, manager–subordinate relationships begin in the social zone and progress to the personal zone after mutual trust has developed.[39] An individual's personal and intimate zones make up a "private bubble" of space that is considered private territory, not to be entered by others unless invited.

Proxemics creates a significant communication barrier when the proxemic behaviors of the sender and receiver differ. For example, assume that, like most Americans, you stand in the social zone while interacting at a social gathering such as a cocktail party. However, in the South American culture, a personal-zone distance is considered more natural in such situations. When a South American businessperson you're talking with at a cocktail party assumes a personal-zone distance, how do you feel? Typically in such a situation, an individual feels so uncomfortable with the person standing "too close" that any verbal communication isn't heard. Conflicting proxemic behavior can also affect each individual's perceptions of the other—you may view the South American as pushy and aggressive; she may see you as cold and impolite.

Time pressures

The pressure of time presents an important barrier to communication. Managers don't have time to communicate frequently with every subordinate. However, time pressures can often lead to far more serious problems than this. *Short-circuiting* is a failure of the formally prescribed communication system that often results from time pressures. What it means is simply that someone has been left out of the formal channel of communication who would normally be included. For example, suppose a salesperson needs a rush order for an important customer and goes directly to the production manager with the request, since the production manager owes the salesperson a favor. Other members of the sales force who get word of this become upset over this preferential treatment and report it to the sales manager. Obviously, the sales manager would know nothing of the "deal," having been short-circuited.

In some cases, going through formal channels is extremely costly or even impossible from a practical standpoint. Consider the impact on a hospital patient if a nurse had to report a critical malfunction in life support equipment to the nursing team leader, who in turn had to report it to the hospital engineer, who would instruct a staff engineer to make the repair.

Communication overload

One vital task performed by a manager is decision making. One of the necessary factors in effective decisions is *information*. The 1990s have often been described as the time when information technology radically changed the corporate landscape.[40] Indeed, as seen in the Close-Up on the development and use of "intranets," technology has great potential to improve both the efficiency and effectiveness of organizational communication.

C L O S E - U P

Intranets Improve Internal Communication

Intranets are improving both the efficiency and effectiveness of internal organizational communication. An intranet brings the visually appealing and interactive technology of the World Wide Web inside the organization to network employees in unlimited ways. The potential of personalized Web pages to improve the effectiveness of management–employee communication also appears to be unlimited. Let's examine some innovative uses of this new technology.

One obvious advantage is the savings that result in printing and physically delivering employee communications. The pharmaceutical firm Eli Lilly saved $400,000 by distributing product information on-line to its offices around the world instead of using mail, fax, and the phone. Motorola Inc., moving its health care provider directory to 700,000 U.S. based employees on-line, saved 8 million pieces of paper and $750,000.

More importantly, the intranet is also improving communication effectiveness. Booz, Allen, and Hamilton, a major consulting firm, built a companywide intranet known as Knowledge On-Line (KOL), whose main purpose is to provide staff all over the world with the organization's best thinking. Chrysler Corporation's Dashboard Intranet simplifies information access to its 40,000 salaried employees. It has increased productivity by enabling users to get at competitive intelligence, human resource information, financial modeling tools, and collaborative workgroup support.

Companies as diverse as Hallmark, IBM, and Rockwell are deploying intranets for uses from financial management to more efficient manufacturing operations. National City Bank, with employees in five midwestern states, developed Gateway, an intranet to foster a sense of community among employees as well as to assist when new banks are purchased in the integration of cultures, product lines, and systems.

These and other organizations are finding that an intranet has tremendous potential as an inexpensive and effective way to communicate within an organization. And not surprisingly, those who have tried it say that the biggest benefits are improved employee communication and increased collaboration between different departments and functions such as marketing, engineering, and research.

Sources: Art Jahnke, "Share Ware," *CIO,* July 1, 1998, p. 10; Lew McCreary, "The Birth of the Do's," *CIO,* July 1, 1998, pp. 44–47; Gene Koprowski, "Intranets Unleashed," *Software Magazine,* August 1997, pp. 76–83; Megan Stantosus, "Banking on the Future," *CIO,* July 1, 1998, pp. 56–60; and Martha Finney, "Harness the Power Within," *HR Magazine,* January 1997, pp. 66–74.

 www.elililly.com, www.mot.com, www2.chrysler.com, www.hallmark.com, www.ibm.com, www.rockwell.com, www.nationalcitybank.com

Figure 16–5

Barriers to Effective Communication

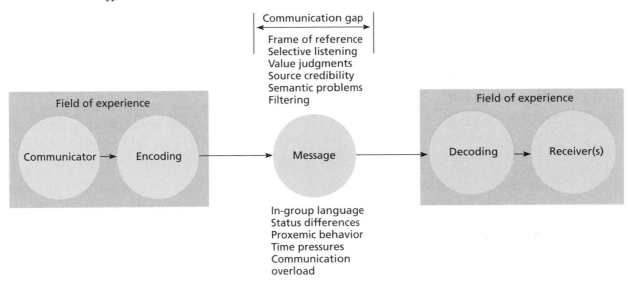

Because of the advances, the difficulty does not lie in generating information. Rather, managers often feel buried by a deluge of information and data. As a result, people can't absorb or adequately respond to all of the messages directed to them. They screen out the majority of messages, which in effect means that these messages are never decoded. Thus, in the area of organizational communication, "more" isn't always "better."

The barriers to communication discussed here, while common, are by no means the only ones. Figure 16–5 illustrates these barriers' impact on the process of communication. Examining each barrier indicates that they are either *within individuals* (e.g., frame of reference, value judgments) or *within organizations* (e.g., in-group language, filtering). This point is important because attempts to improve communication must of necessity focus on changing people and/or changing the organizational structure.

Improving Communication in Organizations

Managers striving to become better communicators must accomplish two separate tasks. First, they must improve their *messages*—the information they wish to transmit. Second, they must seek to improve their own *understanding* of what other people try to communicate to them. In other words, they must become better encoders and decoders. They must strive not only to be understood but also to understand.[41] The following techniques can help accomplish these two important tasks.

Following up

This technique involves assuming that you're misunderstood and, whenever possible, attempting to determine whether your intended meaning was actually received. As we've seen, meaning is often in the mind of the receiver. For example, an accounting unit leader in a government office passes on to accounting staff members notices of openings in other agencies. While long-time employees may understand this as a friendly gesture, a new employee might interpret it as an evaluation of poor performance and a suggestion to leave.

Regulating information flow

Regulating communication can ensure an optimum flow of information to managers, thereby eliminating the barrier of communication overload. Communication can be regulated in both quality and quantity. The idea is based on the *exception principle* of management, which states that only significant deviations from policies and procedures should be brought to the attention of superiors. In formal communication then, superiors should be communicated with only on matters of importance and not for the sake of communication. In other words, executives should be supplied with diagnostic rather than superfluous information.[42]

Utilizing feedback

Earlier the chapter identified feedback as an important element in effective two-way communication. It provides a channel for receiver response that enables the communicator to determine whether the message has been received and has produced the intended response.[43] In face-to-face communication, direct feedback is possible. In downward communication, however, inaccuracies often occur because of insufficient opportunity for feedback from receivers. Distributing a memorandum about an important policy to all employees doesn't guarantee that communication has occurred.

We might expect that feedback in the form of upward communication would be encouraged more in organic organizations, but mechanisms that encourage upward communication are found in many different organizational designs. A healthy organization needs effective upward communication if its downward communication is to have any chance of being effective. The point is that developing and supporting mechanisms for feedback involve far more than following up on communications. Rather, to be effective, feedback needs to be engaging, responsive, and directed toward a desired outcome.[44]

Empathy

Empathy is the ability to put oneself in the other person's role and to assume that individual's viewpoints and emotions. This involves being receiver-oriented rather than communicator-oriented. The form of the communication should depend largely on what is known about the receiver. Empathy requires communicators to place themselves in the shoes of the receiver to anticipate how the message is likely to be decoded.

Too often, managers perceive themselves to be much better communicators than their subordinates perceive them.[45] Managers must understand and appreciate the process of decoding. In decoding, the message is filtered through the receiver's perceptions. For vice presidents to communicate effectively with supervisors, for faculty to communicate effectively with students, and for government administrators to communicate effectively with minority groups, empathy is often an important ingredient. Empathy can reduce many barriers to effective communication. Remember that the greater the gap between the experiences and background of the communicator and the receiver, the greater the effort needed to find a common ground of understanding where fields of experience overlap.

Repetition

Repetition is an accepted principle of learning. Introducing repetition or redundancy into communication (especially that of a technical nature) ensures that if one part of the message is not understood, other parts carry the same message. New employees are often provided with the same basic information in several different forms. Likewise, students receive much redundant information when first entering a university. This ensures that registration procedures, course requirements, and new terms such as *matriculation* and *quality points* are communicated.

Encouraging mutual trust

Time pressures often mean that managers cannot follow up communication and encourage feedback or upward communication every time they communicate. Under such circumstances, an atmosphere of mutual confidence and trust between managers and their subordinates can facilitate communication. Subordinates judge for themselves the quality of their perceived relationship with their superiors. A study of American and Canadian office workers found that only 38 percent of the workers surveyed felt that management was honest with them. Even fewer—27 percent—believed that management cared about them as individuals.[46] Managers who can develop a climate of trust find that following up on each communication is less critical. Because they've fostered high source credibility among subordinates, no loss in understanding results from a failure to follow up on each communication. Some organizations initiate formal programs designed to encourage mutual trust.

Effective timing

Individuals are exposed to thousands of messages daily. Because of the impossibility of taking in all the messages, many are never decoded and received. Managers must realize that while they are attempting to communicate with a receiver, other messages are being received simultaneously. Thus, the message that the manager sends may not be heard. Messages that do not compete with other messages are more likely to be understood.

Because of this problem, many organizations use "retreats" when important policies or changes are being made. A group of executives may be sent to a resort to resolve an important corporate policy issue, or a college department's faculty may retreat to an off-campus site to design a new curriculum.

On an everyday basis, effective communication can be facilitated by properly timing major announcements. The barriers discussed earlier often arise from poor timing that results in distortions and value judgments.

Simplifying language

Complex language has been identified as a major barrier to effective communication. University students often suffer when their teachers use technical jargon that transforms simple concepts into complex puzzles. Government agencies are also known for their often incomprehensible communications. And we have already noted instances where professional people use in-group language in attempting to communicate with individuals outside their group. Managers must remember that effective communication involves transmitting *understanding* as well as information. If the receiver does not understand, then there has been no communication. In fact, many techniques discussed in this section have as their sole purpose the promotion of understanding. Managers must encode messages in words, appeals, and symbols that are meaningful to the receiver.

Effective listening

To improve communication, managers must seek not only to be understood but also to *understand*. This involves listening. One method of encouraging someone to express true feelings, desires, and emotions is to listen. Just listening is not enough; one must

Figure 16–6

Improving Communication in Organizations (Narrowing the Communication Gap)

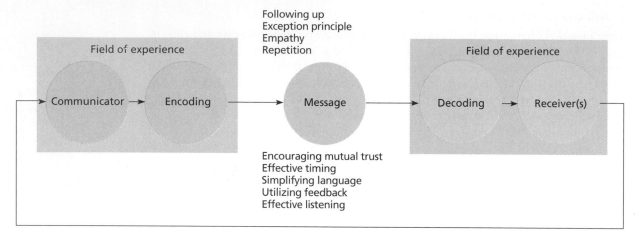

listen with understanding. Can managers develop listening skills? Numerous pointers have been given for effective listening in organizational settings. For example, one writer cites "Ten Commandments for Good Listening": stop talking; put the speaker at ease; show the speaker you want to listen; remove distractions; empathize with the speaker; be patient; hold your temper; go easy on argument and criticism; ask questions; and stop talking.[47] Note that "stop talking" is both the first and the last commandment.

Such guidelines can be useful to managers. More important, however, is the *decision to listen.* Guidelines are useless unless the manager makes the conscious decision to listen. Only after the realization that effective communication involves understanding as well as being understood can guidelines for effective listening become useful.

In conclusion, to find any aspect of a manager's job that does not involve communication would be hard. If everyone in the organization had common points of view, communicating would be easy. Unfortunately, such is not the case—each member comes to the organization with a distinct personality, background, experience, and frame of reference. The structure of the organization itself influences status relationships and the distance (levels) between individuals, which in turn influence the ability of individuals to communicate.

This chapter has described basic elements in the process of communication and what it takes to communicate effectively. These elements are necessary whether the communication is face-to-face or written and communicated vertically, horizontally, or diagonally within an organizational structure. We discussed several common communication barriers and several means to improve communication. Figure 16–6 shows techniques that facilitate more effective communication. Often, time does not permit managers to utilize many of the techniques for improving communication, and skills such as empathy and effective listening are not easy to develop. The figure does, however, illustrate the challenge of communicating effectively and suggests what is required. It shows that communicating involves both transmitting and receiving. Managers must be effective at both; they must understand as well as be understood.

Summary of Key Points

• Communication is the transmission of information and understanding through the use of common symbols.

• The communication process consists of certain basic elements that must always be present if effective communication is to result. These elements are the communicator, the message, the medium, the receiver, and feedback.

• Nonverbal communication is an important source of information about a sender's or receiver's thoughts and feelings. The voice, body expressions, and proxemics are all important mechanisms of nonverbal communication.

• Organizational design and the communication process are inseparable. The design of an organization must provide for communication in three distinct directions: vertical (downward and upward), horizontal, and diagonal.

• The grapevine is an informal communication channel that pervades organizations. In a typical organization, information that's rarely communicated through formal channels is instead passed along through a grapevine.

• Rumors, carried through the grapevine, are an everyday part of organizational life. Regardless of validity, they tend to flourish when they are viewed by the receiver as important, entertaining, and/or ambiguous.

• Communication effectiveness is enhanced when both the sender and receiver utilize feedback and exposure. Balanced use of both is the most effective approach.

• To alleviate the numerous barriers to communication in organizations, managers should follow up on their messages, regulate information flow, utilize feedback, develop empathy, utilize message repetition, encourage mutual trust, simplify their language, effectively time the delivery of their messages, and become effective listeners.

Discussion and Review Questions

1. Describe a situation where you were involved in a communication process that was interrupted by noise. What form did the noise take and in which stage did the noise occur? What were the results?

2. With the increase of diversity in the workplace, discuss the additional issues needing to be addressed that may be present in today's organizations in relation to (1) the communication process and (2) the sending and receiving of nonverbal messages.

3. Consider your own workplace (past or present). Which direction of communication was most lacking? What effect did it have on your productivity and that of the company as a whole?

4. Describe a situation where you heard a rumor through a grapevine. Did the rumor turn out to be true?

5. Provide an example of how an employee might utilize a facade to an organization's detriment.

6. Note a manager/leader that you have worked with (school, job, or other) that had a Type A managerial style. Contrast that person with a familiar Type D manager/leader. What are their differences? How did they affect you or your group's effectiveness?

7. What types of barriers to communication exist in a class setting? How can they be overcome?

8. Describe a situation in which you've been the receiver in a one-way communication process. Give some reasons why certain individuals might not like it. Why might some people prefer it?

9. What, if anything, can managers do to remove barriers to communication that are beyond their direct control?

10. Discuss why organizational design and communication flow are so closely related.

CASE FOR ANALYSIS

Leigh Randell

Leigh Randell is supervisor of in-flight services at the Atlanta base of Omega Airlines, a successful regional air carrier with routes throughout the South and Southwest. In addition to Atlanta, it has bases in six major cities.

Randell's job involves supervision of all in-flight services and personnel at the Atlanta base. She has been with the airline for seven years and in her present job for two years. While preferring flying to a permanent ground

Exhibit 1

Omega, Atlanta: Organization Chart

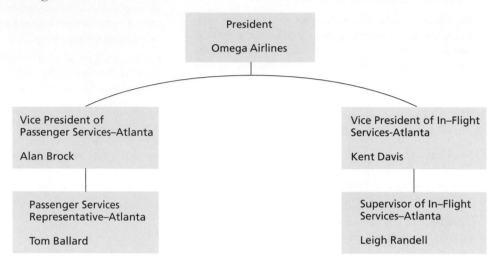

position, she decided to try the management position. In her job, she reports directly to Kent Davis, vice president of in-flight services.

During the past year, Randall has observed what she believes is a great deal of duplication of effort between flight attendants and passenger service personnel in the terminal with respect to paperwork procedures for boarding passengers. This, she believes, has resulted in unnecessary delays in departures of many flights—especially through flights (those that don't originate or terminate in Atlanta). Since most Omega through flights stop in Atlanta, Randell believes that such delayed departures are probably not a major problem at Omega's other bases or at smaller airports. Thus, she has decided to try to coordinate the efforts of flight attendants and passenger service personnel with a simpler, more efficient boarding procedure, thereby reducing ground time and increasing passenger satisfaction through closer adherence to departure times.

In this respect, she has, on three occasions during the past two months, written memos to Tom Ballard, Omega's passenger services representative at the Atlanta base. Each time, Randell has requested information regarding specific procedures, time, and costs for boarding passengers on through flights. She has received no reply from Tom Ballard. His job involves supervision of all passenger service personnel. He has been with Omega for five years, having joined its management training program immediately after

graduating from college. He reports directly to Alan Brock, vice president of passenger services at the Atlanta base. Exhibit 1 presents the organization structure for the Atlanta base.

Last week, Leigh wrote a memo to Kent Davis.

For several months, I have been trying to develop a new method for facilitating the boarding of passengers on through flights by more closely coordinating efforts of In-Flight Services and Passenger Services. The results would be a reduction in clerical work, costs, and ground time and closer adherence to departure times for through flights. Unfortunately, I have received no cooperation at all in my efforts from the passenger services representative. I have made three written requests for information, each of which has been ignored. Needless to say, this has been frustrating to me. While I realize that my beliefs may not always be correct, in this instance I am only trying to initiate something that will be beneficial to everyone involved: Passenger Services, In-Flight Services, and, most important, Omega Airlines. I would like to meet with you to discuss this matter and the possibility of my transferring back to flight duty.

Kent Davis summoned Alan Brock and Tom Ballard to a hastily called conference. Tom Ballard was mildly asked why he had not furnished the information that Randell had requested.

"Too busy," he said. "Her questions were out of sight. There was no time for me to answer this sort of request. I've got a job to do. Besides, I don't report to her."

"But Tom, you don't understand," Kent Davis said. "All Leigh Randell is trying to do is improve the present system of boarding passengers on through flights. She has taken the initiative to work on something that might benefit everyone."

Tom Ballard thought for a moment. "No," he replied, "it didn't look like that to me. You know I've also had ideas on how to improve the system for quite some time. Anyway, she's going about it all wrong."

Discussion Questions

1. What barriers to effective communication do you detect in this case?

2. Is anyone "wrong" in this situation? By what other means could Randell have requested the information from Tom Ballard? What do you think of Tom Ballard's reaction? Why?

3. While communicating information vertically up or down the organization does not present a major problem, why is horizontal and diagonal communication more difficult to attain? What would you recommend that the management of Omega Airlines do to remedy this situation? How would your recommendations improve communication in the organization?

E X P E R I E N T I A L   E X E R C I S E

Perceptual Differences

Objective

To illustrate how people perceive the same situation differently through the process of selective perception.

Related Topics

This exercise aptly demonstrates the wide variety of perceptual differences among people when considering a situation where little factual information is provided. The exercise should also indicate that most people selectively perceive the information they're comfortable with in analyzing a situation. Many will also subconsciously fill in gaps of information with assumptions they suppose are facts.

Starting the Exercise

The instructor will divide the class into groups of four students each. Students will then, as individuals, complete the following quiz. Group members shouldn't converse until everyone has finished.

Completing the Exercise

1. Your instructor will provide the answers to the 15 questions. Score your responses.

2. As a group, discuss your members' responses. Focus your discussion on the following questions:
    a. Why did perceptions differ across members? What factors could account for these differences?
    b. Many people don't perform very well with this quiz. Why? What other factors beyond selective perception can adversely affect performance?

Quiz: The Robbery

The lights in a store had just been turned off by a businessman when a man appeared and demanded money. The owner opened a cash register. The contents of the cash register were scooped up, and the man sped away. A member of the police force was notified promptly.

Answer the following questions about the story by circling T *for true,* F *for false, or* ? *for unknown.*

1.	A man appeared after the owner turned off his store lights.	T	F	?
2.	The robber was a man.	T	F	?
3.	The man who appeared did not demand money.	T	F	?
4.	The man who opened the cash register was the owner.	T	F	?
5.	The store owner scooped up the contents of the cash register and ran away.	T	F	?
6.	Someone opened a cash register.	T	F	?
7.	After the man who demanded money scooped up the contents of the cash register, he ran away.	T	F	?
8.	While the cash register contained money, the story does not state how much.	T	F	?
9.	The robber demanded money of the owner.	T	F	?
10.	A businessman had just turned off the lights when a man appeared in the store.	T	F	?
11.	It was broad daylight when the man appeared.	T	F	?
12.	The man who appeared opened the cash register.	T	F	?
13.	No one demanded money.	T	F	?
14.	The story concerns a series of events in which only three persons are referred to: the owner of the store, a man who demanded money, and a member of the police force.	T	F	?
15.	The following events occurred: someone demanded money, a cash register was opened, its contents were scooped up, and a man dashed out of the store.	T	F	?

Source: William V. Haney, *Communication and Interpersonal Relations: Text and Cases* (Homewood, Ill.: Richard D. Irwin, 1979), pp. 250–51.

Chapter 17

Managing Effective Decision-Making Processes

Learning Objectives

After completing Chapter 17, you should be able to:

Define
The terms *programmed decision* and *nonprogrammed decision*.

Describe
The process of decision making.

Discuss
The major behavioral influences on the process of decision making.

Compare
Group decision making and individual decision making.

Identify
The various methods that managers can use to stimulate creativity in group decision making.

T

his chapter focuses on decision making. The quality of managerial decisions is the yardstick of the manager's effectiveness.[1] Thus, the flow of the preceding chapters leads logically to a discussion of decision making—that is, people behave as *individuals* and as members of *groups,* within an *organizational structure,* and they *communicate* for many reasons. One of the most important reasons is to make decisions. Making effective decisions can be a complex process, relying on all the skills and training a manager possesses. This chapter, therefore, analyzes decision making in terms of how people decide as a consequence of the information they receive both through the organizational structure and through the behavior of important persons and groups.

Types of Decisions

While managers in various organizations may be separated by background, lifestyle, and distance, sooner or later they must all make decisions.[2] As discussed throughout this book, debate continues on whether managers should encourage subordinates to participate in decision making.[3] Likewise, depending on the organization's size and overall technical complexity, opportunities to involve subordinates in the decision process may vary.[4] However, regardless of organizational variations and the degree of employee participation, managers are ultimately responsible for decision outcomes. That is, they face a situation involving several alternatives, and their decision involves a comparison of alternatives and an evaluation of the outcome. In this section, we move beyond a general definition of a decision and present a system for classifying various decisions.

Specialists in decision making have developed several ways of classifying decisions. Similar for the most part, these systems differ mainly in terminology. We shall use the widely adopted system suggested by Herbert Simon.[5] It distinguishes between two types of decisions: programmed and nonprogrammed.

Programmed Decisions

Specific procedures developed for repetitive and routine problems.

Nonprogrammed Decisions

Decisions required by unique and complex management problems.

1. **Programmed decisions.** If a particular situation occurs often, a routine procedure usually can be worked out for solving it. Thus, decisions are *programmed* to the extent that problems are repetitive and routine and a definite procedure has been developed for handling them.

2. **Nonprogrammed decisions.** Decisions are *nonprogrammed* when they are novel and unstructured. No established procedure exists for handling the problem, either because it has not arisen in exactly the same manner before or because it is complex or extremely important. Such problems deserve special treatment.

These two classifications, while broad, make important distinctions. On the one hand, organizational managers face great numbers of programmed decisions in their daily operations. Such decisions should be treated without expending unnecessary organizational resources on them. On the other hand, nonprogrammed decisions must be properly identified as such because they form the basis for allocating billions of dollars of resources in our economy every year. Table 17–1 breaks down the different types of decisions, with examples of each type in different organizations. It indicates that programmed and nonprogrammed decisions apply to distinctly different problems and require different procedures.

Unfortunately, we know very little about the human process involved in unprogrammed decisions.[6] Traditionally, to make programmed decisions, managers use rules, standard operating procedures, and the structure of the organization that develops specific procedures for handling problems. More recently, operations researchers have facilitated such decisions through the development of mathematical models. In contrast, managers make nonprogrammed decisions by general problem-solving processes, judgment, intuition, and creativity.[7] Informal relationships between managers, as well as formal ones, may be utilized to handle such ambiguous problems.[8] For example, a number of studies have suggested that Japanese organizations can be highly effective at processing information and taking action by relying on unplanned interaction around problems rather than on formal procedures and problem solving. To date, the advances in modern technology haven't improved nonprogrammed decision making nearly as much as they've improved programmed decision making.[9] The Close-Up "Falling in Love with Technology" tells us that while some advances have been made, especially with respect to programmed decisions, we must be careful to evaluate the contributions of technology to decision making.

Table 17–1 Comparison of Types of Decisions		PROGRAMMED DECISIONS	NONPROGRAMMED DECISIONS
	Problem	Frequent, repetitive, routine. Much certainty regarding cause and effect relationships.	Novel, unstructured. Much uncertainty regarding cause and effect relationships.
	Procedure	Dependence on policies, rules, and definite procedures.	Necessity for creativity, intuition, tolerance for ambiguity, creative problem solving.
	Examples:		
	Business firm	Periodic reorders of inventory.	Diversification into new products and markets.
	University	Necessary grade point average for good academic standing.	Construction of new classroom facilities.
	Health care	Procedure for admitting patients.	Purchase of experimental equipment.
	Government	Merit system for promotion of state employees.	Reorganization of state government agencies.

Ideally, top management's main concern should be nonprogrammed decisions, while first-level managers should be concerned with programmed decisions. Middle managers in most organizations concentrate mostly on programmed decisions, although in some cases they participate in nonprogrammed decisions. In other words, the nature, frequency, and degree of certainty surrounding a problem should dictate at what level of management the decision should be made.

Obviously, problems arise in organizations where top management expends much time and effort on programmed decisions. One unfortunate result is a neglect of long-range planning. It's subordinated to other activities whether the organization is successful or is having problems. Success justifies continuing the policies and practices that achieved it; if the organization experiences difficulty, its current problems have first priority and occupy the time of top management. In either case, long-range planning ends up being neglected. Neglect of long-range planning usually results in an overemphasis on short-run control and, therefore, less delegation of authority to lower levels of management. This often has adverse effects on employee motivation and satisfaction.

The Decision-Making Process

Decisions should be thought of as means rather than ends. They are the *organizational mechanisms* by which an attempt is made to achieve a desired state. They are, in effect, an *organizational response* to a problem. Every decision is the outcome of a dynamic process that is influenced by a multitude of forces. Although this process is diagrammed in Figure 17–1, it is not a fixed procedure. It is a sequential process rather than a series of steps.[10] This enables us to examine each element in the normal progression that leads to a decision.

Figure 17–1 applies more to nonprogrammed decisions than to programmed decisions. Problems that occur infrequently, with a great deal of uncertainty and risk surrounding the outcome, require that the manager utilize the entire process. For problems

Decision

Means to achieve some result or to solve some problem; outcome of a process influenced by many forces.

Falling in Love with Technology

It is easy for managers to become enamored with technology. It is easy to admire it for its own sake as well as for the unquestionable productivity gains that it makes possible. But it is also important—in fact, more important—to look further for an evaluation of the real value it delivers. The real potential value of technology will not be realized unless it enables managers to improve the quality of their decisions. It must assist managers in bringing their own expertise to bear on important decisions in their areas and allow them to make better decisions. The challenge to improve the quality of decisions is a difficult one for corporate information systems. The first challenge is to determine what information is relevant. Once determined, the relevant information needs to be routed to those managers who require it. Finally, all of these activities have to be accomplished as quickly and cost efficiently as possible. What follows are some examples of decision-support systems that are improving the quality of decisions and using technology to its full potential.

Sabre Decision Technologies Inc. (SDT), the information developer for American Airlines, developed "Aircrews," a software program that helps the airline make crew assignments for its 4,000 daily flights from a pool of 30,000 crew members. The system assigns crews by weighing variables such as crew location, flying time, weather, union rules, and federal regulations. All in all, there are 20 to 30 million variables for deciding a crew flight assignment, which results in billions of combinations. Clearly, it cannot be done manually. In fact, 20 million pairings need to be generated to reach an optimal decision.

In addition to making daily and weekly flight assignments, the system also looks ahead to help determine the long-term staffing needs over a five-year period. It has worked so well that the system has been purchased by other organizations such as Federal Express, US Air, British Airways, and Delta Airlines. It has saved American Airlines that occur frequently, the entire process is not necessary. If a policy is established to handle such problems, managers don't need to develop and evaluate alternatives each time a problem of this kind arises.

Establishing specific goals and objectives and measuring results

Organizations need goals and objectives in each area where performance influences effectiveness. Adequately established goals and objectives will dictate which results must be achieved and which measures indicate whether those results have been achieved. As part of the goal and objective-setting process, top management must communicate their tolerance for experimentation and failure on the part of subordinates.[11] In the absence of such communication, middle and lower-level managers will attempt to zero-out risk, a situation that involves avoiding any potential failures (and corresponding successes), thus ensuring the organization of mediocre results.

Identifying problems

A necessary condition for a decision is a problem.[12] That is, if problems did not exist, there would be no need for decisions. The decision maker is a problem solver, charged with either selecting from available alternatives or inventing an alternative different in meaningful ways from previously existing alternatives.[13] The existence of a problem is indicated by a gap between the organization's goals and objectives and the levels of actual performance. Thus, a gap of 20 percent between a sales volume objective and sales volume actually achieved indicates a problem.

Identifying the exact problem can be hindered by certain factors:

1. *Perceptual problems.* Our individual perceptions may protect or defend us from unpleasant facts. Negative information may be selectively perceived to distort its true meaning; it may also be totally ignored. For example, a college dean may fail to identify increasing class sizes as a problem while at the same time being sensitive to problems

over $20 million and is expected to save the other airlines even more.

A decision-support system named GIS (geographical information system) was developed for an oil company that was planning an onshore and offshore pipeline in the Gulf of Mexico. The system assisted the company in eventually locating the 214-mile pipeline in the most cost-effective way based on landcover type, wetland distribution, and closeness to other environmentally sensitive resources.

Finally, NCR Corp is targeting the Internet service provider with a system it claims will solve the customer service problems that have been an important issue for Internet businesses. The new system, which is called SmartEC Decision System, is targeted at what NCR describes as Internet service businesses. The system correlates Internet activity data with business operational data and external reference data to provide users with comprehensive customer intelligence information.

The brief examples provided direct our attention to the tremendous potential value of technology for improving both the efficiency and effectiveness of managerial decisions. And it is on these criteria that the value of technology in decision making must ultimately be evaluated, not the glitz of the technology itself.

Source: "NCR Launches DSS for ISP Care," *America's Network*, April 15, 1998, p. 45; Dawn R. Schott and Jon A. Schmidt, "Merged GIS, GPS Data Assist Siting for Gulf Gas Line," *Oil and Gas Journal*, June 29, 1998, pp. 80–84; and Ann Saccomano, "Same Goal, Different Objectives in Search for Better Decision Support Systems," *Traffic World*, April 24, 1995, pp. 37–38.

www.Sabre.com

www.americanair.com

www.fedex.com

www.USAIR.com

www.british-airways.com

www.delta-air.com

www.NCR.com/java

Figure 17–1

The Decision-Making Process

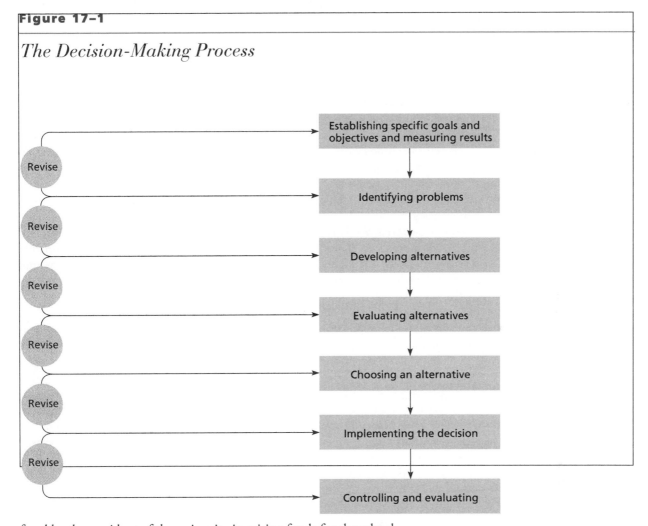

faced by the president of the university in raising funds for the school.

2.   *Defining problems in terms of solutions.* This is really a form of jumping to conclusions. For example, a sales manager may say, "The decrease in profits is due to our poor product quality," which suggests a particular solution: the improvement of product quality in the production department. Certainly, other solutions may be possible. Perhaps the sales force has been inadequately selected or trained. Perhaps competitors have a less expensive product. Regardless, one must seek to identify the real cause of problems through careful analysis.

3.   *Identifying symptoms as problems.* "Our problem is a 32-percent decline in orders." While it is certainly true that orders have declined, the decline is really only a symptom of the true problem. The manager must identify the *cause* of the decline in order to find the real problem.

Problems are usually of three types: opportunity, crisis, and routine. Crisis and routine problems present themselves and must be attended to by the managers.[14] Opportunities, in contrast, must usually be found; they await discovery. Often they go unnoticed and are eventually lost by an inattentive manager. Because most crises and routine problems, by their very nature, demand immediate attention, a manager may spend a great deal of time handling them and not have time to pursue important new opportunities.

Many well-managed organizations try to draw attention away from crises and routine problems and toward longer-range issues through planning activities and goal-setting programs.

Developing alternatives

Before a decision is made, feasible alternatives (potential solutions to the problem) should be developed, and the possible consequences of each alternative should be considered. For example, a sales manager may identify an inadequately trained sales force as the cause of declining sales. The sales manager would then identify possible alternatives for solving the problem, such as (1) a sales training program conducted at the home office by management, (2) a sales training program conducted by a professional training organization at a site away from the home office, and (3) more intense on-the-job training.

Developing alternatives is really a search process in which the relevant internal and external environments of the organization are investigated to provide information that can be developed into possible alternatives. Obviously, this search is conducted within certain time and cost constraints; only so much effort can be devoted to developing alternatives.[15]

However, sufficient effort should be made to develop a wide range of alternatives. Contrary to what you might think, there's a positive link between the number of alternatives considered and the speed with which decisions can be reached.[16] Not generating enough detailed and varied alternatives can actually wind up costing both time and resources, the very commodities organizations seek to conserve. One means to broaden the development of alternatives is through the use of scenario analysis.[17] Scenarios compel managers to consider what could be, not what has been. Managers explore different future business patterns, not extrapolations of historic behavior. Scenario analysis allows managers to compensate for tunnel vision—the inability to think in abstract patterns.[18] The major advantage of scenario-based development of alternatives is that it allows decision makers to uncover new alternatives that would have been overlooked under traditional alternative generation practices.

Evaluating alternatives

Once alternatives have been developed, they must be evaluated and compared. In every decision situation, the objective in making a decision is to select the alternative that will produce the most favorable outcomes and the least unfavorable outcomes. This again points up the need for objectives and goals. In selecting among alternatives, the decision maker should be guided by previously established goals and objectives. The alternative-outcome relationship is based on three possible conditions:

1. *Certainty.* The decision maker has complete knowledge of the probability of the outcome of each alternative.
2. *Uncertainty.* The decision maker has absolutely no knowledge of the probability of the outcome of each alternative.
3. *Risk.* The decision maker has some probabilistic estimate of the outcomes of each alternative.

Decision making under conditions of risk is probably the most common situation.[19] It is in evaluating alternatives under these conditions that statisticians and operations researchers have made important contributions to decision making. Their methods have proved especially useful in the analysis and ranking of alternatives, especially in the area of game theory where decision makers put themselves in the shoes of others, trying out all the potential reactions to their actions prior to the decision being made.[20]

Choosing an alternative

The purpose in selecting an alternative is to solve a problem to achieve a predetermined objective. This point is an important one. It means that a decision is not an end in itself but only a means to an end. While the decision maker chooses the alternative that is expected to result in achieving the objective, the selection of that alternative should not be seen as an isolated act. If it is, the factors that led to and lead from the decision are likely to be excluded. Specifically, the steps following the decision should include implementation, control, and evaluation. The critical point is that decision making is more than an act of choosing; it is a dynamic process.

Unfortunately for most managers, an alternative rarely achieves the desired objective without having some positive or negative impact on another objective. Situations often exist where two objectives cannot be fully achieved simultaneously. If one objective is *optimized,* the other is *suboptimized.* For example, if production in a business is optimized, employee morale may be suboptimized, or vice versa. A hospital superintendent may optimize a short-run objective such as maintenance costs at the expense of a long-run objective such as high-quality patient care. Thus, the multiplicity of organizational objectives complicates the real world of the decision makers forcing them, in effect, to continually be wondering "what-if."[21]

In certain situations, an organizational objective may also be at the expense of a societal objective. This is clear in the rise of ecology groups, environmentalists, and the consumer movement. Apparently, these groups question the priorities (organizational against societal) of certain organizational decision makers. In any case, whether an organizational objective conflicts with another organizational objective or with a societal objective, the values of the decision maker strongly influence the alternative chosen. Individual values were discussed earlier, and their influence on the decision-making process should be clear.

In managerial decision making, optimal solutions are often impossible. The decision maker cannot possibly know all of the available alternatives, the consequences of each alternative, and the probability of these consequences occurring.[22] Thus, rather than being an optimizer, the decision maker is a *satisficer,* selecting the alternative that meets an acceptable (satisfactory) standard.

Implementing the decision

Any decision that is not implemented is little more than an abstraction. In other words, a decision must be effectively implemented to achieve the objective for which it was made. It is entirely possible for a "good" decision to be hurt by poor implementation. In this sense, implementation may be more important than the actual choice of the alternative.

In most situations, implementing decisions involves people, so the test of a decision's soundness is the behavior of the people affected by the decision. Subordinates can't be manipulated in the same manner as other resources. A technically sound decision can easily be undermined by dissatisfied subordinates. Thus, a manager's job is not only to choose good solutions but also to transform such solutions into behavior in the organization. This is done by effectively communicating with the appropriate individuals and groups.[23]

Control and evaluation

Effective management involves periodic measurement of results. Actual results are compared with planned results (the objective), and changes must be made if deviations exist. Here again, we see the importance of measurable objectives. Without them, there is no way to judge performance. Changes, if necessary, must be made in the solution chosen, in its implementation, or in the original objective if it is deemed unattainable. If the original objective must be revised, then the entire decision-making process is reactivated. The important point is that once a decision is implemented, a manager cannot assume that the outcome will meet the original objective. Some system of control and evaluation is needed to make sure the actual results are consistent with the results planned when the decision was made.

Behavioral Influences on Individual Decision Making

Several behavioral factors influence the decision-making process. Some affect only certain aspects of the process, while others influence the entire process. However, each may have an impact and therefore must be understood to fully appreciate the decision-making process in organizations. Four individual behavioral factors—values, personality, propensity for risk, and potential for dissonance—are discussed in this section. Each has a significant impact on the decision-making process.

Values

Values

Basic guidelines and beliefs that a decision maker uses when confronted with a situation requiring choice.

In the context of decision making, **values** are the guidelines a person uses when confronted with a situation in which a choice must be made. Values are acquired early in life and are a basic (often taken for granted) part of an individual's thoughts. Values' influence on the decision-making process is profound:

In *establishing objectives,* value judgments must be made regarding the selection of opportunities and the assignment of priorities.

In *developing alternatives,* value judgments about the various possibilities are necessary.

In *choosing an alternative,* the values of the decision maker influence which alternative is chosen.

In *implementing a decision,* value judgments are necessary in choosing the means for implementation.

In the *control* and *evaluation* phase, value judgments cannot be avoided when corrective action is decided on and taken.

Clearly, values pervade the decision-making process, encompassing not only the individual's economic and legal responsibilities but his ethical responsibilities as well.[24] They're reflected in the decision maker's behavior before making the decision, in making the decision, and in putting the decision into effect.[25] Indeed, some researchers state that alternatives are relevant only as a means of achieving managerial values.[26] The Close-Up, "Nobody Wins with Unethical Decisions" illustrates the cumulative negative effects of unethical choices by managers.

Personality

Decision makers are influenced by many psychological forces, both conscious and subconscious. One of the most important of these forces is personality. Decision makers' personalities are strongly reflected in their choices. Studies that have examined the effect of personality on the process of decision making have generally focused on three types of variables:[27]

1. *Personality variables*—the attitudes, beliefs, and needs of the individual.

2. *Situational variables*—external, observable situations in which individuals find themselves.

3. *Interactional variables*—the individual's momentary state that results from the interaction of a specific situation with characteristics of the individual's personality.

The most important conclusions concerning the influence of personality on the decision-making process are:

C L O S E — U P

Nobody Wins with Unethical Decisions

Unethical behavior rarely just "happens"—it takes a conscious decision. When managers make a choice to act unethically, the consequences are felt by the organization, its shareholders, employees, and customers. Following are accounts of two organizations that have been accused of unethical decision making in the 1990s.

In 1995, Archer Daniels Midland (ADM) was one of the top five companies in the food industry. It shared the spotlight with such organizations as Philip Morris, Conagra, Sara Lee, and IBP. In July of that year, an antitrust investigation of the firm was undertaken. Agreements had reportedly been made among several grain-producing companies, including ADM, that led to accusations of price-fixing for several product categories including sweeteners and food and feed additives.

The accusations had a damaging effect on the credibility of the commodities market and ADM itself. Smaller companies were unable to compete with the pricing schemes of ADM and other large producers. When news of the investigation broke, some investment services began to recommend that ADM shareholders sell their stock, and the company's stock value was adversely affected for some time.

The unfortunate ending to the episode came in 1998, when ADM made some highly publicized agreements with the U.S. Department of Agriculture and the Justice Department to settle the price-fixing charges. One former executive has already been sentenced to nine years in prison. ADM pleaded guilty to price-fixing and paid a $100 million fine.

In 1995, Bausch & Lomb (B&L) announced that the Securities and Exchange Commission was investigating the company's marketing operations for inaccurate reporting of distributor inventories. The problem surfaced when B&L reported a 37 percent decline in profit form 1993 to 1994. It seems that a December 1993 sales strategy encouraged 32 of B&L's independent distributors to purchase two-year inventories of contact lenses. That allowed the company to show a huge increase in sales for 1993. However, it caught up to them in 1994 when sales plummeted because of "presold" inventory. As huge year-end losses emerged for 1994, shareholders became very angry and filed a class action suit accusing the company of misrepresenting its financial condition.

As a result, B&L suffered some serious financial problems. In 1997 the CEO resigned, and after a two-year SEC investigation, as of this writing, the company is close to an out-of-court settlement with its shareholders.

While both ADM and B&L suffered financially because of the investigations, each also suffered irreparable loss of shareholder and public trust. At some point, an individual manager or a group of managers rendered an unethical decision that has and will continue to cost these companies and all their stockholders for quite some time.

Sources: Jeffrey Marshall, "Yes, with Strings Attached," *US Banker,* May 1, 1998, p. 17; Ronald Henkoff, "ADMs Whitacre Goes to Jail," *Fortune,* March 30, 1998; Mark Maremount and Larry Light, "Bausch and Lomb May See an Out," *Business Week,* February 3, 1997, p. 6; and Mark Maremount, "Blind Ambition: How the Pursuit of Results Got Out of Hand at Bausch and Lomb," *Business Week,* October 23, 1995, pp. 78–92.

www.admworld.com/   www.saralee.com/

www.pmdocs.com/   www.IBP.com/

www.conagra.com/   www.bausch.com/

1. One person is not likely to be equally proficient in all aspects of the decision-making process. Some people do better in one part of the process, while others do better in another part.

2. Certain characteristics, such as intelligence, are associated with different phases of the decision-making process.

3. The relationship of personality to the decision-making process may vary for different groups on the basis of such factors as sex, social status, and cultural background.

4. Individuals facing important and ambiguous decisions may be influenced heavily by peers' opinions.

An interesting study examined the importance of cultural influences on decision-making style differences between Japanese and Australian college students.[28] In Japan, a group orientation exists, while in Australia, the common cultural pattern emphasizes an individual orientation. The results confirmed the importance of the cultural influence. Japanese students reported greater use of decision processes or behaviors associated with the involvement and influence of others, while Australian students reported greater use of decision processes associated with self-reliance and personal ability. In general, the personality traits of the decision maker combine with certain situational and interactional variables to influence the decision-making process.

Propensity for risk

From personal experience, we're all undoubtedly aware that decision makers vary greatly in their propensity for taking risks. This one specific aspect of personality strongly influences the decision-making process. A decision maker with a low aversion to risk establishes different objectives, evaluates alternatives differently, and selects different alternatives than a decision maker in the same situation who has a high aversion to risk. The latter attempts to make choices where the risk or uncertainty is low or where the certainty of the outcome is high. The best managers need to tread a fine line between making ill-conceived, arbitrary decisions based purely on instinct (low aversion to risk) and becoming too obsessed with a reliance on numbers, analyses, and reports (high aversion to risk).[29] As we'll discuss later in the chapter, many people are bolder and more innovative and advocate greater risk-taking in groups than as individuals. Apparently, such people are more willing to accept risk as members of a group.

Potential for dissonance

Much attention has focused on the forces that influence the decision maker before a decision is made and that impact the decision itself. Only recently has attention been given to what happens after a decision has been made. Specifically, behavioral scientists have focused attention on *postdecision anxiety.*

Cognitive Dissonance

Anxiety that occurs when there is conflict between an individual's beliefs and reality. Most individuals are motivated to reduce dissonance and achieve consonance.

Such anxiety is related to what Leon Festinger called **cognitive dissonance** over 35 years ago and what researchers today term *regret theory.*[30] This theory states that there is often a lack of consistency, or harmony, among an individual's various cognitions (attitudes, beliefs, etc.) after a decision has been made. As a result, the decision maker has doubts and second thoughts about the choice. In addition, the intensity of the anxiety is likely to be greater in the presence of any of the following conditions:

1. The decision is psychologically and/or financially important.

2. There are a number of forgone alternatives.

3. The forgone alternatives have many favorable features.

Dissonance can, of course, be reduced by admitting that a mistake has been made. Unfortunately, many individuals are reluctant to admit that they've made a wrong decision. These individuals are more likely to reduce their dissonance by using one or more of the following methods:

1. Seek information that supports the wisdom of their decisions.
2. Selectively perceive (distort) information in a way that supports their decisions.
3. Adopt a less favorable view of the forgone alternatives.
4. Minimize the importance of the negative aspects of the decisions and exaggerate the importance of the positive aspects.

While each of us may resort to some of this behavior in our personal decision making, a great deal of such behavior could easily harm organizational effectiveness.

Personality, specifically the level of self-confidence and persuasibility, heavily influences potential for dissonance. In fact, all of the behavioral influences are closely interrelated and are only isolated here for purposes of discussion.[31]

Group Decision Making

Until now, this chapter has focused on individuals making decisions. In most organizations, however, a great deal of decision making is achieved through committees, teams, task forces, and other groups. Managers frequently face situations in which they must seek and combine judgments in group meetings. This is especially true for nonprogrammed problems, which are novel and involve much uncertainty regarding the outcome. In most organizations, decisions on such problems are rarely made by one individual on a regular basis. The increased complexity of many of these problems requires specialized knowledge in numerous fields—knowledge usually not possessed by one person. This requirement, coupled with the reality that the decisions made must eventually be accepted and implemented by many units throughout the organization, has increased the use of the collective approach to the decision-making process. As a result, many managers spend as much as 80 percent of their working time in committee meetings.

In addition to interorganizational meetings, managers are increasingly being called upon to participate in collaborative efforts between organizations.[32] Collaboration involves "a process of joint decision making among key stakeholders of a problem domain about the future of that domain."[33] Managers participate in many forms of collaborative decision-making efforts, including those that involve dealings with other for-profit organizations and those that consist of partnering with nonprofit or government organizations. Some collaborations concentrate on advancing a shared decision among stakeholders, some focus on solving specific problems, and others are directed toward resolving conflicts among stakeholders.

Individual versus group decision making

Considerable debate has taken place over the relative effectiveness of individual versus group decision making. Groups usually take more time to reach a decision than individuals do, but bringing specialists and experts together has benefits. The mutually reinforcing impact of their interaction results in better decisions, especially when a high degree of diversity among backgrounds exists.[34] In fact, a great deal of research has shown that consensus decisions with five or more participants are superior to individual, majority vote, and leader decisions.[35]

Unfortunately, open discussion can be negatively influenced by behavioral factors, such as the pressure to conform. Such pressure may be the influence of a dominant personality in the group, "status incongruity" may cause lower-status participants to be inhibited by higher-status participants and to "go along" even though they believe that their own ideas are superior, or certain participants may attempt to exert influence based on the perception that they are experts in the problem area.[36]

This perception of expertise also inhibits group consideration of outside assistance. Group members may show a negative bias toward advice and guidance given by non-group members, regardless of value, preferring instead to consider only internally generated solutions to problems.[37]

Certain decisions appear to be better made by groups, while others appear better suited to individual decision making. Nonprogrammed decisions appear to be better suited to group decision making. Such decisions usually call for pooled talent in arriving at a solution; also, the decisions are so important that they are usually made by top managers and to a somewhat lesser extent by middle managers.

In terms of the decision-making process itself, the following points concerning group processes for nonprogrammed decisions can be made:

1. In *establishing objectives,* groups are probably superior to individuals because of the greater amount of knowledge available to groups.

2. In *identifying alternatives,* the individual efforts of group members encourage a broad search in various functional areas of the organization.

3. In *evaluating alternatives,* the collective judgment of the group, with its wider range of viewpoints, seems superior to that of the individual decision maker.

4. In *choosing an alternative,* group interaction and the achievement of consensus usually result in the acceptance of more risk than would be accepted by an individual decision maker. Also, the group decision is more likely to be accepted as a result of the participation of those affected by its consequences.

5. *Implementing a decision,* whether or not it was made by a group, is usually accomplished by individual managers. Thus, individuals bear responsibility for implementing the group's decision.

Figure 17–2 summarizes the research findings on group decision making. It shows the probable relationship between the quality of a decision and the method utilized to reach the decision. It indicates that as we move from individual to consensus decision making, the quality of the decision improves. Also, each successive method involves a higher level of mutual influence by group members. Thus, for a complex problem requiring pooled knowledge, the quality of the decision is likely to be higher as the group moves toward consensus.

Techniques for stimulating creativity in group decision making

Because groups are better suited than individuals to making nonprogrammed decisions, an atmosphere fostering group creativity should be developed. In this respect, group decision making may be similar to brainstorming. Discussion must be free-flowing and spontaneous, all group members must participate, and the evaluation of individual ideas must be suspended in the beginning to encourage participation. However, a decision must be reached, and this is where group decision making differs from brainstorming.

Group decision making probably is preferable to individual decision making in many instances. However, you may have heard the statement "A camel is a racehorse designed by a committee." While the necessity and benefits of group decision making are recog-

Figure 17–2

Probable Relationship between Quality of Group Decision and Method Utilized

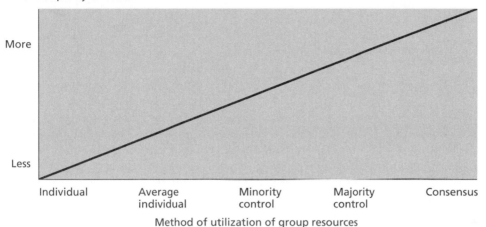

nized, it also can present numerous problems, some of which have already been noted. Practicing managers need specific techniques that enable them to increase the benefits from group decision making while reducing the problems associated with it.

Increasing the creative capability of a group is especially necessary when individuals from diverse sectors of the organization must pool their judgments to create a satisfactory course of action for the organization. When subordinates and peers believe that the manager in charge of the group is essentially nonbiased or "on their side," group members may express their viewpoints more freely and feel less compelled to protect themselves from potentially nonsupportive or retaliatory responses.[38] When properly utilized, three techniques—brainstorming, the Delphi process, and the nominal group technique—have been extremely useful in increasing the group's creative capability in generating ideas, understanding problems, and reaching better decisions.

BRAINSTORMING   In many situations, groups are expected to produce creative or imaginative solutions to organizational problems. In such instances, **brainstorming** often enhances the creative output of the group. Brainstorming includes a strict series of rules to promote the generation of ideas while at the same time removing members' inhibitions that usually stymie face-to-face groups. The basic rules are:

Brainstorming

A technique that promotes creativity by encouraging idea generation through non-critical discussion.

No idea is too ridiculous. Group members are encouraged to state any extreme or outlandish idea.

Each idea presented belongs to the group, not to the person stating it. In this way, group members utilize and build on the ideas of others.

No idea can be criticized. The purpose of the session is to generate, not evaluate, ideas.

Brainstorming is widely used in advertising, where it's apparently effective. In some other fields, it has been less successful. Brainstorming groups normally produce fewer ideas than do the equivalent number of individuals working by themselves, and there's no evaluation or ranking of the ideas generated.[39] Thus, the group never really concludes the problem-solving process.

DELPHI PROCESS   This technique involves soliciting and comparing anonymous judgments on the topic of interest through a set of sequential questionnaires interspersed with summarized information and feedback of opinions from earlier responses.[40]

Delphi Process

A technique that promotes creativity by using anonymous judgment of ideas to reach a consensus decision.

The **Delphi process** retains the advantage of having several judges while removing the biasing effects that might occur during face-to-face interaction. The basic approach has been to collect anonymous judgments by mail questionnaire. For example, the members independently generate their ideas to answer the first questionnaire and return it. The staff members summarize the responses as the group consensus and feed this summary back, along with a second questionnaire for reassessment. Based on this feedback, respondents independently evaluate their earlier responses. The underlying belief is that the consensus estimate results in a better decision after several rounds of anonymous group judgment. However, while continuing the procedure for several rounds is possible, studies have shown essentially no significant change after the second round of estimation.

www.ama.org

An interesting application of the Delphi process was undertaken by the American Marketing Association to determine the international issues most likely to have significant impact on marketing in the year 2000.[41] Twenty-nine experts on international marketing participated in the study. Major issues the experts identified included the environment, globalization, regional trading blocks, internationalization of service industries, and rising foreign direct investment.

NOMINAL GROUP TECHNIQUE (NGT)   NGT has gained increasing recognition in health, social service, education, industry, and government organizations.[42] The term **nominal group technique** was adopted by earlier researchers to refer to processes that bring people together but don't allow them to communicate verbally. Thus, the collection of people is a group "nominally" (in name only).

Nominal Group Technique (NGT)

A technique that promotes creativity by bringing people together in a very structured meeting that allows little verbal communication. Group decision is the mathematically pooled outcome of individual votes.

Basically, NGT is a structured group meeting in which 7 to 10 individuals sit around a table but don't speak to one another. Each person writes ideas on a pad of paper. After five minutes, a structured sharing of ideas takes place. Each person presents one idea. A person designated as recorder writes the ideas on a flip chart in full view of the entire group. This continues until all participants indicate that they have no further ideas to share. There is still no discussion.

The output of the first phase is a list of ideas (usually between 18 and 25). The next phase involves structured discussion in which each idea receives attention before a vote is taken. This is achieved by asking for clarification or stating the degree of support for each idea listed on the flip chart. The last stage involves independent voting in which each participant, in private, selects priorities by ranking or voting. The group decision is the mathematically pooled outcome of the individual votes.

Both the Delphi process and NGT have proved to be more productive than brainstorming.[43] Each has had an excellent success record. Basic differences between the Delphi process and NGT are:

1. Delphi participants are typically anonymous to one another, while NGT participants become acquainted.

2. NGT participants meet face-to-face around a table, while Delphi participants are physically distant and never meet.

3. In the Delphi process, all communication between participants is by way of written questionnaires and feedback from the monitoring staff. In NGT, participants communicate directly.[44]

Practical considerations, of course, often influence which technique is used. For example, such factors as the number of available working hours, costs, and the physical proximity of participants influence selection of a technique.

Rather than to make readers experts in the Delphi process or NGT, this section has aimed to indicate the frequency and importance of group decision making in every organization. The three techniques discussed are practical devices for improving the effectiveness of group decisions.

Decision making is a responsibility shared by all managers, regardless of functional area or management level. Every day, they are required to make decisions that shape the future of their organizations as well as their own futures. Some of these decisions may have a strong impact on the organization's success, while others are less crucial. However, all decisions have some effect (positive or negative, large or small) on the organization. The quality of these decisions is the yardstick of managerial effectiveness. In summary, we remind the reader that decision making is a skill that is gained through experience of trial and error.[45] In other words, one must make some wrong decisions to learn how to make right ones.

Summary of Key Points

- Decision making is a fundamental process in organizations. Managers make decisions on the basis of the information (communication) they receive through the organization structure and the behavior of individuals and groups within it.

- Decision making distinguishes managers from nonmanagers. The quality of managers' decisions determines their effectiveness as managers.

- Decisions may be classified as programmed or nonprogrammed, depending on the problem. Most programmed decisions should be made at the first level in the organization, while nonprogrammed decisions should be made mostly by top management.

- Decision making should not be thought of as an end but as a means to achieve organizational goals and objectives. Decisions are organizational responses to problems.

- Decision making should be viewed as a multiphased process in which the actual choice is only one phase. The preceding phases are establishing goals, identifying problems, developing alternatives, and evaluating alternatives.

- The decision-making process is influenced by numerous environmental and behavioral factors. Because of different values, perceptions, and personalities, different decision makers may not select identical alternatives in the same situation.

- A great deal of nonprogrammed decision making is carried on in group situations. Much evidence supports the claim that in most instances, group decisions are superior to individual decisions. Three techniques (brainstorming, the Delphi process, and the nominal group technique) improve the effectiveness of group decisions. The management of collective decision making must be a vital concern for future managers.

Discussion and Review Questions

1. Can you think of a specific upper-level management position where you would make mainly programmed decisions? What about one where you would be making mostly nonprogrammed decisions? What factors make these type positions favor one type of decision making over another (i.e., the industry, function, or another aspect)?

2. When looking at the decision-making process (Figure 17–1), do you feel any one step is more important than the others? If so, why?

3. Describe a situation you've encountered where a decision made by an individual would have been better made by a group. Why do you feel this way?

4. Which stage of the decision-making process would *groupthink* affect most? Which stage(s) may not exist at all in a groupthink situation? Why?

5. Describe a situation where someone else made a poor decision that adversely affected you. Why was such a decision made?

6. Some people equate values and ethics. If you were a member of a group and you felt the group was making an unethical decision or one that conflicted with your values, what would you do? How far would you go to stop the unethical action?

7. Describe a situation where you were forced to make a decision where your values helped make the final choice.

8. Brainstorming can be a very effective method for stimulating creativity for group decision making. Describe a situation where you either used or could have used brain-storming to come up with a creative idea. How did the brainstorming begin or how would you have begun the process?

9. What is your attitude toward risk? Has that attitude ever influenced a decision you made? What are the implications of your attitude toward risk?

10. Think of a corporate executive who, you believe, is a good decision maker. What traits make this executive effective?

CASE FOR ANALYSIS

Breaking the Rules

Nancy Taggart worked in the customer service department at the Xemas Company. The Xemas Company manufactured industrial air conditioning systems and replacement parts for these systems. Xemas sold its products to large regional distributors which, in turn, supplied and supported independent dealers throughout the United States and Canada.

One night, Nancy received a call from one of Xemas's dealers who seemed unduly agitated. The dealer said he had a customer who needed a part for his air-conditioning system right away and the dealer didn't have the part in stock. He claimed he had tried to reach his distributor for the past two hours, but was unable to get through on the phone. He asked if Nancy could send the part overnight and then bill the distributor. The charge would then be included on the invoice the distributor sent the dealer at the end of the month.

Since it was past the distributor's normal operating hours, Nancy knew she couldn't reach anyone there. Furthermore, Nancy knew something was amiss, as Xemas had discontinued this type of shipping and billing practice because distributors had complained. They wanted to control all shipments to reduce the chance of selling to a bad credit risk.

But even though Nancy knew the rules, she decided to break them, based on the seemingly urgent nature of the situation The dealer said the customer needed the part immediately. Nancy decided customer service was the most important issue involved in the situation, so she sent the part out promptly.

The next day, the local distributor was called. It turned out the dealer wasn't a regular customer of the distributor. Because of this situation, the distributor refused to pay for the part. While Xemas would try to get the dealer to pay directly to them, for the time being the company was out $150, the cost of the part. To make sure the books balanced, Nancy wrote out a personal check for $150 to cover the cost of the part and sent it to billing.

Within days, Nancy received a phone call from one of the firm's executive vice presidents, Ramon Hernandez. Ramon told Nancy that he had received a call from a supervisor in the billing department. The person he spoke to was irate and insisted that something he done about this employee, Nancy Taggart, who had broken company rules. Ramon then asked Nancy for an explanation for her actions. After hearing Nancy's story, Ramon stated that he agreed with the billing supervisor concerning the seriousness of the situation, and that actions did indeed need to be taken. He informed Nancy that she would hear from him the next day regarding those actions.

The next evening, when Nancy arrived at work, a letter awaited her from Ramon. With a feeling of dread, Nancy opened the letter. Inside was a check for $150. Attached to the check was a note from Ramon. The note stated that Nancy was going to be given both a raise and a preferred parking spot.

Discussion Questions

1. Why was Nancy rewarded for breaking the rules?

2. Describe what type of decision Nancy had to make. What decision alternatives were available to her besides the one she chose?

3. What types of behavioral factors might have influenced Nancy's decision?

Sources: Adapted from David Armstrong. "Management by Storytelling," *Executive Female,* May–June 1992, p. 77; David E. Bowen and Edward E. Lawler III, "The Empowerment of Service Workers," *Sloan Management Review,* Spring 1992, pp. 31–39; Leonard L. Berry and A. Parasuraman, "Services Marketing Starts from Within," *Marketing Management,* Winter 1992, pp. 25–34.

E X P E R I E N T I A L   E X E R C I S E

Lost on the Moon: A Group Decision Exercise

Objective

To come as close as possible to the "best solution" as determined by experts of the National Aeronautics and Space Administration (NASA).

Related Topics

Motivation, individual differences, and group development are important topics related to this exercise.

Starting the Exercise

After reading the following scenario, you will, first individually and then as a member of a team, rank the importance of items available for carrying out your mission.

The Scenario

Your spaceship has just crash-landed on the moon. You were scheduled to rendezvous with a mother ship 200 miles away on the lighted surface of the moon, but the rough landing has ruined your ship and all of the equipment aboard, except for the 15 items listed below.

Your crew's survival depends on reaching the mother ship, so you must choose the most critical items available for the 200-mile trip. Your task is to rank the 15 items in terms of their importance for survival. Place number 1 by the most important item, number 2 by the second most important, and so on through number 15, the least important.

WORK SHEET ITEMS	1 NASA'S RANKS	2 YOUR RANKS	3 ERROR POINTS	4 GROUP RANKS	5 ERROR POINTS
Box of matches	———	———	———	———	———
Food concentrate	———	———	———	———	———
Fifty feet of nylon rope	———	———	———	———	———
Parachute silk	———	———	———	———	———
Solar-powered portable heating unit	———	———	———	———	———
Two .45-caliber pistols	———	———	———	———	———
One case of dehydrated milk	———	———	———	———	———
Two 100-pound tanks of oxygen	———	———	———	———	———
Stellar map (of the moon's constellation)	———	———	———	———	———
Self-inflating life raft	———	———	———	———	———
Magnetic compass	———	———	———	———	———
Five gallons of water	———	———	———	———	———
Signal flares	———	———	———	———	———
First-aid kit containing injection needles	———	———	———	———	———
Solar-powered FM receiver-transmitter	———	———	———	———	———
Total error points	Individual ———		Group ———		

Completing the Exercise

Phase I: 15 minutes.   Read the scenario. Then, in column 2 (Your Ranks) of the work sheet, assign priorities to the 15 items listed. Use a pencil since you may wish to change your rankings. Somewhere on the sheet, you may wish to note your logic for each ranking.

Phase II: 25 minutes.   Your instructor will assign you to a team. The task of each team is to arrive at a consensus on the rankings. Share your individual solutions and reach a consensus—the ranking for each of the 15 items that best satisfies all team members. Thus, by the end of phase II, all members of the team should have the same set of rankings in column 4 (Group Ranks). Do not change your individual rankings in column 2.

Phase III: 10 minutes.   Your instructor will provide you with the "best solution" to the problem—that is, the set of rankings determined by the NASA experts, along with their reasoning. Each person should note this set of rankings in column 1 (NASA's Ranks). (Note: While it is fun to debate the experts' rankings and their reasoning, remember that the objective of the game is to learn more about decision making, not how to survive on the moon!)

Phase IV (evaluation): 15 minutes.   Now, see how well you did individually and as a team. First, find your individual score by taking, for each item, the absolute difference between your ranks (column 2) and NASA's ranks (column 1) and writing it in the first error points column (column 3). Thus, if you ranked "Box of matches" 3 and NASA ranked it 8, you would put a 5 in column 3, across from "Box of matches." Then, add the error points in column 3 and write the total at the bottom in the space for individual total error points.

Next, score your group performance in the same way, this time taking the absolute differences between group ranks (column 4) and NASA's ranks (column 1) and writing them in the second error points column (column 5). Add the group error points and write the total in the space provided. (Note that all members of the team have the same group error points.)

Finally, prepare three pieces of information to be submitted when your instructor calls on your team:

1. Average individual total error points (the average of all group members' individual totals). One team member should add these figures and divide by the number of team members to get the average.
2. Group total error points, as shown on each group member's work sheet.
3. Number of team members who had fewer individual total error points than the group total error points.

Using this information, your instructor will evaluate the results of the exercise and discuss group versus individual performance. Together, you will then explore the implications of this exercise for the group decision-making process.

Chapter 18

Managing Organizational Change and Development

Learning Objectives

After completing Chapter 18, you should be able to:

Define
The concept and practice of organizational development.

Describe
Sources of change and alternative change management approaches.

Discuss
The ethical issues that arise in organizational development practice.

Compare
Alternative interventions that management can implement to improve performance.

Identify
The important steps in organizational development programs.

As managers contemplate the futures of their organizations as the 21st century looms, they can't escape the inevitability of change. Indeed, the word *change* has been the most obvious promise of political candidates during local and national election campaigns of the 1990s. *Change* is certainly among the most frequently used words on the business pages of every newspaper in the world. Not only have entire countries and empires gone through dramatic and wrenching changes, but so have great companies such as IBM, General Motors, and Ford. The USSR no longer exists, but neither does Pan-American Airlines. So it makes a great deal of sense for this text devoted to the preparation of future managers to address the issues associated with managing change.

Well-known business writers state that contemporary business organizations confront changing circumstances that put bygone eras of change to shame by comparison. The combination of global competition, computer-assisted manufacturing methods, and instant communications has implications more far-reaching than anything since the beginning of the Industrial Revolution.[1] Popular literature including best-sellers warns managers that their organizations' futures depend on their ability to master change.[2] Other authors state that change is a pervasive, persistent, and permanent condition for all organizations.

Effective managers must view managing change as an integral responsibility, rather than as a peripheral one.[3] But we must accept the reality that not all organizations will successfully make the appropriate changes. Those with the best chance for success are relatively small and compete in industries in which research and development expenditures have traditionally been relatively high and barriers to entry are relatively low. Such firms in these industries have changed to survive and they are likely to be the survivors in the 21st century.[4]

This chapter explores issues associated with managing change through the application of **organizational development (OD)**. Our point of view is that the important management responsibility of managing change can best be undertaken and accomplished by applying organizational development process and interventions.

Organizational Development

The process of preparing for and managing change in organizational settings.

Alternative Change Management Approaches

Managers can undertake organizational change in various ways. In many instances the change process occurs at the expense of short-term losses in exchange for long-term benefits.[5] One extensive review of the literature identified several approaches that managers can use to manage planned change.[6] Although the terms applied to the different approaches vary from author to author and from proponent to proponent, the underlying theme is the same. Regardless of the terms used, the approaches range from the application of power, in any of its forms, to bring about change to the application of reason. Midway between these two extremes is the approach that relies upon reeducation.

Managing change through power

The *application of power* to bring about change implies the use of coercion. Managers have access to power and can use their power to coerce nonmanagers to change in the direction they desire. Managers can implement power through their control over rewards and sanctions. They can determine the conditions of employment including promotion and advancement. Consequently, through their access to these bases of power, managers can bring to bear considerable influence in an organization.

The application of power often manifests autocratic leadership, and contemporary organizations do not generally encourage managers to engage in such leadership behavior. In times past, autocratic management has been a factor in the rise of labor unions as counterweights to the arbitrary use of managerial power. Except in crisis situations when the very existence of the organization is at stake, power is not a favored approach for bringing about change.

Managing change through reason

The *application of reason* to bring about change is based on the dissemination of information prior to the intended change. The underlying assumption is that reason alone will prevail and that the participants and parties to the change will all make the rational choice. The reason-based approach appeals to the sensibilities of those who take a Utopian view of organizational worlds. But the reality of organizations requires that we recognize the existence of individual motives and needs, group norms and sanctions, and the fact that organizations exist as social as well as work units—all of which means that reason alone won't be sufficient to bring about change.

Managing change through reeducation

The middle ground approach relies upon *reeducation* to improve the functioning of the organization. Reeducation implies a particular set of activities that recognizes that neither power nor reason can bring about desirable change. This set of activities has been the subject of much research and application and is generally understood to be the essence of organizational development.[7]

Organizational Development

The literature and practice of organizational development cannot be conveniently classified because of the yet unsettled nature of this aspect of organizational behavior. Various concepts and theories and their meanings and interpretations are subject to considerable disagreement. One definition of *organizational development* refers to "a specific set of change interventions, skills, activities, tools, or techniques that are used to help people and organizations to be more effective."[8] But despite this relatively simple statement, little agreement exists regarding what is to be included in the specific set or from whose perspective one is to judge effectiveness.

The fact that organizational development is a process that brings about change in a social system raises the issue of the change agent (the individual or group who becomes the catalyst for change). Are change agents necessary for organizational development to take place? Once we recognize that organizational development involves substantial changes in how individuals think, believe, and act, we can appreciate the necessity of someone to play the role of change agent. But who should play the role? Existing managers? New managers? Or individuals hired specifically for that purpose? Depending on the situation, any of these can be called upon to orchestrate the organizational development process.[9]

Managers who implement OD programs are committed to making fundamental changes in organizational behavior. At the heart of the process are learning principles that enable individuals to unlearn old behaviors and learn new ones. The classic relearning sequence of unfreezing, moving, and refreezing is implemented in the OD approach to change.[10]

Learning Principles in the OD Context

To better understand how changes are brought about in individuals, we must comprehend the various principles of learning discussed in Chapter 6. Managers can design a theoretically sound OD program and not achieve any of the anticipated results because they overlooked the importance of providing motivation, reinforcement, and feedback to employees. These principles of learning serve to unfreeze old learning, instill new learning, and refreeze that new learning.

Unfreezing old learning requires people who want to learn new ways to think and act. Unfreezing deals directly with resistance to change.[11] Individuals may not accept that they need more skill in a particular job or more understanding of the problems of other units of the firm. Some people recognize this need and are receptive to experiences that will aid them in developing new skills or new empathies. Others reject the need or play it down, because learning is to them an admission that they aren't completely competent in their jobs. These kinds of people face the prospect of change with different expectations and motivations. Determining the expectations and motivations of people isn't easy. It is, however, a task that managers must undertake to manage change; it's management's responsibility to show employees why they should want to change.

Movement to new learning requires training, demonstration, and empowerment. Training nonmanagerial employees hasn't been a high priority among American corporations, but recent losses of market shares to foreign competitors that invest greater resources in training have encouraged American firms to make training a regular part of their employees' assignments. Through training and demonstration of the appropriateness of that training, employees can be empowered to take on behaviors they previously had only vaguely imagined possible. The new behaviors must be carefully and sensitively taught.

Refreezing the learned behavior occurs through the application of reinforcement and feedback. These two principles suggest that when people receive positive rewards, information, or feelings for doing something, they're more likely to do the same thing in a similar situation. The other side of the coin involves the impact of punishment for a particular response. Punishment will decrease the probability of doing the same thing at another time. The principle, then, implies that it would be easier to achieve successful change through the use of positive rewards. Reinforcement can also occur when the knowledge or skill acquired in a training program is imparted through a refresher course.

Management must guard against the possibility that what a person has learned at a training site is lost when that person is transferred to the actual work site. If things have gone well, only a minimum amount will be lost in this necessary transfer. A possible strategy for keeping the loss to a minimum is to make the training situation similar to the actual workplace environment. Another strategy is to reward the newly learned behavior. If the colleagues and superiors of newly trained people approve new ideas or new skills, these people will be encouraged to continue to behave in the new way.

If colleagues and superiors behave negatively, the newly trained people will be discouraged from persisting with attempts to use what they've learned. This is one reason why it has been suggested that superiors be trained before subordinates. The superior, if trained and motivated, can serve as a reinforcer and feedback source for the subordinate who has left the training confines and is now back on the job.

Change Agents in Organizational Development: Forms of Intervention

Change Agent

A person or group who enters an ongoing organization or part of the organization for the purpose of facilitating the process of change.

Because managers tend to seek answers in traditional solutions, the intervention of an outsider is necessary. The intervener, or **change agent,** brings a different perspective to the situation and challenges the status quo. The success of any change program rests heavily on the quality and workability of the relationship between the change agent and the key decision makers within the organization. Thus, the form of intervention is a crucial consideration.[12]

To intervene is to enter into an ongoing organization, or relationship among persons or departments, for the purpose of helping them improve their effectiveness. A number of forms of intervention are used in organizations.

External change agents

External change agents are temporary employees of the organization since they're engaged only for the duration of the change process. They originate in a variety of organizational types including universities, consulting firms, and training agencies. Many large organizations have individuals located at central offices who take temporary assignments with line units that are contemplating organizational development. At the conclusion of the change program, the change agent returns to headquarters.

The usual external change agent is a university professor or private consultant who has training and experience in the behavioral sciences. Such an individual will be contacted by the organization and be engaged after agreement is reached on the conditions of the relationship. Ordinarily, the change agent will have graduate degrees in specialties that focus on individual and group behavior in organizational settings. With this kind of training, the external change agent has the perspective to facilitate the change process.

Internal change agents

The internal change agent is an individual working for the organization who knows something about its problems.[13] The usual internal change agent is a recently appointed manager of an organization that has a record of poor performance; often, the individual takes the job with the expectation that major change is necessary. How successful internal change agents undertake their OD roles has been extensively studied in recent years. Individuals such as Michael Blumenthal and Lee Iacocca have been closely scrutinized by OD theorists and practitioners.[14]

External-internal change agents

Some organizations use a combination external-internal change team to intervene and develop programs. This approach attempts to use the resources and knowledge base of both external and internal change agents. It involves designating an individual or small group within the organization to serve with the external change agent as spearheads of the change effort. The internal group often comes from the personnel unit, but it can also be a group of top managers. As a general rule, an external change agent will actively solicit the visible support of top management as a way to emphasize the importance of the OD effort.[15]

Each of the three forms of intervention has advantages and disadvantages. The external change agent is often viewed as an outsider. When this belief is held by employees inside the company, there's need to establish rapport between the change agent and decision makers. The change agent's views on the problems faced by the organization are often different from the decision maker's views, which leads to problems in establishing rapport. Differences in viewpoints often result in mistrust of the external change agent by the policymakers or a segment of the policymakers. Offsetting these disadvantages is the external change agent's ability to refocus the organization's relationship with the changing environmental demands. The external agent has a comparative advantage over the internal change agent when significant strategic changes must be evaluated.[16]

The internal change agent is often viewed as being more closely associated with one unit or group of individuals than with any other. This perceived favoritism leads to resistance to change by those who aren't included in the internal change agent's circle of close friends and its personnel, and this knowledge can be valuable in preparing for and implementing change. The internal change agent can often serve as the champion for change because of enlightened understanding of the organization's capability and personal persistence.[17]

The third type of intervention, the combination external-internal team, is the rarest, but it seems to have an excellent chance for success. In this type of intervention, the outsider's objectivity and professional knowledge are blended with the insider's knowledge of the organization and its human resources. This blending of knowledge often results in increased trust and confidence among the parties involved. The combination external-internal team's ability to communicate and develop a more positive rapport can reduce resistance to any forthcoming change.

A Model for Managing Organizational Development

The process of managing change through organizational development can be approached systematically. The several steps of OD can be linked in a logical way as suggested in Figure 18–1. The model consists of specific steps generally acknowledged to be essential to successful change management.[18] A manager considers each of them, either explicitly or implicitly, to undertake an OD program. Prospects of initiating successful change can be enhanced when managers actively support the effort and demonstrate that support by implementing systematic procedures that give substance to the OD process.[19]

Figure 18–1

Model for the Management of Organizational Development

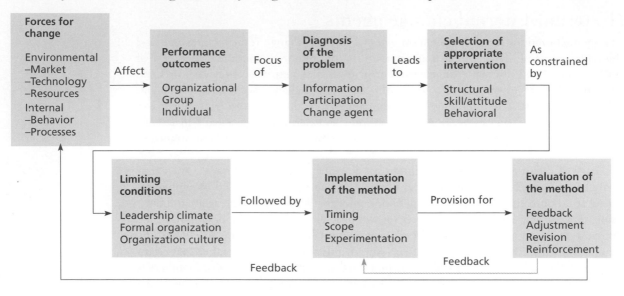

The model indicates that forces for change continually act on the organization; this assumption reflects the dynamic character of the modern world. At the same time, it's the manager's responsibility to sort out the information that reflects the magnitude of change forces.[20] The information is the basis for recognizing when change is needed; it's equally desirable to recognize when change isn't needed. But once managers recognize that something is malfunctioning, they must diagnose the problem and identify relevant alternative techniques.

Finally, the manager must implement the change and monitor the change process and change results. The model includes feedback to the implementation step and to the forces-for-change step. These feedback loops suggest that the change process itself must be monitored and evaluated. The mode of implementation may be faulty and may lead to poor results, but responsive action could correct the situation. Moreover, the feedback loop to the initial step recognizes that no change is final. A new situation is created within which problems and issues will emerge; a new setting is created that will itself become subject to change. The model suggests no final solution; rather, it emphasizes that the modern manager operates in a dynamic setting wherein the only certainty is change itself.

Forces for Change

The forces for change can be classified conveniently into two groups: environmental forces and internal forces. Environmental forces are beyond management's control. Internal forces operate inside the firm and are generally within the control of management.

Environmental forces

Organizations seldom undertake significant change without a strong shock from their environment.[21] The external environment includes many economic, technological, and social/political forces that can trigger the change process. Those who study and practice organizational change agree that these environmental triggers are necessary but not sufficient to initiate change. Change also involves managers who are aware of the change and who take action.

The manager of a business has historically been concerned with reacting to *economic forces*. Competitors introduce new products, increase their advertising, reduce their prices, or increase their customer service. In each case, a response is required unless the manager is content to permit the erosion of her profit and market share. At the same time, changes occur in customer tastes and incomes. The firm's products may no longer have customer appeal; customers may be able to purchase less expensive, higher-quality forms of the same products.

The second source of environmental change forces is *technology*. The knowledge explosion has introduced new technology for nearly every business function. Computers have made possible high-speed data processing and the solution to complex production problems. New machines and new processes have revolutionized how many products are manufactured and distributed. Computer technology and automation have affected not only the technical conditions of work, but the social conditions as well.[22] New occupations have been created, and others have been eliminated. Slowness to adopt new technology that reduces cost and improves quality will show up in the financial statements sooner or later.[23] Technological advance is a permanent fixture in the business world. As a force for change, it will continue to demand attention.

The third source of environmental change forces is *social* and *political* change. Business managers must be tuned in to the great movements over which they have no control but which, in time, influence their firm's fate. Sophisticated mass communications and international markets create great potential for business, but they're also great threats to managers who can't understand what's going on.[24] Finally, the relationship between government and business becomes much closer as regulations are imposed and relaxed. The accompanying Close-Up describes one reaction to change that AT&T has undertaken as a consequence of deregulation of the communication industry.

Comprehending implications of external forces requires *organizational learning* processes.[25] These processes, now being studied in many organizations, involve the capacity to absorb new information, process that information in the light of previous experience, and act on the information in new and potentially risky ways. But only through such learning experiences will organizations be prepared for the 21st century.

Internal forces

Internal forces for change, which occur within the organization, can usually be traced to process and behavioral problems. The process problems include breakdowns in decision making and communications. Decisions aren't being made, are made too late, or are of poor quality. Communications are short-circuited, redundant, or simply inadequate. Tasks aren't undertaken or aren't completed because the person responsible did not get the word. Because of inadequate or nonexistent communications, a customer order isn't filled, a grievance isn't processed, or an invoice isn't filed and the supplier isn't paid. Interpersonal and interdepartmental conflicts reflect breakdowns in organizational processes.

Low levels of morale and high levels of absenteeism and turnover are symptoms of behavioral problems that must be diagnosed. A wildcat strike or a walkout may be the most tangible sign of a problem, yet such tactics are usually employed because they rouse management to action. A certain level of employee discontent exists in most organizations—it's dangerous to ignore employee complaints and suggestions. But the process of change includes the *recognition* phase—the point where management must decide to act or not to act.

In many organizations, the need for change goes unrecognized until some major catastrophe occurs. The employees strike or seek the recognition of a union before the management finally recognizes the need for action. Whether it takes a whisper or a shout, the need for change must be recognized by some means; and once that need has been recognized, the exact nature of the problem must be diagnosed. If the problem isn't properly understood, the impact of change on people can be extremely negative.

Diagnosis of a Problem

Change agents facilitate the diagnostic phase by gathering, interpreting, and presenting data. Although the accuracy of data is extremely important, how the data are interpreted and presented is equally important. Interpretation and presentation are generally accomplished in one of two ways. First, the data are discussed with a group of top managers, who are asked to make their own diagnosis of the information; or, second, change agents may present their own diagnoses without making explicit their frameworks for analyzing the data. A difficulty with the first approach is that top management tends to see each problem separately. Each manager views his problem as being the most important and fails to recognize other problem areas. The second approach has inherent problems of communication. External change agents often have difficulty with the second approach because they become immersed in theory and various conceptual frameworks that are less realistic than the managers would like.

C L O S E — U P

AT&T Responds to Changes in the Competitive Environment through the Creation of Innovative Alternative Workplaces

Deregulated organizations face much different competitive environments than when regulated. They must make appropriate changes in their organization structures to respond to the demands of these different environments. Since deregulation, AT&T has been undergoing changes that have altered nearly every aspect of its organization and strategy. These changes reflect AT&T's responses to the necessity to compete in markets that reward fast adoption of new technology and adaptation to fickle customer demand. AT&T's organization structure at the time of deregulation proved incapable of bringing about appropriate behavior. AT&T had a top-heavy bureaucracy, which created unnecessary blocks to creativity and initiative. AT&T's management began efforts to flatten the organization and bring top managers closer to the customer.

Lower-level managers were to have more authority to respond to customer issues.

The change hasn't been without costs, as reflected in employee layoffs and early retirements. But to stay the course is essential, according to company spokespersons. To combat the effects of these traumatic changes, AT&T has implemented policies giving managers and employees personal stakes in the businesses they run. Their salaries and advancement opportunities are tied to customer satisfaction. Managers who direct the change effort claim to have no grand design for what AT&T will eventually look like, but they insist that it must continue its efforts to create smaller, customer-oriented units.

Sources: Mahlon Apgar IV, "The Alternative Workplace: Changing Where and How People Work," *Harvard Business Review,* May/June 1998, pp. 121–130; Dennis T. Jaffe and Cynthia D. Scott, "How to Link Personal Values with Team Values," *Training and Development,* March 1998, pp. 24–30; Barry F. Dambach and Braden R. Allenby, "Implementing Design for Environment at AT&T," *Total Quality Environmental Management,* Spring 1995, pp. 51–62.

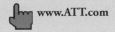 **www.ATT.com**

Appropriate action is necessarily preceded by diagnosis of the problem's symptoms. Experience and judgment are critical to this phase unless the problem is readily apparent to all observers. Ordinarily, however, managers can disagree on the nature of the problem. There's no formula for accurate diagnosis, but the following questions point the manager in the right direction:

1. What is the problem as distinct from the symptoms of the problem?
2. What must be changed to resolve the problem?
3. What outcomes (objectives) are expected from the change, and how will those outcomes be measured?

The answers to these questions can come from information ordinarily found in the organization's information system. Or it may be necessary to generate ad hoc information through the creation of committees or task forces.[26] Meetings between managers and employees provide a variety of viewpoints that can be sifted through by a smaller group. Interviewing key personnel is an important problem-finding method. Another diagnostic approach that obtains broader-based information is the attitude survey.

The survey is a useful diagnostic approach if the potential focus of change is the total organization. If smaller units or entities are the focus of change, the survey technique may not be a reliable source of information. For example, if the focus of change is a relatively small work group, diagnosis of the problem is better accomplished through individual interviews followed by group discussion of the interview data. Consequently, the group becomes actively involved in sharing and interpreting perception of problems. However, the attitude survey can pose difficulties for organizations with relatively low levels of trust in management's sincerity to use the information in constructive ways.

Identification of individual employees' problems comes about through interviews and personnel department information. Consistently low performance evaluations indicate such problems, and it's often necessary to go into greater detail. Identifying individuals' problems is far more difficult than identifying organizational problems. Thus, the diagnostic process must stress the use of precise and reliable information.

To summarize, the data collection process can tap information in several ways. Five different approaches are useful for assorted purposes.[27]

1. Questionnaire data can be collected from large numbers of people.
2. Direct observations can be taken of actual workplace behavior.
3. Selected individuals in key positions can be interviewed.
4. Workshops can be arranged with groups to explore different perceptions of problems.
5. Documents and records of the organization can be examined for archival and current information.

Alternative Interventions

An **intervention** is a specific action that a change agent takes to focus the change process. Although the term has a generally used meaning, it has a specific meaning in the context of organizational development where it refers to a formal activity. Choice of a particular intervention depends on the nature of the problem that management has diagnosed. Management must determine which alternative is most likely to produce the desired outcome, whether it be improvement in skills, attitudes, behavior, or structure. As we've noted, diagnosis of the problem includes specifying the outcome that management desires from the change.

Intervention

A specific action or program undertaken to focus the change process on particular targets.

The literature of organization development recognizes that different interventions have different effects on organizations, groups, and individuals. The term *depth of intended change* refers to the magnitude of the problem to be addressed and the significance of the change required to address the problem.

Depth of intended change

Depth of intended change refers to the scope and intensity of the organizational development efforts.[28] The idea is depicted in Figure 18–2, which likens the organization to an iceberg. This analogy draws attention to two important components: the *formal* and *informal* aspects of organizations. The formal components of an organization are like that part of an iceberg that's above water; the informal components lie below water, unseen, but there nevertheless. As Figure 18–2 shows, the formal components are observable, rational, and oriented to structural factors. On the other hand, the informal components are not observable to all people, affective, and oriented to process and behavioral factors.

Figure 18–2

The Organizational Iceberg

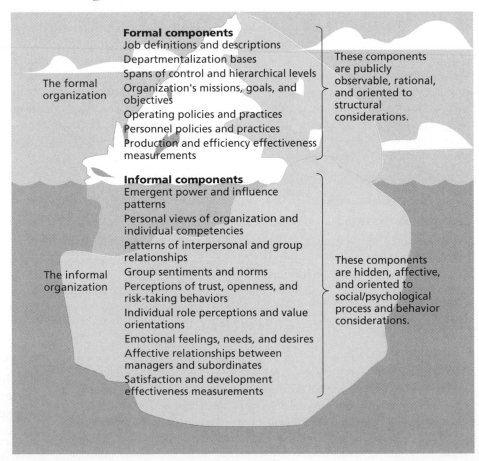

Formal components
Job definitions and descriptions
Departmentalization bases
Spans of control and hierarchical levels
Organization's missions, goals, and objectives
Operating policies and practices
Personnel policies and practices
Production and efficiency effectiveness measurements

The formal organization

These components are publicly observable, rational, and oriented to structural considerations.

Informal components
Emergent power and influence patterns
Personal views of organization and individual competencies
Patterns of interpersonal and group relationships
Group sentiments and norms
Perceptions of trust, openness, and risk-taking behaviors
Individual role perceptions and value orientations
Emotional feelings, needs, and desires
Affective relationships between managers and subordinates
Satisfaction and development effectiveness measurements

The informal organization

These components are hidden, affective, and oriented to social/psychological process and behavior considerations.

Figure 18–3

Targets of Organizational Development and Some Widely Used Interventions

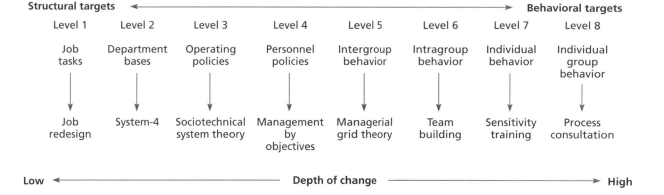

Generally speaking, the greater the scope and intensity of the problem, the more likely it is that the problem will be found in the informal components. Thus, depth of intended change refers to how far management must go into the organization iceberg to solve the problem. At one extreme are problems with the structure of the organization. Managers can solve such problems by changing job definitions, departmentalization bases, spans of control, and delegated authority. At the other extreme are problems with the behavior of groups and individuals. These problems are related to personal views, value orientations, feelings, and sentiments as well as activities, sentiments, and roles within and among groups. And while these behaviors can certainly be affected by changes in structure, they're ordinarily deep-seated and management must confront them more directly. The greater the depth of intervention, the greater the risk of failure and the higher the cost of change.[29]

Targets of interventions

The relationship between source of problem and degree of intended change is illustrated in Figure 18–3. It suggests that there are eight levels, or targets, of an OD program. As the target moves from left to right and, consequently, moves deeper into the organization, the OD program becomes more person- and group-centered, relying more upon socio-psychological and less upon technical-economic knowledge. Levels 1 through 4 involve formal components, including structure, policies, and practices of the organization. Levels 5 through 8 involve informal components including the behavior of groups and individuals. For each of these levels, one or more OD interventions can be possible solutions. Only after the problem and its level are diagnosed should the intervention be selected.

Contemporary practitioners of organizational development classify interventions according to their intended depth. They use the term *technostructural* to refer to interventions in the formal components of organizations and *human process* to refer to those in the informal components. *Multifaceted* interventions intervene in multiple components, both formal and informal, in the organization. We'll use the focus of interventions (i.e., *formal, informal,* and *multiple*) to classify and discuss interventions in the remainder of this chapter since this language is less cumbersome than professional practitioners' terminology.[30]

FORMAL-TARGET INTERVENTIONS   The depth of these interventions is ordinarily restricted to levels 1 through 4. Thus, they target the formal components of the organization for change. However, within this group of interventions, the depth of change can vary from changing jobs to changing the entire organizational structure. For example, interventions such as job enlargement, job enrichment, and job redesign focus on changing job range and depth as we noted in Chapter 14.[31] Interventions such as System-4 change the nature of the organization by changing departmental bases, increasing authority, and emphasizing participative, group-centered management. Sociotechnical system theory (STS) focuses on the relationships between people and technology and causes management to reconsider operations and operating policies.

Management by objectives (MBO) changes how the management relates to individuals by delegating more authority for goal setting. Personnel practices and policies change to reflect the changed relationships among managers and their subordinates. These interventions focus on formal components of the organization, although their effects often spill over into the informal components.

INFORMAL-TARGET INTERVENTIONS   Interventions in this group focus on levels 5 through 8, targeting informal components of the organization for change. Individual and group characteristics such as role expectations, group norms and sanctions, interactions, sentiments, and attitudes are the targets of this family of interventions. The theory and practice of organizational development originated in these interventions and they reflect the preoccupation of OD with individual and group dynamics. Typical interventions include managerial grid, team building, process consultation, and sensitivity training as well as third-party interventions, survey feedback, and structured laboratory training. Organizations are using these interventions to deal with a variety of issues confronting them, including their increasingly diverse workforces. The Close-Up at the bottom of page 457 describes some of the ways organizations deal with diversity through organization development.

MULTITARGET INTERVENTIONS   This grouping acknowledges that interventions are often undertaken in combination.[32] For example, attitude survey feedback and MBO can be used in a single OD program. The increasing use of multitarget interventions indicates a growing awareness of the interrelationships between the formal and informal components of an organization. The combination of two or more types of interventions has a greater chance of improving performance than does the use of any one intervention.[33]

The most popular intervention of the 1990s has been total quality management (TQM). This multitarget intervention attempts to transform organizations by changing the very essence of their formal and informal components. The contemporary and future manager must be familiar with the ideas of the proponents of TQM.[34] TQM can involve a near-total transformation of an organization's formal and informal components including the underlying culture.[35] Moreover, the ideas of the experts who propose TQM as a solution to America's declining competitiveness in global markets emphasize the necessity of organizational development principles, particularly employee involvement, as the means for implementing TQM.[36]

www.xerox.com

Motorola, Ford Motor Company, Procter & Gamble, IBM, and Xerox are but a few of the important large and small organizations that have implemented TQM and, consequently, profoundly transformed their organizations.[37] These organizations can't be said to have totally recovered from the problems that beset them during the 1980s. For example, IBM has yet to regain its position as the global leader of the computer industry. Nevertheless, IBM remains committed to TQM as its best chance. On a larger scale of endorsement, the U.S. government has acknowledged TQM's importance by establishing the Baldrige Award to recognize firms that make the greatest progress toward implementing TQM.[38]

TQM has as many meanings and definitions as there are organizations implementing it. But the overriding sense of TQM endorses the importance of fact-based decision making, quality products and services, and employee-centered management through empowerment and participation.[39] At the formal level of the organization, TQM requires complete job redesign to include self-directed work teams where possible, organic organization structure, and cross-functional coordinative groups. At the informal level, TQM requires trust and commitment to the organization and its mission, cooperation rather than competition among individuals and groups, and honesty in the reconciliation of differences. To bring about these profound changes requires multiple interventions managed according to the principles described in this chapter. TQM is organizational development first and a management practice second.

The idea that organizational development involves multilevels and multifunctions coincides with the conclusions of systems theory. All parts of an organization are connected to all other parts; change in one involves changes in all. Effective organizational development requires accurate diagnosis of problems, selection of appropriate targets for change, and the application of appropriate, usually multiple, OD methods. The desired outcome of OD is an organization whose separate parts are directed toward common purposes. Integrated, multimethod OD programs are promising means to achieve that outcome.

CLOSE—UP

American Organizations Deal with Diversity through Organizational Development

American organizations have recognized that the composition of their workforce is beginning to reflect the composition of American society. Diversity of culture, religion, national origin, race, and gender now characterizes the employment rolls of all but the most isolated organization. In recognition of this fact of organizational life, organizations have turned to organizational development interventions to help employees learn to deal effectively with their fellow employees as well as a diverse population of suppliers and customers. For example, the Monsanto Company has devised a well-publicized organizational development effort that prepares its employees to cope successfully with differences between employees. The program alerts new and veteran employees to become aware of subtle forms of discrimination when dealing with other people and to develop skills to help employees confront differences and, at the same time, get on with doing business.

McDonald's Corporation undertook a determined effort in 1981 to recruit and hire mentally and physically challenged individuals. The program aims to find useful employment for individuals who might otherwise be unable to contributed their talents. McDonald's found during the course of its program that it was necessary to help other store employees understand what it means to be a disabled restaurant employee. The company discovered organizational development to be quite useful for this purpose.

New York City has long been recognized for its diverse population. Recently, the New York City Police Department implemented sensitivity training to help police officers relate to the ever-increasing diversity of the city's population, the police department's constituency. Sensitivity training coincided with the department's new initiative to focus police efforts at community levels throughout the city.

Sources: Julie Miller, "Resort Understands Diversity," *Hotel and Motel Management,* September 1997, pp. 50–51; Thomas Diamante and Leo Giglio, "Managing a Diverse Workforce: Training as a Cultural Intervention Strategy," *Leadership and Organizational Development Journal,* vol 15, no. 2 (1994), pp. 13–17; and Alan M. Webber, "Crime and Management: An Interview with New York City Police Commissioner, Lee P. Brown," *Harvard Business Review,* May–June 1991, pp. 110–26.

www.monsanto.com

www.mcdonalds.com

www.newyorkcity.com

Overcoming Limiting Conditions

The selection of any developmental intervention should be based on diagnosis of the problem, but the choice is tempered by certain conditions that exist at the time. Scholars identify three sources of influence on the outcome of management development programs that can be generalized to cover the entire range of organizational development interventions: leadership climate, formal organization, and organizational culture.

Leadership climate

Leadership Climate

The nature of the work environment in an organization that results from the leadership style and administrative practices of managers.

The nature of the work environment that results from the leadership style and administrative practices of managers is termed the **leadership climate.** It can greatly affect an OD program. Any OD program that lacks management's support and commitment has only a slim chance of success.[40] We can also understand that the style of leadership may itself be the subject of change. For example, total quality management (TQM) attempts to move managers toward a certain style—open, supportive, and group-centered. But we must recognize that participants may be unable to adopt such styles if the styles aren't compatible with their own manager's style.[41]

Formal organization

Formal Organization

The philosophy, policies, structure, and systems of control of an organization.

The **formal organization** includes the philosophy and policies of top management, as well as legal precedent, organizational structure, and the systems of control. Of course, each of these sources of impact may itself be the focus of a change effort. The important point is that a change in one must be compatible with all of the others.[42] It may be possible to design organizations that not only facilitate change, but actually welcome it.[43]

Organizational culture

Organizational Culture

The pervasive system of values, beliefs, and norms that exists in any organization. The organizational culture can encourage or discourage effectiveness, depending on the nature of the values, beliefs, and norms.

As we've learned, **organizational culture** refers to the pattern of beliefs resulting from group norms, values, and informal activities.[44] The impact of traditional behavior that's sanctioned by group norms but not formally acknowledged was first documented in the Hawthorne studies. A proposed change in work methods or the installation of an automated device can run counter to the expectations and attitudes of the work group, and if such is the case, the OD strategy must anticipate the resulting resistance.[45]

Implementing OD that doesn't consider the constraints imposed by prevailing conditions within the present organization may, of course, amplify the problem that triggered the developmental process. If OD is implemented in this way, the potential for subsequent problems is greater than would ordinarily be expected. Taken together, the prevailing conditions constitute the climate for change, and they can be positive or negative.

Implementing the Intervention

The implementation of the OD intervention has two dimensions: *timing* and *scope*. Timing refers to the selection of the appropriate time at which to initiate the intervention. Scope refers to the selection of the appropriate scale. Timing depends on a number of factors, particularly the organization's operating cycle and the groundwork preceding the OD program. Certainly, if a program is of considerable magnitude, it's desirable that it not compete with day-to-day operations; thus, the change might well be implemented during a slack period. On the other hand, if the program is critical to the organization's survival, immediate implementation is in order. The scope of the program depends on the strategy. The program may be implemented throughout the organization. Or it may be phased into the organization level by level or department by department. The optimum strategy uses a phased approach, which limits the scope but provides feedback for each subsequent implementation.

The intervention that's finally selected is usually not implemented on a grand scale. Rather, it's implemented on a small scale in various units throughout the organization. For example, an MBO program can be implemented in one unit or at one level at a time. The objective is to experiment with the intervention (that is, to test the validity of the diagnosed solution). As management learns from each successive implementation, the total program is strengthened. Not even the most detailed planning can anticipate all the consequences of implementing a particular intervention. Thus, it's necessary to experiment and search for new information that can bear on the program.

As the experimental attempts provide positive signals that the program is preceding as planned, there's a reinforcement effect. Personnel will be encouraged to accept the change required of them and to enlarge their own efforts' scope. Acceptance of the change is facilitated by its positive results.

Evaluating the Program

An OD program represents an expenditure of organizational resources in exchange for some desired result. The resources take the form of money and time that have alternative uses. The result is in the form of increased organizational effectiveness: production, efficiency, and satisfaction in the short run; adaptiveness and development in the intermediate run; survival in the long run. Accordingly, some provision must be made to evaluate the program in terms of expenditures and results. In addition to providing information to evaluate a specific organizational development program, evaluation provides a literature that can be accessed by others who are deciding whether to undertake OD. Reviews of the relative efficacy of OD interventions appear regularly.[46] The evaluation phase has two problems to overcome: obtaining data that measure the desired results and determining the expected trend of improvement over time.

The acquisition of information that measures the sought-after result is the easier problem to solve, although it certainly doesn't lend itself to naive solutions. As we've come to understand, the stimulus for change is the deterioration of effectiveness criteria that management has traced to structural and behavioral causes. The criteria may be any number of effectiveness indicators, including profit, sales volume, absenteeism, turnover, scrappage, or costs. The major source of feedback for those variables is the organization's information system. But if the change includes the expectation that employee satisfaction must be improved, the usual sources of information are limited, if not invalid. It's quite possible for a change to induce increased production at the expense of declining employee satisfaction. Thus, if the manager relies on the naive assumption that production and satisfaction are directly related, the change may be incorrectly judged successful when cost and profit improve.[47]

To avoid the danger of overreliance on production data, the manager can generate ad hoc information that measures employee satisfaction. The benchmark for evaluation would be available if an attitude survey was used in the diagnosis phase. The definition of acceptable improvement is difficult when evaluating attitudinal data, since the matter of how much more positive employees' attitudes should be is quite different from the matter of how much more productive should they be. Nevertheless, for a complete analysis of results, attitudinal measurements must be combined with production and other effectiveness measurements.

In a practical sense, an OD program's effectiveness can't be evaluated if objectives haven't been established before it's implemented. A program undertaken to make the organization "a better place to work" or to develop the "full potential of the employees" can't be evaluated. If, on the other hand, measurable criteria that are valid indicators of "better places to work" and "full employee potential" are collected during the diagnostic phase and subsequently tracked as the program is undertaken, bases for evaluation exist. A considerable body of literature describes methods of evaluation, and managers of OD programs should consult it for guidance in program evaluation.

Generally, an evaluation model would follow the six steps of evaluative research:

1. Determining the objectives of the program.

2. Describing the activities undertaken to achieve the objectives.

3. Measuring the effects of the program.

4. Establishing baseline points against which changes can be compared.

5. Controlling extraneous factors, preferably through use of a control group.

6. Detecting unanticipated consequences.

Application of these six steps isn't always possible. For example, managers don't always specify objectives in precise terms, and control groups may be difficult to establish. Nevertheless, the difficulties of evaluation shouldn't discourage attempts to evaluate.

The Ethical Issues of Organizational Development

Organizational development is a managerial technique for implementing major changes in organizations. As a practice intended to bring about change, OD involves applying powerful behavioral science knowledge by a change agent to bring about performance improvements. The ethical issues of organizational development turn on the power relationships among the various participants in the change effort.[48] At the most fundamental level, critics note that OD takes as given the existing power relationships in the organization since the change effort is initiated by managers. As a managerial technique, OD necessarily implements managerial values regardless of the values of the change agent. OD is inherently unethical because it restricts the range of values that can legitimately be considered in bringing about the change. Even though OD may bring about performance improvements in the organization, the basic power relationships remain unchanged.

Opportunities for unethical behavior can be seen in OD-related activities. For example, the purposes of a particular OD intervention can be misrepresented to the participants in order to win their participation. Managers may say that they want to implement MBO to provide greater employee participation when in fact they're attracted to MBO as a means of performance evaluation that holds individuals responsible for results rather than activities. A second OD activity involves data analysis. Change agents collect and analyze data to diagnose the nature of the problem and to evaluate the solution. The change agents' allegiance to the people who hire them, the organization's managers, will inevitably lead to misuse when the data conflict with managers' preferences. Data indicative of management incompetence can be misused so as to indicate employee incompetence. Finally, OD involves manipulation of individuals without informed consent. Employees who are subjects of OD interventions aren't given the choice to participate, particularly when the focus of the change is group and organizational performance. Manipulation can in fact turn into coercion when the individual must choose between participating in the process or being fired.

Thus, the argument for the unethical nature of OD proceeds from the recognition that OD inherently reflects but one possible set of values, managerial values. As a consequence, OD activities that involve ethical choices will always be guided by the underlying values even when those choices involve misrepresentation, misuse, and manipulation.

Those who dispute the argument that organizational development is inherently unethical point out that every act has ethical implications, but only because the action is taken by an individual. Machines aren't capable of unethical behavior; people are more than capable of unethical as well as ethical behavior. OD is no more or less unethical than any other management technique. The fact that OD implements managerial values to the exclusion of others isn't unique to OD. By that argument, management is itself unethical since it reflects the value system of the larger society of which it's part. But there's recognition even among the proponents of OD that special care must be taken to protect against the abuse of powerful knowledge that OD change agents apply.

The best protection against misrepresentation, misuse, and manipulation is managers who create and foster an organizational culture that encourages ethical behavior. Such a culture would begin with top management's formal declaration that ethical behavior is the norm and that in all actions, individuals—including OD practitioners—are to conduct themselves in an ethical manner even when such conduct may be costly to the organization in economic and technical terms. Through the actions of top management, ethical behavior can become part of the everyday activities and decisions of everyone in the organization.

Codes of ethics are suggested means for institutionalizing ethical behavior. Top management demonstrates its commitment to the code through its daily behavior. In addition, the organization reinforces ethical behavior through punishment and rewards. Deviants are dealt with swiftly and adherents are rewarded consistently. The performance evaluation system can be a very important mechanism for demonstrating management's commitment to ethical behavior.

Thus, OD is not unethical. But individuals can be unethical if rewarded for unethical behavior. Consequently, management must create an environment that fosters ethical conduct. In such an environment, OD can proceed in an ethical manner.

Some Guidelines for Managing Change through OD

What then can managers do when they recognize the need to change their organization through organizational development interventions? Although no absolute guarantees can assure success in every instance, the accumulated experience of people involved with organizational development offers some guidelines. We share the views of one such individual, William G. Dyer, who has spent 30 years assisting organizations reach their potential effectiveness. He states that the following conditions must be present if the OD intervention is to have some chance of bringing about the desired change:[49]

1. Management and all those involved must have high and visible commitment to the effort.

2. People who are involved need to have advance information that enables them to know what is to happen and why they are to do what they are to do.

3. The effort (especially the evaluation and reward systems) must be connected to other parts of the organization.

4. The effort needs to be directed by line managers and assisted by a change agent if necessary.

5. The effort must be based on good diagnosis and must be consistent with the conditions in the organization.

6. Management must remain committed to the effort throughout all its steps, from diagnosis through implementation and evaluation.

7. Evaluation is essential and must consist of more than asking people how they felt about the effort.

8. People must see clearly the relationship between the effort and the organization's mission and goals.

9. The change agent, if used, must be clearly competent.

These nine conditions combine the important points we've made in this chapter. Taking them together, we can see that organizational development is a significant undertaking and that managers should go about it in a systematic way. The model for managing change offers a systematic process for realizing the nine conditions for success that Dyer states are necessary, but not sufficient, for bringing about organizational effectiveness.

Of crucial consideration is managers' role in the OD process. Although Dyer's nine steps include the activities of competent change agents, they also clearly include an active role for managers. They must support all the required activities, be involved, and even direct the effort. As the 1990s progress, we should expect to see even greater commitment and involvement of managers in OD processes.[50]

Summary of Key Points

- The need to consider organizational development arises from changes in the inter- and extraorganizational environment. Changes in input, output, technological, and scientific subenvironments may indicate the need to consider the feasibility of a long-term, systematically managed program for changing the structure, process, and behavior of the organization. Even in the absence of environmental changes, organizational processes and behavior may become dysfunctional for achieving organizational effectiveness.

- The diagnosis of present and potential problems involves the collection of information that reflects the level of organizational effectiveness. Data that measure the current state of production, efficiency, satisfaction, adaptiveness, and development must be gathered and analyzed. The purpose of diagnosis is to trace the causes of the problem. In addition to serving as the basis for problem identification, the diagnostic data also establish the basis for subsequent evaluation of the organizational development effort.

- To diagnose the problem, managers can consider these analytical questions:

1. What is the problem as distinct from its symptoms?

2. What must be changed to resolve the problem?

3. What outcomes are expected, and how will these outcomes be measured?

- The managerial response to these questions should be stated in terms of criteria that reflect organizational effectiveness. Measurable outcomes such as production, efficiency, satisfaction, adaptiveness, and development must be linked to skill, attitudinal, behavioral, and structural changes necessitated by problem identification.

- Through diagnosis, management associates the problem with skill, attitudinal, behavioral, and structural causes and selects the appropriate intervention. If employee participation is inappropriate because the necessary preconditions don't exist, management must unilaterally define the problem and select the appropriate method. Whether the problem is related to skill or attitudinal, behavioral, or structural causes, the strategy must include provision for learning principles.

- The last step of the OD process is the evaluation procedure. The ideal situation would be to structure the procedure in the manner of an experimental design. That is, the end results should be operationally defined, and measurements should be taken, before and after, both in the organization undergoing development and in a second organization (the control group). If the scope of the program is limited to a subunit, a second subunit could serve as a control group. An evaluation not only enables management to account for its use of resources but also provides feedback. Based on this feedback, corrections can be taken in the implementation phase.

Discussion and Review Questions

1. Identify the existing forces for change acting on your college. Compare these forces to those acting on a firm where you work or have worked. What are the important differences among these forces? Which are more powerful: the environmental or internal forces? Which organization seems more responsive to these forces for change?

2. Explain the concept *organization intervention* and why any particular management or organizational change can be considered an intervention.

3. Might some managers attempt to implement a particular intervention, such as TQM, without first diagnosing whether the intervention would be appropriate for their organization's problems? What would explain this behavior?

4. Explain why OD programs to bring about significant change often must use more than one form of intervention.

5. Evaluate the ethical issues associated with downsizing an organization by reducing its labor force to increase the organization's long-run chance of survival. What other ethical issues can you identify in the practice of organizational development as you understand it thus far?

6. Describe the relationships among the steps of the change model depicted in this chapter and the process of unfreezing–movement–refreezing. Which steps of the model are related to which elements of the relearning process?

7. How would you go about designing a training program that would cause managers in a small firm to recognize the need to change the way they manage if their industry has become more competitive in recent years?

8. What would be the characteristics of an organization or situation for which the use of reason would be an effective approach for managing change? Are such organizations and situations relatively rare?

9. Explain the difficulties that you would encounter in attempting to obtain diagnostic information from members of two groups who believe that they're competing for scarce resources.

10. Explain why an OD program should be evaluated and why such an evaluation is so difficult to do.

C A S E   F O R   A N A L Y S I S

Managing Change at FMC Corporation

FMC Corporation is a major international producer of machinery and chemicals for industry, agriculture, and government. From the company's headquarters in Chicago, top management directs 28,000 employees in 118 factories and mines in 29 states and 15 other nations. During the 1980s, FMC faced increasingly stiff domestic and international competition. Top management realized that the firm's survival depended on implementing modern manufacturing technology and information systems. They also recognized the importance of developing an organizational culture that encouraged innovation and risk taking.

FMC's management information system (MIS) became the focus of attention when an organization-wide attitude survey indicated considerable dissatisfaction with MIS services. MIS consisted of some 800 professionals throughout the organization. For some time, managers of MIS units had been aware of their inability to fully meet the demands for increasingly complex information technology applications. The attitude survey results documented the extent of dissatisfaction with MIS services and made it evident that corrective action was necessary. MIS management's immediate response to the problem was to announce that "user satisfaction" was the primary goal for all MIS units throughout FMC. Consequently, MIS's entire energies focused on that goal; in a short time, user satisfaction began to increase.

MIS managers throughout FMC achieved the goal by becoming increasingly task directed. They planned project activities and schedules without consulting the people who were to do the work. To meet the planned deadlines, overtime became the rule rather than the exception. Managers viewed employees' reluctance to work overtime as disloyalty to the unit. Centralization of authority created delays, as decisions had to move up and down the hierarchy. Meeting the goal of user satisfaction while maintaining employee satisfaction became increasingly difficult.

Two years after implementing the program to improve user satisfaction, employees' dissatisfaction surfaced in a meeting of MIS managers and employees. The meeting was one of the scheduled quarterly meetings referred to as "town hall" meetings in the MIS units. Top management used this particular meeting to report the improved results in achieving user satisfaction and to congratulate employees on their accomplishment. One employee chose this same meeting to voice concern for the costs of the accomplishment in deteriorating employee satisfaction, as evidenced by management's apparent lack of concern for employees' needs. The discussion that followed indicated that performance levels were, in fact, beginning to slip and that employee turnover was increasing.

Discussion of problems during the town hall meeting stimulated MIS management to appoint an employee task force to design and administer an attitude survey specifically for MIS. Survey results revealed that employee dissatisfaction and turnover were making it more and more difficult, if not impossible, to meet the ever growing demands for high-level information technology applications in FMC. If the problem was not resolved, line units in FMC would begin to turn to external vendors for MIS services. After discussions with a consultant in organizational development, the MIS director decided to focus on the survey results at the annual planning meeting he held with the 11 managers who reported directly to him.

In previous years, the planning meetings had established goals and performance measures for the upcoming year. But this year, the director and the consultant believed that employee concerns must be addressed. They were certain that solutions could be found if the 11 managers focused on new ways to manage people. Specifically, the director wanted managers to define MIS's mission and philosophy to include beliefs about service to customers, the worth of the individual, and operational cost effectiveness and performance. As a result of four days of intensive and often heated discussions, the group-prepared statement of MIS's mission and philosophy embodied values that gave purpose and direction to efforts to adopt and implement it throughout the country.

To implement the mission and philosophy, significant changes were required in performance review, career development, policy and procedures, and managerial behavior. To guide the change effort, the director formed a steering committee of managers and supervisors. The steering committee then broke into four task groups to tackle each of the four areas. Because of the prevailing management styles in MIS, these task groups were unskilled in teamwork and team skills. The consultant facilitated training in team building; soon thereafter, the four groups were under way.

The task groups completed their work and made 78 recommendations for changing the performance review processes, career development practices, administrative policies and procedures, and daily management behavior. Among the more significant changes implemented were the training of managers in performance evaluation, training in team building, decentralization of authority, and active participation of employees in decision making. All of these changes were consistent with MIS's statement of mission and philosophy.

Four years after the initial attitude survey, many of the significant changes were in place. A follow-up attitude survey confirmed that employee satisfaction had increased and that turnover had decreased. MIS managers also pointed to renewed commitment to meet user needs as evidence that progress had been made in improving MIS's performance.

Discussion Questions

1. Was the second FMC change effort successful? If so, what did it do right? If not, what did it do wrong?

2. Which roles did the attitude surveys play in the change effort?

3. What depth of intervention was necessary to change FMC's MIS function in order to improve its performance? What was the alternative to change? Did management have a choice in the matter?

Source: Edmund J. Metz, "Managing Change toward a Leading-Edge Information Culture," *Organizational Dynamics,* Autumn 1986, pp. 28–40.

www.FMC.com

Alternative Ways to Initiate Change

Objective

To evaluate alternative ways to initiate training in the face of possible resistance from both the employees and their supervisors.

Related Topics

Individual, group, and leadership theories are relevant, along with ideas and concepts from organizational change and development.

Starting the Exercise

The instructor will divide the class into groups of five to seven. The groups should read the scenario below and decide which of the five alternatives the manager should implement. Although other alternatives are possible, evaluate only those indicated. Each group will prepare and present an oral report justifying its choice.

Scenario

A manager faces a problem involving mistakes employees are making. The mistakes occur in nearly every department of the plant in which this particular operation is performed. The manager believes that a training program is necessary to help employees perform better and reduce the errors. He believes that supervisors who report to him will defend existing procedures because the introduction of a training program could imply criticism of the way they've been operating. The manager also thinks that the supervisors fear resistance by employees afraid of not doing well in the training program. Given these facts and considerations, the manager believes that he has five alternative ways to initiate the needed change:

1. To the agenda of the weekly meeting with the supervisors, add a recommendation that training be undertaken.

2. Talk to the supervisors individually and get their ideas about what to do before bringing up the issue in the weekly meeting.

3. Ask the corporate training staff to come to the plant, assess the training needs, and develop a program to address those needs.

4. Tell the supervisors that the training is in the interests of the company, and that they are expected to support it with enthusiasm.

5. Appoint a team of supervisors to study the matter thoroughly and to bring a recommendation to the weekly meeting.

Completing the Exercise

Phase I: 30 minutes.   Each group of five to seven students should read the scenario, evaluate the five alternatives, and prepare an oral report defending its choice.

Phase II: 30 minutes.   As a class, discuss the choices made by the groups as well as their reasons for picking a particular alternative.

Source: Based on Leslie W. Rue and Lloyd L. Byars, *Management,* 5th ed. (Homewood, Ill.: Richard D. Irwin, 1989), p. 526.

Motorola: Building the Organization

Almost everyone could rattle off a long list of businesses that are considered successful. They come in all sizes, shapes, and levels of advancement. You probably encounter many products and services of well known businesses each day. Yet a deeper understanding of how these businesses work is sometimes more difficult to obtain. Many companies enjoy a sudden boom of success only to fade into obscurity after a brief time. Others are able to prepare for the future and position themselves to adapt to changes in technology. Foresight, and the ability to adapt to change are what gives an organization the edge over its competition in the present and in the future.

In 1928 Paul Galvin started a small company to manufacture a battery eliminator for radios. The battery eliminator enabled consumers to operate radios directly from household current, rather than from the cumbersome battery supplied with most early radios. Galvin's next invention was a radio for automobiles. It was the concept of marrying sound and motion that provided Galvin with a name for his company—Motorola. Today Motorola is recognized as one of the world leaders in the communications industry.

From day one Paul Galvin knew that the key to success was recognizing customers' needs. Finding ways to fill these needs at Motorola involves a commitment to total customer satisfaction, constant renewal of knowledge and skills, and the ability to see the future. On a trip to Europe in the 1930s, for example, Galvin became convinced that a war of major proportions was about to develop. From this observation, Galvin foresaw a need for mobile communications. Back at home, Motorola began work on what was to become the handy-talkie, a hand-held, two-way radio that set the pace for the company's future.

At the time of Galvin's death in 1959, Motorola was the leader in military, space, and commercial communications. The company had also built its first semiconductor facility, and was a growing force in consumer electronics. Bob Galvin, Paul's son, took Motorola into international markets in the 1960s and the company began to shift its focus away from consumer electronics. Motorola's television business was sold in the mid 1970s as the company again shifted focus and moved more into electronics and communications. By 1990 Motorola had become the premiere, worldwide supplier of cellular telephones. Changing with the times is a way of life at Motorola.

E. David Metz of Motorola's Semiconductor Products Sector, said: "Our factories today, if they're going to be competitive, have to be sensitive to and respond to the opportunities to make and produce a product that people will want to buy tomorrow. They may get tired of today's model and the people who are making those new products may have to learn to use new tools or use older tools in a new way."

It's important for any organization to be able to measure success. This is often easiest to gauge by looking at some of the indicators of business success. Like all businesses, Motorola is concerned with financial performance. However, it goes much further than that. Motorola uses the following indicators of business success:

- Achieving financial performance.
- Meeting customer needs and values.
- Building quality products and services.
- Encouraging innovation and creativity.
- Gaining employee commitment.

Managers study indicators such as sales revenues, net profits, and return on investments. They also look at how these indicators change over time. Meeting customer needs and values is also a way to measure performance. Since Motorola is in the communication business, knowing the communication needs of its customers and filling those needs is of great importance. Quality is another defining indicator of a company's success. Since 1928 Motorola has had to reinvent itself every decade, although the company's commitment to quality and to its employees remains legendary.

Due to its large size and varied areas of specialized technology, Motorola is divided into a number of business sectors. Each is responsible for a different arm of Motorola communication technology. These sectors are:

- Semiconductor Products.
- Cellular Subscribers.
- Cellular Networks and Space.
- Land Mobile Products.
- Messaging, Information, and Media.
- Automotive, Component, Computer, and Energy Sector.

Companywide the culture at Motorola is definitely one where quality is the norm. Motorola is recognized worldwide for producing products that never fail. In addition to this, Motorola is consistently listed as one of the best companies to work for in the United States.

Increasingly, today's businesses must focus on the quality and value of their products and services. Most customers just won't tolerate low quality. Companies like Motorola have made quality the foundation for their future. They have formalized plans and programs for promoting and ensuring a quality focus. For example, Motorola University was established in 1981 to provide training that secures these quality ideals companywide. This training emphasizes the organization's goals while providing learning environments where employees can keep abreast of the changes in communication technology. At a company like Motorola, where the international marketplace is an important one, flexibility is a requirement for employees and the organization as a whole.

Roger Bertelson, Managing Director in Malaysia, said: "Our workforce is going have to accept the fact that they need to be flexible. They are going to have to be a more educated workforce and they are going to have to be more adaptable to change. Because a changing environment is part of manufacturing as it is today."

Another indicator of success is the encouragement of innovation and creativity. With new technologies being developed all the time, the only way a business can stay on top and compete is to be creative and innovative. Employee commitment is yet another prime indicator of success. The dedication of its employees enables Motorola to continue to produce top quality, leading edge products and technology. When quality is of the essence, highly motivated employees are a must. Just listen to the comments of some of Motorola's valuable employees:

"Commitment at Motorola, and I'll speak for the cellular construction group, is honestly the middle name."

"People here are all self-starters and they always take the initiative to do their own job and try to fulfill their duties and responsibilities."

"My belief is that if the people are good at what they do then they will respond to being given increasingly more difficult tasks to perform."

"I must exceed customer expectations. I want to leave the customer delighted with our services."

"I find that this company conducts its business in an honorable fashion and that is something that I can always be proud of."

Success in business depends on many factors. The ability to recognize or even predict customer needs is a solid place to start. The next step is to deliver a quality product or service to the customer. But most challenging of all, the company must be able to make changes and adapt to changes in technology and customer needs to remain competitive for the long run. Measuring success by looking at key indicators can help a business stay on the right track.

Motorola has enjoyed success because it has a business structure in place that was built on adaptation and reorganization. The company and its products are different than they were 10, 20, or 30 years ago. By having to reinvent itself every decade, Motorola is able to move with the many changes and advancements in communication technologies. Motorola expects to adapt and time and time again it has proven to be up to the challenge.

Critical Thinking Questions

1. What is the purpose of Motorola University? In what ways do you think Motorola University provides training that differs from a regular university? Why do you think so many companies have developed their own universities?

2. Managers must study the key indicators of success in order to determine the health of a business. Why do you think these indicators need to be studied both in the present and over time? Are there any indicators of success that you think are important that were not mentioned in this video? Explain.

3. The videotape states that businesses must be able to foresee the future in order to be successful. How do you think it's possible for a business to do this? What tools might a business use to "foresee the future?"

Procedures and Techniques for Studying Organizations: Behavior, Structure, Processes

Sources of knowledge about organizations

The vast majority of the research reports and writing on organizations is contained in technical publications known as journals. Some of these journals, such as the *Academy of Management Review,* are devoted entirely to topics of management and organization, while such journals as *Organizational Behavior and Human Decision Processes* are devoted largely to results of laboratory studies. Such journals as *Harvard Business Review* and *Business Management* are general business journals, while *American Sociological Review* and *Journal of Applied Psychology* are general behavioral science journals. These general business and behavioral science journals often contain articles of interest to management students.

Table A–1 presents a selective list of journals providing information, data, and discussion about what is occurring within and among organizations. This knowledge base provides managers with available research information that could prove useful in their own organizations or situations.[1]

HISTORY The oldest approach to the study of organizations is through the history of organizations, societies, and institutions. Organizations are as old as human history. Throughout time, people have joined with others to accomplish their goals—first in families, later in tribes and other more sophisticated political units. Ancient peoples constructed pyramids, temples, and ships; they created systems of government, farming, commerce, and warfare. For example, Greek historians tell us that it took 100,000 men to build the Great Pyramid of Khufu in Egypt. The project took over 20 years to complete. It was almost as high as the Washington Monument and had a base that would cover eight football fields. Remember, these people had no construction equipment or computers. One thing they did have, though, was *organization.* While these "joint efforts" did not have formal names such as XYZ Corporation, the idea of "getting organized" was quite widespread throughout early civilizations. The literature of the times refers to such managerial concepts as planning, staff assistance, division of labor, control, and leadership.[2]

Table A–1

Selected Sources of Writing and Research about Organizations

1. *Academy of Management Executive*	20. *Journal of Applied Psychology*
2. *Academy of Management Journal*	21. *Journal of Business Ethics*
3. *Academy of Management Review*	22. *Journal of Business Strategy*
4. *Administrative Science Quarterly*	23. *Journal of International Business Studies*
5. *Advanced Management Journal*	24. *Journal of Management Studies*
6. *Business Horizons*	25. *Management Review*
7. *Business Management*	26. *Management Science*
8. *California Management Review*	27. *Organizational Behavior and Human Decision Processes*
9. *Columbia Journal of World Business*	28. *Organizational Dynamics*
10. *Compensation & Benefits Review*	29. *Personnel Journal*
11. *Fortune*	30. *Personnel Psychology*
12. *Harvard Business Review*	31. *Public Administration Review*
13. *Health Psychology*	32. *Public Personnel Management*
14. *HR Magazine*	33. *Sloan Management Review*
15. *Human Relations*	34. *Strategic Management Journal*
16. *Human Resource Planning*	35. *Training*
17. *Industrial and Labor Relations Review*	36. *Training & Development*
18. *Industrial Management Review*	
19. *Journal of Applied Behavioral Science*	

The administration of the vast Roman Empire required the application of organization and management concepts. In fact, it has been said that "the real secret of the greatness of the Romans was their genius for organization."[3] This is because the Romans used certain principles of organization to coordinate the diverse activities of the empire.

If judged by age alone, the Roman Catholic Church would have to be considered the most effective organization of all time. While its success is the result of many factors, one of these factors is certainly the effectiveness of its organization and management. For example, a hierarchy of authority, a territorial organization, specialization of activities by function, and use of the staff principle were integral parts of early church organization.

Finally, and not surprisingly, some important concepts and practices in modern organizations can be traced to military organizations. Like the church, military organizations were faced with problems of managing large, geographically dispersed groups and adopted the concept of staff as an advisory function for line personnel early on.

Knowledge of the history of organizations in earlier societies can be useful for the future manager. In fact, many of the early concepts and practices are being utilized successfully today. But we may ask whether heavy reliance on the past is a good guide to the present and future.[4] We shall see that time and organizational setting have much to do with what works in management.

EXPERIENCE   Some of the earliest books on management and organizations were written by successful practitioners. Most of these individuals were business executives, and their writings focused on how it was for them during their time with one or more companies. They usually put forward certain general principles or practices that had worked well for them. Although using the writings and experiences of practitioners sounds "practical," it has drawbacks. Successful managers are susceptible to the same perceptual phenomena as the rest of us. Their accounts are therefore based on their own preconceptions and biases. No matter how objective the approach, experiential accounts may not be entirely complete or accurate. They may also be superficial, since they are often after-the-fact reflections of situations in which, when the events were occurring, the managers had little time to think about how or why an action was taken. As a result, suggestions in such accounts are often oversimplified. Finally, as with history, what worked yesterday may not work today or tomorrow.[5]

SCIENCE   A major focus in this book is the behavioral sciences that have produced theory, research, and generalizations concerning the behavior, structure, and processes of organizations. Behavioral scientists' interest in the problems of organizations is relatively new, becoming popular in the early 1950s. At that time, an organization known as the Foundation for Research on Human Behavior was established to promote and support behavioral science research in business, government, and other organizations.

Many advocates of the scientific approach believe that practicing managers and teachers have accepted prevalent practices and principles without the benefit of scientific validation. They believe that scientific procedures should be used to validate practice whenever possible. Because of their work, many of the earlier practices and principles have been discounted or modified, and others have been validated.

Behavioral sciences research and methods

RESEARCH   Present research in the behavioral sciences varies greatly with respect to the scope and methods used. One common thread among the various disciplines is the study of human behavior through the use of scientific procedures. Thus, it's necessary to examine the nature of science as it's applied to human behavior.

Some critics believe that a science of human behavior is unattainable and that the scientific procedures used to gain knowledge in the physical sciences cannot be adapted to the study of humans, especially humans in organizations. While this is not the appropriate place to become involved in these arguments, we believe that the scientific approach can be applied to management and organizational studies.[6] Furthermore, as we have already pointed out, means other than scientific procedures have provided important knowledge concerning people in organizations.

When asked about nonscientific ideas, physical scientists generally reply. "There's no evidence for anything like that." They point out, for example, that it is difficult to believe in the existence of UFOs when no artifact of extraterrestrial origin has been found. This argument is not very convincing. After all, physical scientists also speculate about ideas that are, as yet, unconfirmed by empirical evidence. If they didn't, progress would slow down or simply stop.[7]

The manager draws from the behavioral sciences just as the physician draws from the biological sciences. The manager must know what to expect from the behavioral sciences, their strengths and weaknesses, just as the physician must know what to expect from bacteriology and how it can serve as a diagnostic tool. However, the manager, like the physician, is a practitioner who must make decisions in the present, whether or not science has all the answers. Neither can wait until he finds them before acting.[8] Neither the physical nor the behavioral scientists has all the answers.

THE SCIENTIFIC APPROACH   Most current philosophers of science define science by what they consider to be its one universal and unique feature: *method*. The greatest advantage of the scientific approach is its characteristic of *self-correction*, which no other method of attaining knowledge has.[9] The approach is an objective, systematic, and controlled process with built-in checks all along the way to knowledge. These checks control and verify the scientist's activities and conclusions to enable the attainment of knowledge independent of the scientist's own biases and preconceptions.

Most scientists agree that rather than use a single scientific method, scientists can and do use several methods. Thus, it probably makes more sense to say that there is a scientific *approach*.

Table A–2   Characteristics of the Scientific Approach

1. Procedures are public. A scientific report contains a complete description of what was done, to enable other researchers in the field to follow each step of the investigation as if they were actually present.

2. Definitions are precise. The procedures used, the variables measured, and how they were measured must be clearly stated. For example, if examining motivation among employees in a given plant, researchers must define what is meant by motivation and how it was measured (for example, number of units produced, number of absences).

3. Data collection is objective. Objectivity is a key feature of the scientific approach. Bias in collecting and interpreting data has no place in science.

4. Findings must be replicable. This enables another interested researcher to test the results of a study by attempting to reproduce them.

5. The approach is systematic and cumulative. This relates to one of the underlying purposes of science, to develop a unified body of knowledge.

6. The purposes are explanation, understanding, and prediction. All scientists want to know "why" and "how." If they determine "why" and "how" and are able to provide proof, they can then predict the particular conditions under which specific events (human behavior in the case of behavioral sciences) will occur. Prediction is the ultimate objective of behavioral science, as it is of all science.

Source: Bernard Berelson and Gary A. Steiner, *Human Behavior: An Inventory of Scientific Findings* (New York: Harcourt Brace Jovanovich, 1964), pp. 16–18.

Table A–2 summarizes the major characteristics of this approach. While only an "ideal" science would exhibit all of them, they are nevertheless the hallmarks of the scientific approach. They exhibit the basic nature—objective, systematic, controlled—of the scientific approach, which enables others to have confidence in research results. What is important is the overall fundamental idea that the scientific approach is a controlled rational process.

Throughout the book organizational behavior terms, issues, and analyses were used in clarifying how people behave in organizations. A scientific language or vocabulary was used to better understand human resources. Assumptions, propositions, and hypotheses about behavior were interjected and formed the basis of debates, controversy, and understanding about OB. For example, the Hawthorne researchers hypothesized originally that, "if workers received appropriate rest breaks, then productivity would increase." The hypothesis is a predictive statement presented in an "If—Then" context. If (rest break)—Then (productivity increase). This hypothesis was not supported in the Hawthorne studies.

The hypothesis in OB research typically illustrates a linkage between what is referred to as an independent variable (presumed to affect a dependent variable) and a dependent variable. The dependent variable is what the researcher is attempting to understand or explain. Rest pauses were independent variables that supposedly affected productivity, the dependent variable.

METHODS OF INQUIRY   *How do* behavioral scientists gain knowledge about the functioning of organizations? Just as physical scientists have certain tools and methods for obtaining information, so too do behavioral scientists. These are usually referred to as *research designs*. In broad terms, three basic designs are used by behavioral scientists: the case study, the field study, and the experiment.

Case study

A case study attempts to examine numerous characteristics of one or more people, usually over an extended time period. For years, anthropologists have studied the customs and behavior of various groups by actually living among them. Some organizational researchers have done the same thing. They have actually worked and socialized with the groups of employees that they were studying.[10] The reports on such investigations are usually in the form of a case study. For example, a sociologist might report the key factors and incidents that led to a strike by a group of blue-collar workers.

The chief limitations of the case study approach for gaining knowledge about the functioning of organizations are:

1. Rarely can two cases be meaningfully compared in essential characteristics. In other words, in another firm of another size, the same factors might not have resulted in a strike.

2. Rarely can case studies be repeated or their findings verified.

3. The significance of the findings is left to the subjective interpretation of the researcher. Like the practitioner, the researcher attempts to describe reality, but it is reality as perceived by one person (or a very small group). The researcher's training, biases, and preconceptions can inadvertently distort the report. A psychologist may give an entirely different view of a group of blue-collar workers than would be given by a sociologist.

4. Since the results of a case study are based on a sample of one, the ability to generalize from them may be limited.[11]

Despite these limitations, the case study is widely used as a method of studying organizations. It is extremely valuable in answering exploratory questions.

Field study

Attempting to add more reality and rigor to the study of organizations, behavioral scientists have developed several systematic field research techniques, such as personal interviews, observation, archival data, and questionnaire surveys. They use these methods, individually or in combination, to investigate current practices or events. With these methods, unlike some other methods, the researcher does not rely entirely on what the subjects say. She may personally interview other people in the organization—fellow workers, subordinates, and superiors—to gain a more balanced view before drawing conclusions.[12] In addition, archival data, records, charts, and statistics on file may be used to analyze a problem or hypothesis.

A popular field-study technique involves the use of expertly prepared questionnaires. Not only are such questionnaires less subject to unintentional distortion than personal interviews, but they also enable the researcher to greatly increase the number of individuals participating. Figure A–1 presents part of a questionnaire used in organizations to evaluate ratee perceptions of a performance-appraisal interview program. The questionnaire enables the collection of data on particular characteristics that are of interest (for example, equity, accuracy, and clarity). The seven-point scale measures ratee perceptions of the

degree to which the performance appraisal interviews possess a given characteristic.

In most cases, surveys are limited to a description of the current state of the situation. However, if researchers are aware of factors that may account for survey findings, they can make conjectural statements (known as hypotheses) about the relationship between two or more factors and relate the survey data to those factors. Thus, instead of just describing ratee perceptions of performance evaluation, the researchers could make finer distinctions (for example, distinctions regarding job tenure, salary level, or education) among groups of ratees. Comparisons and statistical tests could then be applied to determine differences, similarities, or relationships. Finally, *longitudinal* studies involving observations made over time are used to describe changes that have taken place. Thus, in the

Figure A–1

Scale for Assessing GANAT Appraisal Interviews

Part A: Appraisal Interview
The following items deal with the formal appraisal interview used in conjunction with the GANAT project program. Please circle the number that best describes your opinion of the most recent interview session.

	Very False						Very True
1. The appraisal interview covered my entire job.	1	2	3	4	5	6	7
2. The discussion of my performance during the appraisal interview was covered equitably.	1	2	3	4	5	6	7
3. The appraisal interview was accurately conducted.	1	2	3	4	5	6	7
4. I didn't have to ask for any clarification.	1	2	3	4	5	6	7
5. The interview was fair in every respect.	1	2	3	4	5	6	7
6. The interview really raised my anxiety level.	1	2	3	4	5	6	7
7. The interview's purpose was simply not clear to me.	1	2	3	4	5	6	7
8. The appraisal interview really made me think about working smarter on the job.	1	2	3	4	5	6	7
9. The appraisal interview was encouraging to me personally.	1	2	3	4	5	6	7
10. I dreaded the actual interview itself.	1	2	3	4	5	6	7
11. The boss was totally aboveboard in all phases of the interview.	1	2	3	4	5	6	7
12. The interview gave me some direction and purpose.	1	2	3	4	5	6	7
13. The interview really pinpointed areas for improvement.	1	2	3	4	5	6	7
14. The interview was disorganized and frustrating.	1	2	3	4	5	6	7
15. I disliked the interview because the intent was not clear.	1	2	3	4	5	6	7
16. The appraisal interviewer (boss) was not well trained.	1	2	3	4	5	6	7
17. The interview has been my guide for correcting weaknesses.	1	2	3	4	5	6	7
18. I understood the meaning of each performance area better after the interview.	1	2	3	4	5	6	7
19. The interview time was too rushed.	1	2	3	4	5	6	7
20. I received no advance notice about the interview.	1	2	3	4	5	6	7
21. During the interview, my performance was fairly analyzed.	1	2	3	4	5	6	7
22. I was often upset because the interview data were not accurate.	1	2	3	4	5	6	7
23. My record, as it was introduced in the interview, contained no errors.	1	2	3	4	5	6	7

Source: This interview appraisal form was developed by John M. Ivancevich and sponsored by research funds provided by the GANAT Company.

situation described here, we can become aware of changes in overall ratee perceptions of appraisal interviews over time as well as those relating to individual managers.[13]

Despite advantages over many of the other methods of gaining knowledge about organizations, field studies are not without problems. Here again, researchers have training, interests, and expectations that they bring with them.[14] Thus, a researcher may inadvertently ignore a vital technological factor while concentrating on only behavioral factors in a study of employee morale. Also, the fact that a researcher is present may influence how the individual responds. This weakness of field studies has long been recognized and is noted in some of the earliest field research in organizations.

Experiment

The experiment is potentially the most rigorous of scientific techniques. For an investigation to be considered an experiment, it must contain two elements: manipulation of some variable (independent variable) and observation or measurement of the results (dependent variable) while maintaining all other factors unchanged. Thus, in an organization, a behavioral scientist could change one organizational factor and observe the results while attempting to keep everything else unchanged in one of two general types of experiments.[15]

In a *laboratory experiment,* the researcher creates the environment. For example, a management researcher may work with a small voluntary group in a classroom. The group may be students or managers. If a student sample is used, it is important to determine (1) if the population of interest is similar to the student sample and (2) if research results can be generalized from a student sample to organizational employees.[16] Samples in a laboratory experiment may be asked to communicate, perform tasks, or make decisions under different sets of conditions designated by the researcher. The laboratory setting permits the researcher to closely control the conditions under which observations are made. The intention is to isolate the relevant variables and to measure the response of dependent variables when the independent variable is manipulated. Laboratory experiments are useful when the conditions required to test a hypothesis are not practically or readily obtainable in natural situations and when the situation to be studied can be replicated under laboratory conditions. For such situations, many schools of business have behavioral science laboratories where such experimentation is done.

In a *field experiment,* the investigator attempts to manipulate and control variables in the natural setting rather than in a laboratory. Early experiments in organizations included manipulating physical working conditions such as rest periods, refreshments, and lighting. Today, behavioral scientists attempt to manipulate a host of additional factors.[17] For example, a training program might be introduced for one group of managers but not for another. Comparisons of performance, attitudes, and so on could be obtained later, either at one point or at several different points (a longitudinal study), to determine what effect (if any) the training program had on the managers' performances and attitudes.

The experimental design is especially appealing to many researchers because it is the prototype of the scientific approach. It is the ideal toward which every science strives. However, while its potential is still great, it has not yet produced a great breadth of knowledge about the functioning of organizations. Laboratory experiments suffer the risk of artificiality: the results of such experiments often do not extend to real organizations. Teams of business administration or psychology students working on decision problems may provide a great deal of information for researchers. Unfortunately, extreme caution must be used in determining whether this knowledge can be extended to a group of managers or nonmanagers making decisions under severe time constraints.[18]

Field experiments also have drawbacks. First, researchers cannot control every possible influencing factor (even if they knew them all), as they can in a laboratory. Also, here again, the presence of a researcher may make people behave differently, especially if they are aware that they are participating in an experiment. Experimentation in the behavioral sciences and, more specifically, in organizations is a complex matter.[19]

In a *true experiment,* the researcher has complete control over the experiment: the who, what, when, where, and how. A *quasi experiment,* however, is one in which the researcher lacks the degree of control over conditions that is possible in a true experiment. In the vast majority of organizational studies, complete control is impossible. Thus, quasi experiments are typically the rule when organizational behavior is studied via an experiment.

Finally, with each method of inquiry utilized by behavioral scientists, some *measurement* is usually necessary. Knowledge, to be meaningful, must often be compared with or related to something else. As a result, research questions (hypotheses) are usually stated to show how differences in magnitude of some variable are related to differences in the magnitude of some other variable.

The variables studied are measured by research instruments. Those instruments may be psychological tests, such as personality or intelligence tests; questionnaires designed to obtain attitudes or other information, such as the questionnaire shown in Figure A–1; or, in some cases, electronic devices to measure eye movement or blood pressure.

That a research instrument be both *reliable* and *valid* is very important. Reliability is the consistency of the measure. In other words, repeated measures with the same instrument should produce the same results or scores. Validity is concerned with whether the research instrument actually measures what it is supposed to be measuring.[20] A research instrument may be reliable but not valid. For example, a test designed to measure intelligence could yield consistent scores over a large number of people but not be measuring intelligence.

Research designs

Experiments to study organizational behavior utilize a number of designs. To illustrate some of the available designs, we use the example of a training program being offered to a group of first-line supervisors. Suppose that the task of the researcher is to design an experiment that permits the assessment of the degree to which the program influenced the performance of the supervisors. We use the following symbols in our discussion:[21]

S = The subjects (that is, the managers or workers participating in the experiment).

O = The observation and measurement devices used by the researcher (that is, ratings of supervisors' performance by superiors).

X = The experimental treatment, the manipulated variable (that is, the training program).

R = The randomization process.

ONE-SHOT DESIGN

If we assume that all supervisors go through the training program, the researchers will have difficulty evaluating it. This is because the researchers cannot compare the group with another group that did not undergo the training program. This design, called a *one-shot design,* is diagrammed as

$$X O$$

The letter X stands for the experimental treatment (that is, the training program), the letter O for the observation of performance on the job. The measure of performance could be in the form of an average score based on ratings of superiors. However, the researchers can in no way determine whether performance was influenced at all by the training program. This experimental design is rarely used because of its weaknesses.

ONE-GROUP PRETEST–POSTTEST DESIGN

The previous design can be improved on by first gathering performance data on the supervisors, instituting the training program, and then remeasuring their performance. This is diagrammed as

$$O_1 X O_2$$

Thus, a pretest is given in time period 1, the program is administered, and a posttest is administered in time period 2. If $O_2 > O_1$, the differences can be attributed to the training program. Numerous factors can confound the results obtained with this design. For example, if new equipment has been installed between $O_2 > O_1$, this could explain the differences in the performance scores. Thus, a *history* factor may have influenced the results. The most recurrent factors that could also influence results are listed along with their definitions in Table A–3.[22] Examination of the table indicates that results achieved in this design may be confounded by *maturation* (the supervisors may learn to do a better job between $O_2 > O_1$, which would increase their performance regardless of training), *testing* (the measure of performance in O_1 may make the supervisors aware that they are being evaluated, which may make them work harder and increase their performance), and *instrumentation* (if the performance observations are made at different times of the day, the results could be influenced by fatigue). Each of these factors offers explanations for changes in performance other than the training program. Obviously, this design can be improved.

STATIC-GROUP COMPARISON DESIGN

In this design, half of the supervisors would be allowed to enroll for the training. Once the enrollment reached 50 percent of the supervisors, the training program would begin. After some period of time, the group of supervisors who enrolled in the program would be compared with those who did not enroll. This design is diagrammed as

$$X O$$
$$O$$

The addition of a *control* group (comparison group) has eliminated many of the error factors associated with the first two designs. However, since the supervisors were not randomly assigned to each group, the supervisors who enrolled may very possibly be the more highly motivated or more intelligent supervisors. Thus, *selection* is a major problem with this design. Because the subjects were not randomly assigned to the experimental group (undergoing training) and the control group (no training), differences may exist between the two groups that are not related to the training.

The three designs discussed thus far (one-shot, one-group pretest–posttest, static-group comparisons) have been described as "pseudo-experimental" or "quasi-experimental" designs. When true experimentation cannot be achieved, these designs (especially the last two) are preferred over no research at all or over relying on personal opinion. The next three designs can be considered true experimental designs because the researcher has complete control over the situation, determining precisely who will participate in the experiment and which subjects will or will not receive the experimental treatment.

PRETEST–POSTTEST CONTROL GROUP DESIGN

This design, one of the simplest forms of true experimentation used in the study of human behavior, is diagrammed as

$$R O_1 X O_2$$
$$R O_1 \quad O_2$$

It is similar to the one-group pretest–posttest design except that a control group has been added and the participants have been randomly assigned to both groups, as indicated by R. Which group is to receive the training (experimental group) and which will not (control group) is also randomly determined. The two groups may be said to be equivalent at the time of the initial observations and at the time the final observations are made; they are different only in that one group has received training while the other has not. In other words, if the change from O_1 to O_2 is greater in the experimental group than in the control group, we can attribute the difference to the training program rather than selection, testing, maturation, and so forth.

The major weakness of the pretest–posttest control group design is one of *interaction* (selection and treatment), where individuals are aware that they are participating in an experiment. In other words, being observed the first time makes all of the participants work more diligently, both those who are in the training group and those who are in the control group. Hence,

Table A–3	FACTOR	DEFINITION
Recurring Sources of Error in Experimental Studies	1. History	Events other than the experimental treatment (X) that occurred between pretest and posttest.
	2. Maturation	Changes in the subject group with the passage of time that are not associated with the experimental treatment (X).
	3. Testing	Changes in the performance of the subjects because measurement of their performance makes them aware that they are part of an experiment (that is, measures often alter what is being measured).
	4. Instrumentation	Changes in the measures of participants' performance that are the result of changes in the measurement instruments or the conditions under which the measuring is done (for example, wear on machinery, boredom, fatigue on the part of the observers).
	5. Selection	When participants are assigned to experimental and control groups on any basis other than random assignment. Any selection method other than random assignment will result in systematic biases that will result in differences between groups that are unrelated to the effects of the experimental treatment (X).
	6. Mortality	If some participants drop out of the experiment before it is completed, the experimental and control groups may not be comparable.
	7. Interaction effects	Any of the above factors may interact with the experimental treatment, resulting in confounding effects on the results. For example, the types of individuals withdrawing from a study (mortality) may differ for the experimental group and the control group.

the participants in the training program are more receptive to training because of the pretest. This problem of interaction can be overcome by using a posttest-only control group design.

POSTTEST-ONLY CONTROL GROUP DESIGN In this design, the participants are randomly assigned to two groups, the training is administered to one group, and the scores on the posttests are compared (performance evaluated). It is diagrammed as

$$R\ X\ O$$
$$R\ \ \ O$$

This eliminates the problem of the previous design by not administering a pretest. However, the dependent variable (performance) is an ultimate rather than a relative measure of achievement. Also, the researcher does not have a group that was pretested and posttested without receiving the experimental treatment (training program). Such a group can provide valuable information on the effects of history, maturation, instrumentation, and so on. However, where a pretest is difficult to obtain or where its use is likely to make the participants aware that an experiment is being carried on, this approach may be much preferred to the pretest–posttest control group design.

SOLOMON FOUR-GROUP DESIGN This design, which combines the previous two designs, is the most desirable of all the designs examined here. It is diagrammed as

$$\text{Group 1}\quad R\ O_1\ X\ O_2$$
$$\text{Group 2}\quad R\ O_1\ \ \ O_2$$
$$\text{Group 3}\quad R\ X\ \ \ O_2$$
$$\text{Group 4}\quad R\ \ \ \ \ O_2$$

Where gain or change in behavior is the desired dependent variable, this design should be used. While it does not control any more sources of invalid results, it permits the estimation

of the extent of the effects of some sources of error. In our example, supervisors are randomly assigned to four groups, two of which will receive the training, one with a pretest and one without. Therefore, the researcher can examine, among other things, the effects of history (group 1 to group 2), testing (group 2 to group 4), and testing–treatment interaction (group 2 to group 3). Clearly, this design is the most complex, because it utilizes more participants, and is more costly. The added value of the extra information will have to be compared to the additional costs.[23]

Qualitative research

Instead of using experimental designs and concentrating on measurement issues, some researchers also use qualitative research procedures. The notion of applying qualitative research methods to studying behavior within organizations has been addressed in leading research outlets.[24] The term *qualitative methods* describes an array of interpretative techniques that attempt to describe and clarify the meaning of naturally occurring phenomena. It is, by design, rather open-ended and interpretative. The researcher's interpretation and description are the significant data collection acts in a qualitative study. In essence, qualitative data are defined as those (1) whose meanings are subjective, (2) that are rarely quantifiable, and (3) that are difficult to use in making quantitative comparisons.

The quantitative approach to organizational behavior research is exemplified by precise definitions, control groups, objective data collection, use of the scientific method, and replicable findings. These characteristics, presented in Table A–2, stress the importance of reliability, validity, and accurate measurement. On the other hand, qualitative research is more concerned with the meaning of what is observed. Since organizations are so complex, a range of quantitative and qualitative techniques can be used side by side to learn about individual, group, and organizational behavior.[25]

Qualitative methodology uses the experience and intuition of the researcher to describe the organizational processes and structures being studied. The data collected by a qualitative researcher require her to become very close to the situation or problem being studied. For example, a qualitative method used by anthropologists is the *ethnographic method:*[26] the researcher typically studies a phenomenon for long periods of time as a *participant-observer,* becoming part of the situation in order to feel what it is like for the people in that situation. The researcher becomes totally immersed in other people's realities.[27]

Participant observation is usually supplemented by various quantitative data collection tools such as structured interviews and self-report questionnaires. A variety of techniques are used so that the researcher can cross-check the results obtained from observation and recorded in field notes.

In training researchers in the ethnographic method, a common practice is to place them in unfamiliar settings. A researcher may sit with and listen to workers on a production line, ride around in a police car to observe police officers, or do cleanup work in a surgical operating room. The training is designed to improve the researcher's ability to record, categorize, and code what is being observed.

An example of qualitative research involvement is presented in John Van Maanen's participant-observer study of a big-city police department. He went through police academy training and then accompanied police officers on their daily rounds; he functioned with police officers in daily encounters. Thus, he was able to provide vivid descriptions of police work.[28]

Other qualitative techniques include content analysis (e.g., the researcher's interpretation of field notes), informal interviewing, archival data surveys and historical analysis, and the use of unobtrusive measures (e.g., data whose collection is not influenced by a researcher's presence). An example of the last would be the wear and tear on a couch in a cardiologist's office. The original measure of the Type A behavior pattern in Chapter 8 was the wear and tear on the edges of the couch where patients sat while waiting for an appointment with the physician. Wear and tear was assumed to suggest anxiety and hyperactive behavior. Qualitative research appears to rely more on multiple sources of data than on any one source. The current research literature suggests the following characteristics associated with qualitative research.[29]

1. *Analytical induction.* Qualitative research begins with the close-up, firsthand inspection of organizational life.

2. *Proximity.* Researchers desire to witness firsthand what is being studied. If the application of rewards is being studied, the researcher would want to observe episodes of reward distribution.

3. *Ordinary behavior.* The topics of research interest should be ordinary, normal, routine behaviors.

4. *Descriptive emphasis.* Qualitative research seeks descriptions for what is occurring in any given place and time. The aim is to disclose and reveal, not merely to order data and to predict.

5. *Shrinking variance.* Qualitative research is geared toward the explanation of similarity and coherence. There is a greater emphasis on commonality and on things shared in organizational settings than on things not shared.

6. *Consumer enlightenment.* The consumer of qualitative research could be a manager. A major objective is to enlighten without causing confusion. Providing coherent and logically persuasive commentary accomplishes this.

Researchers and managers do not have to choose either quantitative or qualitative research data and interpretation. Convincing and relevant arguments exist for using more than one method of research when studying organizational behavior. Quantitative and qualitative research methods and procedures have much to offer practicing managers. Blending and integrating quantitative and qualitative research are what researchers and managers must do in the years ahead to better understand, cope with, and modify organizational behavior.

ABC analysis The analysis of antecedents, behavior, and consequences when investigating work- or job-related issues.

Ability A trait, biological or learned, that permits a person to do something mental or physical.

Affect The emotional segment of an attitude.

Attitudes Mental states of readiness for need arousal.

Attribution The process of perceiving the causes of behavior and outcomes.

Attribution leadership theory A theory of the relationship between individual perception and interpersonal behavior. The theory suggests that understanding of and the ability to predict how people will react to events are enhanced by knowing their causal explanation for those events.

Authority Formal power a person holds because of her position in the organization hierarchy. The recognition of authority is necessary for organizational effectiveness and is a cost of organizational membership.

Banking time off A reward practice of allowing employees to build up time-off credits for such things as good performance or attendance. Employees then receive the time off in addition to regular vacation time granted by the organization.

Behavior Anything that a person does, such as talking, walking, thinking, or daydreaming. The action that results from an attitude.

Behavior modification An approach to motivation that uses the principles of operant conditioning, achieving individual learning by reinforcement. This term can be used interchangeably with the term *organizational behavior modification*.

Behavioral self-management (BSM) A process whereby a person is faced with

immediate response alternatives involving different consequences. The person selects or modifies his behavior by managing cognitive processes, causes, or consequences.

Benchmarking A standard of excellence or achievement against which a firm's products or practices are measured or judged.

Boundary-spanning role The role of an individual who must relate to two different systems, usually an organization and some part of its environment.

Brainstorming The generation of ideas in a group through noncritical discussion.

Cafeteria-style fringe benefits The employee is allowed to develop and allocate a personally attractive fringe benefit package. The employee is informed of what the total fringe benefits allowed will be and then distributes the benefits according to her preferences.

Centralization A dimension of organizational structure that refers to the extent to which top management retains authority to make decisions.

Change agents A person or group who enters an ongoing organization or part of the organization for the purpose of facilitating the process of change.

Charismatic leadership The ability to influence followers based on a supernatural gift and powers that are attractive. Followers enjoy being with the charismatic leader because they feel inspired, correct, and important.

Cognition This is basically what individuals know about themselves and their environment. Cognition implies a conscious process of acquiring knowledge. The perception, opinion, or belief segment of an argument.

Cognitive dissonance A mental state of anxiety that occurs when there is a con-

flict among an individual's various cognitions (for example, attitudes and beliefs) after a decision has been made.

Cohesiveness The strength of group members' desires to remain in the group, and their commitment to the group.

Command group The group of subordinates who report to one particular manager. The command group is specified by the formal organization chart.

Commitment A sense of identification, involvement, and loyalty expressed by an employee toward the company.

Communication The transmission of information and understanding through the use of common symbols, verbal and/or nonverbal.

Complexity A dimension of organizational structure that refers to the number of different jobs, units, and authority levels within an organization.

Confucian dynamism The extent to which people believe in the importance of the values of persistence, status, thrift, and feeling shame and the unimportance of the values of personal stability, face saving, respect for tradition, and reciprocation of favors and gifts.

Conscious goals The main goals that a person is striving for and is aware of when directing behavior.

Consideration Acts of the leader that show supportive concern for the followers in a group.

Content motivation theories Theories that focus on the factors within a person that energize, direct, sustain, and stop behavior.

Contingency approach to management This approach to management states that there is no one best way to manage in every situation but that managers must find different ways that fit different situations.

Contingency design theory An approach to organization design that states that the effective structure depends on factors in the situation, including technology, environmental uncertainty, and strategic choice.

Cross-cultural management The study of the behavior of individuals in organizations around the world.

Culture shock cycle A three-phase cycle (fascination and interest, frustration and confusion, and adaptation) which most individuals experience when sent to another culture.

Decision A means to achieve some result or to solve some problem. The outcome of a process that is influenced by many forces.

Decision commitment The degree to which subordinates accept a particular decision. Participation in decisions often tends to increase the commitment of subordinates.

Decision quality An important criterion in the Vroom-Yetton model that refers to the objective aspects of a decision that influence subordinates' performance, aside from any direct impact on motivation.

Delegation of authority The process by which authority is distributed downward in an organization.

Delphi process A technique used to improve group decision making that involves the solicitation and comparison of anonymous judgments on the topic of interest through a set of sequential questionnaires interspersed with summarized information and feedback of opinions from earlier responses.

Departmentalization The process in which an organization is structurally divided. Some of the more publicized divisions are by function, territory, product, customer, and project.

Diagonal communication Communication that cuts across functions and levels in an organization; important when members cannot communicate through other channels.

Differentiation An important concept in the Lawrence and Lorsch research that refers to the process by which subunits in an organization develop particular attributes in response to the requirements imposed by their particular subenvironments. The greater the differences among the subunits' attributes, the greater is the differentiation.

Dispositional attributions Emphasize some aspect of the individual, such as ability or skill, to explain behavior.

Diversity Used to describe human qualities such as race, gender, and ethnicity that are different from our own and outside the groups to which we belong.

Division of labor The process of dividing work into relatively specialized jobs to achieve advantages of specialization.

Downward communication Communication that flows from individuals in higher levels of the organization's hierarchy to those in lower levels.

Dysfunctional conflict Any confrontation or interaction between groups that hinders the achievement of organizational goals.

Employee-centered leader A person who only generally supervises the work of others, permitting them a sense of autonomy.

Equity theory of motivation A theory that examines discrepancies within a person after the person has compared her input/output ratio to that of a reference person.

ERG theory of motivation A theory developed and tested by Alderfer that categorizes needs as existence, relatedness, and growth.

Expatriate manager A manager from the firm's home nation who's on a foreign assignment.

Expectancy The perceived likelihood that a particular act will be followed by a particular outcome.

Expectancy theory of motivation A theory in which the employee is faced with a set of first-level outcomes and selects an outcome based on how this choice is related to second-level outcomes. The preferences of the individual are based on the strength (valence) of desire to achieve a second-level state and the perception of the relationship between first- and second-level outcomes.

Extinction In a learning situation, the decline in the response rate because of non-reinforcement.

Extrinsic rewards Rewards external to the job, such as pay, promotion, or fringe benefits.

Flexible manufacturing technology (FMT) Modern manufacturing methods that combine computer and robot to achieve high levels of production as well as high levels of flexibility.

Formal group A group formed by management to accomplish the goals of the organization.

Formal organization The philosophy, policies, structure, and systems of control of an organization.

Formalization A dimension of organization structure that refers to the extent to which rules, procedures, and other guides to action are written and enforced.

Functional conflict A confrontation between groups that enhances and benefits the organization's performance.

Functional job analysis (FJA) A method of job analysis that focuses on the worker's specific job activities, methods, machines, and output. Widely used to analyze and classify jobs.

Gainsharing An innovative reward strategy wherein employees share in the financial rewards of achieving set objectives.

Global corporation An enterprise structured so that national boundaries become blurred.

Globalization The interdependency of transportation, distribution, communication, and economic networks across international borders.

Goal A specific target that an individual is trying to achieve; a goal is the target (object) of an action.

Goal approach to effectiveness A perspective on effectiveness that emphasizes the central role of goal achievement as the criterion for assessing effectiveness.

Goal commitment The amount of effort that is actually used to achieve a goal.

Goal difficulty The degree of proficiency or the level of goal performance that is sought.

Goal setting The process of establishing goals. In many cases, goal setting involves a superior and subordinate working together to set the subordinate's goals for a specified period of time.

Goal specificity The degree of quantitative precision (clarity) of the goal.

Group Two or more employees who interact with one another in such a manner that the behavior and/or performance of one member is influenced by the behavior and/or performance of other members.

Groupthink The deterioration of the mental efficiency, reality testing, and moral judgment of the individual members of a group in the interest of group solidarity.

Herzberg's two-factor theory of motivation The view that job satisfaction results from the presence of intrinsic motivators and that job dissatisfaction stems from not having extrinsic factors.

Horizontal communication Communication that flows across functions in an organization; necessary for coordinating and integrating diverse organizational functions.

Host country nationals Workers from the local population.

Humanistic personality theories Theories that place emphasis on the growth and self-actualization of people.

Individual differences Individuals are similar, but they are also unique. The study of individual differences such as attitudes, perceptions, and abilities helps a manager explain differences in performance levels.

Individualism–collectivism Individualism emphasizes pursuit of individual goals, needs, and success. Collectivism emphasizes group need, satisfaction, and performance.

Informal group A group formed by individuals and developed around common interests and friendships rather than around a deliberate design.

Initiating structure Leadership acts that imply the structuring of job tasks and responsibilities for followers.

Instrumentality In the expectancy theory of motivation, the relationship between first- and second-level outcomes.

Integration A concept in the Lawrence and Lorsch research that refers to the process of achieving unity of effort among the organization's various subsystems. The techniques for achieving integration range from rules and procedures to plans, to mutual adjustment.

Interpersonal communication Communication that flows from individual to individual in face-to-face and group settings.

Interpersonal rewards Extrinsic rewards such as receiving recognition or being able to interact socially on the job.

Interpersonal style The way in which an individual prefers to relate to others.

Intervention A specific action or program undertaken to focus the change process on particular targets.

Intrinsic rewards Rewards that are part of the job itself. The responsibility, challenge, and feedback characteristics of the job are intrinsic rewards.

Job analysis The process of defining and studying a job in terms of behavior and specifying education and training needed to perform the job.

Job-centered leader A person who closely supervises and observes the work of others.

Job content The specific activities required in a job.

Job context The physical environment and other working conditions, along with other factors considered to be extrinsic to a job.

Job depth The amount of control that an individual has to alter or influence the job and the surrounding environment.

Job description A summary statement of what an employee actually does on the job.

Job descriptive index A popular and widely used 72-item scale that measures five job satisfaction dimensions.

Job design The process by which managers decide individual job tasks and authority.

Job enlargement An administrative action that involves increasing the range of a job by increasing the number of tasks. Supposedly, this action results in better performance and a more satisfied workforce.

Job enrichment An approach, developed by Herzberg, that involves increasing the individual's discretion to select activities and outcomes. It seeks to improve task efficiency and human satisfaction by means of building into people's jobs greater scope for personal achievement and recognition, more challenging and responsible work, and more opportunity for individual advancement and growth.

Job range The number of operations that a job occupant performs to complete a task.

Job redesign Redesigning the jobs of individuals, usually along the lines suggested by the job characteristics model of job design, in order to improve performance. May be used as an intervention in organizational development.

Job relationships The interpersonal relationships required or made possible on a job.

Job requirements Factors such as education, experience, degrees, licenses, and other personal characteristics required to perform a job.

Job rotation A form of training that involves moving an employee from one workstation to another. In addition to achieving the training objectives, this procedure is also designed to reduce boredom.

Job satisfaction The attitude that workers have about their jobs. It results from their perception of the jobs.

Leader–member relations A factor in the Fiedler contingency model that refers to the degree of confidence, trust, and respect that the leader obtains from followers.

Leadership An attempt to use noncoercive types of influence to motivate individuals to accomplish some goal.

Leadership climate The nature of the work environment in an organization that results from the leadership style and administrative practices of managers.

Learned needs theory A theory that proposes that a person with a strong need will be motivated to use appropriate behaviors to satisfy the need. A person's needs are learned from the culture of a society.

Learning The process by which a relatively enduring change in behavior occurs as a result of practice.

Locus of control A personality characteristic that describes people who see the control of their lives as coming from inside themselves as *internalizers*. People who believe that their lives are controlled by external factors are *externalizers*.

Masculinity–femininity High masculinity in a culture designates assertiveness, dominance, and independence. High femininity in a culture designates interdependence, compassion, and emotional opinions.

Matrix organization An organizational design that superimposes a product- or project-based design on an existing function-based design.

Mechanistic model of organizational design The type of organizational design that emphasizes the importance of production and efficiency. It is highly formalized, centralized, and complex.

Mentor A relationship that exists when an older employee helps a younger person learn the job, the systems procedures, and the rituals of the organization.

Merit rating A formal rating system that is applied to hourly paid employees.

Minnesota Multiphasic Personality Inventory (MMPI) A widely used inventory for assessing personality.

Motivation A concept that describes the forces acting on or within an employee that initiate and direct behavior.

Multinational corporations (MNCs) Firms that do business in more than one country.

Multiple roles Roles individuals play simultaneously because they occupy many different positions in a variety of institutions and organizations.

Myers-Briggs type indicator (MBTI) A scale that assesses personality or cognitive style. The respondent's answers are scored and interpreted to classify her as extroverted or introverted, sensory or intuitive, thinking or feeling, and perceiving or judging. Sixteen different personality types are possible.

National culture A set of values, attitudes, beliefs, and norms shared by a majority of the inhabitants of a country.

Need for power (n pow) A person's desire to have an impact on others. The impact can occur from such behaviors as strong action, producing emotion, or concern for reputation.

Need hierarchy model Maslow assumed that the needs of a person depend on what he already has. This in a sense means that a satisfied need is not a motivator. Human needs organized in a hierarchy of importance are classified as physiological, safety, belongingness, esteem, and self-actualization.

Needs Deficiencies that an individual experiences at a particular point in time.

Negative reinforcement Reinforcement that strengthens a response because the response removes some painful or unpleasant stimulus or enables the organism to avoid it.

Nominal group technique (NGT) A technique to improve group decision making that brings people together in a very structured meeting that does not allow for much verbal communication. The group decision is the mathematically pooled outcome of individual votes.

Nonprogrammed decisions Decisions required for unique and complex management problems.

Nonverbal communication Messages sent with body posture, facial expressions, and head and eye movements.

Norms Generally agreed-upon standards of individual and group behavior that have developed as a result of member interaction over time.

Operant conditioning Learning that occurs as a consequence of behavior.

Operants Behaviors amenable to control by altering the consequences (rewards and punishments) that follow them.

Organic model of organization The organizational design that emphasizes the importance of adaptability and development. It is relatively informal, decentralized, and simple.

Organizational behavior The study of human behavior, attitudes, and performance within an organizational setting; drawing on theory, methods, and principles from such disciplines as psychology, sociology, and cultural anthropology to learn about *individual* perceptions, values, learning capacities, and actions while working in *groups* and within the total *organization;* analyzing the external environment's effect on the organization and its human resources, missions, objectives, and strategies.

Organizational behavior modification (OBM) An operant approach to organization behavior. This term is used interchangeably with the term *behavior modification.*

Organizational culture The pervasive system of values, beliefs, and norms that exists in any organization. The organizational culture can encourage or discourage effectiveness, depending on the nature of the values, beliefs, and norms.

Organizational design A specific organizational structure that results from managers' decisions and actions. Also, the process by which managers choose among alternative frameworks of jobs and departments.

Organizational development (OD) The process of preparing for and managing change in organizational settings.

Organizations Institutions that enable society to pursue goals that could not be achieved by individuals acting alone.

Organization structure The formal pattern of how people and jobs are grouped in an organization. The organization structure is often illustrated by an organization chart.

Parent country nationals Individuals sent from the country in which the firm is headquartered. Often called *expatriates*.

Path–goal leadership model A theory that suggests that a leader needs to influence the followers' perceptions of work goals, self-development goals, and paths to goal attainment. The foundation for the model is the expectancy motivation theory.

Perceived job content The characteristics of a job that define its general nature as perceived by the person who does the job.

Perception The process by which an individual gives meaning to the environment. It involves organizing and interpreting various stimuli into a psychological experience.

Personality A stable set of characteristics and tendencies that determine commonalities and differences in the behavior of people.

Personality test A test used to measure the emotional, motivational, interpersonal, and attitude characteristics that make up a person's personality.

Person–role conflict A type of conflict that occurs when the requirements of a position violate the basic values, attitudes, and needs of the individual occupying the position.

Political behavior Behavior outside the normal power system designed to benefit an individual or a subunit.

Pooled interdependence Interdependence that requires no interaction between groups because each group, in effect, performs separately.

Position analysis questionnaire (PAQ) A method of job analysis that takes into account human characteristics as well as task and technological factors of job and job classes.

Position power A factor in the Fiedler contingency model that refers to the power inherent in the leadership position.

Positive reinforcement Action that increases the likelihood of a particular behavior.

Power distance The degree to which members of a society accept differences in power and status among themselves.

Process motivation theories Theories that describe and analyze how behavior is energized, directed, sustained, and stopped.

Processes Those activities that breathe life into the organization structure. Common processes are communication, performance evaluation, decision making, socialization, and career development.

Programmed decisions Situations in which specific procedures have been developed for repetitive and routine problems.

Psychodynamic personality theories Freudian approach that discusses the id, superego, and ego. Special emphasis is placed on unconscious determinants of behavior.

Punishment An uncomfortable consequence for a particular behavior response or the removal of a desirable reinforcer because of a particular behavior response. Managers can punish by application or by removal.

Pygmalion effect The enhanced learning or performance that results from others having positive expectations of us.

Quality of work life (QWL) Management philosophy that enhances employee dignity, introduces cultural change, and provides opportunities for growth and development.

Readiness The follower's skills and willingness to do a job.

Reciprocal causation The argument that follower behavior causes leader behavior and that leader behavior causes follower behavior.

Reciprocal interdependence Interdependence that requires the output of each group in an organization to serve as input to other groups in the organization.

Recognition Management acknowledgment of work well done.

Referent power Power based on charisma due to personality or style of behavior.

Role An organized set of behaviors expected of an individual in a specific position.

Role conflict Stressor that arises when a person receives incompatible messages regarding appropriate role behavior.

Role set Individuals' expectations for the behavior of a person in a particular role. The more expectations, the more complex is the role set.

Self-efficacy The belief that one can perform adequately in a situation. Self-efficacy has three dimensions: magnitude, strength, and generality.

Sequential interdependence Interdependence that requires one group to complete its task before another group can complete its task.

Situational attributions Attributions that emphasize the environment's effect on behavior.

Situational theories of leadership An approach to leadership that advocates that leaders understand their own behavior, the behavior of their subordinates, and the situation before utilizing a particular leadership style. This approach requires the leader to have diagnostic skills in human behavior.

Skill-based pay Wages paid at a rate calculated and based on the skills employees possess and display in performing their jobs.

Skills Task-related competencies.

Social learning The extension of Skinner's work initiated by noted psychologist Albert Bandura. Bandura views behavior as a function of a continuous interaction between cognitive (person), behavioral, and environmental determinants. Contrary to Skinner, Bandura believes that cognitive functioning must not be ignored in explaining and modifying behavior.

Socialization Refers to the processes by which members learn the cultural values, norms, beliefs, and required behavior that permit them to be effective contributors to the organization.

Span of control The number of subordinates reporting to a specific superior. The span is a factor that affects the shape and height of an organizational structure.

Stereotype A set of beliefs that one has about a group of other individuals.

Strategic contingency An event or activity that is extremely important for accomplishing organizational goals. Among the strategic contingencies of subunits are the ability to cope with uncertainty, centrality, and substitutability.

Structure The established patterns of interacting in an organization and of coordinating the technology and human assets of the organization.

Substitutability Extent to which other subunits can perform the job or task of a subunit.

Superordinate goals Goals that cannot be achieved without the cooperation of the conflicting groups.

Systems A grouping of elements that individually establish relationships with each other and that interact with their environment both as individuals and as a collective.

Task structure A factor in the Fiedler contingency model that refers to how structured a job is with regard to requirements, problem-solving alternatives, and feedback on how correctly the job has been accomplished.

Team building Encouraging people who work together to meet as a group to identify common goals, improve communications, and resolve conflicts. A traditional intervention focusing on work groups; has been given renewed interest as organizations rediscover the power of team effort.

Technology An important concept that can have many definitions in specific instances but that generally refers to actions, physical and mental, that an individual performs upon some object, person, or problem to change it in some way.

Thematic apperception test (TAT) A projective test that uses a person's analysis of pictures to evaluate such individual differences as need for achievement, need for power, and need for affiliation.

Third country nationals Employees from a country other than where the parent company is headquartered.

Trait personality theories Theories based on the premise that predispositions direct the behavior of an individual in a consistent pattern.

Trait theory of leadership Theory that attempts to identify specific characteristics (physical, mental, personality) associated with leadership success. Relies on research that relates various traits to certain success criteria.

Transactional leadership A leader who identifies what followers want or prefer and helps them achieve the level of performance that results in rewards that satisfy them.

Transformational leadership The ability to inspire and motivate followers to achieve results that are greater than originally planned and are for internal rewards.

Type A managers Managers who are aloof and cold toward others and are often autocratic leaders. Consequently, they are ineffective interpersonal communicators.

Type B managers Managers who seek good relationships with subordinates but are unable to express their feelings. Consequently, they are usually ineffective interpersonal communicators.

Type C managers Managers more interested in their own opinions than in those of others. Consequently, they are usually ineffective interpersonal communicators.

Type D managers Managers who feel free to express their feelings to others and to have others express their feelings; the most effective interpersonal communicators.

Uncertainty avoidance The degree to which people are comfortable with ambiguous situations and with the inability to predict future events with accuracy.

Upward communication Upward communication flows from individuals at lower levels of the organization structure to those at higher levels. Among the most common upward communication flows are suggestion boxes, group meetings, and appeal or grievance procedures.

Valence The strength of a person's preference for a particular outcome.

Values The guidelines and beliefs that a person uses when confronted with a situation in which a choice must be made.

Vroom-Yetton leadership model A leadership model that specifies which leadership decision-making procedures are most effective in each of several different situations. Two of the proposed leadership styles are autocratic (AI and AII); two are consultative (CI and CII); and one is oriented toward joint decisions (decisions made by the leader and the group, GII).

Whistle-blowing The process in which an employee, because of personal opinions, values, or ethical standards, concludes that an organization needs to change its behavior or practices and informs an outsider, bypassing the organization's authority system.

Work module An important characteristic of job redesign strategies that involves creating whole tasks so that the individual senses the completion of an entire job.

CHAPTER 1

1. Harry S. Dent Jr. *The Roaring 2000s* (New York: Simon & Schuster, 1998).

2. Sumantra Ghoshad and Christopher A. Bartlett, *The Individualized Corporation* (New York: Harper Business, 1997), pp. 7–8.

3. Michael A. Hitt, "Presidential Address: Twenty-First-Century Organizations: Business Firms, Business Schools, and The Academy," *Academy of Management Review,* April 1998, pp. 218–224.

4. Edward E. Lawler III, Alan M. Mohman Jr., Susan A. Mohrman, Gerald E. Ledford Jr., Thomas G. Cummings, and Associates, *Doing Research That Is Useful for Theory and Practice* (San Francisco: Jossey-Bass, 1985).

5. The authors have adapted and utilized this model for classroom and training use in domestic and international settings.

6. Taylor Cox Jr. and Ruby L. Beale, *Developing Competency to Manage Diversity* (San Francisco: Berrett-Koehler, 1997).

7. Durward K. Sobek III, Jeffrey K. Liker, and Allen C. Ward, "Another Look at How Toyota Integrates Product Development," *Harvard Business Review,* July–August, 1998, pp. 36–49.

8. Anne Faircloth, "The Best Retailer You've Never Heard Of," *Fortune,* March 16, 1998, pp. 110–12.

9. A. R. Elangovan and Debra L. Shapiro, "Betrayal of Trust in Organizations," *Academy of Management Review,* July 1998, pp. 547–566.

10. Verne E. Henderson, *What's Ethical in Business?* (New York: McGraw-Hill, 1991), pp. 37–90.

11. Carl Anderson, "Values-based Management," *Academy of Management Executives,* November 1997, pp. 25–46.

12. Joseph W. Weiss, *Business Ethics* (Belmont, CA: Wadsworth, 1994), p. 53.

13. Edwin C. Nevis, Anthony J. Dibella, and Janet M. Gould, "Understanding Organizations as Learning Systems," *Sloan Management Review,* Winter 1995, pp. 73–85.

14. Arie Y. Lewin and John W. Minton, "Determining Organizational Effectiveness: Another Look and an Agenda for Research," *Management Science,* May 1986, p. 514.

15. John R. Kimberly and David B. Rottman, "Environment, Organization, and Effectiveness: A Biographical Approach," *Journal of Management Studies,* November 1987, pp. 595–622.

16. Robert S. Kaplan and David P. Norton, "The Balanced Scorecard–Measures That Drive Performance," *Harvard Business Review,* January–February 1992, pp. 71–79.

17. Discussions of the history of management thought can be found in Daniel A. Wren, *The Evolution of Management Thought* (New York: Ronald Press, 1972); Claude S. George Jr., *The History of Management Thought* (Englewood Cliffs, N.J.: Prentice-Hall, 1968); and W. Jack Duncan, *Great Ideas in Management: Lessons from the Founders and Foundation of Management Practice* (San Francisco: Jossey-Bass, 1988).

18. The term *Classical School of Management* refers to the ideas developed by a group of practitioners who wrote of their experiences in management. Notable contributors to these ideas include Frederick W. Taylor, *Principles of Management* (New York: Harper & Row, 1911); Henri Fayol, *General and Industrial Management,* trans. J. A. Conbrough (Geneva: International Management Institute, 1929); James D. Mooney, *The Principles of Organization* (New York: Harper & Row, 1947); and James D. Mooney, *The Elements of Administration* (New York: Harper & Row, 1944).

19. Henry Mintzberg, *The Nature of Managerial Work* (Englewood Cliffs, N.J.: Prentice-Hall, 1980).

20. Peter F. Drucker, "Management's New Paradigms," *Forbes,* October 5, 1998, pp. 152–177.

21. Allen I. Kraut, Patricia R. Pedigo, D. Douglas McKenna, and Marvin D. Dunnette, "The Role of the Manager: What's Really Important in Different Management Jobs," *Academy of Management Executive,* November 1989, pp. 286–93.

22. Robert E. Quinn, *Beyond Rational Management* (San Francisco: Jossey-Bass, 1988).

23. William A. Band, *Touchstone: Ten New Ideas Revolutionizing Business* (New York: Wiley, 1994), pp. 59–62.

24. Henry Mintzberg, "Organization Design: Fashion or Fit?" *Harvard Business Review,* January–February 1981, pp. 103–16.

25. Alan Levinson, "You Won't Recognize Me: Predictions about Changes in Top-Management Characteristics," *Academy of Management Executive,* May 1988, pp. 119–25.

26. Alan B. Thomas, "Does Leadership Make a Difference to Organizational Performance?" *Administrative Science Quarterly,* September 1988, pp. 388–400.

27. Harlow B. Cohen, "The Performance Paradox," *Academy of Management Executive,* August 1998, pp. 30–40.

28. Stephen Stasser, J. D. Eveland, Gaylord Cummins, O. Lynn Denison, and John H. Romani, "Conceptualizing the Goal and System Models of Organizational Effectiveness," *Journal of Management Studies,* July 1981, p. 323, Kim Cameron, "Critical Questions in Assessing Organizational Effectiveness," *Organizational Dynamics,* Autumn 1980, pp. 66–80, identifies two other approaches: the internal process approach and the strategic constituencies approach. The former can be subsumed under the systems theory approach and the latter is a special case of the multiple-goal approach.

29. Michael Keeley, "Impartiality and Participant-Interest Theories of Organizational Effectiveness," *Administrative Science Quarterly,* March 1984, p. 1.

30. Chester I. Barnard, *The Functions of the Executive* (Cambridge, Mass.: Harvard University Press, 1938), p. 55.

31. Edwin A. Locke and Gary P. Latham, *A Theory of Goal-Setting and Task Performance* (Upper Saddle River, NJ: Prentice-Hall, 1990).

32. Terry Connolly, Edward J. Conlon, and Stuart Jay Deutsch, "Organizational Effectiveness: A Multiple-Constituency Approach," *Academy of Management Review,* April 1980, p. 212.

33. James L. Price and Charles W. Mueller, *Handbook of Organizational Measurement* (Marshfield, Mass.: Pitman, 1986), pp. 128–30.

34. Ibid, pp. 132–34.

35. Steven Cavaleri and Krysztof Obloj, *Management Systems: A Global Perspective* (Belmont, Calif.: Wadsworth, 1993), pp. 15–16.

36. John L. Peterson, *The Road to 2015* (Corte Madera, Calif.: Waite Group Press, 1994), pp. 4–6.

37. Robert Donmoyer, Michael Imber, and James J. Scheukrich eds., *The Knowledge Base in Educational Administration: Multiple Perspectives* (Albany, NY: State University of New York, 1995), pp. 1–10.

38. Amitai Etzioni, "Two Approaches to Organizational Analysis: A Critique and a Suggestion," in *Assessment of Organizational Effectiveness,* ed. Jaisingh Ghorpade (Santa Monica, Calif.: Goodyear, 1971), p. 36.

39. James H. Davis, F. David Schoorman, and Lex Donaldson, "Toward a Stewardship Theory of Management," *Academy of Management Review,* January 1997, pp. 20–47.

40. Connolly et al., "Organizational Effectiveness."

41. James D. Westphal and Edward J. Zajac, "The Symbolic Management of Stockholders: Corporate Governance Reforms and Shareholder Reactions," *Administrative Science Quarterly,* March 1998, pp. 127–153.

42. Anne S. Tsui, "An Empirical Examination of the Multiple-Constituency Model of Organizational Effectiveness," *Proceedings of the Academy of Management,* 1989, pp. 188–92.

43. Richard K. Lester, *The Productivity Edge: How U.S. Industries Are Pointing the Way to a New Era of Economic Growth* (New York: W. W. Norton, 1998).

44. Ram Charan, "Managing through the Chaos," *Fortune,* November 23, 1998, pp. 283–90.

CHAPTER 2

1. Kim S. Cameron and Robert E. Quinn, *Diagnosing and Changing Organizational Culture* (Reading, MA: Addison Wesley, 1999) and Harrison M. Trice and Janice M. Beyer, *The Cultures of Work Organizations* (Englewood Cliffs, NJ: Prentice-Hall, 1993).

2. Gary Hoover, Alta Campbell, and Patricia S. Spain, eds., *Profiles of Over 500 Major Corporations* (Austin, TX: Reference Press, 1996), p. 317.

3. A. M. Pettegrew, "On Studying Cultures," *Administrative Science Quarterly,* 1979, pp. 579–81.

4. D. Jongeward, *Everybody Wins: Transactional Analysis Applied to Organizations* (Reading, MA: Addison-Wesley, 1973).

5. Edgar H. Schein, *Organizational Culture and Leadership* (San Francisco: Jossey-Bass, 1985), p. 9.

6. "What Makes a Company Great?" *Fortune,* October 26, 1998, p. 218.

7. Geert Hofstede, *Cultures and Organizations* (New York: McGraw-Hill, 1991), pp. 8–10.

8. Mary Jo Hatch, "Dynamics of Organizational Culture," *Academy of Management Review* (October 1993), pp. 657–93.

9. M. Schultz, *On Studying Organizational Culture: Diagnosis and Understanding* (New York: W. de Gruyter, 1995).

10. G. S. Saffold III, "Culture Traits, Strength, and Organizational Performance: Moving beyond Strong Culture," *Academy of Management Review,* October 1988, pp. 546–58.

11. Anne B. Fisher, "Where Companies Rank in Their Industries," *Fortune,* March 4, 1996, p. F-2.

12. Malcolm Fleschner, "Flying High: Motivation at Southwest Airlines," *Personal Selling Power,* March 1994, pp. 74–79.

13. Keom L. Freiberg, "The Heart and Spirit of Transformation Leadership: A Qualitative Case Study of Herb Kelleher's Passion for Southwest Airlines," doctoral dissertation, University of San Diego, 1987, p. 234.

14. Peg C. Neuhauser, *Corporate Legends and Lore* (New York: McGraw-Hill 1993).

15. Peter C. Reynolds, "Imposing a Corporate Culture," *Psychology Today,* March 1987, pp. 33–38.

16. Schein, *Organizational Culture and Leadership,* pp. 83–89.

17. Markus Hauser, "Organizational Culture and Innovativeness of Firms: An Integrative View," *International Journal of Technology Management,* Spring, 1998, pp. 239–55.

18. Vijay Sathe, "Implications of Corporate Culture: A Manager's Guide to Action," *Organizational Dynamics,* Autumn 1983, pp. 4–13.

19. Charles A. O'Reilly III, Jennifer Chatman, and David F. Caldwell, "People and Organizational Culture: A Profile Comparison to Assessing Person–Organization Fit," *Academy of Management Journal,* September 1991, pp. 487–516.

20. Hugh P. Gunz, R. Michael Jelland, and Martin G. Evans, "New Strategy Wrong Managers? What You Need to Know About Career Streams," *Academy of Management Executive,* May 1989, pp. 21–37.

21. John P. Wanous, Arnon E. Reichers, and S. D. Malik, "Organizational Socialization and Group Development: Toward an Integrative Perspective," *Academy of Management Review,* October 1984, pp. 670–83. This article reviews the widely accepted models of socialization.

22. These stages are identified by Daniel C. Feldman, "A Contingency Theory of Socialization," *Administrative Science Quarterly,* September 1967, pp. 434–35. The following discussion is based heavily on this work as well as on Daniel C. Feldman, "A Practical Program for Employee Socialization," *Organizational Dynamics,* Autumn 1976, pp. 64–80; and Daniel C. Feldman, "The Multiple Socialization of Organization Members," *Academy of Management Review,* June 1981, pp. 309–18.

23. Emmanuel Ogbonna and Lloyd C. Harris, "Organizational Culture: It's Not What You Think," *Journal of General Management,* Spring 1998, pp. 35–48.

24. Dawn Infuse, "Creating a Culture of Caring That Pays Off," *Personnel Journal,* August 1995, 70–77.

25. James C. Collins and Jerry I. Porras, *"Built To Last,"* New York: Harper Collins, 1995.

26. Gareth R. Jones, "Psychological Orientation and the Process of Organizational Socialization: An Interactionist Perspective," *Academy of Management Review,* July 1983, pp. 464–74.

27. J. Van Maanen, "People Processing: Strategies for Organizational Socialization," *Organizational Dynamics,* Summer 1978, pp. 18–36.

28. The following discussion reflects the research findings of Feldman, "A Practical Program."

29. Douglas T. Hall and Francine S. Hall, "What's New in Career Management," *Organizational Dynamics,* Summer 1976, pp. 21–27.

30. R. Recardo and J. Jolly, "Organizational Culture and Teams," *SAM Advanced Management Journal,* Spring, 1997, pp. 4–7.

31. Barbara Addison Reid, "Mentorships Ensure Equal Opportunity," *Personnel Journal,* November 1994, 122–23; and R. J. Burke and C. A. McKeen, "Mentoring in Organizations: Implications for Women," *Journal of Ethics,* April–May, 1990, p. 322.

32. Kathy E. Kram, "Phases of the Mentor Relationship," *Academy of Management Journal,* December 1983, pp. 608–25.

33. James A. Wilson and Nancy S. Elman, "Organizational Benefits of Mentoring," *Academy of Management Executive,* November 1990, pp. 88–94.

34. Ibid., p. 90.

35. Ronald D. Brown, "The Role of Identification in Mentoring Female Proteges," *Group and Organization Studies,* March–June 1986, p. 72.

36. Taylor Cox Jr. and Ruby L. Beale, *Developing Competency to Manage Diversity* (San Francisco: Berrett-Koehler, 1997).

37. Charles Fishman, "Whole Foods Teams," *Fast Company,* April–May, 1996, pp. 102–11.

38. Taylor Cox Jr., "The Multicultural Organization," *The Academy of Management Executive,* May 1991, pp. 34–47.

39. David Jamieson and Julie O'Mara, *Managing Workforce 2000* (San Francisco: Jossey-Bass, 1991), pp. 84–89.

40. Dawn Anfuso, "Diversity Keeps Newspaper up With the Times," *Personnel Journal,* July 1995, 30–41. Charles Garfield, *Second to None* (Homewood, Ill.: Business One Irwin, 1992), pp. 283–85.

41. Pushkala Prasad, Albert J. Mills, Michael Elmes, and Anshuman Prasad, eds., *Managing the Organizational Melting Pot: Dilemmas of Workforce Diversity* (Thousand Oaks, CA: Sage, 1997).

42. Gareth Morgan, *Images of Organization: The Executive Edition* (New York: Wiley, 1998).

CHAPTER 3

1. Harry G. Barkema and Freek Vermeulen, "International Expansion through Start-up or Acquisition: A Learning Perspective," *Academy of Management Journal,* February 1998, pp. 7–26.

2. Tony Morden, "International Culture and Management," *Management Decision,* 1995, pp. 16–21.

3. Robert B. Reich, *The Work of Nations: Preparing Ourselves for 21st Century Capitalism* (New York: Knopf, 1991), p. 7.

4. Theodore Levitt, "The Globalization of Markets," *Harvard Business Review,* May–June 1983, p. 94.

5. Nancy J. Adler, *International Dimensions of Organizational Behavior* (Boston: PWS-Kent, 1991), pp. 3–10; Charles Gancel, "Inter Cultural Management Associates, ICM: ICM Management Training in Russia, Traps and Gaps," *Journal of Management Development,* 1995, pp. 15–26.

6. Julian Birkenshaw and Neil Hood, "Multinational Subsidiary Evolution: Capability and Charter Change In Foreign-Owned Subsidiary Companies," *Academy of Management Review,* October 1998, pp. 773–95.

7. John F. Milliman, Stephen Nason, Kevin Lowe, Nam-Hyeon Kim, and Paul Huo, "An Empirical Study of Performance Appraisal Practices in Japan, Korea, Taiwan and the U.S.," *Academy of Management Journal,* 1995, pp. 182–86; Stephen McKenna, "The Business Impact of Management Attitudes Towards Dealing with Conflict: A Cross-Cultural Assessment," *Journal of Managerial Psychology,* 1995, pp. 22–27.

8. Adler, p. 11.

9. C. K. Prahalud and Kenneth Lieberthal, "The End of Corporate Imperialism," *Harvard Business Review,* July–August 1998, pp. 69–79.

10. Ibid., p. 74.

11. Robert B. Giloth, ed., *Jobs and Economic Development: Strategies and Practice* (Thousand Oaks, CA: Sage, 1998).

12. Teresa J. Domzal and Lynette S. Unger, "Emerging Positioning Strategies in Global Marketing," *Journal of Consumer Marketing,* Fall 1987, pp. 23–40.

13. Douglas Lamont, *Winning Worldwide* (Homewood, IL.: Business One Irwin, 1991), p. 26.

14. Rick Yan, "Short-Term Results: The Litmus Test for Success in China," *Harvard Business Review,* September–October, 1998, pp. 61–75.

15. Eric K. Hatch, "Cross Cultural Team Building and Training," *Journal for Quality and Participation,* March 1995, pp. 44–49.

16. Charles W. Hill, *International Business: Competing in the Global Marketplace* (Chicago: Irwin, 1997).

17. Laura Miller, "Two Aspects of Japanese and American Co-Worker Interaction: Giving Instructions and Creating Rapport," *Journal of Applied Behavior Science,* June 1995, pp. 141–61.

18. Johnson Edosomwam, "The Baldrige Award: Focus on Total Customer Satisfaction," *Industrial Engineering,* July 1991, pp. 20–24.

19. F. M. Scherer, *International High-Technology Competition* (Cambridge, Mass.: Harvard University Press, 1992), p. 55.

20. Neil Weinberg, "A Fable of Two Companies," *Forbes,* November 30, 1998, pp. 122–27.

21. P. Christopher Earley, "East Meets West Meets Mideast: Further Explorations of Collectivistic and Individualistic Work Groups," *Academy of Management Journal,* April 1993, pp. 319–48.

22. Adler, *International Dimensions,* p. 27.

23. Ashley Dunn, "Cross-Cultural Misunderstandings," *Los Angeles Times,* May 28, 1989, pp. 12, 19.

24. The description of these four dimensions is based on Geert Hofstede, *Culture's Consequences: International Differences in Work-Related Values* (Beverly Hills, Calif.: Sage, 1980); Geert Hofstede, "The Cultural Relativity of Organizational Practices and Theories," *Journal of International Business Studies,* Fall 1983, pp. 75–89; and Geert Hofstede, "Motivation, Leadership, and Organization: Do American Theories Apply Abroad?" *Organizational Dynamics* (1980), pp. 42–63.

25. Simeha Ronen, *Comparative and Multinational Management* (New York: Wiley, 1986), pp. 266–67.

26. Geert Hofstede and Michael H. Bond, "The Confucius Connection: From Cultural Roots to Economic Growth," *Organizational Dynamics,* Spring 1988, pp. 4–21.

27. Geert Hofstede, "Cultural Constraints in Management Theories," paper presented at annual meeting of National Academy of Management, Las Vegas, Nev., August 11, 1992, pp. 1–21; Norman B. Bryan, Ephraim R. McClean, Stanley J. Smits, and Janice M. Burn, "Work Perceptions among Hong Kong and United States I/S Workers: A Cross-Cultural Comparison," *Journal of End User Computing,* Fall 1995, pp. 22–29; Andrew D. Brown and Michael Humphreys, "International Cultural Differences in Public Sector Management," *International Journal of Public Sector Management,* 1995, pp. 5–23.

28. Geert Hofstede, *Cultures and Organizations: Software of the Mind* (New York: McGraw-Hill, 1991).

29. Susumu Ueno and Uma Sekaran, "The Influence of Culture on Budget Control Practices in the U.S.A. and Japan: An Empirical Study," *Journal of International Business,* Winter 1992, pp. 659–74.

30. Irene K. H. Chew and Joseph Putti, "Relationship on Work-Related Values of Singaporean and Japanese Managers in Singapore," *Human Relations,* October 1995, pp. 1149–1170.

31. Harrison M. Trice and Janice M. Beyer, *Cultures of Work Organizations* (Englewood Cliffs, NJ: Prentice-Hall, 1993), p. 338.

32. A. Laurent, "The Cultural Diversity of Western Conceptions of Management," *International Studies of Management and Organizations,* Spring–Summer 1983, pp. 75–96.

33. James H. Donnelly Jr., James L. Gibson, and John M. Ivancevich, *Fundamentals of Management,* 10th ed. (New York: Irwin–McGraw Hill, 1998), pp. 70–71.

34. James Champy, "Deeper Accountability," *Forbes,* November 30, 1998, p. 108.

35. Dora C. Lau and J. Keith Murnighan, "Demographic Diversity and Faultlines: The Compositional Dynamics of Organizational Groups," *Academy of Management Review,* April 1998, pp. 325–40.

36. Susan Moffat, "Should You Work for the Japanese?" *Fortune,* December 3, 1990, p. 107.

37. J. Stewart Black, Mark Mendenhall, and Gary Obbou, "Toward a Comprehensive Model of International Adjustment: An Integration of Multiple Theoretical Perspectives," *Academy of Management Review,* April 1991, pp. 291–317; Roger Darby, "Developing the Euro-Manager: Managing in a Multicultural Environment," *European Business Review,* 1995, pp. 13–15; Mike Edkins. "Making the Move from West to East," *Personnel Management,* June 29, 1995, pp. 34–37.

38. Chao C. Chen, Xiao-Ping Chen, and James R. Meindl, "How Can Cooperation Be Fostered? The Cultural Effects of Individualism-Collectivism," *Academy of Management Review,* April 1998, pp. 285–304.

39. J. Stewart Black and Gregory K. Stephens, "The Influence of the Spouse on American Expatriate Adjustment and Intent to Stay in Pacific Rim Overseas Assignments," *Journal of Management,* December 1989, p. 228.

40. Ibid.; Richard G. Linowes, "The Japanese Manager's Traumatic Entry into the United States: Understanding the American–Japanese Cultural Divide," *Academy of Management Executive,* November 1993, pp. 21–38; Joyce Osland, "Working Abroad: A Hero's Adventure," *Training and Development,* November 1995, pp. 47–51.

41. Cassandra Hayes, "Can a New Frontier Boost Your Career?" *Black Enterprise,* May 1995, pp. 71–74.

42. Black and Mendenhall, "Cross-Cultural Training Effectiveness," pp. 113–36.

43. P. Christopher Earley, "Intercultural Training for Managers: A Comparison of Documentary and Interpersonal Methods," *Academy of Management Journal,* December 1987, pp. 685–98.

44. Rosalie Tung, "Selecting and Training Procedures of U.S., European, and Japanese Multinationals," *California Management Review,* Fall 1982, pp. 51–71; and R. L. Desatnick and M. L. Bennett, *Human Resource Management in the Multinational Company* (New York: Nichols, 1978).

45. Ibid.

46. Charlene Solomon, "Repatriation: Up, Down or Out?" *Personnel Journal,* January 1995, pp. 28–30.

47. Steven L. Wartick and Donna J. Wood, *International Business and Society* (Malden, MA: Blackwell, 1998).

48. Spencer Ante, "All The World's a Stage," *Business 2.0,* December 1998, p. 107.

CHAPTER 4

1. Jack Scarborough, *The Origin of Cultural Differences and Their Impact on Management* (Westport, CT: Quorum, 1998).

2. David A. Nadler and Janet L. Spencer, *Executive Teams* (San Francisco: Jossey-Bass, 1998).

3. Mitchell G. Ash, "Cultural Contexts and Scientific Changes in Psychology," *American Psychologist,* February 1992, pp. 198–207; and Kurt Levin, "Environmental Forecast in Child Behavior and Development," in *Handbook of Child Psychology,* ed. C. Murchison (Worcester, Mass.: Clark University Press, 1931), pp. 94–127.

4. Daniel A. Wren and Ronald G. Greenwood, *Management Innovators: The People and Ideas That Have Shaped Modern Business* (New York: Oxford University Press, 1998).

5. Gerald W. Faust, Richard I. Lyles, and Will Phillips, *Responsible Managers Get Results: How the Best Find Solutions—Not Excuses* (New York: Amacom, 1998).

6. Malcolm James Ree, Thomas R. Carretta and Mark S. Teachout, "Role of Ability and Prior Job Knowledge in Complex Training Performance," *Journal of Applied Psychology,* December 1995, pp. 721–30.

7. Marvin D. Dunnette, "Aptitudes, Abilities, and Skills," in *Handbook of Industrial and Organizational Psychology,* ed. Marvin D. Dunnette (Skokie, Ill.: Rand McNally, 1976), pp. 481–82.

8. Ulric Neisser, Gwyneth Boodoo, Thomas J. Bouchard, A. Wade Boykin, Nathan Brody, Stephen J. Ceci, Diane F. Halpern, John C. Loehlin, Robert Perloff, Robert J. Sternberg, and Susana Urbana, "Intelligence: Knowns and Unknowns," *American Psychologist,* February 1996, pp. 77–101, Robert J. Sternberg, Richard K. Wagner, Wendy M. Williams, and Joseph A. Horvath, "Testing Common Sense," *American Psychologist,* November 1995, pp. 912–27.

9. For a complete discussion of job analysis, see John M. Ivancevich, *Human Resource Management: Foundations of Personnel* (Homewood, Ill.: Richard D. Irwin, 1998), pp. 167–86.

10. C. Thomas Dortch, "Job–Person Match," *Personnel,* June 1989, pp. 48–57.

11. Belle Rose Ragins, Backley Townsend, and Mary Mathis, "Gender Gap in the Executive Suite: CEOs and Female Executives Report on Breaking the Glass Ceiling," *Academy of Management Executive,* February 1998, pp. 28–42.

12. D. Farrell and C. L. Stamm, "Meta-Analysis of the Correlates of Employee Absence," *Human Relations,* Spring 1983, pp. 211–27.

13. J. S. Hyde, E. Fenema, and S. J. Lamon, "Gender Differences in Mathematical Performance: A Meta-Analysis," *Psychological Bulletin,* March 1990, pp. 139–55.

14. Marilyn Loden and Judy R. Rosener, *Workforce America* (Homewood, Ill.: Business One Irwin, 1991).

15. Stella M. Nkomo, "The Emperor Has No Clothes: Rewriting Race in Organizations," *Academy of Management Review,* July 1992, pp. 487–513.

16. Michael E. Barak, David A. Cherin, and Sherry Berkman, "Organizational and Personal Dimensions in Diversity Climate: Ethnic and Gender Differences in Employee Perceptions," *Journal of Applied Behavioral Science,* March 1998, pp. 82–104.

17. Nigel Nicholson, "How Hardwired Is Human Behavior?" *Harvard Business Review,* July–August 1998, pp. 134–47.

18. David Krech, Richard S. Crutchfield, and E. L. Ballachey, *Individual and Society* (New York: McGraw-Hill, 1962), p. 20.

19. Heather M. McLean and Rudolf Kalin, "Congruence between Self-Image and Occupational Stereotypes in Students Entering Gender-Dominated Occupations," *Canadian Journal of Behavioral Science,* January 1994, pp. 142–62.

20. J. M. Darley and P. H. Gross, "A Hypothesis-Confirming Bias in Labeling Effects," *Journal of Personality and Social Psychology,* January 1983, pp. 20–33.

21. Benson Rosen and Thomas H. Jerdee, "The Influence of Age Stereotypes on Managerial Decisions," *Journal of Applied Psychology,* August 1976, pp. 428–32.

22. E. G. Olson, "The Workplace Is High on the Court's Docket," *Business Week,* October 10, 1988, pp. 88–89.

23. Joel Lefkowitz, "Sex-Related Differences in Job Attitudes and Dispositional Variables: Now You See Them . . ." *Academy of Management Journal,* April 1994, pp. 323–49; Reba Rowe and William E. Snizek, "Gender Differences in Work Values: Perpetuating the Myth," *Work and Occupations,* May 1995, pp. 215–29.

24. R. D. Norman, "The Interrelationships among Acceptance—Rejection, Self-Other Identity, Insight into Self, and Realistic Perception of Others," *Journal of Social Psychology,* May 1953, pp. 205–35.

25. J. Bossom and Abraham H. Maslow, "Security of Judges as a Factor in Impressions of Warmth in Others," *Journal of Abnormal and Social Psychology,* July 1957, pp. 147–48.

26. K. T. Omivake, "The Relation between Acceptance of Self and Acceptance of Others Shown by Three Personality Inventories," *Journal of Consulting Psychology,* December 1954, pp. 443–46.

27. J. Anthony Deutsch, W. G. Young, and T. J. Kalogeris, "The Stomach Signals Satiety," *Science,* April 1978, pp. 23–33.

28. H. H. Kelley, *Attribution in Social Interaction* (New York: General Learning Press, 1971).

29. Daniel T. Gilbert and Patrick S. Malone, "The Correspondence Bias," *Psychological Bulletin,* January 1995, pp. 21–38.

30. Paul T. Lewis, "A Naturalistic Test of Two Fundamental Propositions: Correspondence Bias and the Actor-Observer Hypothesis," *Journal of Personality,* March 1995, pp. 87–111.

31. William S. Silver, Terence R. Mitchell, and Marilyn E. Gist, "Responses to Successful and Unsuccessful Performance: The Moderating Effect of Self-efficacy on the Relationship between Performance and Attributions," *Organizational Behavior & Human Decision Processes,* 1995, pp. 286–99; Richard Z. Gooding and Angelo J. Kinicki, "Interpreting Event Causes: The Complementary Role of Categorization and Attribution Processes," *Journal of Management Studies,* 1995, pp. 1–22; C. R. Snyder and R. L. Higgins, "Excuses: Their Effective Role in the Negotiation of Reality," *Psychological Bulletin,* 1988, pp. 23–35.

32. Martin Fishbein and Isek Ajzen, *Belief, Attitude, Intention, and Behavior: An Introduction to Theory and Research* (Reading, Mass.: Addison-Wesley, 1975).

33. J. J. Rosenberg, "A Structural Theory of Attitudes," *Public Opinion Quarterly,* Summer 1960, pp. 319–40.

34. H. W. Dickson and Elliot McGinnies, "Affectivity and Arousal of Attitudes as Measured by Galvanic Skin Responses," *American Journal of Psychology,* October 1966, pp. 584–89.

35. Leon Festinger, *A Theory of Cognitive Dissonance* (Evanston, Ill.: Row, Peterson, 1957).

36. Andrew J. Elliot and Patricia G. Devine, "On the Motivational Nature of Cognitive Dissonance: Dissonance as Psychological Discomfort," *Journal of Personality and Social Psychology,* September 1994, pp. 382–94.

37. Roy Lewicki, Daniel J. McAllister, and Robert J. Bies, "Trust and Distrust: New Relationships and Realities," *Academy of Management Review,* July 1998, pp. 438–58.

38. Ibid.

39. Charles R. Morris, "The Coming Global Boom," *Atlantic Monthly,* October 1989, pp. 51–64; Stanley Hoffman, "What Should We Do in the World?" *Atlantic Monthly,* October 1989, pp. 84–96.

40. H. C. Kelman, "Process of Opinion Change," *Public Opinion Quarterly,* Spring 1961, pp. 57–78.

41. R. A. Osterhouse and T. C. Brock, "Distraction Increases Yielding to Propaganda by Inhibiting Counterarguing," *Journal of Personality and Social Psychology,* March 1977, pp. 344–58.

42. E. Spranger, *Types of Men* (Halle, Germany: Max Niemeyer Verlag, 1928). Quoted in V. S. Flowers et al., *Managerial Values for Working* (New York: American Management Association, 1975), p. 11.

43. Flowers and associates undertook a study of American Management Association members. Questionnaires were mailed to 4,998 members, and the researchers were able to use 1,707 replies. Based on these results and other studies, the author's state that the impact of values on managerial and nonmanagerial behavior is sufficiently important to account for some variation in the relative effectiveness of managers.

44. Fred E. Fiedler, *A Theory of Leadership Effectiveness* (New York: McGraw-Hill, 1967).

45. J. Senger, "Managers' Perceptions of Subordinates' Competence as a Function of Personal Value Orientations," *Academy of Management Journal,* December 1971, pp. 415–24.

46. For example, see Flowers et al., *Managerial Values;* Renato Tagiuri, "Value Orientations and Relationships of Managers and Scientists," *Administrative Science Quarterly,* June 1965, pp. 39–51.

47. U.S. firms have increasingly tended to use foreign nationals to manage overseas offices. This has created a concern for understanding the impact of culture on managers' values. See W. T. Whitely and George W. England, "A Comparison of Value Systems of Managers in the U.S.A., Japan, Korea, India, and Australia," in *Proceedings of the Thirty-Fourth Annual Meeting of the Academy of Management,* 1974, p. 11; R. B. Peterson, "A Cross-Cultural Perspective of Supervisory Values," *Academy of Management Journal,* March 1972, pp. 105–17.

48. P. C. Smith, L. M. Kendall, and Charles L. Hulin, *The Measurement of Satisfaction in Work and Retirement* (Skokie, Ill.: Rand McNally, 1969).

49. Yoav Ganzach, "Intelligence and Job Satisfaction," *Academy of Management Journal,* October 1998, pp. 526–39.

50. Anonymous, "U.S. Workers Remain Upbeat Despite Ongoing Restructurings," *HR Focus,* March 1995, p. 17; Michael Reinemer, "Work Happy," *American Demographics,* July 1995, pp. 26–30+; Amy Aronson, "A Shaky Economy, or Just Frazzled Nerves?" *Working Woman,* April 1995, p. 16.

51. Charles N. Greene, "The Satisfaction–Performance Controversy," *Business Horizons,* October 1972, pp. 31–41.

52. Victor H. Vroom, *Work and Motivation* (New York: John Wiley & Sons, 1964).

53. Dennis W. Organ, "A Reappraisal and Reinterpretation of the Satisfaction–Causes–Performance Hypothesis," *Academy of Management Review,* January 1977, pp. 46–53.

54. Dennis W. Organ and Mary Konovsky, "Cognitive versus Affective Determinants of Organizational Citizenship Behavior," *Journal of Applied Psychology,* February 1989, pp. 157–64.

55. Chi-Sum Wong, Chun Hui, and Kenneth S. Law, "Causal Relationship between Attitudinal Antecedents to Turnover," *Academy of Management Journal* (Best Papers Proceedings), 1995, pp. 342–346.

56. Mark Fichman, "Motivational Consequences of Absence and Attendance: Proportional Hazard Estimation of a Dynamic Motivation Model," *Journal of Applied Psychology,* February 1988, pp. 119–34.

57. This definition is based on Salvatore R. Maddi, *Personality Theories: A Comparative Analysis* (Homewood, Ill.: Dorsey Press, 1989), p. 63.

58. Raymond B. Cattell, *Personality and Mood by Questionnaire* (San Francisco: Jossey-Bass, 1973); Raymond B. Cattell, *The Scientific Analysis of Personality* (Chicago: Aldine, 1966).

59. Ibid.

60. Sigmund Freud, "Psychopathology of Everyday Life," in *The Complete Psychological Works of Sigmund Freud* (Standard Edition), ed. J. Strachey (London: Hogarth Press, 1960), originally published in S. Freud, *The Psychopathology of Everyday Life* (New York: Macmillan, 1904).

61. Philip G. Zimbardo, *Psychology and Life* (Glenview, Ill.: Scott, Foresman, 1985), p. 382.

62. Carl Rogers, *On Personal Power: Inner Strength and Its Revolutionary Impact* (New York: Delacorte, 1977).

63. Anne Anastasi, *Psychological Testing* (New York: Macmillan, 1976), chaps. 17–19.

64. Julian B. Rotter, "Generalized Expectancies for Internal versus External Control of Reinforcement," *Psychological Monographs* 1, no. 609 (1966), p. 80.

65. T. R. Mitchell, C. M. Smyser, and S. E. Weed, "Locus of Control: Supervision and Work Satisfaction," *Academy of Management Journal,* September 1975, pp. 23–31.

66. Carl R. Anderson, "Locus of Control, Coping Behaviors, and Performance in a Stress Setting: A Longitudinal Study," *Journal of Applied Psychology,* August 1977, pp. 446–51.

67. Janice Langan-Fox and Susanna Roth, "Achievement Motivation and Female Entrepreneurs," *Journal of Occupational & Organizational Psychology,* September 1995, pp. 209–18; David Johnson and Rosa Suet Fan Ma, "A Method for Selecting and Training Entrants on New Business Start-Up Programmes," *International Small Business Journal,* April–June 1995, pp. 80–84; Kelly G. Shaver, "The Entrepreneurial Personality Myth," *Business & Economic Review,* April–June 1995, pp. 20–23.

68. B. Strickland, "Internal–External Control Expectancies: From Contingency to Creativity," *American Psychologist,* January 1989, pp. 1–12.

69. Michael Frese, Wolfgang Kring, Andrea Soose, and Jeannette Zempel, "Personal Initiative at Work: Differences Between East and West Germany," *Academy of Management Journal,* February 1996, pp. 37–63.

70. Stephen R. Hawk, "Locus of Control and Computer Attitude: The Effect of User Involvement," *Computers in Human Behavior,* Spring 1988, pp. 199–206.

71. Kevin Daniels and Andrew Guppy, "Occupational Stress, Social Support, Job Control, and Psychological Well-Being," *Human Relations,* December 1994, pp. 1523–44; Adrian Furnham and Barrie Gunter, "Biographical and Personality Predictors of Organizational Climate," *Psychologia,* December 1994, pp. 199–210.

72. Jacqueline M. Hooper and Louis Veneziano, "Distinguishing Starters from Nonstarters in an Employee Physical Activity Incentive Program," *Health Education Quarterly,* February 1995, pp. 49–60; K. A. Wallston and B. S. Wallston, "Health Locus of Control Scales," in *Research with the Locus of Control Construct: Assessment Methods,* ed. H. M. Lefcourt (New York: Academic Press, 1981), pp. 189–243.

73. A. Bandura, *Social Learning Theory* (Englewood Cliffs, N.J.: Prentice-Hall, 1977); and A. Bandura, "Self-Efficacy," *Psychological Review,* 1977, pp. 191–215.

74. A. Bandura, "Self-Efficacy Mechanism in Human Behavior," *American Psychologist,* February 1982, pp. 122–47.

75. Janina C. Latack, Angelo J. Kinicki, and Gregory E. Prussia, "An Integrative Process Model of Coping with Job Loss," *Academy of Management Review,* April 1995, pp. 311–42.

76. Sam Walton, *Made in America* (New York: Doubleday, 1992).

77. Dov Eden and Yaakov Zuk, "Seasickness as a Self-Fulfilling Prophecy: Raising Self-Efficacy to Boost Performance at Sea," *Journal of Applied Psychology,* October 1995, pp. 628–35; Jeanette A. Davy, Joe S. Anderson, and Nicholas DiMarco, "Outcome Comparisons of Formal Outplacement Services and Informal Support," *Human Resource Development Quarterly,* Fall 1995, pp. 275–88.

78. Alan M. Saks, "Longitudinal Field Investigation of the Moderating and Mediating Effects of Self-Efficacy on the Relationship between Training and Newcomer Adjustment," *Journal of Applied Psychology,* April 1995, pp. 211–25.

79. Marilyn E. Gist and Terence R. Mitchell, "Self-Efficacy: A Theoretical Analysis of Its Determinants and Malleability," *Academy of Management Review,* April 1992, pp. 183–211.

80. William S. Silver, Terence R. Mitchell, and Marilyn E. Gist, "Responses to Successful and Unsuccessful Performance: The Moderating Effect of Self-Efficacy on the Relationship Between Performance and Attributions," *Organizational Behavior & Human Decision Processes,* 1995, pp. 286–99.

81. P. Christopher Earley, "Self or Group? Cultural Effects of Training on Self-Efficacy and Performance," *Administrative Science Quarterly,* March 1994, pp. 89–117.

82. Marilyn E. Gist, "Self-Efficacy: Implications for Organizational Behavior and Human Resource Management," *Academy of Management Review,* July 1987, pp. 472–85.

83. Richard Christie and Florence L. Geis, eds., *Studies in Machiavellianism* (New York: Academic Press, 1970).

84. Myron Gable and Frank Dangello, "Locus of Control, Machiavellianism, and Managerial Job Performance," *Journal of Psychology,* September 1994, pp. 599–608; John R. Sparks, "Machiavellianism and Personal Success in Marketing: The Moderating Role of Latitude for Improvisation," *Journal of the Academy of Marketing Science,* Fall 1994, pp. 393–400.

85. R. G. Vleeming, "Machiavellianism: A Preliminary Review," *Psychological Reports,* February 1979, pp. 295–310.

86. James M. Higgins, "Innovation: The Core Competence," *Planning Review,* November/December 1995, pp. 32–35.

87. Anonymous, "How to Squeeze Great Ideas Out of Your Team," *Supervisory Management,* November 1995, p. 11; Anonymous, "Deeply Embedded Management Values at 3M," *Sloan Management Review,* Fall 1995, p. 20; L. D. DeSimone, George N. Hatsopoulos, William F. O Brien, Bill Harris, and Charles P. Holt, "How Can Big Companies Keep the Entrepreneurial Spirit Alive?" *Harvard Business Review,* November/December 1995 pp. 183–92.

88. Lewis M. Terman and Melita Oden, *The Gifted Child at Mid-life* (Stanford, Calif.: Stanford University Press, 1959).

89. Stanley S. Gryskiewicz, "Restructuring for Innovation," *Issues and Observations,* November 1981, p. 1; Isaac Asimov, "Creativity Will Dominate Our Time after the Concepts of Work and Fun Have Been Blurred by Technology," *Personnel Administrator,* December 1983, p. 42; Jay Hall, "Americans Know How to be Productive if Managers Will Let Them," *Organizational Dynamics,* Winter 1994, pp. 33–46.

90. E. T. Smith, "Are You Creative?" *Business Week,* September 30, 1985, pp. 80–84.

91. Michael A. Wallach and Nathan Kogan, *Modes of Thinking in Young Children* (New York: Holt, Rinehart & Winston, 1965).

92. Min Basadur, "Managing Creativity: A Japanese Model," *Academy of Management Executive,* May 1992, pp. 29–42.

93. Gryskiewicz, "Restructuring," p. 3; Leonard M. S. Yong, "Managing Creative People," *Journal of Creative Behavior,* 1994, pp. 16–20.

94. F. H. Barron, *Creativity and Personal Freedom* (New York: Van Nostrand Reinhold, 1968); Donald W. MacKinnon, "Personality and the Realization of the Creative Potential," *American Psychologist,* March 1963, pp. 273–81.

95. R. Glaser, "Education and Thinking: The Role of Knowledge," *American Psychologist,* February 1984, pp. 93–104.

96. Some of the most contemporary work on psychological contracts is provided by Denise M. Rousseau, *Psychological Contracts in Organizations* (Thousand Oaks, CA: Sage, 1995) and Denise M. Rousseau, "Psychological and Implied Contracts," *Employee Responsibility and Rights Journal,* Spring 1989, pp. 121–39.

97. Ibid.

98. Carl Shapiro and Hal R. Varian, *Information Rules: A Strategy Guide to the Network Economy* (Cambridge, MA: Harvard Business School Press, 1998).

99. Elizabeth W. Morrison and Sandra L. Robinson, "When Employees Feel Betrayed: A Model of How Psychological Contract Violation Develops," *Academy of Management Review,* January 1997, pp. 226–56.

100. Denise M. Rousseau, Sam B. Setkin, Ronald S. Burt, and Colin Camerer, "Not So Different After All: A Cross-Discipline View of Trust," *Academy of Management Review,* July 1998, pp. 393–404.

101. Ibid.

102. Sandra L. Robinson, M. S. Kratz, and Denise M. Rousseau, "Changing Obligations and the Psychological Contract: A Longitudinal Perspective," *Academy of Management Journal,* January 1994, pp. 137–52 and Sandra L. Robinson and Denise M. Rousseau, "Violating the Psychological Contract: Not the Exception but the Norm," *Journal of Organizational Behavior,* April 1994, pp. 245–59.

103. Ellen M. Whitener, Susan E. Brodt, M. Audrey Koreguard, and Jon M. Weiner, "Managers as Initiators of Trust: An Exchange Relationship Framework for Understanding Managerial Trustworthy Behavior," *Academy of Management Review,* July 1998, pp. 513–39.

CHAPTER 5

1. Jason A. Colquitt and Marcia J. Simmering, "Conscientiousness, Goal Orientation, and Motivation to Learn During the Learning Process: A Longitudinal Study," *Journal of Applied Psychology,* August 1998, pp. 654–65.

2. John P. Campbell, Marvin D. Dunnette, Edward E. Lawler III, and Karl E. Weick, *Managerial Behavior, Performance and Effectiveness* (New York: McGraw-Hill, 1970), p. 340.

3. John W. Atkinson, *An Introduction to Motivation* (New York: Van Nostrand Reinhold, 1964).

4. Dalbir Bindra, *Motivation: A Systematic Reinterpretation* (New York: Ronald Press, 1959).

5. Marshall R. Jones, ed., *Nebraska Symposium on Motivation* (Lincoln: University of Nebraska Press, 1955), p. 14.

6. Mark Bernstein, "John Patterson Rang Up Success with the Incorruptible Cashier," *Smithsonian,* June 1989, pp. 150–66.

7. "Great Moments in Workstyle," *Inc.,* January 1986, pp. 52–53.

8. Shaker A. Zahra and Hugh M. O'Neill, "Charting the Landscape of Global Competition: Reflections on Emerging Organizational Challenges and Their Implications for Senior Executives," *Academy of Management Executive,* November 1998, pp. 12–21.

9. George T. Milkovich and Jerry M. Newman, *Compensation,* (Burr Ridge, IL: Irwin/McGraw-Hill, 1999), p. 274.

10. Richard M. Hodgetts, "A Conversation with Donald F. Hastings of the Lincoln Electric Company," *Organizational Dynamics,* Winter 1997, pp. 68–74.

11. Ryh-song Yea and John J. Lawrence, "Individualism and Confucian Dynamism: A Note on Hofstede's Cultural Root to Economic Growth," *Organizational Dynamics,* Winter 1995, pp. 655–669.

12. A. Bennett, "American Culture Is Often a Puzzle for Foreign Managers in the U.S.," *The Wall Street Journal,* February 12, 1986, p. 29.

13. Lennie Copeland and Lewis Griggs, *Going International* (New York: Random House, 1985).

14. Lyman W. Porter, "A Study of Perceived Need Satisfaction in Bottom and Middle Management Jobs," *Journal of Applied Psychology,* February 1961, pp. 1–10.

15. Lyman W. Porter, *Organizational Patterns of Managerial Job Attitudes* (New York: American Foundation for Management Research, 1964).

16. Lyman W. Porter, "Job Attitudes in Management: Perceived Deficiencies in Need Fulfillment as a Function of Size of the Company," *Journal of Applied Psychology,* December 1963, pp. 386–97.

17. John M. Ivancevich, "Perceived Need Satisfactions of Domestic versus Overseas Managers," *Journal of Applied Psychology,* August 1969, pp. 274–78.

18. Edward E. Lawler III and J. L. Suttle, "A Causal Correlation Test of the Need Hierarchy Concept," *Organizational Behavior and Human Performance,* April 1972, pp. 265–87; Douglas T. Hall and K. E. Nougaim, "An Examination of Maslow's Need Hierarchy in an Organizational Setting," *Organizational Behavior and Human Performance,* February 1968, pp. 12–35; Neher, Andrew, "Maslow's Theory of Motivation: A Critique," *Journal of Humanistic Psychology,* Summer 1991, pp. 89–112.

19. Abraham H. Maslow, "Critique of Self-Actualization Theory," *Journal of Humanistic Education and Development,* March 1991, pp. 103–08.

20. Clayton P. Alderfer, "An Empirical Test of a Need Theory of Human Needs," *Organizational Behavior and Human Performance,* April 1969, pp. 142–75.

21. Clayton P. Alderfer, *Existence, Relatedness, and Growth: Human Needs in Organizational Settings* (New York: Free Press, 1972).

22. Anne Tsui, Jane L. Pearce, Lyman W. Porter, and Angela M. Tripoli, "Alternative Approaches to the Employee–Organization Relationship: Does Investment in Employees Pay Off?" *Academy of Management Journal,* December 1997, pp. 1089–1121.

23. Barry M. Staw, N. E. Bell, and J. A. Clausen, "The Dispositional Approach to Job Attitudes," *Administrative Science Quarterly,* March 1986, p. 56.

24. Clayton P. Alderfer, "A Critique of Salancik and Pfeffer's Examination of Need-Satisfaction Theories," *Administrative Science Quarterly,* December 1977, pp. 658–69.

25. Clayton P. Alderfer and Richard A. Guzzo, "Life Expectancies and Adults' Enduring Strength of Desires in Organizations," *Administrative Science Quarterly,* September 1979, pp. 347–61.

26. J. P. Wanous and A. Zwany, "A Cross-Sectional Test of Need Hierarchy Theory," *Organizational Behavior and Human Performance,* February 1977, pp. 78–97.

27. Jeremy B. Fox, K. Dow Scott, and Joan M. Donohue, "An Investigation into Pay Valence and Performance in a Pay-for-Performance Field Setting," *Journal of Organizational Behavior,* August 1993, pp. 687–93.

28. Frederick Herzberg, B. Mausner, and B. Synderman, *The Motivation to Work* (New York: John Wiley & Sons, 1959).

29. R. J. House and L. Wigdor, "Herzberg's Dual-Factor Theory of Job Satisfaction and Motivation: A Review of the Empirical Evidence and a Criticism," *Personnel Psychology,* Winter 1967, pp. 369–80; J. Schneider and Edwin Locke, "A Critique of Herzberg's Classification System and a Suggested Revision," *Organizational Behavior and Human Performance,* July 1971, pp. 441–58.

30. Abraham K. Korman, *Industrial and Organizational Psychology* (Englewood Cliffs, N.J.: Prentice-Hall, 1971), pp. 148–50.

31. Edward E. Lawler III, *Motivation in Work Organizations* (Monterey, Calif.: Brooks/Cole, 1973), p. 72.

32. Miriam Lacey, "Rewards Can Cost Nothing? Yes They Can . . . Really!" *Journal for Quality and Participation,* June 1994, pp. 6–8.; Don Merit, "What Really Motivates You?" *American Printer,* January 1995, p. 74.

33. In discussing motivation applications with numerous managers in Europe, the Pacific Rim, and Latin America, the Herzberg explanation is referred to more often than any other theory. Herzberg's writings and explanations have found their way into many countries.

34. Isaac O. Adigun and Geoffrey M. Stephenson, "Sources of Job Motivation and Satisfaction among British and Nigerian Employees," *Journal of Social Psychology,* June 1992, pp. 369–76.

35. David C. McClelland, "Business Drive and National Achievement," *Harvard Business Review,* July–August 1962, pp. 99–112.

36. R. Murray, *Thematic Apperception Test Pictures and Manual* (Cambridge, Mass.: Harvard University Press, 1943).

37. David C. McClelland, *Motivational Trends in Society* (Morristown, N.J.: General Learning Press, 1971).

38. McClelland, "Business Drive." McClelland proposes that a society's economic growth is based on the level of need achievement inherent in its population.

39. David C. McClelland, "Toward a Theory of Motive Acquisition," *American Psychologist,* May 1965, pp. 321–33.

40. David C. McClelland and D. Burnham, "Power Is the Great Motivator," *Harvard Business Review,* March–April 1976, pp. 100–11.

41. W. V. Meyer, "Achievement Motive Research," in *Nebraska Symposium on Motivation,* ed. William J. Arnold (Lincoln: University of Nebraska Press, 1968).

42. Barbara Parker and Leonard H. Chusmir, "Development and Validation of a Life-Success Measures Scale," *Psychological Reports,* 1992, pp. 627–37.

43. David C. McClelland, "Managing Motivation to Expand Human Freedom," *American Psychologist,* March 1978, pp. 201–10.

44. David C. McClelland, "Retrospective Commentary," *Harvard Business Review,* January–February 1995, pp. 138–9.

45. Bruce D. Kirkcaldy, Adrian Furnham, and Richard Lynn, "Individual Differences in Work Attitudes," *Personality and Individual Differences,* 13, no. 1 (1992), pp. 49–55.

46. U. J. Weirsma, "Gender Differences in Attribute Preferences: Work–Home Role Conflict and Job Level as Mediating Variables," *Journal of Occupational Psychology,* 63 (1990), pp. 231–43; James E. Long, "The Effects of Tastes and Motivation on Individual Income," *Industrial and Labor Relations Review,* January 1995, pp. 338–51.

47. Ruth L. Jacobs and David C. McClelland, "Moving up the Corporate Ladder: A Longitudinal Study of the Leadership Motive Pattern and Managerial Success in Women and Men. "Special Issue:" Issues in the Assessment of Managerial and Executive Leadership," *Consulting Psychology Journal Practice and Research,* Winter 1994, pp. 32–41.

48. William D. Spangler, "Validity of Questionnaire and TAT Measures of Need for Achievement: Two Meta-Analyses," *Psychological Bulletin,* July 1992, pp. 140–54.

49. P. D. Machungiva and N. Schmitt, "Work Motivation in a Developing Country," *Journal of Applied Psychology,* February 1983, pp. 31–42.

50. McClelland, "Business Drive."

51. Dawn Anfuso, "PepsiCo Shares Power and Wealth with Workers," *Personnel Journal,* June 1995, pp. 42–49.

CHAPTER 6

1. Aaron Bernstein, "We Really Want To Stay," *Business Week,* June 22, 1998, pp. 67–72.

2. Albert Bandura, *Social Learning Theory* (Englewood Cliffs, N.J.: Prentice-Hall, 1977), p. vii.

3. Robert Wood and Albert Bandura, "Social Cognitive Theory of Organizational Management," *Academy of Management Review,* July 1989, pp. 361–84.

4. For an excellent and concise discussion of social learning theory as applied to organizations, see Robert Kreitner and Fred Luthans, "A Social Learning Approach to Behavioral Management: Radical Behaviorists 'Mellowing Out'," *Organizational Dynamics,* Autumn 1984, pp. 47–65.

5. Albert Bandura, "Self-Efficacy: Toward a Unifying Theory of Behavioral Change," *Psychological Review,* 1977, pp. 191–215.

6. Nancy G. Boyd and George S. Vozikis, "The Influence of Self-Efficacy on the Development of Entrepreneurial Intentions and Actions," *Entrepreneurship: Theory and Practice,* Summer 1994, pp. 63–77; Tracy McDonald and Marc Siegall, "The Effects of Technological Self-Efficacy and Job Focus on Job Performance, Attitudes, and Withdrawal Behaviors," *Journal of Psychology,* September 1992, pp. 465–75; Golnaz Sadri and Ivan T. Robertson, "Self-Efficacy and Work-Related Behaviour: A Review and Meta-Analysis," *Applied Psychology: An International Review,* April 1993, pp. 139–52.

7. Edwin A. Locke, E. Frederick, Cynthia Lee, and Philip Bobko, "The Effect of Self-Efficacy, Goals, and Task Strategies on Task Performance," *Journal of Applied Psychology,* 1984, pp. 241–51.

8. P. Christopher Earley, "Self or Group? Cultural Effects of Training on Self-Efficacy and Performance," *Administrative Science Quarterly,* March 1994, pp. 89–117.

9. Dov Eden, "Leadership and Expectations: Pygmalion Effects and Other Self-Fulfilling Prophecies in Organizations," *Leadership Quarterly,* Winter 1992, pp. 271–305; Marilyn E. Gist, "Self-Efficacy: Implications in Organizational Behavior and Human Resource Management," *Academy of Management Review,* July 1987, pp. 472–85; Paul Loftus, "Expect Yourself," *Canadian Banker,* January/February 1995, pp. 31–33; Matt Oechsli, "Pygmalion Revisited," *Managers Magazine,* March 1994, pp. 16–21.

10. Taly Dvir, Dov Eden and Michal L. Banjo, "Self-Fulfilling Prophecy and Gender: Can Women Be Pygmalion and Galatea?" *Journal of Applied Psychology,* April 1995, pp. 253–70.

11. W. Clay Hamner, "Reinforcement Theory and Contingency Management in Organizational Settings," in *Organizational Behavior and Management: A Contingency Approach,* ed. Henry L. Tosi and W. Clay Hamner (Chicago: St. Clair, 1974), pp. 86–112.

12. B. F. Skinner, "Whatever Happened to Psychology and the Science of Behavior," *American Psychologist,* August 1987, pp. 780–86.

13. Fred Luthans, *Organizational Behavior* (New York: McGraw-Hill, 1998), pp. 244–46.

14. Ibid., p. 244.

15. Jorma Saari, "When Does Behaviour Modification Prevent Accidents?" *Leadership & Organization Development Journal,* 1994, pp. 11–15.

16. Lee Ginsburg and Neil Miller, "Value-Driven Management," *Business Horizons,* May–June 1992, pp. 23–27.

17. Malia Boyd, "Motivating on a Dime," *Performance,* March 1995, pp. 62–65; David Packard, *The HP Way: How Bill Hewlett and I Built Our Company* (New York: HarperBusiness, 1995).

18. Shelly Branch, "You Hired 'Em, But Can You Keep 'Em?" *Fortune,* November 9, 1998, pp. 247–50.

19. Linda Klebe Trevino, "The Social Effects of Punishment in Organizations: A Justice Perspective," *Academy of Management Review,* October 1992, pp. 647–76.

20. Edward L. Thorndike, *Animal Intelligence* (New York: Macmillan, 1911), p. 244.

21. Alexander D. Stajkovic and Fred Luthans, "A Meta-Analysis of The Effects of Organizational Behavior Modification on Task Performance, 1975–1995," *Academy of Management Journal,* 40 1997, pp. 1122–49.

22. Two excellent and very similar behavior modification problem-solving processes are found in L. M. Miller, *Behavior Management* (New York: John Wiley & Sons, 1978), pp. 64–66; Luthans, *Organizational Behavior,* pp. 270–89.

23. Fred Luthans and J. Schweizer, "How Behavior Modification Techniques Can Improve Total Organizational Performance," *Management Review,* September 1979, pp. 43–50.

24. Thomas K. Connellan, *How to Improve Human Performance: Behaviorism in Business and Industry* (New York: Harper & Row, 1978), pp. 48–75.

25. Luthans, *Organizational Behavior,* p. 245.

26. Connellan, *How to Improve Human Performance,* p. 51.

27. P. Nick Blanchard and James W. Thacker, *Effective Training* (Englewood Cliffs, NJ: Prentice-Hall, 1999), pp. 253–54.

28. Kirk O'Hara, C. Merle Johnson, and Terry A. Beehr, "Organizational Behavior Management in the Private Sector: A Review of Empirical Research and Recommendations for Further Investigation," *Academy of Management Review,* October 1985, pp. 848–64.

29. Edwin A. Locke, "The Myths of Behavior Mod in Organizations," *Academy of Management Review,* October 1977, pp. 543–53. In addition to Locke's critique of operant conditioning, also see Jerry L. Gray, "The Myths of the Myths about Behavior Mod in Organizations: A Reply to Locke's Criticisms of Behavior Modification," *Academy of Management Review,* January 1979, pp. 121–29; M. Parmerlee and C. Schwenk, "Radical Behaviorism: Misconceptions in the Locke-Gray Debate," *Academy of Management Review,* October 1979, pp. 601–07.

30. David J. Cherrington, "Follow Through on Award Programs," *HR Magazine,* April 1992, pp. 52–55.

31. Dianne H. B. Welsh, Fred Luthans, and Steven M. Sommer, "Managing Russian Factory Workers: The Impact of U.S.-Based Behavioral and Participative Techniques," *Academy of Management Journal,* February 1993, pp. 58–79.

32. Albert Bandura, *Social Learning Theory* (Englewood Cliffs, N.J.: Prentice-Hall, 1977); Carolyn Hughes and John W. Lloyd, "An Analysis of Self-Management," *Journal of Behavioral Education,* December 1993, pp. 405–25.

33. C. E. Thoreson and Michael J. Mahoney, *Behavioral Self-Control* (New York: Holt, Rinehart & Winston, 1974), p. 12.

34. Louise E. Parker and Richard H. Price, "Empowered Managers and Empowered Workers: The Effects of Managerial Support and Managerial Perceived Control on Workers' Sense of Control over Decision Making," *Human Relations,* August 1994, pp. 911–28; Robert C. Ford and Myron D. Fottler, "Empowerment: A Matter of Degree," *Academy of Management Executive,* August 1995, pp. 21–29.

35. Charles C. Manz, "Self-Leadership: Toward an Expanded Theory of Self-Influence Processes in Organizations," *Academy of Management Review,* July 1986, pp. 585–600.

36. Colette A. Frayne and J. Michael Geringer, "A Social Cognitive Approach to Examining Joint Venture General Manager Performance," *Group and Organization Management,* June 1994, pp. 240–62.

37. Frederick H. Kanfer, "Self-Management Methods," in *Helping People Change: A Textbook of Methods,* ed. Frederick H. Kanfer and Arnold P. Goldstein (New York: Pergamon, 1980), p. 339.

38. Victor H. Vroom, *Work and Motivation* (New York: John Wiley & Sons, 1964); Cynthia Lee and P. Christopher Earley, Comparative Peer Evaluations of Organizational Behavior Theories," *Organization Development Journal,* Winter 1992, pp. 37–42.

39. David A. Nadler and Edward E. Lawler III, "Motivation: A Diagnostic Approach," in *Perspectives on Behavior in Organizations,* ed. J. Richard Hackman, Edward E. Lawler III, and Lyman W. Porter (New York: McGraw-Hill, 1977), pp. 26–38; Edwin A. Locke, "Personnel Attitudes and Motivation," *Annual Review of Psychology,* 1973, pp. 457–80; Ken C. Snead and Adrian M. Harrell, "An Application of Expectancy Theory to Explain a Manager's Intention to Use a Decision Support System," *Decision Sciences,* July/August 1994, pp. 499–513.

40. Jeremy B. Fox, K. Dow Scott and Joan M. Donohue, "An Investigation into Pay Valence and Performance in a Pay-for-Performance Field Setting," *Journal of Organizational Behavior,* 1993, pp. 687–93.

41. Dennis W. Organ and Thomas S. Bateman, *Organizational Behavior: An Applied Psychological Approach* (Plano, Tex.: Business Publications, 1986).

42. Carol J. Loomis, "Mr. Lipp Has a Little List," *Fortune,* January 11, 1999, pp. 86–88.

43. James A. Shepperd, "Productivity Loss in Performance Groups: A Motivation Analysis," *Psychological Bulletin,* January 1993, pp. 67–81.

44. Stephen D. Mastrofski, R. Richard Ritti and Jeffrey B. Snipes, "Expectancy Theory and Police Productivity in DUI Enforcement," *Law and Society Review,* 1994, pp. 113–48.

45. Robert D. Pritchard and P. J. DeLeo, "Experimental Test of the Valence—Instrumentality Relationships in Job Performance," *Journal of Applied Psychology,* April 1973, pp. 264–79.

46. H. Garland, "Relation of Effort-Performance Expectancy to Performance in Goal Setting Experiences," *Journal of Applied Psychology,* 68 (1984), pp. 79–84.

47. John P. Campbell and Robert D. Pritchard, "Motivation Theory in Industrial and Organizational Psychology," in *Handbook of Industrial and Organizational Psychology,* ed. Marvin D. Dunnette (Skokie, Ill.: Rand McNally, 1976), pp. 84–95.

48. Nora Wood, "What Motivates Best?" *Sales & Marketing Management,* September 1998, pp. 70–78.

49. Jeffrey Pfeffer, "Producing Sustainable Competitive Advantage through the Effective Management of People," *Academy of Management Executive,* February 1995, pp. 55–69.

50. J. Stacey Adams, "Toward an Understanding of Equity," *Journal of Abnormal and Social Psychology,* November 1963, pp. 422–36.

51. Richard C. Husemann, John D. Hatfield, and Edward W. Miles, "A New Perspective on Equity Theory: The Equity Sensitivity Construct," *Academy of Management Review,* April 1987, pp. 222–34.

52. P. S. Goodman and A. Friedman, "An Examination of Adam's Theory of Inequity," *Administrative Science Quarterly,* December 1971, pp. 271–88; Linda S. Perry, "Effects of Inequity on Job Satisfaction and Self-Evaluation in a National Sample of African-American Workers," *Journal of Social Psychology,* August 1993, pp. 565–73.

53. Jerald Greenberg, "Equity and Workplace Status: A Field Experiment," *Journal of Applied Psychology,* November 1988, pp. 606–13.

54. Ronald J. Deluga, "Supervisor Trust Building, Leader–Member Exchange and Organizational Citizenship Behaviour," *Journal of Occupational & Organizational Psychology,* December 1994, pp. 315–26.

55. Eugene P. Sheehan, "The Effects of Turnover on the Productivity of Those Who Stay," *Journal of Social Psychology,* October 1993, pp. 699–706; M. Audrey Korsgaard, David M. Schweiger, and Harry J. Sapienza, "Building Commitment, Attachment, and Trust in Strategic Decision-Making Teams: The Role of Procedural Justice," *Academy of Management Journal,* February 1995, pp. 60–84.

56. Edwin A. Locke, "The Nature and Causes of Job Satisfaction," in *Handbook of Industrial and Organizational Psychology,* ed. Marvin D. Dunnette (Skokie, Ill.: Rand McNally, 1976), pp. 1297–349.

57. Robert Vecchio, "Predicting Worker Performance in Inequitable Settings," *Academy of Management Review,* January 1982, pp. 103–10.

58. Richard A. Cosier and Daniel R. Dalton, "Equity Theory and Time: A Reformulation," *Academy of Management Review,* April 1983, pp. 311–19.

59. Robert Folger, "Reformulating the Preconditions of Resentment: A Referent Cognitions Model," in *Social Comparison, Justice, and Relative Deprivation: Theoretical, Empirical, and Policy Perspectives,* ed. John C. Masters and William P. Smith (Hillsdale, N.J.: Erlbaum & Associates, 1987), pp. 153–215.

60. Russell Cropanzano and Robert Folger, "Referent Cognitions and Task Division Autonomy: Beyond Equity Theory," *Journal of Applied Psychology,* April 1989, pp. 293–99.

61. Robert Folger and Mary A. Konovsky, "Efforts of Procedural and Distributive Justice on Reactions to Pay Raise Decisions," *Academy of Management Journal,* March 1989, pp. 115–30.

62. Oded Shenkar and Mary Ann von Glinow, "Paradoxes of Organizational Theory and Research: Using the Case of China to Illustrate National Contingency," *Management Science,* January 1994, pp. 56–71.

63. Edwin A. Locke, "Toward a Theory of Task Motivation and Incentives," *Organizational Behavior and Human Performance,* May 1968, pp. 157–89.

64. Thomas A. Ryan, *Intentional Behavior* (New York: Ronald Press, 1970), p. 95.

65. Mark E. Tubbs and Steven E. Ekeberg, "The Role of Intentions in Work Motivation: Implications for Goal-Setting Theory and Research," *Academy of Management Review,* January 1991, pp. 180–99.

66. M. D. Cooper, R. A. Phillips, V. J. Sutherland and P. J. Makin, "Reducing Accidents Using Goal Setting and Feedback: A Field Study," *Journal of Occupational and Organizational Psychology,* September 1994, pp. 219–40.

67. Frederick W. Taylor, *The Principles of Scientific Management* (New York: W. W. Norton, 1947).

68. Edwin A. Locke, K. N. Shaw, L. M. Saari, and Gary P. Latham, "Goal Setting and Task Performance: 1969–1980," *Psychological Bulletin,* July 1981, p. 129.

69. Edwin A. Locke, "The Ubiquity of the Technique of Goal Setting in Theories of and Approaches to Employee Motivation," *Academy of Management Review,* July 1978, p. 600.

70. Anthony J. Mento, Robert P. Steel, and Ronald J. Karren, "A Meta-Analytic Study of the Effects of Goal Setting on Task Performance: 1966–1984," *Organizational Behavior and Human Decision Processes,* February 1987, p. 53.

71. Locke, "Toward a Theory."

72. For a complete analysis, see Locke et al., "Goal Setting."

73. Ibid.

74. Gary P. Latham and J. J. Baldes, "The Practical Significance of Locke's Theory of Goal Setting," *Journal of Applied Psychology,* February 1975, pp. 122–24.

75. Ibid., p. 124.

76. Locke et al., "Goal Setting"; Patricia M. Wright, John R. Hollenbeck, Samantha Wolf, and Gary C. McMahan, "The Effects of Varying Goal Difficulty Operationalizations on Goal Setting Outcomes and Processes," *Organizational Behavior and Human Decision Processes,* January 1995, pp. 28–43.

77. A. Zander and T. T. Newcomb, "Goal Levels of Aspirations in United Fund Campaigns," *Journal of Personality and Social Psychology,* June 1967, pp. 157–62.

78. Charles Ames, "Sales Soft? Profits Flat? It's Time to Rethink Your Business," *Fortune,* June 26, 1995, pp. 143–46.

79. Miriam Erez, P. Christopher Earley, and Charles L. Hulin, "The Impact of Participation on Goal Acceptance and Performance: A Two-Step Model," *Academy of Management Journal,* March 1985, pp. 50–66. Also Miriam Erez and Frederick H. Kanfer, "The Role of Goal Acceptance in Goal Setting and Task Performance," *Academy of Management Review,* 1983, pp. 454–63.

80. Edwin A. Locke and Gary P. Latham, *Goal Setting: A Motivational Technique That Works* (Englewood Cliffs, N.J.: Prentice-Hall, 1984), p. 22.

81. Gary P. Latham, Miriam Erez, and Edwin A. Locke, "Resolving Scientific Disputes by the Joint Design of Crucial Experiments by the Antagonists: Application to the Erez–Latham Dispute Regarding Participation in Goal Setting," *Journal of Applied Psychology,* November 1988, pp. 753–72.

82. Edwin A. Locke, ed., *Generalizing from Laboratory to Field Settings* (Lexington, Mass.: Lexington Books, 1986).

83. John M. Ivancevich and J. Timothy McMahon, "Education as a Moderator of Goal-Setting Effectiveness," *Journal of Vocational Behavior,* August 1977, pp. 83–94.

84. Gary P. Latham and Gary A. Yukl, "Assigned versus Participative Goal Setting with Educated and Uneducated Wood Workers," *Journal of Applied Psychology,* June 1975, pp. 299–302.

85. Miriam Erez and R. Arad, "Participative Goal Setting: Social, Motivational, and Cognitive Factors," *Journal of Applied Psychology,* 1986, pp. 591–97.

86. Edwin A. Locke, Ken G. Smith, Miriam Erez, Dong-Ok Chah, and Adam Schaffer, "The Effects of Intra-Individual Goal Conflict on Performance," *Journal of Management,* Spring 1994, pp. 67–91.

87. Frank J. Landy and W. S. Becker, "Motivation Theory Reconsidered," in *Research in Organizational Behavior,* ed. Larry L. Cummings and B. M. Stewart (Greenwich, Conn.: JAI Press, 1987), p. 33.

CHAPTER 7

1. Thomas B. Wilson, "Is It Time to Eliminate the Piece Rate Incentive System?" *Compensation and Benefits Review,* March–April 1992, pp. 43–49.

2. Jude T. Rich, "Meeting the Global Challenge: A Measurement and Reward Program for the Future," *Compensation and Benefits Review,* July–August 1992, pp. 26–29.

3. Edward E. Lawler III, "Reward Systems," in *Improving Life at Work,* ed. J. Richard Hackman and J. L. Suttle (Santa Monica, Calif.: Goodyear, 1977), pp. 163–226.

4. Terence R. Mitchell, "Motivation: New Directions for Theory, Research, and Practice," *Academy of Management Review,* January 1982, pp. 80–88.

5. Lawler, "Reward Systems," p. 168.

6. Richard A. Guzzo, "Types of Rewards, Cognitions and Work Motivation," *Academy of Management Review,* January 1979, pp. 75–86.

7. R. L. Opsahl and Marvin D. Dunnette, "The Role of Financial Compensation in Industrial Motivation," *Psychological Bulletin,* August 1966, p. 114.

8. Hugh J. Arnold, "Task Performance, Perceived Competence, and Attributed Cause of Performance as Determinants of Intrinsic Motivation," *Organizational Behavior and Human Decision Process,* December 1985, pp. 876–86.

9. Andrew R. Brownstein and Morris J. Panner, "Who Should Set CEO Pay? The Press? Congress? Shareholders?" *Harvard Business Review,* May–June 1992, pp. 28–38.

10. Douglas M. Cowherd and David I. Levine, "Product Quality and Pay Equity between Lower-Level Employees and Top Management: An Investigation of Distributive Justice," *Administrative Science Quarterly,* June 1992, pp. 302–20.

11. Michael Verespej, "Pay-for-Skills: Its Time Has Come," *Industry Week,* June 15, 1992, pp. 22–30.

12. Dallas L. Salisbury, "Introduction: The Value of Benefits," in *Controlling the Costs of Employee Benefits* (New York: Conference Board, 1992), no. 1004, p. 8.

13. *Recognizing Quality Achievement: Noncash Awards Program* (New York: Conference Board, 1992), no. 1008, pp. 1–54.

14. David C. McClelland, *The Achieving Society* (New York: Van Nostrand Reinhold, 1961).

15. Daniel C. Feldman and Hugh J. Arnold, *Managing Individual and Group Behavior in Organizations* (New York: McGraw-Hill, 1983), p. 164.

16. Edward L. Deci, "The Effects of Externally Mediated Rewards on Intrinsic Motivation," *Journal of Personality and Social Psychology,* 1971, vol. 31, pp. 105–15. Also Edward L. Deci, *Intrinsic Motivation* (New York: Plenum, 1975).

17. Barry M. Staw, *Intrinsic and Extrinsic Motivation* (Morristown, N.J.: General Learning Press, 1975).

18. Barry M. Staw, "The Attitudinal and Behavioral Consequences of Changing a Major Organizational Reward," *Journal of Personality and Social Psychology,* June 1974, pp. 742–51.

19. Cynthia D. Fisher, "The Effects of Personal Control, Competence, and Extrinsic Reward Systems on Intrinsic Motivation," *Organizational Behavior and Human Performance,* June 1978, pp. 273–87. Also James S. Phillips and Robert G. Lord, "Determinants of Intrinsic Motivation: Locus of Control and

Competence Information as Components of Deci's Cognitive Evaluation Theory," *Journal of Applied Psychology,* April 1980, pp. 211–18.

20. K. B. Boone and Larry L. Cummings, "Cognitive Evaluation Theory: An Experimental Test of Processes and Outcomes," *Organizational Behavior and Human Performance,* December 1981, pp. 289–310.

21. E. M. Lopez, "A Test of Deci's Cognitive Evaluation Theory in an Organizational Setting." Paper presented at the 39th annual convention of the Academy of Management, Atlanta, Georgia, August 1979.

22. Dan R. Dalton, Daniel M. Krackhardt, and Lyman W. Porter, "Functional Turnover: An Empirical Assessment," *Journal of Applied Psychology,* December 1981, pp. 716–21.

23. Dan R. Dalton and W. D. Tudor, "Turnover: A Lucrative Hard Dollar Phenomenon," *Academy of Management Review,* April 1982, p. 212.

24. E. J. Brennan, "Merit Pay: Balance the Old Rich and the New Poor," *Personnel Journal,* May 1985, pp. 82–84.

25. Gary Johns and N. Nicholson, "The Meanings of Absence: New Strategies for Theory and Research," in *Research in Organizational Behavior,* ed. Barry M. Staw and Larry L. Cummings (Greenwich, Conn.: JAI Press, 1982), pp. 127–72.

26. Dan R. Dalton and Debra J. Mesch, "On the Extent and Reduction of Avoidable Absenteeism: An Assessment of Absence Policy Provisions," *Journal of Applied Psychology,* December 1991, pp. 810–17.

27. Fred Luthans, H. S. McCaul, and N. G. Dowd, "Organizational Commitment: A Comparison of American, Japanese, and Korean Employees," *Academy of Management Journal,* March 1985, pp. 213–19.

28. B. Buchanan, "To Walk an Extra Mile: The Whats, Whens, and Whys of Organizational Commitment," *Organizational Dynamics,* Spring 1975, pp. 67–80.

29. Richard T. Mowday, Lyman W. Porter, and Richard M. Steers, *Employee-Organization Linkages* (New York: Academic Press, 1982).

30. J. P. Curry, D. S. Wakefield, James L. Price, and Charles W. Mueller, "On the Causal Ordering of Job Satisfaction and Organizational Commitment," *Academy of Management Journal,* December 1986, pp. 847–58.

31. J. H. Shea, "Cautions about Cafeteria-Style Benefit Plans," *Personnel Journal,* January 1981, p. 37.

32. Lawler, "Reward Systems," p. 182.

33. Richard L. Bunning, "Models for Skill-Based Pay Plans," *HR Magazine,* February 1992, pp. 62–64.

34. Verespej, "Pay for Skills," p. 23.

35. Fred Luthans and M. L. Fox, "Update on Skill-Based Pay," *Personnel,* March 1989, pp. 26, 28.

36. R. L. Bunning, "Skill-Based Pay," *Personnel Administrator,* June 1989, pp. 65–70.

37. Luthans and Fox, "Update," p. 28.

38. David Beck, "Implementing a Gainsharing Plan: What Companies Need to Know," *Compensation and Benefits,* January–February 1992, pp. 21–33.

39. Nancy J. Perry, "Here Come Richer, Riskier Pay Plans," *Fortune,* December 19, 1988, pp. 52, 54.

40. Ibid., p. 54.

41. T. L. Ross, L. Hatcher, and R. A. Ross, "From Piecework to Companywide Gainsharing," *Management Review,* May 1989, pp. 22–26; Perry, "Here Come Richer," p. 54.

42. Tracy E. Benson, "Quality and Teamwork Get a Leg Up," *Industry Week,* April 6, 1992, pp. 66–68.

43. Rebecca Sisco, "Put Your Money Where Your Teams Are," *Training,* June 1992, pp. 41–45.

44. Thomas F. O'Boyle, "Working Together," *The Wall Street Journal,* June 5, 1992, pp. A1, A5.

CHAPTER 8

1. Marvin E. Shaw, *Group Dynamics* (New York: McGraw-Hill, 1981).

2. Deborah L. Gladstein, "Group in Context: A Model of Task Group Effectiveness," *Administrative Science Quarterly,* December 1984, pp. 499–517.

3. Connie J. G. Gersick, "Marking Time: Predictable Transitions in Task Groups," *Academy of Management Journal,* June 1989, pp. 274–309.

4. Kerwyn K. Smith and David N. Berg, *Paradoxes of Group Life* (San Francisco: Jossey-Bass, 1987).

5. R. T. Hussein, "Informal Groups, Leadership, and Productivity," *Leadership and Organization Development Journal,* vol. 10, no. 1, 1989, pp. 9–16.

6. G. Meyer, "The Company You Keep Affects Your Attitude Toward the Company," *Academy of Management Executive,* August 1994, pp. 101–2.

7. Seth Alcorn, "Understanding Groups at Work," *Personnel,* August 1989, pp. 28–36.

8. Linda N. Jewell and H. Joseph Reitz, *Group Effectiveness in Organizations* (Glenview, Ill.: Scott, Foresman, 1981). This excellent comprehensive work is devoted entirely to the subject of groups in organizational settings.

9. P. K. Lunt, "The Perceived Causal Structure of Loneliness," *Journal of Personality and Social Psychology,* July 1991, pp. 26–34.

10. Beverly Geber, "Guerrilla Teams: Friend or Foe," *Training,* June 1994, pp. 36–39.

11. K. W. Mossholder, A. G. Bedeian, and A. A. Armenakis, "Group Process—Work Outcome Relationships: A Note on the Moderating Effects of Self-Esteem," *Academy of Management Journal,* September 1982, pp. 575–85.

12. See Larry Hirschhorn, *The Workplace Within: Psychodynamics of Organizational Life* (Cambridge, Mass.: MIT Press, 1988).

13. J. M. Nicholas, "Interpersonal and Group Behavior Skills Training for Crews on Space Stations," *Aviation, Space, and Environmental Medicine,* June 1989, pp. 603–8.

14. P. Amsa, "Organizational Culture and Work Group Behavior: An Empirical Study," *Journal of Management Studies,* May 1986, pp. 347–62.

15. Jill Kanin-Lovers and Jeff Boyle, "Team Incentives as a Core Management Process," *Journal of Compensation & Benefits,* July/August 1994, pp. 57–60.

16. Sharif Caudron, "Tie Individual Pay to Team Success," *Personnel Journal,* October 1994, pp. 40–46.

17. S. E. Gross and S. Safier, "Unleash the Power of Teams with Tailored Pay," *Journal of Compensation & Benefits,* July/August 1995, pp. 27–31.

18. Colleen Cooper and Mary Ploor, "The Challenges that Make or Break a Group," *Training and Development Journal,* April 1986, pp. 31–33; Connie J. G. Gersick, "Time and Transition in Work Teams: Toward a New Model of Group Development," *Academy of Management Journal,* March 1988, pp. 9–41.

19. One early analysis of group development identified four stages similar to the ones discussed here. The author appropriately labeled the four stages as *forming, storming, norming,* and *performing.* Each stage is characterized by features and activities similar to our approach. See B. W. Tuckman, "Development Sequence in Small Groups," *Psychological Bulletin,* November 1965, pp. 384–99.

20. See Steve Buchholz, Thomas Roth, and Karen Hess, eds., *Creating the High Performance Team* (San Francisco: Jossey-Bass, 1988), for several discussions.

21. "Open Communication and the Team," *Supervisory Management,* October 1994, p. 8.

22. W. E. Watson, L. K. Michaelsen, and W. Sharp, "Member Competence, Group Interaction, and Group Decision Making: A Longitudinal Study," *Journal of Applied Psychology,* December 1991, pp. 803–9.

23. E. E. Adams, "Quality Circle Performance," *Journal of Management,* March 1991, pp. 35–49.

24. Briance Mascarenhas, "Strategic Group Dynamics," *Academy of Management Journal,* June 1989, pp. 333–52.

25. See Barry Wellman and S. D. Berkowitz, eds., *Social Structures: A Network Approach* (New York: Cambridge University Press, 1988), for several discussions and examples.

26. A good reference on this and related topics is Dennis W. Organ, *Organizational Citizenship Behavior: The Good Soldier Syndrome* (Lexington, Mass.: Lexington Books, 1988).

27. Daniel C. Feldman, "The Development and Enforcement of Group Norms," *Academy of Management Review,* January 1984, pp. 47–53.

28. Adapted from Robert F. Allen and Saul Plotnick, "Confronting the Shadow Organization: How to Detect and Defeat Negative Norms," *Organizational Dynamics,* Spring 1973, pp. 6–10.

29. Florence Stone, "How to Be Part of a High-Performing Team," *Supervisory Management,* November 1994, pp. 12–13.

30. Nicole Steckler and Nanette Fondas, "Building Team Leader Effectiveness: A Diagnostic Tool," *Organizational Dynamics,* Winter 1995, pp. 20–35.

31. J. D. O'Brian, "The Informal Leader in Project Teams," *Supervisory Management,* June 1992, p. 12.

32. F. P. Flores, "Team Building and Leadership," *Supervisory Management,* April 1992, p. 8.

33. "The Team Non-Player," *Supervisory Management,* October 1994, p. 9.

34. G. Milite, "Developing a Team Culture," *Supervisory Management,* May 1992, p. 12.

35. "Even in Self-Managed Teams, There Has to Be a Leader," *Supervisory Management,* December 1994, p. 7.

36. K. A. Bollen and R. H. Hoyle, "Perceived Cohesion: A Conceptual and Empirical Examination," *Social Forces,* December 1990, pp. 479–504.

37. C. Cartwright and A. Zander, *Group Dynamics: Research and Theory* (New York: Harper & Row, 1968).

38. Irving Janis, *Victims of Groupthink: A Psychological Study of Foreign Policy Decisions and Fiascos* (Boston: Houghton Mifflin, 1973).

39. G. E. Burton, "The Measurement of Distortion Tendencies Induced by the Win–Lose Nature of In-Group Loyalty," *Small Group Research,* February 1990, pp. 128–41.

40. G. Moorhead, R. Ference, and C. P. Neck, "Group Decision Fiascos Continue: Space Shuttle Challenger and a Revised Groupthink Framework," *Human Relations,* June 1991, pp. 539–50.

41. The section on teams is based largely on discussions provided in John H. Zenger, E. Musselwhite, K. Hurson, and C. Perrin, *Leading Teams: Mastering the New Role* (Burr Ridge, Ill.: Richard D. Irwin, 1994); D. E. Hitchcock and M. L. Willard, *Why Teams Fail* (Burr Ridge, Ill.: Richard D. Irwin, 1995); J. D. Orsburn, L. Moran, E. Musselwhite, and J. H. Zenger, *Self-Directed Work Teams* (Burr Ridge, Ill.: Irwin Publishing, 1990); J. R. Katzenbach and D. K. Smith, *The Wisdom of Teams* (Boston, Mass.: Harvard Business School Press, 1993); J. H. Donnelly Jr., J. L. Gibson, and J. M. Ivancevich, *Fundamentals of Management* (Burr Ridge, Ill.: Irwin Publishing, 1995), pp. 499–500; and S. P. Robbins and D. A. DeCenzo, *Fundamentals of Management* (Englewood Cliffs, N.J.: Prentice-Hall, 1995), pp. 255–63. For a more thorough coverage of teams, readers are advised to consult these sources.

42. M. J. Stevens and M. A. Campion, "The Knowledge, Skill, and Ability Requirements for Teamwork: Implications for Human Resource Management," *Journal of Management,* vol. 20, no. 2, 1994, pp. 503–30 and "Teams Aren't Only an American Phenomenon," *Supervisory Management,* vol. 40, no. 2, 1995, p. 2.

43. J. O'Brian, "Cross-Functional Teams Build a Big Picture Attitude, *Supervisory Management,* vol. 39, no. 10, 1994, pp. 1–2.

44. W. A. Pasmore and S. Mlot, "Developing Self-Managing Work Teams: An Approach to Successful Integration," *Compensation & Benefits Review,* vol. 26, no. 4, 1994, pp. 15–23.

45. D. Abrams and R. Brown, "Self-Consciousness and Social Identity: Self-Regulation as a Group Member," *Social Psychology Quarterly,* December 1989, pp. 311–18.

46. For an analysis of some of the organizational implications of this type of conflict, see L. Roos and F. Starke, "Roles in Organizations," in *Handbook of Organizational Design,* ed. W. Starbuck and P. Nystrom (Oxford, England: Oxford University Press, 1980).

47. Jeffrey H. Greenhaus and Nicholas J. Beutell, "Sources of Conflict between Work and Family Roles," *Academy of Management Review,* January 1985, pp. 76–88.

48. Susan E. Jackson, Sheldon Zedeck, and Elizabeth Summers, "Family Life Disruptions: Effects of Job-Induced Structural and Emotional Interference," *Academy of Management Journal,* September 1985, pp. 574–86.

49. John M. Ivancevich and James H. Donnelly Jr., "A Study of Role Clarity and Need for Clarity for Three Occupational Groups," *Academy of Management Journal,* March 1974, pp. 28–36; L. Chonko, "The Relationship of Span of Control to Sales Representatives' Experienced Role Conflict and Role Ambiguity," *Academy of Management Journal,* June 1982, pp. 452–56; P. J. Nicholson, Jr., and S. C. Goh, "The Relationship of Organization Structure and Interpersonal Attitudes to Role Conflict and Ambiguity in Different Work Environments," *Academy of Management Journal,* March 1983, pp. 148–56.

CHAPTER 9

1. Clayton Alderfer and Ken J. Smith, "Studying Intergroup Relations Embedded in Organizations," *Administrative Science Quarterly,* March 1982, pp. 35–64; P. K. Edwards, *Conflict at Work* (New York: Basil Blackwell, 1987).

2. For a review of research on interpersonal conflict, see C. Morrill and C. K. Thomas, "Organizational Conflict Management as Disputing Process: The Problem of Social Escalation," *Human Communication Research,* March 1992, pp. 400–28.

3. Stephen P. Robbins, *Managing Organizational Conflict* (Englewood Cliffs, N.J.: Prentice-Hall, 1974); Robert E. Quinn, *Beyond Rational Management: Mastering the Paradoxes and Competing Demands of High Performance* (San Francisco: Jossey-Bass, 1988).

4. J. Thompson, *Organizations in Action* (New York: McGraw-Hill, 1967).

5. For example, see C. B. Chapman, D. F. Cooper, and M. J. Page, *Management for Engineers* (New York: John Wiley & Sons, 1987).

6. See D. J. Wood and B. Gray, "Toward a Comprehensive Theory of Collaboration," *Journal of Applied Behavioral Science,* June 1991, pp. 139–62, for a comprehensive review of situations where groups and organizations can choose to engage in either conflict or collaboration.

7. A. Mummendey, B. Simon, C. Dietzke, M. Grunert, G. Haeger, S. Kessler, S. Lettgen, and S. Schaferhoff, "Categorization Is Not Enough: Intergroup Discrimination in Negative Outcome Allocation," *Journal of Experimental Social Psychology,* vol. 28, 1992, pp. 125–44.

8. Karen A. Brown and Terence R. Mitchell, "Influence of Task Interdependence and Number of Poor Performers on Diagnosis of Causes of Poor Performance," *Academy of Management Journal,* June 1986, pp. 412–23; Reed E. Nelson, "The Strength of Strong Ties: Social Networks and Intergroup Conflict in Organizations," *Academy of Management Journal,* June 1989, pp. 377–401.

9. Line–staff conflict has been the subject of a great deal of research for over four decades. For representative examples, see J. A. Balasco and J. A. Alutto, "Line and Staff Conflicts: Some Empirical Insights," *Academy of Management Journal,* March 1969, p. 469–77; J. E. Sorenson and T. L. Sorenson, "The Conflict of Professionals in Bureaucratic Organizations," *Administrative Science Quarterly,* March 1974, pp. 98–106.

10. The classic work is Muzafer Sherif and Carolyn Sherif, *Groups in Harmony and Tension* (New York: Harper & Row, 1953). In a study conducted among groups in a boys' camp, they stimulated conflict between the groups and observed the changes in group behavior.

11. Edgar Schein, "Intergroup Problems in Organizations," in *Organization Development: Theory, Practice, Research,* 2nd ed., ed. Wendell French, Cecil Bell, and Robert Zawacki (Plano, Tex.: Business Publications, 1983), pp. 106–10.

12. M. A. Rahim, J. E. Garrett, and G. F. Buntzman, "Ethics of Managing Interpersonal Conflict in Organizations," *Journal of Business Ethics,* vol. 11, 1992, pp. 423–32.

13. William L. Ury, Jeanne M. Brett, and Stephen Goldberg, *Getting Disputes Resolved: Designing Systems to Cut the Costs of Conflict* (San Francisco: Jossey-Bass, 1988).

14. J. Firth, "A Proactive Approach to Conflict Resolution," *Supervisory Management,* November 1991, p. 3.

15. M. O. Stephenson, Jr., and G. M. Pops, "Conflict Resolution Methods and the Policy Process," *Public Administration Review,* September–October 1989, pp. 463–73.

16. Also see Robbins, *Managing Organizational Conflict,* pp. 67–77; M. Afzalur Rahim, ed., *Managing Conflict: An Interdisciplinary Approach* (New York: Praeger, 1989).

17. Muzafer Sherif and Carolyn Sherif, *Social Psychology* (New York: Harper & Row, 1969), pp. 228–62. Sherif and Sherif conducted sociopsychological experiments to determine effective ways of resolving conflict. Based on this research, they developed the concept of superordinate goals.

18. D. H. Weiss, "Barriers Created by Team Leaders," *Supervisory Management,* May 1992, pp. 6–8.

19. G. Milite, "When the Team Becomes Too Human," *Supervisory Management,* May 1992, p. 9.

20. For a discussion of the link between conflict management strategies and concern for the needs of others, see G. S. Hammock and D. R. Richardson, "Aggression as One Response to Conflict," *Journal of Applied Social Psychology,* vol. 22, no. 4, 1992, pp. 298–311.

21. M. A. Neale and Max H. Bazerman, "The Effects of Framing and Negotiator Overconfidence on Bargaining Behavior and Outcomes," *Academy of Management Journal,* March 1985, pp. 34–49.

22. D. A. Lax and J. K. Sebenius, *The Manager as Negotiator* (New York: Free Press, 1986), chap. 1.

23. T. Anderson, "Step into My Parlor: A Survey of Strategies and Techniques for Effective Negotiation," *Business Horizons,* May–June 1992, pp. 71–76.

24. Lax and Sebenius, *The Manager as Negotiator.*

25. M. Zetlin, "The Art of Negotiating," *Success!,* June 1986, pp. 34–39.

26. R. Dawson, "Resolving Angry Disagreements," *Supervisory Management,* January 1989, pp. 13–16.

27. J. Grenig, "Better Communication Spells Success in Negotiations," *Impact,* December 2, 1985, pp. 6–7.

28. Zetlin, "The Art of Negotiating."

29. Ibid.

30. C. W. Barlow and G. P. Eisen, *Purchasing Negotiations* (Boston: CBI Publishing, 1983), chap. 5.

31. J. A. Wall Jr., and M. W. Blum, "Negotiations," *Journal of Management,* vol. 17, 1991, pp. 273–303.

32. G. Dangot-Simpkin, "Eight Attitudes to Develop to Hone Your Negotiating Skills," *Supervisory Management,* February 1992, p. 10.

33. Barlow and Eisen, *Purchasing Negotiations.*

34. D. G. Pruitt, J. M. Magenau, E. Konar-Goldband, and P. J. Carnevale, "Effects of Trust, Aspiration, and Gender on Negotiation Tactics," *Journal of Personality and Social Psychology* 38, no. 1, 1980, pp. 9–22.

35. J. D'O'Brian, "Negotiating with Peers: Consensus Not Power," *Supervisory Management,* January 1992, p. 4.

36. G. R. Shell, "When Is It Legal to Lie in Negotiations?" *Sloan Management Review,* Spring 1991, pp. 93–101.

37. Grenig, "Better Communication."

38. L. G. Greenhaigh, "Secrets of Managing People Much, Much More Effectively," *Boardroom Reports,* November 1, 1989, pp. 13–14.

39. B. Rodgers, *The IBM Way: Insights into the World's Most Successful Organization* (New York: Harper & Row, 1986).

40. "The Payoff from Teamwork," *Business Week,* July 10, 1989, pp. 56–60.

41. A Desreumaux, "OD Practices in France: Part I," *Leadership and Organization Development Journal,* vol. 6, no. 4, 1985, p. 29; A Desremaux, "OD Practices in France: Part II," *Leadership and Organization Development Journal,* vol. 7, no. 1, 1986, pp. 10–14; and Joanne C. Preston and Terry R. Armstrong, "Team Building in South Africa: Cross Cultural Synergy in Action," *Public Administration Quarterly,* Spring 1991, pp. 65–82.

42. Richard W. Woodman and John J. Sherwood, "Effects of Team Development Intervention: A Field Experiment," *Journal of Applied Behavioral Science,* April–May–June 1980, pp. 211–17; and R. Wayne Boss, "Organizational Development in the Health-Care Field: A Confrontational Team Building Design," *Journal of Health and Human Resources Administration,* Summer 1983, pp. 72–91.

43. Paul D. Howes and Michael B. Jones, "Impact of 1992 on Benefits and Compensation Plans," *Journal of Compensation and Benefits,* January–February 1990, pp. 229–32.

44. Richard L. Hughes, William E. Rosenbach, and William H. Clover, "Team Development in Intact, Ongoing Work Group," *Group and Organizational Studies,* June 1983, pp. 161–81.

45. Bernard A. Rausch, "Dupont Transforms a Division's Culture," *Management Review,* March 1989, pp. 37–42.

46. Adapted from Jack D. Orsburn, Linda Moran, Ed Musselwhite, John H. Zenger, and Craig Perrin, *Self-Directed Work Teams,* (Burr Ridge, Ill.: Irwin Professional Publishing, 1990), p. 23; and Darcy E. Hitchcock and Marsha L. Willard, *Why Teams Can Fail* (Burr Ridge, Ill.: Irwin Professional Publishing, 1995), chaps. 2–3.

47. R. M. Marsh, "The Difference between Participation and Power in Japanese Factories," *Industrial and Labor Relations Review,* January 1992, pp. 250–57.

48. Robbins, *Managing Organizational Conflict,* chap. 9.

CHAPTER 10

1. See Iain Mangham, *Power and Performance in Organizations* (New York: Basil Blackwell, 1988), for a discussion of power in organizations.

2. J. Pfeffer, "Understanding Power in Organizations," *California Management Review,* Winter 1992, pp. 29–50.

3. Anthony T. Cobb, "Political Diagnosis: Applications in Organizational Development," *Academy of Management Review,* July 1986, pp. 482–96.

4. Robert Dahl, "The Concept of Power," *Behavioral Science,* July 1957, pp. 202–3.

5. "The Perils of Inadequate Leadership," *Harvard Business Review,* September/October 1994, p. 137.

6. Max Weber, *Theory of Social and Economic Organization* (New York: Free Press, 1947), pp. 324–28.

7. Henry Mintzberg, *Power in and around Organizations* (Englewood Cliffs, N.J.: Prentice-Hall, 1983), p. 5; Henry Mintzberg, "Power and Organization Life Cycles," *Academy of Management Review,* April 1984, pp. 207–24.

8. John R. P. French and Bertram Raven, "The Basis of Social Power," in *Studies in Social Power,* ed. D. Cartwright (Ann Arbor: Institute for Social Research, University of Michigan, 1959), pp. 150–67.

9. A. Halcrow, "Rules of the Game," *Personnel Journal,* March 1995, p. 4.

10. J. Blasi, J. Gasawat, and D. Kruse, "Employees and Managers as Shareholders," *Human Resource Planning,* Vol. 17, no. 4, 1994, pp. 57–67.

11. A. J. Vogl, "Tough Guy," *Across the Board.* February 1995, pp. 15–19.

12. A. J. Stahelski, D. E. Frost, and M. E. Patch, "Uses of Socially Dependent Bases of Power: French and Raven's Theory Applied to Workgroup Leadership," *Journal of Applied Social Psychology,* March 1989, pp. 283–97.

13. J. Warham, "Eight Steps to Charisma," *Across the Board,* April 1994, pp. 49–50.

14. G. Yukl and C. M. Falbe, "Importance of Different Power Sources in Downward and Lateral Relations," *Journal of Applied Psychology,* June 1991, pp. 416–23.

15. J. A. Halpert, "The Dimensionality of Charisma," *Journal of Business and Psychology,* Summer 1990, pp. 399–410; and A. M. Rahim, "Relationships of Leader Power to Compliance and Satisfaction with Supervision: Evidence from a National Sample of Managers," *Journal of Management,* December 1989, pp. 545–56.

16. B. R. Ragins and E. Sundstrom, "Gender and Perceived Power in Manager–Subordinate Relations," *Journal of Occupational Psychology,* December 1990, pp. 273–87.

17. E. A. Fagenson, "Perceived Masculine and Feminine Attributes Examined as a Function of Individuals' Sex and Level in the Organizational Power Hierarchy: A Test of Four Theoretical Perspectives," *Journal of Applied Psychology,* April 1990, pp. 204–11.

18. David Kipnis, *The Powerholders* (Chicago: University of Chicago Press, 1976), pp. 149–56. Kipnis doesn't present these characteristics as fitting all power seekers but only as a summarization of the negative face of power seekers.

19. David C. McClelland, *Power: The Inner Experience* (New York: Irvington, 1975), p. 7.

20. D. McClelland and D. Burnham, "Power Is the Great Motivator," *Harvard Business Review,* January/February 1995, pp. 126–39.

21. J. T. Knippen and T. B. Green, "Dealing with an Insecure Boss," *Supervisory Management,* March 1995, p. 14.

22. Jeffrey Pfeffer, *Power in Organizations* (Marshfield, Mass.: Pitman, 1981), p. 117; Dean Tjosvold, "Power and Social Context in Superior–Subordinate Interaction," *Organizational Behavior and Human Decision Processes,* Summer 1985, pp. 281–93.

23. Pfeffer, *Power,* pp. 104–22; Rosabeth M. Kanter, "Power Failures in Management Circuits," *Harvard Business Review,* July–August 1979, pp. 65–75; Hugh R. Taylor, "Power at Work," *Personnel Journal,* April 1986, pp. 42–49.

24. R. Kanter, "Power Failures."

25. David Ulrich and Jay B. Barney, "Perspectives in Organizations: Resource Dependence, Efficiency, and Population," *Academy of Management Review,* July 1984, pp. 471–81.

26. For a study of dependency between organizations, see Steven S. Skinner, James H. Donnelly Jr., and John M. Ivancevich, "Effects of Transactional Form on Environmental Linkages and Power-Dependence Relations," *Academy of Management Journal,* September 1987, pp. 577–88.

27. For a discussion of the resource issue in a nonbusiness setting, see William McKinley, Joseph L. C. Cheng, and Allen G. Schnick, "Perception of Resource Criticality in Times of Resource Scarcity: The Case of University Departments," *Academy of Management Journal,* September 1986, pp. 621–31.

28. R. N. Ashkenas, "Beyond Fads: How Leaders Drive Change with Results," *Human Resource Planning,* vol. 17, no. 2, 1994, pp. 25–44.

29. J. T. Knippen and T. B. Green, "What to Do about a Boss Who Makes Decisions Too Fast," *Supervisory Management,* April 1994, p. 6.

30. L. Landes, "The Myth and Misdirection of Employee Empowerment," *Training,* March 1994, p. 116.

31. J. Dobos, M. H. Bahniul, and S. E. Kogler Hill, "Power Gaining Communication Strategies and Career Success," *The Southern Communication Journal,* Fall 1991, pp. 35–48.

32. R. Tagiuri, "Ten Essential Behaviors," *Harvard Business Review,* January/February 1995, pp. 10–11 and "The Danger of Becoming Overdependent on a Staff Member," *Supervisory Management,* July 1995, p. 4.

33. Gary Yukl and Tom Taber, "The Effective Use of Managerial Power," *Personnel,* March–April 1983, pp. 37–44; Henry Mintzberg, "The Organization of Political Arena," *Journal of Management Studies,* March 1985, pp. 135–54.

34. Lyman W. Porter, Robert W. Allen, and H. L. Angee, "The Politics of Upward Influence in Organizations," in *Research in Organizational Behavior,* ed. Larry L. Cummings and Barry M. Staw (Greenwich, Conn.: JAI Press, 1981), pp. 181–216.

35. For excellent discussions of upward influence, see L. Atwater, P. Roush, and A. Fischtal, "The Influence of Upward Feedback on Self- and Follower Ratings of Leadership," *Personnel Psychology,* Spring 1995, pp. 35–59.

36. For an interesting discussion of this and related topics, see Robert C. Liden and Terence R. Mitchell, "Ingratiating Behaviors in Organizational Settings," *Academy of Management Review,* October 1988, pp. 572–87.

37. R. P. Vecchio and M. Sussman, "Choice of Influence Tactics: Individual and Organizational Determinants," *Journal of Organizational Behavior,* vol. 12, 1991, pp. 73–80.

38. Michel Crozier, *The Bureaucratic Phenomenon* (Chicago: University of Chicago Press, 1964).

39. C. R. Hinnings, D. J. Hickson, J. M. Pennings, and R. E. Schneck, "Structural Conditions of Intraorganizational Power," *Administrative Science Quarterly,* March 1974, pp. 22–44.

40. D. J. Hickson, C. R. Hinnings, C. A. Lee, R. E. Schneck, and J. M. Pennings, "A Strategic Contingency Theory of Intraorganizational Power," *Administrative Science Quarterly,* June 1971, pp. 216–29.

41. Hinnings et al., "Structural Conditions," p. 39.

42. Richard L. Daft, *Organization Theory and Design* (St. Paul, Minn.: West, 1983), pp. 392–98. This source contains an excellent discussion of the strategic contingency perspective in terms of managerial and organizational theory. Daft concisely presents the original Hickson et al. theory and research.

43. Hinnings et al., "Structural Conditions," p. 41.

44. Ibid., p. 40.

45. C. S. Saunders, "The Strategic Contingencies Theory of Power: Multiple Perspectives," *Journal of Management Studies,* January 1990, pp. 1–18.

46. Stanley Milgram, "Behavioral Study of Obedience," *Journal of Abnormal and Social Psychology,* October 1963, pp. 371–78; Stanley Milgram, *Obedience to Authority* (New York: Harper & Row, 1974). For a more recent discussion of the concept of obedience, see N. Woolsey, B. Gary, and G. Hamilton, "The Power of Obedience," *Administrative Science Quarterly,* December 1984, pp. 540–49.

47. Milgram, "Behavioral Study," p. 377.

48. K. Macher, "The Politics of People," *Personnel Journal,* January 1986, pp. 50–53.

49. Dan L. Madison, Robert W. Allen, Lyman W. Porter, Patricia A. Renwick, and Bronston T. Mayes, "Organizational Politics: An Exploration of Managers' Perceptions," *Human Relations,* February 1980, pp. 79–100; Jeffrey Gantz and Victor V. Murray, "The Experience of Workplace Politics," *Academy of Management Journal,* June 1980, pp. 237–51; Robert W. Allen, Dan L. Madison, Lyman W. Porter, Patricia A. Renwick, and Bronston T. Mayes, "Organizational Politics: Tactics and Characteristics of Its Actors," *California Management Review,* 1979, pp. 77–83.

50. George Strauss, "Tactics of the Lateral Relationship: The Purchasing Agent," *Administrative Science Quarterly,* 1962, pp. 161–86.

51. Allen et al., "Organizational Politics."

52. For a complete description of the profile of a political manager, see C. Kirchmeyer, "A Profile of Managers Active in Office Politics," *Basic and Applied Social Psychology,* September 1990, pp. 339–56.

53. B. E. Ashforth and R. T. Lee, "Defensive Behavior in Organizations: A Preliminary Model," *Human Relations,* July 1990, pp. 621–48.

54. For a complete and interesting discussion of political games, refer to Mintzberg, *Power in and around Organizations,* chap. 13.

55. William B. Stevenson, Jane L. Pearce, and Lyman W. Porter, "The Concept of Coalition in Organization Theory and Research," *Academy of Management Review,* April 1985, pp. 256–68.

56. M. P. Miceli, J. P. Near, "Whistleblowing: Reaping the Benefits," *Academy of Management Executive,* August 1994, pp. 65–72.

57. Marcia P. Miceli and Janet P. Near, "The Incidence of Wrongdoing, Whistle-Blowing, and Retaliation: Results of a Naturally Occurring Field Experiment," *Employee Responsibilities and Rights Journal,* June 1989, pp. 91–108.

58. Gerald F. Cavanagh, Denis J. Moberg, and Manuel Velasquez, "The Ethics of Organizational Politics," *Academy of Management Review,* July 1981, pp. 363–74; Manuel Velasquez, Denis J. Moberg, and Gerald F. Cavanagh, "Organizational Statesmanship and Dirty Politics." Also see "Collegians Speak Out on Ethical Issues," *Collegiate Edition Marketing News,* January 1988, pp. 1, 4.

CHAPTER 11

1. Bernard M. Bass, *Stogdill's Handbook of Leadership* (New York: Free Press, 1990), p. 21.

2. Richard A. Barker, "How Can We Train Leaders If We Do Not Know What Leadership Is?" *Human Relations,* April 1997, pp. 343–62.

3. For example, see Ricardo Sember, "Managing without Managers," *Harvard Business Review,* September–October 1989, pp. 76–84 for the view that leaders are often not needed and Steven R. Davis, Jay H. Lucas, and Donald R. Marcotte, "GM Links Better Leaders to Better Business," *Workforce,* April 1998, pp. 62–68 for the contrary view.

4. Jill L. Shearer, "Lessons in Leadership," *Healthcare Executive,* March/April 1998, pp. 12–17; George B. Weathers, "Seventy-five Years of Leadership," *Management Review,* May 1998, p. 23; and Robert N. Frerichs, "Learning from Successful High-Tech CEO's," *Directors and Boards,* Spring 1998, p. 41.

5. Ralph M. Stogdill, *Handbook of Leadership* (New York: Free Press, 1974), pp. 43–44.

6. Edwin E. Ghiselli, *Exploration in Managerial Talent* (Santa Monica, Calif.: Goodyear, 1971) and Rob R. Meijer, "Consistency of Rest Behaviour and Individual Differences in Precision Prediction," *Journal of Occupational and Organizational Psychology,* June 1998, pp. 147–60 for a report of recent method validation studies.

7. Michael S. Frank, "The Essence of Leadership," *Public Personnel Management,* Fall 1993, pp. 381–89 reviews this literature.

8. Edwin E. Ghiselli, "The Validity of Management Traits in Relation to Occupational Level," *Personnel Psychology,* Summer 1963, pp. 109–13.

9. Shelley A. Kirkpatrick and Edwin A. Locke, "Leadership: Do Traits Matter?" *The Executive,* May 1991, pp. 48–60 and Andrew Kinder and Ivan T. Robertson, "Do You Have the Personality to Be a Leader?" *Leadership and Organizational Development,* vol. 15, no. 1 (1994), pp. 3–12.

10. Peter A. Topping, "On Being a Leader," *Business & Economic Review,* April–June 1997, pp. 14–16.

11. Kirkpatrick and Locke, "Leadership: Do Traits Matter?"

12. Ralph M. Stogdill, "Personal Factors Associated With Leadership," *Journal of Applied Psychology,* January, 1948 p. 72.

13. Rensis Likert, *New Patterns of Management* (New York: McGraw-Hill, 1961).

14. For a review of the studies, see Stogdill, *Handbook of Leadership,* chap. 11. Also see E. A. Fleishman, "The Measurement of Leadership Attitudes in Industry," *Journal of Applied Psychology,* June 1953, pp. 153–58; C. L. Shartle, *Executive Performance and Leadership* (Englewood Cliffs, N.J.: Prentice-Hall, 1956); E. A. Fleishman, E. F. Harris, and H. E. Burtt, *Leadership and Supervision in Industry* (Columbus: Bureau of Educational Research, Ohio State University, 1955).

15. Fleishman et al., *Leadership and Supervision.*

16. G. H. Dobbins and S. J. Platz, "Sex Differences in Leadership: How Real Are They?" *Academy of Management Review,* January 1986, pp. 118–27.

17. E. A. Fleishman, "Twenty Years of Consideration and Structure," in *Current Developments in the Study of Leadership,* ed. E. A. Fleishman and J. C. Hunt (Carbondale: Southern Illinois University Press, 1973).

18. G. Bellman, *The Quest for Staff Leadership* (Glenview, Ill.: Scott, Foresman, 1986).

19. D. K. Carew, E. Parisi-Carew, and K. H. Blanchard, "Group Development and Situational Leadership: A Model for Managing Groups," *Training and Development Journal,* June 1986, pp. 46–50.

20. The discussion that follows is based on R. Tannenbaum and W. H. Schmidt, "How to Choose a Leadership Pattern," *Harvard Business Review,* May–June 1973, pp. 162–80.

21. Ibid., p. 180.

22. Fred E. Fiedler, *A Theory of Leadership Effectiveness* (New York: McGraw-Hill, 1967).

23. Fred E. Fiedler and M. M. Chemers, *Leadership and Effective Management* (Glenview, Ill.: Scott, Foresman, 1974).

24. Fred E. Fiedler, "How Do You Make Leaders More Effective: New Answers to an Old Puzzle," *Organizational Dynamics,* Autumn 1972, pp. 3–8.

25. Fred E. Fiedler and M. M. Chemers, *Improving Leadership Effectiveness: The LEADER MATCH Concept* (New York: John Wiley & Sons, 1984).

26. G. Graen, J. B. Orris, and K. M. Alvares, "Contingency Model of Leadership Effectiveness: Some Experimental Results," *Journal of Applied Psychology,* June 1971, pp. 196–201.

27. Chester A. Schriesheim, Bennett J. Tepper, and Linda A. Tetrault, "Least-Preferred Co-Worker Scale, Situational Control, and Leadership Effectiveness: A Meta-Analysis of Contingency Model Performance Predictions," *Journal of Applied Psychology,* August, 1994, pp. 561–73.

28. J. Kelly, *Organizational Behavior: Its Data, First Principles, and Applications* (Homewood, Ill.: Richard D. Irwin, 1980), p. 367.

29. Robert J. House, "A Path-Goal Theory of Leadership Effectiveness," *Administrative Science Quarterly,* September 1971, pp. 321–39; Robert J. House and Terence R. Mitchell, "Path-Goal Theory of Leadership," *Journal of Contemporary Business,* Autumn 1974, pp. 81–98.

30. M. G. Evans, "The Effects of Supervisory Behavior on the Path-Goal Relationship," *Organizational Behavior and Human Performance,* May 1970, pp. 277–98.

31. Robert J. House and G. Dessler, "The Path-Goal Theory of Leadership: Some Post Hoc and A Priori Tests," in *Contingency Approaches to Leadership,* ed. J. G. Hunt (Carbondale: Southern Illinois University Press, 1974).

32. Robert T. Keller, "A Test of the Path-Goal Theory of Leadership with Need for Clarity as a Moderator in Research and Development Organizations," *Journal of Applied Psychology,* April 1989, pp. 208–12.

33. House and Mitchell, "The Path-Goal Theory," p. 84.

34. House and Dessler, "The Path-Goal Theory."

35. C. Greene, "Questions of Causation in the Path-Goal Theory of Leadership," *Academy of Management Journal,* March 1979, pp. 22–41.

36. C. A. Schriesheim and A. DeNisi, "Task Dimensions as Moderators of the Effects of Instrumental Leadership: A Two-Sample Replicated Test of Path-Goal Leadership Theory," *Journal of Applied Psychology,* October 1981, pp. 589–97.

37. Originally published in Paul Hersey and Kenneth H. Blanchard, *Management of Organizational Behavior: Utilizing Human Resources* (Englewood Cliffs, N.J.: Prentice-Hall, 1969). Now in 6th edition, which discussed readiness.

38. Gary Yukl and Cecilia M. Falbe, "Importance of Different Power Sources in Downward and Lateral Relations," *Journal of Applied Psychology,* June 1991, pp. 416–23.

39. John F. Monoky, "What's Your Management Style?" *Industrial Distribution,* June 1998, p. 142, and Kenneth H. Blanchard and Bob Nelson, "Recognition and Reward," *Executive Excellence,* April 1997, p. 15.

40. The Leader Behavior Analysis scales and instructions are available from Blanchard Training and Development, Inc., 125 State Place, Escondido, Calif. 92025. See John K. Butler, "Assessing the Situations of the LEAD," *Organization Development Journal,* Winter, 1993, pp. 33–42.

41. William R. Norris and Robert Vecchio, "Situational Leadership: A Replication," *Group and Organization Management,* September, 1992, pp. 331–342, and Warren Blank, John R. Weitzel, and Stephen G. Green, "A Test of the Situational Theory," *Personnel Psychology,* Fall 1990, pp. 579–97.

42. George Graen, "Role-Making Processes with Complex Organizations," in *Handbook of Industrial Organizational Psychology,* ed. M. D. Dunnette (Chicago: Rand McNally, 1976), pp. 1210–59. Charlotte R. Gerstner and David V. Day provide an excellent summary of contemporary research related to LMX theory in "Meta-Analytic Review of Leader–Member Exchange Theory: Correlates and Construct Issues," *Journal of Applied Psychology,* December 1997, pp. 827–44.

43. George Graen, R. Liden, and W. Hoel, "Role of Leadership in the Employee Withdrawal Process," *Journal of Applied Psychology,* 1982, pp. 868–72.

44. Steve W. J. Kozlowski and Mary L. Doherty, "Integration of Climate and Leadership Examination of a Neglected Issue," *Journal of Applied Psychology,* August 1989, pp. 546–53.

45. Antoinette S. Phillips and Arthur G. Bedeian, "Leader–Follower Exchange Quality: The Role of Personal and Interpersonal Attributes," *Academy of Management Journal,* August 1994, pp. 990–1001.

46. Ronald J. Deluga, "Supervisory Trust-Building, Leader–Member Exchange and Organizational Citizenship Behavior," *Journal of Occupational and Organizational Psychology,* December 1994, pp. 315–326.

CHAPTER 12

1. Andrew J. DuBrin, *Leadership: Research Findings, Practice, and Skills* (Boston: Houghton Mifflin, 1995) pp. 5–9.

2. Milam Moravec, Jan Johannessen, and Thor A. Hjelmas, "The Well-Managed Self-Managed Team, *Management Review,* June 1998, pp. 56–60.

3. Tom Peters, *Thriving on Chaos* (New York: Knopf, 1987), p. 264.

4. Karen Boehnke, Andrea C. DiStefano, Joseph J. DiStefano, and Nick Bontis, "Leadership for Extraordinary Performance," *Business Quarterly,* Summer 1997, pp. 56–63.

5. Victor Vroom and Philip Yetton, *Leadership and Decision Making* (Pittsburgh: University of Pittsburgh Press, 1973).

6. Victor H. Vroom and Arthur G. Jago, *The New Leadership: Managing Participation in Organizations* (Englewood Cliffs, N.J.: Prentice-Hall, 1988).

7. Victor H. Vroom and Arthur G. Jago, "On the Validity of the Vroom-Yetton Model," *Journal of Applied Psychology,* April 1978, pp. 151–62; R. H. G. Field, "A Test of the Vroom-Yetton Normative Model of Leadership," *Journal of Applied Psychology,* October 1982, pp. 523–32; Arthur G. Jago and Victor H. Vroom, "Predicting Leader Behavior from a Measure of Behavior Intent," *Academy of Management Journal,* December 1987, pp. 715–21;

William R. Pasewark and Jerry R. Strawser. "Subordinate Participation in Audit Budgeting Decisions," *Decision Sciences,* March/April 1994, pp. 281–299.

8. Victor H. Vroom and Arthur G. Jago, *The New Leadership: Cases and Manuals for Use in Leadership Training* (New Haven, Conn.: Yale University Press, 1987). Authors retain all rights for decision trees, cases, and computer software.

9. W. Bohnisch, Arthur G. Jago, and G. Reber, "Zur interkulturellen Validitat des Vroom/Yetton Models," *Bebriebsivirtschaft,* 1987, pp. 85–93.

10. C. Margerison and R. Gluf, "Leadership Decision-Making: An Empirical Test of the Vroom and Yetton Model," *Journal of Management Studies,* 1979, pp. 45–55.

11. John B. Kelley, "The Validity and Usefulness of Theories in an Emerging Science," *Academy of Management Review,* 1984, pp. 296–306. See F. William Brown and Kenn Finstuen, "The Use of Participation in Decision Making: A Consideration of the Vroom-Yetton and Vroom-Jago Normative Models," *Journal of Behavioral Decision Making,* September 1993, pp. 207–19.

12. Marvin D. Dunnette and Leaetta M. Hough, eds., *Handbook of Industrial and Organizational Psychology,* (Palo Alto, CA: Consulting Psychologists Press, 1992), pp. 165–68.

13. Gary Yukl, *Leadership in Organizations* (Englewood Cliffs, NJ: Prentice-Hall, Inc., 1994), pp. 241–2; S. G. Green and Terence R. Mitchell, "Attributional Processes of Leaders in Leader–Member Interactions," *Organizational Behavior and Human Performance,* June 1979, pp. 429–58.

14. Terence R. Mitchell, S. C. Green, and Robert E. Wood, "An Attributional Model of Leadership and the Poor Performing Subordinate: Development and Validation," in *Research in Organizational Behavior,* ed. Barry M. Staw and Larry L. Cummings (Greenwich, Conn.: JAI Press, 1981).

15. Henry P. Sims Jr. and Peter Lorenzi, *The New Leadership Paradigm* (Newburg Park, Calif.: Sage, 1992), p. 221; James C. McElroy, "Attribution Theory Applied to Leadership," *Journal of Managerial Issues,* Spring, 1991, pp. 90–106.

16. Terence P. Mitchell and Robert E. Wood, "An Empirical Test of an Attributional Model of Leader's Responses to Poor Performance," in *Academy of Management Proceedings,* ed. Richard C. Huseman, 1979, pp. 94–98.

17. G. H. Dobbins, E. C. Pence, J. A. Organ, and J. A. Sgro, "The Effects of Sex of the Leader and Sex of the Subordinate on the Use of Organizational Control Policy," *Organizational Behavior and Human Performance,* December 1983, pp. 325–43.

18. Mark J. Martinko, ed., *Attribution Theory: An Organizational Perspective* (Boca Raton, FL.: Saint Lucie Press, 1995).

19. Robert E. Ployhart and Ann Marie Ryan, "Toward an Explanation of Applicant Reactions: An Examination of Organizational Justice and Attribution Frameworks," *Organizational Behavior and Human Decision Processes,* December 1997, pp. 308–35.

20. William S. Silver, Terence R. Mitchell, and Marilyn E. Gist, "Responses to Successful and Unsuccessful Performance: The Moderating Effects of Self-Efficacy on the Relationship Between Performance and Attributions," *Organizational Behavior and Human Decision Processes,* June, 1995, pp. 286–99.

21. C. N. Greene, "The Reciprocal Nature of Influence between Leader and Subordinate," *Journal of Applied Psychology,* April 1975, pp. 187–93.

22. Nancy DiTomaso, "Weber's Social History and Etzioni's Structural Theory of Charisma in Organizations: Implications for Thinking about Charismatic Leadership," *Leadership Quarterly,* vol. 4, no. 3 (1993), pp. 257–75.

23. John Sculley, "Sculley's Lessons from Inside Apple," *Fortune,* September 14, 1987, pp. 108–11. Also see James C. Collins and Jerry I. Porras, "Building a Visionary Company," *California Management Review,* Winter 1995, pp. 80–100.

24. Boas Shamir, Eliav Zakay, Esther Breinen, and Micha Popper, "Correlates of Charismatic Leader Behavior in Military Units: Subordinate's Attitudes, Unit Characteristics, and Superiors' Appraisals of Leader Performance," *Academy of Management Journal,* August 1998, pp. 387–409.

25. Robert J. House, "A 1976 Theory of Charismatic Leadership," in *Leadership: The Cutting Edge,* ed. J. G. Hunt and L. L. Larson (Carbondale: Southern Illinois University Press, 1977), pp. 189–207.

26. His views of charismatic leadership are clearly presented in Jay A. Conger, *The Charismatic Leader* (San Francisco: Jossey-Bass, 1989) and Jay A. Conger and Rabindra N. Kanunga, "Charismatic Leadership in Organizations: Perceived Behavioral Attributes and Their Measurement," *Journal of Organizational Behavior,* September 1994, pp. 439–52.

27. William L. Gardner and Bruce J. Avolio, "The Charismatic Relationship: A Dramaturgical Perspective," *Academy of Management Review,* January 1998, pp. 12–58.

28. Jay A. Conger, "The Necessary Art of Persuasion," *Harvard Business Review,* May/June 1998, pp. 84–95; Bernard M. Bass, *Leadership Performance beyond Expectations* (New York: Academic Press, 1985); Warren G. Bennis and Burt Nanus, *Leaders* (New York: Harper & Row, 1985).

29. J. M. Bryson, "A Perspective on Planning and Crisis in the Public Sector," *Strategic Management Journal,* 1981, pp. 181–96.

30. S. Fink, *Crisis Management* (New York: AMACOM, 1986); Ian I. Mitroff, Paul Shrivastava, and Firdaus E. Udivadia, "Effective Crisis Management," *Academy of Management Executive,* November 1987, pp. 283–92.

31. Badrinnaryan Shankar Pawar and Kenneth K. Eastman, "The Nature and Implications of Contextual Influences on Transformational Leadership: A Conceptual Examination," *Academy of Management Review,* January 1997, pp. 80–109.

32. B. Hedberg, "How Organizations Learn and Unlearn," in *Handbook of Organizational Design,* ed. P. C. Nystrom and W. H. Starbuck (London: Oxford University Press, 1980), pp. 3–37.

33. Daniel Sankowsky, "The Charismatic Leader as Narcissist: Understanding the Abuse of Power," *Organizational Dynamics,* Spring 1995, pp. 57–71; Jane M. Howell and Bruce J. Avolio, "The Ethics of Charismatic Leadership: Submission or Liberation?" *The Executive,* May 1992, pp. 43–54.

34. Allan H. Church and Janine Waclawski, "The Relationship between Individual Personality Orientation and Executive Leadership Behaviour," *Journal of Occupational and Organizational Psychology,* June 1998, pp. 99–125.

35. D. Yankelovich and J. Immerivoki, *Putting the Work Ethic to Work* (New York: Public Agenda Foundation, 1983).

36. J. C. Wofford, Vicki Goodwin, and J. Lee Whittington, "A Field Study of a Cognitive Approach to Understanding Transformational and Transactional Leadership," *Leadership Quarterly,* vol. 9, no. 1 (1998) pp. 55–84. James M. Burns, *Leadership* (New York: Harper & Row, 1978) popularized the distinction in this classic work.

37. Bruce J. Avolio and Bernard M. Bass, "Transformational Leadership, Charisma, and Beyond," in *Emerging Leadership Vistas,* ed. James G. Hunt, B. Rajaram Baliga, H. Peter Dachler, and Chester A. Schriesheim (Lexington, Mass.: Lexington Books, 1988), pp. 29–49.

38. Jay Clarke, "Disney World Grows Like Pinocchio's Nose," *Houston Chronicle,* March 6, 1988, p. 9.

39. Ross Groves, *The Disney Touch* (Homewood, Ill.: Business One Irwin, 1991).

40. Bass, *Leadership Performance;* Deanne N. Den Hartog, Muijap Van, J. Jaap, and Paul L. Koopman, "Transactional versus Transformational Leadership: An Analysis of the MLQ," *Journal of Occupational and Organizational Psychology,* March 1997, pp. 19–34 test and extend the underlying methodology to identify these two leadership patterns.

41. Ibid., p. 31.

42. Jan P. Howell, Peter W. Dorfman, and Steven Kerr, "Moderator Variables in Leadership Research," *Academy of Management Review,* January 1986, pp. 88–102.

43. Steven Kerr and John M. Jermier, "Substitutes for Leadership: Their Meaning and Measurement," *Organizational Behavior and Human Performance,* December 1978, pp. 376–403; Scott Williams, "Personality and Self-Leadership," *Human Resource Management Review,* Summer 1997, pp. 139–55.

44. Ibid.

45. Richard S. Lapidus, James A. Chonko, and Lawrence R. Chonko, "Stressors, Leadership Substitutes, and Relations with Supervision," *Industrial Marketing Management,* May 1997, pp. 255–69.

CHAPTER 13

1. Christopher Gresov and Robert Drazin, "Equifinality: Functional Equivalence in Organization Design," *Academy of Management Review,* April 1997, pp. 403–28.

2. L. Ubo Sitter, J. Frisco den Hertog, and Ben Dankbar, "From Complex Organizations with Simple Jobs to Simple Organizations with Complex Jobs," *Human Relations,* May 1997, pp. 497–534.

3. William A. Nowlin, "Restructuring in Manufacturing: Management, Work, and Labor Relations," *Industrial Management,* November–December 1990, pp. 5–9.

4. Dean Minderman, "Big Blues" *Credit Union Management,* February 1995, pp. 15–17; "Surprise! The New IBM Really Looks New," *Business Week,* May 18, 1992, pp. 124, 126.

5. Margaret R. Davis and David A. Weckler, *A Practical Guide to Organization Design* (Menlo Park, CA: Crisp Publications, 1997)

6. Ronald A. Heiner, "Imperfect Decisions in Organizations: Toward a Theory of Internal Structures," *Journal of Economic Behavior and Organization,* January 1988, pp. 25–44.

7. Greg R. Oldham and J. Richard Hackman, "Relationship between Organizational Structure and Employee Reactions: Comparing Alternative Frameworks," *Administrative Science Quarterly,* March 1981, pp. 66–83.

8. James C. Dumville and Francisco A. Torano, "Division of Labor, Efficient? Empirical Evidence to Support the Argument," *SAM Advanced Management Journal,* Spring 1997, pp. 16–20.

9. Donald J. Campbell, "Task Complexity: A Review and Analysis," *Academy of Management Review,* January 1988, pp. 40–52.

10. "No More Mr. Nice Guy at P&G—Not by a Long Shot," *Business Week,* February 3, 1992, pp. 54–55.

11. James R. Treece and John Templeman, "Jack Smith Is Already on a Tear at GM," *Business Week,* May 11, 1992, p. 37.

12. Joseph T. Mahoney, "The Adoption of the Multidivisional Form of Organization: A Contingency Approach," *Journal of Management,* January 1992, pp. 49–72.

13. Frank Cornish, "Building a Customer-Oriented Organization," *Long-Range Planning,* June 1988, pp. 105–107.

14. Michael Maccoby, "Transforming R&D Services at Bell Labs," *Research-Technology Management,* January–February 1992, pp. 46–49.

15. Jay R. Galbraith and Robert K. Kazanjian, "Organizing to Implement Strategies of Diversity and Globalization: The Role of Matrix Organizations," *Human Resource Management,* Spring 1986, pp. 37–54.

16. Mohammed K. El-Najdawi and Matthew J. Liberatore, "Matrix Management Effectiveness: An Update for Research and Engineering Organizations," *Project Management Journal,* March 1997, pp. 25–31.

17. Paul B. de Laat, "Matrix Management of Projects and Power Struggles: A Case Study of an R&D Laboratory," *Human Relations,* September 1994, pp. 1089–1119.

18. Christopher A. Bartlett and Sumantra Ghosal, "Organizing for Worldwide Effectiveness: The Transactional Solution," *California Management Review,* Fall 1988, pp. 54–74; James K. McCollum and J. Daniel Sherman, "The Effects of Matrix Organization Size and Number of Project Assignments on Performance," *IEEE Transactions on Engineering Management,* February 1991, pp. 75–78.

19. Mohammed M. Habib and Bart Victor, "Strategy, Structure, and Performance of U.S. Manufacturing and Service MNCs: A Comparative Analysis," *Strategic Management Journal,* November 1991, pp. 589–606.

20. Roger Banks, "Is Asia Different? Defining a Strategy to Serve Multi-National Clients in the Region," *Marketing & Research Today,* February 1997, pp. 4–11.

21. Wilber J. Prezzano, "Kodak Sharpens Its Focus on Quality," *Management Review,* May 1989, pp. 39–41.

22. Richard D. Whitley, "Eastern Asian Enterprise Structures and the Comparative Analysis of Forms of Business Organization," *Organization Studies,* vol. 11, no. 1 (1990), pp. 47–74; M. P. Kriger, and E. E. Solomon, "Strategic Mindsets and Decision-Making Autonomy in U.S. and Japanese MNCs," *Management International Review,* vol. 32, no. 4 (1992), pp. 327–43.

23. Manfred Kling and Charles Davies, "Organization Redesign of DND's Material Group: Operation Excellence," *Optimum,* vol. 27, no. 4 (1997), pp. 25–33.

24. Ann Altaffer, "First-Line Managers: Measuring Their Span of Control," *Nursing Management,* July 1998, pp. 36–40.

25. Karen E. Mishra, Gretchen M. Spreitzer, and Aneil K. Mishra, "Preserving Employee Morale During Downsizing," *Sloan Management Review,* Winter 1998, pp. 83–95.

26. David H. Freedman, "Corps Values," *Inc.,* April 1998, pp. 54–66.

27. Jeffrey A. Alexander, "Adaptive Change in Corporate Control Practices," *Academy of Management Journal,* March 1991, pp. 162–93.

28. Carolyn G. Friese, Paula J. Fleurant, Sandra S. Hillman, and Kathryn T. Ulmen, "Nursing Council: Coordination within Decentralization," *Nursing Management,* March 1998, pp. 40–41.

29. Deone Zell, *Changing by Design: Organizational Innovation at Hewlett-Packard* (Ithaca, NY: Cornell University Press, 1997).

30. Abraham Seidmann and Arun Sundararajan, "Competing in Information-Intensive Services: Analyzing the Impact of Task Consolidation and Employee Empowerment," *Journal of Management Information Systems,* Fall 1997, pp. 33–56.

31. Robert W. Hetherington, "The Effects of Formalization on Departments of a Multi-Hospital System," *Journal of Management Studies,* March 1991, pp. 103–41.

32. Phoebe M. Carillo and Richard E. Kopelman, "Organization Structure and Productivity," *Group and Organization Studies,* March 1991, pp. 44–59.

CHAPTER 14

1. Richard E. Kopelman, "Job Redesign and Productivity: A Review of the Evidence," *National Productivity Review,* Summer 1985, p. 239.

2. Randy Hodson, "Group Relations at Work: Solidarity, Conflict, and Relations with Management," *Work and Occupations,* November 1997, pp. 426–52.

3. Paul Osterman, "How Common Is Workplace Transformation and Who Adopts it?" *Industrial and Labor Relations Review,* January 1994, pp. 173–88.

4. Marvin R. Weisbord, *Productive Workplaces: Organizing and Managing for Dignity, Meaning and Community* (San Francisco: Jossey-Bass, 1987).

5. Susan G. Cohen, Lei Chang, and Gerald E. Ledford Jr., "A Hierarchical Construct of Self-Management Leadership and Its Relationship to Quality of Work Life and Perceived Work Group Effectiveness," *Personnel Psychology,* Summer 1997, pp. 275–308.

6. Barry M. Staw, Robert I. Sutton, and Lisa H. Pelled, "Employee Positive Emotion and Favorable Outcomes at the Workplace, *Organization Science,* February 1994, pp. 51–71.

7. Jean Ann Seago, "Five Pitfalls of Work Redesign in Acute Care," *Nursing Management,* October 1997, pp. 49–50.

8. Kenneth W. Thomas and Betty A. Velthouse, "Cognitive Elements of Empowerment: An 'Interpretive' Model of Intrinsic Task Motivation," *Academy of Management Review,* October 1990, pp. 666–81.

9. Joan R. Rentach and Robert P. Steel, "Testing the Durability of Job Characterstics as Predictors of Absenteeism over a Six-Year Period," *Personnel Psychology,* Spring 1998, pp. 163–90.

10. Menachem Rosner and Louis Putterman, "Factors behind the Supply and Demand for Less Alienating Work, and Some International Illustrations," *Journal of Economic Studies,* vol. 18, no. 1 (1991), pp. 18–41.

11. Frank Shipper and Charles C. Manz, "Employee Self-Management without Formally Designated Teams: An Alternative Road to Empowerment," *Organizational Dynamics,* Winter 1992, pp. 48–61.

12. Robert J. Vandenberg and Charles E. Lance, "Examining the Causal Order of Job Satisfaction and Organizational Commitment," *Journal of Management,* March 1992, pp. 153–67.

13. Glenn Bassett, "The Case Against Job Satisfaction," *Business Horizons,* May/June 1994, pp. 61–68; Jill Kanin-Lovers and Gordon Spunich, "Compensation and the Job Satisfaction Equation," *Journal of Compensation and Benefits,* January–February 1992, pp. 54–57.

14. Robert Dowless, "Motivating Salespeople: One Order of Empowerment: Hold the Carrots," *Training,* February 1992, pp. 16, 73–74.

15. Frederick P. Morgeson and Michael A. Campion, "Social and Cognitive Sources of Potential Inaccuracy in Job Analysis," *Journal of Applied Psychology,* October 1997, pp. 627–55, and James P. Clifford, "Job Analysis: Why Do It, and How Should It Be Done?" *Public Personnel Management,* Summer 1994, pp. 321–340.

16. G. Jonathan Meng, "Using Job Descriptions, Performance and Pay Innovations to Support Quality," *National Productivity Review,* Spring 1992, pp. 247–55.

17. U.S. Dept. of Labor, *Dictionary of Occupational Titles,* 4th ed. (Washington, D.C.: U.S. Government Printing Office, 1977).

18. Edward L. Levine, Doris M. Maye, Ronald A. Ulm, and Thomas R. Gordon, "A Methodology for Developing and Validating Minimum Qualifications," *Personnel Psychology,* Winter 1997, pp. 1009–23.

19. Jai V. Ghorpade, *Job Analysis: A Handbook for the Human Resource Director* (Englewood Cliffs, N.J.: Prentice-Hall, 1988).

20. The literature of scientific management is voluminous. The original works and the subsequent criticisms and interpretations would make a large volume. Of special significance are the works of the principal authors, including Frederick W. Taylor, *Principles of Scientific Management* (New York: Harper & Row, 1911); Harrington Emerson, *The Twelve Principles of Efficiency* (New York: Engineering Magazine, 1913); Henry L. Gantt, *Industrial Leadership* (New Haven, Conn.: Yale University Press, 1916); Frank B. Gilbreth, *Motion Study* (New York: D. Van Nostrand, 1911); and Lillian M. Gilbreth, *The Psychology of Management* (New York: Sturgis & Walton, 1914).

21. Taylor, *Principles,* pp. 36–37.

22. Greg L. Stewart and Kenneth P. Carson, "Moving Beyond the Mechanistic Model: An Alternative Approach to Staffing for Contemporary Organizations," *Human Resource Management Review,* Summer 1997, pp. 157–84.

23. Douglas R. May and Catherine E. Schwoerer, "Employee Health by Design: Using Employee Involvement Teams in Ergonomic Job Redesign," *Personnel Psychology,* Winter 1994, pp. 861–76; Larry Reynolds, "Ergonomic Concerns Stiffen Rules Regarding VDT Use," *Personnel,* April 1991, pp. 1–2.

24. Theodore W. Braun, "Ergonomics: The Safety Science of the 1990's" *Risk Management,* October 1994, pp. 54–60.

25. Chi-Sum Wong, Chun Hui, and Kenneth S. Law, "A Longitudinal Study of the Job Perception–Job Satisfaction Relationship: A Test of the Three Alternative Specifications," *Journal of Occupational and Organizational Psychology,* June 1998, pp. 127–46.

26. Patrick H. Raymark, Mark J. Schmit, and Robert M. Guion, "Identifying Potentially Useful Personality Constructs for Employee Selection," *Personnel Psychology,* Autumn 1997, pp. 723–36.

27. Juan I. Sanchez, Alina Samora, and Chockalingam Viaweavaran, "Moderators of Agreement between Incumbent and Non-Incumbent Ratings of Job Characteristics," *Journal of Occupational and Organizational Psychology,* September 1997, pp. 209–18.

28. J. Richard Hackman and Edward W. Lawler III, "Employee Reactions to Job Characteristics," *Journal of Applied Psychology,* June 1971, pp. 259–86; and J. Richard Hackman and Greg R. Oldham, "Development of the Job Diagnostic Survey," *Journal of Applied Psychology,* April 1975, pp. 159–70.

29. Robert P. Steel and Joan R. Rentach, "The Dispositional Model of Job Attitudes Revisited: Findings of a 10-Year Study," *Journal of Applied Psychology,* December 1997, pp. 873–79.

30. Gregory B. Northcraft, Terri L. Griffith, and Christina E. Shalley, "Building Top Management Muscle in a Slow Growth Environment," *Academy of Management Executive,* February 1992, pp. 32–41.

31. Michael A. Campion, Lisa Cheraskin, and Michael J. Stevens, "Career-Related Antecedents and Outcomes of Job Rotation," *Academy of Management Journal,* December 1994, pp. 1518–42.

32. Michael A. Campion and Carol L. McClelland, "Follow-Up and Extension of the Interdisciplinary Costs and Benefits of Enlarged Jobs," *Journal of Applied Psychology,* June 1993, pp. 339–51; Michael A. Campion and Carol L. McClelland, "Interdisciplinary Examination of the Costs and Benefits of Enlarged Jobs: A Job Design Quasi-Experiment," *Journal of Applied Psychology,* April 1991, pp. 186–98.

33. Lance Hazzard, Joe Mautz, and Denver Wrightman, "Job Rotation Cuts Cumulative Trauma Cases," *Personnel Journal,* February 1992, pp. 29–32.

34. Don Nichols, "Taking Participative Management to the Limit," *Management Review,* August 1987, pp. 28–32; and Bob Deierlein, "Team Cuts Costs," *Fleet Equipment,* April 1990, pp. 28–30.

35. Charles R. Walker and Robert H. Guest, *The Man on the Assembly Line* (Cambridge, Mass.: Harvard University Press, 1952).

36. J. Richard Hackman, Greg Oldham, Robert Janson, and Kenneth Purdy, "New Strategy for Job Enrichment," *California Management Review,* Summer 1975, pp. 57–71; and J. Richard Hackman and Greg Oldham, "Development of the Job Diagnostic Survey," *Journal of Applied Psychology,* April 1975, pp. 159–70.

37. J. Richard Hackman and Greg Oldham, *Work Redesign* (Reading, Mass.: Addison-Wesley, 1980).

38. Tom D. Taber and Elisabeth Taylor, "A Review and Evaluation of the Psychometric Properties of the Job Diagnostic Survey," *Personnel Psychology,* Autumn 1990, pp. 467–500.

39. Gary Johns, Jia L. Xie, and Yongqing Fang, "Mediating and Moderating Effects in Job Design," *Journal of Management,* December 1992, pp. 657–76.

40. Ricky W. Griffin, "Effects of Work Redesign on Employee Perceptions, Attitudes, and Behaviors: A Long-Term Investigation," *Academy of Management Journal,* June 1991, pp. 425–35.

41. Larry A. Pace and Eileen P. Kelly, "TQM at Xerox," *International Journal of Technology Management,* vol. 16, nos. 4–6 (1998), pp. 326–35 and Joseph Fiorelli and Richard Feller, "Re-Engineering TQM and Work Redesign: An Integrative Approach to Continuous Organizational Excellence," *Public Administration Quarterly,* Spring 1994, pp. 54–63.

42. Lloyd Dobyns and Clare Crawford-Mason, *Quality or Else: The Revolution in World Business* (Boston: Houghton Mifflin, 1991); E. Craig McGee, "The Convergence of Total Quality and Work Design," *Journal of Quality & Participation,* March 1993, pp. 90–96.

43. Willem Niepce and Eric Molleman, "Work Design Issues in Lean Production from a Sociotechnical Systems Perspective: Neo-Taylorism or the Next Step in Sociotechnical Design?" *Human Relations,* March 1998, pp. 259–87.

44. George S. Easton and Sherry L. Jarrell, "The Effects of Total Quality Management on Corporate Performance: An Empirical Investigation," *Journal of Business,* April 1998, pp. 253–307 and Tom Christensen, "A High-Involvement Redesign," *Quality Progress,* May 1993, pp. 105–8.

45. Eric Trist, "The Evolution of Sociotechnical Systems," Occasional Paper (Ontario Quality of Working Life Centre, June 1981); William M. Fox, "Sociotechnical System Principles and Guidelines," *Journal of Applied Behavioral Science,* March 1995, pp. 91–105.

46. Fred Emery, "Participative Design: Effective, Flexible and Successful," *Journal of Quality and Participation,* January/February 1995, pp. 6–9.

47. A. B. Shani and James A. Sena, "Information Technology and the Integration of Change: Sociotechnical System Approach," *Journal of Applied Behavioral Science,* June 1994, pp. 247–70.

CHAPTER 15

1. Tom Burns and G. M. Stalker, *The Management of Innovation* (London: Tavistock, 1961), are largely responsible for the terms *mechanistic* and *organic.*

2. Henri Fayol, *General and Industrial Management,* trans. J. A. Conbrough (Geneva: International Management Institute, 1929). The more widely circulated translation is that of Constance Storrs (London: Pitman, 1949).

3. James D. Mooney and Allan C. Reiley, *Onward Industry* (New York: Harper & Row, 1939); Revised in James D. Mooney, *The Principles of Organization* (New York: Harper & Row, 1947).

4. Henry C. Metcalf and Lyndall Urwick, eds., *Dynamic Administration: The Collected Papers of Mary Parker Follett* (New York: Harper & Row, 1940).

5. Lyndall Urwick, *The Elements of Administration* (New York: Harper & Row, 1944).

6. Michael Crozier, *The Bureaucratic Phenomenon* (Chicago: University of Chicago Press, 1964), p. 3.

7. Max Weber, *The Theory of Social and Economic Organization,* trans. A. M. Henderson and Talcott Parsons (New York: Oxford University Press, 1947).

8. Ibid., p. 334.

9. *From Max Weber: Essays in Sociology,* trans. H. H. Gerth and C. W. Mills (New York: Oxford University Press, 1946), p. 214.

10. Kent C. Nelson, "Efficiency Wasn't Enough, So We Learned How to Dance," *Computerworld,* March 23, 1992, p. 33; and Richard B. Chase and Nicholas J. Aquilano, *Operations Management* (Homewood, Ill.: Richard D. Irwin, 1992), p. 533.

11. Rensis Likert, *New Patterns of Management* (New York: McGraw-Hill, 1961); and Rensis Likert, *The Human Organization* (New York: McGraw-Hill, 1967).

12. Greg L. Stewart and Kenneth P. Carson, "Moving Beyond the Mechanistic Model," *Human Resource Management Review,* Summer 1997, pp. 157–84, and Leigh Buchanan, "Organic Restructuring," *CIO,* September 1994, pp. 66–76.

13. Donald J. McNerney, "Compensation Case Study: Rewarding Team Performance and Individual Skillbuilding," *HR Focus,* January 1995, pp. 1, 4.; Dennis H. Pillsbury, "Team Concept Makes Vorpagel #1 for AAL," *Life & Health Insurance Sales,* October 1993, pp. 10–11; and Fred Luthans, "A Conversation with Charles Dull," *Organizational Dynamics,* Summer 1993, pp. 57–70.

14. Charles Perrow, "A Framework for the Comparative Analysis of Organizations," *American Sociological Review,* April 1967, p. 195. See Michael Withey, Richard L. Daft, and William H. Cooper, "Measures of Perrow's Work-Unit Technology: An Empirical Assessment and a New Scale," *Academy of Management Journal,* March 1983, pp. 45–63.

15. Joan Woodward, *Industrial Organization: Theory and Practice* (London: Oxford University Press, 1965).

16. Ibid., p. 35.

17. J. J. Rackham, "Automation and Technical Change—The Implications for the Management Process," *Organizational Structure and Design,* ed. Gene W. Dalton, Paul R. Lawrence, and Jay W. Lorsch (Homewood, Ill.: Richard D. Irwin, and Dorsey Press, 1970), p. 299.

18. Joan Woodward, *Management and Technology: Problems of Progress in Industry,* No. 3 (London: Her Majesty's Stationery Office, 1958), pp. 4–30; and Gary A. Yukl and Kenneth N. Wexley, eds., *Readings in Organizational and Industrial Psychology* (New York: Oxford University Press, 1971), p. 19.

19. Patricia L. Nemetz and Louis W. Fry, "Flexible Manufacturing Organizations: Implications for Strategy Formulation and Organization Design," *Academy of Management Review,* October 1988, pp. 627–38.

20. Richard B. Chase and David A. Garvin, "The Service Factory," *Harvard Business Review,* July–August 1989, pp. 61–69.

21. Mary Jo Maffei and Jack Meredith, "The Organization Side of Flexible Manufacturing Technology," *International Journal of Operations & Production,* vol. 14, no. 8 (1994), pp. 17–34.

22. Paul R. Lawrence and Jay W. Lorsch, "Differentiation and Integration in Complex Organizations," *Administrative Science Quarterly,* June 1967, pp. 1–47; Jay W. Lorsch, *Product Innovation and Organization* (New York: Macmillan, 1965); Paul R. Lawrence and Jay W. Lorsch, *Organization and Environment* (Homewood, Ill.: Richard D. Irwin, 1969); and Paul R. Lawrence, "The Harvard Organization and Environment Research Program," in *Perspectives on Organization Design and Behavior,* ed. Andrew H. Van de Ven and William Joyce (New York: Wiley Interscience, 1981), pp. 311–37.

23. Lawrence and Lorsch, *Organization and Environment,* p. 16.

24. Lawrence and Lorsch, "Differentiation and Integration in Complex Organizations," pp. 3–4.

25. James D. Thompson, *Organizations in Action* (New York: McGraw-Hill, 1967), p. 56.

26. Lawrence and Lorsch, "Differentiation and Integration in Complex Organizations," pp. 7–8.

27. John T. Drea, "Perceived Environmental Uncertainty: Planning Implications for Small Banks," *American Business Review,* January 1997, pp. 49–56.

28. Donald D. Bergh and Michael W. Lawless, "Portfolio Restructuring and Limits to Hierarchical Governance: The Effects of Environmental Uncertainty and Diversification Strategy," *Organization Science,* January/February 1998, pp. 87–102.

29. James L. Heskett, *Managing in the Service Economy* (Boston: Harvard Business School Press, 1986); and D. Keith Denton, "Customer-Focused Management," *HR Magazine,* August 1990, pp. 62–63, 66–67.

30. Martin P. Charns, "Organization Design of Integrated Delivery Systems," *Hospital and Health Services Administration,* Fall 1997, pp. 411–32.

31. The development of theory relating information process and organization structure has been discussed in various sources. The most publicized sources are Jay Galbraith, *Designing Complex Organizations* (Reading, Mass.: Addison-Wesley, 1973); and Jay Galbraith, *Organization Design* (Reading, Mass.: Addison-Wesley, 1977).

32. Shouhong Wang, "Impact of Information Processing on Organizations," *Human Resources Management,* vol. 16, no. 2 (1997), pp. 83–90.

33. Miles H. Overholt, "Flexible Organizations: Using Organization Design as a Competitive Advantage," *Human Resource Planning,* vol. 20, no. 1 (1997), pp. 22–32.

34. Lorin M. Hitt and Erik Brynjolfsson, "Information Technology and Internal Firm Organization," *Journal of Management Information Systems,* Fall 1997, pp. 81–101.

35. Joseph L. C. Cheng and Idalene F. Kesner, "Organizational Slack and Response to Environmental Shifts," *Journal of Management,* vol. 23, no. 1 (1997), pp. 1–18.

36. Raymond E. Miles, Charles C. Snow, John A. Malthus, Grant Miles, and Henry J. Coleman Jr., "Organizing in the Knowledge Era: Anticipating the Cellular Form," *Academy of Management Executive,* November 1997, pp. 7–20.

37. Abbe Mowshowitz, "Virtual Organization: A Vision of Management in the Information Age," *Information Society,* October–December 1994, pp. 267–288; Heather Ogilvie, "At the Core, It's the Virtual Organization," *Journal of Business Strategy,* September/October 1994, p. 29; "Learning from Japan," *Business Week,* January 27, 1992, pp. 52–55, 58–59.

38. Marc J. Dollinger, "Environmental Boundary Spanning and Information Processing Effects on Organizational Performance," *Academy of Management Journal,* June 1984, pp. 351–68.

39. Ram Charan, "How Networks Reshape Organizations—For Results," *Harvard Business Review,* September–October 1991, pp. 104–15.

40. James W. Frederickson, "The Strategic Decision Process and Organizational Structure," *Academy of Management Review,* April 1986, pp. 280–97.

41. Alfred Chandler, *Strategy and Structure* (Cambridge, Mass.: MIT Press, 1962).

42. Dennis P. Slevin and Jeffrey G. Covin, "Strategy Formation Patterns, Performance, and the Significance of Context," *Journal of Management,* vol. 23, no. 2 (1997), pp. 189–209.

43. Herman L. Boschken, "Strategy and Structure: Reconceiving the Relationship," *Journal of Management,* March 1990, pp. 135–50.

44. Anthony M. Townsend, Samuel DeMarie, and Anthony R. Hendrickson, "Virtual Teams: Technology and the Workplace of the Future," *Academy of Management Executive,* August 1998, pp. 17–29.

45. William F. Joyce, Victor E. McGee, and John W. Slocum Jr., "Designing Lateral Organizations: An Analysis of the Benefits, Costs, and Enablers of Nonhierarchical Organizational Forms," *Decision Sciences,* Winter 1997, pp. 1–25.

CHAPTER 16

1. Klaus Krippendorf, "An Epistemological Foundation for Communication," *Journal of Communication,* Summer 1984, pp. 21–36.

2. M. J. Papa and E. E. Graham, "The Impact of Diagnosing Skill Deficiencies and Assessment-Based Communication Training on Managerial Performance," *Communication Education,* October 1991, pp. 368–84.

3. These five questions were first suggested in H. D. Lasswell, *Power and Personality* (New York: W. W. Norton, 1948), pp. 37–51.

4. Claude Shannon and Warren Weaver, *The Mathematical Theory of Communication* (Urbana: University of Illinois Press, 1948); Wilbur Schramm, "How Communication Works," in *The Process and Effects of Mass Communication,* ed. Wilbur Schramm (Urbana: University of Illinois Press, 1953), pp. 3–26. These works are considered classics in the field of communication.

5. Susan Ashford, "Feedback-Seeking in Individual Adaptation: A Resource Perspective," *Academy of Management Journal,* September 1986, pp. 465–87.

6. Dale A. Level, Jr., and William P. Galle, Jr., *Managerial Communications* (Plano, Tex.: Business Publications, 1988).

7. For a detailed review of research associated with nonverbal communication, see B. M. DePaulo, "Nonverbal Behavior and Self-Presentation," *Psychological Bulletin,* vol. 11, no. 2, 1992, pp. 203–43.

8. J. K. Burgoon, T. Birk, and M. Pfau, "Nonverbal Behaviors, Persuasion, and Credibility," *Human Communication Research,* Fall 1990, pp. 140–69.

9. Paul Ekman and W. V. Friesen, *Unmasking the Face* (Englewood Cliffs, N.J.: Prentice-Hall, 1975).

10. Level and Galle, *Managerial Communications,* p. 66.

11. Barnum and N. Wolniansky, "Taking Cues from Body Language (International Business Transactions)," *Management Review,* June 1989, pp. 59–60.

12. D. Matsumoto, "American–Japanese Cultural Differences in the Recognition of Universal Facial Expressions," *Journal of Cross-Cultural Psychology,* March 1992, pp. 72–84.

13. Nicholas Smeed, "A Boon to Employee Communications: Letters of Understanding," *Personnel,* April 1985, pp. 50–53.

14. G. F. Kohut and A. H. Segars, "The President's Letter to Stockholders: An Examination of Corporate Communication Strategy," *Journal of Business Communication,* Winter 1992, pp. 7–21.

15. Randall Poe, "Can We Talk?" *Across the Board,* May 1994, pp. 16–23.

16. J. W. Smither, M. London, R. R. Reilly, and R. E. Millsap, "An Examination of an Upward Feedback Program Over Time," *Personnel Psychology,* Spring 1995, pp. 1–34.

17. Charles E. Beck and Elizabeth A. Beck, "The Manager's Open Door and the Communication Climate," *Business Horizons,* January–February 1986, pp. 15–19.

18. Allan D. Frank, "Trends in Communication: Who Talks to Whom?" *Personnel,* December 1985, pp. 41–47.

19. For two excellent examples of company efforts to enhance communication (and the pitfalls of such attempts), see Ruth G. Newman, "Polaroid Develops a Communications System—But Not Instantly," *Management Review,* January 1990, pp. 34–39; M. M. Petty, James F. Cashman, Anson Seers, Robert L. Stevenson, Charles W. Barker, and Grady Cook, "Better Communication at General Motors," *Personnel Journal,* September 1989, pp. 40ff.

20. M. Erez, "Interpersonal Communication Systems in Organizations, and Their Relationships to Cultural Values, Productivity, and Innovation: The Case of Japanese Corporations," *Applied Psychology: An International Review,* vol. 41, no. 1, 1992, pp. 43–64.

21. David Cathmoir Nicloo, "Acknowledge and Use Your Grapevine," *Management Decision,* vol. 32, no. 6, 1994, pp. 25–30.

22. K. M. Watson, "An Analysis of Communication Patterns: A Method for Discriminating Leader and Subordinate Roles," *Academy of Management Journal,* June 1982, pp. 107–22.

23. Robert Levy, "Tilting at the Rumor Mill," *Dun's Review,* December 1981, pp. 52–54.

24. Abebowale, Akande, and Funmilayo Odewale, "One More Time: How to Stop Company Rumors," *Leadership and Organizational Journal,* vol. 15, no. 4, 1994, pp. 27–30.

25. R. L. Rosnow, "Psychology in Rumor Reconsidered," *Psychological Bulletin,* May 1980, pp. 578–91.

26. Frederick Koenig, *Rumor in the Marketplace* (Dover, Mass.: Auburn House, 1985).

27. J. Mishra, "Managing the Grapevine," *Public Personnel Management,* Summer 1990, pp. 213–28.

28. Ibid.

29. Fred Luthans and Janet K. Larsen, "How Managers Really Communicate," *Human Relations* 39, no. 2, 1986, pp. 161–78. See also Larry E. Penley and Brian Hawkins, "Studying Interpersonal Communication in Organizations: A Leadership Application," *Academy of Management Journal,* June 1985, pp. 309–26.

30. Joseph Luft, "The Johari Window," *Human Relations and Training News,* January 1961, pp. 6–7. The discussion here is based on a later adaptation. See James Hall, "Communication Revisited," *California Management Review,* Fall 1973, pp. 56–67.

31. Walter D. St. John, "You Are What You Communicate," *Personnel Journal,* October 1985, pp. 40–43.

32. Watson, "An Analysis of Communication Patterns," p. 111.

33. F. W. Nickols, "How to Figure Out What to Do," *Training,* August 1991, pp. 31–34, 39.

34. Owen Hargie and Dennis Tourish, "Communication Skills Training: Management Manipulation or Personal Development?" *Human Relations,* November 1994, pp. 1377–89.

35. Robert E. Kaplan, Wilfred H. Drath, and Joan R. Kofodimos, "Why Some Managers Don't Get the Message," *Across the Board,* September 1985, pp. 63–69.

36. William Hennefrund, "Fear of Feedback," *Association Management,* March 1986, pp. 80–83.

37. Chris Argyris, "Good Communication That Blocks Learning," *Harvard Business Review,* July/August 1994, pp. 77–85.

38. Edward Hall, *The Hidden Dimension* (Garden City, N.Y.: Doubleday, 1966).

39. Phillip L. Hunsaker, "Communicating Better: There's No Proxy for Proxemics," *Business,* March–April 1980, pp. 41–48.

40. Liz Thach and Richard W. Woodman, "Organizational Change and Information Technology: Managing on the Edge of Cyberspace," *Organizational Dynamics,* Summer 1994, pp. 30–46.

41. Ernest G. Bormann, "Symbolic Convergence Theory: A Communication Formulation," *Journal of Communication,* Fall 1985, pp. 128–38.

42. Peter F. Drucker, "The Information Executives Truly Need," *Harvard Business Review,* January/February 1995, pp. 54–62.

43. Robert C. Liden and Terence R. Mitchell, "Reactions to Feedback: The Role of Attributions," *Academy of Management Journal,* June 1985, pp. 291–308.

44. Harriet V. Lawrence and Albert K. Wiswell, "Feedback Is a Two-Way Street," *Training & Development,* July 1995, pp. 49–52.

45. M. E. Schnake, Michael P. Dumler, Dan Cochran, and Timothy Barnett, "Effects of Differences in Superior and Subordinate Perceptions of Superior's Communication Practices," *Journal of Business Communication,* Winter 1990, pp. 37–50.

46. G. W. Kemper, "Managing Corporate Communication in Turbulent Times," *IABC Communication World,* May–June 1992.

47. Keith Davis, *Human Behavior at Work* (New York: McGraw-Hill, 1980), p. 394.

CHAPTER 17

1. Bernard M. Bass, *Organizational Decision Making* (Homewood, Ill.: Richard D. Irwin, 1983).

2. Danny Samson, *Managerial Decision Making* (Homewood, Ill.: Richard D. Irwin, 1988).

3. See John L. Cotton, David A. Vollrath, and Kirk L. Froggatt, "Employee Participation: Diverse Forms and Different Outcomes," *Academy of Management Review,* January 1988, pp. 8–22.

4. Patrick E. Connor, "Decision-Making Participation Patterns: The Role of Organizational Context," *Academy of Management Journal,* March 1992, pp. 218–31.

5. Herbert A. Simon, *The New Science of Management Decision* (New York: Harper & Row, 1960), pp. 5–6.

6. Neil M. Agnew and John L. Brown, "Executive Judgment: The Intuition/Rational Ratio," *Personnel,* December 1985, pp. 48–54.

7. Stephen D. Brookfield, *Developing Critical Thinkers; Challenging Adults to Explore Alternative Ways of Thinking* (San Francisco: Jossey-Bass, 1987).

8. William B. Stevenson and Mary C. Gilly, "Information Processing and Problem Solving: The Migration of Problems through Formal Positions and Networks of Ties," *Academy of Management Journal,* March 1991, pp. 918–28.

9. Weston Agor, "The Logic of Intuition: How Top Executives Make Important Decisions," *Organizational Dynamics,* Winter 1986, pp. 5–18.

10. Paul C. Nutt, "Types of Organizational Decision Processes," *Administrative Science Quarterly,* September 1984, pp. 414–50; S. Pokras, *Strategic Problem Solving and Decision Making* (Los Altos, Calif.: Crisp, 1989).

11. Norman Augustine, "Is Any Risk Acceptable Today?" *Across the Board,* May 1994, pp. 14–15.

12. Russell L. Ackoff, *The Art of Problem Solving* (New York: John Wiley & Sons, 1987).

13. Allen R. Solem, "Some Applications of Problem-Solving versus Decision-Making to Management," *Journal of Business and Psychology,* Spring 1992, pp. 401–11.

14. Dean Tjosvold, "Effects of Crisis Orientation on Managers' Approach to Controversy in Decision Making," *Academy of Management Journal,* March 1984, pp. 130–38.

15. Paul Shrivastava, "Knowledge Systems for Strategic Decision Making," *Journal of Applied Behavioral Science,* Winter 1985, pp. 95–108.

16. William Q. Judge and Alex Miller, "Antecedents and Outcomes of Decision Speed in Different Environmental Contexts," *Academy of Management Journal,* June 1991, pp. 449–63.

17. David H. Mason, "Scenario-Based Planning: Decision Model for the Learning Organization," *Planning Review,* March/April 1994, pp. 6–11.

18. Paul J. Shoemaker, "Scenario Planning: A Tool for Strategic Thinking," *Sloan Management Review,* Winter 1995, pp. 25–40.

19. Kenneth R. MacCrimmon and Donald A. Wehrung, *The Management of Uncertainty: Taking Risks* (New York: Free Press, 1986).

20. For a detailed explanation of game theory, see Adam Brandenburger and Barry Nalebuff, "The Right Game: Use Game Theory to Shape Strategy," *Harvard Business Review,* July/August 1995, pp. 57–71.

21. Jeffrey E. Kottemann, Fred D. Davis, and William E. Remus, "Computer-Assisted Decision Making: Performance, Beliefs, and the Illusion of Control," *Organizational Behavior and Human Decision Processes,* January, 1994, pp. 26–37.

22. Paul Shrivastava and I. I. Mitroff, "Enhancing Organizational Research Utilization: The Role of Decision Makers' Assumptions," *Academy of Management Review,* January 1984, pp. 18–26.

23. Charles R. Schwenk, *The Essence of Strategic Decision Making* (Lexington, Mass.: Lexington Books, 1988).

24. Kelly C. Strong and G. Dale Meyer, "An Integrative Descriptive Model of Ethical Decision Making," *Journal of Business Ethics,* September 1992, pp. 89–94.

25. Linda Klebe Trevino, "Ethical Decision Making in Organizations: A Person-Situation Interactional Model," *Academy of Management Review,* July 1986, pp. 601–17.

26. Ralph L. Keeney, "Creativity in Decision Making with Value-Focused Thinking," *Sloan Management Review,* Summer 1994, pp. 33–41.

27. P. A. Renwick and H. Tosi, "The Effects of Sex, Marital Status, and Educational Background on Selected Decisions," *Academy of Management Journal,* March 1978, pp. 93–103; A. A. Abdel-Halim, "Effects of Task and Personality Characteristics on Subordinate Responses to Participative Decision Making," *Academy of Management Journal,* September 1983, pp. 477–84. For an interesting cross-cultural study, see Frank Heller, Peter Drenth, Paul Koopman, and Veljko Rus, *Decisions in Organizations: A Three Country Comparative Study* (Newbury Park, Calif.: Sage, 1988).

28. Mark H. Radford, Leon Mann, Yasuyuki Ohta, and Yoshibumi Nakane, "Differences between Australian and Japanese Students in Reported Use of Decision Process," *International Journal of Psychology,* vol. 26, no. 1, 1991, pp. 35–52.

29. Ann Langley, "Between Paralysis by Analysis and Extinction by Instinct," *Sloan Management Review,* Spring 1995, pp. 63–76.

30. Leon Festinger, *A Theory of Cognitive Dissonance* (New York: Harper & Row, 1957), Chap. 1; Richard P. Larrick and Terry L. Boles, "Avoiding Regret in Decisions with Feedback: A Negotiation Example," *Organizational Behavior & Decision Process,* July 1995, pp. 87–97.

31. J. Richard Harrison and James C. March, "Decision Making and Postdecision Surprises," *Administrative Science Quarterly,* March 1984, pp. 26–42. Also see James C. March, *Decisions and Organizations* (New York: Basil Blackwell, 1988).

32. Jeanne M. Logsdon, "Interests and Interdependence in the Formation of Social Problem-Solving Collaborations," *Journal of Applied Behavioral Science,* March 1991, pp. 23–37.

33. For examples, see B. Gray, *Collaborating: Finding Common Ground for Multi-Party Problems* (San Francisco: Jossey-Bass, 1989).

34. Martha L. Maznevski, "Understanding Our Differences: Performance in Decision-Making Groups with Diverse Members," *Human Relations,* May 1994, pp. 531–32.

35. For examples, see Barry M. Staw, "The Escalation of Commitment to a Course of Action," *Academy of Management Review,* October 1981, pp. 577–88; Max H. Bazerman and Alan Appelman, "Escalation of Commitment in Individual and Group Decision Making," *Organizational Behavior and Human Decision Process,* Spring 1984, pp. 141–52; Barbara Bird, "Implementing Entrepreneurial Ideas: The Case for Intention," *Academy of Management Review,* July 1988, pp. 442–53; Warren E. Watson, Larry K. Michaelsen, and Walt Sharp, "Member Competence, Group Interaction, and Group Decision-Making: A Longitudinal Study," *Journal of Applied Psychology,* December 1991, pp. 803–9.

36. Richard A. Guzzo and James A. Waters, "The Expression of Affect and the Performance of Decision Making Groups," *Journal of Applied Psychology,* February 1982, pp. 67–74; Dean Tjosvold and R. H. G. Field, "Effects of Social Context on Consensus and Majority Vote Decision Making," *Academy of Management Journal,* September 1983, pp. 500–06; Fredrick C. Miner, Jr., "Group versus Individual Decision Making: An Investigation of Performance Measures, Decision Strategies, and Process Losses/Gains," *Organizational Behavior and Human Decision Processes,* Winter 1984, pp. 112–24.

37. Diane M. Mackie, M. Cecilia Gastardo-Conaco, and John J. Skelly, "Knowledge of the Advocated Position and the Processing of In-Group and Out-Group Persuasive Messages," *Personality and Social Psychology Bulletin,* April 1992, pp. 145–51.

38. Kathleen J. Krone, "A Comparison of Organizational, Structural, and Relationship Effects on Subordinates' Upward Influence Choices," *Communication Quarterly,* Winter 1992, pp. 1–15.

39. R. Brent Gallupe, Lana M. Bastianutti, and William H. Cooper, "Unblocking Brainstorms," *Journal of Applied Psychology,* February 1991, pp. 137–42.

40. Norman Dalkey, *The Delphi Method: An Experimental Study of Group Opinion* (Santa Monica, Calif.: Rand Corporation, 1969). This is the classic groundbreaking work on the Delphi method.

41. "Study Spots Global Marketing Trends (Global Marketing 2000: Future Trends and Their Implications, A Delphi Study)," *Marketing News,* October 14, 1991, p. 9.

42. See Andre L. Delbecq, Andrew H. Van de Ven, and David H. Gustafson, *Group Techniques for Program Planning* (Glenview, Ill.: Scott, Foresman, 1975), for a work devoted entirely to techniques for group decision making.

43. Brian Mullen, Craig Johnson, and Eduardo Salas, "Productivity Loss in Brainstorming Groups: A Meta-Analytic Integration," *Basic and Applied Social Psychology,* March 1991, pp. 3–23.

44. Delbecq, Van de Ven, and Gustafson, *Group Techniques for Program Planning,* p. 18.

45. "Making Good Decisions," *Supervisory Management,* January 1995, pp. 10–11.

CHAPTER 18

1. Rosabeth Moss Kanter, Barry A. Stein, and Todd Jick, *The Challenge of Organizational Change: How Companies Experience It and Leaders Guide It* (New York: Free Press, 1992).

2. Leon Martel, *Mastering Change* (New York: New American Library, 1987).

3. Danny Miller, "What Happens after Success: The Perils of Excellence," *Journal of Management Studies,* May 1994, pp. 325–58.

4. Laurie W. Pant, "An Investigation of Industry and Firm Structural Characterstics in Corporate Turnaround," *Journal of Management Studies,* November 1991, pp. 623–43.

5. Cynthia Hardy and Franca Redivo, "Power and Organizational Development: A Framework for Organizational Change," *Journal of General Management,* Winter 1994, pp. 29–41.

6. Louise Lovelady, "Change Strategies and the Use of OD Consultants to Facilitate Change: Part I," *Leadership and Organizational Development Journal,* vol. 5, no. 2, 1984, pp. 3–5.

7. Susan A. Mohrman, Allan M. Mohrman Jr., and Gerald E. Ledford Jr., "Interventions That Change Organizations," in *Large Scale Organizational Change,* ed. Allan M. Mohrman Jr., Susan A. Mohrman, Gerald E. Ledford Jr., Thomas G. Cummings, Edward E. Lawler, III, and Associates (San Francisco: Jossey-Bass, 1989), p. 146.

8. Ellen Fagenson and W. Warner Burke, "The Current Activities and Skills of Organization Development Practitioners," *Proceedings of the Academy of Management,* 1989, p. 251.

9. Manual London, *Change Agents* (San Francisco: Jossey-Bass, 1988), pp. 41–70.

10. Kurt Lewin, "Group Decisions and Social Change," in *Readings in Social Psychology,* ed. Eleanor E. Maccobby, Theodore M. Newcomb, and Eugene L. Hartley (New York: Holt, Rinehart & Winston, 1958).

11. Janet Cegelka, "Yes, People Will Really Have to Change," *Journal of Quality and Participation,* September 1994, pp. 72–77.

12. Ed Kur, "Why Some Successful Change Agents Last and Other Don't," *Employment Relations Today,* Spring 1998, pp. 39–59; Jay Klaggee, "The Reinvention Trail: An Account of One Agency's Quality Journey," *Public Administration Quarterly,* Winter 1997, pp. 433–48.

13. Stephen C. Harper, "The Manager as Change Agent: 'Hell No' to the Status Quo," *Industrial Management,* May–June 1989, pp. 8–11.

14. Noel M. Tichy and David Ulrich, "The Challenge of Revitalization," *New Management,* Winter 1985, pp. 53–59.

15. Michael Beer and Anna Elise Walton, "Organization Change and Development," in *Organization Development: Theory, Practice, and Research,* ed. Wendell L. French, Cecil H. Bell Jr., and Robert A. Zawacki (Homewood, Ill.: Richard D. Irwin, 1989), p. 73.

16. Ari Ginsberg and Eric Abrahamson, "Champions of Change and Strategic Shifts: The Role of Internal and External Change Advocates," *Journal of Management Studies,* March 1991, pp. 173–90.

17. Jane M. Howell and Christopher A. Higgins, "Champions of Change: Identifying, Understanding, and Supporting Champions of Technological Innovations," *Organizational Dynamics,* Summer 1990, pp. 40–55.

18. Donald L. Kirkpatrick, *How to Manage Change Effectively* (San Francisco: Jossey-Bass, 1985), pp. 101–06.

19. J. J. Murphy, "Reappraising MBO," *Leadership and Organization Development,* vol. 4, no. 4, 1983, pp. 22–27.

20. Ralph H. Kilmann, "Toward a Complete Program for Corporate Transformation," in *Corporate Transformation,* ed. Ralph H. Kilmann, Teresa Joyce Covin, and Associates (San Francisco: Jossey-Bass, 1989), pp. 302–29.

21. Tichy and Ulrich, "The Challenge of Revitalization," p. 54.

22. Morten Levin, "Technology Transfer in Organizational Development," *International Journal of Technology Management,* vol. 14, nos. 2, 3, 4 (1997).

23. Michael S. Morton, "The 1990s Research Program: Implications for Management and the Emerging Organization," *Decision Support Systems,* November 1994, pp. 251–56.

24. Huibert de Man, *Organizational Change in Its Context: A Theoretical and Empirical Study of the Linkages between Organizational Change Projects and Their Administrative, Strategic, and Institutional Environment* (Delft, The Netherlands: Eburon, 1988).

25. Peter M. Senge, "The Leader's New Work: Building Learning Organizations," *Sloan Management Review,* Fall 1990, pp. 13–23; and Peter M. Senge, *The Fifth Discipline: The Art and Practice of the Learning Organization* (New York: Doubleday, 1990); Calhoun W. Wick and Lu Stanton Leon, "From Ideas to Action: Creating a Learning Organization," *Human Resource Management,* Summer 1995, pp. 299–311.

26. Gordon L. Lippitt, Peter Longseth, and Jack Mossop, *Implementing Organizational Change* (San Francisco: Josey-Bass, 1985), pp. 53–74.

27. Noel M. Tichy, *Managing Strategic Change* (New York: John Wiley and Sons, 1983), pp. 162–64.

28. The relationship between depth of organization and intended change is popularly termed *depth of intervention.* We have chosen to term it *degree of intended change* to highlight the issues associated with change rather than those related to intervention. See Roger Harrison, "Choosing the Depth of Organizational Intervention," *Journal of Applied Behavioral Science,* April–May 1970, pp. 181–202, for the original discussion of the concept and more recently Wendell L. French and Cecil H. Bell Jr., *Organizational Development: Behavioral Science Interventions for Organizational Improvement* (Englewood Cliffs, N.J.: Prentice-Hall, 1984).

29. Noel M. Tichy, "GE's Crotonville: A Staging Ground for Corporate Revolution," *Academy of Management Executive,* May 1989, p. 102.

30. Allan H. Church, W. Warner Burke, and Donald F. Van Eynde, "Values, Motives, and Interventions of Organization Development Practitioners," *Group & Organization Management,* May 1994 pp. 5–50; and Ellen A. Fagenson and W. Warner Burke, "Organization Development Practitioners' Activities and Interventions in Organizations in the 1980s," *Journal of Applied Behavioral Science,* vol. 26, no. 3, 1990, pp. 285–97.

31. Joseph B. Mosca, "The Restructuring of Jobs for the Year 2000," *Public Personnel Management,* Spring 1997, pp. 43–59.

32. David A. Nadler and Michael L. Tushman, "Organizational Frame Bending: Principles for Managing Reorientation," *Academy of Management Executive,* August 1989, p. 201.

33. Neuman et al., "Organizational Development Interventions."

34. Philip B. Crosby, *Quality Is Free: The Art of Making Quality Certain* (New York: McGraw-Hill, 1977); W. Edwards Deming, *Out of the Crisis* (Cambridge, Mass.: MIT Center for Advanced Engineering Study, 1986); Kaoru Ishikawa, *What Is Total Quality Control? The Japanese Way* (Englewood Cliffs, N.J.: Prentice-Hall, 1985); Joseph M. Juran, *Juran on Leadership for Quality* (New York: Free Press, 1989).

35. Cesar Camison, "Total Quality Management and Cultural Change: A Model of Organizational Development," *International Journal of Technology Management,* vol. 16, nos. 4–6, (1998), pp. 479–93; Marshall Sashkin and Kenneth J. Kiser, *Total Quality Management* (Seabrook, Md.: Ducochon Press, 1992).

36. Edward E. Lawler III, Susan Mohrman, and Gerald E. Ledford Jr., "The Fortune 1,000 and Total Quality," *Journal of Quality and Participation,* September 1992, pp. 6–10.

37. U.S. General Accounting Office, *Management Practices: U.S. Companies Improve Performance through Quality Efforts* (Washington, D.C.: GAO Printing Office, 1991).

38. David A. Garvin, "How the Baldrige Award Really Works," *Harvard Business Review,* November–December 1991, pp. 80–93.

39. Warren H. Schmidt and Jerome P. Finnigan, *The Race without a Finish Line: America's Quest for Total Quality* (San Francisco: Jossey-Bass, 1992).

40. Noel M. Tichy, "GE's Crotonville: A Staging Ground for Corporate Revolution," *Academy of Management Executive,* May 1989, pp. 99–106.

41. Gary G. Whitney, "Vectors for TQM Change," *Journal for Quality and Participation,* October–November 1992, pp. 40–44.

42. Yoram Ziera and Joyce Avedisian, "Organizational Planned Change: Assessing the Chances for Success," *Organizational Dynamics,* Spring 1989, pp. 31–45.

43. Russell L. Ackoff, "The Circular Organization: An Update," *Academy of Management Executive,* February 1989, pp. 11–16.

44. J. Stephen Ott, *The Organizational Culture Perspective* (Pacific Palisades, Calif.: Brooks/Cole, 1989).

45. Ivan Perlaki, "Organizational Development in Eastern Europe: Learning to Build Culture-Specific OD Theories," *Journal of Applied Behavioral Science,* September 1994, pp. 297–312.

46. John M. Nicholas, "The Comparative Impact of Organization Developments on Hard Criteria Measures," *Academy of Management Review,* October 1982, pp. 531–43; Anthony P. Raia and Newton Margulies, "Organizational Development: Issues, Trends, and Prospects," in *Human Systems Development,* ed. Robert Tannenbaum, Newton Margulies, Fred Massarik, and Associates (San Francisco: Jossey-Bass, 1985), pp. 246–72; and George A. Neuman, Jack E. Edwards, and Nambury S. Raju, "Organizational Development Interventions: A Meta-Analysis of Their Effects on Satisfaction and Other Attitudes," *Personnel Psychology,* Autumn 1989, pp. 461–89, are reviews.

47. Bernard A. Rausch, "Dupont Transforms a Division's Culture," *Management Review,* March 1989, pp. 37–42.

48. Gary Zajac, "Reinventing Government and Reaffirming Ethics: Implications for Organizational Development in the Public Service," *Public Administration Quarterly,* Winter 1997, pp. 385–404; C. M. Dick Deaner, "A Model of Organization Development Ethics," *Public Administration Quarterly,* Winter 1994, pp. 435–446.

49. William G. Dyer, "Team Building: A Microcosm of the Past, Present, and Future of O.D.," *Academy of Management OD Newsletter,* Winter 1989, pp. 7–8.

50. Michael Beer and Anna Elise Walton, "Organization Change and Development," in *Annual Review of Psychology,* ed. Mark Rosenzweig and Lyman W. Porter (Palo Alto, Calif.: Annual Review, 1987), pp. 339–67.

APPENDIX

1. David W. Stewart, *Secondary Research: Information Sources and Methods* (Beverly Hills, Calif.: Sage Publications, 1984).

2. C. S. George Jr., *The History of Management Thought* (Englewood Cliffs, N.J.: Prentice-Hall, 1968).

3. J. D. Mooney, *The Principles of Management* (New York: Harper & Row, 1939).

4. Robert S. Goodman and Evonne Jonas Kruger, "Data Dredging or Legitimate Research Method: Historiography and Its Potential for Management Research," *Academy of Management Review,* April 1988, pp. 315–25.

5. W. H. Gruber and J. S. Niles, "Research and Experience in Management," *Business Horizons,* Fall 1973, pp. 15–24.

6. A similar debate has taken place for years over the issue of whether management is a science. For relevant discussions, interested readers should consult R. E. Gribbons and S. D. Hunt, "Is Management a Science?" *Academy of Management Review,* January 1978, pp. 139–43; O. Behling, "The Case for the Natural Science Model for Research in Organizational Behavior and Organization Theory," *Academy of Management Review,* October 1980, pp. 483–90.

7. John Brockman, *Doing Science* (Englewood Cliffs, N.J.: Prentice-Hall, 1991), p. 155.

8. Edward E. Lawler III, A. M. Mohrman, S. A. Mohrman, G. E. Ledford Jr., and T. G. Cummings, *Doing Research That Is Useful for Theory and Practice* (San Francisco: Jossey-Bass, 1985).

9. F. N. Kerlinger, *Foundations of Behavioral Research* (New York: Holt, Rinehart & Winston, 1973).

10. Robert K. Yin, *Case Study Research: Design and Methods* (Beverly Hills, Calif.: Sage, 1984).

11. Kathleen M. Eisenhardt, "Building Theories from Case Study Research," *Academy of Management Review,* October 1989, pp. 532–50.

12. G. R. Salancik, "Field Simulations for Organizational Behavior Research," *Administrative Science Quarterly,* December 1979, pp. 638–49.

13. The design of surveys and the development and administration of questionnaires are better left to trained individuals if valid results are to be obtained. Interested readers might consult S. Sudman and N. M. Bradburn, *Asking Questions: A Practical Guide to Questionnaire Design* (San Francisco: Jossey-Bass, 1982).

14. For an excellent article on the relationship between what researchers want to see and what they do see, consult G. Nettler, "Wanting and Knowing," *American Behavioral Scientist,* July 1973, pp. 5–26.

15. For a volume devoted entirely to experiments in organizations, see W. M. Evan, ed., *Organizational Experiments: Laboratory and Field Research* (New York: Harper & Row, 1971).

16. M. E. Gordon, L. A. Slade, and N. S. Schmitt, "The Science of the Sophomore Revisited: From Conjecture to Empiricism," *Academy of Management Review,* January 1986, pp. 191–207.

17. See an account of the classic Hawthorne studies in F. J. Roethlisberger and W. J. Dickson, *Management and the Worker* (Boston: Harvard Business School, 1939). The original purpose of the studies, which were conducted at the Chicago Hawthorne Plant of Western Electric, was to investigate the relationship between productivity and physical working conditions.

18. Karl E. Weick, "Laboratory Experimentation with Organizations: A Reappraisal," *Academy of Management Review,* January 1977, pp. 123–27.

19. J. P. Campbell, "Labs, Fields, and Straw Issues," in *Generalizing from Laboratory to Field Settings,* ed. Edwin A. Locke (Lexington, Mass.: Lexington Books, 1986), pp. 269–74.

20. James L. Price and Charles W. Mueller, *Handbook of Organizational Measurement* (Marshfield, Mass.: Pitman, 1986).

21. R. H. Helmstader, *Research Concepts in Human Behavior* (New York: Appleton-Century-Crofts, 1970); D. W. Emery, *Business Research Methods* (Homewood, Ill.: Richard D. Irwin, 1980).

22. Ibid.

23. Kerlinger, *Foundations,* pp. 300–376; Emery, *Business Research,* pp. 330–65.

24. John Van Maanen, ed., *Qualitative Methodology* (Beverly Hills, Calif.: Sage, 1983).

25. R. L. Daft, "Learning the Craft of Organizational Research," *Academy of Management Review,* October 1983, pp. 539–46.

26. A. F. C. Wallace, "Paradigmatic Processes in Cultural Change," *American Anthropologist,* 1972, pp. 467–78.

27. Catherine Marshall and Gretchen B. Rossman, *Designing Qualitative Research* (Newbury Park, Calif.: Sage, 1989), pp. 79–83.

28. John Van Maanen, J. M. Dobbs Jr., and R. R. Faulkner, *Varieties of Qualitative Research* (Beverly Hills, Calif.: Sage, 1982).

29. Van Maanen, *Qualitative Methodology,* pp. 255–56.

Name Index

Company Index

Subject Index